AGAINST THE GATES OF HELL
The Life & Times of Henry Perry,
a Christian Missionary in a Moslem Land

Gordon and Diana Severance

**With a Foreword by
Timothy George**

WIPF & STOCK · Eugene, Oregon

Wipf and Stock Publishers
199 W 8th Ave, Suite 3
Eugene, OR 97401

Against the Gates of Hell
The Life & Times of Henry Perry,
A Christian Missionary in a Moslem World
By Severance, Gordon and Severance, Diana
Copyright©2003 by Severance, Gordon
ISBN 13: 978-62032-525-4
Publication date 10/1/2012
Previously published by University Press of America, 2003

"I will build my church, and the gates of hell shall not prevail against it."
Matthew 16:18

"We must give great weight to the judgment of the missionaries. They stand at the front. They have faced danger. They have walked in the valley of the shadow of death. They have felt the power of the gates of hell."
Reverend Judson Smith,
ABCFM Foreign Secretary (1896)

CONTENTS

Maps		v
Foreword by Dr. Timothy George		xi
Preface		xiii
Acknowledgments		xvii
Prologue		1
1 The Beginning of Wisdom	(1838-1856)	5
2 Planted by Rivers of Water	(1856-1866)	23
3 Compelled by the Love of Christ	(1866-1869)	51
4 Fellowship of His Suffering	(1870-1876)	81
5 Dangers in the Wilderness	(1876-1881)	107
6 Bearing the Cross	(1882-1886)	141
7 A Fruitful Field	(1886-1892)	169
8 Crafty Counsel	(1893-1894)	189
9 Rulers of the Darkness of This Age	(1894-1896)	211
10 A Bruised Reed	(1896-1901)	245
11 Building the Wall in Troublous Times	(1901-1909)	279
12 A Vessel unto Honor	(1909-1914)	309
13 To Live is Christ, to Die is Gain	(1915-1930)	335
Epilogue: Cast Down but Not Destroyed		369
Appendix A: Armenian Massacres, Fall 1895		381
Appendix B: The Unrelenting Struggle against Genocide		383
Bibliography		415
About the Authors		433
Index		435

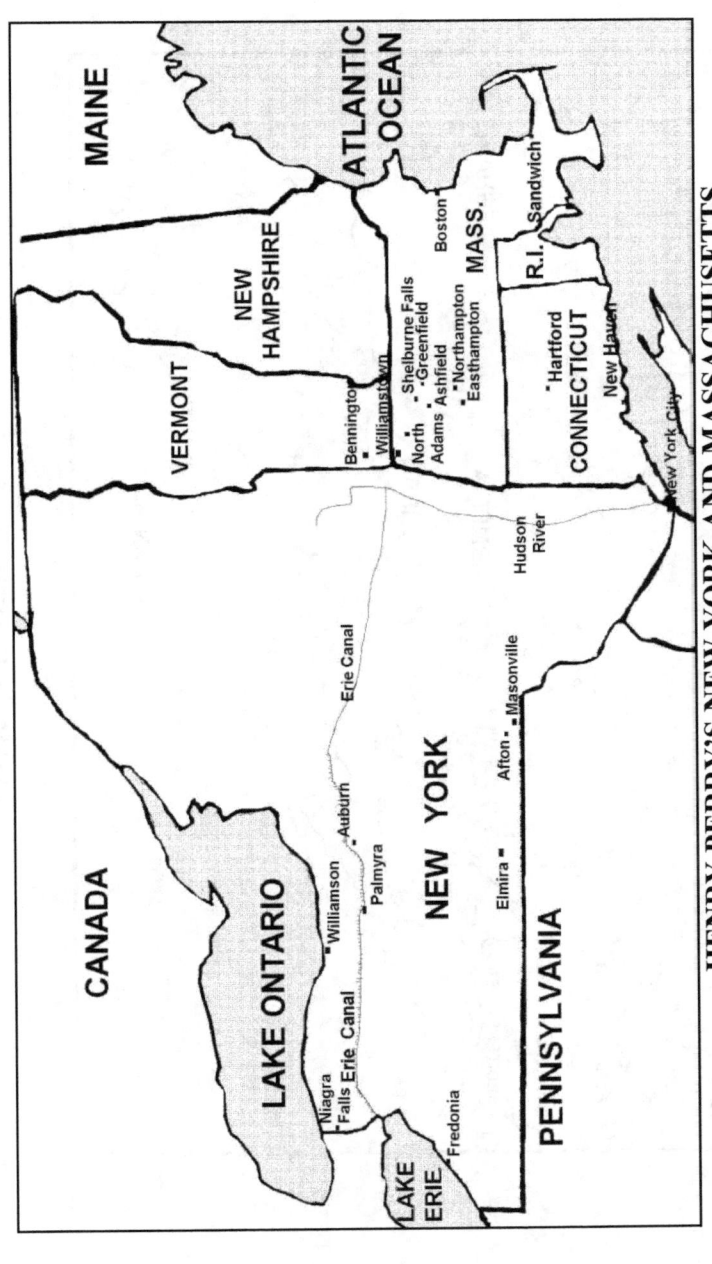

HENRY PERRY'S NEW YORK AND MASSACHUSETTS

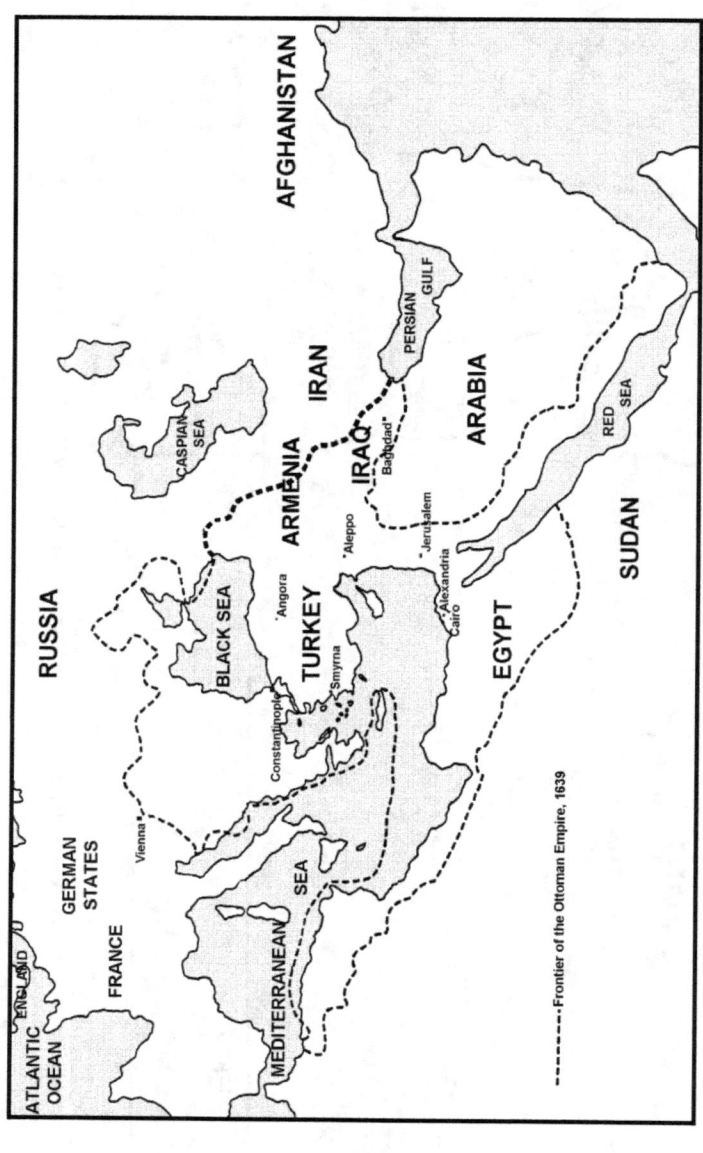

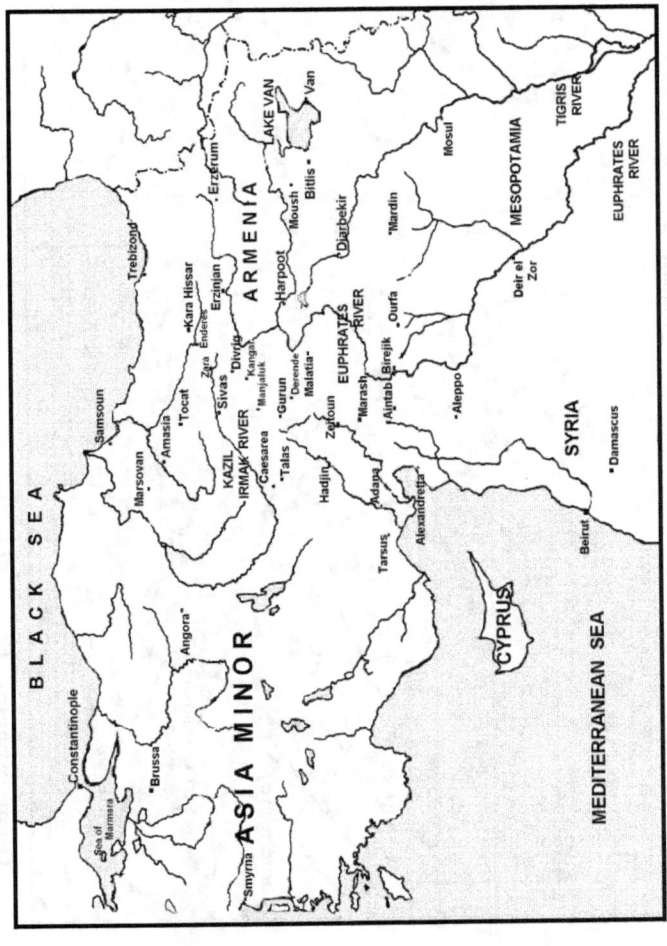

SITES OF MISSIONARY ACTIVITY IN OTTOMAN TURKEY

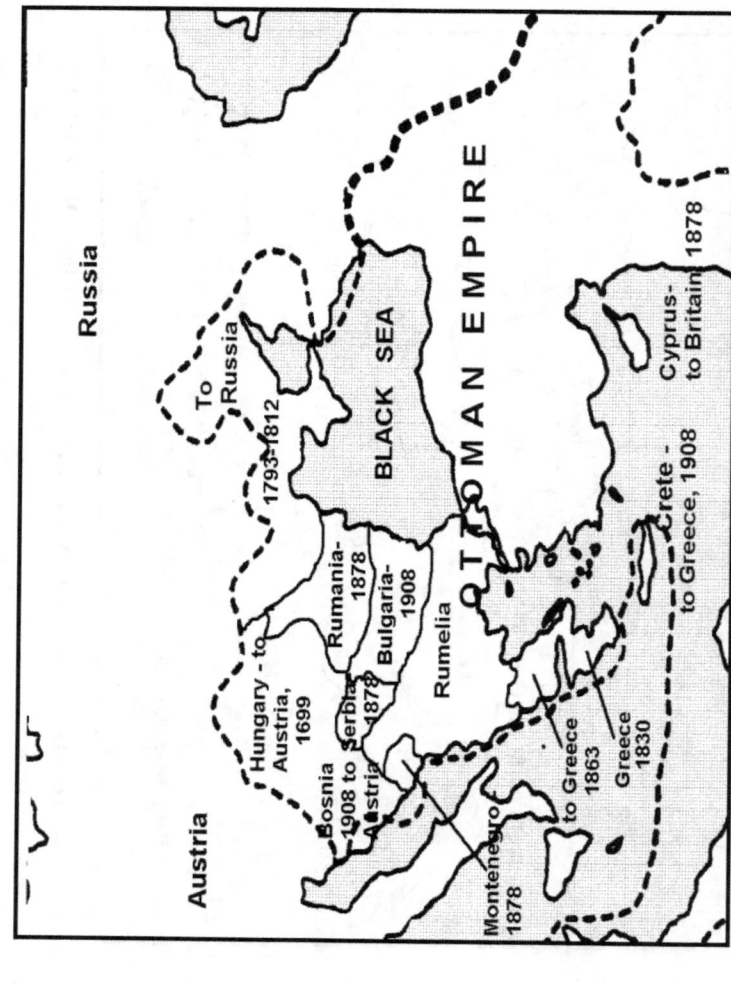

Dismemberment of the Ottoman Empire in Europe, 1683-1909

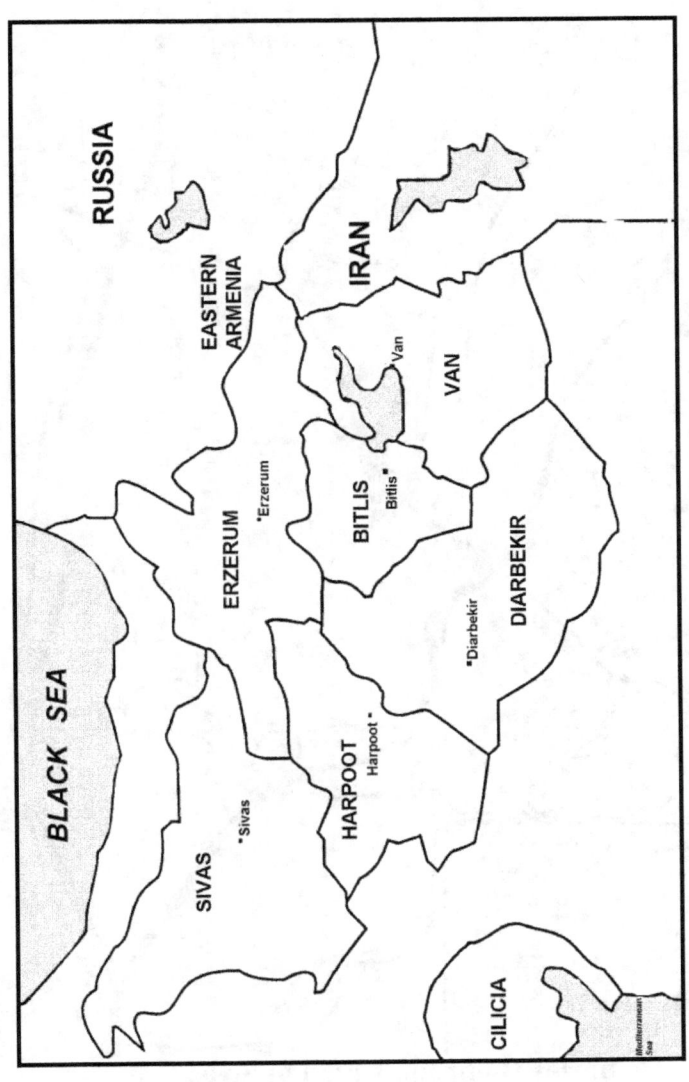

Cilicia and the Six Vilayets of Western Armenia, within the Ottoman Empire, in the Second Half of the Nineteenth Century

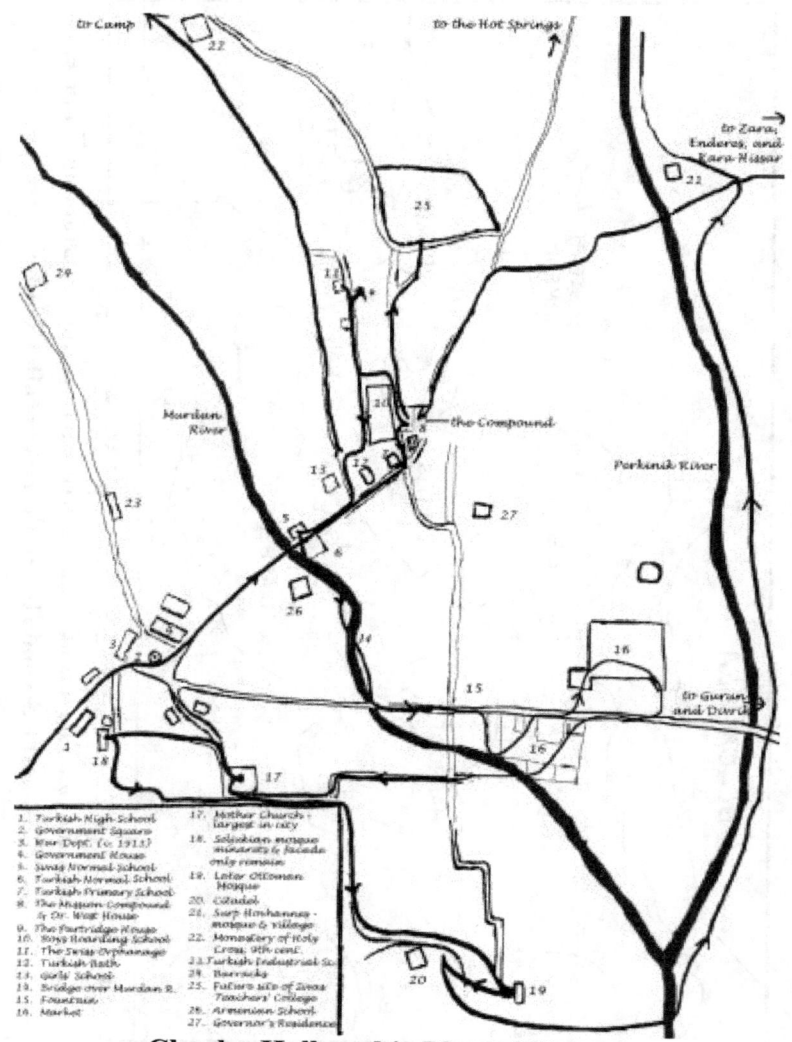

Charles Holbrook's Plan of Sivas
From ABCFM archives in Houghton Library, Harvard University, ABC 77.1 (29.6)

FOREWORD

The noted historian of Christian missions, Kenneth Scott Latourette, once described the 1800's as "the greatest century" that Christianity has ever known. He was referring to the prodigious creativity, expansion and development of the world Christian movement which took place between the French Revolution and the beginning of World War I. At the vanguard of this expansive Christian outreach were the evangelical Protestant missionaries who fanned out across the globe to preach the Gospel, plant churches, translate the Scriptures, establish schools and hospitals, and care for the poor and displaced. This book recounts the story of Henry Perry, one of the most notable and admirable figures in the missionary saga.

From the standpoint of missionary history, the "great century" of Christian witness really began in 1793 when William Carey, a shoemaker-pastor from England, set sail from Dover on a Danish ship headed for India. It lasted until 1910 when Christian leaders from around the world gathered in Edinburgh for the historic missionary conference that marked the beginning of the modern ecumenical movement. Henry Perry was born four years after Carey died and his own life and calling were in many ways an extension of Carey's vision and work. Both men demonstrated unstinted devotion to the people they were called to serve. Both suffered great personal and family losses and both remained steadfast in the face of enormous difficulties that would have leveled any ordinary person.

This book tells the compelling story of Henry Perry, his missionary labors in the ancient land of Armenia, his comings and goings across the Atlantic, the death of five daughters and then his beloved wife in

Turkey, his resilience and courage as a follower of Jesus Christ. But this book also introduces us to the turbulent times in which Henry Perry lived. His love and devotion to the Armenian people were stretched to the point of anguish by the terrible fate that befell those with whom he had shared so much of his life. Perry personally witnessed the slaughter of thousands of Armenians at the hands of the Turks in 1895. He also followed closely the Armenian holocaust that shocked the world two decades later when one and one-half million Armenians were killed in the first genocide of the twentieth century. In the midst of these bloody events, Perry never wavered in his love and concern for the homeless and helpless, the orphans and widows, indeed for all who suffered and perished. The Armenian massacres involved issues of geopolitics that Perry and his fellow missionaries could not control. He never saw his role as that of a political activist, much less as an ambassador of an alien culture or civilization. He would have agreed with Lesslie Newbigin, a twentieth-century missionary to India, that at the very heart of the biblical vision "is not an imperial power but the slain Lamb."

Many of the issues Perry struggled with in his day have strangely become contemporary again in our own time. Terrorism, ethnic cleansing, economic upheaval, the boiling pot of Middle Eastern politics, the civilizational clash between Christendom and Islam – the same ferment was stirring in the waning days of the Ottoman Empire. We cannot well understand our own times without looking closely at those of Henry Perry.

Still, there is a note of equanimity, even serenity, that comes through to us in the letters and journals of Henry Perry. How did he manage to live through such shocking and terrible times with what St. Paul once called "a peace that passes understanding?" The overriding theme that resounds throughout Perry's life is: *hope*.

Near the end of his life, Perry gave himself to the study of biblical prophecy, seeking better to understand from the Scriptures of old how the purposes of God were unfolding in the drama of history. This, I suggest, was not an old man's escape from reality but rather an expression of trust in the One who promised to make all things new.

Timothy George is dean of Beeson Divinity School of Samford University and an executive editor of *Christianity Today*.

PREFACE

English writer L.P. Hartley once commented that understanding the past is like trying to understand a foreign country. One of the best ways to unlock the mysterious "foreign land" of the past is to read the letters and diaries of those who lived in yesteryear. Such intimate records (which email has stolen from our times) reveal the thoughts and emotions of people who lived during events now remote from us. A treasure trove of such letters and diaries can be found in the archives of the American Board of Commissioners of Foreign Missions (ABCFM), housed at Harvard University's Houghton Library.

Organized in 1810, the ABCFM was the first American foreign missions society and sent out an army of missionaries to Hawaii, China, India, Sri Lanka, Japan, southern Africa, Turkey, and Syria. Besides work in evangelism and Bible translation, the missionaries developed schools, hospitals, and orphanages. In many parts of the world, the American Board's missionaries were the only face-to-face contact foreigners had with Americans. The Board's monthly *Missionary Herald* became a kind of Christian *National Geographic*, bringing news and pictures of foreign lands to the American people (Gilbert Grosvenor, long time president and editor of *National Geographic*, was born in Constantinople, where his father was a professor at Robert College, closely affiliated with the ABCFM missions. Many of the authors of the early *National Geographic* articles were missionaries.). Amazingly, the ABCFM's home office in Boston preserved every letter and official report of its missionaries. Today, these provide priceless insights into the activities of these Americans abroad, brilliant descriptions of the foreign cultures they served, and sometimes thoughtful reflections about the results of the meeting of American and foreign cultures.

One of the largest of the ABCFM's mission fields was the Ottoman Empire, and it was in Ottoman Turkey that Henry T. Perry worked from 1866-1913. In addition to his voluminous correspondence of fifty years, the ABCFM archives preserve Perry's half-century of diaries. Perry's letters and journals provide an eyewitness account of the last years of the Ottoman Empire, years that are the foundation for the modern Middle East. Here too are historical testimonies of Moslem/Christian relations that have assumed renewed importance since the events of September 11, 2001. From Perry's letters and diaries we learn the riveting story of one man's life and ministry during the explosion of Christian missions in nineteenth century America.

Indeed, Henry Perry's life becomes a window into important aspects of nineteenth century American culture. With ancestral roots in New England Puritanism, Henry grew up in western Massachusetts under the influence of the Second Great Awakening. His hometown of Ashfield also produced Mary Lyon, who went on to found Mt. Holyoke College, a source for many female missionaries and educators in the nineteenth century. Henry's missionary call came in Williamstown, Massachusetts, at the 1856 Haystack Jubilee celebrating the beginning of American foreign missions. At Williams College Henry came under the influence of President Mark Hopkins, who thought Christian character the most important mark of the Williams graduate. In seminary Henry ministered to the workers of the Erie Canal. Coming to manhood during the Civil War, his first pastorate was in Rolla, Missouri, where Buffalo Bill still did business with the U.S. Government. It was in Rolla that Henry met Jeanne, who was eager to share his missionary life. Before the young couple left for the mission field, Henry preached in Boston's historic Old South Church.

In Turkey, Henry found himself living in an exotic land, traveling over ancient Roman roads as he ministered where the ancient Hittites and Assyrians once ruled. The archaeological remains of these ancient peoples were just being discovered in Henry's day. The discoveries reinforced the realization that he was living in a Bible land --the land where Abraham's Haran could still be seen. Henry's diaries are full of detailed, poetic descriptions of the land and people. During his fifty years in Turkey, he traveled over 30,000 miles on horseback, bringing the Gospel to isolated villages, sometimes over the same robber-infested mountains traveled by St. Paul. With a love and concern for the betterment of the people of Turkey, Henry founded a remarkable system of schools in his mission station of Sivas, including the first school in Turkey specifically for the training of teachers. Fluent in Turkish, he often negotiated with the local government for the protection of the Christian community. His beloved Jeanne shared fully in the mission work, using her musical talents and love of children to reach out to the women and young people.

Henry's diaries and letters are also very personal, revealing the joy of Christian ministry as well as sorrow and heartache, as one by one, Henry and Jeanne's five young daughters died in Turkey. Then Jeanne herself died shortly after the birth of her last child. Alone in a foreign land with a young son and infant daughter, Henry poured out his heart in his diary, writing of both his moments of despair and his comfort found in the Scriptures and in prayer. The pathos of his reflections bring a very personal side to the missionary enterprise.

At the end of the nineteenth century, Turkey was known as the "sick man of Europe" and was often at the center of European negotiations and secret diplomacy. The United States was not involved in these European intrigues, however, and the American missionaries in Turkey were recognized by the Turks and Europeans alike as selflessly working to help the people of the Ottoman Empire. When Sultan Abdul Hamid II orchestrated the massacre of thousands of Armenian Christians in 1895, the American missionaries on the scene provided the relief that prevented thousands more from meeting their deaths. In Henry Perry's own mission of Sivas, many were martyred for their Christian faith. Henry's diaries and letters provide another eyewitness account of the massacres, which the Turkish government persistently denies.

Relief aid soon poured in from people in England, Switzerland, and the United States. Clara Barton herself, then seventy-five, led a relief team to Turkey to help the persecuted Armenians. It was only the second overseas mission for the American Red Cross, which Miss Barton had founded fifteen years before. Henry administered over $150,000 in international relief aid sent to the suffering and starving Armenians who had survived the massacres. He established orphanages for the children and work programs to help the widows become self-supporting. All this was done in addition to his continued work in the schools and churches of Sivas.

Henry left Turkey after nearly fifty years of service, before the even greater atrocities of the 1915 holocaust fell on the Armenian people of Turkey. Though he was spared witnessing this first genocide of the twentieth century, some of his co-workers remained in Sivas. One of them, Mary Graffam, actually accompanied the victims on their death march and witnessed the horror of ethnic cleansing, which killed over a million and a half Armenians. The scores of American missionaries who witnessed these events provide more testimony to the incontrovertible fact of the Armenian genocide.

Henry's diaries and letters describe the horrors of the massacres, the Christian witness of the martyrs, and his own Christian commitment to love friend and enemy alike, even as he faithfully struggled against the gates of hell. His life is an example of how we can face the clash of civilizations in our own day.

Reformation Day, 2002
Soli Dei Gloria

ACKNOWLEDGMENTS

Our gratitude and thanks go out to the many people and libraries who helped us immeasurably in researching Henry Perry's life and times. Araxi Palmer, the Armenian orphan adopted by Mary Hubbard, shared with us many of the Hubbard photos from Sivas as well as her boundless enthusiasm for our project. Norma Harris provided not only her vast background in Ashfield's history but also record books with some notes in Henry Perry's own hand. Rick Teller, archivist of the Williston Northampton School, graciously sent invaluable material from the school's copious archives covering Perry's attendance there. Gary Lind-Sinanian of the Armenian Library and Museum of America familiarized us with the library's vast resources on the Armenians and their life in Turkey. Dr. Levon Chorbajian of the Zoryan Institute was most helpful in sharing the vast Armenian oral history collection of the Institute. Aris Sevag of the *Armenian Reporter* provided valuable information on the city of Sivas. Frank Stone shared with us his research on the American missionary schools in Turkey. Reverend Dr. David Hilborn and Colin B. Sanders of London's Evangelical Alliance graciously opened the society's archives to us. John Ulrich was most helpful locating additional material in the Houghton's ABCFM archives when we were in Texas. Several Perry descendants, especially Carlton Spencer Severance, Kay Floyd, Bruce Severance, and Dale Severance, shared with us Perry documents, books, and photos in their possession.

Portions of chapters 8, 9, 13, and Appendix B appeared as "Pattern for Genocide" in the January/February 2003 issue of *The New England Journal of History*.

The staff of historical societies and institutions, both large and small, readily responded to our numerous inquiries, including the Williams College Archives and Special Collections; Mt. Holyoke College Archives and Special Collections; Presbyterian Historical Society; The State Historical Society of Missouri; the First Presbyterian Church of Rolla, Missouri; Phelps County, Missouri Historical Society; Historical Museum of the D.R. Barker Library, Fredonia, New York; The Auburn Center for the Study of Theological Education; the Stewart Memorial Library of Coe College in Cedar Rapids, Iowa; the Presbyterian Church of Williamson, New York; the Hazel Braugh Records Center of the American Red Cross in Falls Church, Virginia, and the New York State Military Museum. The interlibrary loan department of the Cypress Creek Library amazingly brought numerous nineteenth century resources into our hands. The staffs of the Day Mission Library at the Yale Divinity School Library, the Andover/Harvard Theological Library, the Bridwell Library at Southern Methodist University, the Costeneda Library of the University of Texas and Rice University's Fondren Library were all unfailingly helpful. Indispensable, however, were the librarians, especially Emily Walhout, at Harvard's Houghton Library, where Henry Perry's diaries and letters are located. The archivists of the United Church Board for World Ministries of the United Church of Christ, successor to the ABCFM, were most helpful in helping us begin our research, as well as giving consul at crucial junctures along the way. Quotations from the ABCFM archives are reprinted with permission of Wider Church Ministries of the United Church of Christ and the Houghton Library, Harvard University.

Dr. Richard Hovannisian graciously reviewed the manuscript; we deeply appreciate his critique based upon his imminent scholarship in Armenian studies. His insights and expertise greatly improved the work.

We extend special thanks to Gordon Ohanesian for his help with the details of the epilogue, and our heartfelt gratitude goes out to Franklin Ohanesian for sharing the tragic story of his family. The Ohanesians were among the nearly two million other Armenians who were forced into the horrors of the Turkish death march of 1915. How Franklin and four others of his family survived the brutality of the Turkish deportations and later rose to places of respect and recognition in America is a testimony to God's Providence and man's courage against staggering odds. Again, Franklin, we thank you!

PROLOGUE

As the first traces of the sun streaked across the eastern sky, a lone rider carefully zigzagged down the rocky Ourfa hills to the broad plain stretching endlessly to the south. A long journey still ahead, Henry Perry eased the reins of his gray Arabian. Instantly Prince surged forward in a steady canter. Suddenly the stallion's hoofs clattered loudly upon stone pavement hidden from view under a thin layer of sand. "Another Roman road," Perry mused to himself. "In this part of the country, they all go where I'm going—toward Antioch."[1] Riding circuit for three years, he had learned to recognize the cut of these ancient highways that crisscrossed Asia Minor.

By noon Perry had reached the Euphrates, crossing on the log ferry near Biredjik. On the far side, he rode to a clump of trees by the river and thoughtfully watched Prince drink the cool water. It reminded him: he hadn't had a good bath in five days. Stripping off his clothes, he plunged into the river, luxuriating in its freshness. Taking cheese and *lavash* from his saddlebag, he ate while resting in the shade. Then swinging his tall frame back into the saddle, he was once more on the long road toward Antioch.

With miles to go, Perry relaxed, letting Prince set his own steady pace. There was time to think on a monotonous ride in the desert; and Perry, on that April day in 1870, was indeed thinking. Finished with seminary, ordained as a minister, and having served three years as a missionary in Turkey, it was not surprising that on that day, as on every day, Perry was thinking about the Almighty. Gazing at the breathtaking scenery around him, he was awestruck by the majesty of God's creation. As he rode south, to his left was the great Arabian Desert, and

> At the edge of the horizon could be seen a small...mound with a tower upon it. This is Haran 15 miles distant on a perfectly level plain. Extensive ruins, and a beautiful spring of water are found there. It is the place where the father of Abraham died...On the right, toward the East, is the Amanus range of mountains, towering high and rocky... all the way from Marash to Antioch...All the lands of that outlook are of new interest to me from the fact that they are included in those of [God's] Promise to Abraham.[2]

Perry carefully recorded his thoughts and experiences in his diary during that April journey. What he wrote on 17,000 other days during nearly 50 years in the mission field of Turkey suggests what his other thoughts might have been. Riding toward Antioch, he undoubtedly was thinking of it as the city where Jesus' followers were first called "Christians." It was here that the Apostle Paul and Barnabas met and decided to go to Cyprus. The trips Perry made from Antioch up the Roman highways to Cappadocia reminded him he was traveling roads over which Paul had surely walked. Even as he crossed the Euphrates, Perry could have wondered if the elephants leaving Noah's Ark on Mount Ararat 200 miles upstream (Gen. 8:4) had multiplied into herds, followed down the mighty river, crossed Palestine, and moved into Egypt, feeding along the Nile and spreading out over Africa. Or his mind might have wandered 300 miles south to the land of Galilee where Jesus said to Peter, "I will build my church and the gates of hell will not prevail against it" (Matthew 16:18). In Perry's heart, that promise to Peter was also a promise to him. On that promise he was staking his career—yes, even his life! Perry might have wondered how the gates of hell could possibly ever be aligned against his small mission to Turkey. Little could he dream, as he rode south on the Antioch road next to the great Arabian Desert, that the forces of hell itself would indeed drive tens of thousands of Armenian Christians out into this very place to die—that the world would come to see their martyrdom as the twentieth century's first great holocaust. Certainly when he first chose to become a missionary in the peaceful Berkshire Hills of Massachusetts, Henry Perry could never have foreseen the struggle he would wage against the gates of hell.

[1] Henry T. Perry. *Diary*, August 30, 1873, ABC 47.13, from the American Board of Commissioners of Foreign Missions archive, Houghton Library of Harvard University, hereinafter cited as the ABCFM archives. Publication from the H.T. Perry diaries and other materials from the ABCFM archives is by permission of the Houghton Library, Harvard University. 39 volumes of diaries are in the H.T. Perry collection, ABC 47.13. Hereinafter the diary entries are simply cited according to date.

[2] *Diary,* April 4, 1870. The Promise to Abraham Perry referred to is in Genesis 15:18, "Unto thy seed have I given this land, from the river of Egypt unto the great river, the river Euphrates."

1
THE BEGINNING OF WISDOM
(1838-1856)

*"The fear of the Lord is the beginning of wisdom,
And the knowledge of the Holy One is understanding."*
Proverbs 9:10

Thunderclouds moved over the college town of Williamstown, Massachusetts, threatening to dampen the festive Jubilee celebration. On this warm, summer day, August 5, 1856, hundreds from around the globe had gathered at Williams College to celebrate the fiftieth anniversary of the birth of Christian foreign missions in the United States. As the rains came and the celebration moved from the open air to the old white church on the hill, the crowds couldn't help but remark how similar the weather was to that important day fifty years before.

In 1806, Christian revival had swept through Williamstown, and many college students enthusiastically embraced the Christian faith and Biblical truth. Samuel J. Mills, a college freshman, had converted to Christianity in 1801, and came to Williams with a great seriousness about his religious life. During the 1806 religious awakening, he became increasingly convinced that Christians had a duty to carry the gospel message to all peoples of the world. Mills' passion for reaching the peoples of Asia with the gospel of Jesus Christ had been encouraged by the writings and examples of England's William Carey. In 1792, Carey had published his famous *Enquiry,* urging English Christians to follow Jesus' command to preach the gospel to all nations, especially to people in the lands of Asia and the Pacific who had never heard of Christ.[1] Carey, later hailed as the "Father of Modern Missions," followed his words with action and set off with his family for

India to preach the gospel where Christ's name was not known. Samuel Mills had come to share Carey's burden for the pagans in other lands. One summer day in 1806, he invited several Williams students to join him for prayer in Sloan's meadow, near the College. Impending rain probably kept some away, but James Richards, Francis Robbins, Harvey Loomis, and Byram Green joined Mills at the grove for prayer. As Mills unburdened his heart, he was surprised and gratified that several of the other young men also had a concern for developing missions to foreign lands. Suddenly, a summer thunderstorm unleashed a cloudburst of rain on the men, sending them scurrying for shelter inside a haystack. As the rain fell, Mills and his haystack companions eagerly talked and prayed about bringing the light of the gospel to those in spiritual darkness in Asia. Perhaps Mills even encouragingly quoted William Carey's famous "Expect great things from God; attempt great things for God."[2] The men prayed together under the haystack and closed with a hymn.

During the warm months they continued to meet in the grove for prayer, always praying for foreign missions.[3] In 1808, the students formed a missionary society at Williams College, not for the purpose of sending others, but for going abroad themselves. The Society of the Brethren, as the organization was first called, took as its motto "We can do it if we will." This student organization was actually the first foreign missionary society in the United States. The constitution of the society powerfully revealed its members' burden for foreign missions:

> The object of this Society shall be to effect, <u>in the person of its members</u>, a mission to the heathen. No person shall be admitted who is under engagement of any kind which shall be incompatible with going on a mission to the heathen.
> Each member shall keep absolutely free from every engagement, which, after his prayerful attention and after consultation with the brethren, shall be deemed incompatible with the objects of this Society; and shall hold himself ready to go on a mission when and where duty may call.[4]

When Samuel Mills, Gordon Hall, and James Richards graduated from Williams and attended Andover Seminary, they met other students who also desired to create missions abroad and among the American natives in the unsettled lands of the far west. In 1810, the students petitioned the Congregationalists of Massachusetts to organize a foreign mission society, and the American Board of Commissioners for

Foreign Missions (ABCFM) was formed. The ABCFM was the first American foreign mission society. Presbyterians, Congregationalists, and other reformed denominations used the Board as their missionary agency. In 1812, the Board sent out Adoniram Judson, Samuel Nott, Samuel Newell, Gordon Hall, Luther Rice, and their wives to establish a mission to India. By the end of the decade, the ABCFM had also established missions in Ceylon, Hawaii, Palestine, and among the Cherokee and Choctaw Indians.[5]

Looking back, it seemed clear that the haystack prayer meeting had been the "Birthplace of American Missions." When Byram Green returned to Williams College in 1854, he was able to point out exactly where the famous haystack had stood. The Alumni purchased the spot and ten acres of surrounding land for a "Mission Park," and a Jubilee Celebration was organized. On the morning of August 5, 1856, a memorial haystack had been prepared on the historic site. In a grove of trees, comfortable seats were waiting for the arriving crowd of missionaries, clergymen, and public officials. At that moment, the darkening clouds overhead burst forth in a downpour. Some might have thought the rainstorm was a Providential reminder of how important that haystack prayer meeting of 1806 was to world missions.

Though rain forced the meeting to move inside the church, the spirits of the crowd refused to be dampened. Certainly the excitement of eighteen year old Henry Perry remained high. William A. Lloyd, Perry's teacher at Sanderson Academy in Ashfield, had invited him to be his guest at the Missionary Jubilee. Perry was very happy for the invitation and eager to make the most of it. As the people crowded into the church, he found a place to stand near the speaker's platform, and though the speeches and ceremony lasted for six hours, he never grew tired.[6] In back of the speaker's platform were large maps showing the location of ABCFM missions around the globe.

The Honorable David Dudley Field of New York presided over the proceedings and gave the introductory address, reviewing the history of the haystack prayer meeting and the foundation of the ABCFM.[7] He noted that Samuel Mills and his friends had been poor, and the times seemed unpropitious for such a grand missionary scheme. War raged in Europe. Prussia was fighting France, and America itself was on the verge of war. Undaunted by these troubling signs, "these young men went forth to a conquest more glorious than the conquests of Alexander."[8] Fifty years later the ABCFM had over one hundred stations around the world, and plans were made to plant a tree for every missionary station on the globe at the new Missions Park.

Williams Professor Albert Hopkins delivered the Jubilee Address. Professor Hopkins reviewed the times and the men of the haystack meeting and examined their bearing on the great problem of converting the entire world to Christ:

> The men of the haystack taught a dull, material age, the value of ideas; that an age is glorious, not in proportion to its material wealth, but in proportion as it finds its life in thought and principles...[9]

Not only were the men who formed the missionary society at Williams men of ideas, they were men of deeds. Many had expressed concern about the lost souls in Africa, but Mills went to Africa. Many had prayed for the heathen in far off lands; but Hall, Richards, and Rice went personally to carry the gospel to them. Now, fifty years later, Hopkins challenged the Jubilee listeners to follow the lead of the haystack men and convert the entire world to Christ. Men and women who preached Christ by the examples of their very lives and character should be sent to the mission field. Missionary teams who were mighty in Scriptures, filled with the Holy Spirit, and discerning of the world around them were needed to shine as light in the dark places of the world.[10]

After the singing of hymns, Albert's brother, Williams' College President Mark Hopkins, delivered an address. If Albert Hopkins' speech had opened young Henry Perry's eyes to the needs of foreign missions, Mark Hopkins' words seemed to Henry a personal call to be a missionary:

> May we not hope that here the purpose shall be formed by many to take up the sickle and reap in that harvest whose field is the world? May there not be many who shall kneel on yonder spot, and pray as Mills and his associates prayed, and devote themselves to the cause of God and men as they devoted themselves? The cause of Christ is the great general issue in this world. For that I wish this college to stand.[11]

Though Henry stood immovable throughout President Hopkins's address, his heart and soul were deeply stirred by every word. Like the men of the haystack meeting fifty years before, he knew the cause of Christ was the central issue in the world, and he felt called to be among those bringing the gospel message to foreign lands. The remaining nine speakers, along with the hymns and prayers, only deepened Henry's call. A passion for the foreign mission field began to grow within him.

Rufus Anderson, Senior Secretary of the ABCFM, spoke of standing less than a year before at Antioch in Syria, where the early church had sent out the first Christian missionaries. Anderson called Williams College the Antioch of the Western Hemisphere, because it was here in this place that the first personal commitments of men for missions were made. In the fifty years since its founding, the ABCFM had sent out 358 ordained missionaries, as well as 26 physicians, 138 lay helpers, and 616 female assistants. Over 600 native helpers were also supported in the field. In 1811 the new organization received $1000 for the support of missions; in 1855 $310,000 was received. Missionaries were sent to Hawaii, Micronesia, China, Ceylon, India, Persia, Syria, Lebanon, Turkey, Greece, Africa, and the western wilderness of America. Anderson concluded by noting that God continued to govern the world, controlling the movements of men and nations to extend His kingdom.

The Board's missionaries came from all denominations, including Baptists, Congregationalists, Presbyterians, and Episcopalians. Reverend Stephen Tying, an Episcopalian from New York, challenged his hearers to remember the central message of missions:

> We have no differences in this work. We have one great message to deliver, one great work to accomplish, one great harvest to reap. A free salvation for sinners in the blood of Jesus, the only-begotten Son of God is our message. The gathering of converted souls to Christ is our work. The building of a spiritual Church with new-born souls, in the enclosures of grace and glory, is our final harvest.

Reverend Tying also warned against the identification of material advances of civilization with Christianity:

> I think there is an alarming tendency to ... look at the temporal elevation of a savage community, and a melioration of the outward and social evils of the present life, as a real extension and operation of the Gospel. The preacher at home and the missionary abroad, are both exposed to this delusion; and we must guard against it. Let us never mistake the progress of outward advancement in the present life, for that real conversion of soul which is still indispensable for the salvation of another.[12]

Bringing railroads and industrialization to a developing country could not awaken a sleeping soul. What was needed everywhere was a simple, powerful preaching of the gospel.

Emory Washburn, a Williams alumnus and former governor of Massachusetts, recognized the Providence of God in the establishment of the ABCFM and the expansion of foreign missions:

> No one can contemplate, for a moment, the history of the missionary enterprise in this country, without being struck by the economy of the divine Providence ... by which the great work of Christianizing the Pagan world was here conceived and undertaken. Friendless, feeble, unknown to the world, ... they gave the first impulse to an enterprise, compared with which the conquests of an Alexander or a Genghis Khan were but the work of a day. It was Providence working out anew its great designs by the humblest of instrumentalities.

Though the organizers of the ABCFM were few and feeble, they were able to accomplish what could not be accomplished by the nation itself. Without armies or political connections they planted schools, churches and institutions which bore the fruits of a moral culture. Washburn contrasted two important events launched in February 1812. One was Napoleon's advance against Russia; the other was the ABCFM's first missionaries setting sail for India. One began with a great show of success and ended in failure; the other did not draw attention to itself, but the enterprise still grows and succeeds.[13] Reverend Gordon Hall, whose father of the same name was an early missionary from Williams who had died in India, asserted that if Bunker Hill deserved its monument as one of the opening scenes of the American Revolution, then the spot of the haystack meeting deserved a monument, for here was the origin of the ABCFM, an organization "destined to revolutionize nations."[14]

Speaker after speaker deepened Henry Perry's conviction that his place in life was on the foreign mission field. As the hours passed, Perry never tired of standing and listening to the parade of godly men celebrating the missionary work of the past fifty years. Some said the Lord's Prayer in Tamil or Arabic. Reverend Hiram Bingham, pioneer missionary to Hawaii, sang a hymn in Hawaiian. Could the young Perry have imagined that one day he would become a co-worker with the distinguished Elias Riggs of Constantinople when Riggs spoke of the growing work among the Armenians in Turkey? Perry heard for the first time of Aintab, Turkey, where the first missionary was driven away with stones, but in 1856 a church of 167 and a congregation of seven or eight hundred flourished. Could he have dreamed that within ten years Aintab would be his first mission station?

Throughout his life Henry Perry looked back to that day of the Haystack Jubilee Celebration as the day of his call to the mission field. Over seventy years later, in a March 12, 1928 letter to Williams College, Henry recalled that momentous day:

> My interest was so great that I was not wearied by so many hours of continuous standing and my decision for the mission service was first reached there.
>
> On account of the rain the Haystack Service was held in the old White Church on the hill, near the Greylock Hotel.
>
> In the crowded assembly the boy will choose his standing place between the speaker's platform and the pews. I was near the Presiding Officer Hon. David Dudley Field of New York, whom I loved to watch. Facing me and back from the Speakers on the platform, were hung the Mission Maps.
>
> The outlook of that meeting...was that, as we enter another half century.... we shall go "forth to preach everywhere the Lord working with us..."[15]

Though Henry's call to the mission field came during the Jubilee Celebration at Williams, his boyhood at the nearby Massachusetts town of Ashfield had encouraged his receptivity to a call to missions. Ashfield was nestled in the beautiful hills of western Massachusetts. The English had first settled the Ashfield area in the 1740s, when the region was still threatened by Indian attacks during the colonial wars between the French and the English.[16] When hostilities between the two countries again broke out in 1754, the ten to fifteen families in Ashfield moved to safer settlements to the east for 2 or 3 years. Only after building a protective fort and receiving a company of nine soldiers as guards did the settlers return in 1757.

In 1762, the town proprietors called Jacob Sherwin of Hebron, Connecticut to pastor the newly organized Congregational Church. Reverend Sherwin, a graduate of Yale College, became the church's first pastor the following year. Reverend Sherwin's sister, Hannah, had married David Perry in Hebron, Connecticut in 1761, and some years later Hannah and David moved to Ashfield.[17]

David Perry was the fourth generation of his family to live in Massachusetts. During the 1630's widow Sarah Perry and her five children had immigrated from Devonshire, England to Plymouth, Massachusetts as part of the Great Migration of Puritans. Though 13,000 came to Massachusetts in those years, the 1630's immigration to Massachusetts came to be called "Great" not simply for the numbers involved, but because of the unique character of the settlements the Puritans formed. Religious convictions were foremost to these immigrants, and they came to New England for conscience's sake. Puritans believed the English church should be cleansed of the extra-Biblical traditions and practices that were obscuring the purity of the Gospel. Usually well-educated and prosperous merchants or landholders, the Puritans in England for a time tried to work through Parliament to change royal policies. When King Charles I dissolved Parliament in 1629, he deprived the Puritans of any way to legitimately protest, and thousands decided to move to the American wilderness to establish a more Biblical society. Economically the well-off Puritans had more to lose than gain by immigrating, but they looked to benefits more in the next world than in this. It would be better to undergo hardship and form a Biblical society in America than to be comfortable in England without being able to worship the Lord according to His Word. Because of their strong religious purpose, the Puritan settlements were organized into towns, with the meeting house or church at the center of the town both geographically and spiritually.[18]

The first Perrys in America settled in Sandwich, Massachusetts, where they were active in the affairs of the town and the Congregational Church.[19] As the town lands in eastern Massachusetts were divided, members of the second and third generations of the earliest settlers began moving westward to establish new settlements. Thus began the inexorable westward migration that continued until the end of the nineteenth century. Henry Perry's great-grandfather David, born in Sandwich, Massachusetts in 1729, lived for a time in Hebron, Connecticut and then near Springfield, Massachusetts before moving to Ashfield. Several of David and Hannah Perry's children moved into western New York searching for better farmland.[20] John Perry was apparently the youngest of David's children and remained in Ashfield with his parents.

The hard, rocky soil of Ashfield made it unsuitable for large scale farming, yet through diversification farmers were able to provide for their families. In the summer, corn and hay were grown for the cattle and sheep that were the livelihood for many. Apples and apple cider production provided income in the fall. The surrounding hardwood forests of oak, birch, beech, ash, hickory, and maple supplied lumber for numerous sawmills in the winter months, and maple sugar was produced in the spring. Though summers were warm and humid, the winters were frigid, with temperatures often in the single digits and occasionally plummeting to -20^0F. Snow covered the ground from December to April and often blocked the roads in February and March. The soil and weather combined to make hard work a necessity and strong character an important aid to enduring the rigors of living on the western Massachusetts frontier.[21]

In 1792 John Perry married Eunice Cooledge in Leyden, Massachusetts and established his home in Ashfield. The couple had nine children. When they came of age, several of the children moved to western New York, as did many Ashfield young people. The hills around Ashfield simply could not provide for everyone in the next generation, and many looked westward for better farmlands. Though the days of the Puritan descendants were consumed with the hard labor of establishing farms in a frontier area, their thoughts were frequently on eternity and the things of the spirit. The things of this world might occupy their time but never consumed their thoughts. This was true of the Perrys who moved westward as well as Henry's own father, Alvan.

Alvan Perry, the sixth of John and Eunice Perry's nine children, was born in Ashfield in 1806. He seems to have been the scholar of the family. Education had always been important in Ashfield, and Alvan did well in the Ashfield schools. In his later Ashfield schooling his teacher was Mary Lyon, later a leader in female education and founder of Mount Holyoke College. After completing his own schooling, Alvan taught for several years in the Ashfield common schools. He was very successful in governing his classes and on several occasions was called upon to complete terms at which other teachers had failed. The teacher's salary was small, however, and in 1832, Alvan went to Shelburne, nine miles from Ashfield, to open a store. The account books still exist, and they provide an interesting record of daily business activity.[22] In June 1832, for example, the account books reveal that items sold included buckram, padding, stay laces, wicking, ginger, cake soap, suspenders, codfish, silk twist, calico, combs, and iron spoons. The very listing of items conveys something of the time period.

Like his brothers in western New York, Alvan worked hard, but he did not become consumed with his business affairs; he always maintained a keen interest in the things of the spirit. This world was fleeting, and Alvan's eyes were fixed on eternity.[23] His extant letters from Shelburne to his parents in Ashfield are not only filled with news about his daily life; but include spiritual reflections about the need to be prepared to face his Creator at any moment, for no one knew the length of his life.

In 1834, Alvan moved his store to Ashfield and married Sarah Ann Sanderson. Sarah Ann's ancestors had also been part of the Puritan Great Migration to America in the 1630's. Immigrant Thomas Sanderson had been the first silversmith in Massachusetts and had minted the pine tree shilling. Sarah Ann's grandparents were prominent citizens of Whately, Massachusetts. Grandfather Col. Josiah Allis had been a militiaman in the Revolutionary war, a representative to the Massachusetts legislature after the war, and a delegate to the Massachusetts State Convention to ratify the Federal Constitution in 1788.[24] Sarah's parents, Chester and Anna Allis Sanderson, had moved to Ashfield shortly after their marriage. Chester was active in the affairs of the Ashfield community, serving as justice of the peace, town treasurer for six years, selectman for five years, and twice representing Ashfield in the General Court. Chester's brother, Reverend Alvan Sanderson, became a pastor of Ashfield's Congregational Church in 1808, but left the pastorate seven and a half years later because of consumption. Reverend Sanderson had a passion for missions and serving others. He used his funds to further support Christian ministry and to establish an academy in Ashfield. In 1821, four years after his death at the age of 37, Sanderson Academy was established in Ashfield for the education of both girls and boys. In coming years the Academy became an important educational institution in the town.

After their marriage, Alvan and Sarah Ann ran a store in Ashfield. Alvan also prepared Essences, especially peppermint, for the peddlers of those days. In the 1830's Ashfield had a population of around 1730. In addition to 5 stores, the town had 250 houses, 4 churches, 13 schools, 1 academy, 3 taverns, 2 gristmills, 9 sawmills, 3 clothier shops, 3 carding machines, 2 machines for turning broom handles, 5 blacksmith shops, and 2 tanneries. Alvan was active in the life of the town. With his interest in education and his strong Christian faith, he became a deacon in the Congregational Church and was assistant superintendent of the Sabbath School. For fifteen years he was also on the town's School Committee and later became a trustee of the Sanderson Academy. From 1845 to 1851, he served as a town selectman. Sarah wisely managed the affairs of her home and was a loving mother for the two Perry children, Sarah Ann, born in 1835, and Henry Thomas, born May 6, 1838.

Soon after Henry's birth, circumstances drew Alvan back to farming on his father's farm. One day a rusty nail from the store window shutter pierced Alvan's hand, and from it he developed a severe case of lockjaw. The case was so critical that the doctor decided Alvan must leave his work in the store and go on a farm. Alvan leased the store in town and bought eighty acres of the ancestral Perry property from his brother John.[25] The farm was a perfect place for a boy to grow up, and over eighty-five years later Henry fondly recalled those early years:

> On my father's Farm in the Eastern part of Ashfield, Mass., at the head of a valley opening toward Deerfield, and overlooking a cross-section of the Connecticut river-basin, with sharp protecting hills in the north and west, - I had the first experience of this world, which I can remember. Occasional ridges of black fire-rock revealed the fact that the springs of water among the hills were abundant, clear, and cool. Grass-covered fields and meadows, the hillsides for pasture, and strips of forest, occupied their third of the farm.
>
> The little white house with its barn and sheds, were built among maple and apple trees, on an elevated plot of ground, as if fitted by nature for them. From this point of observation Mt. Monadnock (100 miles away) can be clearly seen above the horizon in good weather.
>
> Near the street gate was a cozy three-cornered triangle, with a road leading from each corner. On one side was the primitive road over the hills from Deerfield to Albany in the times of the Indian trails. The connection southward was to Northampton and New York. Deerfield and Greenfield on the east; Chesterfield and Westfield southward; Plainsfield and Pittsfield on the west...[26]

Henry flourished on the farm. His grandmother noted he ran everywhere out of doors, never walked, and he relished the fresh, seasonal food the farm produced.

As Alvan developed the farm, he always did so with the encouragement that all was being done for "Alvan Perry and Son." He had a quiet, assured way of telling Henry,

> Henry, if we work this farm well, we can turn 80 or 100 fat sheep every spring for the Boston Market; two or three fat cows in summer,

and one or two of our hogs. Our own hay, grain, and milk will do this, and for all we want.[27]

This kind of leading was all Henry needed to enthusiastically do his share of the work. Until he was fifteen, Henry and his father enjoyed working the farm together. At ten Henry was able to work alone in the hay fields, hitching up Charley the horse to the hayrack, riding down to the pasture by the spring, mowing the grass and fern, and then bringing it up to dry near the barn. Every morning in winter, however cold the weather, Henry was at the barn to feed the animals. When the buyers came in April and bought the sheep for the Boston market, the payment was always in cash bills. Henry remembered,

> Father would bring and spread them on the table for us to play with, comparing the engravers work, and the values. It was a reward to make us feel, that we had helped in the work, by which this money had come to the family.[28]

Regardless of how much work there was to be done on the farm or in the store, Alvan Perry never missed morning devotions with Sarah Ann and the children. Theirs was a "happy, Christian, Puritan home."[29] Regularly they read the Bible through, each person reading a verse until a chapter was finished. Alvan's prayer was not too long, and Henry never found the morning exercises tedious. In the evenings around the kitchen fire the family also read Bunyan's *Pilgrim's Progress*, Washington Irving, or Sunday School books aloud. Undoubtedly stories of ancestors from colonial times and the Revolutionary period were also retold when the larger family gathered together. Sunday services and Sabbath school were a regular part of the Perry family's life, as was the Wednesday prayer meeting. The spiritual example Alvan set made a strong impression on young Henry, and Henry's respect and admiration for his father remained deep throughout his life.

Henry's love and respect for his mother were also unfaltering. In later years he recalled that her loving disposition was manifest in everything she did:

> It was the unbreakable bond, which held our family together. It was her prevailing temper, to the extent that she never indulged in scolding. I say never because with all my shortcomings, I cannot remember that she ever scolded me. She would show grief, and express regret; but she did not lose self-control, even to say much in the way of

reproof. I think suffering love is the strongest possible motive which can call children to obedience.[30]

Though from an early age Henry helped his father in the farming activities, he also readily helped his mother with carding wool or sewing, gaining skills with a needle and thread that would be quite useful in later years.

In her daily life Henry's mother clearly showed her Christian character, delighting in prayer and the study of the Holy Scriptures. She kept her house in good order:

> From garret to cellar. No piles of incomplete pieces of work were left to mar the place anywhere! In the morning when the children must be sent a mile and a half to school, the breakfast and worship were never allowed to be late...On Sunday mornings she had all the garments for the worship at church selected, placed in the row for each and warm. Without hurry or bustle we were off for riding or walking a mile and a half to the church "on the hill," in time to arrive without failure to our place.[31]

Growing up, Henry loved the outdoors. He was very fond of fishing in the various brooks near the farm, and "the pickerel of the Ashfield pond were an easy prey." Grandpa Sanderson gave Henry a shotgun for hunting, and he sometimes brought grey squirrels to his mother for cooking. He wouldn't shoot the red squirrels because they were too small and not as good for food. Hours were spent with his dog Major. Henry would hide, and Major would run to find him. Sometimes Henry would try to cover his scent by running in the brooks. Henry enjoyed the water and swam like a fish. Once when he and his cousin Elon were swimming in the Ashfield lake, Elon went out in the deep water near the lake outlet where the current was strong and began to sink. Henry grabbed him with one arm and struggled to swim to shore with him. It was a severe struggle. Henry brought Elon to safety, then fainted on the bank of the pond.

Henry's best friend, Henry Boice, lived on an adjoining farm, and the two Henrys enjoyed many outdoor adventures together. They would meet early in the morning to gather chestnuts. They knew how to jar the trees to bring the chestnuts down and could easily bring home a half a peck of chestnuts. The boys could spend hours in the woods gathering berries. However, in 1850, after a brief illness, Henry Boice died. This was Henry Perry's first experience with death, and he was deeply grieved. The death of his boyhood friend was an important preparation for Henry becoming a Christian a few years later. He began to understand life was to be lived for eternity, not just the here and now. Henry's sister, Sarah Ann, had become a Christian earlier and encouraged Henry in his Christian faith: "She it was, who took me by the hand and led me to the pastor's 'inquiry meeting.'"[32] Henry's Christian faith and commitment became the consuming passion of his life, as it was to his parents and had been to his Puritan forebears.

For his early schooling Henry attended the Beldingville common school in Ashfield. Such schools often had one teacher with twenty-five or thirty pupils ranging in ages from five to twenty-one. School was held six months during the year; the rest of the time the children were needed to help on the family farms. Uncle Daniel and Aunt Almira Williams' farm adjoined the Perry farm, and Henry and his sister Sarah Ann walked to school with cousins Harriet and Elon. Sarah Ann studied harder than Henry and was the best scholar in all the schools. Henry was very proud of his sister; her constant goodness to him made it impossible for him to tease her. Sometimes Alvan Perry taught school in the winter, and he would take the children with him in his sleigh. The children were tucked into the bottom of the sleigh to keep warm. Sometimes they tumbled out, but they never were hurt. Throughout his life Henry kept in his memory an unfailing picture of his father at the Beldingville School:

> He had a very strong will, combined with a tactful patience and wisdom. As in his school so in our house, his word was obeyed as a matter of course...a little twelve inch ruler in his hand; usually walking about the crowded school room, in full charge of his little workshop, quick in movement; of pleasant, helpful countenance; accurate and efficient.[33]

It was amazing that Alvan could keep up the farm, teach school, and actively participate in the affairs of the church and community, but Alvan's health had steadily improved over the years. In 1853 he decided to again re-open his store in Ashfield on the main street and repaired the second story for the family dwelling. Fifteen year-old Henry was in charge of the farm that winter, and Alvan went to Boston to purchase goods for the store. Alvan moved the family to town in the summer of 1854. "Alvan Perry and Son" was now a mercantile business and no longer a farming enterprise. Alvan carefully taught Henry the principles of double-entry bookkeeping, and Henry kept much of the store's accounts. It would be experience that would stand him in good stead in years to come.

When Henry completed his common school education, he attended Sanderson Academy, where Alvan was a trustee, and then Shelburne Falls Academy in 1855. As the only son, Henry was preparing to enter into business with his father in Ashfield.

In March of 1856, while at the Shelburne Falls Academy, Henry realized he was getting the measles, and he walked the nine miles from Shelburne to Ashfield to be at home during the illness. By April Henry was recovering, but his mother became severely ill from the measles she had contracted from him. Her fever was high, and there was a great concern about her recovery. What joy there was when Alvan came into Henry's room and awakened him one night with the news that his mother's fever had broken and the danger had passed. Undoubtedly father and son joined in a prayer of thanksgiving for Sarah Ann's recovery.[34]

It was during the summer of 1856, that William Lloyd, Henry's former teacher at Sanderson Academy and then a student at Williams College, invited Henry to the Jubilee Celebration at Williams. Attending the Haystack Jubilee became a turning point in Henry's life. Here he heard God's call to the mission field so clearly there was no turning back. The family farm and store in Ashfield, though dear as childhood memories, had no hold on Henry's future; he was called to serve in foreign lands. Williams College, with its missionary-minded President, Mark Hopkins, seemed the best school to prepare him for missionary life. In the winter of 1856, Henry went to Williston Academy to prepare himself for Williams.

---

[1] The full name of Carey's work was *An Enquiry into the Obligation of Christians to Use Means for the Conversion of the Heathen.*
[2] Timothy George. *Faithful Witness.* Christian History Institute, 1998, 32.
[3] In 1854 Byram Green wrote Professor Albert Hopkins a letter describing the details of the famous haystack prayer meeting. The letter is reprinted in *Proceedings of the Missionary Jubilee Held at Williams College.* Boston: T.R. Marium & Son, 1856, 7-9. John Nelson, Calvin Bushnell, Rufus Pomeroy, Samuel Ware, Edwin Dwight, and Ezra Fisk were among those to join the original group.

[4] *Proceedings of the Missionary Jubilee*, 9; "Haystack Prayer Meeting," *Dictionary of Christianity in America* (eds. Daniel G. Reed, Robert D. Linder, Bruce K. Shelley, Harry S. Stout), Downers Grove, Illinois: Intervarsity Press, 1990, 515.

[5] "Condensed Sketch of the American Board of Commissioners of Foreign Missions," *The Missionary Herald*, vol. 81, October 1885, 387-388. Prior to the ABCFM there had been American missions to the American Indians, but little concern with foreign missions. Though the ABCFM's early years did focus on American Indian missions, it also became actively involved in numerous foreign missions.

[6] On January 21, 1866, the Congregational Church at Williamstown was destroyed by fire. The current church on the hill was then built.

[7] David Dudley Field was a distinguished lawyer and graduate of Williams, 1825. He was very active in legal reform. His reformed civil, criminal, and penal law codes were adopted in numerous states, in whole or in part. He also wrote "Outlines of an International Code" which was highly respected. "Field, David Dudley," *Appleton's Cyclopedia of American Biography* (ed. James Grant Wilson and John Fiske), vol. 2. New York: D. Appleton & Co., 1887, 447-448.

[8] *Proceedings of the Missionary Jubilee*, 13.

[9] *Proceedings of the Missionary Jubilee*, 36.

[10] *Proceedings of the Missionary Jubilee*, 28-29.

[11] *Proceedings of the Missionary Jubilee*, 52. In his personal copy of the Jubilee proceedings that Perry purchased when he became a student at Williams College, this passage in Mark Hopkins' address was marked. It must have been a part of the proceedings that led Perry to feel called to the mission field.

[12] *Proceedings of the Missionary Jubilee*, 67-69. Henry Perry later marked these quotes from Reverend Tying's address in his copy of the *Proceedings*.

[13] *Proceedings of the Missionary Jubilee*, 73-75.

[14] *Proceedings of the Missionary Jubilee*, 90.

[15] Henry T. Perry on "The Haystack Centennial," March 12, 1928, in Williams College Archives.

[16] The settlement was originally called Huntstown, in honor of Captain Ephraim Hunt of Weymouth, who had been sent on an expedition into Canada during King Williams War in 1690. In 1736 members of the expedition were tardily paid for their services with grants of land in the newly organized town, though none of the original grantees ever lived there. When Huntsdown was incorporated in 1765, Governor Bernard renamed the town Ashfield after Lord Thurlow Ashfield of England. Frederick G. Howes. *History of the Town of Ashfield*. Ashfield, 1983 reprint of 1910 edition, 15-23, 73-74.

[17] *History of Ashfield*, 20-21, 34; "Ezra Perry of Sandwich, Massachusetts," *New England Genealogical Register*, October 1961, 185. Reverend Sherwin's father, also Jacob Sherwin, had been a Proprietor and clerk of the town of Ashfield since the 1730's.

[18] Virginia De John Anderson. *New England's Generation: The Great Migration and the Formation of Society and Culture in the 17th Century.* Cambridge University Press, 1993.

[19] Sarah Perry, widow of Edmund Perry, came to Massachusetts with her children Ezra, Margaret, Hannah, Edward, and Deborah. One of Edward Perry's descendants was Commodore O.H. Perry of War of 1812 fame. Sandwich town records indicate Ezra Perry made donations for the repair of the meetinghouse and served in the militia in the 1650's. His descendants include President Franklin Delano Roosevelt, General Douglas MacArthur, the first wife of Teddy Roosevelt, and Henry T. Perry. Lydia Brownson and MacLean McLean. "Ezra Perry of Sandwich, Massachusetts," *New England Genealogical Register*, April 1961, 86-96.

[20] On September 9, 1829, one of David and Hannah's children, Hannah Perry Alexander, born 1761/62, wrote a letter from "Macdonaugh," in western New York, to her brother John Perry in Ashfield. A grandmother by this time, Hannah's health was not good, and she longed to see her relatives. Her letter reflects the difficult life of frontier farmers in this period as well as the new textile machinery bringing industrialism to New England: "...you rote David [probably John's son] was coming up. I hope you will come to. I want to see you all and I want you should go and see my children...the grasshoppers are destroying crops very mutch. We have got a poor garden. There was a great Drouth the first part of the Summer. Hay is light. Stock is cheap. We have got one hog two pigs a poor year for shugar last Spring. I like the people and place here verry mutch. We have meetings within a few rods of us. I never took more comfort in visiting than now. I wish you would come up this fall and bring your wife. I want to sea her verry mutch. We have a carding machine 100 rods from our house. A fulling mill 100 rods from here. The first of August they carded 27 hundred wt. We have got 6 sheep. We are in a good country for water. You must come and eat some of our watermelons we have so many. I wish to be remembered to all...." Letter in authors' possession.

[21] J. Ritchie Garrison. *Landscape and Material Life in Franklin County, Massachusetts, 1770-1810.* Knoxville: University of Tennessee Press, 1991; Josiah Gilbert Holland. *History of Western Massachusetts*, vol. 2, part 3. Springfield: Samuel Bowles & Co., 1855; *Inventory of Town and City Archives of Massachusetts. No. 6 – Franklin Co.*, Vol. 1 – Ashfield. Boston, Massachusetts: Historical Records Survey (WPA), 1940; *History of the Connecticut Valley in Massachusetts*, Vol. 2 Philadelphia: Louis H. Everts, 1879.

[22] Norma Harris of Ashfield currently owns the account books. The earliest book was purchased by Alvan's grandfather, David Perry, July 15, 1794, and was given to his son, John Perry, October 24, 1807. The early records contain personal accounts of the farm, cider making, and specific work done, such as a coverlet woven. In notes Henry T. Perry added to the ledger in 1926, he wrote, "These books of my father's accounts are especially valuable since they show in part in this peculiar way, the history of the Family from starting in his store in Shelburne till the Appointment to the Custom House in Boston in 1861."

[23] July 19, 1832 letter from Alvan Perry to parents in authors' possession.

[24] D.A.R. records, National number 246887.

[25] Franklin County Register of Deeds Book 103, page 274.

[26] Henry T. Perry. "A Part of the Story of My Youth on the Farm," February 1920, 1-2. Manuscript in possession of Dale Severance.

[27] "Story of My Youth," 5.

[28] "Story of My Youth," 5.

[29] "Story of My Youth," 3.

[30] "Story of My Youth," 11.

[31] "Story of My Youth," 12-13.

[32] "Story of My Youth," 21.

[33] "Story of My Youth," 6, 18.

[34] When reviewing the family account books years later, in January 1923, Henry T. Perry made a note in the account books about his walking home from Shelburne with the measles and his mother's severe illness.

2
PLANTED BY RIVERS OF WATER
(1856-1866)

"Blessed is the man who walks not in the counsel of the ungodly, nor stands in the path of sinners, nor sits in the seat of the scornful; but his delight is in the law of the Lord, and in His law he meditates day and night. He shall be like a tree planted by the rivers of water, that brings forth its fruit in its season, whose leaf also shall not wither, and whatever he does shall prosper."
Psalm 1:1-3

Samuel Williston had established Williston Academy in Easthampton, twenty miles from Ashfield, in 1841.[1] As a college preparatory school, Williston had a strong classical department that drilled students in the Greek and Latin languages central to the college studies of the day. However, learning was not an end in itself at Williston. Samuel Williston strongly believed

> that the primary and principal object of the Institution, is the glory of God in the extension of the Christian religion, and in the promotion of true virtue and piety among men; that the discipline of the mind in all its noble faculties is, and should be deemed next in importance.

Each day school exercises opened and closed with Scripture reading and prayer, and at least once a week a lecture in the Bible was given.[2]

With its strong Christian influence and classical program, Williston was the ideal preparatory school for young Henry Perry. In the fall of 1856, Henry packed his trunk and made the twenty mile wagon trip from his home in Ashfield to Easthampton. Although students could arrange room and board at the Williston dormitory, they could save money by living and working in private homes. Perry lost no time in locating Mrs. Leonard, a widow living near the school, and agreed to chop her firewood and cultivate her vegetable garden plus pay $3.50 weekly in exchange for room and board, including washing. Mrs. Leonard was a good cook who, as Perry put it, knew how to meet the needs of the "inward man, with pork and beans, pudding, pie, etc., etc."[3]

The day after his arrival, Perry began Greek and Latin classes. Student recitations in each class lasted two hours, with the professor calling upon the young scholars to translate assigned passages. The shame of not being prepared was sufficient to motivate students to ever-harder study:

> I have to confess on the record today I had a poor Greek lesson. Spending most of my time for study on Xenophon's *Anabasis*, I had but imperfectly learned the grammar lesson, and when called up on it, I could not recite. I came home with a determination to have a perfect lesson on the morrow (5-29-1857).

In addition to Greek and Latin, there were classes in arithmetic and geography. In the middle year, there were more advanced Greek and Latin translation, algebra, English and rhetoric. In the senior year, there were more Latin (Virgil), ancient geography-history, and Euclid.

The keen scholarly competition at Williston quickly spurred the students into developing a perfectionist's outlook:

> I did as well as I expected [on my examinations] though not as well as I ought to have done (7-27-1857).

> I shall always feel determined to have better lessons than I have done and strive to make improvements (4-17-1857).

> I feel very much the want of a better command of language, both in conversation and in public speaking. I am resolved to pay particular attention to this important branch of my education (2-13-1857).

At first young Henry didn't like school. Then, later, he wrote:

> The mind is a queer thing. The more that is required of it, the more it will accomplish, provided sufficient rest is given at the proper time (6-25-1857).

It sometimes seems hard to confine one's mind to study so much, but it is my present chosen employment. I think it is best I should, and it comes much easier than it used to, and I like it better the more I study (4-28-1857).

The mind needs to be disciplined and educated. This is a good opportunity and I hope and trust I shall be successful (5-1-1857).

The eighteen year old Perry also realized the importance of an education and was thankful for it: "While studying and enjoying my comfortable quarters, I often think of those who are suffering, and I thank God that He has granted me so many blessings" (1-19-1857).

The regimen at Williston was rigorous and not for the faint of heart. Averaging six to seven hours of sleep, Perry rose at 5 a.m. and studied until breakfast, then chopped wood until the bell for the first classes. Last classes were over by 2 p.m., after which there was more study and work to be done. The strictness and intense study did not discourage Perry; he had come to Williston anticipating discipline and hard study. In winter, when temperatures often ranged between 10 and 30 degrees below zero, Perry noted that it took all of one's time to keep warm. He averaged two hours a day sawing and chopping wood for five elderly people, constantly laboring at woodpiles which kept the fires burning through the cold winter. On January 6, 1857, while outside, Perry "found it rather cold, the thermometer being 20 degrees below zero, but sawing was good exercise." In mid-February, it was more of the same: "was sawing wood when the sun rose and when it set also." But there was a bright side to the cold weather: "I find I can study and improve my mind ... better than in warm weather" (1-24-1857).

The abundance of studies or chores never caused Henry to lose sight of the ultimate spiritual purposes for which Williston was established, or to which Henry himself had devoted his life. He regularly spent at least a half an hour in the morning and in the evening in Bible study, prayer, and memorizing Scripture. He consistently sought

the blessings of God upon every undertaking I may engage in, and not to let a day pass without prayer and of reading Scriptures (12-26-1856).

All day long I have been pouring over Latin and Greek books. I hope I shall never forget to spend every morning and evening a half hour in reading of the Scripture, meditation, and prayer. For unless the blessing of God attends me, all my Latin and Greek will be of no avail (1-5-1857).

Tuesday nights there was a one-hour young men's prayer meeting which Henry often led. Another Saturday night prayer meeting was led by different teachers, but most frequently by Mr. L.T. Phillips, teacher of mathematics and natural philosophy. Each spring classes were dismissed on Williston's annual day of fasting and prayer for the national and state governments and for the schools and colleges. Students were expected to attend all three church activities on Sunday: a preaching service in the morning, a Sabbath school for Bible study in the afternoon, and another preaching service in the evening. Henry always looked forward to these Sabbath day activities as important to his spiritual growth and development. The Sabbath was a sacred day set apart for spiritual renewal and worshipping the Lord; Henry took seriously the activities of the day. The Sunday of December 21, 1856 he wrote in his diary:

> I think this has been a profitable day with me. Thought much about my consecration to God and gave myself anew to Him, and resolved to spend my life in His service in whatever sphere he may choose to place me. To follow as strictly as possible, the leadings of Providence, and do my duty. I attended the Bible Class in the morning at 9 ½ o'clock at the Chapel hall in the Seminary. Meetings all day at the Sabbath School. At six met at Blakesly and in our rooms [after that we] picked members of our class and had a prayer meeting.

On Sunday, March 8, 1857, Henry wrote:

> Another holy precious Sabbath has passed by with all its many privileges for the improvement of which I must give an account on the day of judgment. Oh! That I might live a better and a holier life and improve better the great privileges which I enjoy. I have today attended three services at church, and also the Bible class this morning at which Mr. Clark occupied the time with some good remarks from Proverbs 22:1: "A good name is rather to be chosen than great riches, and loving favour rather than silver and gold."[4]

Henry was a member of two societies at Williston, the Adelphi and the student Missionary Society. The Adelphi was a debating society that developed the students' skills in oratory, extemporaneous debate, and parliamentary procedure. The maxim of the society was printed on all its programs: "Philosophy, wisdom and liberty support each other. He who will not reason is a bigot; he who cannot is a fool; he who does not is a slave."[5] The closing years of the 1850's were tense ones for the nation, and Williston students were eager to debate the social, political, and moral questions of the day. The Whig Party went to everlasting defeat in 1852. In 1854 the Republican Party arose, and Kansas became a battle ground between the free soil and slavery forces. Issues of personal freedom and human rights became most important, and students of the Adelphi eagerly debated the issues. Debate topics of the day included:

> *Resolved*, that the Democratic Policy of Free Trade and Popular Sovereignty is detrimental to the interests of the United States.
> *Resolved*, that the course of the United States in the war with Mexico was unjustifiable.
> *Resolved*, that the odium cast upon the name of Aaron Burr is justifiable.[6]

The *Adelphi Records* show Perry taking an active part in the debates of the society. He debated the affirmative side of the following questions:

> Is Capital Punishment Justifiable?
> *Resolved*, that the world is advancing in moral improvement.
> *Resolved*, that the <u>land</u> exhibits greater wonder than the <u>water</u>.
> *Resolved*, that pride and ambition has caused more evil than ignorance and superstition.

He debated the negative side of the following:

> Is temptation ever the least excuse for crime?
> Were the principles advocated by the American Party correct?
> *Resolved*, that poetry asserts a greater influence upon the Human Character than prose.
> *Resolved*, that the importation of slaves to the United States has been injurious to the African race.[7]

At one meeting Henry also presented a "Eulogy on the Marquis de LaFayette." The Adelphi had a small library; from it Henry borrowed William Cowper's poems and D'Augbigne's *History of the Reformation* for some extra-curricular reading.

As a prospective missionary, it was only natural for Henry to be active in the Society for Missionary Inquiry. In February 1857, he joined the society by paying the 25-cent admittance fee for membership. By the time of their annual meeting, the students had raised over $100. They appropriated $60 for the Home Missions Society and sent $40 to the American Board of Commissioners for Foreign Missions. Samuel Williston was a corporate member of the ABCFM, and missionary enterprises were part of the Christian concerns of his Seminary's leadership. One of Henry Perry's fellow students at Williston was Henry Goodell, who was born of missionary parents and raised in Constantinople. Goodell undoubtedly gave Perry first hand information about Turkey, the country that would be the setting for his future missionary work.

On the occasions when Perry was not studying, working, or involved in prayer meetings and devotions, he found enjoyment in simple pleasures – swimming in the pond, fishing, hiking to the top of Mt. Tom or Mt. Holyoke, gathering walnuts, or ice skating. On July 4 he enjoyed listening to the patriotic orators in the village square and watching the fireworks. On one occasion Perry and a fellow student took three young ladies sailing on the pond for about an hour. Perry recorded in his diary, "We enjoyed it much, or at least I did" (6-3-1857).

Letters and packages from home always brightened Henry's day and earned a notice in his diary. Letters from loving parents and from sister Sarah Ann were a critical lifeline of emotional, financial, and material support.[8] On January 23, 1857 Henry recorded:

> I received a bundle from home today containing a new vest and shirt, a study robe, necktie, butter nut meats, which I suppose Father cracked, apples, and also a letter from Father. It really made my heart glad to receive such tokens of affection from home.

Henry also corresponded regularly with Pastor Clarke in Ashfield and Mr. Lloyd, the mentor who had taken him to the Jubilee at Williams. He always appreciated the good advice given by those who had taken an interest in him.

In the spring of 1857, Williston suffered a disastrous fire that Henry described in a letter to his parents:

> March 5, 1857
> Dear Parents,
> Doubtless by this time you are expecting a letter from me, and perhaps the more after hearing, as you probably will before this

reaches you, that we have lost the wood Seminary by fire. I came home as usual from the rhetorical exercises yesterday afternoon and thought I would exercise a short time at my "wood pile" before commencing the morrow's lessons. I had worked about an hour and was just going home to my room when I heard the alarm of fire and the bell commenced ringing and upon looking toward the seminary I saw a dense cloud of black smoke coming from the "L" part of the building. I went down as quickly as possible and commenced helping the students get out their things—the seminary furniture, etc. It was all bustle and confusion I tell you.... There were five or six students who were out at the time the fire commenced, and who lost all they had in their rooms, and in two cases at least...all they had in the world except what they wore at the time. One of these, a Mr. Porter, is a member of the Middle Class, ...he has no father, was boarding himself, and working his way along, and lost over $100 worth of clothing, books, etc. which were all destroyed and which was all he possessed anywhere. I presume measures will be taken to help him with some others. The building burned from 4 to 7 o'clock when it was even with the ground. It was largely insured and no great loss, but attended by considerable inconvenience. ...[9]

Later in the same letter Henry mentioned that he had received an invitation to call at Dr. Clark's, Williston's principal, through Miss Ellen, a friend of Dr. Clark's daughter. Miss Ellen suggested Henry call before the public Adelphi meeting. Henry wrote his parents, "I suppose that I may form an acquaintance with the ladies there and so company them home on that evening, but I am not going to, and if I do call before then I am not going to invite them, would you? They go in the first company here and I mistrust they would not care to have me."

The Williston school year consisted of three terms: fall, winter and spring/summer. During the ten weeks of vacation between the terms, Henry went home to Ashfield where he again helped out in his father's store and on the farms of his Uncle William and his Grandfather Sanderson. Once before going home he bought a supply of suspenders at a good price in Easthampton that he was able to mark up and sell at a profit in Ashfield. Besides helping keep the accounts and clerking at the store, Henry worked at hoeing potatoes, haying, harvesting corn, harvesting maple sap, and sawing wood. Henry enjoyed vigorous outdoor activity, writing at one point in his diary, "Work! Work!, I like to work!" (5-20-1857). A lanky six-footer, Henry was a great walker and enjoyed walking around the hills and valleys of Ashfield to visit friends and relatives and help on the farms where needed. He thought nothing of walking "over the hill" eight miles to visit Cousin Hattie at Shelburne Falls, then leaving at 6:30 p.m. to walk the eight miles home, and arriving at 9 p.m.

When Henry's father had brought him to Williston in the fall of 1856, the headmaster would not allow Henry to be placed with the 1858 graduating class, but by working hard, Henry completed his course at Williston and graduated in 1858. He even had an honor placed on his senior oration, an English version of an extract of Sallust's speech of Mimmius.[10] Henry applied to attend Williams College, whose President, Mark Hopkins, Henry held in the highest regard. Mr. John Phillips, who had taught Henry mathematics at Williston, had just transferred to Williams College where he was Professor of Greek. Professor Phillips spoke very highly of Henry Perry's record at Williston, and Perry's admission to Williams College was assured.[11]

Williams College, established in 1791, was located forty miles from Ashfield in the town of Williamstown, an isolated community of 2000 people nestled in the Hoosac Valley, encircled by the Berkshire Hills. Though founded as a secular institution by men from Yale, the college had repeatedly been swept by spiritual revivals, including that which touched the young men of the famous 1806 Haystack Prayer Meeting. In 1836, Mark Hopkins became President of the college and began to place his special stamp on the institution, giving it a strong Christian mission.

For Mark Hopkins, religious influence was more important than classroom instruction. Classroom instruction only molded the intellect, but religion formed moral character. In his 1836 inaugural address, Hopkins had stated his belief that, "The true and permanent interests of men can be promoted only in connection with religion." The character of the regulations and the very spirit of Williams College should be formed with "a regard to man as an immortal, accountable, and redeemable being." Young people must be taught to meet the evil in the world, but kept from the "fascination of the serpent" until taught to recognize his fangs.[12] Hopkins found men for his faculty who were devout and dedicated to the religious, not just intellectual, development of the students. Mark's younger brother Albert, who taught natural philosophy, prayed that the college might have a religious revival at least once every four years. For thirty-five years he conducted noonday prayer meetings for students; he also built one of the first astronomical observatories at any American college. Arthur Perry, professor of history (not related to Henry T. Perry) wrote in his diary in 1850, "I mean to be a good scholar, but I hope I shall remember that scholarship is nothing, that all worldly good is nothing compared with heavenly good."[13]

Mark Hopkins was chaplain as well as President, and his weekly addresses spoke to the students' spiritual education. Hopkins regularly invited students to his home and discussed with them the spiritual condition of their souls. His sentiment was, "What is education if it does not lead the mind to its true good? How much better to be a ploughboy and a Christian, than be a vicious, sensual, conceited collegian!"[14] Williams was recognized as a college that turned out gentlemen who were not snobs, and both students and the wider community respected Mark Hopkins. In 1849, Hopkins was elected to the Massachusetts Board of Education, and in 1857, he became President of the ABCFM. James Garfield, a Williams alumnus and later President of the United States, defined a university as "a student at one end of a log and Mark Hopkins at the other."[15] The great respect students had for President Hopkins continued throughout their lives. In 1876, James Garfield wrote Hopkins from the House of Representatives, "I state only the simple truth, when I say that your approval is more precious to me than that of any other man in the world."[16] Henry Perry was to be similarly influenced by Hopkins while at Williams. Throughout his many years in Turkey, Hopkins' portrait was on the wall of Perry's study.

Young Perry had to work hard and live frugally in order to attend Williams. The summer of 1858, he worked in the hayfields around Ashfield to earn money. Then in September he shipped his trunk to the College and walked the forty miles to save the stagecoach fare.[17] Life at Williams was simple. The dormitory rooms were bare and cold with no carpets or wallpaper. The Williams College curriculum was basically inherited from Yale and in Perry's day remained the traditional course of studies emphasizing Latin, Greek, mathematics, and moral and intellectual philosophy. The main purpose of this education was to discipline the mind and help form a balanced character. A study of the classics was thought to best discipline memory, judgment, reason, and taste. During Mark Hopkins' Presidency, Williams College resisted the Transcendentalist, Unitarian spirit of Harvard as well as the growing tendency for colleges to become schools for professional training. President Hopkins and the Williams faculty still believed a liberal education was the training of man to be what God intended he should be. Unless this deep and serious view is retained, the business of education will degenerate into a mere trade. Men will cease to work with God and for Him, and will work for money.[18]

Henry Perry's extracurricular activities at Williams reflected his serious nature and his consistent purpose to become a missionary. He continued to sharpen his speaking and debating skills in the Adelphic Union and joined the Lyceum of Natural History and the Mills Theological Society. The latter held weekly meetings dedicated to prayer, missionary reports, strengthening one another in good works, and the reading of essays on theology or Biblical subjects. Henry studied hard during the college terms, returning to Ashfield during breaks to work in the fields, accumulating more funds for college.

Even before her 1858 graduation from Mt. Holyoke, Henry's sister Sarah Ann had been teaching at a girls' school in Mount Vernon, Ohio. Late in 1859, she returned home to marry Ashfield native William Pitt Porter. Son of a minister, Porter was graduated from Williams College in 1848 and taught school for several years before being admitted to the Massachusetts bar in 1856. Sarah Ann and her new husband settled at Elmwood, a lovely home in North Adams, Massachusetts, between Ashfield and Williamstown.[19] Henry's decision to be a missionary coupled with Sarah's marriage and move to another town caused their father to leave the store in Ashfield and find another line of work. Alvan saw no need to continue in the business if the store was not going to be passed on to his children. With his experience as a merchant and through the help of his brother-in-law Henry Dawes, U.S. Representative from Massachusetts, Alvan obtained a position in the Customs House in Boston.[20] Alvan and Sarah Perry kept their house in Ashfield, but moved to Boston where they rented a place on Beacon Hill.

The day before spring vacation of Henry's junior year, on April 15, 1861, news of the capture of Fort Sumter by the Southerners reached Williamstown. There was intense excitement, and most of the students were ready to enlist in the Union cause immediately. When school resumed on May 13, the entire junior class, as did the other classes, formed a military company and elected officers. For several weeks every day after two o'clock, and again after supper, the students drilled and marched for half an hour. They wrote the Massachusetts governor asking for weapons; but on June 3, a note from the Governor arrived saying that was impossible, since too few arms were available. Interest in drilling gradually subsided, but a number of students left college to enlist in the army.[21] Henry was as stirred by the war as other young men were, but he chose to complete his last year of college before deciding to enlist.

Perry undoubtedly looked forward to his senior year, not only because it was the culmination of four years of arduous study, but also because of the moral and intellectual philosophy course all seniors took with President Hopkins. Perry's classmate and friend Samuel C. Armstrong wrote his mother September 14, 1861:

> The coming year is frought with responsibility and yet pleasure. It must tell heavily on our after lives ... We are treated like and feel like men now and must quit ourselves like men. Soon the greatest mind in New England will take and train us.[22]

Armstrong had wanted to go to Yale, but his father insisted he attend Williams simply to be exposed to Mark Hopkins. In 1882, Armstrong wrote a friend, "For a man's own upbuilding, which is, after all, the great thing, Dr. Hopkins' teaching is the best human help I know. I owe much to him, and feel it more every year."[23] Hopkins' senior course in moral philosophy encouraged students to understand the universal character of Christianity and the universal reach of God's laws. Using ideas found in the writings of William Paley and Joseph Butler in England, Hopkins showed how man's reason in nature corresponded with Scriptures. Hopkins integrated the entire college curriculum, including science, politics, ethics, aesthetics, economics, and theology, into a Christian world-view which he challenged his students to embrace. Hopkins' skill as a teacher was that he made his students think and formulate their own Christian positions, not simply learn by rote. Repeatedly Hopkins' question to the class was "What do you think?"

Henry Perry and most students found the senior year under Hopkins left an indelible imprint. Mark Hopkins labored tirelessly with these students, forging their malleable minds in the crucible of critical thinking. As iron sharpens iron he honed their intellects to graduate onto the cutting edge of history and as leaders in their world.

Every Saturday forenoon the senior class also met to study the Westminster Confession. Originally this had been part of the studies at Yale, though no longer. President Hopkins admitted that Williams was probably the only college that kept the Westminster Confession or something analogous as part of its college instruction, yet this was part of preparing young men for what God wanted them to be.

In addition to his continued participation in the Adelphic Union and the Mills Theological Society, Perry was librarian and treasurer of the Franklin Library, where students obtained course textbooks. This would not be the last time Perry's talents at bookkeeping learned in the Ashfield store would gain him a treasurer's post.

As his senior year drew to a close and the war between the north and south intensified, Perry contemplated enlisting in the army. Several of his fellow classmates, including Samuel Armstrong, were planning to enlist. Armstrong, the son of missionary parents, had been raised in Hawaii; from him Perry had learned much not only about Hawaii, but also about being a missionary in a foreign land.[24] Armstrong and many other Williams students believed strongly in the justness of the North's moral cause and were eager to play a part in the war.[25] Henry Perry considered postponing his seminary studies and enlisting in the cause. His father encouraged him to carefully consider his decision. He should consider the "leadings of providence" into the ministry. He had already spent six years preparing for this. Was the call of his country greater than the call of the Church? – "Hundreds are ready and willing to fight the battles of the country; where one is willing to work in the vineyard of our Lord." Alvan encouraged Henry to complete his preparation for the ministry; then he would be better prepared to serve his country:

> Henry after this wicked Rebellion shall have been suppressed by force of arms (which I hope will soon be done) the spirit of bitterness and hatred ... will not be in the least abated. And nothing but the Spirit of the Gospel will bring the contending parties to assimilate. Now I hope you may be fitted and ready to enter upon this work for it certainly must rest upon the young men.[26]

Apparently after talking with Uncle Dawes and carefully considering the advice of his parents, Henry decided to carry out his plans to attend seminary after graduation from Williams. The call to the mission field remained uppermost in Henry's life.

At last graduation day came on August 3, 1862. Perry had an oration at the Adelphic Union Exhibition and was Jackson Orator during his senior year. He also delivered an oration at the Commencement. Perry's Williams' class of 1862, composed of fifty-five students, was an outstanding one in many ways. The young men valued scholarship, and many were committed Christians. The class produced twenty clergymen, thirteen lawyers, eleven physicians, and sixteen teachers (some of whom were also clergymen). The four years at Williams had done much to prepare Henry Perry for his missionary work, but three more years of training still lay ahead.

Within a month after Williams' commencement, Henry Perry began his theological studies at Auburn Seminary in western New York. In the colonial period and the early days of the United States, ministers had been trained in the studies of pastors or at Harvard and other colleges. In the early 1800's, however, Harvard was moving away from its original Christian position. When Unitarian Henry Ware was appointed to Harvard's Hollis Chair of divinity in 1805, Christians began to establish seminaries specifically for theological studies. Andover Theological Seminary was established in Massachusetts in 1808; Princeton Seminary opened in New Jersey in 1812; and Auburn Theological Seminary was established in western New York in 1818. Though the earliest missionaries of the ABCFM as well as many of Williams' ministerial students in Henry's day attended Andover Seminary, Henry's father advised him not to attend the school. Alvan believed that an acceptance of German Biblical criticism was beginning to undermine Andover's doctrinal position, and he felt Auburn Seminary better adhered to Biblical truth.[27]

Henry arrived at Auburn in September 1862, a time when the war to preserve the Union was not going well; Lincoln had yet to find a general who could win a battle for him. On September 17 the army fought a bloody stalemate at Antietam Creek near Sharpsburg, Maryland. 23,500 brave soldiers, north and south, died in one day. After the battle Lincoln issued his Emancipation Proclamation to free all the slaves in the rebel states. The slavery issue was on Henry's mind as well. In November 1862, he noted:

> The time will come when all men shall be free and equal. One day is with God as a 1000 years...The length of time occupied in coming to it will not change the result. One thing seems to me certain. God will not permit this world to come to an end till this principle is worked out. Work manfully for it therefore and be not impatient.[28]

Henry's cousin and playmate Elon Williams had enlisted in Co. E of 52 Reg. Massachusetts; he became one of the casualties of the war on September 23, 1863.[29] With the country in the throes of a dreadful Civil War and affecting his own family, Henry tried to concentrate on his theological studies, preparing for spiritual conflicts and, unknown to him at the time, bloodshed and tragedy even worse than his country was then enduring.

At Auburn Henry studied under men who were not only scholars, but also had personal experience in the pastorate and Christian ministry. Courses included church history, Christian theology, Biblical criticism, rhetoric and homiletics.[30] In the summers Henry provided pulpit supply for various ministers throughout western New York. During the summer of 1863, the Sailors Missionary Society sent Henry to work with the tow boys on the Erie Canal.

The Erie Canal, opened thirty-eight years earlier, had been one of early America's great commercial achievements. In 1817, De Witt Clinton had been elected governor of New York on a pledge to build the canal. Completed in 1825, westerners along the Great Lakes could then send their produce on barges through the waterway to the Hudson River and on down to New York harbor, where the world's sailing ships were eagerly waiting. In turn, manufactured goods from New England and abroad could reach the Great Lakes region on the return route. The 363-mile canal was an engineering wonder, with a surface width of 40 feet, and 82 locks providing a lift of nearly 700 feet. Largely as a result of the ever-growing commerce on the Erie Canal, New York eventually pushed past Boston as America's major port city. Perry would see this transition in his lifetime. On his first trip to Europe he took a sailing ship from Boston; in later years he always went to and from Europe via steamers based in New York harbor. Travel was surprisingly fast through the Erie Canal. In its earlier years, it was the chief mode of transportation between New York and Buffalo, for both passenger and freight traffic. Leaving Buffalo, lighter boats, towed by frequent relays of trotting horses, could reach the Hudson River in less than four days. The chief work of the tow boys was to manage the horse teams alongside the canal's towpath.

Since its earliest days the canal had been a haven for vice and immorality. Boat workers were notorious for drinking, swearing, whoring, and gambling. The canal seemed a magnet for delinquents. A large portion of the workforce was composed of orphans and children who began working the canal at eleven or twelve years old. The Second Great Awakening of the 1830's and following had encouraged reforms among the canal workers, and a number of missionary societies had worked among the tow boat workers for decades. Converted boatmen usually left the canal for elsewhere, but others in need of evangelization and Christian teaching soon filled their places. Henry preached to the canal workers, distributed tracts, and placed Bibles wherever the boatmen spent their leisure time, from horse barns to grog shops. He learned how to handle the taunts, curses, and probably the fists and knives of the boatmen.[31] Palmyra, New York was on the center of the section of Canal he was assigned to work, and Henry became life-long friends with Reverend and Mrs. Horace Eaton, pastor of the Presbyterian church in Palmyra.

By May 1865, Henry completed his seminary studies and was ready to embark on his life's work. The Civil War had ended a month earlier, so Henry would not be needed to enlist as a chaplain in the army. He sent his application for missionary service to the American Board offices, and Secretary Treat invited him to visit Boston for an interview. In his interview, Henry was encouraged by Secretary Treat and by the dignified Rufus Anderson, who had been foreign secretary of the ABCFM since 1826, and whom Henry had heard speak at the Haystack Jubilee in 1856. Anderson had done much to shape the mission policy of the Board, advocating strengthening self-governing local churches and ordination of native pastors. He retired in 1866, and Henry Perry always was thankful his missionary service had begun under Anderson's supervision.

Rufus Anderson established the mission policy and philosophy under which Henry would operate throughout his missionary career. Anderson strongly believed that the missionary's purpose was to carry the message of Christ, not western culture, throughout the world. A firm believer in God's sovereign working in the hearts of men, Anderson taught that the missionary was only the planter; the harvest belonged to God. The missionary was not to export civilization or his own peculiarities of church doctrine to foreign lands. If schools were established, their purpose should be to train native Christian workers, and they should be conducted in the native language, not English. The preaching of the missionary should be as an itinerant preacher. Native pastors should be established in all the local churches, and the native population, not the mission board, should support them. Once self-supporting churches with native pastors had been firmly established in a region, the missionary should go home or move to another field. The missionary's goal, in short, was to establish a self-supporting, self-governing, and self-propagating church. In developing the missionary policy of the ABCFM, Anderson sought to follow the pattern of the apostles in the first century Church.[32]

On November 18, 1865, the American Board accepted Henry Perry as part of the Central Turkey Mission. December 20, in North Adams, Massachusetts, he was ordained by the mentor he so much admired, President Mark Hopkins, of Williams College. Dr. Horace Eaton of Palmyra preached the sermon on Colossians 1:24, "Filling up that which remains of the Affliction of Christ, in my flesh for His body's sake, which is the church." It was a Scripture and sermon Henry would often reflect upon during his years in Turkey.[33] After years of hard work, Henry Perry had completed his training. He was ready to fulfill the dream of missionary service Hopkins himself had helped create in him almost ten years before at the Haystack Jubilee.

While the American Board was arranging the details for Perry's missionary service in Turkey, Perry was assigned to a home mission in Rolla, Missouri, a rough section of Missouri's western frontier. When Perry arrived in January 1866, Rolla was still very much a frontier town, though settlers had been coming to that part of Missouri since the early 1800's. About 1810, Daniel Boone's son had built a sawmill near what would become the town of Rolla, but the moving force that created Rolla as an organized town was the railroad. In 1851, the Pacific Railroad of Missouri, starting from Saint Louis, had begun laying the track west of the Mississippi. Progress was slow. By 1858, three years before the Civil War, the railroad had only reached 100 miles west of the Mississippi. Railroad officials succeeded in urging local settlers to organize a town in the oak forest and thicket and have it designated the seat of Phelps County. One man originally wanted to call the town "Hardscrabble," but a North Carolinian with a southern brogue suggested "Raleigh," after Sir Walter Raleigh. His suggestion was adopted, and the town was spelled just as he pronounced it – "Rolla."

Rolla's first town council met in February 1861; at the same time the county held a convocation of whether to join the South in secession. Though the vote was "not yet," southern sympathies increased with the southern capture of Fort Sumter. Even so, Rolla remained in Union hands throughout the war. As the terminus for the Pacific Railroad, the town was heavily guarded, and Fort Wyman was built for its protection. During the war, Buffalo Bill and Wild Bill Hickok were in Rolla organizing ox wagon teams to carry supplies to the Army immediately to the west in Indian Territory.[34] Union armies stationed here marched off to numerous western battles.

As if the horrors of war were not enough, two months after the war was over a great fire swept through Rolla destroying forty buildings.

Smallpox and cholera then broke out, and the 6000 inhabitants were reduced to 600.[35] Among those who died in the epidemic was Reverend Williston Jones, first pastor of Rolla's Presbyterian Church. The First Presbyterian Church of Rolla had been organized in 1864, with a charter membership of twelve. While Henry Perry was in Rolla, and for its first five years, the Church met in the Phelps County Courthouse. Perry would spend nine months in Rolla "preaching and picking up the war-wrecked relics of Presbyterian churches."[36]

In January 1866, when Henry Perry stepped off the train at the end of the line in Rolla, he was entering an area that for more than a decade had been perhaps the hottest cauldron of hate, hostility, and heartbreak anywhere in America. Throughout the 1850s, the Kansas-Missouri border wars had raged over the issue of slavery. Open conflict and bloodshed broke out when Congress enacted the Kansas-Nebraska Act of 1854. This legislation provided that the people themselves would decide whether new states entering the Union from the Kansas-Nebraska territory would be slave or free. The Kansas-Nebraska Act spurred northern abolitionists to send settlers into the Kansas and Nebraska territories so that when the popular vote came, the new states entering the Union would be free. The Southern pro-slavery forces sent their emissaries into the territories to ensure that the territories would become slave states. Hostilities soon erupted into guerrilla warfare along the border between Missouri and Kansas Territory until the American press described the whole area as "Bleeding Kansas."

The Civil War only intensified the hatred and savagery in southwest Missouri and all along the Missouri border with Kansas Territory. In addition to hostilities between regular Union and Confederate armies, the commanding generals of both sides periodically authorized murderous raids by underground civilian groups. Missouri guerrillas in civilian attire, called "bushwhackers," regularly attacked Union targets throughout the war. Similarly, their free state counterparts, the "Kansas Jay-hawkers," mounted a steady barrage of sabotage activity in Confederate territory. As the conflict dragged on, civilians increasingly viewed their next-door neighbors with suspicion and distrust. Appomattox may have ended formal hostilities, but it did not end bloodshed in the vicinity of Rolla. Though Missouri had remained a Union state throughout the War, many Missourians fought for the South. After the war was over, Confederate soldiers returning to their Missouri homes were often shot or hanged by "Regulators" intent on keeping "Rebels" out of the state.[37]

When Henry arrived in Rolla, he saw the ashes of what was once a bustling frontier town and death and destruction at every turn. Nearly everyone the young pastor met on the street was still mourning the loss of a relative or friend that had died in the plagues. Among those living in this border state he encountered the still-smoldering hatred between families – some with rancor against the South, others bitter toward the North – and all being fueled by the venom between returning "Yankee" and "Reb" soldiers. Henry undoubtedly recalled his father's words at the beginning of the war – that when it was over, there would be so much hatred between North and South that only the gospel of Jesus Christ could heal the wounds.

The young pastor's duty was clear. Perry plunged energetically into the work of healing the mental and spiritual wounds of the frontier area. He preached funerals for the dead, prayed with the mourners, and counseled the gospel to returning veterans. He rode far into the outlying countryside to listen to the settlers' problems, pray with them, and minister the gospel to them. Yet he never lost sight of his ultimate goal of foreign missionary work. The ABCFM, recognizing the help a wife would be on the mission field, preferred not to send out missionaries unless they were married. The American Board encouraged Perry to marry before going to Turkey. Apparently Perry had proposed marriage to a lady back East and anticipated her joining him in missionary work, but his expectations proved in vain. In March 1866, Perry was uncertain as to what course to take and wrote Reverend Clark, Secretary of the ABCFM, that he was ready to go to Turkey as a single man for the present, as soon as an opening was available:

> My hope to serve the missions cause in Central Turkey is not shaken in the least by this experience. I am not despondent, for I do not believe to have the right to be betrayed into discouragement by any of these things. But I may as well confess that I am disgusted, and would gladly undertake the mission work just as I am, and at once, if it were best.[38]

Perry broached the possibility with Reverend Clark of continuing to the East after the May meeting of the General Assembly in St. Louis and waiting for the first opening in Turkey.

Though Reverend Clark gave his approval to the plan, a surprising series of events caused Henry to return to Rolla after the St. Louis meeting. Elizabeth Jones, widow of Reverend Williston Jones, the pastor who preceded Henry at Rolla, had remained in the town after her husband's death. The Joneses had two adopted daughters, Emilie and Jeanne Hannah. Emilie had immigrated to America from Germany with her father when she was six years old. When her father fell ill and could no longer care for her, the Reverend and Mrs. Jones took Emilie into their family and surrounded her with love and spiritual warmth. They encouraged her mental inquisitiveness and provided her with a good education.[39] Jeanne Hannah was born in Cedar Falls, Iowa on March 14, 1848, the third of four daughters born to John and Barbara Welsheimer. In the early 1850's John and his brother Fred went to California in the gold rush and died there; they were buried at the cemetery at Sutter's Creek. Barbara Welsheimer was unable to care for her four young daughters, and they were sent to stay with different families. Williston and Elizabeth Jones took Jeanne Hannah and adopted her as they had Emilie.[40]

Williston and Elizabeth Jones brought up Emilie and Jeanne in a loving Christian home. Reverend Jones had a missionary spirit and immediately after graduating from Lane Seminary in 1844, became an itinerant evangelist in Illinois. After he married Elizabeth, Reverend Jones moved to Cedar Rapids where he worked diligently to establish the Presbyterian church there. He was a model pastor always concerned about the souls of his people. George Carroll, a young man in Reverend Jones' church, later recalled his pastoral activities:

> Every house was visited, no matter how poor or humble its occupants, and every member of his congregation was faithfully dealt with. He reproved, rebuked, exhorted, questioned, urged, entreated, encouraged, sympathized with, and in every possible way tried to get men and women to live for Christ and Him alone. In season and out of season he presented the subject of religion and urged men to accept the Saviour... he believed that the religion of Christ was the most important of all subjects, and, therefore, that it was always seasonable and proper to talk about it and act in view of it. He believed that it was far better to talk with men about their souls at seasons that seemed a little inopportune than to neglect it altogether, as some of us are apt to do.[41]

Reverend Jones daily held family devotions with Elizabeth, Emilie, and Jeanne. Singing was an important part of their daily worship, as well as Bible reading and explanations. Family worship ended with prayers by each of the family members. When traveling on his itinerant ministry, Reverend Jones also held family devotions with whatever family had boarded him for the night. He had a great skill in dealing with young Christians and helping develop their character. A great lover of sacred music, Reverend Jones often had large singing classes for the young people. Not only did they enjoy the singing and learning elementary music principles, but they also were challenged by Reverend Jones' comments on the spiritual sentiments of the hymns. Jeanne especially enjoyed singing, and both she and Emilie readily shared their parents' love of the gospel.

In 1851, Reverend and Mrs. Jones established a school in their home to prepare young men for college. When Reverend Jones went to Buffalo, New York for a General Assembly meeting in 1853, he sought out donors to provide college scholarships for some of the men he had schooled. How surprised he was when Daniel Coe encouraged him to establish a college in Cedar Rapids and provided the funds to buy the land for the institution. Coe College continues a strong liberal arts institution today.

With the church and college firmly established in Cedar Rapids, in 1856, Reverend Jones moved his family to Iowa Falls. He had a passion for establishing new churches in the western lands and traveled all over the region of Iowa Falls telling the Gospel Story. In 1865 the *New York Evangelist* carried a notice for a minister in Rolla, Missouri, "a promising field of labor for some faithful minister who was not afraid of hard work and self-denial." It was just such a work as Reverend Jones thrived upon, and he eagerly accepted Rolla as his new mission field; Mrs. Jones, Emilie, and Jeanne joined him in the move west.

In Rolla, Reverend Jones labored tirelessly among the people of the war-torn and cholera-ravaged town. Interest in the gospel was intense when he was stricken by disease. The Joneses had just bought a house in Rolla, and Reverend Jones was carried into the house on his sickbed. On November 20, 1865 he died. His last words, characteristic of his life, were "May all be converted."[42] Elizabeth Jones and her daughters remained in Rolla to help the new pastor continue the Christian ministry showing so much promise there.[43]

When Henry came to Rolla in January 1866, Emilie and Jeanne were attending Western Female Seminary in Oxford, Ohio. Western Female Seminary was founded in 1853 as the "western" offshoot of Mt. Holyoke in Massachusetts; it continued Mt. Holyoke's missionary zeal and goal of low-cost yet high quality education for women.[44]

When Emilie and Jeanne returned to Rolla in March 1866, Henry knew he had met kindred spirits. Their love of learning, their strong

Christian faith, and their desire to serve the Lord in some useful sphere of work matched Henry's own spirit. He felt very much at home with Mrs. Jones and her daughters, but he was especially taken with Jeanne. He shared with her his call to the mission field, describing the powerful impact the Haystack Jubilee had on him ten years earlier. Jeanne was very sympathetic with Henry's desire to bring the Gospel and Christian truth to a people in spiritual darkness and blindness. The difficulties or hardships of the missionary life had no fears for her. By May 1866, Henry proposed marriage to Jeanne, and she and her mother looked favorably on the proposal.

Henry sensed that Jeanne from the first understood him in a way even most of his friends did not. She understood his spiritual goals and the dissatisfaction he often felt that his present accomplishments did not match his lofty ideals. She understood how the Gospel met the longings of his soul and gave an impulse to all his actions. Henry had a strong desire for a soulmate and friend who could share with him the real-life questions and issues as well as allow his affectionate nature to find expression. Beyond his own needs and considerations, Henry saw in Jeanne an abundance of love for others and many gifts which suited her for the missionary life. Henry wrote to Jeanne:

> ...if there is anything in me which can reach you and make you happy and contribute to the exercise of Christian gifts, your confidence and society and love shall be to me a treasure of which I feel myself unworthy.

For her part, in Henry Jeanne saw

> A noble spirit – and a heart of which I feel myself unworthy but which if I do ever call mine I shall prize as Heavens best gift. His heart is bound up in the work of Saving Souls, is a noble Christian man and able to take a high position in life.[45]

Henry was as amazed as anyone at this turn of events. In a June letter to the ABCFM's Reverend Clark, Henry described the circumstances to have occurred "in a manner as unaccountable to me as it was unanticipated and as naturally as the breath of heaven which 'bloweth where it listeth'..."[46] Though Jeanne was only nineteen, her spirit had been prepared for mission work since childhood. Her parents had shown a heart for missions at home and constantly reached out to others in Christian love. The ABCFM's annual board meeting was scheduled for Pittsfield, Massachusetts at the end of September. Henry hoped to attend the meeting with his new bride, and he trusted a position for them in Central Turkey would be assigned at that time. Though it was difficult for Jeanne to leave her dear mother, with the distinct possibility she might never see her again, she welcomed the call to missions and to sharing life with the soul mate she had found in Henry.

The summer in Rolla was a busy time as Henry continued his gospel ministry among the people. Jeanne taught school, and both prepared for a September wedding. Mrs. Jones was full of advice and helpfulness as Jeanne made preparations to set up her first home in a distant land. All three ladies of the Jones household were busy sewing clothes for Jeanne and items for her home. The American Board also gave suggestions and guidance for the move to Turkey, including what housekeeping items needed to be acquired in the States and what could be obtained abroad. Jeanne and Henry took long horseback rides together as Jeanne began to share Henry's ministry and make pastoral visits with him. The horseback riding skills would be useful in Turkey.

Fifty years later Henry Perry, looking back over his early life, missionary call, preparation for the ministry, and marriage to Jeanne, could not help but recognize God's guiding hand:

> I was happy in having been led to put my life into the hand of my Lord, and seek first of all to do His will. The discipline of His guidance was severe sometimes, but needful; for the temptations were many, and it was not always easy to live by faith for the Unseen, by the guidance of God's Word and His Spirit.[47]

At last September came. The church had a farewell service for Perry on Sunday September 16. Three days later, Henry and Jeanne were married before taking the train to St. Louis. Friends escorted the newlyweds to the depot. Mrs. Jones and Emilie rode with the Perrys to the halfway station before returning to Rolla. At St. Louis, more friends greeted the couple with enthusiasm and escorted them to their hotel. The newlyweds sent a telegram to Mrs. Jones - "Perry victorious; Jeanne most Glorious; Galt House uproarious!"[48]

[1] *Constitution of Williston Seminary*, 1845, 5 (in Williston Northampton School Archives). The Constitution's complete statement of purpose is as follows: "Believing, that the image and glory of an all-wise and holy God are most brightly reflected in the knowledge and holiness of his rational creatures, and that the best interests of our country, the church and the world are all involved in the intelligence, virtue, and piety of the rising generation; desiring also, if possible, to bring into existence some permanent agency, that shall live, when I am dead, and extend my usefulness to remote ages, I have thought I could in no other way more effectually serve God or my fellow-men than by devoting a portion of the property he has given me, to the establishment and ample endowment of an Institution, for the intellectual, moral and religious education of youth."

[2] *Constitution of Williston Seminary*, 15-16.

[3] During his time at Williston, Henry Perry kept a diary, now in the possession of Carlton Spencer Severance. All descriptions of Perry's life at Williston are taken from this dairy, unless otherwise noted.

[4] Mr. Josiah Clark was principal at Williston during Henry's years there. Saturated with the ancient languages and their literature, he delighted in teaching the Senior Class. He knew how to lead the boys into the classics, encouraging their discernment and admiration for the ancients. Mr. Clark's very life was an admirable model to the students; attendance at his Sunday Bible studies was always large. Joseph Henry Sawyer. *A History of Williston Seminary*. 1917, 106-150.

[5] *A History of Williston Seminary*, 126-127.

[6] *A History of Williston Seminary*, 127.

[7] Rick Teller, Williston's archivist, graciously culled this information from the *Adelphi Records*. Other debate topics during Perry's years at Williston reveal something of the concerns of the day:

Is a dissolution of the United States under any circumstances preferable to Union?

Which afford the greater field for eloquence, the pulpit or the bar?

Is the preaching of politics from the pulpit justifiable?

Has any nation a right to isolate herself from the world?

Should the main end of punishment be the reformation of the criminal or the prevention of the crime?

Which is productive of the most evil, intemperance or slavery?

Resolved that a country residence is more favorable to intellectual and moral improvement than a city residence.

Resolved that the right of suffrage ought to be extended to the ladies.

Is it expedient to annex Cuba to the United States?

Resolved that the gun barrel is more detrimental to human life than the rum barrel.

Has the moral influence of the United States on the whole been salutary to the world?

Is deception ever advisable?
Was the decision of the Supreme Court in the Dred Scott case constitutionally right?
Ought common schools to be supported by direct taxation?

[8] While Henry was at Williston, Sarah Ann taught at Mt. Vernon, Ohio and attended Mt. Holyoke Seminary. She was a graduate of Mt. Holyoke's class of 1858.

[9] Henry T. Perry to parents, March 5, 1857 in Williston Northampton School Archives.

[10] Henry T. Perry to Jean Severance, May 24, 1928, letter in possession of Carlton Spencer Severance; Williston Seminary. "Order of Exercises at the Annual Exhibition," July 27, 1858. Program in Williston Northampton School Archives.

[11] Henry T. Perry to Professor B.B. Snowden, August 12, 1916, in Williston Northampton School Archives.

[12] Frederick Rudolph. *Mark Hopkins and the Log.* New Haven: Yale University Press, 1956, 17.

[13] *Mark Hopkins and the Log,* 150.

[14] *Mark Hopkins and the Log,* 93.

[15] M.A. DeWolfe Howe. *Classic Shades: Five Leaders of Learning and Their Colleges.* Boston: Little, Brown & Co., 1928, 85.

[16] *Classic Shades,* 104.

[17] Jean Hannah Perry Severance, Henry's daughter, later recounted this story to her sons Carlton Spencer Severance and Gordon Barker Severance.

[18] Mark Hopkins. *Religious Teaching and Worship* (Sermon for Dedication of the New Chapel, September 22, 1859). Boston, 1859, 11-12.

[19] "Class Letters" in Mount Holyoke Archives; Joseph Sawyer. *Williston Seminary Alumni Records,* 1875, 64 (Class of 1845 information on William Pitt Porter).

[20] Henry Dawes married Sarah Ann Perry's sister, Electra Sanderson. Admitted to the Massachusetts bar in 1842, Dawes soon became active in politics, serving in the state legislature and senate and as a member of the 1853 state Constitutional Convention. For a time Henry Dawes and William Porter, Henry Perry's brother-in-law, were law partners in North Adams. Dawes served in the U.S. Congress from 1857 to 1873, where he served as Chairman of the Committee on Ways and Means and inaugurated the measure for completion of the Washington Monument. In 1875 he succeeded Charles Sumner in the Senate and was re-elected in 1881 and 1887. He was largely responsible for the legislature creating a system for Indian education. "Dawes, Henry," *Appleton's Cyclopedia of American Biography,* vol. 2, 107-108.

[21] George L. Raymond. *Fiftieth Anniversary Report of the Williams College Class of '62,* 17 (in Williams College Archives).

[22] *Mark Hopkins and the Log,* 46.

[23] *Report of Williams College Class of '62,* 25.

[24] In a 1917 letter to his son-in-law Carlton Severance, who was then working in Hawaii, Henry Perry wrote of his interest in Hawaiian missions, which he had learned more of in college: "What interesting memories attach to those former Mission Stations! ... only wishing that I might be with you to see that famous country, and study the outcome from the GOSPEL service wrought by the Missionaries. Much did I read of them in my youth: especially being interested in Reverend Titus Coan of Hilo, whom I had the pleasure to meet and hear his story when at College. Some parts of it were thrilling, perhaps from his skill in telling... Also in College Sam'l Armstrong was a classmate and personal friend, who became famous in his work for the black people at Hampton Va. Charming were his stories of the "Islands." Also "President" W'm. D. Alexander of Oahu College was at "Williams", who greatly interested me, the more from his Christian Character..." Henry T. Perry to Carlton Severance, April 10, 1917, letter in authors' possession.

[25] Samuel Armstrong, born in the Hawaiian Islands in 1839, enlisted in the army immediately after his graduation from Williams. He later became Lt. Col. 9th U.S. Colored troop and then Brig. Gen. of colored troops in Texas. After the war Armstrong was Asst. Commissioner of the Freedman's Bureau at Fortress Monroe. He resigned in 1867 to establish Hampton Institute for the education of ex-slaves and to help prepare Indians for American citizenship. Applying what he had seen in Hawaii of missionary education for the natives, Armstrong combined moral, mental, and industrial education, and Hampton Institute became a model school for others around the country. Armstrong tried to teach the students at Hampton to think, just as Hopkins had taught him and the students at Williams. Armstrong's own character influenced many. Booker T. Washington, one of Hampton's most distinguished graduates, described Armstrong as "a great man – the noblest, rarest human being that it has ever been my privilege to meet." *Report of Williams College Class of '62*, 24-25.

[26] Alvan Perry to Sarah Ann Perry, July 22, 1862; Alvan Perry to Henry Perry, July 28, 1862. Letters in authors' possession. Alvan did not specify in the letter what his "Ailment" was, but possibly Alvan suffered from severe headaches, as his son Henry did throughout his life.

[27] Amasa Edwards Park, Abbot Professor of Christian Theology (1847-1880) at Andover, strongly resisted German Biblical criticism throughout the 1860's and 1870's, but other faculty members followed a liberal emphasis. When Park retired in 1881, the "Andover Controversy" erupted over the erosion of orthodoxy at the Seminary. "Andover Controversy" and "Andover Seminary" in Daniel G. Reid, ed. *Dictionary of Christianity in America*. Downers Grove, Illinois, 1990, 61; Elwyn Allen Smith. *The Presbyterian Ministry in American Culture (1700-1900)*. Philadelphia: Westminster Press, 1962, 107-111, 163; "Auburn Theological Seminary," Alfred Niven, ed. *Encyclopedia of the Presbyterian Church in the United States of America*. Philadelphia:Presbyterian Publishing Co., 1884, 44-46.

[28] Note signed "H.T. Perry" on page 14 in college notebook, back pages of which were used 60 years later for Perry's "Story of My Youth."
[29] Burial marker in Ashfield Plain Cemetery.
[30] John Quincy Adams. *A History of Auburn Theological Seminary, 1818-1918*. Auburn, New York: Auburn Seminary Press, 1918, 117-128, 177-179.
[31] Carol Sheriff. *The Artificial River. The Erie Canal and the Paradox of Progress, 1817-1862*. Hill & Wong, 1996, 138-155.
[32] William R. Hutchison. *Errand to the World: American Protestant Thought and Foreign Missions*. Chicago: University of Chicago Press, 1987, 79-82. Anderson's policy was well illustrated and developed in Reverend C.H. Wheeler's *Ten Years on the Euphrates – or Primitive Missionary Policy Illustrated*. Boston: American Tract Society, 1868.

Rufus Anderson's emphasis on "self-supporting, self-governing, and self-propagating" churches was carried by the missionaries throughout the globe, including China. The Chinese Communists later transformed this into the Three Self Movement, twisting "the formula into a means of disassociating the church from the 'foreign influence' of orthodox Christian teaching and conforming it to government ideology." Mindy Belz. "Caesar's Seminary," *World*. Vol. 16, no. 3, January 27, 2001.
[33] *Diary*, December 22, 1867. Henry Perry's collection of diaries during his missionary service is among the ABCFM archives in the Houghton Library of Harvard University, ABC 47.13.
[34] William F. Cody. *The Life of Hon. William F. Cody, known as Buffalo Bill. An Autobiography*. Lincoln, Nebraska: University of Nebraska Press, 1978, 131.
[35] *Phelps County: Our Centennial Book*. Phelps County, Missouri, 1957, 7-21, 69-79.
[36] Henry T. Perry to Publisher of ABCFM [of *Missionary Herald*] from Sivas, Turkey, January 18, 1906, ABC 16.9.3, Vol. 37, No. 40. Unless otherwise noted, all future letters are from the ABCFM archives in the Houghton Library of Harvard University.
[37] Joseph G. Rosa. *Wild Bill Hickok: The Man and His Myth*. University Press of Kansas, 1996, 43-47, 81.
[38] Henry T. Perry to Rev. N.G. Clark, March 28, 1866, ABC 16.9.5, Vol. 2, No. 135.
[39] Emily Jones, "A Chapter in Life," June 8, 1870. Manuscript in possession of Carlton Spencer Severance; Jean Perry Severance, "Obituary of Emilie J. Barker, M.D.," typescript in authors' possession.

[40] *Welsheimer Genealogy*, 59-62. In *Diary*, January 16, 1867, Henry Perry wrote, "I may as well explain without further delay, the reason why I have so persistently written my wife's first name Jeanne instead of Jennie. Her first name as given by her own mother was Hannah Jane. When she became my wife, I preferred the name Jean to Jennie; and therefore write it Jeanne. This I much used during her lifetime; and in the case of her daughter, it was simple to ring it down to Jean."

[41] Rev. George R. Carroll, "Memorial Tribute to Rev. Williston Jones, Our First Pastor," *Fortieth Anniversary of the First Presbyterian Church of Cedar Rapids, Iowa.* Cedar Rapids, Iowa: Daily Republican Printing and Banking House, 1888, 20.

[42] Erik McKinley Erikkson. *Cedar Rapids Collegiate Institute and Its Founders, 1853-1866.* Cedar Rapids, Iowa: Coe College, 1928, 66.

[43] Though it is not documented, it is quite likely that when Henry came to Rolla he boarded with Mrs. Jones. Since the Joneses had purchased a house in Rolla, it would have been logical for the new pastor to lodge with the previous pastor's widow.

[44] Undated brochure from Western College Alumnae Association.

[45] Jeannie Jones letter from Rolla, Missouri, May 29, 1866, in authors' possession. In this letter, apparently writing to one of her natural sisters, with whom Jeannie always kept in touch, Jeannie describes her impression of Henry, Henry's proposal to her, and quotes from a letter he wrote her from St. Louis to reveal some of his own thoughts.

[46] Henry T. Perry to Rev. Clark, June 6, 1866, ABC. 16.9.5, No., 137.

[47] Henry Perry to Carlton Severance, June 15, 1916, letter in authors' possession.

[48] *Diary*, September 19, 1866.

3
COMPELLED BY THE LOVE OF CHRIST
(1866-1869)

"For the love of Christ compels us, because we judge thus: that if One died for all, then all died, and He died for all, that those who live should live no longer for themselves, but for Him who died for them and rose again."
II Corinthians 5:14

Henry Perry had kept a journal throughout his years at Williston, but the habit lapsed during the years of intense study at Williams and Auburn. As his new life began with Jeanne, Henry resumed his diary and continued it throughout his missionary years. Everyday events and often personal thoughts were chronicled for almost fifty years, making it possible to examine his life a century later and see the world through his eyes.

Jeanne and Henry had two months of whirlwind activity in Massachusetts and New York before embarking on their missionary adventure. Early September 20, 1866, they left St. Louis by morning train for Boston, leaving the next day for Niagara Falls, one of the nineteenth century's favorite honeymoon spots. Henry had visited the Falls several times when working with the Erie Canal tow boys; sharing the experience with Jeanne doubled his pleasure. The newlyweds spent an entire day at Niagara Falls. The weather was fine, and it was a great joy to watch "that wonderful display of Nature's power."[1]

Henry was eager to introduce Jeanne to his family and friends and show her as much of Massachusetts and western New York as possible. The Perrys spent their first Sunday together in Palmyra, New York, at the church of Dr. Horace Eaton, then they traveled on to North Adams, Massachusetts. There the Perrys stayed at "Elmwood," the lovely home of Perry's sister Sarah and her husband William Porter. Sarah made them feel very much at home, and Henry enjoyed seeing his Jeanne take her place with the rest of the family. The Porter children, Allie and Harriette, gave added joy to the family gathering as only toddlers can. Allie was four and little Harriette just a year old. One month after Harriette was born, a five-year-old daughter, named Sarah Sanderson, had died of diphtheria. The loss of dear children would be a repeated sorrow for both Sarah and Henry in coming years; it was good such future sorrows were hidden from them.

Henry's parents came to "Elmwood" from Boston, and the entire Perry family had a quiet visit and rest together as they welcomed Jeanne into the family. Perry recorded in his diary, "It was our joy of our dear Lord's blessing!"[2] At the end of the week Henry and Jeanne went to Pittsfield, Massachusetts for the ABCFM annual board meeting. They stayed with Aunt Electra Dawes, whose house was overflowing with missionaries for the meeting. Jeanne and Henry had to sleep on a little bed made up for them in Aunt Electra's large pantry, but it was a wonderful opportunity to meet the missionary delegates! Many gave words of advice and encouragement to the young couple just setting out for the mission field. The wife of Congressman William Dodge, one of Aunt Electra's guests, gave Jeanne a fine leather traveling bag.[3]

The Perrys spent the first week in October in Ashfield, visiting and receiving visits from relatives. Henry also received invitations to preach in both North Adams and Ashfield. Alvan, Henry's father, had to return to work in Boston, but Henry's mother stayed in Ashfield to be with Henry and Jeanne before their all too soon departure for Turkey. As an only son, with primary responsibility to care for his parents if need arose, it was difficult for Henry to leave for a distant land. Only a conviction that this was the Lord's leading led him to take such steps. Alvan, also convinced that this was the Lord's leading, cheerfully gave his blessing to Henry's missionary plans. After selling his Ashfield business and beginning work at Boston's Customs house, Alvan and Sarah Ann had found an apartment in Pemberton Square on Boston's Beacon Hill, not far from the ABCFM offices. They would be able to keep in close contact with all the news received from Turkey. The ABCFM also agreed that if Mrs. Perry needed Henry's help, he would be released from his missionary service and allowed to return to Massachusetts.

October 20, Jeanne, Henry, and his mother left Ashfield and journeyed to Boston by train. Only a month and the young missionaries would leave for Turkey. Alvan had found adjoining rooms for Henry and Jeanne in the apartment house where he and Sarah Ann lived. There the four were able to live together as a family, and Henry was able to spend time with his dear parents before his departure. Jeanne had a beautiful voice and loved to sing. During their few weeks in Boston, Henry arranged for her to take lessons from a vocalist with the Conservatory of Music. It was a rare opportunity, and Henry delighted in the joy on her face each morning as she started for the Conservatory with music in hand! While Jeanne was away, Henry spent time with his mother, telling her of his many experiences on the Missouri frontier and occasionally taking her out.

Alvan and Sarah Ann were members of Boston's Old South Church, where Alvan was also a deacon. One Sunday in November Henry was invited to preach in the historic church where in 1773 Sam Adams held meetings leading to the Boston Tea Party. Henry's sermon, "Promise and Oath" was based on Hebrews 6:18, "That by two immutable things, in which it is impossible for God to lie, we may have a strong encouragement, who have fled for refuge to lay hold of the hope set before us." Using God's promise to Abraham, "Unto thy seed I will give this land" (Genesis 12:7) as an illustration, Perry showed how the Christian can be doubly secure in the promises of God. God not only made the promise to Abraham, but he made it under an oath, swearing by His name to bless Abraham according to all He had promised (Genesis 22:16). Therefore, Perry said, we have double security in the Bible. It is not only God's Word, but He has also sworn an oath that His Word is true.[4]

By the end of November, the time for final farewells had come. On November 21, a special meeting of the Prudential Committee of the ABCFM was held in Boston to send off the missionaries. Sarah Ann and William Porter came for the farewell. When the time for embarkation came, Alvan escorted Jeanne to the *Java*, and Mrs. Perry accompanied Henry, with many of their friends following. As the sailing-steamer pulled away from Boston and the waving hands faded, Jeanne and Henry did not know how many of their loved ones they would ever see again. In his diary Perry wrote, "The call of our Precious Lord, was our comfort."[5]

Reverend Simon Calhoun, a missionary to Syria, was a fatherly companion for the Perrys on their voyage. He often held morning prayers with them and preached Sundays at the ship's service. Also traveling with them was Miss Merriam, a missionary from Springfield, Massachusetts going to Constantinople. The rolling of the ship made Jeanne and many other passengers sick, confining them to their cabins, but Henry was not affected. Off the coast of Ireland the south winds were so strong that the sails were hoisted to steady the ship. At nights, heads rolled on their pillows like everything else on board unless something was packed to hold the item in place!

December 4, 1866, the *Java* landed in England, and the missionary party made its way to London. Miss Merriam fell ill in London, and the group had to delay its departure for France. Jeanne and Henry used the delay to explore the London sites – the Tower of London, Westminster Abbey, Windsor Palace, and various chapels. They also made important contacts with fellow Christians in England by visiting the Turkish Mission Aid Society and the Evangelical Alliance.[6] September 9th they visited the Congregational Church of Reverend Binney, where Henry was invited to speak. Both Henry and Jeanne were interested in visiting the Ragged Schools, a charity established to educate the London poor and share with them the good news of Jesus Christ. Throughout their travels, sightseeing and visiting, Henry's admiration of Jeanne grew:

> Jeanne is in good health and full of animation in all that she does. She is proving herself to be indeed a Missionary. Since our marriage instead of going on a wedding tour we have been in the public eye!! Comparing her with so many others, and from a missionary point of view, I admire (more than ever before) her good manner, good sense, and care for the honor of the cause of missions.[7]

The Perrys, Mr. Calhoun, and Miss Merriam booked passage to sail from Marseilles, France to Turkey on December 18. On the 14th they left behind the white cliffs of Dover and began their travel through France. For a day they took a carriage and toured Paris, seeing the Egyptian obelisk from Thebes, Napoleon's Triumphal Arch, and other sites of historical interest. The foursome visited the Louvre, where Jeanne was fascinated with everything. They all were very weary at the end of their whirlwind day in Paris!

While waiting for the steamer in Marseilles, Mr. Calhoun suggested Henry buy a white, ventilator hat to use in Turkey, which he did for

$2.50. The trip through the Mediterranean was both relaxing and exciting. For Henry and Jeanne, it was a ten-day review of European history. With the telescope they could see Garabaldi's home in Corsica. Just below Messina was Reggio, the country Paul spoke of on his way to Rome after his shipwreck. Jeanne especially enjoyed watching the shoreline at night with a full moon and the stars glistening above. When the steamer approached the southern cape of Greece, the winds picked up. Both Jeanne and Miss Merriam became seasick as the wind and the current tossed the steamer about. On Christmas Eve the ship was able to take refuge in the harbor of Melos until the storm passed. The storm cleared, and on Christmas day, the steamer sailed into the Aegean Sea. Henry used his classical atlas to follow their course through the islands, and Jeanne enjoyed recalling the islands' history with her husband. The aged apostle John had been a prisoner on the island of Patmos, where he wrote the Biblical book of Revelation. Many of the islands had been involved in the ancient Peloponessian and Persian Wars. Kos was the birthplace of the physician Hippocrates; Samos was a famous ancient commercial and shipping center; and Khios was the home of noted ancient Greek poets and sculptors. The ship stopped at Smyrna, where Henry and Jeanne first met Turkish people. Here Miss Merriam disembarked to continue to Constantinople. Henry and Jeanne continued on for three more days to Alexandretta. With Mr. Calhoun they spent time in prayer as they neared their own mission field, a land rich in Biblical and secular history.

Historically the land of Turkey was called Asia Minor; the Turks called the area Anatolia, meaning "the dawn." Whatever the name, it was here that the ancient Hittities had their kingdom and where Homer's Troy was located. The land was an ancient crossroads between east and west. Persia's King Xerxes had marched westward across Asia Minor when he invaded Greece; the Macedonian Alexander the Great had moved eastward across the same land in his conquests of Persia. In the century before Christ, the Romans had conquered the land. The apostle Paul was born in Tarsus, a city in southern Asia Minor, and he traveled throughout Asia Minor on his earlier missionary journeys. When Constantine became Roman emperor in the fourth century, he moved the Empire's capital to Byzantium, across the Bosphorus from Asia Minor, and called the city Constantinople. Christianity had so spread throughout Anatolia that Constantine himself adopted it, and it soon became the religion of the Empire. When the western Roman Empire collapsed, Constantinople continued as the capital of the eastern or Byzantine Empire. In the Byzantine Empire, Christianity was wedded to the pomp and manners of an oriental court. Gradually the Biblical gospel lost its vitality as it became submerged in a political and religious labyrinth of archaic ritual.

In the sixth century, the Byzantine Empire included not only Asia Minor but also most of the lands touching the Mediterranean Sea. In the seventh century, Arabs, inspired by the new religion of Islam, conquered Palestine, Syria, Mesopotamia, and Egypt, reducing the size of the Byzantine Empire. The Arab Moslems repeatedly invaded Asia Minor and besieged Constantinople several times. Though weakened, the Byzantine Empire endured. In the eleventh and twelfth centuries the nomadic Seljuk Turks invaded and ravaged much of eastern and central Anatolia. In the fourteenth century, the Turk Osman conquered northwest Anatolia and gained control over the Byzantine financial, administrative, and military systems. Osman gave his name to the Ottoman Turks, who controlled Asia Minor and much of the Middle East into the twentieth century. In 1453, the Ottomans conquered Constantinople. With Constantinople's fall, the Byzantine Empire came to an end. The Moslem Turks controlled the lands where Christianity began and first flourished.

At its height under Suleimann the Magnificent, the Ottoman Empire controlled southeastern Europe, Asia Minor, the Middle East, Egypt, and North Africa. In 1529 the Turks besieged Vienna, and Christian Europe feared the Moslem forces would advance even further west. A series of wars in the following centuries, however, weakened the Empire, and pieces began to break away. Greece was the first to gain independence in 1829. The dissolution was slow, however, and the Empire was not finally dissolved until the end of World War I.

Early in its history the ABCFM made plans to send missionaries to the Ottoman Empire's Bible lands. The land of Abraham, Isaac, and Jacob, the land where Jesus ministered, and the lands where Paul preached the Risen Lord were all part of the Moslem Ottoman Empire. Certainly these lands needed to again hear the clear truths of the Bible. In November 1819, a month after the first missionaries were sent to the Sandwich or Hawaiian Islands, Levi Parsons and Pliny Fisk set sail from Boston on the first ABCFM mission to the Bible lands. In 1820 they arrived in Smyrna in Asia Minor, where they established a temporary base.

The complexity of working in the Ottoman lands was little understood when the missionaries first entered upon their work. The Ottoman government was a theocracy, inextricably connected to the Moslem religion. The Ottoman sultan had the title "caliph" and was considered the successor to Mohammed. For a Moslem to convert to another religion and forsake Islam was not just a personal decision, but was considered an attack on the government itself. An equally troubling problem was the poverty that seemed to envelop most of the people in the Empire. All these issues would need to be faced by the missionaries in coming decades.

Ultimately Parsons and Fisk hoped to establish a mission to the Jews in Jerusalem. At the time, it was thought that the Ottoman Empire would soon disappear and Jews from around the world would return to Palestine. A Christian mission in Jerusalem would be ideally located for evangelizing the Jewish people. However, when Parsons and Fisk arrived in Jerusalem there were few Jews there, and they had little interest in the Christian message. The missionaries did meet some Armenian pilgrims who were very interested in a better understanding of the Bible and the Christian faith. Back in Smyrna, Fisk wrote to the ABCFM in Boston recommending a mission to the Armenians in Turkey.[8]

The Armenians were an ancient people who claimed descent from Haik, son of Togarmah, and a great-grandson of Noah through his son Japheth.[9] The Hebrew for Armenia is Ararat; and Mt. Ararat, where Noah's ark landed after the great flood, was a central place in the Armenian homeland between the Black and Caspian Seas.[10] Aram, seventh king of the Haik dynasty, was thought to be a contemporary of Isaac and Jacob. The land of Armenia was a pathway for merchants and conquering armies between Europe and Asia, and Armenia was often under foreign rule – by the Assyrians, Medes, Persians, Greeks, Parthians, and Romans. Whatever the controlling empire, Armenians remained renowned as merchants and traders. The Old Testament prophet Ezekiel described the commercial activity of Tyre and noted that the merchants from Togarmah (a synonym for Armenia) brought horses and mules to trade there.[11]

Armenian tradition said that the Apostle Bartholomew first preached the Christian gospel to the Armenians. When, in the fourth century Gregory "the Illuminator" powerfully preached the Gospel among the Armenians; around 301 A.D., King Tiridates embraced Christianity and had his people do the same; Tiridates ordered heathen temples and altars thrown down and churches built in their place. An alphabet was developed, and the Bible was translated into Armenian.

Armenia became the first Christian nation. Though the Armenians became scattered throughout Persia, Turkey, and southern Russia, they clung to their national Armenian Church, which was independent of both the Roman Catholic and Greek Orthodox churches. Foreigners often called the Armenian Church the Gregorian Church, after Gregory the Illuminator. Armenians themselves called their Church the Church of the Illuminator. Over the centuries of invasions and migrations, the Armenian Church guarded its independence and became an important institution preserving the Armenian sense of nationhood.[12]

Though the ABCFM was eager to explore Pliny Fisk's recommendation of a mission to the Armenians, the Greek War for Independence and the Russo-Turkish War (1828-1829) prevented development of the mission for a time. When the wars ended in 1829, William Goodell opened a mission station in Constantinople, where there were approximately 100,000 Armenians (Goodell's son, Henry, was a classmate of Henry Perry's at Williston Academy). The following year, the ABCFM sent Eli Smith and Henry Otis Dwight to explore the eastern parts of the Turkish Empire. Dressed in oriental clothes, Smith and Dwight traveled from Constantinople to Persia, collecting a wealth of information on the geography, culture, and peoples of the Empire. In all their travels they did not meet one evangelical Christian. Though the Christians in the Ottoman lands continued to risk much by persevering in their faith, it seemed to Smith and Dwight that the Oriental churches had lost much of their Christian message and no longer understood the Scriptures.

Smith and Dwight found the Armenian peoples to be highly industrious, thrifty, and temperate. They were the bankers of the Empire as well as the leaders in commerce and industry. The Armenian church remained an important part of their lives, but the church's ritual was in the ancient Armenian, which to the Armenians in the nineteenth century was as incomprehensible as medieval English would be to a modern American. Yet the Armenians had a deep reverence for the Word of God and were eager to learn about the Bible and Christian truths. With over a million and a half Armenians scattered throughout Turkey, it seemed that a mission to the Armenians could be a training center for evangelists and teachers to the rest of Turkey and the eastern lands.[13]

After his explorations of Turkey, Henry Dwight asked to be assigned work among the Armenians. He studied their language and history and yearned to see a revival and reformation of their Christian faith. He worked to provide schools and textbooks so Armenians could better understand their Christian faith and heritage. In organizing missions to the Armenians, neither Dwight nor anyone at the ABCFM aimed originally to organize Protestant evangelical churches among them or try to Americanize them. Dwight recognized that:

> These brethren are still Armenian, and I trust that they will remain so. I see no reason why we should wish them to become anything else. We want to see them truly enlightened; we want to see them studying the Scriptures; and we want to see their characters transformed by the power of the divine spirit; but we have no desire that they should become Americans or Lutherans, or Congregationalists or Presbyterians or anything else but true Christians.[14]

The goal was to provide the Scriptures, promote education, and encourage a truly converted Christian peoples.

Soon after Smith's and Dwight's exploratory journey through Turkey, the ABCFM established mission stations at Urumia, Trebizond, and Erzerum, and strengthened its missionary presence in Constantinople. When Reverend Cyrus Hamlin left for Turkey in 1839, the Prudential Committee of the ABCFM instructed him:

> The object of our missions to the Oriental Churches is, first, to revive the knowledge and spirit of the Gospel among them, and, secondly, by this means to operate upon the Mohammedans. These Churches must be reformed. The fire of a pure Christianity must be rekindled upon those Christian altars. In all the professedly Christian communities of western Asia there must be living examples of the holy, happy influence of the religion of Jesus. The Oriental Churches need assistance from their brethren abroad. Our object is not to subvert them; not to pull down, and build up anew. You are not sent among these churches to proselyte. Let the Armenian remain an Armenian, if he will, the Greek a Greek, the Nestorian a Nestorian, the Oriental an Oriental. It is not the rites, ceremonies, and superstitions of those people that you, a foreigner and a stranger, can attack to the best advantage; these will be corrected as a thing of course when your main work is accomplished. Your great business is with the fundamental doctrines and duties of the Gospel. The work will be mainly carried on and accomplished by the already existing and increasing body of evangelical native Christians.[15]

The missionaries were most concerned with establishing truth among the people, not with attacking the Armenian Church. Among the missionaries' first task was translating the Bible into modern Armenian, Turkish, and Turkish-Armenian, so the people could read the Scriptures.[16] Some in the Gregorian Church began to recognize the need for reform, and in the early 1830's they organized an Evangelical Union to further reform efforts. As more and more Armenians read the tracts and literature distributed by the missionaries and flocked to the schools established by the ABCFM, and as Armenian pastors became educated and taught their people an evangelical Biblical faith, the hierarchy of the Gregorian Church began to rise in opposition. In 1839, the Armenian patriarch banned the reading of missionary material and threatened excommunication to any member of the Congregation who associated with the Protestants. The missionaries were denounced as "Satanic heresiarchs from the caverns of hell and the abyss of the northern ocean."[17] The Egyptian-Turkish War, ending with the sultan's defeat, briefly interrupted the growing persecution. The young Sultan Abdul Medjid issued a charter of civil protection and religious liberty. By the mid-1840's, however, a new Armenian Patriarch excommunicated the Armenians associating with the American missionaries. Evangelical Armenians were stoned in the streets, unjustly imprisoned, ejected from their shops, and their houses were plundered. Such persecution and excommunication presented not only religious, but also severe political problems to these Armenians.

At the beginning of Ottoman rule in 1453, when Sultan Mehmed conquered Constantinople, he proclaimed that the vanquished peoples should return to their homes and continue in their occupations and religion. Sultan Mehmed had a new Patriarch of the Greek Church chosen who was to represent the Greek community in its relations with the Ottoman States. The Greeks had inhabited western Turkey since the days of Homer and continued to be a strong minority under the Turks. The Patriarch was to have judicial authority within the Greek community over marriages, divorce, wills, and other local legal issues. Other religious communities or <u>millets</u> were also allowed in this way to preserve their own traditions under Ottoman rule. By the end of the nineteenth century, the Sublime Porte, as the Ottoman government was called, recognized the Greek Orthodox, Greek Melkite, Maronite, Gregorian Armenian, Catholic Armenian, Syrian Jacobite, Orthodox Coptic, Orthodox Chaldean, Catholic Chaldean, and Jews as separate <u>millets</u>.[18] The Ottoman Empire was a Moslem state, but Moslem religious laws were not to be enforced on the non-Moslem communities. When evangelical Armenian Christians were excommunicated from the Gregorian Church, they were perforce outside the millet system of the Ottoman Empire. This deprived them of any legal status and prevented them legally from owning property, marrying, and even receiving a death certificate at death (which would affect their heirs).[19]

Some evangelical Protestants excommunicated from the Gregorian Church recanted and became secret evangelicals while remaining in the Gregorian Church. Others maintained their faith, suffered persecution, and by their very boldness drew more to the gospel. Soon Protestant Evangelical Armenian Churches were organized in Constantinople, Nicomedia, Adabazar, and Trebizond. All the churches were under native pastors. In 1850, the sultan recognized the Protestants as a new <u>millet</u>. While the recognition gave the Protestants legal status, it also restricted them. As a millet they had authority within their own community, but they were not to "molest" the other millets and take members from them. The millet system did not support evangelism or proselytism.

The spread of the Gospel message could not be contained, however. The ABCFM missionaries, not themselves members of the millet, continued their evangelism and educational work; and native Christians established Bible societies to distribute the Scriptures in the villages. In 1853, the Crimean War between Turkey and Russia brought turmoil to the region, but the spiritual reformation among the Armenians continued, and a call went out for more missionaries. Schools, colleges, and seminaries, as well as additional mission stations, were established to help carry out the spiritual reformation of the Armenian people. In 1854, British Christians organized the Turkish Mission Aid Society to financially assist the American Board in its work in the Ottoman Empire.[20]

In 1860, the American Board divided its Turkey operations into three Missions – the Western, the Central, and the Eastern. There were 23 stations, over 100 missionaries, and 40 native pastors with evangelical churches.[21] In 1853, A.H. Layard, famed excavator of Nineveh and Babylon and Britain's ambassador to Turkey, had told the British Parliament there was no important place in Turkey which had not felt the influence of the Christian reformation led by the American missionaries. In 1860, the Earl of Shaftsbury, speaking to the Turkish Aid Society in London, said,

> I do not believe that in the whole history of missions, I do not believe that in the history of diplomacy, or in the history of any negotiation carried on between man and man, we can find anything equal the wisdom, the soundness, and the pure Evangelical truth of the men

who constitute the America mission. I have said it twenty times before, and I will say it again, - for the expression appropriately conveys my meaning, - that they are a marvelous combination of common sense and piety.[22]

The missionaries in Turkey had established the highest degree of character and integrity, manifesting an unselfishness, uprightness, and honor that the world had rarely seen. Henry and Jeanne Perry, praying about their new missionary work as they sailed to Alexandretta, were about to join an illustrious group of men and women in the service of the Gospel.

At Alexandretta Mr. Calhoun helped Henry and Jeanne prepare for their land journey by horseback to Aleppo and hired a native servant to accompany them. Originally a missionary had been sent to meet the Perrys at Alexandretta; but, since the telegraph had not yet been built in that part of Turkey, there had been no way of notifying him of the 10-day delay in London when Miss Merriam was ill. Mr. Adams had come to Alexandretta the previous week, but when the Perrys did not arrive, he returned to Aintab! Neither Henry nor Jeanne yet knew Turkish, but the only way forward was with the help of the Turkish guide. The horseback riding on the Missouri frontier had helped prepare Henry and Jeannne for the three-day ride to Aleppo. On New Year's Day 1867, they crossed the Amanus Mountains on horseback and turned east on the Syrian plain to Aleppo. The weather was good, and there was no discomfort from the heat. Henry was so excited at being in Turkey, that at one point he got on his knees to kiss the soil. Here was the long anticipated land for his mission work. He had been called to this land to preach the Gospel of Christ.

At Aleppo Henry and Jeanne sought out the American counsel, but he was out of the city. They were relieved when an Armenian woman came up to them in the streets, spoke to them in English, and invited them to be guests in her house! Henry and Jeanne looked forward to the first Lord's day in their new land, so they left Aleppo and traveled across the plain to reach Killis, where Reverend Tomas was the native pastor of the large Protestant Church there. Though Henry and Jeanne could not understand Turkish, and Reverend Tomas and his wife could not understand English, the four Christians were able to understand each other. One way they communicated was for the Tomases to point to a verse in their Turkish Bible and the Perrys would find the verse in the English Bible. The Perrys then answered by pointing to a verse in their English Bible, which the Tomases would find in their Turkish

Bible. By exchanging verses in this way, their souls were knit more closely in the Lord:

> It is curiously wonderful how much Christians with their Bibles can communicate with each other; The hand of Christian fellowship is strong. We there were happy in singing together. Jeanne was charming.[23]

After some difficult negotiations for a servant and horses, the Perrys set out on a three-day journey through treeless hills and valleys to Aintab, their first mission station.[24] As Henry and Jeanne traveled through what was to be their new home, they undoubtedly were fascinated by the sights and sounds met along the way. As a later colleague of Henry's wrote during his first travels in Turkey:

> ...it is the odd groups you will pass every now and then along the road that will doubtless interest you most. Far off down the road a long black line, like a marching army, creeps slowly along with a strange, swaying, rhythmic motion; and if it is your first one, your heart will give a jump as you suddenly recognize that it is a caravan of camels loaded high with huge boxes and bales of goods. As the long string of disdainfully posed noses passes by you in solemn, sleepy dignity, you realize at last that you are really in the east, travelling an ancient caravan route!
>
> Our commonest fellow-traveller will be the donkey; by twos or threes or scores, laden with everything conceivable, from watermelons or huge copper kettles to haystacks or complete household outfits with the baby's cradle on top! Sometimes he will come singly bearing on his back a sleepy old *hoja* in his snow-white turban and cloak of many colors, his bare feet stuck out at a comical angle balancing heelless slippers precariously on the upturned toes, with a faded umbrella poised above his placid face and patriarchal beard. Behind him perhaps will trudge his wife on foot, wrapped in a big white sheet and carrying a baby in her arms![25]

Located 600 miles southeast of Constantinople, Aintab was one of the ABCFM's most promising mission stations. The city had a population of 35,000, mostly Turks, but about one third of the population was Armenian. Reverend Azariah Smith, M.D., first indirectly brought the Gospel to Aintab in 1844 in his travels when he gave a copy of the New Testament to an Armenian priest going to Aintab. Reverend Smith later sent Bedros, a colporteur, into the region with books and tracts to sell and distribute.[26] Bedros reported considerable interest in Christianity, and many desired religious instruction. Several missionaries visited Aintab, including Mr. Johnson, who after two months was ordered from the city, insulted and stoned by the people as he left. Dr. Smith arrived the same month during a cholera epidemic. The help and aid he gave the people earned their respect, and in January 1848, he organized a church of eight members. That spring Doctor and Mrs. Benjamin Schneider came from their work in Broosa, near Constantinople, to help Dr. Smith minister in Aintab. The large stone church erected in 1850, was paid for in large part by donations from the native people. It was the first building for Christian worship erected in the Ottoman Empire on a new site since the Turks had come to power. That the people were willing to support a pastor and much of the church building themselves was remarkable in a community where the average laborer earned 13 cents a day and a carpenter earned 32 cents a day. Under Dr. Schneider's ministry, the Aintab church flourished. By the time Perry arrived, the church, with 360 members, had an average Sunday attendance of 100. Though poor, the people themselves supported their native pastors and established a Home Missionary Society to bring the Scriptures to surrounding communities. Seven common schools and one high school had been established, all supported by the people themselves. A theological school was also established to train the native pastors and preachers as well as teachers and colporteurs. Even the Gregorian church in Aintab became more evangelical and increased its Bible teaching under the missionary influence.[27]

The church at Aintab had become so large that in 1865, it was divided into a second church, a native pastor was chosen, and grounds for a new church building were sought. By the time the Perrys arrived, several outstations connected with Aintab had been established. In Marash to the northwest, two self-supporting churches and five schools were flourishing. In areas farther afield, Ourfa, Aleppo, Antioch, and Adana, churches with native pastors had also been established. Other villages, such as Bitias, Kessal, Diabekir, and Hassan Beyli, had pockets of Christians.

When they first arrived, Jeanne and Henry stayed with Dr. and Mrs. Schneider, who welcomed the young couple with fatherly and motherly affection. Dr. Schneider had lost his two sons in the Civil War, and he took Henry and Jeanne into the vacant place in his heart. The Perrys were given the best guestroom. Jeanne's lovely singing especially ministered to Dr. Schneider's grief for his sons; her singing "But the Healer was there" often comforted him.[28]

The two months Jeanne and Henry stayed with the Schneiders, waiting for their boxes with their household items, was a special time of training for the young missionaries. They were able to see first-hand the lives and activities of a missionary couple so completely dedicated to missionary service. Dr. Schneider had been in Turkey since 1834. His fluency in the Turkish language was such that the native people marveled at his mastery of the idioms and nuances of the language. A superb scholar, Dr. Schneider also had a humble spirit that caused him to reach out to all classes with the love of Christ. His life was one of powerful dependence on his God for sustenance, strength, wisdom, and direction. In 1856, Dr. Schneider's wife, Eliza, died in Aintab. On a trip to the United States in 1858, Dr. Schneider married Eliza's sister, Susan, and returned to the Aintab mission with his new wife.[29]

When the Perrys arrived, Susan Schneider immediately took Jeanne under her wing. Together the two went visiting the Armenian Christian women. Mrs. Schneider was able to counsel and minister to the women in Turkish, while Jeanne sang hymns to them in Turkish. Without knowing or understanding the language, Jeanne had a ministry among the people. Henry, however, had to struggle to learn the Turkish language. Accustomed to preaching every Sunday, he felt muzzled by not being able to yet speak the language of the people. Daily, Henry worked with his Turkish teacher, studied his grammar, and pored over the Turkish Bible. It was frustrating to be in the longed-for mission field, but unable to preach the Gospel to the people. On January 16, 1867, Henry unloaded his frustration with the language barrier into his journal:

> But my wife has found a field for Service already. By the Gospel hymns in Turkish she is now as if on preaching duty. She sings the Gospel even now. If Jeanne was not my wife I might be tempted to be jealous, that while I am laid aside from preaching till I learn Turkish, she is already in the active service singing the blessed way of Grace in the homes of people, and in the congregations for Christian worship.[30]

In March their boxes arrived, and the Perrys began to move into the house Dr. Schneider had rented for them The house was on the east slope of the hill, at the top was the Aintab church and Dr. Schneider's own home. By Monday, March 4, the Perrys had moved into their home and had the other missionaries in for afternoon tea. For years Henry had been either a boarder or guest in others' homes; it was a happy day to be in a home of his own with Jeanne by his side. In the days ahead, Henry helped get the house in order. The books were arranged in the bookcase, and a stove put up in the study. Henry did a lot of work cleaning out the stable for Prince, the horse bought with money given him by his brother-in-law William Porter. Prince was of Persian origin, "iron grey in color; height medium; his body round; ears small; sensitive; intelligent, quick, legs small; his gait easy, a fast walk and gallop – never trots between the two. The only disappointment that he proves too spirited for the ladies to ride."[31]

Settled in their own home, Henry and Jeanne's days began to develop a pattern of their own. The Perry house faced east, and Henry set his clock and watch by the rising sun. Every morning began with Jeanne and Henry's own personal devotions followed by family worship, which included their servant Garabet and any of the teachers from the schools who might join them. By the end of May Henry was using Armeno-Turkish in family worship and Bible reading. Henry's mornings were spent in studying Turkish with his teacher, while Jeanne often went to visit the Armenian women with Mrs. Schneider. In the afternoons Henry continued his studies, by going to the marketplace to try simple conversations with the people in their own language. Henry and Jeanne often rode out on the plains and hills surrounding Aintab – Henry on Prince and Jeanne on one of the Schneiders' horses or on her white donkey. It was always refreshing to put aside the work of the day and ride together in the clear air of the Aintab countryside. In the evenings Henry and Jeanne spent time in leisure reading, such as from the lives of Henry Martyn or Murray McCheyne, or from the various periodicals they subscribed to, such as *Congregational Review*, *Evangelist*, *Harper's Weekly*, or *Hours at Home*. On some evenings there were missionary or choir meetings. Often there were anniversaries and birthdays to celebrate among the missionary group.

Sundays were always faithfully observed as the Lord's Day in the two Aintab Protestant churches. The Lord's Day pattern in most of the Protestant churches in Turkey was to begin with a prayer meeting for the day's services. A Bible class on a particular Bible passage, with questions and discussions from the men, usually followed. The moral lessons of the Scripture were always clearly discussed. During the Sabbath or Sunday School, young people were taught the Bible and the catechism. During the actual church service, a more formal sermon was given, and the congregation sang a number of hymns. Sometimes the sermon was in Turkish; at other times it was in Armenian. The chapels themselves were very simple structures. The only furniture was usually a pulpit and a low railing down one side of the chapel, to separate the men and the women. The people sat on the floor, as they did in the Gregorian churches and the Turkish mosques. The windows were often covered with oiled paper rather than glass.[32]

It took several months before Henry began to understand the sermons preached in Turkish, though from the first he tried to take notes on what was being said. Because of their unfamiliarity with the language, Henry and Jeanne were given charge of the infant department and took care of forty or so infants and toddlers during the Sunday School hour. On Sunday evenings the missionaries had an English service in one of their homes. One of them read aloud a sermon, and then the group sang hymns and had a time of prayer together. Henry's father had bought the mission an organ, and Jeanne was thrilled to be able to play the hymns at the missionary meetings.

When they established their homes in Turkey, the missionaries introduced many western items into the ancient land. The potato was first planted in 1827 (American ambassador and Southerner Terrell later introduced the sweet potato or yam in the 1890's). The sewing machine and parlor organ were first brought over in 1854, the camera in 1856, and kerosene lighting in 1865. Cyrus Hamlin in Constantinople introduced the use of the sheet-iron stove and a new way of making bread. The integrity, honor, and industry of the missionaries were more important commodities, however, than the latest western developments.[33]

Besides the Schneiders, missionaries at Aintab included Mr. Lucien Adams, whose wife had recently died, and Mr. Philander Powers, who had only recently returned to Turkey after several years pastoring a church in Connecticut. Myra Proctor and Nancy Francis supervised the Aintab Girls' School, which had been established in 1860, and had just moved into its new buildings in November 1866. Counting the Perrys, this made eight ABCFM workers. The Christian leadership of the Protestant Church in Aintab also included two native pastors, one preacher, and six teachers.[34]

In the spring, both the Armenian Evangelical Union and the Central Turkey Mission of the ABCFM held annual meetings. In April Henry and Jeanne made the two-day trip to Marash for the meeting, where they met those working in other parts of the Central Turkey field

– Dr. Andrew Pratt, Mrs. Coffing, Dr. and Mrs. Nutting, and Giles and Emily Montgomery. The Central Turkey Mission, like each Mission of the American Board, was a virtually autonomous administrative unit. It operated in a democratic fashion and with whatever committees it deemed necessary for its mission. The Prudential Committee in Boston determined the funds available to the Mission and what new personnel were to be appointed, but the Mission itself determined the tasks for which each missionary was responsible. The Prudential Committee trusted its missionaries to establish policies and practices that would best commend the gospel to the people and find favor with the home supporters.[35]

Recognizing they were about the Lord's business, not their own, the missionaries began the morning sessions with prayer. The first item of business was then choosing a Treasurer for the Mission, and all eyes turned to Henry Perry. Henry objected that he needed to first learn the language, but the mission was short-handed; and the previous Treasurer, Dr. Pratt, had his time consumed with preaching and writing, as well as being a physician. There seemed little choice, and Henry accepted. Miss Proctor was due a furlough in the United States, and in her absence Henry and Jeanne were assigned the supervision of the Girls' Boarding School in Aintab. Dr. and Mrs. Nutting, who had been at Ourfa, were leaving for Aleppo. Dr. Nutting had caused quite a confusion in the Ourfa church by teaching the theology of Horace Bushnell, who questioned the need for conversion, the importance of Christian doctrine, and the substitutionary atonement in the death of Christ. It was decided that Philander Powers would spend the winter at Ourfa to help heal the divided church there. Henry would join him there part of the time. All in all, Henry's first annual meeting gave him important responsibilities as part of the missionary team in Central Turkey.

The Secretary-Treasurer responsibilities consumed much of Henry's time, time that he preferred to spend learning Turkish so he could preach the Gospel clearly to the people. He maintained all the Mission records, sending copies to Boston and keeping duplicates in Aintab. The bookkeeping he had done in his father's store helped him with the Treasurer records, and his parents sent him a long letter concerning double entry accounts as well as an accounting manual. The Mission Treasurer was responsible not only for the general mission account, but also for the accounts of the individual missionaries assigned to the Central Turkish Mission. It was a tedious bureaucratic job Henry never relished, but also one of great responsibility. Though he often tried to relinquish his role as Treasurer, allowing more time for gospel ministry, Henry was given the roll of Treasurer throughout all his years in Turkey.

By August Henry and Jeanne had moved into the Female Boarding House. So many people helped that moving was easy. Henry began teaching Bible lessons in the boys' schools while continuing to study his Turkish. At every opportunity he improved his language skills to better improve his gospel ministry. The Aintab church had divided the Armenian quarter of the city into sections and sent out teams to present the gospel family to family. Henry, lantern in hand, regularly accompanied a Christian brother on these visits. He described the visitations in a letter to his parents:

> Can I give you a description of our meeting this evening? Go with us along the dark, winding narrow streets of Aintab. After a half-hour's walk we come to a door within which a meeting had been appointed. We knock; it is opened. We pass into a yard surrounded by walls, and from the yard into the room of a family. The room we entered tonight was the home of a poor man; so look in with us upon such a home. Even among the poor of Boston you can have but a meagre idea of what poverty is; but you would find it in any city in Turkey. The father of a large family can earn but a few piasters (each about 4 cents) per day, and most of that must go to pay taxes and rents. Where then is the money coming from, needful to give bread and clothing to his children? We entered a low dark room. A small tin cup, with oil and wick in it, was giving a faint relief from total darkness. In the centre of the room was a box, say a foot and a half high and *two* feet square, covered with a thick blanket of goat's hair. Imagine eight half-clothed children sitting on the floor, all putting their bare limbs under that blanket to get warmth from the pan of coals which it covers. This is all the fire they have from the coldest of the weather. Every thing about the room indicated poverty. Even the father pulled his outer blanket-coat about him to cover his rags.
>
> They prepared a nice place for me to sit at the end of the room – the place of honor – by making a carpet of the best blankets in the house. As usual, I left my boots at the door and took my seat – the brother who conducted the meeting beside me. The mother was still young in years, I should judge; but she told me that her family of children numbered eight. Soon others came in and filled the room. A chapter was read and expounded – the 11th of Hebrews; and all were almost too free in talking about the examples of faith. They sang twice, had several prayers; and we two came away. Leaving the company praying and singing and reading the Scriptures.[36]

As Henry and Jeanne's first anniversary approached, they looked back over the year and praised their loving God for His many blessings. The unalloyed joy they shared was "because our Glorified Lord has bound us with Himself in this way. We have been united in our allegiance to Him. This blessing has been bestowed by the hand of the Heavenly Father, whom for it we praise."[37] Mrs. Schneider prepared a special dinner to celebrate the Perrys' anniversary.

Henry and Jeanne learned to praise God in all circumstances of life. October 22, 1867, Jeanne gave birth to their first child at 2 A.M. Henry recorded in his diary the baby was

> ...to be a treasure, not with us on earth, but in the bliss of Heaven, which is far better. She breathed her last at the hour of birth. Her form was complete in every respect. We took the best possible care of Jeanne, and with bitter grief; yet praising God for His matchless Grace, buried little Hattie at 4 P.M.[38]

This would not be the last time Jeanne and Henry would have a child swiftly removed from their arms; but each time their faith in their loving Father remained unshaken, and they found rest and peace in Him.

The shortage of mission workers and the urgent work to be done did not allow Henry the time for study he wished, but his fluency in Turkish increased, and the people were patient with him. Dr. Schneider gave him special lessons and helped him prepare sermons in Turkish on several occasions. Henry accompanied the Schneiders and Mr. Powers on trips to the out-stations and villages around Aintab. Such journeys were teaching him both the language and valuable lessons from mentors whose years on the mission field gave them priceless experience to share with the younger man. Henry especially admired Dr. Schneider's life of prayer; from him Henry learned that prayer was "the main instrument in missionary operations."[39]

By the fall of 1868, Henry was ready to tour the field of the Central Turkey Mission with Baron Simon, pastor of Aintab's First Church. For five weeks the two traveled over 600 miles on horseback into the Hassan Beyli region, preaching every night in some village. The people were poor and lived off of subsistence farming. The pastor of the church in Hassan Beyli was paid in produce, and Henry's heart was warmed to see the "bags of wheat and flour, and onions, and cotton piled up in the pastor's home in Hassan Beyli – the first fruit of the harvest of tithes this year." Out of their poverty, the people paid half of the pastor's salary and half of the cost of building a parsonage.[40]

Henry also frequently helped Philander Powers in Ourfa, an important town since 1500 B.C. Located on the edge of the Syrian desert, the town had been important during the days of the ancient Hurrians and Hittites. Alexander the Great's Seleucid successors renamed the town Edessa, and it became a center of trade and learning, a place where both goods and ideas were exchanged between east and west. During Roman and Byzantine times, a citadel was located there. The Frankish crusaders rebuilt the citadel as a castle when they conquered the town in 1092, during the First Crusade. For fifty years the Franks made their city the capital of their County of Edessa, until overcome by the Turks.[41] Crossing the river Euphrates at Biridjik, each time Henry rode to Ourfa he thought of God's promises to Abraham, for many believed Abraham came to Ourfa on his way to the Promised Land. Henry's work was to see that the Word of the Gospel be planted in Ourfa. Mr. Powers recognized that Henry was becoming comfortable with conversational Turkish, and encouraged him to speak in the pulpit as if he were speaking to one person. The people were very patient with Henry's early attempts at speaking Turkish. Together Powers and Perry tried to heal the discord brought by Mr. Nuttings' teaching during his time at Ourfa. They encouraged the people in the Scriptures, and the church grew. In the afternoons the two missionaries rode outside the city together. Henry wrote that "The outlook upon the great Arabian plain, from the uplands above Ourfa was very fine, which would never tire us! Especially we noted Haran, where Abraham halted on his way to the land of Promise."[42]

Throughout Henry's travels to the various outstations, Jeanne remained at Aintab, helping at the Female Boarding School, teaching sewing and music to the girls, and ministering with Mrs. Schneider to the Armenian women of the town. When a missionary wife was due to have a baby, such as Mrs. Montgomery of Marash or Mrs. Adams at Adana, Jeanne traveled to help her during her delivery and afterwards. Henry loved and respected Jeanne more deeply than ever. Her fortitude, self-denial and patience in her separations from Henry revealed her love for the Lord and the missionary life to which they both had been called. Yet, Jeanne did find the summer heat debilitating. Henry decided to build a summer place at Kerkhan, outside Aintab. With its higher elevation it was cooler, and Jeanne should be more comfortable there in the summer months. The Montgomeries had a summer home there too. Emily and Jeanne had become like sisters, and it would be easier for Jeanne during Henry's mission travels to have the Montgomeries close by.

Benjamin Schneider had spent over twenty years in Aintab, preaching his first sermon there in 1848 to 25 or 30 individuals and a little church of eight members. By 1869 there were two churches with 373 members and over 1000 attending weekly services. Dr. Schneider had helped establish numerous outstations with five churches and trained over twenty native pastors for Christian ministry. In the summer of 1869, the Schneiders left Aintab and returned to Broosa near Constantinople, where Dr. Schneider had begun his missionary work in 1833. With the Schneiders' departure, the Perrys became the missionaries in charge of the Aintab station and moved into the Schneider home on top of the hill. The people welcomed Jeanne back after her summer's absence and enjoyed having her lovely singing among them again.

Though Henry took a quick trip to Ourfa to purchase two houses with their lands and gardens for a church there, he was able to spend more time in Aintab. In Dr. Schneider's study Henry sometimes felt overwhelmed by his predecessor's influence and power, which still seemed to fill the room. Henry's growing realization that the secret of that power was Dr. Schneider's commitment to prayer reinforced a simple, yet profound conclusion – prayer is the most important factor in the success of a Christian mission:

> I pray for the Pastors, and the Teachers, who cooperate with them ... that the Lord will endue them with His Power of the Holy Spirit, to fill the Assemblies not only, but to call and convince the unbelievers; that the Name of the Lord be Glorified.[43]

In November Henry stayed home attending to the missionary accounts, preparing sermons, writing and receiving a multitude of correspondence with the pastors and teachers in the field, and taking care of Jeanne. Another child was soon due, and Henry did all he could to make Jeanne comfortable. Mrs. Trowbridge from Marash came to help, and Dr. Nutting came from Aleppo. Everything went well, and on November 25, 1869, a daughter was born. Jeanne and Henry both praised the Lord for His goodness. They named their daughter Elizabeth Eunice, after Jeanne's mother, Elizabeth Jones, and Henry's grandmother, Eunice Cooledge, both women "mighty in the faith of Jesus."[44]

As 1870 began, Jeanne and Henry began their third year in Turkey feeling very much at home and joyful with the fruits they could see in their mission field. Henry began the year by reviewing in his diary the condition of the Aintab field under his care:

> The number of Stations and outstations is seventeen, extending through an area of 200 miles in length by 50 in breadth—from the Amanus range of mountains in the west, to the Arabian desert on the east; from the Taurus mountains in the north, to Aleppo and the desert on the south. Of these 17 congregations, 11 have organized churches of which 5 have their own settled pastors...The result of work in so large a field, and so ably supplied has been good. The gain in all parts of this field have been very encouraging.

The missionary work not only included the obvious spiritual and educational responsibilities, but also working with the Turkish government to help the Christians. At one point, Henry went before the Governor to plea for the work of the colporteur, who had been arrested for selling Christian books. Perry explained "that the books he sold were good books, suitable to lead the people to tell the truth and be honest. That the influence of our Bible makes the people better than they are now, was an argument that puzzled not a little the Governor ... By patience instead of irritation I often was able to win my case."[45]

In December, several fillings from Henry's teeth fell out, and it seemed he would lose his teeth while still a young man. American missionaries in Beirut had recently opened a college and medical school there, and Henry wrote to them for advice. Dr. Post told him to come without delay and he could refill the teeth. Jeanne, in her ever-loving and patient way, encouraged Henry to go, so on January 21, 1870, Perry set out from Aintab. His route was overland from Aintab to Alexandretta, and then by steamer to Tripoli and Beirut, a one-way journey of nine days. Henry stayed with Dr. and Mrs. Post almost two weeks. Though missing Jeanne and little Lizzie Eunice terribly, Henry not only had his teeth filled, but was able to share with the Beirut missionaries news of the progress in Turkey, as well as learn first hand about missionary work in Beirut.[46] Dr. Daniel Bliss, President of the College of Beirut, took Henry to visit the newly purchased grounds for the college buildings. Henry noted it was "a beautiful location indeed, on a low promontory overlooking the sea. The area of it is large; and the buildings when complete, will make a fine appearance, as seen from the harbor."[47]

By March 8 Henry was finally able to be at home in Aintab with Jeanne and Lizzie. Much work had accumulated for him in his absence – Treasurer accounts, correspondence with outlying churches, and preparation for meetings of the Armenian Evangelical Union at Ourfa and the annual meeting of the Central Turkey Mission at Antioch. On the way to Ourfa, Henry stopped at the Armenian village of Jebbin to visit a local pastor. Many Kurdish villages were nearby, and Henry tried to share the light of the Gospel with them as well:

> These Kourdish tribes are ignorant, poor, half-naked, and much oppressed by the Turkish Government. Both at Jebbin and among the Kourds, I read and taught the Bible to the limit of my strength. The Kourds readily accept it <u>all</u>; but interpret according to their <u>Pantheistic</u> notions...[48]

The large Kurdish villages each had ruins of a Greek church with its arched doorways and pillars. Many of the village houses had square blocks from the ruined church in their walls. On one of them Henry saw a Greek Christian cross incised. He was saddened as a he thought back upon the church established in the area through the ministry of St. Paul, flourishing for centuries, and now in such a ruined state. But then, the building up of Christ's church was what had brought Henry to Turkey in the first place.

The meeting of the Evangelical Union at Ourfa was encouraging. Native Armenians were preaching the Scriptures and taking positions of leadership in the church. The load was no longer solely on the shoulders of the missionaries. Christ's church did have a renewed presence in Turkey, in spite of the ruined church building Henry had passed along the way.

Henry came back to Aintab just long enough to catch up on his mission work and correspondence, then he took Jeanne and Lizzie to Marash, where they stayed with Emily Montgomery while the men went to Antioch for the annual meeting of the Central Turkey Mission. One of the primary concerns of the meeting was the education and training of native pastors for the growing Christian community. Doctrinal controversies over the new liberalism had already caused much dissension and a church split at Ourfa. Ministers must be equipped to examine issues in the light of Scriptural truth. Giles Montgomery proposed that Henry fill a vacancy at the theological school at Marash, teaching homiletics, pastoral theology, the canon of Scripture, and the preparatory classes of Biblical history.

At first Henry had little interest in the proposal; he already had more than enough work with caring for the Aintab station, being treasurer for the mission, and taking preaching tours to the Armenian, Moslem and Kurdish villages. But, after an evening in prayer, he felt it was the Lord's call to accept the Mission's decision, but with two conditions. First, he must have a part of each year for preaching tours in the villages. Preaching the Gospel was his first love, and he must be allowed to do this. Second, he would continue to be an associate with Henry Marden at Aintab until Mr. Marden had sufficiently acquired the native language (the Mardens had come to their first mission station at Aintab less than six months before).

When he returned to Jeanne, the heat of summer was approaching, and the Perrys moved to their summer home at Kerkhan, about seven miles from Marash. The little four-room home had a bedroom and sitting room upstairs and a kitchen/dining room and Henry's study downstairs. The Montgomery and Trowbridge families had homes higher up the hill, with a group of apricot trees separating them. Through much of the summer Jeanne suffered from malarial fever and little Lizzie was weak and sickly, but the cooler air of Kerkhan brought some relief. Henry wrote, "we all need this quiet summer retreat. Such a burden of work and care we carry, a few weeks of quiet here is needful to save us from breaking."[49] Henry spent the summer preparing for his new teaching responsibilities in the fall. He was eager to begin training preachers for the Gospel ministry in Turkey.

---

[1] *Diary*, September 20, 1866.

[2] *Diary*, September 25, 1866.

[3] William E. Dodge was a member of the U.S. Congress 1866-1867, where he advocated moderate postwar Reconstruction policies. Dodge began his career in the dry-goods business. Along with his father-in-law, Anson Phelps, in 1833, he organized the firm of Phelps, Dodge and Company, a dealer in metals. The company became the largest American importer of metals. Dodge was very civic minded and a firm Christian. He was on the board of the ABCFM and active in numerous other religious and temperance societies. "Dodge, William E.," www.*Britannica.com*.

[4] Henry Perry's sermon notes on "Promise and Oath" are in the possession of Gordon Bruce Severance. On the back of his notes Perry listed the places and dates he gave this sermon: Rolla, Mo, Ashfield, Mass., and Old South Church in Boston in 1866; Williamson, N.Y. July, 1876; Rewritten at Afton, New York, March 1891.

[5] *Diary*, November 21, 1866.

[6] The Evangelical Alliance began in England in 1846, and independent branches were established in France, Canada, Sweden, India, the United States, Portugal, Turkey, and Spain. It became an "umbrella body" for supporting and linking evangelical activity across denominational lines. In its early inception it combated rationalism and popery while supporting Christian education and Sabbath observance. Though abjuring political activity, the Evangelical Alliance soon championed religious liberty, championing the rights of not only evangelical Christians, but also Protestants, Roman Catholics, and Orthodox minorities in places of persecution throughout the world. In 1855 the Evangelical Alliance sent a memorial to the sultan of Turkey appealing to him against the Moslem custom of inflicting death on those who converted to another faith. As a result, the sultan issued to the Vizier a *firman* declaring religious freedom for all subjects, "As all forms of religion are and shall be freely professed in my empire, no subject shall be hindered in the exercise of the religion he professes, nor shall be in any way annoyed on this account..." J.W. Ewing. *Goodly Fellowship: A Centenary Tribute to the Life and Work of the World's Evangelical Alliance, 1846-1946.* London: Marshall, Morgan & Scott, Ltd., 1946. Steve Brady and Harold Rowde, ed. *For Such a Time as This*. Scripture Union, 1996, 149-155. Sadly, the sultan's decree was ignored as Turkish persecution of Christians steadily increased from 1870-1915.

[7] *Diary*, December 12, 1866.

[8] Samuel C. Bartlett. *Historical Sketches of the Missions of the American Board in Turkey.* New York: Arno Press, 1972 (reprint of 1876 edition, published in Boston), 3; Albert Have Lybyer, "America's Missionary Record in Turkey," *Current History* (Vol. XIX, February, 1924), 802-803.

[9] Genesis 10:2-3

[10] II Kings 19:37; Isaiah 37:38

[11] Ezekiel 37:14 and 38:6.

[12] Matthias R. Heilig. *The Story of Armenia.* Dansville, N.Y.: F.A. Owen Publishing Co., 1920; Rev. Joseph K. Greene. *Leavening the Levant.* The Pilgrim Press, 1916, 19-20; Leon Arpee. *A History of Armenian Christianity.* New York: Armenian Missionary Association of America, Inc., 1946, 1-188; Rev. M.P. Parmelee, "The Armenian Church," *The Missionary Herald*, July 1868, 210-212.

[13] William Ellsworth Strong. *The Story of the American Board*. Boston: Pilgrim Press, 1910, 80-91; Bartlett. *Historical Sketches*, 1-6. Claudius Buchanan in his *Christian Researches in Asia* (Boston: Samuel F. Armstrong, 1811), 206 wrote that "A learned author, in a work published about the beginning of the last century (i.e. early 1700's), entitled "The Light of the Gospel, rising on all nations": 'that the Armenian Christians will be most eminently qualified for the office of extending the knowledge of Christianity throughout the nation of Asia...Their general character is that of a wealthy, industrious, and enterprising people...Wherever they colonize, they build churches, and observe the solemnities of the Christian religion in a decorous manner.'" As merchants they could be found from Canton to Constantinople, making them the ideal Christian missionary to the eastern lands. Smith and Dwight were undoubtedly familiar with Buchanan's work. They called their own report *Christian Researches in Armenia.*

[14] Fred Field Goodsell. *They Lived Their Faith: An Almanac of Faith, Hope, and Love.* Boston: American Board of Commissioners for Foreign Mission, 1961, 415.

[15] Greene. *Leavening the Levant*, 99-100.

[16] Turkish-Armenian was the Armenian language written in Arabic script. Interestingly, though the Turkish language itself was usually written in Arabic script, at times it was written in Greek script. There had been movements towards reform within the Gregorian church before the ABCFM missionaries arrived. About 1760, an Armenian priest, familiar with the reformation begun by Martin Luther, wrote a book exposing the errors of the Gregorian church at that time and referring repeatedly to the Bible as the standard by which the church and priests were to be measured. In 1813, six years before the first ABCFM missionary was appointed to Palestine, the British and Foreign Bible Societies began printing copies of the Bible in Armenian. These copies, however, were in the fourth century old Armenian and difficult for most nineteenth century Armenians to understand. Even so, there was a great interest among the Armenians in the Scriptures. The ABCFM very early in the mission began a Bible translation into modern Armenian. Whereas the old Armenian Bible had been translated from the LXX and the Vulgate, the modern Armenian translation was from the Hebrew and Greek. This in itself produced differences of meaning in places. At first the Gregorian Church was adamantly opposed to the modern Armenian translation, claiming it was not the Word of God. After a generation of intense controversy, however, the Gregorian Church accepted the modern Armenian translation. Many Gregorians began reading and understanding the Bible, and a reformation within the church itself began. This reformation was largely due to the influence of the ABCFM missionaries and the Bible translation. J.D. Barton. *Daybreak in Turkey*. Boston: Penguin Press, 1908, 150-154.

[17] Strong. *Story of the American Board*, 92-93; Jeremy Salt. *Imperialism, Evangelism, and the Ottoman Armenian, 1878-1896*. Frank Cass, 1993, 33-35; Bartlett. *Historical Sketches*, 6-9.

[18] "Sublime Porte" is a French translation of the Turkish for "Gate of the Eminent", the official name of the gate giving entrance to the block of buildings in Constantinople that housed the various state departments. In 1930, the city's name was changed from Constantinople to Istanbul.

[19] Lootfy Levonia, "The Millet System in the Middle East," *Muslim World* (Vol. 42, 1952), 90-96; Kamel S. Abu Jaber, "The Millet System in the Nineteenth Century Ottoman Empire," *Muslim World* (Vol. 57. No. 3, July, 1967), 212-223. Richard Hovannisian noted that the millet system brought a certain advantage to minorities: "Most Armenian laymen, for example, were shielded from direct contact with the central government by the official hierarchy of their millet, and the Armenian church, though losing much of its spiritual and intellectual vitality, found it possible to maintain the separate identity of the nation. While the Ottoman Empire was still mighty and expanding, the Armenians enjoyed more peace and security than at any other time since the fall of their medieval kingdoms." "The Armenian Question in the Ottoman Empires," *East European Quarterly*, 6, no. 1, March 1972, 3.

[20] In 1893, the Society was renamed the Bible Lands Mission Aid Society. The Society was nondenominational and included Anglicans, as well as nonconformists. In the last half of the nineteenth century, the Society contributed $335,000 for work in Asia Minor and European Turkey.

[21] Arpee. *History of Armenian Christianity*, 274. There were other missions in Turkey, including Roman Catholics (especially from France), the British Bible Society, Church Missionary Society, the Bible Land's Mission Aid Society, British Syrian Mission Schools and Bible Work, Church of Scotland Mission to the Jews, the Society of Friends, the Irish Presbyterian Mission, the Reformed Presbyterian Mission, and the German Deaconesses. The ABCFM missions, however, were the best organized, widespread, and influential. By the 1890's, there were 250 American missionaries within Turkey's borders. *Armenian Massacres and Turkish Tyranny*, 148-156.

[22] Bartlett. *Historical Sketches*, 15.

[23] *Diary*, January 8, 1867.

[24] Though the town had been known as Aintab since the days of the Hittites, its modern name is "Gazientep." Ataturk changed the name of many of the towns because of the valor in beating off the French in the War for Independence. Marash became "Kahramanmarash (Hero), Aintab became "Gazientep (Warrior), and Ourfa became "Sanliurfa: (Glorious). Since ancient times Aintab has been famous for its pistachio nuts. Dana Facaros and Michael Pauls. *Cadogan Guide to Turkey*. Chester, Conn.: The Globe Pequot Press, 1988, 326.

[25] Charles Holbrook, "Along Turkish Highways," *Envelope Series* (a quarterly of the ABCFM), vol. XIV, no. 4, January 1912, 7, ABC 77.1 (29.6).

[26] Colporteurs were native Christian workers who sold Bibles and Christian tracts in the villages. Bible Readers were another category of workers who went into the villages to interest the people, especially the women, in the Bible by reading it to them with brief explanations.
[27] Joseph Greene. *Leavening the Levant*, 84-86; "Aintab and the Girls' Boarding School," *The Missionary Herald*, vol. LXV, March 1869, 73-75.
[28] *Diary*, January 11, 1867
[29] "Rev. Benjamin Schneider, D.D.," *The Missionary Herald*, vol. LXXIII, December, 1877, 385-389.
[30] *Diary*, January 16, 1867.
[31] *Diary*, June 20, 1867.
[32] *Ten Years on the Euphrates*, 153-161.
[33] David H. Finnie. *Pioneers East.* Cambridge, Massachusetts: Harvard University Press, 1967, 133; Albert Howe Lybyer. "America's Missionary Record in Turkey," *Current History*, XIX (February 1924), 808.
[34] "Central Turkey – Survey of the Missions of the Board," *The Missionary Herald*, January 1867.
[35] Fred Field Goodsell. *You Shall Be My Witnesses.* Boston: ABCFM, 1959, 205-207.
[36] "Central Turkey Mission: Aintab," *The Missionary Herald*, May 1868, 149-150.
[37] *Diary*, September 19, 1867.
[38] *Diary*, October 22, 1867.
[39] *Diary*, June 5, 1868.
[40] "Letter from Mr. Perry, October 19, 1868," *The Missionary Herald*, January 1869, 22-23.
[41] *Cadogen Guide to Turkey*, 328-329.
[42] *Diary*, January 1869.
[43] *Diary*, October 1869.
[44] *Diary*, November 25, 1869; May 21, 1871.
[45] *Diary*, 1870 introduction and January 10, 1870.
[46] Henry described in detail in his diary Dr. Post's method of filling his teeth. First he put wooden wedges in the teeth, rather than filing down the tooth and losing valuable parts of the tooth. This was very painful as the teeth moved and became inflamed. Three days later fillings were put in and a second set of wedges closing the places widened by the first fillings. Then the second fillings were put in. Years later Henry added to his diary that at the age of 85, Dr. Post's fillings were still in place.

Though his trip to Beirut was a longer trip to the dentist than usual, Henry regularly notes throughout his diary when either he or Jeanne visited the dentist. In May 1880, both Jeanne and Henry had dental work throughout much of their stay in Constantinople during the annual meeting. Jeanne took chloroform and had six teeth removed. On June 18, 1881, Henry went to a barber in Sivas to have one of his teeth extracted, and the barber broke off part of his jaw in the process!

[47] *Diary*, February 10, 1870. ABCFM missionaries founded the Syrian Protestant College in 1866; it's now the American Univeersity in Beirut. Even with the financial pressures of the American Civil War, Dr. Daniel Bliss raised the funds and established the college, whose charter was granted by the state of New York. From the beginning the college had a strong emphasis on medical training. The cornerstone of the first building, dedicated in December 1871, expressed the guiding principle of the college:

> This College is for all conditions and classes of men without regard to color, nationality, race, or religion. A man, white, black, or yellow, Christian, Jew, Mohammedan or heathen, may enter and enjoy all the advantages of this institution for three, four, or eight years; and go out believing in one God, in many gods, or in no God. But it will be impossible for anyone to continue with us long without knowing what we believe to be the truth and our reasons for that belief. (www.aub.edu.lb)

In 1920, the college became the American University of Beirut and today is a secular university.

[48] *Diary*, March 30, 1870.
[49] *Diary*, May 30, 1870.

4
FELLOWSHIP OF HIS SUFFERING
(1870-1876)

---

*"that I may know Him and the power of His resurrection,
and the fellowship of His sufferings..."*
Philippians 3:10

The beauty of the Turkish landscape always moved Henry, and he found the natural scenery around Marash magnificent. Located fifty-four miles north of Aintab, Marash lay among the scattered foothills of the Taurus Mountains. Most of the inhabitants of the mountains and valleys around Marash were Moslems, but about 26,000, almost one-third, were Armenians. 10,000 Armenians lived in Marash itself, while the rest lived in thirty surrounding villages.[1]

Marash was one of the oldest cities in Anatolia, first mentioned around the twelfth century B.C. as Marqasi, capital of the Hittite Kingdom of Gurgun. In 711 B.C., Assyrian King Sargon II conquered Gurgun, but Scythians and Persians controlled the area in later centuries. Alexander the Great conquered Marash and its environs in 333 B.C., and at his death the area passed to the Seleucids. Under the Romans the city was known as Germanica, and many Armenians in Henry's day still called the town Kermanig after its Roman name. During ensuing centuries, the Byzantines, Arabs, Armenians, Crusaders, and Seljuks controlled Marash, until it finally came into the hands of the Ottoman Turks in the sixteenth century.[2]

Benjamin Schneider first brought the Gospel to Marash in 1852, under much opposition. One Armenian interested in learning the Scriptures brought Dr. Schneider to his home, but his wife exclaimed, "Why have you brought here that Satan?" Only the protection of the Turkish governor prevented Dr. Schneider from being driven from the town. God's love soon prevailed, however, and a wonderful change could be seen in a few years. One Armenian declared an extra 500 pounds of candles would be used in the winter as the families in Marash read their Bibles together. In 1854, a Protestant church with 16 members was formed. By 1862, the Protestants had increased to 1101 persons. The people were extremely poor, but they gave sacrificially to the support of the church. It was estimated that the entire property of the Protestant community did not exceed $25,000, yet annually they paid taxes amounting to $800 and gave $500 for religious and educational purposes. In 1864 the Central Turkey Mission decided to move the ten year old theological school from Aintab to Marash, where they thought the students would have a good evangelistic impact.[3]

In October 1872, the Perrys completed their move from Aintab to Marash. Working together, Jeanne and Henry soon had their house in order. Their home included a sitting room, dining room, bedroom and study downstairs, and a guest room upstairs. Mrs. Coffing had the remainder of the upstairs rooms.

Mrs. Coffing was one of the many remarkable individuals serving in Turkey. She was born Josephine Lemmert in 1833, in Dresden, Ohio. Her father died when she was ten, and she learned early how to live with hardship and difficulty. Personal courage and bravery must have been in the family blood. Among numerous relatives who fought in the American Civil War, 21 of Josephine's cousins fell in battle. By that time, however, Josephine had married the Reverend Jackson G. Coffing, and in 1857, the couple sailed for Turkey. The Reverend Coffing had worked vigorously in the Sunday School movement in the States, and the Coffings were sent to Turkey to develop the Sunday Schools there. When they arrived in Aintab, forty or fifty children were in the Sunday School. Soon attendance averaged 1400. Even the Moslem donkey boys were singing the gospel children's songs!

In 1861, Reverend Coffing felt his work in Aintab was complete and it was time to move to a field that had not heard the gospel. He and Mrs. Coffing moved to Hadjin, a town in the Taurus Mountains with a population of 20,000. The region was noted for its robbers and murders and was under the power of the chieftain Kazan Oghloo. The Turkish government had no authority over the mountaineers, and Oghloo ruled supreme. When the Coffings began building their house,

Oghloo ordered them to leave. The chieftain feared that if the people became Protestants they would become law-abiding, and his empire of brigandage would collapse. When Mr. Coffing refused to follow Oghloo's order, a mob assembled. The mob forcibly removed Mr. and Mrs. Coffing from their tent and threw all of their possessions into a ravine. The Coffings spent the night in a vineyard and after three days finally returned to Adana.

The following year, in March 1862, when Mr. Coffing was traveling to the annual meeting of the mission, highwaymen rushed from the bush and shot Mr. Coffing and his servant. The servant died instantly, but Mr. Coffing was taken to Alexandretta and died the next morning. The Coffings were extremely devoted to each other, and Mrs. Coffing felt she must remain in Turkey to continue the work they had begun together. She not only ran the Young Ladies' Seminary in Marash, but she regularly made tours into the surrounding mountain villages. Uncomplainingly the little woman stayed in homes filled with filth and vermin for the opportunity of sharing the Gospel with the people.[4]

Mrs. Coffing's life of service and self-denial was a worthy example for Jeanne and Henry as they settled into their new mission station. The Perrys were joining six missionaries already in Marash. Miss Mary Williams assisted Mrs. Coffing in the girls' school, and Revs. T.C. Trowbridge and Giles Montgomery taught in the Theological School with Henry. Their wives, Margaret Trowbridge and Emily Montgomery, were of great help to Jeanne during the difficult days ahead.

Henry worked diligently in preparation for his classes at the seminary. There were no theological textbooks in Armenian, and the students did not understand English well enough to use the English texts. Consequently, Henry had to write all of the lessons out himself. He summarized the key points of the subject for each lesson, then, with the help of a good teacher, translated the summary analysis into Armeno-Turkish. He dictated the summary to the students, and this became their basic text. Henry then lectured on the subject, using illustrations and diagrams, and asking and answering questions. His prayer always was that the Lord would use him to teach His Word and His will. Whatever the specific lesson, "at the fore in the development of every part, is the Person of Our Lord Jesus Christ, the Eternal Son of God, the 'King of Kings and Lord of Lords, Him Let these students preach! Christ and Him Crucified!' in the Spirit of Stephen the Martyr."[5] Many of the theological students Perry taught were later killed in the Armenian massacres. They preached "in the Spirit of Stephen the Martyr" more than Perry could possibly have realized at the time.

With four courses to teach, Henry had to prepare twelve lessons a week. Five of these were written compositions for the students to copy into their notebooks. His lesson preparations consumed much of his time, but Perry relished the study and teaching. There was great joy in training those who would be ministers of the gospel to the people of Turkey.

One of the students at the Marash Preparatory School was Agop Koundakjian, who as a boy had been Perry's first guide to Hassan Beyle. Hassan Beyle was part of the Amanus Mountains, and had been controlled by robber bands for centuries. As they traveled together, Henry talked to thirteen-year-old Agop about Jesus, and the boy became a Christian. Agop eagerly began attending the boys' school at Marash and then studied at the theological school. Perry's ministry in Turkey was beginning to bear fruit.

In addition to teaching in the theological school, Henry continued with his responsibilities as treasurer of the Central Turkey Mission. This involved much bookkeeping, letter-writing to the outstations and Boston, and distribution of funds to the various missionaries. Whenever possible, Henry also visited the surrounding villages and outstations. On occasion Jeanne was able to accompany him. Though often sick, she had a passion and a heart for bringing the gospel to the outlying areas. Her beautiful voice and compassion for the people complimented Henry's gospel teaching. Sometimes Henry went to the nearby villages on Saturday to minister to the people on Sunday. In places where there was no church, Henry found himself a room to stay; a group of people then gathered in his room to hear teaching from the Bible. When one audience had "listened sufficiently" they left, and another group formed to hear Henry's message. Such gospel ministry among the people refreshed Henry after a week of teaching school!

It was a strenuous life, and Langdan Ward, treasurer of the ABCFM in Boston, wrote Henry, "Don't work so as to break down, and be laid aside; for your sake; for our sakes; and for the Master's sake."[6] However, in addition to the pressures of work, added strains were placed on Henry at this time. Henry's mother wrote of his father's severe illness and then of them having to rent another house in Boston. It was difficult being an only son so far from home and unable to help his dear parents. Yet all this had been considered before Henry went to the mission field. At a meeting of the American Board, Dr.

H.H. Jessup of Beirut had told Henry, "It is a matter of trust on God. If the Lord has called you to His vineyard in Turkey, you may trust Him to care for your parents; if they consent to your going. In that case, they will have a share in it." As Henry learned of his father's gradual recovery from his severe illness, he could only exclaim, "How wonderful Our Heavenly Father has cared for us all."[7] Alvan's own continued interest in the mission work was shown in part by his sending $32 in gold to support two of Henry's theological students for seven months.

Henry was also deeply distressed by Jeanne's and little Lizzie's health. Both suffered in the hot climate; Jeanne had contracted malaria and was often feverish and suffering from diarrhea. Lizzie was weak and not flourishing. On May 7, 1871, Lizzie Eunice was baptized in the Perry's sitting room. Dr. and Mrs. Clark of the ABCFM were visiting from Boston, and Dr. Clark baptized the little one as the eight Marash missionaries and several Armenian friends looked on. Jeanne and Henry were impressed with the scene and touched "with deep fervor; and abiding allegiance to Christ, our true Lord and Master."[8]

At the end of May, the Perrys moved to their summer home in Kerkhan to escape the heat. In spite of the change of climate, Lizzie Eunice continued to lose strength. She breathed her last on June 1, 1871; she was only a year and a half. Her weakness and suffering had been so great that in the end it was a relief that the Lord took her to Himself. Mr. Trowbridge prepared a little box, and the ladies prepared the baby for burial. After a brief service in Kerkhan, Henry took the casket on his saddle and rode into Marash. There was another brief service before the baby was buried in the Mission yard, beside others who had gone before. Henry marveled at Jeanne's sweet expression of total trust in God, who sustained her throughout Lizzie's sickness and death. Both Jeanne and Henry were comforted by their firm belief that the Lord had taken their child to give her a place with Him, better than any home on earth could be. God knew best, and they were able to trust Him.

Henry and Jeanne had now buried two babies. Though he had no doubt that the Lord eternally saved those babies who died in infancy, Henry took time to carefully study the Scriptures on the subject, "thus to have the case well-proved for my comfort continuously."[9] Basic to Henry's comfort was that Jesus died for the sins of infants as well as those of a mature age. As they share in Christ's death, so they will share in the resurrection unto life through Him. Those children were lifted to a place of triumph and would be "blameless in the day of our

Lord Jesus Christ" (I Corinthians 1:8-9). Henry was comforted by the blessed hope "that our children who die in infancy have preceded us, in their entrance into the presence and Glory of the King!"[10]

Comfort also came with the birth of another little daughter on July 27, 1871. Jeanne loved children, and the loss of her first two girls increased the joy of the third daughter's arrival. They named the child Mary Schneider, in recognition of missionary Mary Williams' sweet kindness and all the Schneiders had done for them in their first mission station.

When the school term resumed in October, the Perrys returned to Marash. Mary Schneider was never a healthy baby and always seemed weak. Jeanne too continued to suffer from fever and diarrhea. In between attacks she was her animated self, but increasingly her health suffered. It became obvious to Henry that something must be done, but what was unclear. He continually prayed for the Lord's wisdom and direction. On Friday October 20, three-month old Mary Schneider breathed her last. The next day she was buried in the Mission House yard beside Lizzie. The missionaries, native pastors, and others were overflowing in sympathy for Henry and Jeanne, who had now lost three little ones. Yet Henry could say with a trusting faith that they did not count the children lost to them, "Our Dear Lord has them in charge."[11]

Jeanne's own health continued feeble. On a weekend preaching tour to Zeitoun with Mrs. Coffing, Henry was surprised to meet Dr. Henry West of Sivas and urged him to come to Marash to examine Jeanne. Dr. West had come to Sivas in 1859, the first of several physicians the ABCFM sent to Turkey. When he saw Jeanne, the doctor insisted she come to Sivas immediately and be his guest throughout the autumn and winter. He was optimistic that the interior city's elevation and cooler climate would restore Jeanne to health. Within the week, Henry and Jeanne set off on the ten-day journey to Sivas, Henry traveling on horseback and Jeanne in a Maffa. It was a difficult journey through the mountains and across the plains where in ancient times the armies of Greece and Persia had marched. Though several places were noted for robbers and bandits, the Perrys encountered no danger along the way. Jeanne never complained, but throughout the journey she suffered from fever and chills. How joyous they were to see a carriage waiting for them as they began descending the mountains overlooking Sivas.

Henry stayed in Sivas a week to see Jeanne settled with Dr. and Mrs. West before returning to Marash. Little did he realize at the time that Sivas would later become his major field of missionary service. Parting with Jeanne to return to Marash was difficult, but "The joy of it was clear that the Dear Lord was about to restore her health."[12]

On the return journey, Henry rode as far as Gürün with Ed Riggs and had a wonderful visit along the way. Ed's parents, Elias and Martha, had first come to Turkey in 1838. A skilled linguist, Elias Riggs translated the Bible into Armenian and Bulgarian and aided in the translation of the Bible into Turkish. Three of Elias' children, Margaret, Edward, and Charles, continued to serve on the Turkey mission field. Edward Riggs was able to share with Henry some of the family's experiences and insights from their years in Turkey.[13]

Before reaching Marash, while at Albustan for the Sabbath, Henry came down with a fever. His flesh was yellow, and he realized he suffered from jaundice. Nevertheless, he preached to the people in Albustan that Sunday.

Back at Marash, Henry threw himself into his work even more intensely. Teaching at the Seminary, keeping the accounts for the Central Turkey Mission, and preaching in the villages whenever possible consumed his days. He rejoiced in every letter from Jeanne and her reports of improved health, yet sorrow continued with him. November 7, 1871, when Henry and Jeanne were together in Sivas, Alvan Perry had died in Boston. The pastors at Boston's Old South Church and Alvan's friends at the Customs House did everything to help Henry's mother during this time. Sarah Ann moved back to Ashfield and began repairing their home there. Henry wrote his mother:

> May the Lord sustain you, Dear Mother, in all your trial of loneliness! We cannot weep for father; for he has gone to be "like Jesus, for he shall see Him as He is [I John 3:2]." Only for ourselves can we mourn. Like a shock of corn fully ripe, father went up to his reward. To us a work remains e'er we too go thither.[14]

Henry held his father in deep reverence, and the years did not lessen his sense of loss at his father's death. The following year he wrote,

> His memory is still precious and vivid as though it were only yesterday when with a buoyant and brave heart, he sent us forth from Boston to Aintab in 1866. His influence over me in my youth was very positive. I yielded to his judgment and marked his words containing the wisdom which I needed, and since his death the feeling of loss has led me to treasure the teaching of his life. What a blessing

to...have had such a father, to guide and train me...I cannot mourn for him, tho' still oppressed with the feeling of loss, for I hope to meet him soon in the glorified state. "Blessed are the dead who died in the Lord." [Rev. 14:13][15]

Within a year Henry had lost two little girls and his father, and his beloved Jeanne was in poor health in a distant city. It was only natural for Jeanne to write Henry from Sivas asking why the Lord caused them to suffer so. Henry replied, "That we may know Jesus, and the efficacy of His resurrection; and may participate in His sufferings, and be assimilated to His death."[16]

Henry's trials were not only personal; he also had to deal with opposition to the missionaries within the Moslem community:

> One annoyance we have in this Moslem country, especially when we have some of the women with us, is that Moslem boys have the habit of throwing stones...which can be dangerous, especially when they use a sling...When they become too impudent, I have my horse and, if the coast is clear, I quickly make a charge raid at them which they much fear, and I notice that they look out to keep clear of me when I have a horse.[17]

Mrs. Coffing's students had to pass through a Moslem quarter of Marash on the way to school and were often bothered by Moslem boys throwing stones. On one occasion Henry intervened and pounded the offending boy with his cane. Some Moslem men came up, put Henry's hands behind his back and forcibly took him to their Moslem leaders. Under the millet system, since a Moslem was accusing a Christian, Henry appealed to the Governor and applied his right to be represented by a lawyer. Reverend Avedis Constantian, a pastor of the Second Church in Marash, represented Henry. He turned the defense into a charge against the Moslems for attacking Mrs. Coffing's girls. The case was tried before the *mutassarif*, the local sub-*vilayet* governor:

> In the course of the charge against me for the injury of the boy, whose head my fist struck [the lawyer's phraseology], a complaint against the Government of Marash, for insufficient protection, began to be developed. The Governor got nervous, and tried to stop off the complaint.

Mrs. Coffing had already filed a complaint with the Turkish government, and Henry sent a record of the events to the American consul in

Beirut. When the Turkish government realized the American consul might intervene, its attitude changed. Faced with the threat of review by higher authority in Constantinople, the *mutassarif* began to protect the missionaries:

> ...the governor sent for soldiers daily dressed in workmen's clothing, who followed the girls on their way to school. In one day they seized six boys and put their fathers in prison. When this situation was once settled...no further difficulty occurred.[18]

At last spring came, and Henry looked forward to being reunited with Jeanne. The plan was for Jeanne and Dr. West to travel to Constantinople, where Henry would go as a delegate from the Central Mission for the annual meeting in May. Two of the female missionaries from the Central Turkey station were going home, Miss Wood, "having lost her mental balance," and Miss Hollister, being ill. Hattie Powers agreed to accompany the ladies to Boston, while Henry served as the ladies' escort from Central Turkey to Smyrna, where they would catch an English steamer for Liverpool. At Antioch, Henry was overwhelmed by the destruction everywhere from the earthquake a few weeks before. Sunday morning April 2, he had felt his house in Marash shake violently, but the center of the quake had been at Antioch. The stone houses were destroyed, and piles of stone stood where houses once were. Amazingly, the missionary house survived, and none of the missionaries were hurt. The Turks thought the wood-framed house was haunted, so only the Americans would occupy it. However, the flexibility of the wooden frame helped save the house![19]

Though it was only May, the heat in Antioch and on the road to Alexandretta was intense. Often the missionary party had to camp at night in the open air, and Henry contracted malaria. But there was nothing to do but go on. Besides, his Jeanne would be waiting for him in Constantinople. At Alexandretta the group took a Russian steamer for Smyrna, and in Smyrna Henry oversaw the transfer of the ladies' baggage to the Liverpool steamer. It was an exhausting process requiring permits from the U.S. Consul and completion of many government forms. Henry was able, however, to visit the Armenian quarter of Smyrna and the Protestant pastor there, one of Henry's former pupils.

Finally, on May 25, Henry arrived in Constantinople and went to Dr. Pratt's house at Rumali Hissar, near Robert College on the Bosphorus. Dr. Pratt had been the Central Turkey Mission Treasurer before Henry and had founded the Theological School of Marash. He had come to Constantinople to help revise the translation of the Turkish Bible. The Perrys stayed with the Pratts during the Annual Meeting, as did Dr. and Mrs. Schneider. It was a grand reunion with those who had first mentored Henry when he came to Turkey. Even more exciting was Henry's reunion with Jeanne:

> ... I noticed at once how much my Jeanne had recovered in flesh and strength since I left her at Sivas six months ago,
> It was an outburst of praise to God for his grace and healing Mercy that he had arranged for this joyful reunion!...
> What a blessing it is from the Lord, that my wife and I meet here after a separation of six months! To Him also praise, that her health is so much improved since I took her from Marash to Sivas in October 1871. Her patience and her supreme wish to follow the Lord's guidance, however great the self-denial, has been happily proved. To Him be the praise, that he has given one such a wife, who indeed loves the Mission service; and has the gift by singing to impart the message of the Cross...To sing reaches the heart, especially of the Children![20]

Joyous as he was at being again with Jeanne, Henry was very ill. Suffering from malaria and exhaustion, with chills, fever, and a severe headache, he could not attend the first four days of the Missions' conference. With quinine and Jeanne's loving nursing, Henry gradually became better. As he took his much-needed rest, Henry reflected on his missionary work. He recalled Jesus' words in John 15:7, "If ye abide in me, and my words abide in you, ye shall ask what ye will, and it shall be done unto you," and he reflected,

> O, how much we need to keep close to the life and teaching of our glorious Lord! Such crowds of people about who do so much need Him! And we are here in Constantinople and Marash to teach and preach <u>Him</u>, and win by <u>His</u> grace! Let His Holy Spirit breathe through our whole being. Abiding in Christ renews and sanctifies the will; we ask what we will; and he will give it to us.[21]

In spite of Henry's illness, the Perrys' first visit to Constantinople was a time of refreshment, both physically and spiritually. Many leaders of the ABCFM Turkish mission were there, including Drs. Bliss, Riggs, and Washburn. Henry had first heard Dr. Elias Riggs speak seventeen years earlier at the Jubilee Celebration at Williams, where Henry first felt called to be a missionary. Now he was serving with

Riggs in the Turkey field. It was invigorating to see how the Christian work was progressing in the Ottoman Empire's capital and beyond. On Monday, June 10, Henry was well enough to attend the dedication service of the Bible House.

The Bible House was the dream of Dr. Isaac Bliss, who first came to Turkey as a missionary in 1847. Stationed in Erzerum, he was among the first to open up the Euphrates valley to missionary work. His health broke under his tireless labors, however, and he resigned from the ABCFM. The American Bible Society then invited him to be their representative in the Levant. His field included Greece, Egypt, Syria, Mesopotamia, and Persia. Since Constantinople was the port most missionaries landed at before reaching their field, Dr. Bliss saw the need for a Bible House in Constantinople. In 1866, he came to the United States to raise funds for the project, the same time his brother, Daniel, was raising funds to establish the college in Beirut. Though the country was still recovering from the Civil War, Bliss was able to raise sufficient funds for the Bible House from both Christians in the United States and native Christians in Turkey. In 1872 the building was completed and ready for dedication. It was one of the finest and most imposing buildings in Constantinople. Dr. Bliss enthusiastically showed Henry and the other guests through the rooms, outlining the future plans for Bible printing and distribution which the building would house.[22]

On the following Sunday evening Dr. Washburn invited Henry to preach to the boys at Robert College. The College, established in 1863, had already become a beacon of educational excellence throughout the region. Henry was able to speak to the boys in Turkish and made his sermon simple, direct, and short. It was a joy to be able to meet the young men, the leaders of the future, and share the Scriptures with them.

Mrs. Schneider made a point to take Henry and Jeanne in tow to see the city sites, including the mosques and baths. But there were also chores to be done in the metropolis before heading back to the hinterlands. Jeanne needed a lot of dental work done. The Perrys purchased clothing and household goods in Constantinople rather than ordering from Boston as they usually did. Finances were tight from living separately at Marash and Sivas, so they had to limit their purchases. They had their photos taken, wrote long letters to Mrs. Perry at Ashfield, then said their farewells to their Constantinople friends before boarding a French steamer to Samsoun on the Black Sea.

The plan was for the Perrys to spend the summer in Sivas, keeping Jeanne from the summer heat of Marash, then return to Marash in the fall, in time for Henry to resume teaching in the Theological School. The two-week journey from Samsoun to Sivas was especially difficult for Jeanne, suffering from fever and neuralgia. There was not an improved road for travel, and the mules and packhorses traveled slowly along the 220 miles. They spent the first Sunday in Marsovan, where Henry preached in the church. On Wednesday they left for Amasia, a city in a gorge by the riverside. Henry was fascinated by the history of the place and wished he had time to explore. An old castle could be seen on one of the crags overhanging the city. In ancient times, Amasia had been the capital of King Mithradates' Pontus. In 47 B.C., Julius Caesar defeated Pontus' King Pharnaces and uttered his famous phrase, "I came, I saw, I conquered" (*Veni, vidi, vici*). Pontius Pilate was reputedly born in Pontus; Paul's friend and fellow-tentmaker Aquila was also born there (Acts 18).

By the following Sunday the Perrys reached Tocat, an outstation of the Sivas field. Henry again preached in the church. In the orchard near the chapel Henry and Jeanne visited the monument to Henry Martyn, the English missionary to India and Persia who died in Tocat in 1812. His young life full of dedication and devotion to the Savior was an example and challenge to all in missionary service.

Finally, on July 11, 1872, Henry and Jeanne reached Sivas. Ed Riggs and his family were spending the summer in Gürün, so the Perrys, along with Flavia Bliss, lived in their house. Their servant and cook Hagop came from Marash to help them throughout the summer. The Riggs' house was spacious and situated well to catch the breeze. Ed Riggs' study was perfect for Henry. Though he had learned Armeno-Turkish (Turkish using the Armenian alphabet), he realized that was not sufficient. That summer he hired a Moslem teacher to teach him Arabo-Turkish (Turkish with the Arabic alphabet). He worked hard at his studies. As a relief from his work he rode his horse Prince out in the countryside.

Henry found the spiritual outlook at Sivas very different from the thriving churches at Marash. Though the church had a good Armenian pastor, the congregation was small. Those in attendance did not participate in prayer meetings or other Christian service. The missionaries in Sivas, however, worked together in good harmony, and Henry and Jeanne were happy living and ministering with them a few months.[23]

By the first of September, it was time for Henry and Jeanne to leave Sivas and return to their own missionary field in Marash. Along the way, Henry took a side trip to Hadjin for a special ordination service. The doctor feared the side trip would be too much for Jeanne, so she stayed in Albustan, reading and ministering to the women there.

At Hadjin, Henry met Mr. Montgomery, Mrs. Coffing, and others for the ordination service. It was a most amazing and joyous time, especially for Mrs. Coffing, who, with her husband, had been forcibly expelled from the town eleven years before. Now when she approached the city, a mass of people came to welcome her with joy and singing. Mrs. Coffing wrote a friend:

> Can you doubt that these were among the happiest days of my life? Cannot I say that "It is good to wait on the Lord." More than one of those who were formed into the church trace their first impressions to the truth to the hymns sung during that day when the mob pulled our tent down over our heads. "Cast thy bread upon the waters, for thou shalt find it after many days."[24]

Henry too found the organization of the Hadjin church and the ordination of its pastors one of the most joyful occasions he had ever attended. Only the power of God could have produced such a change among the people. Henry recalled that

> four years before, Mr. Montgomery and I preached on a house-top, chiefly to strangers who came to see and hear us. Now they have a regularly organized Protestant community and a church more than one-half self-supporting, a pleasant chapel, a faithful and successful pastor; and the spirit of inquiry is general in the city. The whole neighboring region is cleared of robbers, and in their place the work of evangelization is spreading among the villages.[25]

Henry was happy to return to Albustan and find Jeanne in good health and ready to continue their journey to Marash. Tuesday September 19, Henry and Jeanne enjoyed a quiet day together. Henry enjoyed the rest, visiting with Jeanne, and writing letters. It was the Perrys sixth anniversary, and though

> ...the review of these few years shows much of sickness, suffering, and death, in our home; yet in it all we have been drawn nearer to the precious Saviour; and more into the fellowship of His sufferings. In his way he led us to a more entire consecration of His service: the

years have been laden with soul blessing; and we have feasted upon the heavenly manna and have felt richly compensated.

The Perrys stayed at Albustan through Sunday, and Henry rejoiced to see how much good Jeanne had done among the people during her two weeks there. The way she especially reached out to the children was beautiful to see.

Once back in Marash, Henry resumed his teaching in the Theological School. The school had thirty students, and the spiritual interest in the Marash churches was good. On the weekends Henry continued his practice of riding out into the surrounding villages to preach where there was no pastor. Jeanne often rode with him. For longer preaching tours, an Armenian preacher usually accompanied him. On one two-week tour to the village of Sis, Henry and Pastor Killisle Kevork stayed overnight in a Moslem village. Henry's diary contains his impressions:

> These Moslem villages, see how they live! Two rooms in the house; one for all the animals together, the other for the family. The women do all the work of the fields; the men talk and ride about on their horses: give orders to the women; and give their own time to pleasure. They entertain us as is their custom. We talked of our Lord to them.
> Kevork and I visited the village of Yenzi Kala, which is Armenian; and we were comfortable.[26]

All in all, the winter of 1873, was a good one in Marash. Emily Montgomery and Jeanne were like sisters, and Henry was happy following Giles Montgomery's leadership:

> Somehow at Marash the Lord seemed to rest; and impart the blessing of His Presence. The two Protestant churches with their congregations had become large; and the germ of the Third had been formed. The schools were large and fruitful and the Hand of the Lord was clearly seen in the fine quality of the Theological Students.[27]

But, by the end of April the heat returned. Though they had planned to move to the summer home in Kerkhan, Henry feared Jeanne could not take another summer there. She was with child again, and her health became serious. When Henry wrote to Dr. West for advice, Dr. West said Jeanne must leave immediately for the United States. He would write the American Board and explain the medical necessity.

June 16, 1873, Henry and Jeanne departed Marash for Ashfield. They took sea voyages from Alexandretta to Smyrna and from Smyrna to Liverpool. During their sixteen days in Liverpool they had some wool clothing made, since it was cheaper there. The voyage from Liverpool to New York on the Cunard line took ten days. From New York they took the train to South Deerfield, where they found a two-horse carriage (actually, the carriage had come for a party that did not arrive on that train):

> It was in the afternoon of a most beautiful day of sunshine. The afternoon sunshine through the trees was a special delight to Jeanne who watched it with joy all the way. It was indeed a gleeful ride...O! how quickly the horses had taken us to Ashfield. The street appeared all in its natural beauty! The afternoon sun shone through the green-flowing Maples.
> Mother met us at the door, having received news of our arrival. Joy was in her face; and in our hearts. This was my own and Dear Jeanne's home.[28]

Henry was full of thankfulness and praise to God for the safe journey from Turkey. Jeanne was not ill at all along the way and had only the slightest case of seasickness: "How wonderfully gracious the Lord was that He allowed no storms to overtake us! It was as if His hand was upon us for good all the way. Psalm 17:8, 'Hide me under the shadow of Thy wing.'"[29]

August in Ashfield was beautiful. There was so much to share with Mother – and then there were chores to be done. Regardless of how esteemed Henry might be as a minister or missionary, at home he was his mother's "little boy" with chores to do: "So now Mother fondly called my attention to the fact that the kitchen eaves trough-sink was out of order and needed mending."[30] One Saturday Henry hired a horse and buggy from a neighbor and took Jeanne for a ride among the beautiful hills. Jeanne was delighted with Apple Valley and Little Switzerland; then they rode through Bear Swamp to view in the distance the "saddle Mountains" around Williamstown. Ashfield's quiet made it a perfect place for the "weary, almost worn-out" missionaries to rest from their toil.

Yet, thoughts of Turkey and his work in Marash were never far from Henry's mind. He prayed for the Montgomeries, left alone in the field, and thought perhaps his prayers could be of more help than his presence. Often Henry walked to the cemetery where his father was buried. At the grave stood a monument with an open-Bible and an inscription of John 11:25 "I am the resurrection and the life, he that believeth in me, though he were dead, yet shall he live." Henry always thought of his father with joy:

> I cannot keep him out of my mind here; To review his Christian character; his success as Deacon of the Church here; how his work on the farm (of the old Perry colonial location) was never so urgent that he omitted family prayers. I think of the good times we had when I was a boy on that farm.[31]

With Henry's love for Ashfield, it was fitting that September 17, 1873, in Ashfield, Jeanne gave birth to a son. They named him Alvan Williston, after Henry's and Jeanne's fathers. There was great joy and happiness in the Perry home.

In October Henry went to Boston to consult with the ABCFM about what path he should take. Dr. Clark suggested for Henry to return to Turkey, leaving Jeanne and Alvan in the States for a year and a half. They would have time to gain their strength before rejoining him on the mission field. Henry accepted the plan, asking no questions.

The next three months were times of continued rest at Ashfield, but also days of activity. Days were filled with chopping wood for Mother, mending and preparing trunks for Turkey, prayer meetings, church activities, and lovely moments with Jeanne and Alvan. The afternoon of January 4 1874, Alvan Williston was baptized. Though Jeanne's health seemed better than in Turkey, she still was not well. Hard though it might be, it was obviously the best course for her and baby Alvan to remain behind while Henry resumed his work in Turkey.

On February 7, 1874, Henry sailed from New York on the *S.S. California*. Mrs. Jones, sister Emily, and Jeanne accompanied Henry to the dock. There they met Mrs. T.C. Doremus, founder of the Woman's Union Missionary Society, also saying farewell to some friends. Taking the usual route of connecting ships and trains from New York to London to Paris to Marseilles and Alexandretta, Henry arrived there March 17. The rains made travel difficult, and it was not until March 31 that Henry reached Marash and began unpacking and setting up house. All his friends were glad to see him, and Henry was ready to resume work. Immediately he was involved in annual meetings, preaching in villages, and solving church doctrinal problems. One circuit-preaching trip that spring lasted five weeks. What a joy to have letters from Jeanne and Mother and pictures of Alvan waiting for him when he returned.

While Henry was on a 37-day trip to the Evangelical Union meeting in Adjaman and to encourage churches in Germish and Severek, an arrest was made in Marash that gained international attention. A Moslem by the name of Mustapha had been secretly a Christian for a long time. Ali, his oldest son, and his daughter, Elif, attended the Protestant schools, and Ali had begun attending church. Mustapha began to attend church too, standing firm against the threats of the Moslems. On Sunday, May 3, the incensed Moslems came to Mustapha's door and cried, "Come out... we will kill you." Mustapha replied, "Go report me to the Government," and he went to church with his son. The next day they were summoned before the Governor of the city and confessed they were Christians. That night Mustapha and Ali were arrested, put in chains, and marched on the road to Aleppo under a strong guard. In reporting the case to the ABCFM, Giles Montgomery could not help but exclaim, "This is Turkey, in the nineteenth century! This is the liberty in Turkey, so often boasted of by the Christian press of Europe!"[32]

The Constantinople branch of the Evangelical Alliance presented the case, along with others, to the representatives of the Christian European powers:

> In these repeated acts of persecution, occurring simultaneously with a persistent effort at the Capital to hinder the circulation of the Christian Scriptures, there is manifest a spirit and a purpose on the part of the Turkish Government, which challenges instant attention on the part of the Christian Powers and the Christian public of Europe and the United States.[33]

Yet, there was little public outcry. Later, in a statement Ali wrote to the American missionaries at Smyrna, he told of the repeated imprisonments and pressure to return to Islam. Repeatedly rich men, military officers, and government officials offered payment to Ali and Mustapha to renounce their Christian faith. One official said, "What is this you're doing? I've never heard of such a thing as this. My son, these Protestants are accustomed to give each convert £10. If you have received this money, give it back, and the government will give you double. Come, give this thing up." Ali and Mustapha replied, "We have not accepted the Gospel for silver, or gold, or any such thing, but simply because we hope for salvation in this faith...Man does not live by money or things of that sort."[34]

After Mustapha and Ali were imprisoned thirteen days in Aleppo, Mustapha's wife, who was brought from Marash, joined them. The government detained the couple's three other children in Marash and placed them in the home of a strict Moslem family. Ali and his parents were then brought as prisoners to Istanbul and finally to Smyrna. In Smyrna they were released from prison under strict instructions not to leave Smyrna or attempt to return to Marash. They had been banished to Smyrna for their Christian faith. The Christians in Smyrna took care of them, but pain of separation from their home and the rest of their family remained.

During his tours into the region around Marash, Henry Perry also encountered Moslems coming to faith in "the truth as it is in Jesus." In the Kurdish village of Kuriichai, on the road from Marash to Caesarea, Henry spoke in the home of Vele, who had learned of Christ while working for some Christians in nearby Hadjin. The Kurds gladly heard the Scriptures, and Henry reported to the ABCFM, "This is another example of the way the Lord is working, bringing in here and there one from the Mohammedan faith to his fold."[35]

Back at Marash Henry spent time keeping the accounts of the Central Turkey Mission, corresponding with pastors and ABCFM workers, and preparing his school lessons. He had to prepare two lessons in Hebrew per week plus eleven lectures, five in hermeneutics and exegesis, three in the harmony of the gospels, and three in the history of the Old Testament. In all his work, Henry was comforted by Exodus 33:14, "My presence shall go with you, and I will give you rest." His resolution was to "Let the background of my mind be occupied by the King."[36] Though often lonely and missing his own family, Henry had the feeling "that Christ is with me and therefore I am never alone. In the path of duty I find a comfort of unspeakable value."[37] On February 7, 1875 he wrote his mother:

> I feel thankful that I have been strong and busy this year. Have lost only one day of the 365 by sickness; and as to my work of teaching, there is no letting up from it when Sunday comes. Just now after giving eleven lectures and two recitations per week, I had last Sunday a sermon and a Sunday School class at the Third Church. By taking it easy and spending a little time daily in saddle riding (to keep my head cool) I am thus far in good working order.[38]

Letters from Jeanne were full of love and details of life in Ashfield. She told Henry all the little anecdotes and stories of Alvan, and his prayers intensified for his son when she wrote of his bout with diphtheria. Though his diaries and letters never mentioned it, Henry and Jeanne could not help but wonder how long Alvan would be with them. His three sisters all died before the age of two. Would Alvan soon follow them?

As soon as the school term was over in July, Henry left Marash for the United States. When he packed and stored the furniture, he recognized that "Much is now uncertain; but I trust that the Dear Lord will have work for us to do yet in this country."[39] The future was indeed uncertain. Jeanne's health was still not good; Alvan was weak from two bouts of diphtheria; and Henry's mother might need their care in Ashfield. Yet, Henry boarded the ship at Alexandretta trusting the Lord for direction in the future.

At Smyrna Henry was held in quarantine for a week on an island near the city. A well-traveled Englishman on the steamer had told Henry that when he left the steamer he should wear the Fez and speak only Turkish. He should give his name but not volunteer he was an American. If he did this, the officials wouldn't "jolt you for your money." Henry followed the advice and passed easily to the quarantine:

> The companion of my room in the Quarantine was a business fellow from Smyrna – a Greek. Rather smart in his appearance, but utterly ignorant of the Bible. When we left the steamer, we two were assigned to one of the better rooms, which was light, and not uncomfortable. As for food, I had my little teapot; and we could purchase from a bread and fruit stand, placing the money in a long-handled push shovel. The food we could take from the shovel, as it was pushed out to us. Our health was good, and the quarantine officers took little if any special notice of us.[40]

Once released from quarantine, Henry had a day in Smyrna. He went to the market and bought Broosa silk table spreads and a rug.

July 23, 1875, Henry left Smyrna for Liverpool and felt the Lord had particularly favored him in his accommodations:

> The steamer was loaded so fully that passenger rooms downstairs were filled with small boxes of opium, of which the smell was intoxicating. No travelers could use these rooms. But the captain gave us two-Baldwin and me-one of his officers' room on the upper deck.[41]

Years later, in 1923, when Henry read through his diary for 1875, he still remembered one experience of the voyage which he recorded on a blank page:

> On that freight steamer (which included cattle being left off at Malta) there were no <u>bath</u> rooms!...The custom of the sailors is to wash the decks at the earliest dawn before the light has already come. When we heard the <u>swash</u> of their scrapers and brooms-dropping our nightshirts, just within the door, the sailors would enjoy the <u>fun</u> of what we came for; and would immediately turn their hoses on us. We understood well enough that they would not spare in giving us the rough side of it. It would be quickly done. Escaping and seizing our nightshirts and towels, after a hasty rub, we would return to our beds. No lack of baths on that voyage.[42]

On August 14 Henry landed in New York. On the 16th he went to the depot and bought a train ticket to Springfield, Massachusetts. He didn't have enough money to buy a ticket all the way to South Deerfield, but the conductor passed him through. By 6 p.m. he was in his Ashfield home: "How delightful to be at home again with my precious wife! My patient Mother and darling boy Alvan. Such reunion is by the Lord's great favor to us!"[43]

Henry had overworked himself in Marash and enjoyed a much-needed rest in Ashfield, though he wrestled with what his duty was concerning his future missionary work. At first he was ready to write the ABCFM and resign from missionary work altogether. The doctor insisted Jeanne could not return to the harsh climate of Marash. However, a place in Sivas seemed to be opening up. Dr. Herrick of Marsovan was going to Constantinople to replace Dr. Pratt, and Ed Riggs was going from Sivas to Marsovan to replace Dr. Herrick. Sivas had a much cooler climate than Marash, and there were many surrounding villages in need of the Gospel. But what about Mother? It was Henry's responsibility to care for her in her elder years. Yet her health was good, and she was willing for Henry to spend more years in the mission field until she might more directly require his aid. Tentatively he decided to plan for a move to Sivas, Turkey, after a year's stay in the States to give Jeanne and Alvan the opportunity to gain their strength.

But Henry couldn't remain idly in Ashfield for a year; he must find a temporary pastoral position. Dr. Horace Eaton of Palmyra, New York, Henry's friend and mentor from seminary days, arranged for

Henry's appointment to a Presbyterian church in Williamson, New York, just a few miles west of Palmyra and south of Lake Ontario.

Williamson was east of Rochester, New York and very near Lake Ontario. Its cold climate was a big contrast with the heat of Marash. By the end of November, Henry was noting in his diary that the water froze in his sleeping room. The weather did not cool Henry's zeal, however. He energetically began visiting his congregation, preparing sermons, and studying. Tuesdays he regularly read a chapter of the Scriptures in Hebrew and wrote out an exposition. On Sundays he preached a morning and evening sermon, and there were often meetings during the week in nearby schools where Henry preached. On occasion, the Methodist and Baptist preachers exchanged pulpits with the Presbyterian Perry; there was a congenial relationship between the various Christian pastors in the community.

The Perrys had a set of rooms and the use of the kitchen in Deacon Patrick's home, and they were as happy as could be. The weather continued cold (in February the water froze in the tea kettle on the stove), but it was often perfect for sledding and sleighing. Little Alvan didn't seem to mind the cold, and Henry often pulled him about in his sled. At times a wave of sadness passed over him as he thought that Alvan would never play with his three older sisters.

Though Jeanne's health was improved, she still was often weak. When well, she sang in church and played the organ. The question remained, "Should the Perrys return to Turkey or stay in the States?" Henry enjoyed his pastoral work, and the Williamson congregation would have liked him to stay with them. Yet, both Jeanne and Henry felt called to Turkey. Jeanne thought she would do as well in a cooler climate in Turkey as she did in the States. Mr. Porter, Henry's sister's husband, had died, and Henry hoped Sarah Ann might return to Ashfield and help care for Mother; but Sarah Ann opened a school at North Adams. Henry's mother, however, was willing for Henry and Jeanne to return to Turkey for several more years. She was certain she could find someone to stay with her in her Ashfield house. Should the Perrys stay or go? Henry wrote the ABCFM's Dr. Clark in May 1876:

> Never before have I so completely left the case with the Lord to decide by showing his will whether it be to go or stay. Never before have I been so willing to wait till the time sh'd come when the Lord will make known his will in the case; and never before have I been so confident that whatever decision is reached there will be no mistake about it.[44]

Increasingly the way seemed clear for Henry, Jeanne, and Alvan to go to Sivas, Turkey. During the spring of 1876, as Henry continued to fulfill his pastoral duties at Williamson, the Perrys prepared to return to Turkey. There were trunks and boxes to be repaired, supplies to be purchased, and friends and relatives to visit. There were also the wonderful seasonal activities of spring and summer. Sleighing season ended, and the apple trees began to blossom. Henry and Jeanne attended a brass band concert together in nearby Ontario. The church organized a strawberry festival that all seemed to enjoy.

Then there were the preparations for the Centennial July 4th. Henry worked on a historical sermon for the occasion and visited with older members of the church to learn more about its past. He and Jeanne enjoyed their visit with Mrs. Ledyard, an eighty-seven year old matron who had been a member of the church for 57 years. In spite of a bad headache and a rainy Sabbath, July 2nd Henry delivered his historical sermon. The Tuesday July 4th celebration at Williamson brought everyone out for the parade and patriotic speech by a Col. Wood. The church had a thanksgiving service in the morning, and the evening skies were lit with fireworks. Henry said the day was "a July 4th we shall never soon forget."[45]

The next Sunday was Henry's last at Williamson. News of revolution in Turkey reached the Perrys in June, and Henry questioned the ABCFM about the security of foreign travelers in the country. Though cautious about possible trouble, once he had assessed all available information, Henry did not think the political unrest would prevent his family's return to Turkey. July 5th he wrote Reverend Clark:

> It seems now to be inevitable that there is to be war between Turkey and her Christian subjects. If England does not fight to save Turkey again, the position of the American Missionaries will be a critical, and possibly dangerous one. We do not shrink from it, if it is best to go. Unless I hear from you to the contrary, we shall go on with our preparations to sail in September.[46]

Preparations for the journey filled July, August, and the first of September. There were many visits with friends and relatives and opportunities to help along the way – picking berries, working in the hayfields, chopping wood, and preaching whenever called upon. In North Adams Henry heard his mentor, Dr. Mark Hopkins, preach at Church. Jeanne and Henry's mother enjoyed quilting with the Ashfield ladies.

Henry worked at needed repairs on the Ashfield house and readied his mother for winter. Jeanne and a neighbor were able to go to Greenfield to hear Dwight L. Moody preach and were very interested and impressed by the meeting. Quickly the day came to say goodbye. How many of their friends and relatives would they ever see again?

September 16, 1876, Jeanne, Henry, and little three year old Alvan sailed from New York on the *S.S. Australia*. Stopping a few days in London, they hoped to attend Charles Spurgeon's London Tabernacle, but the church was so full they went instead to Christ's Church and heard Dr. Newman Hall. From London they took the now familiar journey to Paris, Marseilles, Smyrna, and Constantinople. By October 30, 1876, the Perrys arrived in Sivas. They were happy to again be in Turkey and eager to be about the Lord's work.

---

[1] Henry T. Perry, "Marash Station Report," *The Missionary Herald*, August 1872, 243.
[2] Ephraim K. Jernazian. *Judgment unto Truth*. New Brunswick: Transaction Publishers, 1990, 15.
[3] *Leavening the Levant*, 241-242.
[4] Rev. G.H. White. *Mrs. Coffing of Hadjin*. Chicago: Woman's Board of Mission of the Interior, 1888.
[5] *Diary*, October 10, 1870. The books Perry used as the basis for his courses included Dr. Shedds' two-volume *Homiletics* and Samuel Andrews' *Life of Christ Upon the Earth*.
[6] *Diary*, December 1870.
[7] *Diary*, September 20, 1870.
[8] *Diary*, May 7, 1871.
[9] *Diary*, June 6, 1871.
[10] *Diary*, October 21, 1871.
[11] *Diary*, October 21, 1871.
[12] *Diary*, November 13, 1871.
[13] The contributions of Elias Riggs are truly amazing. He had a mastery of Greek, Armeno-Turkish, Bulgarian, Arabic, Latin, Hebrew, Old Syrian, and Coptic. He wrote tracts and texts and composed or wrote over seven hundred hymns. At least thirty-three members of Elias and Martha Riggs' family served on various mission fields throughout the world. The combined years of service for four generations totaled over nine hundred years. *They Lived Their Faith*, 148. For a summary of Elias Riggs' life and contributions see Rev. Henry O. Dwight, "A Mighty Warrior Before the Lord," *The Missionary Herald*, Vol. 97, March 1901, 98-103; Joseph L. Grabill. *Protestant Diplomacy and the Near East: Missionary Influence on American Foreign Policy, 1810-1927*. Minneapolis: University of Minnesota Press, 1971, 21.
[14] *Diary*, April 2, 1872.

[15] *Dairy*, November 7, 1873.
[16] *Diary*, March 3, 1872. Perry was paraphrasing the Apostle Paul in Philippians 3:10, "That I may know him [Christ], and the power of his resurrection, and the fellowship of his sufferings, being made conformable unto his death."
[17] *Diary*, December 31, 1870.
[18] *Diary*, February 7, 1872, November 20, 1872.
[19] *Diary*, April 2, 1872, May 11, 1872.
[20] *Diary*, May 25-26, 1872.
[21] *Diary*, June 10, 1872. Andrew Murray was a favorite author of the Perrys at this time, and the importance of abiding in Christ was an important theme throughout his works.
[22] *Diary*, June 10-12, 1872; Rev. H. Clay Trumbull, "Bible House Building in the Levant," *Christian Herald*, June 18, 1902, 527. Rev. Trumbull concluded his article on the Bible House by saying "the Constantinople Bible House stands as a monument to good Dr. Bliss, while its glad rays stream out as a light to the Gentiles, in the land of the crescent and the shadow of death."
[23] *Diary*, July 17, 1872; August 1872.
[24] Mrs. Coffing, "A Pleasant Contrast," *The Missionary Herald*, May 1873, 169.
[25] Henry Perry, "The Change at Hadjin," *The Missionary Herald*, July 1873, 224.
[26] *Diary*, March 28-April 8, 1873.
[27] *Diary*, April 15, 1873.
[28] *Diary*, July 31, 1873.
[29] *Diary*, August 4, 1873.
[30] *Diary*, August 14, 1873.
[31] *Diary*, August 20, 1873.
[32] Giles Montgomery, "Persecution of a Moslem Convert," *The Missionary Herald*. August 1874, 242.
[33] Quoted in "Central Turkey Mission," *The Missionary Herald*, August 1874, 243. As early as 1867, in a resolution adopted at its annual meeting, the American Board began to urge that the "Christian Governments of Europe and America should take the necessary steps for securing to Christian communities in Turkey the complete enjoyment of their religious rights." *ABCFM Annual Report, 1867*, 13.
[34] "The Persecuted Moslem Converts," *The Missionary Herald*, September 1874, 287.
[35] Henry T. Perry, "A Tour-Hadjin," *The Missionary Herald*, December 1874, 391.
[36] *Diary*, January 16, 1875.
[37] *Diary*, June 5, 1874.
[38] Annotation later made in his *Diary* under February 27, 1875.
[39] *Diary*, May 25, 1875.
[40] *Diary*, July 19, 1875.

[41] *Diary*, July 23, 1875.
[42] *Diary,* added after July 23, 1875.
[43] *Diary*, August 31, 1875.
[44] H.T. Perry to Rev. N.G. Clark, May 12, 1876 from Williamson, New York, ABC 16.9.3, Vol. 7, Part 2, No.   .
[45] *Diary,* July 4, 1876.
[46] H.T. Perry to Rev. N.G. Clark, July 5, 1876, from Williamson, N.Y, ABC 16.9.3, Vol. 7, Part 2.

5
DANGERS IN THE WILDERNESS
(1876-1881)

"I have been in frequent journeys, in danger from rivers, danger from robbers, dangers from my countryman, dangers from the Gentiles, dangers in the city, dangers in the wilderness...dangers among false brethren...I have been in labor and hardship, through many sleepless nights, in hunger and thirst, often without food, in cold and exposure. Apart from such external things, there is the daily pressure upon me of concern for all the churches."
II Corinthians 11:26-28

When the Perrys returned to Turkey in October 1876, the Ottoman Empire was reeling from the burden of internal and international pressures. The Empire had just undergone an internal revolution in the government. Minorities clamored for independence. The European powers maintained a steady stream of diplomatic demands that the sultan implement a series of internal reforms to relieve the oppressed peoples within the Empire. Centuries of internal and foreign problems were boiling to the surface. Since the 1815 Congress of Vienna at the end of the Napoleonic Wars, Europe had been considering the "eastern question" and the impending dissolution of the Turkish Empire. The roots of the problem went back to age-old disputes over control of the trade routes to the Orient and to conflicts between Europe and Asia, Christians and Moslems. Russia, whose Czar Nicholas I had called Turkey a "sick man," anticipated Turkey's dismemberment and hoped to acquire some of its territory for a warm water port on the Mediterranean. Russia furthered its aims by claiming to be the protector of the Christian religion within the Ottoman Empire. Great Britain, especially concerned about protecting its route to India, sought to maintain the integrity of Turkey and resisted any Russian attempts to gain controlling influence in the region. The Crimean War (1853-1856), which ostensibly began between Russia and France over their protection of Holy Places in Jerusalem, soon developed into a European challenge to Russian claims as the protector of Slavs and Orthodox Christians in the Ottoman lands.

When Russia was soundly defeated in the war, it renounced its right to interfere in Turkey's internal affairs and its pretense of protecting Christians in Turkey. During the peace treaty negotiations, Turkey unsuccessfully tried to abrogate the capitulations with European foreign countries. The capitulations were treaties permitting foreign countries to have extraterritorial jurisdiction over their own nationals within the Ottoman Empire. Under the capitulations, European Christians in Turkey were not under Moslem law, but the laws of the European powers. Many of the capitulations dated from the sixteenth and seventeenth centuries, when the sultans were relieved not to have to administer justice to foreign merchants. By the nineteenth century, however, Turkey was beginning to feel the capitulations brought too much foreign interference within its borders.[1] In spite of Turkey's attempts to abrogate the capitulations, they continued in force into the twentieth century, and the European powers pressured the sultan to make important civil reforms within the Empire. As part of the 1856 Treaty of Paris concluding the Crimean War, the sultan issued an edict declaring religious freedom for all subjects and forbade discrimination against and degradation of all non-Muslims.

Any edict for complete religious freedom within the Ottoman Empire, however, went contrary to the foundations of Ottoman law, in which Islam was the ruling religion. The Ottoman Empire at its very base was a theocracy, with the sultan himself a Moslem caliph. Moslems throughout the world, including India, China, and Africa, recognized the Ottoman sultan as the living head of the Moslem faith. Under pressure from European powers, the sultan might proclaim religious freedom, but it was impossible for him to implement his proclamation without disrupting the entire Ottoman legal system. Grand Vizier Ali Pasha asked, "in what country in the world has it been found practicable to efface in a day the efforts of the habits and traditions of ages by a simple change of the law or in the disposition of the Government?"[2] Custom was stronger than codes, and written laws did little to change practices.

Dangers in the Wilderness   109

Russian agents throughout the Balkans encouraged a spirit of pan-Slavism and dissatisfaction with the implementation of promised reforms. With the financial collapse of the Ottoman Empire in 1874, heavier taxes were imposed and discontent intensified. In 1875 the simmering conflict between the Christian and Moslem Slavs of Bosnia and Herzegovina led to their revolt against Ottoman rule. In May 1876, the Bulgarian peasants rose and massacred many Turkish officials. To try to preserve peace in the region, a large fleet of English and other vessels came to the Dardanelles; and the American fleet in the Mediterranean sent vessels into Turkish waters. The English ambassador ordered the captain of the Cunard steamer in Constantinople to keep up steam and be ready to receive any English and Americans who came to him for safety.[3]

By the summer of 1876, as the Perrys were preparing to return to Turkey, the revolt had spread to Montenegro and Serbia. The Serbian army at war with Turkey was led by a Russian general and made up in part of Russian volunteers. As the Turks marched north against Serbia, they took vengeance on the Bulgarians, put down the revolt, and committed such atrocities that western opinion turned against the Turks. Fifteen thousand Bulgarian men, women and children were brutally killed. Though Britain's Prime Minister Benjamin Disraeli continued to support Turkey as a bulwark against Russia's expansive powers, William Gladstone, Disraeli's great rival, wrote a pamphlet urging the Turks be expelled from the European community because of their inhumanity. Gladstone was most concerned about the treatment of Christians in the Ottoman Empire and had encouraged Britain's Evangelical Alliance in 1875, when it sent a deputation to the sultan because of reports of ill treatment of Christians.

Inside Turkey, leaders realized something must be done to prevent total collapse of the Ottoman State and the massive intervention of the European powers. Sultan Abdul Aziz's spending sprees had sent the Empire's debt soaring. He ignored all movements for reform and insanely enforced a glorification of Turkish accomplishments. All Turkish schoolbooks were re-written, deleting every Turkish defeat and eliminating all references to Christianity. Those close to him recognized the sultan was deranged. Under the influence of Medhet Pasha, Sultan Abdul Aziz was deposed and replaced by his nephew Murad V. If possible, Sultan Murad was worse than his uncle. Physicians from Vienna declared Murad, a physically debauched drunken prince, incurably insane; and he was deposed after three months. Murad's brother,

Abdul Hamid II, then came to power. He was to be the last supreme despot of the Ottoman Empire. Duplicity and the massacres that would gain him the name of the "Red Sultan" marked his rule.

The European powers believed reforms must be implemented in Turkey to protect the Christians within the Empire. They scheduled a conference in Constantinople in December 1876, to consider the problem. As the European delegates began their meeting, they heard a 101-gun salute. The Turkish delegate announced, "Gentlemen, the canon you have heard is the signal for the promulgation by the sultan guaranteeing the rights of all subjects of the empire without distinction. In the presence of this great event, I feel that our task is superfluous."[4] The new government was to have three branches of government, a national assembly elected by universal suffrage without distinction of race or religion, and guarantees of religious freedom and civil rights. The Europeans rightly thought this was a trick by the new sultan to prevent any European intervention forcing real reforms on Turkey, but there was little they could do.[5]

Missionaries in Turkey were fully aware of the dangerous times, and one reported in *The Missionary Herald*:

> The excitement here is intense. The Government is in fear of all its Christian subjects, and quite as much so of the old Turks, - all fanatics, all armed or now arming, and all opposed to the Government, to the spirit of progress, to Christians, and to Franks [Europeans]. Public feeling is like a vast powder magazine ... In such a state of things we cannot leave home, nor is it safe to travel.[6]

In August, H.G.O. Dwight wrote from Constantinople that, "the condition of Asia Minor is not pleasant. People treat the Christians with violence everywhere, and in many places they take pleasure in sharpening their large butcher-knives before their eyes, and frightening them with threats."[7]

Henry Perry was aware of the political revolution and the increased persecution of Christians when he sailed for Turkey in 1876, but he and Jeanne both believed the Lord was leading them to Sivas for ministry. The turmoil in the Balkans, Constantinople and eastern Turkey had not reached Sivas, but several changes had occurred at the Sivas mission station since their last stay. Dr. West had died April 1876, and Ed Riggs and his family had been transferred to Marsovan in July. Albert and Emma Hubbard had come to Sivas three years earlier. Albert had graduated from Amherst in 1867 and from Princeton Seminary in 1870.

He served two years as a pastor in Pennsylvania before marrying Emma Spencer in August 25, 1873; he was 32 and she 22. Two days later the couple left for Sivas, Turkey. Dr. and Mrs. West and the Riggs family welcomed the Hubbards to Sivas and helped them adapt to their new home. By the time the Perrys arrived three years later, the Hubbards had added little Florence and Ray to their family and had moved into the home they had built next to Dr. West's home. At first the Perrys stayed with the Hubbards. The Hubbards had been tremendously overworked since the departure of the West and Riggs families and were happy to have the Perrys as neighbors and co-workers in Sivas.

Located 450 miles southeast of Constantinople on the range of mountains and plateaus stretching from the Anti-Taurus to old Armenia, Sivas was the second largest city in Asiatic Turkey. It was the capital of the *vilayet* or province and the residence of the *Vali* or governor.[8] At an altitude of 4420 feet and located on the Murdan Su, a tributary of the Kizil Irmak (Halys River), the ancient city had been the summer residence of the Kings of Pontus. Under the Roman Empire the town took the name of Sebastea, and under the Emperor Diocletian it became the capital of the province of Armenia Minor. At least four major Roman roads converged on the city. During the Byzantine Empire it became, after Caesarea, the richest city of Asia Minor.

In the eleventh century the Seljuk Turks began to move into Persia and Armenia. King Sennekerim was then ruling the Armenian kingdom of Vaspurakan, around Lake Van. Fearing the marauding Turks, he negotiated with the Byzantine Emperor to exchange his kingdom of Vaspurakan for the province of Sivas, agreeing to become a vassal of the Byzantine Emperor. Sennekerim, his nobles, and 400,000 of his subjects (about 1/3 of his former realm) moved to Sivas. This was the origin of the large Armenian population in the province west of Armenia proper. The beautiful white stone bridge with pointed arches still spanning the Kizil Irmak in Perry's day had been built by Sennekerim. Sennekerim's throne and other relics were later kept in the Armenian Monastery of Neshan or the Holy Cross, about one hour from Sivas, and his royal chapel was excellently preserved. As the Turks pursued their westward push, other large groups of Armenians scattered into the Crimea, Cilicia, Moldavia, Poland, and Russia. In 1071, Sivas fell into the hands of the Seljuk Turks, whose decorative architecture still could be seen throughout the town.

At the end of the fourteenth century, when the Turko-Mongol Tamerlane swept through Asia Minor on his rampage of death and destruction, he attacked Sivas. Tamerlane sent word to the defenders that if they opened their gates their lives would be spared. The citizens opened the gates, but the conqueror plundered the city, took many slaves, tortured the rich to reveal their treasures, tied women to their horses and dragged them until dead, and trampled the children under their horses' hooves. He bound 4000 Christian Armenian soldiers with their heads between their legs and buried them alive. The town never recovered from this massacre, and the place of the mass grave, known as the *Sev Hogher* or Black Earth, was still pointed out in Perry's day.

The rich agricultural and pastoral area around Sivas produced wheat and barley, oats and potatoes, cattle, goats, and sheep. It produced more than enough for itself, but primitive transportation made export difficult and unprofitable. Numerous roads did make Sivas an important trade center for less perishable products, however. The road from Constantinople to Erzerum and the Russian frontier passed through Sivas, as did the roads from the Black Sea to Baghdad and the Black Sea to the Mediterranean.[9]

Many of the Armenians in Sivas were occupied in various handicrafts, especially the printing of cotton hangings, making belts, sewing, shoe-making, carpentry, mason's work, blacksmithing, watch-repairing, and in carpet and textile weaving. There were at least thirty such handicrafts, which were sold at large markets at the center of town. The markets were divided into particular trades, with at least 1200 shops in all. The Armenians were leaders in the financial affairs of the Sivas *vilayet*. All the trade of the province was in their hands. Many also were chemists and physicians.[10]

Sivas had notoriously muddy streets. A later missionary colleague of Henry's graphically described the situation:

> The soil here is a very heavy, sticky clay that makes the finest mud in the world: it is really excellent for the mud-bricks of which so many of the houses and walls are built! In the spring as the winter snow melts in the streets and the rains add their quota to the rivers that flow in the streets, the mud will stand on the sidewalks to the depth of two or three inches, - in color and consistency about like pea soup, while on the roads and bare hillsides outside the city the mud is so stiff and thick that you must lift several pounds of it with every step you take. Your rubbers to be of any use at all must be buttoned, tied, or strapped on, and even then getting stuck in the mud is an everyday occurrence, often an every minute occurrence. The spring mud in the streets, however, is the worst. Everybody throws all kinds of

refuse into the street, the sewers often flow in open ditches through the middle of the street, and when covered by an inch of boards often become clogged and overflow. The homeless street dogs which die from exposure to the bitter cold of winter nights often lie for weeks before anybody takes the trouble to remove them. Out of such ingredients the black slime of the streets is composed! When the spring rains cease, the dry air and the hot sun of this high altitude soon convert this mud into beautiful clouds of white dust that whirl through the city streets all summer and fill your eyes, nose, and mouth with fine white powder. Fortunately the sun is so hot that most of the microbes are probably killed.[11]

Christian books and tracts had been the first "missionaries" in Sivas. In 1845, a Protestant shoemaker was beaten, chained, and imprisoned by the resident Armenian priest. In 1849, a Protestant man who had found a Bible in Erzerum was so fearful of persecution that he demanded protection of the government. In 1858 Mr. Philander Powers came from Erzerum and spent six months with the small group of believers who had gathered to read the Bible. A church was organized and several missionaries came to Sivas. For various reasons their stays had been short, and repeated changes in the mission had to some degree prevented the church's sound growth. Yet, the churches in the villages around Sivas grew and flourished. Henry Perry was eager to plunge into this mission field. Tocat, Gürün, Zara, and Kara Hissar would all become familiar towns to him during the next thirty-seven years. With Sivas at the center, this would be his mission field.

Though it would be some weeks before the Perrys were settled in Sivas, within a week after arriving, Henry set out on a month long tour south to Albustan, Gürün and Derende, while Albert Hubbard went east to Divrik. Jeanne and Emma stayed up much of the night preparing food for their husbands to take on their journeys. The Perrys had learned that their shipment of goods from the States was robbed on the way to Sivas, and Henry also hoped to find what remained. In Albustan Henry found the remaining boxes, four of which had been opened but remained as packed. The organ was badly broken, and Henry had to file a claim with the government for damages and for robbery. Throughout his travels to the villages Henry visited schools, attended prayer meetings, encouraged pastors, preached, and exhorted the brethren in their Christian walk. As he rode back to Sivas with a gentle snow beginning to cover the ground, Henry prayed that the seeds he had planted would produce a winter harvest rich in spiritual fruit.

By the middle of December, with the arrival of their boxes from Boston, Jeanne, Henry, and Alvan were able to begin setting up house in Dr. West's old home. Chairs had to be assembled, the stove set up, books unpacked for the library, carpets cut and laid, curtains and pictures hung, and myriad of other chores performed. All of this while they continued the work of the mission. As usual, Henry was appointed Treasurer of the mission station.

One of the immediate problems facing the mission was a real estate dispute that needed to be settled in the Turkish courts. Because Henry was most fluent in Turkish, this responsibility fell on him. He summarized the case as follows:

> A party of the previous chief men of the Protestants had appeared, who claimed the ownership of our chapel. For this purpose they occupied a part of it; putting a family in it. All the deeds of it were in our possession. Dr. West had purchased and built it; putting the property in the name of a man now living at Tocat [foreigners could not then own land in their own names]. We called him up and proved it. The chief men entered the case at the Sivas Government. At that trial I alone was on one side and a row of the [12] chief men were seated against me. NO Decision by the Government was ever made. I was able to renew the Trust Deed to us; and that settled the Case.[12]

The whole legal wrangling went on for two years and consumed much of Henry's time. His *Diary* records numerous meetings, appearances at court, and rescheduling of court dates before the matter died down. The evidence of the case was solidly behind the American Board of Missions, but the government did not want to make a clear ruling in favor of the foreigners, so it made no ruling at all.

The dispute, however, went deeper than an issue over property rights and was part of a schism in the Protestant community at Sivas. Apparently when the Protestant church at Sivas was first organized, many who were nominal Christians but had no evidence of a changed life in Christ were accepted for membership. These expected their children to be baptized, accepted into the church and enjoy Holy Communion without any visible evidence of faith. Refusing to repent of obvious sins, they expected full fellowship in the church. It was this group which claimed the chapel and gardens built by Dr. West as their own. The discord became so heated that the Armenian pastor could no longer bear the pressure and resigned. Henry and Albert Hubbard assumed the preaching duties of the church for a time. Both Perry and

Hubbard agreed that Holy Communion should be suspended until the people repented of their sins and the schism in the church was resolved. By the time the property dispute turned out favorably to the American Board, the protesting group had separated and established its own Sunday services. Their departure restored unity, love, penitence, and prayer to the service in the Protestant chapel.

In pursuing the property settlement in the Turkish courts, Henry was able to deflect some of the animosity of the missionaries' opponents by promising to use the old chapel building for a Normal School to train teachers. Education had become a major element of the ABCFM's work in Turkey. The missionaries had not come to Turkey to establish Protestant churches but to bring life to the Christian church already there. One way of accomplishing this was to establish schools in which the Bible was used to teach reading and Christian principles were included in all areas of instruction. Classical scholar William Ramsay, among many others, had the highest praise for the American Board schools in Turkey:

> Beginning with a prejudice against their work, I was driven by the force of facts and experience to the opinion that the mission has been the strongest, as well as most beneficent, influence in causing the movement toward civilization which has been perceptible among all the peoples of Turkey.[13]

At first the Gregorians opposed the ABCFM schools, and even burned their books. There was also foreign opposition. In Constantinople, a Russian envoy removed a Russian Armenian who was helping the Protestants establish schools. The Ambassador of the Czar told Dr. Schauffler of the American Board, "I might as well tell you now, Mr. Schauffler, that the Emperor of Russia, who is my master, will never allow Protestantism to set its foot in Turkey." Schauffler, a German who had lived in Russia before immigrating to the United States, replied, "Your Excellency, the Kingdom of Christ, who is my Master, will never ask the Emperor of all the Russians where it may set its foot."[14]

The American schools expanded the curriculum well beyond the traditional Ottoman schools in several ways. They included instruction in the sciences of chemistry, physics, biology and astronomy as well as advanced mathematics. Art, music, and drama classes were taught along with physical education and applied subjects such as accounting and agriculture. All of these were innovations in Ottoman education at the time. Because of the high quality of instruction in the missionary schools, Gregorian Armenians as well as Moslems often sent their children to the schools, and the truth of the Gospel had a steady influence on the Sivas community.

In 1873, a high school had been established in Sivas and was directed by Flavia Bliss. Miss Bliss also oversaw common schools in the surrounding villages. For children from villages where there was no school, Miss Bliss formed a girls boarding department. The education of girls was an innovation the missionaries brought to Turkey, and many of the mission stations had established separate schools for girls. This was part of the Christian emphasis on the value and dignity of women as created by God. Eventually the Gregorians and Moslems also established girls' schools. Before the missionaries came, it was hotly debated whether or not girls were even capable of learning to read. The missionaries showed the answer was, "yes."

Shortly after coming to Sivas, Henry became convinced that a boys' high school and normal school to train teachers for the surrounding villages should be established. Perhaps he longed in part for the seminary teaching he had so enjoyed in Marash. There was no financial support for the school, and at first Albert Hubbard was not in favor of the work. Henry, however, was convinced of the importance of a teacher training school and was determined to try, having faith that God would provide a way. Henry's mother sent $30 to help repair Dr. West's old chapel building for use by the school. With much prayer and some fear that students would not be found who could be self-supporting, the first class began the winter of 1877-1878 with four students – Bedros Moughelian, Andon of Ashudi, Hadji Panos of Sivas, and a student from Divrik. Henry taught Bible history and English; the first year others from outside the school often came to hear Henry's lectures on the book of Job. Jeanne taught English and singing, and several Armenians assisted in teaching other subjects.

Though the first year was difficult, interest in the school steadily grew. By the fourth year, 1881-1882, the school opened with twenty students that soon increased to thirty. Students completed courses in algebra, geometry, English, Turkish, and Bible. The school followed the Lancasterian plan popular in New England and used by missionaries in many other fields, from Hawaii to the Cherokee and Choctaw missions. Andrew Bell and Joseph Lancaster, two British educators, developed the plan. Under it a single teacher supervised a large number of students, using more advanced students to monitor the progress of the lower levels. Rewards for good behavior were also an important part of the Lancasterian model.[15] Begun with little support and a simple conviction that a Normal School was needed for the educational betterment of the people of Sivas and the surrounding communities, the Sivas Normal School became the crown of a system of graded schools Henry Perry established in Sivas.[16] In a letter to Dr. Clark, the ABCFM Secretary in Boston, Henry explained the importance of the Sivas schools:

> Now when you consider how very discouraging the state of our Protestant community still is here in Sivas, and that the cost to the Board this year of the whole system of graded schools for running expenses is only about £7.50, and in the work of three years growth, you will see I think it is wise for us to push forward in this line of Education. We are getting a hold in this way upon the <u>families</u> of the vicinity which will greatly aid in the work of the Gospel when the time for fruitage shall come.[17]

Henry asked Dr. Clark and the ABCFM to pray for conversions in the schools and that some would be prepared for the ministry.

In 1881, an assistant to the British Consul in Sivas made a detailed evaluation of the Protestant Armenian, Turk, Gregorian Armenian, Catholic Armenian, and Greek schools in the town. He had the highest praise for the American missionary school:

> This school is in the hands of six American missionaries, who put an amount of enthusiasm and energy into their work that seems to be quite wanting elsewhere in Sivas. The efficiency of elementary schools ought not to be judged of by the performances of a few selected pupils, so much as by the evident pains taken with the real education of the majority of the children in the lower divisions, and it is for this later quality that the Protestant school deserves praise. At the same time, their standard of instruction, which is the highest in the town, has had the good effect of arousing competition among the Gregorian Armenians, and of obliging them to open three new establishments. The Protestant girls' school is altogether without a rival, and many of the leading Gregorian Armenians send their daughters there.
>
> The lesson books are excellent, being often translations of the best American works, and the only school atlases in the town are to be found here.[18]

The educational programs Perry established in Sivas were encouraged by the *Vali* Abbedalin Pasha and spurred the Gregorian Armenians to establish schools of their own. In the early 1870's the Gregorian Armenians of Sivas spent less than $440 a year on education, but by 1880 they were spending $2,640 annually. Their schools increased from four to thirteen, their students from 500 to 1500, and their girls' schools from zero to three. A wealthy Armenian in Sivas told Henry, "you showed us a picture, and looking upon it we began to see it was very beautiful, whereupon we took it to our bosoms, and have been cherishing it every since."[19]

The passion of Henry's heart, so beautifully shared by Jeanne, was for evangelism and building up the church. After weeks of diligent teaching and work in Sivas, Henry eagerly rode out to the villages to preach the Word of Christ and encourage the Christians there. In 1877, for example, Henry made eight visits to the outstations, varying from three to twenty-nine days. About a third of the year, 127 days, was spent visiting and ministering in the villages in the *vilayet* of Sivas. On these trips Henry always traveled with a companion, either an Armenian pastor or colporteur or a local guide and muleteer. When political situations became tense, the government provided a military police, called *zaptieh*, to accompany him. The outstation visits were both evangelistic, presenting the gospel to the unconverted, and important times of ministry to the churches. In churches without pastors, Henry's visits were times of baptisms, weddings, accepting of new church members, and communion.

Fellow missionary Frederick Greene described spending the night in one of the Armenian villages, a scene Henry Perry experienced thousands of times during his years of missionary service:

> On reaching the village where one is to spend the night, he naturally desires at once to see his quarters. After the saddle is removed that it may not be injured in going through the low passages, both horse and traveler are led in by the light of a flickering wick in a cup of linseed oil, which barely suffices to reveal the sooty walls and posts. The guide warns you not to strike your head on that beam, or to step into the puddle on your left; in avoiding the puddle you stumble over something on the right, but your host immediately puts you at ease by saying it was only a calf. He then proceeds to remove a yoke of buffaloes or half a dozen sheep from one obscure corner, and informs you that it is at your disposal. Before you realize what is going on, the corner has been swept, with the effect of raising a stifling dust. In

summer you would prefer the roof to the inside accommodation, but this happy alternative would be impossible in winter. The temperature of these crowded, unventilated, damp compartments — not to mention the fleas – makes you so uncomfortable that sleep is out of the question. A hole in the roof is often the only window, and serves also as a chimney; but in winter this is generally closed...[a] woman is churning a goatskin full of sour milk by jerking it back and forth as it hangs from a beam in the roof. The meal, which consists of fermented milk, boiled wheat or rice, and eggs fried in a sea of butter, is at last served in the middle of the floor, on a round stool. Every article of food is served in a single dish, from which each helps himself, using his fingers for a fork. If the food is liquid, it is eaten by twisting the thin tenacious bread into the form of a spoon, which disappears in the mouth together with what it conveys. The civilized drudgery of dishwashing is thus reduced to the simple process of washing hands, which each one does for himself both before and after the meal. A certain etiquette and kindly feeling refines even these dismal homes, and points to higher ideals than the material condition of the people would indicate.[20]

The village people gladly welcomed the European or American traveler not only because of a courteous respect, but also because they knew they would pay for all they received, and not extort services and goods from them as did the Kurds or Turks.

The missionaries, as did all travelers, carried with them their own bedding, rugs, and utensils for staying at the khans or caravansaries located at intervals of about thirty miles along most of the caravan routes:

They are as a rule stone buildings, with a large open enclosure, surrounded by alcoves, closed or open, according to the climate. In the north, where the winter storms may be severe, there are stables frequently partly underground. The alcoves are for the travelers, the open space for their loads and the stables for the animals, but in case of severe weather the stable also becomes the refuge for the traveler, whether merchant, muleteer or official. In the large cities regular rent is charged, but in the country there is simply a keeper who receives a small fee for furnishing fuel and water, otherwise the place being free for all comers. In some cases there is no keeper at all, the place being left to go to ruin. Most of these buildings in the interior have been put up as acts of merit by wealthy Turks, but with no regular income, and no one to be responsible for them, they have in many places fallen sadly into decay.[21]

Usually the room in the khan had a raised board platform across one side of the room. Travelers brought their own bedding and made up their beds on the boards, liberally sprinkling flea powder all around.[22]

In February 1877, Henry went with the colporteur Kevork Jurjuryan on a twenty-one day tour to Kara Hissar. Kara Hissar was "four days journey northeast of Sivas and three days inland from Kerassum on the Black Sea."[23] Though Kevork had little schooling, in the capacity of a colporteur he was one of the best Armenian preachers. A man of faith, prayer, and hard work, he studied all the books he sold. In addition to the Bible, many Christian classics had been translated into the several native languages of Turkey, including Bunyan's *Pilgrim's Progress*, Doddridge's *Rise and Progress of Religion in the Soul*, Baxter's *Saint's Everlasting Rest*, commentaries, catechisms, hymnbooks, and simple primers. Kevork loved to speak of the Scriptures and preached with a deep voice and convincing eloquence, whether in a dark village room or in a chapel. A native of Sivas, he lived in Enderes and was well known throughout the northern villages of the Sivas *vilayet*.[24]

Traveling on horseback, Henry and Kevork first rode through the broad and fertile valley of the Kizil Irmak (Halys River) east towards Zara. There were over thirty Armenian villages along the way, and the Armenians were feeling the oppression of impending war with Russia. Turkey was drafting soldiers for the war, and as they marched to their assigned destination, the Armenian villages, already suffering under oppressive taxation, had to house and feed them. Henry wrote to Dr. Clark that because of the soldiers, the Armenians

> ... are now quite willing to acknowledge that it is because of their sins that the Lord is bringing calamities upon them, and to receive the Protestant booksellers, for the consolation which they may be able to impart from the Word of God.[25]

Though these were all Gregorian Armenians, and none of the villages had a Protestant congregation, the people were eager to hear the truth.

Outside of Zara, Henry and Kevork overtook four hundred soldiers traveling from Sivas to Erzerum. They traveled with them for a time when they were caught in a blinding snow-storm. Several times the horses lay down in the deep snow, and Henry and Kevork could only get them up by taking off their loads and carrying them themselves.

At least four times along the journey Henry and Kevork met companies of soldier-recruits, about four hundred each. These placed a heavy burden on the regions through which they passed. The recruits were on their way to Erzerum but had no officers with them to establish discipline. The civil authorities in the towns had no authority over them. At liberty to do as they pleased, the men lived off the land and beat the impoverished villagers until food was brought from their meager stores. They openly stole from the villagers, who were already crushed by burdensome taxation.[26] Henry was unharmed by the soldiers because he was a foreigner, but otherwise he was certain that the soldiers would have taken his and Kevork's horses. The despairing villagers didn't know where to look for help. Their despair made them more open to the Word of God and the comfort of the Lord than they had been in years.

On April 24, 1877, Russia, ostensibly impatient with Turkey's promises of reform and claiming protection for Ottoman Christians, declared war on Turkey. Though the war did not come to Sivas, Henry closely followed its causes and progress through telegrams, background reading on Russian and Ottoman history, and close reading of the *London Times*. The Armenian population in eastern Turkey welcomed Russia's help against their Kurdish attackers in the region. By 1878, much of western Armenia (in eastern Turkey) was under Russian control, and the Russian army was near Constantinople. A humiliated Turkey sued for peace, and Russia dictated the terms of the Treaty of San Stefano on March 3, 1878.

Britain realized the importance of maintaining the integrity of the Ottoman Empire to keep Russia from expanding its presence in the region. Britain was concerned both about protecting its access to India and protecting Christians, including Armenians, in the Turkish lands. On June 4, 1878, Britain signed a bilateral agreement with Turkey under which Britain agreed to join the sultan in defending Ottoman Turkey if Russia tried to take any more territory. The sultan agreed to introduce necessary reforms to protect Christians in those territories. To help Britain protect Turkey, the agreement also provided that the island of Cyprus would be administered and occupied by Britain. Britain's purpose was also to administer Cyprus in such a way as to be a model for the administration of Ottoman lands.

Under further pressure from Britain, terms of the Treaty of San Stefano were revised in Berlin in July. Serbia, Romania, and Montenegro were granted independence, and Bulgaria was given autonomy within the Ottoman Empire. For the first time the problem of Armenians within Turkey was formally recognized by the European community. Under Article 61 of the Treaty of Berlin, the Porte was obliged to

> carry out, without further delay, the improvements and reforms demanded by local requirements in provinces inhabited by the Armenians and to guarantee their security against the Circassians and Kurds. It will periodically make known the steps taken to the Powers who will superintend their application.[27]

Facially, Article 61 appeared to give the Armenians greater protection than Article 16 of the San Stefano treaty. However, the new promise to "guarantee their security" was a meaningless shibboleth. The new treaty required withdrawal of the Russian army that was occupying the homelands of the Armenians, leaving no one to protect them from the periodic Kurd and Circassian raids. In place of the vacating Russian army, the European powers gave only vague assurances that the sultan would implement reforms that somehow would be collectively overseen by the European powers.

British Prime Minister Disraeli's government looked upon Turkey as a virtual British protectorate, and British military consuls were stationed throughout the country to insure the implementation of reform. Consul-General Lt. Col. C.W. Wilson was stationed at Sivas and coordinated the work of Vice-Consuls in other *vilayet*s. The consuls often insisted on the removal of corrupt local officials, and the Armenians especially were encouraged that reform would come about.[28] Only time would tell how well the reforms would be implemented. But Perry, whether in Sivas or visiting the villages, refused to discuss political developments outside of missionary circles. He was called to preach the Gospel, not promote government reform.

Whenever her health permitted, Jeanne joined Henry on his preaching tours and helped at the Sivas station. She taught English, music, and sewing in the schools, ministered to the Armenian women, and led singing whenever possible. Every Wednesday she sang with the children. She was an accomplished seamstress and sewed for others as well as herself, making the wedding dress for at least one of the Armenian weddings in Sivas. She loved plants, and whenever Henry went visiting government officials or other local leaders, he often brought a bouquet of flowers from Jeanne's garden as a gift.

Since there were no English schools in the town, each morning Jeanne taught Alvan his lessons, especially reading and math. By the time he was five, Alvan was able to help read in the family's daily devotions. Henry and Jeanne also made American holidays, such as Washington's birthday, Thanksgiving, and July 4th, special for Alvan so he would grow up appreciating his American heritage. In the evenings, history was brought to life as Henry and Jeanne read aloud to Alvan from Charles Coffin's *The Boys of '76* or *Old Times in the Colonies*. On Sunday's Jeanne taught Alvan the catechism and helped him memorize chapters of the Bible.

Jeanne loved children, and besides teaching Alvan, she helped Emma Hubbard with her growing family. Ray and Luke Crescens Hubbard were born before the Perrys arrived in Sivas, but Jeanne helped with the births of Faith in 1880 and the twin boys Loyal George and Royal Chauncy in 1882. Jeanne stayed with Emma for two weeks after the twins were born to help her get on her feet again. The five Hubbard children were always full of energy and adventure, and even Albert called his children "little Indians."

Ray, the oldest Hubbard child, was two years younger than Alvan Perry, but always tried to keep up with him. This proved disastrous in December 1879, when Ray went over to the Perrys to play with Alvan. In a family letter Albert related what happened:

[The Perrys] have there a library with shelves all the way up to the ceiling. Alvan's mother had forbidden him to climb... up on the shelves, but she left the children alone, and Alvan took the opportunity to show Ray how well he could climb. He ascended and descended safely, but Ray following him fell, and screaming with pain was brought back to us.[29]

The arm was dislocated at the elbow and fractured. The American trained doctor in Sivas was unavailable, and the Armenian doctor called wouldn't touch the boy. The arm was swelling all the time. Albert followed a medical book and relocated the bone, but it wouldn't stay put. Other doctors were called in who finally consented to give little four year old Ray ether while the doctors reset and bandaged the arm. It was a terrifying time for all, but little Ray was soon happy with his bandaged hand, confident that "Jesus will make it all well pretty soon."

The ABCFM's policy of establishing married missionaries working as a unit in a central station was a wise one in Turkey. Not only did it necessitate the training of native pastors and teachers to work in the surrounding villages, it had an important influence on the society of the community. By the missionaries actually making their homes in Turkey, with their children being born, and often dying and being buried there, they made a profound impression on the peoples of Turkey, which began to reshape the social system. As James Barton later wrote, "Each station became a social settlement, in which the Christian home was the center and from which wholesome Christian influences were exerted upon all with whom the missionaries came in contact."[30] Certainly the very lives of the Hubbard and Perry families in Sivas influenced many in the *vilayet*.

Jeanne's weakness and poor health made it impossible for her to keep pace with her vibrant will and spiritual energy. She had come to patiently bear her physical suffering without complaining, and she insisted to Henry she did not want to go back to the States for her health. After all, she had not improved that much when she stayed in the States after Alvan was born. The Lord had called them to the mission field in Turkey, and here she wished to remain doing whatever she could in the Lord's vineyard.

On Sunday August 11, 1878, Jeanne gave birth to a fourth daughter, Edith Welsheimer. Emma Hubbard and a local doctor assisted in the birth. Little Edith was a healthy baby with an oval face and dark, bright eyes, but Jeanne continued weak. She had come to think the gypsum in the water of Sivas aggravated her diarrhea and intestinal problems, so the Perrys decided to spend the winter of 1878-1879 in the outstation of Tocat.

Located fifty-seven miles northwest of Sivas, Tocat was in a gorge "which receives the waters from several valleys which bank up the crest of the Chamli Bell Mountain."[31] The mission property was on one of the hills; from it one had a view of most of the city. Dr. Van Lennep, a missionary Henry and Jeanne briefly met in Smyrna in 1866, had built a chapel and parsonage in Tocat, and it was here Henry and Jeanne, along with Alvan and little Edith, lived and ministered. The parsonage had a garden with some 500 fruit trees, and Alvan loved to play there. Here too was the monument that Dr. Van Lennep had erected to the memory of Henry Martyn.

The winter in Tocat was one of repair – repairing the spiritual discipline and piety of the church and repairing the crumbling garden of the mission property. Many of the stone walls of the garden were in disrepair, and Henry enjoyed overseeing the workmen repairing the terraces. Tocat was warm enough in the winter to carry out such work while Sivas was frozen over. The improvements needed in the garden seemed a reflection of the necessary spiritual rebuilding of the foundations of the church at Tocat. Spiritual leadership in the church was weak, but Simon Agha from Marsovan was able to come and provide some native leadership to the congregation. Henry continued to rejoice in Jeanne's quiet influence among the Armenian women and children.

At the end of March the Perrys returned to Sivas. The peach trees were in bloom, and it was time to prepare and plant the spring vegetable garden. Five year old Alvan eagerly helped his father in the garden. When the Hubbards went to Constantinople for the annual meeting, the Perrys stayed at Sivas. The spiritual situation at Sivas was improving, and both the schools and chapel congregation were gaining in strength. A native pastor was still needed, however, and Henry preached regularly in the Sunday morning and evening services. With school out, he used his extra time to read about Africa and the missionary enterprise there encouraged by David Livingstone's explorations.

At the end of June 1879, Henry left for a month-long tour to Gürün, Derende, and Ashude. The road from Sivas to Gürün was a picturesque one, climbing from the Sivas plain, 4500 feet above sea level, to nearly 6600 feet near Gürün:

> ...the whole three days is constantly climbing over bare ridges from the summits of which the view sweeps off in every direction over miles and miles of mountain peaks to the blue and hazy horizon – one vast wilderness of barren rock without sign of human habitation as far as eye can see. But it is a wilderness view to make one's blood leap with the exultant joy of boundless freedom. No forest or snow clad mountains in the world can vie with these barren rocks in richness and beauty of color: the red-brown of iron, the gray-green of copper, the pure white of marble, and dead black of charcoal streak and blend with the grays and browns of granite and limestone to paint a scene of wild but entrancing beauty. Over the chaos of rough, gray crags, eagles circle and swoop. Riotous ridges of rock reach off, break, blend, and blur into the shimmering distance. While above in the sun-swept blue of the sky white clouds of dazzling brightness drift. One can well understand how Jesus loved to go "into the desert places to rest and pray."
>
> But it is not all barren desert, for in between those ridges that look so desolate there are beautiful green valleys and hillsides covered with sheep...[32]

Jeanne, ill with her old complaint, which was irritated by Sivas' limestone water, remained in Sivas as Henry visited the villages. Too weak to travel, she did not complain about Henry's leaving her at Sivas with the children. She was thoroughly submissive to the Lord's will and encouraged Henry in the work to which he was called. While Henry was gone, however, little Edith fell sick. Jeanne wrote Henry of their baby's worsening condition, but the letter never reached him. When he returned home, Alvan met his father at the street gate and said, "Do you know, Edith died and they buried her?" Jeanne came calmly out to meet her husband with a smile and peace on her face only the Lord could bring. Henry could not help but love Jeanne even more for her beautiful trust in the Lord. She committed her children to Him. They were her "treasures in heaven," and she knew her Lord would care for them. Her life was a constant victory over grief and despair. Only the Lord could bring such comfort and joy in the midst of sadness.

Two years later, on October 6, 1881, a fifth daughter, infant Carrie Williams, died in Jeanne's arms while Henry was on a preaching tour to the villages. Jeanne herself was so ill that her own death seemed imminent. She made her will, and Henry was called back to Sivas from his preaching tour. Mercifully, Jeanne slowly recovered. Jeanne always encouraged Henry on his preaching tours, even when she was ill. Though weak, she felt that by sparing him she was making a small contribution to the Lord's work. The love Henry and Jeanne had for the Lord and the mission work was a strong bond that intensified their love for each other. Over forty years later, Henry added these reflections about Jeanne to his diary:

> To complain was not her way at all. Her letters were always clear, simple, and affectionate. Even when twice during my absence the children breathed their last in this world in her arms. On my return she never once spoke an unpleasant word.
>
> Such a wife was the Dear Lord's precious gift to me; and her children in heaven are a blessing to her; and to me in this world. Heavenly Treasures they are. Praise to our Matchless Lord!!
>
> Believers who <u>sing</u> their way in the service of the Lord, express their faith more directly than the preachers who use argument, or even the exposition of Scripture truth. The success in using <u>music</u> as a medium is from the fact that it appeals directly to the heart. This method, confirmed in the case of my Jeanne, made her intensely loyal to her Lord.

In her physical depression at Sivas from an incurable disease, she overcame it by the positive vigor of her faith in Jesus. Every severe attack was followed by a rebound of faith and of praise to the Lord.

As to the loss and disappointment, in the case of the death of our five little girls, she recognized the will of the Saviour in taking them to Himself; and spent no time in vain regrets. Especially was this evident when my <u>delay</u> out on the Sivas-station tours, perhaps fifty-miles saddle-riding distant, led on to finding the little one gone, and the Mother's arms empty, - she had for me not a single word of reproach. She spoke of the detail of the case; and of the sweet comfort by which our precious Jesus had comforted her.

It was in her case her Prize of the Throne. She loved her Enthroned Lord; and when He took her children, she happily gave them to His care. Rev. 3:21, "To him that overcometh will I grant to sit with me in my throne, even as I also overcame, and am set down with my Father in his throne."[33]

Henry and Albert often had requested a doctor at Sivas to replace Dr. West. In March 1880, Dr. and Mrs. Davis became part of the Sivas mission, and the Perrys vacated Dr. West's house for the doctor's use. The Davises, however, brought more turmoil than relief to the mission. Dr. Davis especially resented Treasurer Perry, believing he did not provide him with adequate funds. Emma Hubbard believed Dr. Davis was not sane in some points, and Henry thought his "aptitude for affairs is the nearest to zero of that of any missionary I ever saw."[34] Dr. Davis took his breakfast in bed and stayed in bed until noon. He left his room in time for lunch, then spent the afternoon lounging, smoking, riding, and reading the papers until bedtime. Claiming the climate of Sivas interfered with his health, Dr. Davis moved with his family to Caesarea in July. The missionaries at Caesarea soon had strong evidence that Dr. Davis was addicted to opium, and the American Board recalled him the following year.[35]

Miss Laura Chamberlin had come to Sivas in 1879, to replace Flavia Bliss as head of the Girls' Boarding School, which was using half of Dr. West's house for its facilities. Miss Chamberlin's letters to her family and friends in Vermont were full of all the details of life in Turkey, from the dress of the women, to a description of houses and farming methods, to types of food. These were features of Turkish life all missionaries became familiar with as they labored among the native population.

The Turkish houses in the villages were

...built of brick made with straw, dried in the sun, and when used, they plaster the walls inside and out with the same material, which gives the house the clay-colored appearance; cedar beams, sometimes large, sometimes small, are placed across the wall, then stones, and over all earth is piled up, and often the grass springs up and grows so that you cannot distinguish the houses in the distance scarcely, for they resemble green or clay-colored mounds...The bricks used for houses and walls around them are nearly eight times larger than those made in the United States. Of course the walls are very thick, and in the villages the windows afford but little light...[36]

Farmers used the same tools and methods used since the times of the patriarchs. Miss Chamberlin wrote the Vermont farmers that the plough seen in the fields was the same pictured on ancient monuments. Barley and wheat were the main grains grown. Cracked or bulgur wheat was a popular native food:

It is made with two round stones, a foot in diameter and four inches thick; a hole in one side of the upper stone allows us to put in a stout stick to turn it; the grain is put in a round hole in the middle of the upper stone, and the cracked wheat comes out in the cloth put under the stones to catch it as it comes out between them. This is hard work for one, but two or three young girls like to keep it going rapidly around, and sing their merriest songs as they work...[37]

Mutton was the only meat eaten in the region; no one killed an ox or cow unless it was old, sick or maimed. For many months of the year bread and onions were the main food – and "owert" (yogurt). Miss Chamberlin described "owert" as

... a kind of sour kurd made from either new or skim-milk. It reminds one of the buckwheat pitcher in many families, where the bottom of the pitcher is not seen all winter. To every fresh quantity of milk, a little of the old is added, or the same dish used with the old. It is a favorite dish of the natives, and in some villages you cannot persuade them to sell you new milk, but will keep you waiting an hour, then bring it to you hot from the fire or in the form of this curd. It is very unfortunate for the traveler if he cannot soon learn to like it (and the taste is an acquired one), for often one is compelled to eat it.[38]

Green peas were cooked with the pods all chopped together. Squashes, cucumbers, beets, carrots, eggplant and cabbages were also grown.

Apricots, peaches, plums, and pears grew well. Potatoes had only recently been introduced to the country by an English Consul, but were beginning to be grown in the country. Roots of trees and bushes and dried manure were used for cooking fuel. The women mixed the manure with straw, dried it in the sun, then stacked it near the house, just like cords of wood were stacked in New England or masses of peat in Ireland.

Miss Chamberlin of course was interested in the women's clothing, and especially noted the way the women colored their fingernails with "some garnet material." When she was invited to an afternoon engagement feast and ceremony by one of the Protestant families of Sivas, she described the brightly colored silks and broadcloth clothing of the natives, which contrasted with the simple cambric fabric of the missionaries. Of course the missionary women wore their hats, as all respectable Victorian ladies would. Some of the Turkish women, after inspecting the missionaries, told them they would look quite well without their hats. At last, the Americans removed their hats, and the Turkish women all wanted to feel them. They said the Americans looked much better without "those baskets."

The *Vali* of Sivas in 1879 and early 1880 was an excellent administrator interested in bringing reform to the government. In November 1879, British general-Consul Wilson had a confidential conversation on the subject of reforms at Abeddin Pasha's private residence. The *Vali* had some definite suggestions. First, he believed the *Vali*, *Mutessarifs*, and *Kaimakams* should be good men of integrity. The *Vali* should be allowed to appoint the *Kaimakams*, free from the bribery system of Constantinople. Secondly, he believed the police force needed to be reorganized and made more efficient. He believed villages could be grouped according to religions and Christians could rule Christians and Moslems rule over Moslems. The *Vali* had already submitted to the government plans for an elementary educational system in the villages, a better system for collecting taxes, road improvements, and the introduction of industries, but the government never answered his requests. Wilson had the impression that the *Vali* was somewhat disheartened by the Porte's lack of response. Nevertheless, his efforts had brought order to Sivas and made life and property secure.[39]

In 1880, Abeddin Pasha become Ottoman Minister of Foreign Affairs, and Ismail Hakki Pasha became *Vali* of Sivas. From the best governed, Sivas soon became the worst governed *vilayet* in Anatolia. Hakki Pasha filled important offices with his friends and relatives, drank to excess, and oppressed both Moslems and Christians. He released all but one of the murderers imprisoned by Abeddin Pasha and punished few criminals. On the slightest provocation, however, he would imprison the innocent and not release them until they paid for their freedom.

On October 23, 1880, a riot broke out in Sivas that the *Vali* used to persecute the Armenians. An honorable Armenian merchant and landowner of Sivas was traveling home from his farm to a wedding at his house when armed robbers attacked him. The robbers murdered him with stones and clubs and robbed him of all the profits from the grain he had just sold. His family was told he was slightly wounded, but when they came to take him home, they found only a mutilated corpse. The family reported the murder to the Vali and took the body to the church. When the family returned to their home, they found a thief pillaging their home. They caught him and handed him over to the police, but he escaped. The family went to see the *Vali* at his home as darkness set in. A crowd gathered, and some began to throw stones at the windows of the *Vali*'s house. Though the gathered crowd included Armenians, Turks, and Greeks, the *Vali* accused the Armenians of organizing a riot. He arrested over 25 people, including some of the leading Armenians of the city who were not even in town the evening of the riot. W.J. Richards, British assistant at Sivas, reported:

> Perjury is quite an institution in the country. Whether the soil of Sivas is peculiarly genial to this evil growth I cannot say, but it certainly is a very thriving business here, trade being at present unusually brisk. The prosecution on the part of the Government of those concerned in the late riot has opened up a vast field of employment for those who gain a precarious living by this means.[40]

The British reported that the *Vali* was controlled by Mehmet Ali Effendi, who brought corruption and disorder throughout the *vilayet*.[41] The evidence of injustice, corruption, perjury, and torture of prisoners was clear. The whole incident aroused the Armenians and convinced them that justice was impossible under the present government, and the guilty must suffer with the innocent. Through the efforts of British Consul-general Wilson, Hakki Pasha was removed as Vali in 1882; his rule had brought injustice to both Moslems and Armenians. Yet increasingly, Armenians were giving up hope of British or European help in improving their lot. Unable to obtain support from the European powers to press reforms on the sultan, Britain too began to abandon its efforts.

In the midst of all the political uncertainties, Henry knew that the Gospel was the one source of stability. Henry and Jeanne both relished visiting the villages and speaking personally to the people about salvation in Jesus Christ. Though the Armenian people seemed most receptive to the gospel preaching, the missionaries did not neglect ministering to Kurds, Moslems and Greeks in their villages. The Greek orthodox priests usually would not allow the Protestant missionaries in the Greek villages, but some of the Kurds were more receptive. The Kuzzelbash Kurds had villages in the Sivas *vilayet* northeast from Divrik to Kangal in the south. Colporteurs had distributed Bibles and Christian literature among them; but few could read, and they were not interested in having schools among them. Nevertheless, by 1880, at least fifty Protestant families were scattered among these Kurdish villages. Most of the Kurds were pantheists molded by Moslem tradition. They eagerly accepted all beliefs, but by accepting so many gods, they denied the unique divinity of Christ. Their belief in reincarnation forced them to deny the resurrection. Some Kurds became Protestants for political gain, thinking the Europeans would help them against the oppressive Turks; others genuinely embraced the truth of the gospel and Scripture. Visiting one group of Kurds near Zara, Henry was pleased to see the light of the gospel spreading in Turkey:

> We were treated each evening to a <u>concert</u>: the children of the family singing, for our especial entertainment in Turkish, the hymns "I Need Thee Every Hour," and the "Gates Ajar." I need not say that, though the tune could scarcely be recognized, it sounded out sweetly from the amazing ignorance of the Koordish locality.[42]

When Jeanne discovered that the gypsum in Sivas' water aggravated her intestinal problems, she tried to accompany Henry on more of his preaching tours. Different water, the open air, and "tenting" or camping out in the countryside always seemed to improve her health. Jeanne also quickly developed a warm rapport among the children and women of the villages and was able to minister the gospel of Christ to them, both in song and conversation. In the fall of 1880, Jeanne and Alvan accompanied Henry to Zara for a two-week trip. Jeanne and Alvan stayed in Zara as guests of Hacheh Agas while Henry and Baron Barsam, the pastor from Tocat, visited surrounding Armenian and Kurdish villages.

Perry and Barsam traveled along the upper Halys River east to Erzinjian, staying at a different village each night, preaching the Gospel. They crossed the mountains into the Lycus Valley and called on several village priests before reaching Enderes. They had not traveled on many of the roads before, but found their way asking from village to village. Staying with a prominent Armenian in the village of Keche-Yoordoo, they were warned of a band of Laz robbers who had recently been in the region. After some discussion, they decided to take a guide to lead them back to Zara over an unfrequented mountain pass. Traveling along the mountain road, they passed a Greek village with an ancient Greek church and the ruins of an ancient Roman town. As they climbed higher and entered a forest of pines, they began to follow the ruins of a graded and stone-paved Roman militia road. Perry was so intrigued by the road that he had forgotten about the robbers, when suddenly two men darted from the trees, shooting, and demanding the travelers dismount. Perry was armed with only a small pistol, and since his companions were unarmed, resistance seemed futile. He wished he had a repeating rifle such as he carried the previous year, so he could put up some resistance. After dismounting, Perry and his two companions were bound, blindfolded, and forced to follow the robbers, who now numbered five armed men. After walking only a short distance, the captives were made to sit down while the robbers thoroughly searched them and their saddle bags. They were disappointed in not finding any gold. Since he was at the end of his journey, Perry had little money. The thieves did enjoy eating the watermelon, apples, and bread Perry had bought for Jeanne and Alvan back in Zara. After about two hours, Perry and his companion were released and allowed to go. Henry later wrote his mother a detailed account of the whole affair and concluded:

> We were thankful to the Great Shepherd for caring for us and saving the sheep of His pasture in the time of their danger. Since our escape in September three travelers have been shot dead by robbers in that same locality and their bodies were brought to Zara.
> It seems that the Lord has something more for us to do here yet; so please join us in the prayer that we may do it well.[43]

Like Paul in Asia Minor centuries before, Henry and other missionaries in Turkey were "on frequent journeys, in danger from rivers, dangers from robbers..." (II Corinthians 11:26). Henry could remain calm throughout because he counted it part of his gospel ministry, and he returned to Jeanne and Alvan in Zara with even greater joy! The next day, before leaving for Sivas, Henry and Alvan went down to the river to bathe. Henry thoroughly loved traveling with his family and enjoying such special, though very ordinary, times with his son.

The following summer, Jeanne and Alvan accompanied Henry on tours south to Divrik and Gürün. On June 20, 1881, the three started out with Jeanne mounted on Jim, Alvan on Whitey, and Perry on a "Kurd's horse." The fields were carpeted with flowers, and the Perrys enjoyed picking some of the honeysuckle and flowers. The two overnights on the way to Divrik they tented outside villages. On Sunday Henry preached to about 150 people in the Divrik church on the conversion of St. Paul. The next week they broke ground for a parsonage, and the people helped, as they had on the building of the chapel. The chapel was a two-story building with schoolrooms below and a reception room above. It stood in the center of a large lot of ground on the crest of a hill. The church had been without regular preaching or pastoral care for six years, and errors "like rank weeds in a neglected field" were springing up. The weakness throughout the Sivas field was clearly evident at Divrik. Trained, native pastors to nurture the congregations were needed.

Henry had been reading a collection of Dr. Lyman Beecher's sermons, published in 1842. One sermon especially, "The Building of Waste Places" seemed to speak to the need of the Protestant churches in Turkey. The same causes of the "waste places" in Connecticut churches one hundred years ago seemed to be affecting the churches in Turkey - a low state of piety, infidelity, not requiring a converted life for church membership, and worldly ambitions. Beecher said the supply of evangelists and pastors was necessary to rebuild the churches, and Henry knew this was the solution to the problems of the churches in Turkey. The congregations in the outstations and Sivas itself, with all of their problems, were worth saving; however, native pastors and evangelists must be trained for them. [44]

In Divrik were some excellent Christians

> ...whose prayers daily ascend like incense before the Lord for a revival of his work. One of these, Baron Sahak, is a paralytic dependent for support on the alms of the people and unable to walk, but his knowledge of the Bible and especially its spiritual teachings is very clear, and his faith tested by great trials and through many years of suffering is ever firm and strong. When in Divrik I always call upon him and his faithful wife, and never without feeling myself minis-

tered unto by one of the Lord's poor who is ripening for the Kingdom of Glory.[45]

Gürün was the most prosperous of the Sivas outstations and the only place which had a native pastor, Marderos Beshguturyan. The Gürün church actually had five places of worship along a six-mile length of valley, and Pastor Marderos had long distances to walk in ministry to his people. Not able to afford a horse, for thirteen years the pastor had walked to his preaching places in "the heat and dust of summer and the mud of winter." When opportunity afforded, he also traveled to other churches among the outstations of Sivas and ministered to them. With much patience he entered into the plans and troubles of his people. It was a pleasure for Henry to sit and hear the advice of this godly Armenian about the Sivas district and to share with him in the ministries of the gospel.

Albert Hubbard did not approve of Henry's extensive work in the villages and outstations around Sivas. Because of the schism in the Sivas church and the weakness and worldliness of its leaders, Albert thought the missionaries should focus on building up the central church in Sivas. Henry did not think the evangelization and encouragement of the growing churches in the outlying regions of the province should be neglected. Temperamentally Henry and Albert were opposites, and they sometimes disagreed on the approaches to mission work. Henry had a strong passion for the truth, a serious conviction that he must give his all for Christ's kingdom, and a high sense of duty and responsibility to the tasks at hand. Albert was much more fun-loving and lacked Henry's intensity and organizational abilities. He was especially fond of children and had a special interest in developing the Sunday School in Sivas; Henry recorded in his diary Albert's ability in this area:

> In his addresses to the children (of which there were many in our Sivas Sunday service in the PM) the smile of his face and twinkle in his eye at the point of the Bible Story, would so captivate the attention of the children that the number of them would easily increase.[46]

With so much work to be done, both Henry and Albert asked that another missionary be sent to Sivas. The ABCFM, however, was considering cutting back the missionary forces in Turkey, not increasing them. Henry and Albert had to carry on the work by themselves.

The failure of the ABCFM to send the needed additional missionary to Sivas was in part due to a reconsideration of its missionary presence in Turkey. In 1881 the Prudential Committee in Boston issued a *Memorandum for the Missions in the Turkish Empire*. In it the Prudential Committee noted that the missionary work begun among the Armenians forty years earlier had the purpose of reforming and strengthening the Armenian church, so the Armenian Christians could be illustrations to the rest of Turkey of Christian life and character. The hope was that these Armenian Christians could then become the means of evangelizing all of Turkey. By 1880, among the Armenians there were nearly one hundred evangelical churches with over 6000 members, and thirty-nine schools of higher learning, including Robert College. The many schools for girls had elevated the position of females in Turkey. The students from the schools were a trained group who were able to bring the gospel and the benefits of education to an expanding number in Turkey. It seemed as if the goal of the ABCFM in Turkey had been accomplished, and it was time for the American Board to cut back its involvement among the Armenians in Turkey and use its resources among other gospel-needy peoples. The Armenian Christians must assume more financial responsibility for their native churches and not rely so heavily on American funding. The Otis legacy, which had helped finance a large portion of the missionary activity in Turkey, was declining in amount, and cutbacks in financing the Turkey mission, including the Sivas station, began immediately.

Both the Armenian Christians and the missionaries in Turkey appealed to the ABCFM to consider the precarious position of the Christians in Turkey and not abandon their support. The Russo-Turkish war, famine, and relentless Ottoman oppression had left the Armenians in such grinding poverty that they were not able to support their churches. Though schools and seminaries had been established, they had not yet produced enough trained men to adequately satisfy the need for pastors, evangelists, and teachers in the churches. Unfortunately, some of the best-qualified students went to America or Europe for further study and never returned to their native land. Others had been more interested in the secular aspects of education, neglecting the Gospel and the service of the Church

Among some Armenians there was also dissatisfaction with their treatment by the missionaries. A few missionaries had little respect for the native Armenian preachers and ruled over the Armenian churches. Native pastors had not been allowed to participate in the Mission meetings, even as observers. Some native pastors wanted to be paid the same salary the missionaries were paid, but local churches could never afford such support. The Prudential Committee recommended a plan of cooperation between the native pastors and workers and the missionaries. The missionaries should be the helpers of the native pastors and the native church, and not vice versa. Missionaries and native workers should meet together for prayer, Bible study, and cooperative planning for the churches. Though the pastors and churches could receive funds from the mission budget, at least half of the support for the pastors and church property should be from native sources. Funds from America would still have to be reduced, and the funds would still be managed by the American missionaries, not the native workers. The Prudential Committee did not believe native pastors should control the dispersal of funds donated by Americans to an American organization. With some directive changes in the missionary operation, the Prudential Committee would continue the Turkey mission.[47]

Though the cut in funds made it more difficult for the Sivas station to pursue the aggressive building up of the churches in the villages Henry considered so important, he was very much in accord with the Prudential Committee's recommendations for work in Turkey. The missionary's purpose was not to build his own position, but to help build up the native church, under native pastors supplied by their own congregations. Both Henry and Albert worked with the native pastors and workers in a cooperative manner, and the native workers regularly met with the missionaries in planning the church's activities.

On November 11, 1881, Henry's mother turned seventy, and this brought another important time of decision for the Perrys. Was Henry needed in the States to care for her, or might the Perrys spend a few more years in the Turkey mission? Henry wrote his mother to prayerfully give her answer, and the ABCFM sent concerned friends to Ashfield to personally determine Mrs. Perry's needs. Mrs. Perry wrote her son that her health was still fairly good and she thought she could spare him for his work in Turkey for another five years.

---

[1] J.D. Barton explained the relationship of the capitulations to international law as follows:

Intercourse of the Christian world with Mohammedan countries does not proceed according to the law of nations. International law as practiced by the civilized nations of Christendom is an outgrowth from the communion of ideas existing between them and rests upon a common conception of justice and right. Between the Mohammedans and the Christian nations of Europe and America there exists no such common idea or principle from which could result a true international law. Relations one with the other have, therefore, to be regulated by special 'capitulation' or 'concession' granted by the ruler of the Mohammedan country.

For this reason, even to the present time, the law of nations as known and practiced throughout Christendom has not been applied in the relations existing between Turkey and the Christian Powers. *Daybreak in Turkey*, 241-242.

[2] Vahakn N. Dadrian. *The History of the Armenian Genocide: Ethnic Conflict from the Balkans to Anatolia to the Caucasus.* Providence and Oxford: Berghahn Books, 1995, 33. "Pasha" was an honorary title placed after a name to indicate a high rank or office in.

[3] Edwin W. Martin. *Hubbards of Sivas.* Santa Barbara, California: Fithian Press, 1991, 87-88.

[4] Noel Barber. *The Sultans.* N.Y.: Simon and Schuster, 1973, 168.

[5] Political background to the period is described in Noel Barber. *The Sultans.* N.Y.: Simon and Schuster, 1973, 148-198; Rev. Edwin Bliss. *Turkey and the Armenian Atrocities.* Fresno, California: Mesag Publishing, 1982 reprint of 1896 ed., 185-296; George A. Bournoustian. *A History of the Armenian People*, Vol. II 1500 A.D. to present. Costa Mesa, California: Mazda Publisher, 1993, 88-92; Vahakn N. Dadrian. *The History of the Armenian Genocide.* Providence and Oxford: Burgahn Books, 1995, 3-34; W.M. Ramsay. *Impressions of Turkey During Twelve Years of Wanderings.* N.Y.: G.P. Putnam's Sons, 1897, 150-161; Jeremy Salt. *Imperialism, Evangelism and the Ottoman Armenians 1878-1896.* Frank Cass, 1993; Articles on "Turkey" and "Eastern Question" in *Encyclopedia Britannica*, 1958 ed.

[6] *The Missionary Herald*, July 1876, quoted in *The Hubbards of Sivas,* 87.

[7] Quoted in *Hubbard of Sivas*, 88.

[8] Turkey was divided into states called *vilayets*. The *vilayet* was ruled by a *Vali* or governor-general appointed directly by the sultan. Each vilayet was divided into provinces called *sanjaks*.

[9] Murray's *Handbook of Asia Minor*; Rev. Albert Bryant, "Sivas, Turkey," *The Missionary Herald*, vol. LXV, no. iv, April 1869, 113-114; Antranig Chalabian. *Armenia After the Coming of Islam*. Southfield, Michigan, 1999, 90-93, 327-329; *Leavening the Levant*, 198-199. Dr. Armand E. Bedikian, "Pilgrimage to Sebastia in 1993 and 1994," W. J. Childs, excerpt from "Across Asia Minor on Foot (1917), Henry F. Tozer, excerpt from "Turkish Armenia and Eastern Asia Minor (1886)." And Capt. Fred Burnaby, excerpt from "On Horseback Through Asia Minor (1877)" in *Nor Sebastia*, Vol. 59, No. 180, 1995, 28-39.

[10] Mesrob K. Krikorian. *Armenians in the Service of the Ottoman Empire, 1860-1908*. London, Henley & Boston: Routledge Direct Editions, 55-59.

[11] Charles Holbrook. "Turkey Letter No. 3, being my first, second, third, and sundry succeeding impressions of Sivas and its People." c. 1913, 5-6, ABC 77.1 (29.6).

[12] Notes made in 1920's added to front of *Diary* for 1878.

[13] *Annual Report of the American Board of Commissioners for Foreign Missions*, 1897, xxv.

[14] Frank Stone. *Academies for Anatolia*. Lanham, MD.: University Press of America, 1984, 49-50.

[15] Paul William Harris. *Nothing but Christ: Rufus Anderson and the Ideology of Protestant Foreign Missions*. Oxford University Press, 1999, 20. Harris's book is a very useful introduction to the thought of Rufus Anderson, the Foreign Secretary of the ABCFM who retired in 1866, just as Henry Perry was entering the mission field. Anderson's policies on the role of education and the importance of a self-supporting native pastorate and church continued to influence the ABCFM during Henry's years of missionary service.

Joseph Lancaster was an English Quaker in charge of a Charity School without enough teachers. Around 1798, he developed the very organized system of a teacher teaching the brighter students who taught the younger ones. In 1808, the Royal Lancasterian Institution was established. In 1814, this became the British and Foreign School Society. Dr. Andrew Bell had developed a similar system for use in India in the Anglican missionary schools there. Rev. William Goodell first used this system among the Greeks in Constantinople. *Academies for Anatolia*, 37.

[16] Notes Henry Perry added in 1920's to beginning of *Diary* for 1881; *Leavening the Levant*, 200.

[17] Henry T. Perry to N.G. Clark, March 18, 1881, ABC 16.9.3, Vol. 15, No. 313.

[18] Bilal N. Simsir, ed. *British Documents and Ottoman Armenians*. Ankara: Türk Taril Kurumu Basimivi, 1982, Vol. I, 381.

[19] Henry Perry, "Armenian Schools at Sivas," *The Missionary Herald*, September 1880, 353.

[20] Frederick Davis Greene. *Armenian Massacres or Sword of Mohammed.* Philadelphia & Chicago: International Publishing Co., reprinted by J.C. & A.L. Fawcett, 1990, 159.
[21] Edwin Bliss. *Turkey and the Armenian Atrocities*, 32-33.
[22] Theresa Huntington Ziegler. *Great Need Over the Water.* Ann Arbor, MI: Gomidas Inst., 1998, 41.
[23] Henry T. Perry to Rev. N.G. Clark, Sivas, Feb. 4, 1882, ABC 16.9.3, Vol. 18, No. 46.
[24] Henry T. Perry to Rev. N.G. Clark, Sivas, Jan. 17th, 1884, ABC 16.9.3, Vol. 15, No. 341.
[25] Henry T. Perry to Rev. N.G. Clark, March 20, 1877, ABC 16.9.3, Vol. 7, Part 2; Henry T. Perry. "A Tour from Sivas," *The Missionary Herald*, July 1877, 224.
[26] *The Missionary Herald*, July 1877, 225.
[27] *Imperialism, Evangelism, and the Ottoman Armenians*, 47.
[28] *Impressions of Turkey*, 143-147.
[29] *Hubbards of Sivas*, 122.
[30] *Daybreak in Turkey*, 142.
[31] *Diary*, July 8, 1872.
[32] Charles Holbrook, "Turkey Letter No. 2, being A Rambling Account of my First Tour to Gürün, October 16-28, 1911, 2, ABC 77.1 (29.6).
[33] Notes added to beginning of *Diary* for 1880.
[34] Henry T. Perry to Dr. N.G. Clark, Sivas, August 4, 1880, ABC 16. 9.3, Vol. 7, part 2, No. 442.
[35] *Diary*, March 10, 29-30, 1880, May 3, 1880, July 7, 13, 1880; "Controversy with Dr. Davis," ABC 16.9.3, Western Turkey Missions, Misc., Vol. I.
[36] Laura D. Chamberlin. *Leaves from Her Scrapbook of Her Printed Letters and Articles 1879-1885*. ABC 16.5, Misc. Papers Relating to Near East, Vol.5 1860-1931, Documents and Letters, 156 (Oct. 7, 1879).
[37] *Leaves from Her Scrapbook*, 159 (August 1880).
[38] *Leaves from her Scrapbook*, 161 (August 1880).
[39] *British Documents on Ottoman Armenians*, Vol. 1, 576. A *kaimakam* was a governor of a subdistrict of the Ottoman Empire, or a deputy-governor.
[40] *British Documents on Ottoman Armenians*, vol. 2, 156. Detailed reports of the riot and its aftermath are found on pp. 154-170.
[41] "Effendi" was a general title such as "Mr." or the French "Monsieur."
[42] Henry Perry. "Christian Songs Among the Koords," *The Missionary Herald*, October 1878, 345.
[43] Henry T. Perry to Mother, Sivas, Feb. 17th, 1881, ABC 16.9.3, Vol. 15, No. 313.
[44] Henry T. Perry to Rev. N.G. Clark, Sivas, Dec. 13, 1881, ABC 16.9.3, Vol. 15, No. 320. The 1842 collection of Lyman Beecher's sermons had belonged to Benjamin Schneider, who had given many of his prized books to the younger missionary.

[45] Henry T. Perry to Rev. N.G. Clark, Sivas, Dec. 13, 1881, ABC 16.9.3, Vol. 15, No. 320.
[46] *Diary*, February 11, 1877.
[47] Prudential Committee. *Memorandum for the Missions in the Turkish Empire.* Boston: Beacon Press, 1881; S.M. Minasian. *Correspondence and Other Documents Relating to Troubles in the Turkish Missions of the American Board C.F.M.* N.Y.: Atkin & Prout, 1883; Strong *Story of the American Board*, 385-387. ABC 18.9. "Mission to Armenian, Misc.," Vol. 4 has numerous documents concerning the "Armenian Controversy" of the 1880's.

6
BEARING THE CROSS
(1882-1886)

"Whoever does not carry his own cross and come after Me cannot be My disciple."
Luke 14:17

In the spring of 1882, Jeanne and Alvan accompanied Henry to the annual meeting of the Turkish Mission in Constantinople. Jeanne had not recovered her strength from her serious illness in the fall, but was able to travel to Samsoun in a Maffa and then make the refreshing Black Sea crossing to Constantinople. The road to Samsoun on the Black Sea was always a busy one. It was not unusual to be traveling with donkey or camel trains and buffalo carts. A later missionary at Harpoot was amazed at the noisy carts:

> The wagons they draw are of a primitive type. Two thick, flat pieces of wood are rounded and shaped a little, and an axle is laid upon this foundation. Sometimes a sort of basket-work fence is built up upon the boards — narrow in front and broad behind. They usually leave the wheels ungreased, because they think the noise helps the buffaloes on. The noise is excruciating. You have no idea what shrieks and whines can be produced by one pair of wheels.[1]

At Constantinople the Perrys consulted Dr. Patterson about Jeanne's health. He said she was "starving in the midst of food," and unless relief could be found, her nervous system would soon break down. They decided it was best for Jeanne to remain in Constantinople a few months under the doctor's care while Henry returned to Sivas. Mrs. Schneider had been working in the Bible House in Constantinople since Dr. Schneider's death in 1878; she happily took Jeanne and Alvan into her home.

This was the third time in his missionary career Henry had to leave his wife under the care of a physician and return to his work alone. Though he continued his work in Sivas and toured outstations, Henry missed Jeanne and little Alvan deeply. Unfortunately, nothing the doctor did seemed to help Jeanne. Realizing she had little hope of recovering <u>anywhere</u>, she was eager to return to Henry, Sivas, and whatever of the Lord's work she was able to do there.

Henry planned to work to rebuild the church in Kara Hissar, and for the winter of 1882-1883 he moved Jeanne and Alvan to the village.[2] He not only hoped that they might be able to reinvigorate the church in the town, but he also hoped the fresh air and clear water of Kara Hissar would help restore Jeanne's health. Kara Hissar was not a new mission, so it fell within the guidelines of the Prudential Committee's *Memorandum*. However, the church established ten years earlier with ten families had never had a stable pastor, and the membership had declined, by death or defection, down to two families. Albert Hubbard was not fully in accord with Henry's move to Kara Hissar for several months, leaving the Hubbards alone in Sivas. Henry felt this northeastern section of their station should no longer be neglected. His main hope, however, was that keeping Jeanne away from the Sivas water would improve her health.

Approaching the fortress city of Kara Hissar from the south,

> ... two cliffs of black rock send up their sharp peaks to meet the clouds. A strip of land joins them, with sharp descent on either side to deep valleys. As we ascend the long southern slope the right-hand cliff appears, crowned with its black citadel. About its base is built the old city, the white and mud-colored houses intermingled; ... High in altitude, the climate, though cold, is dry and tempered somewhat by the protecting ridges of rocks which encompass the city on all sides but the southwest. The water, as in all these black-rock formation districts, is good, though little in quantity...
>
> In this city are eight hundred houses of Armenians, and in Tamzara, a large town less than an hour distant, there are two hundred and fifty more. Within less than a day's journey from the city are thirty-six thousand Armenians, among whom the only place at present occupied by a preacher of the gospel is Enderes.[3]

The "Mine of Silver" mentioned by Homer in the *Iliad*, ii.857 was near Kara Hissar, and a British company had just purchased a concession from the Turkish government to begin working it.[4]

By preaching, visiting with the people, and having Bible reading among the women, Henry and Jeanne hoped to expand the church in Kara Hissar. As soon as a native pastor could be found, Henry planned to turn the church over to his direction. Through correspondence with Dr. Barnam of Harpoot, Henry was able to enlist Sarkis Tufinkgian, a teacher from Harpoot trained at Antioch College, to teach in the school already established at Kara Hissar. A Bible Reader then working at Enderes was also coming to the town. Bible Readers were important native workers in ministering to women. They were women who would go into homes and explain the Bible to women. They also taught women to read so that they could begin reading the Bible for themselves.

After much searching, Henry was able to find a house to rent centrally located near the marketplace. With three small rooms, it had two large halls on the first and second floors. The second floor hall could seat sixty people. The Perrys began their work by inviting the townspeople to join them in their own family services in the hall on Sundays. Jeanne had brought her organ from Sivas, and many people were attracted to the services by the music. Between 50 and 100 often attended on Sundays, but few maintained any regular attendance.

Amazingly, a group of Kuzzle-Bash Kurds, who lived two days' journey south of the city, was among the most faithful. They were in town for a month to attend to a lawsuit, and all the time they were there they came to the services in the Perry home. They openly professed their belief in the doctrines of Christianity and purchased several portions of the Scriptures. The *mundir*, or local judge of the Kurds, told Henry that there was a movement of "reform" among the Kurds to reject more of the pagan Koordish rites and accept more of the truths of Christianity. These "Protestant Koords" were not always Protestant in the American or European sense of the term, but they were open to Christian truth.[5]

The work among the women of Kara Hissar was the most successful of the Perrys' ministries. In spite of her ill health, Jeanne worked with the native Bible reader to hold two prayer meetings a week for the women, one in the Perry house and one in another part of the city. The women knew almost nothing about the Gospel, but were ready to listen.[6]

Schools had become an important means of reaching communities with the Gospel, and Henry expected the school at Kara Hissar to create an interest in the Scriptures among the Armenian families. The Turks, however, had come to look with disfavor on the mission schools, fearing they were the cause of growing unrest and revolutionary sentiments among the people. Many of the leaders of the Bulgarian Revolution had been educated at Robert College, and the Turkish government became suspicious of all American-sponsored schools. An article in a Turkish newspaper in Constantinople stated that the American schools were the most pernicious in the empire and urged the authorities to issue a proclamation that no one educated in the American schools could hold any office in, or appointment from, the government. In Kara Hissar the Gregorian Armenians put pressure on students not to attend the mission school and urged the governor to close the school. Never had Henry seen such persistent hatred against the Protestants by the leaders of the Armenian church. Henry and Jeanne both spent weeks in fasting and prayer for permission to continue the school. While permission for the school was being pursued, the Armenian teacher and Henry began a series of weekly lectures to which they invited "the most intelligent people in the city." Sarkis spoke on astronomy, and Henry spoke on Egyptian and Assyrian antiquities. The lectures were well attended, and Henry hoped this would be a means of drawing the listeners into the hearing of the gospel.

In May Henry attended the annual meeting in Constantinople and stayed two weeks beyond the meeting hoping that the U.S. Ambassador to Turkey, General Lew Wallace, would do something about the permission for a school at Kara Hissar. General Wallace, lawyer and Civil War general, had been appointed American ambassador to Turkey by President James Garfield and came to Constantinople in 1881, a year after his popular novel, *Ben Hur,* was published. He had been governor of New Mexico Territory before becoming minister to Turkey. One of his reasons for accepting the post in Constantinople was to acquire background information for a novel on the Byzantine Empire (which he later published in 1893 as the *Prince of India*).[7] Wallace had developed a cordial relationship with the sultan, and Henry hoped he might prevail upon the sultan to allow the Kara Hissar school to remain open.

It was a vain hope. Shortly after Henry arrived back in Kara Hissar, the order came from Constantinople that the school must be closed. Henry had no choice but to close the school and dismiss the teachers: "It was submitting to defeat in the presence of the enemy, but we accepted the situation, confident that the Lord would in some way bring good out of it."[8] The closing of the school coupled with the Hubbards' time to return to the United States for a furlough, caused the Perrys to return to Sivas in July. Baron Barsam Jeurahyan, a former preacher at Tocat and one of Henry's former students from Marash, accepted the position at Kara Hissar and moved his family into the house the Perrys had leased.

On the way back to Sivas the Perrys were able to see first hand the severe effects of the famine on the villagers:

> We could not get the poorest quality even of bread at any price simply because it was not there to be had. The pinched, starved appearance of the villagers was really pitiable. The crops this year have been fortunately good which gives present relief, but farmers pressed by debt are now selling their entire crop for a low price well knowing that they must buy again when winter comes at a much higher rate or else go without bread. The country is getting so poor that even a good crop affords but a temporary relief.[9]

Not only at Kara Hissar, but also throughout the Sivas field the Protestant churches were struggling. Though the Protestant churches remained small and often without a native pastor, the missionaries did have an important influence throughout the community. Especially in Sivas, the old Armenian leaders were beginning to stress the Scripture and hold regular preaching services and prayer meetings. Many of the Armenian services were beginning to adopt some of the characteristics of Protestant services, and the Bible was increasingly read in the Armenian homes. Most of the students in the Sivas schools were from Gregorian Armenian families, and the evangelical training the students received in the schools was beginning to influence the parents. The ABCFM schools were a prime way of spreading the gospel. The Protestant churches seemed to be ebbing as the growing Armenian national movement encouraged the Armenians to remain loyal to the Gregorian church. Remaining in the old church, however, did not preclude seeking a more Biblical Christianity. However, with smaller numbers, it was very difficult for the Protestant churches to totally support the native workers without financial help from abroad. Henry urged the ABCFM not to abandon the native churches in this time of need.

With the Hubbards in the States, responsibility for the Sivas station rested heavily on Henry's shoulders. Laura Chamberlin remained in charge of the Girls' Boarding School, and Susan Blake spread her

Christian influence by going house to house as a Bible Reader. While Laura was efficient in her school affairs, she lacked the common touch with the people. Susan, however, was the perfect missionary. She quickly picked up the vernacular Armenian, and people were attracted to her heartfelt piety and winning manner. With responsibility for the schools and the large Sivas field, Henry relied heavily on native workers. He organized the pastor at Gürün, the four licensed preachers in the field, and representatives from the Tocat and Gürün churches into a committee to direct the work of the churches. Like Paul centuries before, Henry wrote letters to these men and other Christian workers to help develop their Christian perspective on the ministry and deal with the various problems in the churches.

Back in Sivas, Jeanne's health continued to fluctuate between sickness and recovery. The gypsum in the water did have a deleterious effect on her system, and Henry would have preferred to remain with her at Kara Hissar. The absence of the Hubbards, however, compelled the Perrys to stay in Sivas. Years later Henry could look back on these times of Jeanne's illness and say:

> In our service for the Lord Jesus, He teaches us, that we are to follow Him, by the way of His cross. Whoever does not bear his Cross and Come after me, cannot be my disciple (Luke 14:27). There is no exception to this rule. These words stand forever true. Nothing short of this will suffice for the follower of Christ; or satisfy the heart of God. It was His way that Christ on the Cross should bear our sins. We must also share the suffering. Is it possible that the servant should be above his Master? Happy are they who learn by experience to say: No! ...
>
> [Jeanne's] consecration to her Lord, to give to Him all that she had, though the time of it should be brief, appealed to me most deeply. No self-denial was too great for her to make; and I remember with joy the days of fasting and prayer we had together at Kara Hissar, when our work there was ordered by the Turkish Government to be closed. She had learned how to suffer; she learned also how to bear her Savior's Cross and to pray.[10]

September 19 was Henry and Jeanne's fourteenth wedding anniversary. Jeanne made some extra cake and peach pie, "which tasted all the better because seasoned with such precious love."[11]

Henry's diary during the first months back in Sivas reveals busy days for the ministry. There were the treasury accounts to be kept of all the affairs of the mission; payments to be made to missionaries and native workers; lessons to teach in the school and Sunday School; times for Bible study and prayer; correspondence with all the native workers, other missionaries, and the Secretary in Boston; counseling and encouragement for students and Christians in the community; and the maintenance of cordial relations with the Pasha. The government was closing the mission school at Enderes, and Henry repeatedly met with government leaders to try to prevent this. Sometimes Henry mentioned headaches from the stress of work, but a horse ride in the countryside usually helped. Alvan sometimes rode out with him. Henry also enjoyed evenings with his family. Sometimes they all went riding together; at other times Henry and Alvan enjoyed a game of "fox and geese" at home.

Alvan was an enterprising young man with many interests. With his own mercantile background, Henry encouraged Alvan to sell dictionaries to earn some money, and Alvan diligently set to work. He also built himself a bee house to raise bees, helped Henry in the vegetable garden, and raised a goat and a calf. Yet, Alvan apparently had all the mischief and energy of an eleven year old boy. One cryptic diary entry for February 28, 1884, states, "Alvan's fault in putting calf in the girls' school room."

Though Jeanne was often ill, Henry did not specifically mention a partial cause of her illness—she was again with child. It was not a subject spoken of in polite Victorian society, and Henry's diary was appropriately reticent as well. Henry personally cared for Jeanne when she was forced to stay in bed; she preferred his personal touch to all others. Alvan too was a great help and comfort to her.

In mid-April 1884, Henry planned a weeklong conference in Sivas for the native pastors, preachers, and representatives. Only churches that had at least half of the support from the native congregation could send delegates, something the other churches complained of. In spite of her illness, Jeanne insisted on hosting Baron Jovehannes and Baron Vartivar, the delegates from Gürün and Ashude, in her home. She had an interest in the Christian work in their villages and asked about specific members she knew in their churches. Her conversation with them was always full of Christian love and encouragement. The conference covered a wide range of topics, from how to promote revivals to specific development plans for Kara Hissar, Divrik, Derende, Ashude, and other villages. At times cooperation was very close among the seven attending the conference. At other times Henry was surrounded by complaints and demands for more financial support. Henry had a great headache after the Conference, and Jeanne too was exhausted.

Three days after the Conference ended, on Sunday April 27, 1884, Henry joyfully wrote in his diary, "Birth of our little daughter at sunrise, this Lord's day morning. Miss Blake and Dr. Serope with us, the latter part of the night. Mother and daughter both doing well today." The baby was named Jeanne Hannah after her mother, and a wet nurse was found for her. Jeanne herself continued weak, however. In the coming days she had severe stomach pains and neuralgia, with alternating diarrhea and constipation. Dr. Serope regularly visited, but none of his medications were effective. Henry sent a telegram to Dr. Thom of Mardin, but he could not come the long distance. Jeanne had no appetite and grew weaker. Henry or Susan Blake stayed with her constantly, and little Alvan was always eager to do any little errands or chores to make his mother comfortable.

By Friday evening, Jeanne was free of pain and was much more restful. Henry stayed with her throughout the night, reclining on the lounge while she slept. Several times she called him to her side; she was unusually cheerful. About two hours before daylight, Jeanne had another diarrhea spell and felt faint. Henry insisted she take a little brandy, which she finally consented to do. As she lay exhausted on her bed, Jeanne urged Henry to lie down and rest before daybreak. He reluctantly began to leave her bedside when Jeanne pulled him down for a kiss and said, "I have been very impatient these last few days, but now I am going to be pleasanter." Jeanne's remark made Henry hopeful that she was feeling better and was on the road to recovery.

Henry fell into a deep sleep on the lounge, when just before dawn Jeanne's heavy breathing awakened him. Rushing to her side, he found her in a deep swoon, her pulse feeble, and her eyes fixed. Calling Susan Blake into the room, the two tried to revive Jeanne with little effect. Alvan was called into the room and also tried to revive his mother, but she had breathed her last. It was the dawn of May 3, 1884, and she was 37 years old. When Alvan realized his mother had died, he wept as though his heart would break. He took the rings from her finger as a memento.

Susan Blake combed Jeanne's hair, and women came to prepare Jeanne for burial. Henry and Alvan went together to sit awhile by the remains of their beloved wife and mother. Alvan wept freely; but when Henry began to talk to him about the "dead who die in the Lord" and showed him Scriptures about the dead living again, Alvan cheerfully began to speak about what life was like for his mother and his five sisters. The Scriptures comforted both father and son.

Anna Doodoo, the Perrys' house servant, took special care of baby Jean, who slept sweetly while the ceremonies for her mother's burial were being prepared.[12] During the day Henry took Alvan with him and even consulted him about plans for the burial. Some years before, the ABCFM had purchased an acre of land outside the city for a Protestant cemetery. There was a level place there along the stream, with a few willow trees, that Henry and Alvan chose for the burial spot. It was a place of peace and solitude. The two Perry children buried in the Sivas mission yard could also be moved and buried there with their mother.

Back in Sivas, preparations continued, as Susan Blake trained the schoolgirls to sing hymns for the funeral. Early the morning of Sunday, May 4, Susan came over to cut flowers from the pot plants Jeanne had nourished over the winter. At 9:30 in the morning the body was placed in the coffin and brought into the sitting room, where an English service was held. Anna Doodoo brought baby Jean in for the service, and Henry read Scriptures full of Christian hope – Psalm 90:12-17; I Corinthians 15:35-45; Revelation 14:12-13. Henry's explanations of these Scriptures were especially for Alvan, assuring him there is a glorious resurrection for those who die in the Lord. As the people sang the hymn "Asleep in Jesus," Alvan stood looking in the coffin at the face of his mother. After the hymn, he helped his father close the coffin lid as the men came to screw it down.

The coffin was then carried to the chapel for the Armenian service. Susan Blake played the organ and led the singing of the Turkish hymns Jeanne had sung so beautifully. Pastor Marderos, the Gürün pastor, preached the sermon. The chapel was full of people, who followed the coffin outside the city for burial. A group of rowdies joined with the crowd causing noise and confusion along the way to the grave.

All the men of Henry's acquaintance made calls of consolation throughout the Sunday and following days, yet loneliness enveloped him. Jeanne had been ill with great weakness before but had recovered; he had assumed she would on this occasion. She herself had no intimation that death was so near. Alvan was in and out of her room throughout the day before she died. If she had thought death imminent, she would have had special spiritual exhortations for her only son to remember after her death; but there were none.

Anna Doodoo and a wet nurse cared for Jean throughout the day while Susan Blake took the baby at night. Henry cared for the little one in the evenings and on Sunday mornings between services. She was a healthy baby, though somewhat pale. Of course, Henry could not know how long she would be with them. He had already lost five daughters and now his dear, dear Jeanne. Though he tried to continue with his mission work, teaching in the schools, and giving special care to Alvan, often Henry was overwhelmed by despair and loneliness. On Sunday, May 18, two weeks after Jeanne's death, Henry wrote in his diary:

> I awoke in the early morning (Alvan yet sweetly sleeping) to be severely tried with sad thoughts. I seemed to be tempted on every side by this terrible affliction, to yield to the power of discontent, hardness of heart, worldly thoughts, and unrest! I could not get rid of the burden; and it seemed to be hardening, rather than softening me. To trouble these unsympathizing people with my distress is distasteful to them, and only makes matters worse. My weeping eyes, and throbbing head, instead of bringing relief, only made my heart the more sick. I was glad not to preach today, for I seemed totally unfit for it yet the <u>occupation</u> of a sermon, would have prevented this reflective concentration.
>
> I know it – I believe it;
>   I say it fearlessly,
> That God, the highest, mightiest,
>   Forever loveth me.
> At all times, in all places,
>   He standeth at my side;
> He rules the battle's fury,
>   The tempest and the tide. (Paul Gerhardt)
>
> As the day wore on I was able to get around into position. The eternal truths, seemed clearer and brighter, as the desirableness of throwing off at some time this garment of the flesh, became also more apparent.[13]

The following Saturday Henry wrote,

> This was a day of depression in spirit. I could not throw off the load of discouragement, and reproached myself for having so little self-control, in getting my mind back into working order upon mission duty. Spontaneously the impression, that Jeannie is about the house, happy as usual, seems to make false the facts of the last few weeks! Then a … comprehension of the <u>actual</u> sweeps over me, and I am borne off into trouble; only to swing back to halt, and buckle on again the wings of faith.[14]

Henry found consolation in reading Horatio Bonar's *Hymns of Faith and Hope*. Many Scriptures also brought comfort and assurance. He wrote out a whole series of these in his diary:

> O you afflicted, tossed with tempest, *and* not comforted, behold, I will lay thy stones with fair colours, and lay thy foundations with sapphires (Isaiah 54:11); ...
> I will not leave you comfortless: I will come to you (John 14:18);
> As one whom his mother comforteth, so will I comfort you ... (Isaiah 66:13);
> He will swallow up death in victory; and the Lord God will wipe away tears from off all faces ... (Isaiah 25:8);
> For ... thou shalt weep no more: he will be very gracious unto thee at the voice of thy cry; when he shall hear it, he will answer thee...Ye shall have a song, as in the night when a holy solemnity is kept; and gladness of heart, as when one goeth with a pipe to come into the mountain of the Lord, to the mighty One of Israel (Isaiah 30:19, 29).

Letters of comfort and condolence continued to arrive, but they often produced a flood of tears. Emily Montgomery was among those who sent condolences to Henry. She had lived with Jeanne in Marash where their husbands had taught together at the Seminary. She praised Jeanne's energy and efficiency coupled with her tenderness and sweetness of soul. She recalled how U.S. President Arthur's sister, Mrs. Caw, knew and loved Jeanne and delighted in the way she measured success in terms of the fruit one bore for the gospel. One day when Jeanne was at tea with Mrs. Caw, a critical gentleman had remarked, "I should think you had rather live in Beirut, than so far in the interior!," to which Jeanne had immediately replied, "Oh, no! We have a great many more conversions at Marash than they do at Beirut."[15] Wherever she was, Jeanne lived her life for Christ, and without her Henry felt so alone. She had been a constant support to him, and in his diary he repeatedly recorded his sense of loss:

> June 8, 1884: Five weeks in heaven! How I long to know what its experience has been! Is Jeanne thus cut off from us? I could seem to see her at the church again today; Yet the place she was wont to fill knows her now no more...

> June 9, 1884: Oh how blank and desolate all seems! I found myself sighing in the street. Jeanne seemed to be returning with me to the

house as aforetime; but the thot that we should see her no more here, almost crushed me.

June 11, 1884: The morning hour of devotion – Read a sermon recently received by mail on the resurrection by Reverend A.B. Kittridge of Chicago. Felt the need of something to sustain me; for I awoke from sleep in a flood of tears. At work in PM on the accounts; made several mistakes from sheer weariness; and threw them aside for a walk with Alvan to the grave, there to weep again in silence, with none to share the burden of grief except the unseen Savior, who passed through the grave to the Father's glory.

July 16, 1884: Though encouraged by faith, I was racked with unrest. Though sustained by faith and reading of the Scriptures, I was not made happy. I cannot get a victory of the Spirit over the flesh; which shall drive off this terrible feeling of loss and craving for the companionship of the dear one who has gone. My spiritual comforts are something in the far future. They are not realized as here now. In waiting for them my soul does not find the peace and rest which I desire.

The July 1884, issue of *The Missionary Herald* included a page and a half tribute to "Mrs. Jennie H. Perry of Sivas." After a biographical sketch the article noted, "Her life has been one of true devotion to the work of her Master. She enjoyed this service, and wished never to leave it. It is a mysterious Providence which takes her from the field where she seemed so specially needed, and from the missionary circle where she was so much beloved." Mrs. Hubbard wrote,

> Living as we did so near together for seven years, she proved a true missionary sister, rejoicing in all our joy, and sympathetic in every trial. In her own afflictions, which were not a few, - five little daughters having gone home before her, - she showed a most beautiful Christian spirit. She was untiring in teaching the native women cleanliness as well as godliness, her perfect housekeeping being a daily object-lesson before a naturally untidy people. She was a diligent laborer in the Master's vineyard, often going beyond her strength. Our hearts are burdened for ourselves and for Sivas.

The article then quoted a letter received from Henry, written in Sivas May 10, a week following Jeanne's death:

Mrs. Perry's special characteristic was *intense, unselfish devotion*. Her love was ever flowing outward like a stream within even banks, the supply ever full because nourished from the inexhaustible divine fountain. Especially was she sensitively sympathetic with the poor, the afflicted, and the oppressed, and so jealous of their rights as to be impatient, sometimes, with the proud and the oppressor. It was so easy for her to believe and trust, the way to the mercy seat was so familiar and constantly trodden, and the relief which she found there was so uniformly complete, that she never seemed to have any burden of her own to carry. If she ever had any anxiety, it was for the relief of suffering and distress in others. The intensity and unselfish character of her devotion was a constant strain on her physical constitution. While the spirit seemed capable of bearing any burden of love, her thoughtlessness of self caused her to go beyond the power of physical endurance. The activities of the spirit wore out the possibilities of the flesh.

Hers was a life long in experience, though brief in the number of years. There were no moments wasted in doubt, hesitation, or discussion of methods. With a rare discernment of character, a ready use of Scripture, and accustomed to wield influence not only by persuasive words but by the power of song, she made straight for the work to be done in the hearts of the people ...

Mrs. Perry had no fear nor even a physical shrinking from the change of death. To her it was but putting away the image of the earthly when there should be no further use for it, to be reclothed in the image of the heavenly. She had no desire to return to her native land. To teach these poor bigoted people she had come to a land of strangers, and among them she wished a burial place.[16]

When Henry began breaking up housekeeping, selling some of the furniture, and disposing of Jeanne's things, tears again welled up. The selling of the furniture was sheer agony because of its many precious associations. Henry and Jeanne had made friends with their Moslem neighbor, Eomer Effendi, and had both he and his wife in their home for dinner. On numerous occasions Eomer had come to Perry's office to discuss the Koran and Christian Scriptures. He was quite moved when Henry gave him Jeanne's stereoscope and ten photos. Henry came upon a devotional book, *Every Day Text and Hymnbook*, which Jeanne had begun using in 1884. As he read through the underlined sections for January through April, he felt as if he were sharing Jeanne's spiritual thoughts during her last months. One passage she had underlined was the following:

> I do not seek that God shall always make my pathway light,
> I only pray he will hold my hand throughout the night.
> I do not hope to have the thorns removed that pierce my feet:
> I only ask to find His blessed arms, my safe retreat.

Henry found the devotional reading for May 3, the day of Jeanne's death, especially comforting. The text was, "He that loveth me shall be loved of my Father, and I will love him, and will manifest myself to him," followed by the stanza:

> So near, so very near to God
>   I cannot nearer be,
> For in the person of his Son
>   I am as near as He:
> So dear, so very dear to God,
>   I cannot dearer be;
> The love wherewith He loves His Son,
>   That love He gives to me.[17]

Henry's heart reached out more than ever before to his motherless children. His diary is full of references to baby Jean, noting her size, weight, and every precious development. On June 22, 1884, Anna Doodoo dressed baby Jean for her baptism, and Henry and Anna took her to church. A controversy over infant versus adult baptism had plagued the Sivas church, and the Armenian pastor took the opportunity of Jean's christening to preach a long sermon on baptism. But on that particular day, Henry could not concentrate on theological controversy. His thoughts and his heart were filled with prayers for his one little daughter left behind when her mother passed away. In his prayers, Henry "gave the little one back to the Lord, either to speedily take, or long spare as He may choose..."[18] He would not cling too closely to this child, knowing how quickly she could be taken away; the Lord would work His perfect will.

Nevertheless, little Jean continued to expand her hold over her father's heart. In his diary he recorded his delight in her:

> June 30, 1884: Little Jean is as plump and sweet as the roses which are now in bloom in the Garden.
> September 2, 1884: Our little Jean is a sunbeam in the house.
> November 2, 1884: Jean is now six months old; is full in flesh, but pale, almost bears her weight upon her feet, smiles very pleasantly, when spoken to, and wants to be carried about. She is our joy, and

we make the most of her. Uncertain how long we may have her, to love and care for.

January 2, 1885: Little Jean still a delight. Can sit up all her own self on the floor, and amuse herself with her playthings.

January 12, 1885: Jean restless...probably teething.

January 19, 1885: In the evening had quite a frolic with little Jean.

January 23, 1885: Jean much in my room. Said "Papa" very distinctly.

February 18, 1885: Baby Jean is as happy these days as one of the spring birds. She is always calling out for me "papa;" sits in the carriage as we draw her about the halls; without being tied in... and enters with the greatest vigor in the plays of the children, shouting out after them in the ecstasy of delight.

June 9, 1885: Little Jean cunning as can be! Is trying with many falls to learn to walk: wants to kiss Mama's photograph...

June 14, 1885: Little Jean is a special comfort to me on Sundays. She has been creeping all about my room, talking happily about "Mama", "A-van", "Baby", etc.

July 8, 1885: Little Jean in charming health. Is beginning to walk. Calls us to prayers in the morning.

July 28, 1885: Little Jean happy as a bird. I found a pair of new blue shoes for her in the bundle of things which her mother left....

During the summer's heat, city dwellers would go "tenting" beside a cool stream near Sivas. This summer Anna Doodoo took Jean tenting, while Henry remained in town. He rode out in the evenings to visit his precious daughter, camped amid the trees near the convent of St. James. Laura Chamberlin described the tenting custom in her missionary journal:

> In the interior of Turkey we do not have any Coney Island nor Newport; nor even a hotel at any cold springs, but every rich man and well-to-do family have tents, and during the summer go out for from sixteen to twenty-one days for a change of water, as they say...The trees around the convent have been recently set out, but the building itself affords such a deep shade that at midday we can be comfortable on one of the four sides. In the valley below flows a rapid brook bordered with willows. Lending a delightful shade for the barren land, and a natural dam in this brook furnishes a bathing rink where a dozen of us can sport at mid-day when the sun has sufficiently warmed the water. We eat our dinner of bread and cheese, or owert (the sour curd of the country), sew, knit and read, and the day has gone before we are conscious of it, until the lengthening shadows warn us that we must turn to our tents to cook our supper of cracked

wheat, rice, or squash. Before the darkness creeps about us we spread our bed and, after evening devotions, we retire, to be lulled to sleep by the flapping of our tents; sometimes aroused by the firing of guns by our Turkish neighbors to keep off robbers, by the baying of shepherd dogs, or by some belated villager returning from the city, who lifts his voice on the night air in a wild, shrill song, which has more of sound than of melody. [19]

In October 1884, the Hubbards returned to Sivas from their United States furlough. Alvan was almost wild with delight to have the Hubbard boys to play with again. Henry, Jean, and Alvan moved into three upstairs rooms in Dr. West's house, while the Hubbards occupied the remainder. The Perrys took their meals with the Hubbard family, and Emma eagerly helped with the Perry children. She took little Jean with her during the nights and taught Alvan his lessons in the morning with her own children. Henry paid for a wet nurse and Anna Doodoo to care for Jean; he hired Neshan to care for the stables and the outside chores. In September 1884, he was also able to send his mother $50 to pay for help during the winter months.

Remembering how important to him the time was he had spent with his father as a boy, Henry was careful to spend as much time with Alvan as possible. He encouraged him to go with Neshan to plant willow trees and the turf around his mother's grave. Father and son often went riding in the countryside together or out to Jeanne's grave. A month after Jeanne's death, Henry, Alvan, and Baron Krekorv went on a month long tour to Enderes, Kara Hissar, and Divrik. They camped out along the way, and Alvan enjoyed preparing the fire and tea as they made camp. He especially loved riding and taking care of the horse, Jim. On these tours Henry and Alvan had their Saturday's bath in the nearest stream. Sometimes fleas interrupted their sleep, but Henry used flea powder to keep the pests away. When they reached a village for the evening, Alvan enjoyed going to the market and purchasing grain for the horses. Whether at home or on tour, Henry gave Alvan his lessons, though he did hire a tutor to teach Alvan Turkish.

Henry often spent evenings reading to Alvan, whether in Sivas or touring the outstations. When reading Bunyan's *Pilgrim's Progress*, Henry noticed that Alvan was much more interested in the story of Christiana than he had been with Christian, "evidently for the reason that as Christiana was encouraged by her husband's presence in heaven, so he is by the vision of his Mother there."[20]

Besides regular daily devotions with Alvan and the servants, Henry did not neglect observing Sunday as the Lord's Day, as he and Jeanne had always done. After morning services, Henry had Alvan memorize various key chapters of Scripture, such as Isaiah 53, Romans 5, or I Corinthians 15. Some Sundays Alvan memorized a hymn, such as Charles Wesley's "And Can It Be?" Though rearing his children in Moslem Turkey, Henry continued the Puritan practices of Sabbath observance he had known as a boy in New England. Interestingly, most of Henry's diary entries for Sundays begin with "It was a pleasant day." Sundays remained forever special to him.

Sunday, November 9, 1884, was quite an occasion for Alvan; it was the day he wore his first pair of long pants. Henry had ordered new suits for himself and Alvan from Wannamakers, and they both fit quite well. Later in January, when the weather turned exceptionally cold, Henry realized Alvan didn't have enough warm clothing and tried to double up some of his clothes for warmth − "Another instance in which a 'father's love' fails to be 'blended' with a 'mother's care.'"[21] Emma Hubbard later cut out a pair of pants for Alvan out of a pair of Henry's older ones, and Henry sewed them up for Alvan.

Alvan eagerly became part of the escapades and frolic of the large Hubbard family, if not leading them himself. Within a few days of the Hubbards' return, Alvan and the Hubbard boys were caught playing with matches in the attic. One day when Alvan and Ray got into a quarrel and had to be separated, Henry wrote in his diary, "I shall be satisfied when I wake with thy likeness (Psalm 17:15)."[22] However, it was not yet that glorious day in Heaven, and Henry had to face the trials of being a single parent of an eleven year old boy.

Henry always read *The London Times* and kept abreast of international news. Of consuming interest at the time were events in Khartoum, events that directly touched Henry in a number of ways. In 1875, England, under Prime Minister Disraeli, had purchased a large share of the Suez Canal. Former Prime Minister William Gladstone had opposed the move, foreseeing it would involve England with all of Egypt's problems. In 1880, Gladstone began his second term as prime minister, and it was on his watch problems developed. At the end of 1881, Col. Arbi Pasha led a nationalist revolt which the English were able to put down, but in the same year the Sudanese, led by the Mahdi, a Moslem fanatic, rebelled against the Egyptians. After the Treaty of Berlin, England had assumed a policy of aiding Turkey in its reforms in Asia Minor, and a British consulate-general had been established in

Sivas. Sir Charles Wilson and John Donald H. Stewart were among the English stationed there. Troubles in Egypt caused the English to temporarily withdraw from its oversight of the Turkish reforms and concentrate on the rebellions in Egypt. Wilson and Stewart were called from Sivas to the Sudan, and the British consulate in Sivas was closed.

By 1884 the British had decided to evacuate Sudan and sent General Charles Gordon to lead the evacuation. Col. John Stewart, whom Henry had known in Sivas, was Gordon's second in command. A Bible reading man of strong religious faith, General Gordon was a man highly respected in England. As governor-general of Sudan in the 1870's, he had assaulted the Arab slave trade in Africa, which David Livingstone had described as a "monster brooding over Africa." He also sponsored charitable work among the poor in England. His great military prowess in China had added to his fame. Cast in a heroic mold, Gordon could not in good conscience abandon the women and children of the Sudanese capital of Khartoum to be massacred by the Mahdi's Dervishes. Gordon would not retreat, and he called for reinforcements to defend Khartoum. Public opinion in England mounted, and calls that Gordon be saved intensified. Khartoum was besieged for ten months. Days before destruction seemed certain, Gordon sent Colonel Stewart on a steamer down the Nile to Cairo with a last plea for help. The steamship foundered on the rocks; Stewart and his companions were captured and murdered by the Mahdi's forces. Gladstone had at last heeded the cries of the British public, and Sir Charles Wilson, whom Henry also had known in Sivas, was sent to aid Gordon. He and his men arrived at Khartoum January 28, 1885, but it was too late. Two days before, the Mahdi had captured Khartoum and massacred the Anglo-Egyptian garrison and General Gordon.

When reading *The London Times*, Henry went back in his diary and wrote in the dates of Wilson's arrival at Khartoum, information about Stewart's help of Gordon, and the obituary of General Gordon. Knowing Wilson and Stewart made the events surrounding Khartoum touch him personally. He also saw the fall of Khartoum as not just a heroic act, but as one in which the freedom of Africa was at stake. The Arabs had controlled the African slave trade for centuries, and the English were intent on breaking slavery's destructive power. March 9, 1885, Henry wrote in his diary,

> Mail in and interested in the News from the Soudan. Sir Charles Wilson's column falling back from Gubat. I was praying much for

Africa and the Valley of the Nile, that the Lord would make the English army strong there and break down the slave power.[23]

In the spring of 1885, Henry, Alvan, and Susan Blake went to Constantinople together for the annual meeting of the Turkish missions. Though Susan had been most effective and much loved during her four years at the Sivas station, she was leaving the mission to return to the States and marry a pastor, Mr. Childs (Laura Chamberlin said this was very Child-ish!). During the weeklong journey from Sivas to Samsoun, Henry and Susan had many good conversations together — about "our Christian experiences, and Sivas relations and work! Especially talking much of our dear Jeanne, and of the saints in Heaven."[24] In Constantinople, Henry discussed Jeanne's death with Dr. Parmelee, a missionary doctor from Trebizond. Dr. Parmelee thought Jeanne's sudden death had been caused by a blood clot in the heart.

Mrs. Schneider and Susan Blake encouraged Henry to send Alvan to the United States when Susan returned to the States in another week. They both thought the time was right for Alvan to attend school in the States. Henry was too moved to answer, but sought the Lord's direction as to what was best for his son. He awoke refreshed the next morning, but with a heavy feeling as he looked at Alvan in the bed beside him. How could he let Alvan go when he had just lost Jeanne a year ago? Loneliness enveloped him anew. Jeanne still had a place in his heart, and Alvan was so much a part of her. Nevertheless, Mrs. Schneider and Miss Blake were probably right, and Henry decided to have Alvan go to the United States. Alvan was a "dear, good boy," and Henry could "hardly think of parting with him next week!"[25]

The Constantinople conference spent much time on the topic of how to develop interested hearers of the gospel into efficient workers for the church. There was also much interest in cases of Moslems coming to faith in Christ. On the closing day of the conference, there was a special children's meeting that Alvan attended, and a communion service. Henry preached the communion service sermon on Isaiah 42:4, "He shall not fail nor be discouraged, till he have set judgment in the earth: and the isles shall wait for his law." Henry felt as if the Holy Spirit aided him in preaching this encouraging Scripture to the missionaries of Turkey.

The next few days were full of final preparations for Alvan's departure. The Riggs children invited Alvan for a "Goodbye" picnic, and the children were "happy as birds." Henry wrote the necessary letters to

America, had clothes made at the tailors, went to the dentist, and sadly took Alvan on the ship with Miss Blake on May 20. His last evening in Constantiople he spent as guest of Dr. Edwin Grosvenor, professor at Robert College.[26] Dr. Grosvenor and his wife Lillian had twin sons, Gilbert and Edwin. Edwin later became a prominent lawyer, while Gilbert became editor of *The National Geographic Magazine*.[27]

Back at Sivas, Henry was especially consoled by the happiness and health of little Jean. Being so much with Anna Doodoo, Jean often chattered away in a childish Armenian. Henry would have to have Anna interpret for him! Sometimes as he looked at Jean lying in her cradle she looked just like Edith did six years ago – "fair complexion; blue eyes; light hair; round face...upper and lower lips both dimpled..." It saddened him anew to think of Edith's death while he was away and Jeanne left to cope so alone. Sunday, June 7, 1885, Henry noted in his diary,

> Spent considerable time with Jean amusing her. How unconsciously delightful was her way of kissing Mama's photograph! I was glad thinking about it today that Alvan is not here! I miss him, but think that he is much better off there. May the Lord make him His own child!

Though Henry missed Alvan, he knew it was right to send him to the States. In the evenings Henry sometimes put Jean on his saddle and took her for a little ride. Not far out in the countryside were sheep and goats she always enjoyed seeing.

On sleepless nights Henry rode out to Jeanne's grave alone to meditate and pray. He knew God's grace was sufficient in his loneliness, but sometimes he had to struggle to rest peacefully in that truth. Henry also often read poetry as balm to his hurting spirit. He read Tennyson's *In Memoriam, Holy Grail*, and *Fatima*.[28] He read Shakespeare's *King John*, to find Constance's expression of grief and her hope of meeting her boy in the other world. But, most often he read the poems of Elizabeth Barrett Browning. Her poetry often expressed his own love for Jeanne, his grief at her loss, and his faith that the Lord's sovereign purposes would be done. Browning's "Substitution" gave a Christian answer to Henry's loneliness and the silence of Jeanne's voice:

> When some blessed voice that was to you
> Both sound and sweetness, faileth suddenly,
> And silence against which you dare not cry,

> Aches round you like a strong disease and new –
> What hope? what help? What music will undo
> That silence to your sense? Not friendship's sigh –
> Not reason's subtle count; not melody
> Of viols, nor of pipes that Faunus blew.
> Not songs of poets, nor of nightingales
> Whose hearts leap upward through the cypress trees
> To the clear moon! Nor yet the spheric laws
> Self-chanted, - nor the angels' sweet All hails,
> Met in the smile of God; nay, none of these.
> Speak THOU, availing Christ! – and fill this pause.[29]

Increasingly Henry's deep loss drew him ever closer to Christ. He read some of Browning's passionate love sonnets with a spiritual interpretation, as the love between Christ and His Bride, the people of His church. He found that some of the expressions worked very nicely, as he focused on Christ's very personal love for him. Poetry was a "powerful spur to the emotions." Henry found he needed "something of the kind to stimulate the sluggish working of my mind and heart."[30]

Henry's sorrow drew him into a deeper, sweet communion with Christ. He read extensively on Divine Love, both in Scriptures and in Christian writers such as Thomas a'Kempis, Samuel Rutherford, and Philip Brooks, and his life of prayer deepened. His resolve was

> to be a mystic in piety; but a revivalist with the people. A mystic showing it to the people cannot be understood; and is too unpopular to do much good; and a Revivalist without a hidden life in the mystic Christ loses his power. So put the two together, Mystic piety and a true zeal for the Lord's house.[31]

By August 14, 1885, Henry could write to Reverend N.G. Clark in Boston:

> ...this year of my bitter trial and great loneliness has been in other respects the richest one of my life. The sympathizing Saviour has so sustained me that oftentimes I have seemed to have no trial at all to bear. Even the feeling of loneliness has been usually lifted, and the mystic presence of an unseen Friend has abundantly supplied with a surpassing sweetness not only spiritual but even social joys. Work and especially that of preaching and visitation among the people has been easy for me, and my physical health has never been better than

it is now. I rode on horseback last week in the heat of the sun from Zara to Divas 36 miles in ¾ of a day and felt scarcely wearied by it...[32]

Henry's mother was ill in Ashfield and needed his care. Henry determined to leave Sivas in the spring; two-year old Jean was a healthy child who now seemed capable of making the journey. There was much Henry wanted to accomplish in the next few months, however. In the fall of 1885, Henry took a two-week vacation to re-visit the Central Turkey Mission where he and Jeanne had first served in 1866. It was a bitter-sweet trip full of precious memories which accentuated his loss, but also full of encouragement at the progress of the church in the last twenty years. Many remembered Jeanne and her cheerful, sweet ways. Henry seemed powerless to follow her cheerfulness, and he regretted his persistent melancholy. He took time out from his visiting to go to little Lizzie and Mary's graves. He arranged for a stone man to repair the gravestones placed there almost fifteen years before.

Throughout his journey, Henry noticed that the people everywhere were distressed by the agitation of war brought on by the Bulgarian revolution for independence. The Turkish government had called out its reserves, but the people had little interest in the war effort and did not want their men to be forced to fight. Many of those called up attempted to escape military service by running away. Henry could only wonder, "How can any government, especially a weak one, carry on a war in this way by force – alone?"[33]

At Marash Henry stayed with Dr. and Mrs. Marden. Dr. Marden was a genial, practical man and companionable. Though he did not share Henry's interest in literature, he was quite interested in the Hittite ruins and talked about them extensively with Henry as they rode towards Aintab together.[34] Only very recently had some scholars begun to recognize the vast expanse of the ancient Hittite power. The existence of the Hittites was not known from any ancient history source except the Bible, where they were often grouped along with the Amorites, the Jebusites, and the Canaanites (Genesis 23:3-4;Joshua 3:10; Numbers 13:28). Rarely did anyone notice that the Bible also recognized that the Kings of the Hittites were on a par militarily with the Egyptian rulers (II Kings 7:6). In 1880, Archibald Henry Sayce, a thirty-four year old Orientalist, shocked the scholarly community by delivering a lecture in London to the Society for Biblical Archaeology claiming that numerous monuments and inscriptions in a strange hieroglyphic found throughout much of Asia Minor and Northern Syria were from the ancient Hittites. For millennia, no one had thought the Hittites lived in Asia Minor, much less that their empire could have spread from Smyrna to Marash to Hamath in Syria. Soon headlines in newspapers throughout England carried news of the "discovery" of the 3000 year old vanished Hittites.

Dr. Marden undoubtedly told Henry about William Wrights' book, *The Empire of the Hittites*, published just the previous year, in 1884. Wright was an Irish missionary stationed in Damascus who, in cooperation with A.H. Sayce, pulled together the numerous accidental finds of inscriptions, sculptures, and monuments throughout Asia Minor to claim that the Hittites once controlled a large empire. At Marash itself, a majestic lion inscribed with hieroglyphics might once have flanked a palace door. Dr. Marden probably was able to also tell Henry of the three German archaeologists, Otto Puchstein, Karl Humann, and Dr. Felix Luschen, who had visited Zinjirli, less than a day's journey south of Marash, and were planning a major archaeological expedition to that village in the foothills of the Taurus Mountains. Humann was the discoverer and excavator of ancient Pergamon, and on a side-trip from his excavation, Humann and his friends found marvelous carved reliefs at Zinjirli which suggested more Hittite ruins close by. It was exciting for the two missionaries, Marden and Perry, to be traveling through land once part of the empire of these ancient Biblical peoples. Not until at least twelve years later, with William F. Petrie's discovery of the Tel El Amarna tablets and their many references to the Hittites, and Hugh Winckler's excavations at Boghazköy, the Hittite capital about two hundred kilometers west of Sivas, would the full extent of the range and power of the ancient Hittites begin to be realized.

In Albustan, Henry again was overcome by sadness and feelings of inadequacy. He felt so unfit for work in Turkey, he felt like immediately leaving. Reading Isaiah 55 gave him some encouragement. He took a walk for two and a half hours:

> After looking about on the magnificent panorama of Mountains on all sides, the Achan Mts. above Marash; the Zeitoon Mts.; the ridge off towards Burnlin; and the Anti-Taurus with the plains around Albustan with their winding streams...I set up seven stones on the Marash side of the ridge consecrating each with a prayer; and left them there as a memorial.[35]

Surrounded by Turkish mountains, the prophet Isaiah again brought comfort to Henry's soul, as he recalled a favorite verse which always spoke to his missionary heart: "How beautiful upon the mountains are the feet of him that bringeth good tidings, that publisheth peace; that bringeth good tidings of good, that publisheth salvation; that saith unto Zion, Thy God reigneth!"[36]

In the winter, Henry spent several months visiting the outstations and encouraging the churches. The economic condition of the countryside was stark. Farmers and businessmen alike were on the verge of financial ruin. Money had been drained by taxes and was almost nonexistent. When money was not forthcoming, tax gatherers seized land, sheep, bedding, cooking utensils, evaluating them at less than half their value. Government officials were fed continually by bribes.

In his final Sivas Station Annual report before he left Turkey, Henry noted that the severe poverty of the people affected the ability of the Christians in Turkey to fully support their own pastors, schools, and churches. Many of the Armenians and Greeks coming to the full light of the Gospel no longer felt it necessary to become Protestants. In both Armenian and Greek churches there were reformed evangelical parties which rejected the errors of the traditional churches, such as prayers to saints and the Virgin Mary, and looked to the Scriptures for guidance. In many areas the leadership of the older churches allowed evangelical reforms within the churches. Prayer meetings and Bible studies in private homes, previously unknown, had become common. In Sivas especially, though the Protestant church remained small, the influence of the Gospel among the native churches was spreading.

Though Henry was leaving Sivas to care for his mother, he had some hope that he might yet return to Turkey. With that hope, he carefully packed some of the boxes and placed them in the attic of Dr. West's house. When distributing extra items that could not be taken with him, Henry gave Emma Hubbard his horse, Jim. She and Albert would enjoy riding out in the countryside together.

On May 2, 1886, his last Sunday in Sivas, Henry preached on Hebrews 6:18, "The Abundant Consolation," to a full congregation. Many called in the afternoon to wish him goodbye. Especially moved was his Turkish neighbor Eomer Effendi. He shed some tears at their parting and, in his dignified way, kissed Henry on each cheek.

May 3, 1886, Henry and little Jean, accompanied by Anna Doodoo and Laura Chamberlin, left Sivas in a wagon. It was the second anniversary of Jeanne's death, making it a day of excitement mingled with sadness. The little party on the way to Samsoun stopped at Tocat for a day, where again there was a sad parting with the Christians there.

May 6th was Henry's birthday. He felt so much older than he had two years ago. Before Jeanne's death he still felt a young man, but now his hair was turning, and there were stray white hairs in his beard. His whole life was now breaking up in so many ways, but he prayed that somehow the Father could use all for a good result.

---

[1] *Great Need Over the Water*, 41.

[2] Known as Kara Hissar Shaki or Shab Kara Hissar in Henry's day, this is today the town of Shebin Karahisar.

[3] H.T. Perry to Rev. N.G. Clark, from Kara Hissar, September 14, 1882, ABC 16.9.3, Vol. 15, No. 327; "Kara Hissar Re-occupied," *The Missionary Herald*, January, 1883, 25.

[4] Henry and Alvan later visited the mines on July 15th, 1884 and met the Welsh operators. They both talked like Christian men and encouraged the sale of Christian literature to their workers. *Diary*, July 15, 1884.

[5] H.T. Perry, "Kuzzle-Bash Koords," *The Missionary Herald*, June 1883, 221 (From March 6, 1883 letter, H.T. Perry to Rev. N.G. Clark).

[6] "Gleanings from Letters," *The Missionary Herald*, April 1883, 152.

[7] Irving McGee. *"Ben Hur" Wallace: The Life of General Lew Wallace*. Berkeley and Los Angeles: University of California Press, 1947.

[8] H.T. Perry to Rev. N.G. Clark, from Sivas, October 9, 1883, ABC 16.9.3, Vol. 15, No. 336.

[9] H.T. Perry to Rev. N.G. Clark, from Sivas, October 9, 1883, ABC 16.9.3, Vol. 15, No. 336.

[10] *Diary*, 1881 notes added August 1925 at beginning and end of diary.

[11] *Diary*, September 19, 1883.

[12] As with her mother, Henry wrote his daughter's name in several different ways. Sometimes it was "Jennie;" sometimes it was "Jeanne." In this biography, we have consistently called the little girl "Jean," for reasons that will become clear later. To avoid confusion, Perry's quoted diary entries have been made consistent with this practice as well.

[13] *Diary*, May 18, 1884 (Henry Perry's *Diary* from September 1, 1883-December 31, 1884 is in the possession of authors).

[14] *Diary*, May 24, 1884.

[15] *Diary*, written after May 18, 1884.

[16] "Mrs. Jeanne H. Perry, of Sivas," *The Missionary Herald*, July 1884, 266-267.

[17] From a letter to his mother Henry inserted in his diary for February 19, 1885.

[18] *Diary*, June 22, 1884.

[19] *Leaven from Her Scrapbook*, 162-163.

[20] *Diary*, October 22, 1884.

[21] *Diary*, January 8, 1885.

[22] *Diary*, February 16, 1885.
[23] Henry's *Diary* for April 30, 1880, speaks of "Great preparations being made for the Grand dinner for the English guests" and specifically mentions "Capt. Stewart" among the guests. It is unclear whether this was a dinner given by the American missionaries or a more formal dinner elsewhere. Henry refers to the events of Khartoum in his 1885 diary on January 28, February 25, March 2, and March 9. In his *Diary* for February 28, 1913, he mentioned that England had to abandon Turkish reforms because of problems in Egypt, and that Sir Charles Wilson was sent from Turkey to Egypt. See also Rev. A.W. Hubbard, "Sketch of Sivas Station, Western Turkey," *The Missionary Herald*, March 1893; Winston Churchill. *History of the English-Speaking People* (One vol. Ed. By Henry Steele Commager). N.Y.: Pocket Books, 1966, 557-559; Alan Moorhead. *The White Nile*. New York: Harper and Brothers, 1960, 221-280; John H. Waller. *Gordon of Khartoum*. New York: Athenum, 1988.
[24] *Diary*, April 28, 1885.
[25] *Diary*, May 12, 1885.
[26] Cyrus Hamlin founded Robert College in 1863 at Rumeli Hissar near Constantinople. Hamlin had been a missionary with the American Board, but when his plans for a college did not fit in with Board policy, he resigned. He raised funds for an independent college, which he named after its principal donor. Though not directly a part of the ABCFM, Robert College maintained a close association with the missionaries and trained men for Christian work in Turkey. In 1871, an American College for Girls was founded nearby. In 1971 the two schools merged to form a school for Turkish nationals, under the jurisdiction of the Turkish Ministry of Education. The school has operated continuously longer than any other American school outside the United States. It has been renamed and is today called the University of the Bosphorus.
[27] *The Hubbards of Sivas*, 196.
[28] *Diary*, August 18, 1885. Of *Fatima*, Henry wrote, "read it passionately, with my tho't steadily fixed on Christ. Found the exercise profitable; and then said to myself: This is a good element of excellence in the poem; that it is capable of such use without a blur."
[29] "Substitution," in Elizabeth Barrett Browning. *Selected Poems* (ed. Margaret Forster). Baltimore, Maryland: The Johns Hopkins University Press, 1988, 80.
[30] *Dairy*, September 13, 1885.
[31] *Diary*, August 3, 1885.
[32] Henry T. Perry to Rev. N.G. Clark, August 14, 1885, ABC 16.9.3, Vol. 15, No. 349.
[33] *Diary*, October 15, 1885.
[34] *Diary*, October 20, 1885. For a description of the "discovery" of the Hittites, see C.W. Ceram. *The Secret of the Hittites*. N.Y.: Schochen Books, 1973, 21-53.
[35] *Diary*, October 31, 1885.

[36] Isaiah 52:7.

7
A FRUITFUL FIELD
(1886-1893)

"Until the Spirit be poured upon us from on high,
and the wilderness be a fruitful field..."
Isaiah 32:15

At the end of May 1886, after two weeks in Constantinople attending the Annual Meeting, Henry and his two-year-old Jean boarded the *Macedonia* for Liverpool. Arthur Pierce and two daughters of a Mr. Locke brought the missionary party to five. Anna Doodoo, Jean's nurse, went back to Sivas with Laura Chamberlin. Jean cried when Anna left, but she recovered quickly with all the changes of scenes and the newness of the ship. Besides, her dear father surrounded her with his love and care.

As the *Macedonia* neared the harbor of Smyrna, it passed two American ships of war, the *Pensacola* and the *Kearsarge*. Henry was delighted to see the American flag flying off the Turkish coast. While stopping briefly in Smryna, Henry visited the *Kearsarge*. The third captain, Winslow, had been a midshipman on the *Kearsarge* during its engagement with the *Alabama* during the Civil War twenty years before. The American ships were part of a naval blockade to prevent a full-scale war in the region. The Turks had called their possessions in the Balkans Rumelia (the land of the Romans). By the 1878 Berlin treaty, Eastern Rumelia became an autonomous province. In September 1885, Bulgaria annexed Eastern Rumelia, and Greece demanded compensating territory from Turkey. A brief war between Bulgaria and Serbia broke out in the Balkans. To prevent Greece and Turkey from going to war, Britain implemented a naval blockade in May 1886. The

Macedonia passed through the blockading fleet as it made its way through the Aegean Islands. Henry's diary for June 5 reads:

> In the A.M. we passed two ironclads of the blockading fleet; one was Italian, to which we dipped the flag. Smaller torpedo boats were sailing about. Prizes having war material for Greece on board are sent to the harbor of Melos. This is a maneuver against Russia, forcing Greece to disarm and so Russia is kept out of the European States of Turkey. It is under English direction, the Duke of Edinburgh being at the head of the squadron.

A week after leaving Constantinople, the *Macedonia* docked at the island of Malta. As Henry looked out on the island covered with forts, he thought of its tumultuous history. In ancient times the sea-faring Phoenicians had controlled the island. St. Paul was shipwrecked here when being taken to Rome as a prisoner. Later the Moors controlled the island, and then the crusading Knights of St. John held the place against the Turks. During Napoleon's time the French took it from the Knights, then the English took it from the French after the loss of the battles of the Nile. England took the island from the French on the condition that they would not interfere with the Catholic religion of the people.

Henry had a letter of introduction from Mr. Bliss in Constantinople to Reverend George Wise, Minister of the Church of Scotland on Malta. In spite of an attack of lumbago, Henry had dinner with Reverend Wise and found him a "peculiar man" – his talk was full of humor, and he drank wine with his dinner![1] Reverand Wise had been in Malta thirty-two years, yet he had no Maltese in his congregation. Every Sunday he held four services for the British on the island.

Aboard the *Macedonia*, for the first time little Jean was solely Henry's responsibility, and he tried to make the two of them "comfortable; and as far as possible agreeable, and profitable to other people." Henry kept Jean amused by taking her around the ship to see the sights (though this was sometimes difficult when his lumbago made him bend over like an old man). Everyone on board the ship knew Jean and called her "Jean Pasha," just to hear her say the words. Henry's diary entries reveal how much energy the two-year-old required of him:

> <u>June 14, 1886 (Monday, Rounded Cape Vincent, Portugal)</u> Retired early with the "birdie" so as to get my sleep when she (Jean) gets

hers. This habit is necessary to keep me in working order; for the trip
– taking care of Jean day and night without help.
<u>June 15, 1886 (Tuesday, off the coast of Spain)</u> Sea moderate.
Weather fine. Especially by the full moon at night. I was busy all
day with my little charge; could do but little else; She was somewhat
fretful and needed patient care. I did but little; read but little; thought
but little; made no progress in anything; except the trial of a moderate
degree of patience. Had a headache in the PM, arising from a bilious
state: sleep and a lemon, with a scedlitz, put me right.

After a day in Liverpool, on June 24 Henry and Jean boarded the
Adriatic for the trip to America. The *Adriatic* had taken Henry and
Jeanne to America when she was ill in 1873, and Henry again in 1875,
when he came back from Turkey alone. Henry was happy to spend his
time taking care of his precious daughter on this journey; it was good
he was never seasick so that he was able to give his time to Jean. On
the *Adriatic* the children's table was separate and an hour earlier from
the other passengers. Henry regularly fed Jean there, sitting with the
nannies and children of the wealthier passengers. During the day, people with children congregated in the reading room, and there Henry was
able to visit with some of the other passengers, including some Baptist
missionaries and their children from Lagos, Africa. Meeting other
English and Americans made Henry realize how much he had lost so-
cially during his time in Turkey.

July 4, 1886, Henry and Jean arrived in New York. Henry's diary
for that date is blank, except for the note of their arrival in America.
His thoughts and feelings at stepping again on American soil without
his Jeanne, but with his two-year-old daughter by his side, were probably inexpressible. Though the Statue was Liberty was now standing in
New York harbor (it would be dedicated the following October), it remains unmentioned in Henry's diary. Undoubtedly caring for little Jean
and seeing Alvan and his mother in Ashfield consumed all of his
thoughts. In 1923, however, Henry looked back upon his return and
wrote:

    Surely the way of my Lord in training me for Himself has been
wonderful.
    The grief that came to me in 1884 resulted in not a little distrac-
tion. Going to my Lord with it, He gave me an abiding comfort; nevertheless I did not receive in 1885 the fullness of His gift of the Holy
Spirit for service, as it was my joy to have in 1886. In 1885 I was
craving <u>comfort</u> for my own troubled soul. In 1886 I prayed once

more for the Holy Spirit's gift for fruitage in souls born into the Kingdom.

In our Moslem field we were always at work for our pupils and Congregations, beset by exceedingly great difficulties. In this battlefield with the enemy, our discouragements abounded. When overwhelmed, we could only fall back on our Lord, to wait for Him, and see the movement of His hand <u>forward</u>. This was our experience at Kara Hissar-Sharki in 1884. My wife and I, in her life-time there, had our fast-days together for prayer, that our Lord would give His blessing and guidance.

My wife and I believed that our work of service in Turkey, in obedience to His command, is His work. Therefore, He will win by us the victory. He has already won it at Calvary over the hosts of darkness, and over all the power of the enemy.

Our part now is to range ourselves entirely on His side, to stand with Him by faith for the present need, that the Holy Spirit may prove its power.

This view of the case was revived in me in 1886, to the extent that the world about me was filled with the tokens of His presence and uplift.

God's way is perfect. His weapons are still mighty; His power's supreme; and His Church in Christ will be "powerful as an army with banners." There is deliverance thro the Name of the Lord (II Chron. 20). Not by might, nor by power, but by My Spirit, saith the Lord of Hosts (Zech. 4:6).

This lesson I have been learning, and by it, my grief for the loss of my wife had been assuaged. In the joy of His Presence I followed in the way of His will, to bring home my little Jeanne to my Mother in the United States.[2]

Henry had promised his mother six months of his time after he returned to America, and she had a list of things for him to do when he arrived home! The biggest of the projects was a second floor addition to the eastern attachment of the Ashfield house. Henry enjoyed supervising and helping in the work, as well as helping his mother in any other way she wished. The strenuous years in Turkey had taken their toll, and the six months in Ashfield provided needed rest and refreshment. On Sundays Henry preached in surrounding churches, at Conway, South Deerfield, Plainfield, Buckland, and Montague. Often he walked from his mother's house to the cemetery where his father was buried. Here was his special place of prayer, and here he especially prayed for the Lord's direction in his future work.

It had been so long since he had spoken regularly in an American pulpit, Henry felt woefully unfit for a pastoral position. Though he had resigned from the ABCFM to care for his mother, he still valued Reverend Clark's advice and sought his guidance in what path he should take. Should he seek out a pastoral position or was there a foreign immigrant group in the cities he could work with in a missionary fashion? If he were free to move west, he would have liked returning to a missionary church such as he had in Rolla, Missouri. However, this was not practical with the responsibility he had for his mother's care.

Henry finally accepted a call to pastor the small Presbyterian church at Masonville, New York, north of Pennsylvania and near the Susquehanna River. The church was a struggling one with a small membership, and the church building itself was worn out. Henry felt called to bring renewal to the small congregation and the community. May 1, 1887, he began his service in Masonville; on the journey over he bought his first pair of reading spectacles.

Until he could find a place to stay and bring his mother and Jean, Henry boarded with Mrs. and Miss Mandeville, the widowed wife and daughter of the previous pastor. He developed a regular routine of studying in the forenoon and calling on members of his congregation and others in the afternoon. Since many of the people were farmers, Henry often had to walk long distances for his visitations. He found the deep suffering he had experienced enabled him to better help others who were going through times of affliction.

In June, fourteen year old Alvan came to stay with his father, bringing Henry special joy. Since his return from Turkey in 1885, Alvan had been staying in Fredonia, New York with Aunt Jeannie Shearer, his mother's aunt and sister to Grandmother Jones. Aunt Shearer had felt a special bond with Alvan since he was a baby and welcomed the opportunity to care for him when he returned to America. Henry was happy to find Alvan such a good boy, and the two had many special times reading and walking together. Alvan's youthful cheerfulness lifted Henry's spirit. He felt like he could unbend in his conversations with his son as he could with no others.

Franklin Carter, one of Henry's classmates at Williams College, was now President of the College, and he invited Henry to give an address at the Park Missionary Meeting during the June commencement. Henry took Alvan with him, and the lad was quite interested in the long train ride from Albany to Williamstown. President Carter heartily welcomed the Perrys and was eager to hear all about Henry's missionary work in Turkey. Alvan happily played with President Carter's daughter, Francie, and her friends during the various commencement ceremonies, and Henry was pleased that his son behaved himself well. Of the many dignitaries at the commencement, Henry seemed to be the youngest, and he was quite honored to be in their presence. They all seemed eager to hear of Henry's experience in Turkey. Not only did he feel honored, but he felt his responsibility as a minister of Christ.

Before returning to Masonville, Henry went to Ashfield for a brief visit. During that time he helped his mother prepare for her move to Masonville in the fall and spent time with his precious Jean. When Henry returned to Masonville, Alvan returned to Fredonia. Once again Henry was all alone. He totally devoted himself to the work of the ministry and visiting the people in the community. He also spent much time in prayer for a revival in the church.

Henry's teaching and evangelism among the young people in the schools became a prelude to a spiritual revival throughout the community in 1888. Reverend C.B. Personeus, pastor of the Methodist Church, approached Henry about combining their churches for a series of revival meetings. Beginning in January, Perry and Personeus, assisted by two older retired preachers, held services three times a week in their churches; sometimes the Baptists joined in the services. Henry described the revival in a letter to Reverend N.G. Clark:

> The first uplift in power came as by a descending cloud Jan. 20th suddenly, bringing the children and youth of the two Sunday Schools into the inquiry room. Many found peace in the Lord and on subsequent days others followed...The interest then began to spread abroad. The people came <u>packing</u> the church every night...
>
> To such a pitch did the interest rise that we could use the whole packed house as an inquiry room – the people standing while the new converts and others quietly but very earnestly worked with all the unsaved. Thus collecting the seekers to the front we pray with them...Merchants, mill-owners, greyheaded farmers, the profane and the drunkards are among the converts. Family altars have been set up in scores of homes...In the two Sunday schools new classes are formed made up largely of those who a few weeks ago were notorious unbelievers. The old people say that during the past 40 years at least there has never been a revival here of such power as this.[3]

One answer to Henry's prayers for revival was Mr. Brewer:

When I went to Masonville, I was told that I must "beware of Mr. Brewer" (a farmer in the Pine Hill District) for he could "browbeat and silence all the ministers." Therefore, I turned to meet him when working in his field; said nothing of religion or the Bible at that time. Being warned of him, I lost no time in making his acquaintance; and turned for occasional calls with him when he was working, but said to him yet nothing of my message. Thus the time passed until the revival "break" as the Methodists say. In all my country congregations, I made much of District School-House Preaching, and one of the most hopeful of those places was the Pine Hill district. When there at one of our "break" occasions with the young people and children, a tall, stately Mr. Brewer came in, which at first disconcerted me with the thought that he had come for an attack upon us; but I kept straight on with the service. As soon as I dismissed the audience, Mr. Brewer went out, saying nothing to me. At another time not long after, he came again and when the "testimony" was being given, this tall man lifted himself slowly up from the little seat (made for the children) and saying nothing of himself as to the truth, only expressed his pleasure that the meetings were useful for the children. I recognized at once that this was by the Holy Spirit. Among the converts were Mr. Brewer's wife and only child—a daughter. He made no objection, so far as I know, concerning them; and soon after at the Revival services at the Churches, he was fully with us. When the declaration for division was made by the card system, he inscribed for our Presbyterian church. Without much delay he was appointed as Superintendent of our Sunday School, and succeeded well in that office. To God, the Father, the Son, and the Holy Spirit be all the praise!

"All things are possible to him who believeth" Luke 18:27.
The things which are impossible with men are possible with God."

Being a masterly man in his character, he was specially fitted to lead our Sunday School as Superintendent.[4]

In his diary Henry further described these exciting times:

We pastors alternating preached three evening sermons each week. The one who did not preach sat with those singing; to watch the effect of the sermon; and at its close passed through the congregation to call forward the convicted ones to the "anxious seats." Especially he was to get the children; Then closing the doors, we dealt with all cases. In this movement, we depended much on the unity of the churches in the prayer service. Prayer meetings were held daily in our Presbyterian church. At the anxious seat meetings in the Methodist

Church, we led the converts in <u>their praying</u>. It was as if <u>the Lord filled the house</u> with His presence. It was easy to preach.[5]

The choir leaders arranged for special appeals in song, and sometimes it seemed the songs had even more effect on the people than the preaching did.

The revival services continued for almost eight weeks, and the very atmosphere of the town "seemed <u>thrilled</u>." Henry preached with the utmost ease, and the cooperation between the Methodists, Presbyterians, and Baptists, truly reflected their oneness in Christ. All recognized the revival was a movement of God's Spirit among the people, not any work or contrivance of men. By the first of March, there were at least 200 converts. A union meeting was held for the new converts at which neatly printed cards were passed out to be filled in, with the name of the church blank. A majority of the new converts chose to join the Methodist church, but about fifty chose to join the Presbyterians. It was a remarkable addition to a church that had only thirty members when Henry arrived! A few of the new converts choosing to join Henry's church had been raised as Baptists. When the baptism service was held they preferred to be baptized by immersion, rather than the Presbyterian sprinkling. Henry willingly agreed to this and took them down to the river for the ceremony.

Not only did the revival change lives, enlarge the congregation, and encourage Henry; it also became the impetus for remodeling the church building. Though the church building, pulpit, carpets, and cushions were worn and neglected when Henry came to Masonville, Henry said nothing of these things. He simply "preached Christ and Him crucified for sinners."[6] The leaders of the congregation decided on their own to repair the church, and for several weeks the Presbyterian congregation worshipped in other church buildings. The men tore out all the pews, pulpit furniture and carpets, cleaned the pews, and replaced them along with new carpets and pulpit furniture. When the day came for dedicating the building, many from other churches came. Henry was especially animated when he preached his first sermon in the refurbished church from Isaiah 60:13, "I will make the place of my feet glorious." When Henry looked around the church he thought, "As I had done so little for it, I felt greatly humbled; and that the name of the Dear Lord must be exalted!!" How the Lord was to be praised for His work![7]

Henry's mother and Jean had come to Masonville in October 1887, and the Perrys rented a house from a Mr. Gould. Henry was able to have a lady, Jessie, help care for his mother. Mrs. Perry had grown heavy, and it was often difficult for her to get about. Though she was feeble and could not go out much, she rejoiced and prayed over the news of the revival sweeping through the town. She also reproved Henry on some of his reading material! Henry had picked up a set of Chautauqua readings and worked through the exercises as a way of expanding his acquaintance with works of literature.[8] Mrs. Perry thought Henry could better spend his time working on his sermons.

Whatever Henry read, however, whether it was secular material or a devotional book, it always was with an intent to improve his soul to better serve his God. He was especially fascinated with Africa and continuously followed the explorations of Henry M. Stanley. In the 1870's, Stanley not only went on his famous expedition to "find" David Livingstone, but he later explored the waterways of Central Africa and mapped the course of the Congo River. His letters from Uganda called for missionaries and led to the British interest in establishing a protectorate in the region. In January 1887, Stanley led a third African Expedition to aid William McKinnon in establishing a British protectorate in East Equatorial Africa. In July of that year, Henry noted in his diary:

> Mr. Stanley's work in Africa is of a Mighty Magnitude. He marches thru the immense forests; and scatters the wicked Masters of the Slave trade. He prepares the way for the Missionaries, who will follow. Upon his track is laid the needful Railways.[9]

After Stanley's account of his expedition, *In Darkest Africa*, was published in 1890, Henry eagerly read the book. He prayed often and long for Africa, since "The native tribes are unable to save themselves from the Arab horrors of the slave trade."[10] Stanley's book spurred Henry to go through back issues of The *Missionary Herald*, reading articles on Africa and Uganda. In the process, he took out all the pages for the "Young People" and made them into a little book for Jean.

Sunday, May 6, 1888, Henry turned fifty. No one, not even his mother, mentioned the event. Yet, Henry took note of the occasion to resolve "to commemorate this second half century with a more steady habit of prayer and more firm reliance upon it for results."[11] The loss of his Jeanne at times seemed deeper and more vivid than it did four years before. Only the Lord could give him the patience and strength to live for Him.

Henry's ministry in Masonville was a delight, with no trouble or illness but great joy because of the harvest of souls into the church. On a visit, Aunt Electra Dawes recommended that Henry find a place where his mother (Aunt Electra's sister) could be closer to the railway. Masonville was a long way from Ashfield, and Mrs. Perry would have to return to Ashfield by rail for her final resting place. Shortly after Easter, 1888, Henry received a call to become the minister at the church at nearby Afton, New York. Though he did not want to leave Masonville, for his mother's sake it seemed the best move. Afton was a much larger town and had a railroad station, with easy access to Ashfield.

Afton was in the rolling hills of New York, separated into two parts by the broad valley of the Susquehannah River. Henry wrote that the

> parsonage, which the Presbyterians purchased, was situated in a healthful place on the upper terrace of the village. There was a large bedroom on the lower floor which...[mother] could occupy; and a very convenient study room for me upstairs. There was plenty of water, and a large garden, which I could cultivate...It was an ideal place where I, as acting pastor of the Church at Afton, could so comfortably care for my Mother, till her last hours in this world.[12]

Besides his pastoral duties and caring for his mother, Henry devoted much time to Jean, who began attending school in Afton. Henry surrounded Jean with love, but also recognized she was a strong-willed, independent child. He conscientiously worked to bend her will to the right and true. Sometimes she willfully disobeyed his instructions, and several times he caught her in lies to him. He strictly disciplined her, usually by sending her to bed. However, Jean was doing nicely in her piano and sewing lessons.

Henry included Jean in as many of his activities as possible. In January 1891, he took her to hear the Jubilee Singers at Afton's Baptist Church, where for the first time Jean, and possibly Henry, heard the passionate Negro spirituals sung.[13] Jean enjoyed the outdoors, and while Henry worked in his vegetable garden, Jean began raising chickens. Unfortunately, in 1891, ten of her brown Leghorns drowned in a cold rain the evening of July 3rd.

The following July 4th had good weather, however, and Jean enjoyed the day's celebrations with her father. She got to sit on the Celebration Platform with him, since he gave the prayer. After Reverend

Ripley's animated oration, Henry and Jean had dinner, then went to the parade and all the races – including the sack race, the potato race, and the tub race. The day ended with a grand fusillade of guns. Though Jean was a happy child, Henry felt somehow she should be receiving better care.

Alvan was finishing school in Fredonia, and it was an easy train ride for Henry and Jean to visit him. The New York State Normal School at Fredonia provided free tuition to the town taxpayers, so Alvan stayed with Aunt Jennie Shearer to help pay his schooling. Henry could not afford to pay the normal school prices, and Aunt Jennie was happy for Alvan to stay with her. Alvan received excellent training in mathematics, which would help him in business. He seemed to have a good business sense that should see him into a good mercantile position. Even while in school he began selling needles to earn extra money. He politely made certain he would see the mistress of the house, not just the servant girls, and he soon earned all the money he needed. Alvan also began growing grapes, and Henry helped him in the garden during his visits. Aunt Jennie Shearer was like a mother to Alvan, "strong in her Christian character, wise to rebuke when it was needed; patient with him in his impatient ways; praying with him when he needed guidance. And this 'Aunt' Jennie had skill in her way of guidance."[14] Alvan was a good boy, but Henry continued to pray for his conversion. Whenever he visited Alvan in Fredonia, Henry frequently visited the Hubbards, Albert's parents, who had moved to the town from their farm. They were usually able to share with Henry the latest news from Turkey and Sivas.

At Afton, on Friday, October 16, 1891, Sarah Perry quietly passed to her eternal rest. The following Monday she was buried beside her husband Alvan in the Ashfield cemetery. Her Christian character had continued to influence everyone around her to the very end, and Henry always was happy to be able to care for her in her last days.

Only four months before, Henry had met another Christian lady who would have a big impact on his life. In June Henry had attended the annual Missionary Convention at Clifton Springs, New York, east of Rochester. There he was introduced to Mary Ellen Hartwell. Mary had been a classmate of Jeanne's at Western Female Seminary in Oxford, Ohio. She had taught school for a number of years, including at Western Seminary from 1878-1879. She had long had an interest in missions and in 1879, sailed for Bangkok, Siam with the Presbyterian Board.[15] She taught at the Wang Lang Girls' School in the Bangkok

Station for five years, until 1884. Ill health brought on by the tropical heat caused her to return to the United States. Once her health recovered, she worked for the Women's Board in the northwest and then as an officer for the Young Women's Christian Association in Boston. She had a heart for missions and the Lord's work.

Henry and Mary's meeting in Clifton Springs developed into a steady correspondence once Henry returned to Afton and Mary to her work in Boston. Henry could easily imagine Mary by his side on the mission field in Turkey. She could also provide the mother's love and guidance seven-year-old Jean so desperately needed. By September, Henry was writing to "My Mary." After his mother's funeral in mid-October, Henry went from Ashfield to Boston and Auburndale, where he spent several days with Mary. He proposed to her; she accepted; and the two began planning their marriage and their future together in Turkey.

On December 7, Henry left Jean in the care of Mrs. Bridger and returned to Boston, taking a small room in the Bellevue Hotel. The marriage of Henry and Mary took place December 9, 1891, with Alvan acting as Henry's "best man." Mary "was in dignity like a queen. Equal and more to every emergency of the occasion."[16] That evening the Bellevue Hotel transferred Henry to a larger room to share with his new bride.

On the week-long, leisurely journey back to Afton, Henry and Mary stayed with Henry's sister Sarah in North Adams and with Emily Montgomery in New Haven. It was a time of rejoicing among family and friends, and all seemed to approve of Henry's choice of a wife. At Afton, Henry's congregation had prepared a lavish feast inside the manse for the newly weds. The first to welcome Mary was little Jean, who ran to her with outstretched arms, called her, "Mother," and kissed her.

Henry, however, was in severe pain from his lumbago! Lifting and turning his mother during her illness had injured his back, and he had difficulty standing straight. His first Sunday back in Afton, Mary consented to go to church and speak in Henry's place while he stayed in bed. The people seemed to appreciate her words to them, and Henry was thankful for the patience of his congregation with his infirmities.

As 1891 came to a close, Henry looked back with gratitude on the Lord's mercies. While he was caring for his mother, he had prayed the Lord would give him a church where he might "dwell in the house of the Lord...to behold the beauty of the Lord, and to enquire in his temple," and this the Lord had given at Masonville and Afton. The passing of his mother to "rest" and the coming of "my Mary" both were beautifully brought about by the Lord's hand.

By January 1892, Henry and Mary had been accepted by the ABCFM for missionary service to Turkey and were being appointed to Sivas. Henry continued as pastor at Afton through the end of April, but the next few months were full of preparations for the move to Turkey. Henry's diary entry of January 2 is full of an interesting listing of things bought for Turkey:

> 4 pairs of boots; heavy coat, shirts, wool leggings, heavy cotton flannel drawers, towels, overcoat, 1 years' supply of shoes for Jean; 2 hats, glue for furniture, pocket knives; books: 2-volume cyclopedia, 1 concordance, Spurgeon's *Psalms*, Connybeare *Life of St. Paul*, Sheets, garden seeds (lettuce, radishes, parsnips, beans, peas, corn, celery, squash, tomatoes, beets.) 2 boxes of books- total 80 volumes. Pulpit suit, double blanket, cloak, black wool dress, summer silk dress, 4 white shirts, 1 short house coat, 1 umbrella lamp, 1 sofa pillow, 1 water color picture, table ware; ladies' handkerchiefs, pillow, work basket, worsted cape, white Swiss dress, woolen veil, 1 gents wool muffler, student lamp, gents neckties, 17 napkins, 2 suits, nice doll, child's rubbers, shoes, ladies shoes, ladies velvet hat, old table cloth.

The first of May, Henry and Mary left Afton for Washington, D.C., where they were guests of Aunt Electra and Senator Dawes. The Dawes were friends of President and Mrs. Cleveland. Anna Dawes, Henry's cousin, gave the Perrys a tour of the White House, showing them the East Room, the Blue Room, the Green Room, and the conservatory. She also took them for a tour of the Treasury Building and the Capitol. The following day Aunt Electra thought the Perrys should see Mt. Vernon and enlisted a Mr. Angers to accompany them to Washington's home. On Sunday, Henry and Mary attended the Presbyterian Church with Aunt and Uncle Dawes, sitting in a pew very near President Cleveland.

After a delightful week in D.C., the Perrys returned to Ashfield. There was still much for Henry to do in tending to the house since his mother's death six months before. Much of the goods and furniture were carefully stored in the attic so the house could be leased while the Perrys were in Turkey. Henry provided his niece, Ally Porter, with all the necessary papers and authority to handle his affairs in America while he was away.

In July, Henry and Mary went to the missionary conference at Clifton Springs, New York, where they had first met the previous year. It was wonderful to now attend the conference as a missionary team. The speakers refreshed, stimulated, and challenged them for the task before them. Henry thought the sermon by Dr. James Hall Brookes was one of the most memorable he had ever heard: "His power to preach and prove his points by the Word of God, reciting the exact words, and the place of each in the Bible was to me masterful and wonderful."[17] Brookes was a well-known Bible conference speaker, one of the founders of the Niagra Bible Conference, and an influential premillennialist author who believed Christ might return to earth at any moment. Mary knew the Brookes family well and was happy to introduce Henry to them. Another speaker who impressed Henry was Hudson Taylor, whom Mary had earlier met in London. Taylor, founder of China Inland Mission, spoke with power on "abiding in Christ." Henry was also delighted to meet for the first time Reverend W.J. Erdman, another prominent premillennialist and Bible conference speaker. In 1865, when Henry was just graduating from Auburn Seminary, he had "preached for supply" in Reverend Erdman's pulpit in Fayetteville, New York; but he had never met him.

All the speakers at the conference reflected the premillennialism and emphasis on Bible prophecy which was a growing movement among American evangelicals after the Civil War.[18] The Perrys bought a number of books at the conference, including Wilkinson's *Israel My Glory,* and returned to Afton and Masonville to make final preparations for the move to Turkey. Henry left the conference uplifted with a continuing joy:

> The joy of contemplating the coming of the Lord to this world, to complete his Work of judgment, and take His kingdom, filled me more and more. I studied the Scripture and found the proof ample. The conference was to me a great help.[19]

Henry's health was much better than it had been the previous year. His back was healed, and he had no problem with the lifting and hard work involved in moving. August was filled with the last minute preparations for departure, including packing and visiting many friends and relatives. Alvan came to offer his nineteen-year old energy, strength, and gentlemanliness to help in the move. He enjoyed driving Henry, Mary, and Jean on their numerous errands before taking them to the boat in New York. Alvan had grown to manhood during his father's five years in the United States; Henry would miss his son as he again returned to the mission field.

August 27, 1892, Henry, Mary, and eight-year-old Jean boarded the *Etruria* of the Cunard line and began their two-month journey to Sivas. Joining them was Miss McCallum, in charge of the girls' school in Smyrna. Mary and Miss McCallum suffered greatly from seasickness during the voyage to Liverpool, but Henry and daughter Jean fared well and enjoyed the trip. During their three days in London, the Perrys made last minute purchases for Turkey - a set of dinner dishes, an Ulster for Mary, and a supply of rubber goods. In London they heard stories of the cholera epidemic then sweeping from the east.[20] Cholera was increasing in Paris, and it seemed likely there would be long periods of quarantine imposed upon the Perrys during their travels. After prayer and seeking the Lord's guidance, they decided to proceed at once to Marseilles, passing through Paris without a stop. In Marseilles, they purchased some cholera medicine before boarding the *Cambodge* on September 10. The Perrys were among the first to board the steamer and secured good berths before the crowd of refugees from the cholera filled the ship. The steamer was so crowded that at nights cots were set up in the saloon for the overflow of passengers. There was no outbreak of cholera on board the *Cambodge*, but in the Bay of Salamis, off the coast of Greece, the ship was quarantined for five days. Henry spent the time studying the psalms in Turkish and reading the books on prophecy he had picked up at the conference in New York. Jean was happy and seemed to be enjoying her return trip to Turkey. Once the quarantine was over the Perrys were able to spend a day in Athens, visiting the Acropolis, the Temples of Thesus and Jupiter, the Theater of Dionysius, the King's Palace, the Arch of Hadrian, and the Modern Academy.

By September 23, the *Cambodge* docked in Constantinople, and the missionaries of the city happily received the Perrys. Mary had suffered greatly from seasickness on both legs of her sea journey from New York. Henry thought it best to let her enjoy land a bit before making the Black Sea voyage to Samsoun. They stayed with Dr. and Mrs. Frederick Greene and spent the days introducing Mary to Constantinople and the various missionary enterprises there.[21] All the missionaries enjoyed meeting Mary and hearing her tell of her earlier experiences in Siam.

October 1st the Perrys took a Dutch steamer for Samsoun. Henry's old servant Neshan was waiting for them when they landed October 3.

The quarantine had been removed the day before, so Neshan quickly loaded the Perrys on the wagons and began the trip to Sivas. Throughout the journey the Lord seemed very near to Henry, leading him and his family securely towards Sivas. At stops in Marsovan, Amasia, and Tocat along the way, missionaries and Armenians alike welcomed the Perrys home. Jean was full of life and comfortable in returning to the land that she had left when only two. When they reached Sivas, on October 14th, Henry wrote,

> ... the missionaries, the American consul, the students, schoolchildren, former neighbors and friends of the congregation old and young, met us at a lunching place two hours from the city and gave us a very happy greeting. It was indeed a delight to be so heartily welcomed, and a greater delight still to be again at this post of duty in the center of this great province.[22]

The Hubbards were especially happy to see Henry and little Jean again and welcomed Mary to the missionary family. Earlier in the summer the two oldest Hubbard boys, Ray and Crescens, had returned to America for their schooling, but three more children had been born since Henry had left Sivas – Hugh Wells in 1887, Mary in 1890, and Theodore Horace just a few months before the Perrys' arrival. All the children were delighted to have Jean to play with. Albert wrote his sister-in-law, "Mrs. Perry, I think, will be quite an addition to our missionary force. Mr. Perry does make mistakes sometimes, but in affairs of this kind he seems to exercise excellent judgment."[23]

Besides the growth in the Hubbard family, there had been other changes in Sivas since Henry and Jean left in 1886. Mary Brewer had come to Sivas, quickly learned Armenian, and was an excellent evangelist among the women. In November 1886, H.M. Jewett arrived in Sivas to open a U.S. Consul there. Jewett was born in Tocat of missionary parents. After five years in Sivas, he resigned and was replaced by his brother, Dr. Milo Jewett, who had been born in Sivas in 1857. Milo Jewett had received his M.D. from Harvard Medical School and practiced medicine for several years before becoming superintendent of the Danvers Insane Asylum in Boston. He served as superintendent for ten years and during that time published a book on *Sleep and Dreaming*. When Milo's brother resigned his consular post in Sivas, Milo applied for the post. After being accepted, he left his medical position and went to Turkey, arriving in March 1892.[24] Emma Hubbard wrote her sister Hattie, "He seems like a very pleasant young man. He is a doctor and was a physician of the Danvers Lunatic Asylum. A fine preparation for life in this country, was it not? I only wish he had brought a wife with him."[25] Wife or not, Milo Jewett was an earnest Christian with a heart for the sick and suffering. He would become fast friends with both the Perrys and the Hubbards.

By the end of October, the Perrys were in their own home in Sivas, but there was still much work to be done. For one thing, when it rained, the roof leaked – one rainy Sunday Mary stayed home from church to care for the buckets placed throughout the house. And there were still boxes to be unpacked, rooms to settle, curtains to put up. Henry had to refresh his Turkish, and Mary began learning Armenian. Since Mary could not speak the language, Henry helped out more in the kitchen and throughout the house to give instructions to the cook and workers. Henry was again appointed station Treasurer, and the accounts had not been settled since April. Many of the school facilities had fallen into disrepair, and Henry wondered if he should spend the $180 his mother had left for missionary purposes on the school buildings. With all the growing work about him, Henry rejoiced to again be at Sivas. Jean too seemed happy and healthy in Turkey. Henry gave her school lessons while Mary adjusted to the language and life of Sivas. As 1892, grew to a close, Henry prayed for "God's manifestation of Himself in this work in the Turkish Empire."[26] Little could he have imagined what the coming years held in store.

---

[1] *Diary*, June 8-9, 1886. Henry was later told rheumatism was common on the iron ship, because the iron "sweats" and makes everything damp in warm weather.

[2] 1923 note added to *Diary* after July 5, 1886.

[3] H.S. Perry to Rev. N.G. Clark, Masonville, New York, February 20, 1888, ABC 16.9.3, Vol. 15, No. 358.

[4] *Diary*, September 19, 1888.

[5] *Diary*, January 1888. The opening pages of the 1888 diary seem to have been a summary later written by H.T. Perry in the 1920's. The "anxious seat" or "mourners' bench" was the area at the front of the church where people responding to the altar call or gospel presentation went. Seekers or inquirers could here pray and meet with spiritual leaders. The practice of the "anxious seat" developed in the early nineteenth century out of the camp meetings of the Southern frontier and the practices of evangelist C.G. Finney.

[6] *Diary*, September 3, 1888.

[7] Notes at end of 1887 *Diary*, added in 1920's.

[8] The Chautauqua Institution was established in 1874 near Lake Chautauqua, New York, as a center for education, religion, and the arts. The founders, John Hugh Vincent and Lewis Miller, were Methodists who first established the meetings to better train Sunday School teachers. Soon the programs expanded to become a series of programs emphasizing life-long education and learning. "Chautauqua" meetings were organized throughout the country to enrich the education and culture of middle-class Americans. In 1878 the Chautauqua Literary and Scientific Circle (CLSC) was begun. A system of guided readings in the classics of literature and science, the CLSC was originally designed as a 4-year program of reading for those who had not attended college. Soon, however, ministers, lawyers, and doctors were participating in the program. Theodore Morrison. *Chautauqua*. University of Chicago Press, 1974, 12-21, 53-57.

[9] *Diary*, July 2, 1887.

[10] *Dairy*, January 12, 1891.

[11] *Diary*, May 6, 1888; April 13, 1888.

[12] Summary introduction written in 1928 for *Diary*, 1888.

[13] The Jubilee Singers were a group of young black singers, including two former slaves, who in 1871 traveled the country to raise money for Fisk University in Nashville, Tennessee. Fisk had been established in 1866 by the American Missionary Association to help newly freed blacks become educated citizens and Christians. The fund-raising concerts of the Jubilee Singers not only helped the financially struggling university, but acquainted many white audiences with the power of the Negro spiritual. It was through the Jubilee Singers that songs like "Swing Low, Sweet Chariot" and "This Little Light of Mine" became part of American culture.

[14] *Diary*, January 25, 1892.

[15] *Diary, 1891*, Summary introduction written in 1928; "Miss Mary Perry Dies at Ashfield," *Greenfield, Mss. Daily Recorder-Gazette*, January 15, 1935; Herbert R. Swanson correspondence with Diana Severance, February 16, 2000. Mr. Swanson kindly found information on Mary Hartwell in the Eakin family Papers at the Payap University Archives, Chiang Mai, Thailand. Mary Hartwell went to Siam ten years after the more famous Mary Langdon had been a tutor to the King of Siam's children (which inspired the musical play and film "The King and I"). The same king continued on the throne of Siam while Mary Hartwell was there.

[16] *Diary*, December 9, 1891.

[17] *Diary*, July 8, 1892; "Brookes, James Hall (1830-1897)," *Dictionary of Christianity in America*, 191.

[18] Throughout much of the seventeenth through nineteenth centuries in America, postmillennialism was the predominant eschatological perspective. Under this belief, the church would continue to improve and expand until a millennial age would be ushered in on the earth, after which Christ would return. Under this optimistic view, the United States and the Christian religion predominant there was to have a major role in expanding Christianity throughout the world. Many of the early leaders of the nineteenth century Protestant missionary movement were postmillennialists. After the Civil War, the optimism of the postmillennialists waned, and the premillennialists gained prominence. Under this view, there would be a series of physical, political, and religious catastrophes upon the earth that would end with Christ's Second Coming, after which He would usher in a millennial kingdom, or a thousand-year reign.

[19] *Diary*, July 10, 1892.

[20] Cholera was endemic to India and Asia, and in 1891, a serious outbreak of the disease was spread from India to Europe by pilgrims returning from Mecca. The outbreak was especially severe in European Russia, and it was during this outbreak that composer Peter Ilich Tschaikovsky died of the disease. "Cholera," *Encyclopedia Britannica*, 1958 ed.

[21] Born in Turkey, Fredrick Davis Greene was a missionary in Van for four years before ill health required his return to America. After the 1895-1896 Armenian massacres, he wrote *Armenian Massacres or the Sword of Mohammed*, giving a "full account of the Turkish people, their history, government, manners, customs, and strange religious beliefs."

[22] H.T. Perry to Rev. Judson Smith, Sivas, Turkey, November 4th, 1892, ABC 16.9.3, Vol. 25, Part 2, No. 392. Rev. Judson Smith served as foreign secretary to the American Board from 1884-1906. Prior to his service with the Board, he was professor of ecclesiastical history at Oberlin Theological Seminary. *They Lived Their Faith*, 272-273.

[23] Albert Hubbard to Hattie and Horace [Pond], Sivas, November 26, 1892. Letter in possession of Araxi Palmer.

[24] U.S. State Department Archives: RG59, Stack 250, Row 19 Compt.29, Shelf 1 – Box 1462, Ref. 123J55.

[25] *Hubbards in Sivas*, 209.

[26] *Diary*, November 20, 1892.

8
CRAFTY COUNSEL
(1893-1894)

"For behold, Your enemies make a tumult;
And those who hate you have lifted up their head.
They have taken crafty counsel against Your people,
And consulted together against Your sheltered ones.
They have said, 'Come and let us cut them off from being a na-
tion...'"
(Psalm 83:2-5)

After a January journey to Tocat, Henry returned to Sivas to face a number of emergencies. A stray street dog bit him in early February; the bite flared up, and the doctor ordered him pretty much off of his feet. On March 3, an earthquake shook the house around 2 a.m. The house quivered, and the closet door in Henry's room swung back and forth. The noise woke Neshan, the Perrys' faithful servant. He thought someone was fooling around with the knob on his door, and he went all through the house looking for the intruder, but found no one!

More serious than any of these occurrences were the persistent rumors and evidence of political troubles brewing. When Britain and Europe no longer actively pressed Turkey for governmental reforms, some Armenians began to try to promote disturbances to provoke European intervention. Some Russian Armenians systematically began to organize committees in towns throughout the Armenian *vilayet*s, which in some areas became a kind of shadow government. Such was the case at Marsovan and Amasia, where two Russian Armenians, Shimavan and Harautune Thoumaian, organized a committee to arouse the resident Armenians. They used threats and violence to assert their control. The committee forbade the Armenians from going to the government with complaints, and those Armenians who did so were often killed. In August 1893, a shoemaker at Marsovan who told the government about the committee was murdered in open daylight. He was the eighth or ninth person in Marsovan killed in this way. The *Vali* began arresting many leading Armenians to try to get at the root of the problem, promising to release the prisoners if the Russian refugees leading the committee were brought to him and identified. The Turks complained of the stoppage of business because of the large number of Armenian shopkeepers imprisoned.[1]

On January 2, 1893, Simon Dzeroonian, an American Bible Society colporteur from Sivas, stopped for the night at Charkushia, a village with only a few evangelical Christians. For two nights Simon met with about fifteen people for prayer meeting. The Turkish officials decided that there must be some treason being plotted in the meetings and arrested the colporteur and all those attending the meetings.

A few days later, on January 6, placards were posted throughout the provinces of Sivas and Angora appealing to both Armenians and Moslems to rise up against the bribery of officials, the disappearance of law, and the fall of justice. The colporteur and the Christians at the prayer meeting were held responsible for the placards and brought to Sivas, where they remained in prison. The Sivas prison was soon filled with hundreds of prisoners accused of fomenting rebellion and treason against the government. Most of the prisoners were Armenians, though there were some Moslems imprisoned as well. These blamed the Christians for bringing such trouble upon them. Marderos Kalousdian, the Protestant preacher at Gemerek, was among the prisoners.[2]

Because of his fluency in Turkish, Henry often visited the *Vali* in Sivas and pled for the Christians' release. He and Albert visited the prisoners, encouraged them, and brought them food. One day Henry brought the colporteur's boys with him to the prison so they could bring food to their father and see him. When the boys saw their father in jail, they began to cry, and Simon fell to the ground overcome with weakness and sorrow. Through Henry's intercession, the Vali promised to pardon Simon and give him his freedom.[3]

The case of two fellow-prisoners of the Sivas colporteur, Professors Thoumaian and Kayayan of the American College at Marsovan, gained international attention. When the incendiary placards appeared against the government, Khosanu Pasha, chief gendarme at Marsovan, charged the American College with their authorship. Since Marsovan College had a cyclostyle like the placards were printed on, the pasha accused the college of seditious activity. Thoumaian was also the name of the Russian leader of the Armenian committee in Marsovan, making it easier to associate Professor Thoumaian with the seditious placards. The Pasha was not a particularly noble individual, however. He was an ex-brigand who had been found guilty of murder by a Turkish court before he was given his position in Sivas.

On February 1, the building being erected for a girls' school in Marsovan was burned to the ground. The Turks blamed the college officials, saying they were trying to incite the Armenians to revolt or they wanted to cover up that they had been hiding arms and ammunition in the buildings. These were the charges the Turks sent to Constantinople. An order soon came from Constantinople to close down the Marsovan College. Henry was in Divrik at the time, and the *Vali* called for him to return and go to Marsovan to help deal with the problem. Consul Jewett refused to close the American College. Representatives from the U.S. Legation in Constantinople and the Turkish Foreign office came to investigate the American college's role in Marsovan's political opposition to the sultan. When the Turkish government investigated the Pasha's charges, they acquitted the college of any involvement in the placard affair and proved that the Pasha himself had been the instigator. Unrest continued throughout the province, however. At the end of February, someone set fire to the Protestant chapel in Sivas with kerosene and pine pitch, but the fire was discovered and extinguished without too much damage.

In spite of the clearance of Marsovan College in any rebellion, Professors Thoumaian and Kayayan remained not only in prison, but also in chains. Gemerk's pastor, Marderos Kalousdian, had been pardoned along with Simon the colporteur, but was not released. He refused to sign a paper affirming what he thought were false charges against Professor Thoumaian and refused to pay a bribe. With their necks and hands in chains, the Christian prisoners were taken from Sivas to prison in Angora. The petty officials treated them cruelly along the way.

The Turkish government claimed to have no doubt about the guilt of the Marsovan professors. The substance of their case was that when visiting Gemerek and Bookhan one and a half years ago, the two exhorted their Armenian friends to begin arming themselves to resist the government. Later, an ostensible photographer representing a "London Society" came to organize a resistance committee in the villages. In January the seditious placards came to the Armenians in the village under a fictitious name that the *Vali* said he knew was the seal of Professor Thoumaian. Henry could never find any evidence how the Vali knew this. Nor was there any evidence that the Professors were members of any resistance organization. Though Henry believed the men might have been indiscreet in their speech, he could not find any evidence of the seditious activity of which they had been accused. He began to think the vehemence with which the *Vali* asserted his claims testified to the weakness of his case, and that the evidence against the two men was circumstantial or manufactured. It was difficult in Turkey to find out the facts.[4] As a Frenchmen once wrote, "In Turkey, both facts and women are veiled."

At their trial the two Christian Armenians had no opportunity to provide an alibi or complain of the tortures they received in prison. As evidence of Professor Thoumaian's seditious intent, the Turks cited a sermon he had preached on the text, "Awake! thou that sleepest," saying he was arousing the people to rebellion. The two Marsovan professors were condemned to death. The Gemerek pastor was sentenced to fifteen years in prison.

The story of the two Marsovan professors was followed attentively by the U.S., German, and British governments. Ambassadors of all three countries used their influence to secure the professors' release. The Earl of Rosebury, British Secretary of State for Foreign Affairs, saw the issue as one of religious liberty. He contended that when the Turkish government arrested and condemned teachers, preachers, and Christians for sedition against the government without any proof, Turkey was not fulfilling its treaty obligations concerning the religious liberty of all its subjects. Because of international pressure, Turkey agreed to release the two professors, but they were exiled from the country. They went to England, where the House of Commons and many British leaders became more concerned about Turkey's anti-Christian policies.[5] These policies had a long history and would impact future missionary work in Turkey.

Henry was one of approximately 175 ABCFM missionaries in Turkey. By the last quarter of the nineteenth century, American missionary activities in Turkey began to bear fruit. Biblical Protestantism had been introduced to a strong and growing Armenian constituency. Thousands of Armenian Christian children were attending a vast network of schools that the missionaries had founded. The American Board of Commissioners of Foreign Missions (ABCFM) had planted scores of churches throughout the six eastern *vilayets*. The circuit riding preaching of Perry and the other missionaries was giving way to church services conducted by local native pastors, many of whom had been trained in the ABCFM theological seminary at Marash where Perry had taught. Hospitals, such as the one at Marsovan, also reached out to help the sick in the community.

But even as the educational and spiritual life of Protestant Armenians improved significantly, the lot of *all* Armenians in Turkey had steadily deteriorated under the oppressive misrule of the corrupt and ruthless Turkish sultans. The last of these, Abdul Hamid II (1842-1918), had come to power in 1876. His continuous persecution of the Armenian minority fueled growing concern among European nations over what came to be called the "Armenian Question," namely, "What should European nations do to stop the mistreatment of Turkey's Armenian Christian minority?"[6] The Ottoman Empire had steadily lost territory through a series of external wars and internal revolts. Territorial decline was accompanied by economic decline. Under the sultan's lavish court spending, the Empire had developed the habit of regularly defaulting on loans advanced by European individuals and government. The Empire was unable to compete with the capitalistic industrial systems of the west.

At the same time, the sultan was ambivalent towards modernization and reform. By the outbreak of World War I in 1914, although European nations had modernized, Constantinople remained a medieval city, largely due to the whims of Sultan Abdul Hamid II. As long as he remained on the throne, he prohibited the introduction of electric lights or the telephone. He had heard that streetcars and electricity were associated with a "dynamo," and he believed it had something to do with dynamite, the archenemy of rulers. Likewise, the sultan prohibited the introduction of rubber tires because once a bomb had been thrown from a carriage fitted with them, causing him to see a dangerous relationship between bombs and rubber tires.[7] Yet, he did encourage large-scale public works to develop roads, railroad and telegraph lines.

The Ottoman Empire's decline coincided with a rising spirit of cultural and political awareness among the sultan's subject peoples. Encouraged into war by some of the European powers, most of the Balkan provinces had gained independence from Ottoman rule. However, inside the empire, the Armenian and other Christian minorities continued to face persecution. When news of such grievances reached European nations, the Europeans promptly protested to the Sublime Porte, greatly annoying the sultan.

Over the centuries, there were many crosscurrents in the ebb and flow of the sultan's relationship with his Armenians. But in the closing years of the nineteenth century, three major factors accounted for the crescendo of Turkish oppression of Armenians: (l) From its inception, the Ottoman Empire was an Islamic theocracy ideologically hostile to Christianity; (2) With a million Armenians residing across the border in Russia, the sultan feared that in the event of another war, his own Armenian subjects would defect to Russia, causing a further loss of territory; and (3) The appearance of a small group of Armenian revolutionists operating throughout central Turkey, accompanied by the defensive use of firearms by Armenian peasants trying to protect themselves from marauding bands of Kurds, Circassians, and Turks in the eastern provinces, gave the sultan an excuse to crush swiftly and brutally tens of thousands of innocent Armenians along with the guilty. These three factors accounting for growing persecution of Armenians in Turkey warrant closer scrutiny to better understand the trying times that Perry faced.

The first factor causing Turkey's government to persecute the Armenians was that *the Ottoman Empire, from its inception, was an Islamic theocracy ideologically hostile to Christianity.* The sultan was not only the head of state, but also the religious leader of the empire. With the title of Caliph (meaning "successor to Mohammed"), the sultan was duty-bound to uphold the Islamic religious law [Ş*eriat* or *Sharia*], which was structured around the Koran.

The *sharia* declared the religious and social superiority of Moslems over peoples of all other religions. Under *sharia*, those who refused to convert to Islam were to be killed. However, since the Ottoman conquerors were at first a minority in their own empire, they followed a *dhimmi* system. The *ahl al-dhimmi* were a "protected people," whose lives were spared, though they were viewed by their Moslem overlords as *gaiour* (cattle) and their lives were restricted. The lives of the *dhimmi*, who included Jews and Christians, were spared only if they paid ransom money or a special tax. If they refused or could not pay the tax, the Moslems had the rights of *jihad* and could kill them, force their conversion to Islam, or enslave them. The *dhimmi* could only exercise their religion in private and had to wear special clothing to show their inferior status to the Moslems. The *kharaj* was the special tax on non-Moslems for their right to practice their religion.

The *sharat* was collected from Armenians for the "privilege" of being allowed to wear a Christian headband. The *dhimmis* had no legal protection in the Ottoman legal system. Christian testimony was not recognized, especially against a Moslem.[8] The *sharia* also imposed political duties on the sultan-Caliph to carry out its precepts while ruling the country, overseeing the administrative branches of government, and the court system.[9] Specific provisions of the Koran provided important clues to the mind-set of the ruling Turkish sultans, the army, the paramilitary forces and bureaucratic officials concerning how to treat their non-Islamic vassals. The Koran encouraged its followers to wage holy war[10] *(jihad)* against non-Moslems and quoted Mohammed as commanding Moslems to battle

> against the non-believers and to be severe unto them.[11] ... And when the months wherein ye are not allowed to attack them shall be past, kill the idolaters wheresoever ye shall find them, and take them prisoners, and besiege them, and lay wait for them in every convenient place.[12]

Other Koran provisions described with prophetic accuracy the Ottoman Turks' brutal persecution of their Armenian minority:

> When ye encounter the unbelievers, strike off their heads, until ye have made a great slaughter among them;[13] Ye are also forbidden to take to wife free women who are married, except those women whom your right hand shall possess as slaves.[14]

In the last half of the nineteenth century, England, France, and Russia, nations with large Christian populations, exerted varying degrees of diplomatic pressure on the sultan to stop mistreating his minorities. In February 1856, to persuade its European allies to allow Turkey to participate in the peace conference after the Crimean War against Russia, a "Christian" power, Sultan Medjid (1839-1861) issued the *Hatti Humayoun*. One authority described the *Hatti Humayoun* as "the most notable proclamation ever issued by a Moslem ruler."[15] Had its provisions been assiduously implemented, it would have ushered in highly significant reforms. For example, it provided that in courts of law, testimony of Christian and Moslem witnesses would be given equal weight; and that suits between Moslems and non-Moslems were to be tried before "mixed tribunals." Turkey did participate in the Congress of Paris after the Crimean War, and the Peace Treaty signed March 30, 1856 included the provisions of the *Hatti Sherif,* an earlier decree by which sultan Abdul Medjid ostensibly extended to the "non-Mussulman" the same protections and access to justice enjoyed by Moslems. However, at the very time of the Treaty of Paris, the enforcement of these rights was virtually nullified by a provision that European powers could not use the treaty as an excuse to intervene between the sultan and his subjects.

In 1861, Abdul Medjid died and his brother, Abdul Aziz, began his reign as sultan (1861-1876). Unfortunately, promises of reform were little more than window dressing, and the old discriminatory system continued in the rural provinces as well as in urban areas.[16] British Consul J.G. Taylor, reporting from Erzerum in 1869, observed that the Armenians throughout the eastern provinces complained bitterly against the sultan's rule "with ample cause" due to the "wretched system of Turkish provincial administration, the unequal imposition of taxes, scandalous methods of levying them, ... persistent denial or miscarriage of justice, and practical disavowal of the Christians' claims to be treated with the same consideration and respect as their equals among the Muslims."[17] Twenty years later, unequal justice before the courts was still a cornerstone of Turkish law. In 1881, Mr. Chermside, British Vice-Consul at Sivas, wrote that though Christian testimony was theoretically accepted in the courts, tradition, sympathy, and education prejudiced the officials against it.[18]

The Vice-Consul at Erzerum, Mr. Everett, had a similar evaluation: "The first consideration of the administration of justice is the amount of money that can be extorted from an individual, and the second is his creed. The only doubt as to the morality of the Turkish magistrates appears to be whether they are more corrupt than fanatical, or more fanatical than corrupt."[19] Turkish denial of equal justice in the courts to Armenian Christians was a policy clearly based on religious discrimination. If a Muslim abandoned Islam, he immediately lost his preferential standing in the courts, as well as his exemption from many taxes, and other privileges. In addition, he was subject to arrest and imprisonment as a criminal. Apostasy from Islam was treason to the sultan. Religious superiority over Christians was a Moslem principle firmly imbedded in Turkish rule.

Many Turks came to believe the American missionary schools and their western education would destroy the Islamic Turkish nation. One patriotic Turkish official in one of the large eastern provinces asserted that

The progress in education and general intelligence of the Armenians and other Christians in the interior of our country is of the gravest import to us. Our Mohammedan peasantry know nothing, and they are learning nothing. If the present condition is allowed to continue, in twenty years Christian peasants will be their rulers. I consider it my mission to remedy this evil by informing these simple-minded Muslims of their danger and arousing them to escape it. Wherever I go I harangue the Muslims on their danger of becoming servants of the Christians and the need of waking up to progress themselves.[20]

Many Turkish leaders believed that if Turkey was to maintain its greatness, uniformity of religion had to be maintained and the Christian sects eliminated. Because of this, numerous administrative measures were issued to suppress education among the Christians. Books were censored, schools were closed, and permits for schools were denied. Schools were forbidden to use books imported from abroad, and Turkey's officials generally prevented the printing of books above the elementary grade level.

The second factor causing the Turkish government to persecute Armenians was that with *a million Armenians residing across the border in Russia, the sultan feared that if war again should break out between the two countries (which happened with the advent of World War I), his own Armenian subjects would defect to Russia, causing a further loss of territory.*[21] Russia's successes in the periodic nineteenth century wars arising from boundary disputes had steadily moved its frontier to the west.[22] By the 1890s there were an estimated million or more Armenians living on the Russian side of the boundary and nearly two million Armenians living on the Turkish side.[23] Since the ancient Armenian homelands lay on both sides of the frontier, Armenians would suffer regardless of who might win in a Russo-Turkish conflict.[24]

As far back as the mid-1870s there had been growing resentment of Bulgarian Christians against Turkish Moslem rule, a situation that Russia encouraged and exploited politically. In 1877, Russia declared war on the Ottoman Empire, claiming, among other reasons, that she was protecting the Bulgarian Christians against Turkish tyranny. As the war raged on Turkey's eastern front against Russia, the sultan used the conflict as a cover under which the plundering Kurds accelerated persecution of the unarmed minority of Armenian civilians living in the war zone. During the early stages of the war, Armenian deputies complained to the Ottoman Parliament that even as Armenian soldiers were defending the Ottoman fatherland in battle, thousands of unarmed civilian Armenians were being attacked and killed by fully armed Kurds supported by regular and irregular Turkish troops.

The Armenian deputies, joined by Greek and even Turkish legislators, noted that provincial governors (*valis*) and local leaders (*mutesarrifs*) aided the Kurds by ignoring complaints against them. If an offending Kurd was arrested, upon payment of a bribe, he was set free. It was also charged that the central government of the sultan had impliedly assented to the Kurdish killing of the Armenians by failing to enforce the laws or take disciplinary action against the killers. The sultan's response was to dismiss the legislature. Only later did the Armenian deputies learn the sultan's real reason for tolerating the pillaging Kurds: they would be needed to repress the Armenians in event they should rise up in the eastern *vilayets*.[25] This was not the last time that war would be used as a cover for massacre.

In the 1878 Treaty of Berlin following the Russo-Turkish war, article 61 had made the Armenian Question a matter of international concern.[26] It had mandated that the Sublime Porte reform its treatment of the Armenians and make known to the European powers its progress in the reforms. All lands covered by the treaty, the new Balkan nations as well as the entire Ottoman Empire, were to have *complete religious liberty*. A European Commission was created to oversee the sultan's establishment of various administrative reforms in specified areas of the Ottoman Empire, including all districts inhabited by Armenians. Sadly, the glowing plans and promises for the Armenians in the Treaty of Berlin remained simply that – plans and promises.

The sultan organized, armed, and directed Kurds and Circassians to increase their raiding, plundering and killing of Armenians in the eastern *vilayets*, particularly in the areas that Russia had ceded back to Turkey under the Treaty of Berlin. Kurdish cavalry troops, *Hamidieh* Regiments, were to specifically deal with any Armenian uprising. In 1892, a British military attaché reported that thirty-seven regiments of five hundred men each had been organized and thirteen were in the process of formation. Trained by regular army officers and ostensibly organized to protect the Russian frontier, the *Hamidieh* pillaged and plundered at will.[27] Although the European powers increased the number of consulates in the eastern provinces to oversee the reforms more effectively, all they could do was report the increasing havoc wrought by the Kurdish tribesmen.[28] In 1880, the British Consul had reported from Van that there were widespread Kurdish robberies of

Armenians, encouraged by the Ottoman government which had "given up" any attempt to punish the guilty. In European capitals, the ministries were flooded with similar reports of "ill-treatment," "oppression," and "killings;" but they took no action. Oppressed by intolerable land laws and crushed by the weight of taxes, many Armenians simply left the eastern *vilayets*; Kurds and Turks who were exempt from such despotic laws and taxes quickly replaced them.[29]

The third factor causing the sultan and Turkish governing officials to increase persecution of all Armenians, particularly after the Treaty of Berlin, was *the appearance of a small group of Armenian revolutionsts*. By 1881, the European powers had become obsessed with the race to divide and colonize Africa, and were giving less attention to the Armenian Question. But the activists envisioned a possible precedent for an Armenian state in the Treaty's recognition of complete autonomy in Bulgaria and total independence from Ottoman rule for Serbia and Montenegro. In the new European Commission's focus on equal rights for Armenians, the activists believed a new day of freedom had dawned, perhaps even the beginning of a Republic of Armenia.

Three Armenian political movements arose in Turkey in the last half of the nineteenth century: (1) The *Armenakan Party*, founded in Van in 1885, did not seek independence, but greater economic and political equality for Turkish Armenians; (2) the *Hunchakian Revoutionary Party*, organized in Geneva in 1887 by seven Russian Armenians, sought independence for Turkish Armenia; and (3) the Armenian Revolutionary Federation, or *Dashnaktsutiun*, organized in Tiflis in 1890, also sought greater economic and political freedom for Armenians.[30] It is noteworthy that the Hunchakian and Dashnaktsutiun parties were formed, not by Turkish Armenians, but largely as the result of outside Russian influence.[31] Many of the revolutionary leaders had been trained in the universities of Paris and Geneva.

The European powers' growing pressure upon the sultan to expedite "reforms" by completely equalizing the religious and political rights of Moslems and Christians spurred some Armenian activists to consider using force. The Hunchakian's rationale was simple: Greek, Serb, and Bulgarian nationalistic movements had attracted sufficient European sympathy and support to bring about independence. Why couldn't the Armenians do the same? Such lofty plans were doomed by two fatal miscalculations: (1) It was erroneously assumed that Europe would ascribe the same strategic, military, and diplomatic importance to the six eastern Armenian *vilayets* of Turkey as they had to Greece, the Balkans, and Bulgaria, all of which were contiguous to Europe; and (2) During the 1890s, both Russia and the Western European powers had separately concluded that their respective national interests were best advanced by maintaining the territorial status quo of the Ottoman empire. Balance-of-power criteria were a part of these decisions. The Russian Cabinet of Lobanov-Rostovsky had little interest in the plight of Ottoman Armenians, although it was very much interested in the land of Turkish Armenia *without* its Armenian occupants.[32] Russia also feared that its million Armenian citizens could defect to a new independent Armenia just across the border, or worse yet, revolt and annex the Russian land where they resided to a new Armenian state.[33]

In the West, England was already committed by the Cyprus Convention and Treaty of Berlin to preserve Turkish territorial integrity. In exchange, the British Admiralty had the valuable right to occupy Cyprus as a naval base, which commanded both the Dardenelles and Suez. The Government now had to balance the concession of Cyprus by the sultan against a few persistent revolutionary complaints that he was not protecting his Armenians from Kurdish raids. England took the path of expedience; it would do no more than apply periodic pressure on the sultan to institute the "reforms" he had promised. Even with its Christian constituencies crying out against Turkish oppression of Armenians, the British government saw no diplomatic advantage in risking war to aid and abet a few vocal rebels agitating for Armenian independence. More importantly, it served England's national interest to avoid antagonizing a sultan who was powerful enough to control the Dardanelles and the Bosphorus. He might some day be of help in keeping Russian naval forces bottled up in the Black Sea, an additional protection for England's Suez trade route. In England's view, an independent Armenian state might also tip the balance-of-power toward Russia, which already had a large Armenian population.

As provocations and injustices against the Armenians continued, zealots began to see armed conflict as a necessary option. Armenians continued to be victimized by the old abuses: unjust treatment in the courts, Turkish use of extortion and physical violence in the collection of taxes, and the old *Kishlak* system which gave the Kurds the right to quarter themselves and their flocks in the Armenian villages, usually at the expense of the Armenians.[34]

The Armenian revolutionaries did not lack issues to incite popular anger against the growing violence of the marauding Kurds in the eastern *vilayets*. Yet, the zeal of the activists for revolt was never shared by the vast majority of Armenians, whose loyalty to the government had won them the praise of generations of sultans as the "faithful community."[35] Their leaders preferred to peacefully petition the government to defend them against the threat of corrupt officials or marauding tribes who endangered their lives and property. Perhaps the most remarkable characteristic of the Armenian peoples in the period between the Treaty of Berlin and the early twentieth century, was their loyalty to Turkish rule. The eminent historian, Arnold Toynbee, then of the British Foreign Office wrote:

> The Armenians, during the centuries they have been under Turkish rule, have been characterized by the extraordinary patience with which they have borne that rule, and by their unrequited fidelity to the Turkish government. Indeed, they have long ago earned in Turkey the name of the "Loyal Race". [36]

As events unfolded, the ironic outcome of the small Armenian independence movement was that it gave the sultan and government officials convenient cover and excuse to persecute, and attempt to liquidate, all Armenians.

In spite of the growing political turmoil, Henry and the other missionaries remained non-political. They saw their mission as a spiritual mission to souls, minds, and hearts, not a political mission to change the Turkish government. Yet, they had to work within the framework of the Turkish government to accomplish their spiritual goals. Growing restrictions on the Christian schools complicated the missionaries' work.[37]

The *Hatti Humayoun* of 1856 had authorized the Christians to open schools on the condition that the method of instruction and choice of teachers be submitted to Ottoman authorities. Schools were an important part of almost every mission station the ABCFM had established in Turkey. They had raised the standard of education throughout the land and encouraged the native populations to expand their educational programs. The Turks, however, had become suspicious of the American schools. Many of the Bulgarian revolutionists had trained at Robert College and the missionary schools. The missionary schools and colleges had made many young people increasingly aware of the social equality and political freedom enjoyed in American and the more advanced European countries. The Turks began to fear the American schools were a threat to Turkish institutions. In an 1892 edict no new schools were allowed to open, and all previously established schools had to ask for continuance permits. Sale of real estate to Christians was not allowed unless they agreed not to use the property for school purposes. The edict also prohibited government officers from employing anyone who had graduated from any school other than a government school. This effectively closed a job in government service to graduates of a Christian college.[38]

In spite of these restrictions, Henry was able to expand the Sivas Normal School building, and he did so at the suggestion of the *Vali* in Sivas! The school definitely needed a larger building, but no new permits for school buildings were being issued. In order to get rid of a crook in the street near the school, the government planned to widen the street, making it eight meters broad. This required taking 3.5 meters from the Sivas School even as other houses on the street were being torn down, Henry went to speak to the *Vali* about the matter, describing how the school would be useless if the wall had to be moved that distance. The *Vali* cheerfully suggested that the missionaries simply build the building expanding back from the street into the yard and adding an additional story. The *Vali* gave his word that this would be allowed without an official written permit! All the American missionaries and Consul Jewett realized the wonderful opportunity given them to rebuild the school. This was obviously an opportunity from the Lord. Henry made plans to begin the rebuilding at once, drawing on his personal funds until the ABCFM could approve the project. High officials of the city tried to prevent the rebuilding, but the *Vali* kept his word and allowed the Normal School to be rebuilt. Henry carried on all the negotiations with the government and oversaw the entire construction, sometimes with as many as thirty workers on the project. Henry seemed to live at the building site, insuring that the work be completed as speedily as possible.

The building was 37 x 30 feet upon a basement of cut stone fronting the widened street. The basement was two feet higher than the previous one and designed to be used for the industrial department. Here the boys could learn carpentry and blacksmithing skills and support themselves at the boarding school. Two stories for schoolrooms were built above the basement.[39]

In September Emma Hubbard and her six children left for the United States. Ray and Luke were already in school there, but it was time to place the next oldest children in school as well. Because of the political uncertainty in the country, Albert planned to stay in Turkey until the following spring, not wanting to leave the Perrys alone to face any major problems that might arise. In a letter to Reverend Smith in Boston, Mary Perry described the 1893 year drawing to a close:

> There have been many weeks, of suspense during the past twelve months, - such suspense as comes to those who, having been suddenly cast by the waves of circumstances upon a volcanic shore, live in momentary expectation of <u>another eruption,</u> but know not <u>just where</u> the pent up fires will burst forth. We hope that the year to come, may be more quiet.[40]

Before Albert Hubbard left in the spring, Henry spent almost two months touring the outstations, though the weather was at its coldest. During the January Week of Prayer, he stayed in Gürün, one of the most pleasant of all the villages and having the most mature of the congregations.[41] The town itself was "in a small canyon – a winding belt of orchards and gardens, between dry barren cliffs, extending east toward the Euphrates basin. Through the oasis, and supplying its irrigation, flows a beautiful stream of clear water well supplied with fish." Henry thought highly of Gürün's Pastor Chevron and his wife. The pastor, educated at Harpoot, was:

> enthusiastic in his work, able to organize and push, and is a practical and vigorous preacher. His congregations are always full, from which we may infer that his sermons provide what the people need...he has a faithful wife, a graduate of Harpoot College, who is an excellent helpmeet for him. She is doing work among the women and girls of his congregation, teaching her S. School class and counseling them in an affectionate and intelligent manner.[42]

The pastor arranged four meetings a day for Henry, and he rejoiced at the number of young people attentive to the things of Christ.

Wherever he went, however, Henry found the cold intensified the hunger of the people: "Bread, bread, bread is the constant and disturbing cry."[43] Several years of poor harvests had produced the specter of famine throughout the land. Though the ABCFM's policy had encouraged native support of local pastors, churches, and schools, Henry recognized that the people were giving all they could from their impoverished circumstances. Since the ABCFM had been forced to cut back on its financing of schools and native workers in Turkey, Henry decided to support the pastor at Zara from his own salary.

Henry visited the villages in the wintertime because the villagers were not working in the fields and could be more attentive to the preaching of the Scripture. Travel could be hazardous, however. The winter of 1894-1895, was especially so. Mary wrote Dr. Judson Smith that on Henry and Miss Brewer's trip to Divrik, the severity of the snowstorm turned a three-day journey into five days:

> There was a driving snow in their faces, as they approached the summit – and when it was reached, the wind was so violent, that Miss Brewer was compelled to dismount, and crawl on her hands and knees, over the cliffs![44]

On an earlier occasion, Henry recounted traveling up a mountain in deep snow behind a muletrain of 100 mules loaded with grain. "Only one" slipped under the load and fell twenty feet down the steep banks. Henry found the Kurdish muleteers very interesting. In the midst of a "thousand difficulties," they seemed unmindful of their hard life or the harshness of the travel conditions.[45]

Traveling in snowstorms and all kinds of weather, Henry had long since learned to sleep in whatever accommodations could be found. On one trip to Divrik, Henry described riding on the back of a black mule:

> ...slowly...over the ridge through the scrub oak hills, to the long valley leading to the mountain which we crossed in a snow storm. Then came the night in the goat room. The numerous trains on the road during the day filled all the larger rooms in the khan, and ours was the one devoted to the servants and the goats. My head was so near them that they nibbled my hair....[46]

In between preaching tours, Henry had to arrange for a new roof for the double house of the Girls' School and his own house. For several years he had tried to repair the leaky zinc roof, but in February the roof cracked under the weight of the thawing snow, badly flooding the third story, where many of the girls slept. In spite of the ABCFM's policy of financial retrenchment, Henry had to request emergency expenses to repair the roof, at the same time completing work on the Normal School.

Albert had planned to leave Sivas for the United States in the spring, but on April 16th a cholera epidemic came to Sivas, which had not seen the disease for forty years. It took the city by surprise, and

Albert stayed to help the Perrys minister to the people during the crisis. *The Missionary Herald* summarized Albert's report of the epidemic:

> The outbreak of the epidemic occurred suddenly about the middle of April, and the people were wholly unprepared for its advent. During the last week of April there were from thirty to forty deaths daily, out of a population of about 43,000. None of the missionaries, except Mrs. Perry, had seen cases of cholera before, but they immediately prepared for service. Even the Normal School boys were instructed in the use of Dr. Cyrus Hamlin's "cholera remedies" and proved very serviceable.[47]

Many of the people in the city trustingly turned to the missionaries for help. Albert was even called to prescribe treatment for boys in the Gregorian Orphan Asylum. Because of Henry's fluency in Turkish, many Turks, as well as Armenians, appealed to him for help. The missionary houses almost became "open dispensaries," and for two months it seemed the missionaries' entire time was devoted to caring for the thousands of sick. At the height of the epidemic, there were 175 deaths a day. Mary Perry estimated 1500-2000 people died, but by mid-May the cholera seemed to be decreasing, with about ten deaths a day.

The people had been gripped by fear as they faced the quick and sudden death the cholera brought. The calm, patient care provided by the missionaries won widespread respect among the population. Many who had once thought of the missionaries only as "infidels" turned to them to save their lives. A daily prayer meeting sprang up among the Armenian women, attended by 300-400. As often was the case, physical suffering bore spiritual fruit. Throughout Sivas, especially among the Gregorian Armenians, there was an increased interest in the Gospel and the Bible's truths.

Once the cholera epidemic had passed, Albert Hubbard left for the United States. Though there were signs of political unrest, the Perrys would have to manage the Sivas station alone. Little could anyone have imagined the terror that would come to Sivas and Turkey in Albert's absence.

---

[1] *British Documents on Ottoman Armenians*, Vo. 3, 250-252, 270-272.
[2] "Constantinople Branch," *Evangelical Christendom*, Vol. 34, n.s., March 1, 1893, 92.

[3] Henry T. Perry to Rev. Judson Smith, March 6 & 18, 1893, ABC 16.9.3, Vol. 25, Part 2, Nos. 394-35; *Diary,* March 5, 12-14, 1893. One of the Armenians imprisoned for a time in Sivas whom Perry helped was the pastor from Marsovan, H.M. Knodjian. His account of his imprisonment and the massacres in Sivas and Ourfa are found in H.M. Knodjian. *The Eternal Struggle: a word picture of Armenia's fight for freedom.* Fresno: Republican Printing n.d. (http://www.archive.org/details/eternalstrugglew00knadiala).

[4] Henry T. Perry to Rev. Judson Smith, March 18, 1893; *Diary,* March 21, 1893, April 12, 1893, May 20, 1893.

[5] "Religious Persecution in Armenia," *Evangelical Christendom*, vol. 34, n.s., April 1, 1893, 127; "Relgious Persecution in Turkey," *Evangelical Christendom*, vol. 34, n.s., June 1, 1893, 191-192; "Religious Persecution in Armenia," *Evangelical Christendom*, vol. 34, n.s., August 1, 1893, 252-253; *Hubbards of Sivas*, 215-219. Pastor Kalousdian was sent to prison in Syria. Under pressure from the British, he was pardoned and released in 1895.

[6] Richard H. Hovannisian, "The Armenian Question, 1878-1923" in The Peoples' Tribunal. *A Crime of Silence: The Armenian Genocide.* Bath, England: Zed Books, Ltd., 1985, 12.

[7] H.G. Dwight. "Life in Constantinople," *The National Geographic Magazine*, Vol. 26, no. 6, December 1914, 521.

[8] Bat Y'or. *The Decline of Eastern Christianity under Islam: From Jihad to Dhimmitude.* Fairleigh Dickinson University Press, 1996; Vahakn N. Dadrian. *The History of the Armenian Genocide.* Providence: Berghahn Books, 1995, 5; "The Armenian Question, 1878-1923," *A Crime of Silence: The Armenian Genocide,* 12.

[9] *History of the Armenian Genocide,* 4.

[10] The traditional Muslim division of the world into the *dar al-harb* (House of War) and *dar al-Islam* (House of Islam), a world of "them" and "us," has not been repudiated in the current third millennium; rather this view is characteristic of many Islamic countries in the world today. Cf. Reuel Marc Gerecht, "Even in the House of Khatami, Americans Aren't Welcome," *Wall Street Journal,* February 24, 2000, A-18.Mr. Gerecht is a former Middle East specialist in the CIA's Directorate of Operations. Under the pseudonym Edward Shirley, he is the author of *Know Thy Enemy: A Spy's Journey into Revolutionary Iran.* Farrar, Straus & Giroux, 1997. The Moslem division of the world into *dar al-harb* and *dar al-Islam* was clearly stated by associates of the terrorists in the September 11, 2001 attacks on the United States.

[11] *Koran,* Ch. IX.73, as quoted in *History of Armenian Genocide,* 4.

[12] *Koran,* Chapter IX.5.

[13] *Koran,* Chapter XLVII.4.

[14] *Koran,* Chapter IV. 24.

[15] *Turkey and Armenian Atrocities,* 271.

[16] *Turkey and the Armenian Atrocities*, 296-297.

[17] Antranig Chalabian. *Armenia After the Coming of Islam*. Southfield, Michigan: 1999, 463; Manoug Somakian. *Empires in Conflict: Armenia and the Great Powers, 1895-1920*. New York: I.B.Tauris Pub., 1995, 13. Ottoman taxation was ruthless, oppressive, and discriminatory against the Armenians who were required to pay taxes for:

1. *Kharaj*	--	levied only on non-Muslims for the right to practice their own religion (Turks and Kurds were exempt from this tax).
2. *Surat*	--	War tax.
3. *Avariz*	--	Emergency tax, supposedly payable only in times of emergency, but actually it was collected every year.
4. *Djeib akchesi*	--	(pocket-money tax) collected for the sultan when he went to war.
5. *Tibn* [straw]	--	collected for feeding the horses of the pashas (generals).
6. *Ordu* [army]	--	collected when the pashas went to war.
7. *Sharaat*	--	collected for being allowed to wear a Christian head band. Turks and Kurds wearing turbans were tax-exempt.
8. *Shira*	--	levied for the right to drink or possess wine at home; collected from every Serb, Armenian, Greek, Bulgarian, Albanian, Assyrian, Jew, etc. whether he drank or not, whether he possessed it in his home or not (Muslims were exempted, since in theory Muslims abstained from alcohol).

"Tax farming" was one infamous method of collecting taxes which the Ottomans borrowed from ancient Rome. The sultan would sell to a local tax collector the privilege of collecting as much taxes as possible from the local peasants in exchange for a lump sum in advance. Cf. *Crime of Silence*, 12.

[18] *Blue Book*, Turkey, No.8 (1881), 57-110, quoted by M. Rolin Jaequemyns. *Armenia, the Armenians, and the Treaties*. London: John Heywood, 1881, 74-76.

[19] *Blue Book*, Turkey, No. 8 (1881) as quoted by M. Rolin-Jaequemyns, *Armenia, the Armenians, and the Treaties*, 74-76.

[20] Quoted in "Anti-Christian Legislation in Turkey," *Evangelical Christendom*, Vol. 34, n.s., September 1, 1893, 267.

[21] G.S. Graber. *Caravans to Oblivion: The Armenian Genocide, 1915*. New York: John Wiley & Sons, Inc., 1996, 58. These are population estimates as of the outbreak of the First World War in 1914. The numbers would be somewhat smaller in the 1890s. During the period from 1890-1914, approximately an equal number of Armenians lived in Turkey as lived across the frontier in Russia.

[22] Manoug Joseph Somakian, *Empires in Conflict: Armenia and the Great Powers, 1895-1920*. New York: I.B.Taurus Publishers, 1995, 1-2.

[23] While debate has raged on the size of the Armenian population in the six eastern vilayets in Turkey, a preponderance of evidence indicates that in the l890s, Armenians were in a majority in all of the vilayets except Sivas, and that in 1895 the number of Armenians in Turkey was well over one million. *Empires in Conflict*, 3-4, quoting *Report on the Population of Asia Minor* by Colonel William Everett, June 1895.

[24] "The Armenian Question, 1878-1923," *Crime of Silence*, 19.

[25] *History of the Armenian Genocide*, 45-47.

[26] *Empires in Conflict*, 10.

[27] A.O. Sarkissian. "Concert Diplomacy and the Armenians, 1890-1897," *Studies in Diplomatic History and Historiography*. London: Longman, Green & Co., Ltd., 1961, 58.

[28] *Crime of Silence*, 15.

[29] *Empires in Conflict*, 14.

[30] *The Armenian Genocide in Perspective,"* 27.

[31] *Empires in Conflict*, 16.

[32] *Empires in Conflict*, 16, 23.

[33] *Empires in Conflict*, 16.

[34] *Empires in Conflict*, 13.

[35] *Crime of Silence*, 13.

[36] *Empires in Conflict*, 15.

[37] Indubitably the presence of the American missionaries brought tension to Turkey. With their love of freedom rooted in the Protestant reformation and the American Revolution, the missionaries could not help but teach the importance of individual dignity and liberty in their schools. That the Americans would not go beyond teaching and actively help the Armenians achieve political liberty and independence irritated some Armenian activists. On the other hand, Turkish officials understood the missionary teachings on Christian liberty to be a threat to the Moslem state.

[38] "Anti-Christian Legislation in Turkey," 269.

[39] Henry T. Perry to Rev. Judson Smith, October 7, 1893, October 21, 1893; Mary H. Perry to Rev. Judson Smith, October 31, 1893, ABC 16.9.3, Vol. 25, Part 2.

[40] Mary H. Perry to Rev. Judson Smith, October 31, 1893, ABC 16.9.3, Vol. 25, Part 2, No. 453.

[41] The Universal Week of Prayer had its origins with the Evangelical Alliance. When the British organization was formed in 1846, one of its first resolutions was "that the week beginning with the first Lord's Day of January in each year be observed by the members and friends of the Alliance throughout the world as a season for concert in prayer on behalf of the grand objects contemplated by the Alliance." As the Evangelical Alliance's influence and related organizations expanded, the concert of prayer the first week in January became an international event. Each day of the week came to be dedicated to a particular topic. Beginning with Monday, the topics were Thanksgiving and Humiliation; the

Church Universal; Nations and Their Rulers; Foreign Missions; Families, Educational Establishments, and the Young; Home Missions and the Jews. Revivals often followed the week of prayer.

Henry Perry would have agreed with the article in *Evangelical Christendom* that "When clergy, ministers, and laymen of all denominations unite at the commencement of each year in prayer, forgetting the differences which separate them, anxious only to gather together at the Throne of Grace to plea for the Lord's blessing upon His Church and upon the world, we may surely expect that the Universal Week of Prayer will be followed by rich blessing, in the deepening of the spiritual life of those who are Christians, and the awakening of some who have hitherto remained indifferent to His claims upon them."
"The Universal Week of Prayer," *Evangelical Christendom*, January 1906, 132-133.

[42] Henry Perry to Rev. Judson Smith, October 12, 1895, ABC 16.9.3, Vol. 25, Part 2.

[43] *Diary*, February 26, 1894.

[44] Mary H. Perry to Rev. Judson Smith, March 9, 1895, ABC 16.9.3, Vol. 25, Part 2.

[45] Henry T. Perry to Rev. Judson Smith, May 16, 1894, ABC 16.9.3, Vol. 25, Part 2.

[46] *Diary*, March 17, 1894.

[47] "Editorial Paragraphs," *The Missionary Herald*, Vol. 90, July, 1894, 272.

Monument established at Williams College in 1856 commemorating the 1806 prayer meeting as the birthplace of American foreign missions, It was at this Jubilee Celebration that Henry Perry felt called to become a missionary. Photo courtesy of Williams College.

Alvan and Sarah Ann Perry, Henry's parents, were devout Christians whom Henry held in the highest regard.

Henry Dawes, Perry's uncle, was active in state politics before serving in the U.S. Congress from Massachusetts from 1857 to 1873. As Chairman of the Ways and Means Committee, he inaugurated the completion of the Washington Monument. He succeeded Charles Sumner as Senator and sponsored the Dawes Act, which provided for individual, rather than tribal, ownership of land by native Americans.

Henry Perry as a student at Williams College.
Photo courtesy of Williams College.

In 1866, Henry and Jeanne had their photos taken in Pittsfield, Massachusetts, shortly after their wedding in Rolla, Missouri.

Interior of First Church, Aintab. Note there are no seats in the center. People were accustomed to sit on the carpeted floor, with the women on one side of the church, and the men on the other. The pulpit, where the Bible was preached, was the focal point of the church. Photo from the ABCFM archives in the Houghton Library, Harvard University. ABC 78.2 (17:12).

Scenes of life in Turkey: oxen and man hauling wheat; donkey at grinding stone; two women grinding. Photos by Herman Kreider, *Missionary Herald*. vol. 126, 1930, 384.

Harbor of Smyrna on Turkey's west coast, 1872.
Photo courtesy of Araxi Palmer

Robert College, locate at Rumeli Hissar near Constantinople, founded by Cyrus Hamlin in 1863. The College maintained a close association with the ABCFM and trained men for Christian work in the Ottoman Empire. Perry was friends with the President and professors and often preached in the college chapel when in Constantinople.
Photo from James Barton's *Daybreak in Turkey*.

Constantinople as Henry would have known it. The Galata bridge on the left connected old Stamboul, from which the photo was taken, with the European quarter. The domed Hagia Sophia is to the right of the Galata Bridge near the Port of Constantinople.

Albert and Emma Hubbard, fellow missionaries with the Perrys in Sivas.
Photos courtesy of Araxi Palmer.

Scenes from Sivas bazaar: Shopkeeper's home; selling bread; wood vendor.
Photos courtesy of Araxi Palmer.

Stone bridge with pointed arches spans Kizil Irmak as one lieaves Sivas on the road to Caesarea. Photo taken in 1910.

Seljuk gateway in Sivas. Photo from ABCFM picture collection in Houghton Library, Harvard University, ABC 78.2 (18.8).

View of street of American missionary compound in Sivas.

Parsonage at Tocat. Henry stayed here with Jeanne and Alvan in 1880. He enjoyed building up the garden walls and orchard surrounding the parsonage. Photo in the ABCFM archives in the Houghton Library, Harvard University, ABC 78.2 (18.11).

When not staying with a local family, Henry would stay in a khan or caravansary on his outstation travels. The open alcoves seen in the photos were used by the travelers. Here they stored their rugs and merchandise in good weather. What appear to be platforms are the roofs of the stables, which are half underground. In the time of storm or in winter, most travelers occupied the platforms in these stables.
Photo from E.M. Bliss' *Turkey and the Armenian Atrocities*.

Kurdish Encampment. The black tents were those of the Kurdish tribes who spent the winter in the mountain villages and came down for the spring and summer to feed their flocks on the plain. Often Armenian villagers were forced to house the Kurds in winter. In the Bible these tents are often spoken of as the "tents of Kedar," In his missionary travels Henry sometimes stayed with the Kurdish tribesmen and shared eagerly the Gospel with them.
Photo from E.M. Bless' *Turkey and the Armenian Atrocities*.

Jean Perry, at two years old, with her Armenian nurse, Annie Doodoo.

Below: Newlyweds Henry and Mary Perry had their photograph taken with the children in 1892, before they returned to Turkey. Alvan was eighteen and Jean was seven.

Top photo: Mission house built by Dr. West in Sivas, lived in by Henry and Jeanne Perry until he death in 1884, after which Emma and Albert Hubbard and their family moved into the ample dwelling. Middle photo is Albert's business office, where e met with both Armenians and Turks on business. Perry had a similar office in his home. Below is Emma Hubbard sitting in the rocker in the parlor of their house.
Photos courtesy of Araxi Palmer

The Armenian massacres created numerous orphans and refugees. After the massacres, the American missionaries in Turkey immediately stepped in to establish orphanages and help with the relief. Henry Perry became the administrator for relief in the Sivas region. Top: Sivas orphans
Below: Refugees in Sivas begging for food.
Photos courtesy of Araxi Palmer

Part of the orphanage program established in the Sivas district included teaching the young people marketable trades or skills. Girls were taught sewing, cooking, weaving, cloth and rugmaking. Boys learned cabinetmaking, shoemaking, tailoring, and bookbinding. Perry especially enjoyed overseeing the carpentry shop, pictured here.

Armenian monastery of Neshan or the Holy Cross was located about an hour from Sivas. After the massacres, a boys orphanage was established at the monastery. This was one of six orphanages in the Sivas region which the American missionaries oversaw.

Photos courtesy of Araxi Palmer

Henry Perry ready to visit the outstations, accompanied by a government zaptieh. The horse is probably Hubble, given to the missionaries by the Red Cross.

Henry and Mary Perry, 1901.
Mary Perry photo from ABCFM archives in the
Houghton Library, harvard University, ABC 8.2
(18.8)

Sivas Normal School and the nearby Protestant Church. Perry established the Normal School to train teachers shortly after he came to Sivas. The Normal School was the first institution in Turkey devoted completely to the training of teachers. The Bible was an important part of the curriculum.

Below: American girls School in Sivas. The ABCFM was a leader in promoting female education in Turkey. Girls were taught Bible, needlework, and music as well as given a good basic education.

Photos from the ABCFM archives in the Houghton Library, Harvard University. ABC 78.2 (18.11, 18.8)

In June 1912 Perry was awarded the D.D. degree by Williams College. His children Jean and Alvan joined him for the occasion. In this photo of dignitaries at the event, Perry is in the middle of the top row.
Photo courtesy of Williams College

Perry, on the right with his white beard, stands out in the gathering of Armenian pastors and students at the grave of Henry Martyn in Tocat at the Centennial Celebration of his death on October 16, 1912. Three years later most of these would be killed in the horrors of 1915.
Missionary Herald, vol. 109, 1913, 32.

The atrocities of 1894-96 against the Armenians were surpassed by the deportations and horrors of 1915. The Turks readily punished by hanging those who would not forsake their Christian faith.

Turkish soldiers with Armenian skeletons. Hundreds of thousands of Armenians died during the long forced marches into the desert.
Photos courtesy of Araxi Palmer

Since ancient times, caravans regularly traversed Turkey. When relief was brought to Sivas after the Holocaust of 1915, it was by camel train.

Camels bringing Near Eastern Relief waiting to be unloaded in Sivas.
Photos courtesy of Araxi Palmer.

With the deportations, killings, and deaths of 1915, normal missionary work came to a halt in Sivas and throughout Turkey. The missionary buildings in Sivas were used for orphanages. Above: Orphans in Sivas receive a bath; hygiene and sanitation were important in the orphanages. Below: Teaching the children to play in the compound of one of the Sivas orphanages. Normal missionary work came to a halt after the 1915 deportations, killings, and deaths; the missionary buildings in Sivas were used for orphanages. After having endured such horror, it was important
Photos from *Missionary Herald,* vol. 116, April 1920, 169,171.

Above: Portrait of Henry Perry made by famed photographer Pirie MacDonald in 1911.

Left: Henry Perry in Ashfield, May 6, 1928. During the 1920s, Perry carefully went through his diaries during his years in Turkey, annotating explanations where necessary, and rebinding them before presenting them to the ABCFM.

Ohanasian family while still in Aleppo, before the Armenian Holocaust of 1915 forced them from their homes. The father and oldest son were killed on the deportations. The grandmother and two youngest children died on the march. Franklin Ohanasian is the young boy standing in the center. He was 7 years old in 1915.

As a teacher in Sacramento in the 1920's. Jean Perry Severance befriended Franklin. With her own background in Armenian, she was able to help Franklin learn English and become accustomed to his new land of America.

9
RULERS OF THE DARKNESS OF THIS AGE
(1894-1896)

"For we do not wrestle against flesh and blood, but against principalities, against powers, against the rulers of the darkness of this age, against spiritual wickedness in high places."
Ephesians 6:12

With the Hubbards away in the States, the business of maintaining the Sivas mission fell doubly on Henry and Mary Perry's shoulders. There were letters to write, accounts to keep, classes to teach, villages to visit, sermons to prepare, government relations to negotiate, lessons to give Jean, and the rebuilding of the schools to supervise. It was easy to become consumed with work and chores. Throughout his journal, however, Henry prayed that he never lose his spiritual focus. The Old Testament verse of Micah 6:8 especially challenged him: "He has told you, O man, what is good; and what does the Lord require of you but to do justly, and to love mercy, and to walk humbly with your God?" Thinking on this Scripture, Henry wrote in his diary:

> What a high ideal! To walk with God amid the mists and mysteries, through the din and the strife of battle, at last to emerge into His light; His love, His life at Home with Him. May we all so walk and so arrive! ... In all our work of teaching and preaching, unless we are animated and indwelt by the Divine Spirit, our work will be in vain. May He lead us, that our works may be filled with His Power!

With all the pressures of work, Henry often felt inadequate. There was so much more he would like to do than he was able to do. Here again he found comfort in the Scriptures:

> The love of Christ, which passeth knowledge, Ephesians 3:19. How comforting it is that our Lord knows us thoroughly! How comforting to hear Him say to Peter: "Thou art Simon, son of Jonah!" He knows all that was in Peter and could say: "I have prayed for thee that thy faith fail not" [Luke 22:32] He knows how we fail Him so much, when we are so pushed with these business and building items.[1]

Political clouds continued to darken as 1894 drew to a close. When Henry visited Tocat in November, many of the Armenian women called on him to help them get their sons and brothers out of prison. The Tocat pastor was imprisoned and in chains for allegedly preaching sedition. Henry knew the charges against the men were false and vainly appealed to the Pasha for the pastor's release. The Pasha told Henry, "You had better change your man; you can find a better. He is guilty and you will do well to believe it." Thankfully, the preacher was freed after five months in prison. When Henry left Tocat to return to Sivas, for the first time he had to get the seals of the Protestant millet, the police, and the military before his *tiskere*, or permission to travel, was granted.

Consul Jewett warned Henry that political forces might increasingly hinder his missionary activities, and news of troubles elsewhere in Turkey began to reach Sivas. In August and September 1894, Sassoun, west of Lake Van in the eastern province of Bitlis, was washed in blood after a tax protest by Armenian peasants. Peasants in the Talori district of Sassoun had told the governing *kaimakam* that they would not continue to pay the official Ottoman tax (*hafir*) unless he ended the unofficial tax the Kurds exacted from them as the price of "protection." When the governor and his *zaptiehs* arrived to enforce the tax, the Armenians decided they had a moral duty to resist tyrannical rule and drove the oppressors out. This was the excuse the Ottoman government needed. It immediately called in the *Hamidieh*. The Kurds, acting in concert with the *zaptiehs*, and supported by Turkish army troops, attacked the Armenian villagers. There followed a widespread massacre of several thousand Armenian men, women, and children, mostly under cover of darkness.[2]

Often, Armenians were provoked in some small incident which was then used as a pretext to justify massive retaliation against the general Armenian population. For example, the Kurds stole several oxen from Armenian villages near Moush, and when the Armenians tracked their oxen to the Kurdish tents, they found one ox had already been butchered. They asked for the others, but were refused. The Armenians left, but returned with a larger group to reclaim their cattle. Fighting broke out, and several were killed on each side. The Kurds took their dead bodies to the government at Moush and said the region was filled with Armenian and foreign soldiers. The government immediately gathered eight regiments, while 20,000 Kurds and 500 Kurdish cavalry (*Hamidieh*) came to Moush. The Turkish troops kept out of sight while the Armenians repulsed the Kurds several times. Small groups of Turks entered the villages saying they would protect the villagers, and they were quartered in the Armenian houses. In the night the Turks arose and slew the sleeping men, women, and children. The butchery begun in Moush continued throughout Sassoun from mid-August to mid-September. The Pasha came from Erzinjan with the sultan's *firman* to eliminate the rebel Armenians.[3] No distinctions were made in the villages for those who paid their taxes or not. A priest and leading men from one village came out with their tax receipts declaring their loyalty, but everyone in the village was killed.[4]

Reverend Frederick Greene, a missionary for four years in the Lake Van area of eastern Turkey, carefully recorded eyewitness accounts of the Sassoun massacre, as described to him by survivors:

> A number of able-bodied young Armenians were captured, bound, covered with brushwood and burned alive. A number of Armenians, variously estimated, but less than a hundred, surrendered themselves and pled for mercy. Many of them were shot down on the spot and the remainder was dispatched with sword and bayonet.
>
> A lot of women, variously estimated from 60 to 160 in number, were shut up in a church, and the soldiers were "let loose" among them. Many of them were outraged to death and the remainder dispatched with the sword and bayonet. A lot of young women were collected as spoils of war. Two stories are told. 1. That they were carried off to the harems of their Moslem captors. 2. That they were offered Islam and the harems of their Moslem captors, --refusing, they were slaughtered. In another village fifty women were set aside and urged to change their faith and enter Turkish harems, but they indignantly refused to deny Christ, preferring the fate of their fathers and husbands. Children were placed in a row, one behind another,

and a bullet fired down the line, apparently to see how many could be dispatched with one bullet. Infants and small children were piled one on the other and their heads struck off. Children were frequently held up by the hair and cut in two. ... Houses were surrounded by soldiers, set on fire, and the inmates forced back into the flames at the point of the bayonet as they tried to escape. [5]

Other missionaries and the American and European consuls echoed Reverend Greene's outrage until the public and press clamored for the European powers to enforce the Treaty of Berlin's mandate for the sultan to initiate genuine "reforms" protecting the Armenians. However, the sultan's government had developed reliable propaganda techniques to diffuse international outrage. The sultan's first official response to media inquiries and diplomatic protests was routine denial. Later, after trustworthy eyewitness testimony had established the truth, the propaganda was revised to assert that the local Sassoun governor had restrained and punished Armenian aggression against the Kurds. England's Gladstone noted that the force of facts shattered the sultan's denials. An estimated twenty-seven villages and between six and ten thousand Armenian men, women, and children were annihilated in the Sassoun massacre.[6]

Another defensive twist widely used by the Sublime Porte's press corps was to contend that all killing in local areas was without the sultan's knowledge or authority, that the massacres were beyond his capacity to control. However, after a six-month English-French-Russian board of inquiry into the Sassoun massacre, British Vice-Consul Shipley's report found that "the Armenians were massacred without distinction of age or sex; ...were absolutely hunted like wild beasts, being killed wherever they were met, and ... it was not so much the ...suppression of a pseudo revolt which was desired by the Turkish authorities, as the extermination, pure and simple [of the Armenians in Sassoun]."[7]

When England inquired about the mass killings, the sultan and the Sublime Porte promptly went into denial, a posture repeatedly assumed by the Ottoman government. But the truth in such matters was impossible to conceal. British Consul Graves confirmed the massacre with reports from actual participants:

> Suleiman, a Turkish ex-sergeant, in regard to the massacres of Armenians at Sassoun, confirmed [to me] that the story of the

nocturnal butcheries was true. Suleiman was told to act as a butcher, and says that the whole slaughter was about 5,000 persons.[8]

Reverend Judson Smith wrote Henry of the American outpouring of concern for affairs in Turkey:

> The situation in Turkey gives us no small anxiety. I have never known such intense feeling in our country or in England with regard to the situation abroad as is now felt over affairs in Turkey. It is surprising that the Turkish government does not understand the situation more clearly and feel the necessity of at once making a change and putting itself in the right and disowning these acts, which seem in reprobation.[9]

After almost fifteen years of quiescence, England, France, and Russia again took up the Armenian Question, and stridently demanded the sultan initiate the promised "reforms." However, Germany's Kaiser, already harboring ideas of a land route to India through Turkey on a German-constructed Berlin-to-Baghdad railway, remained neutral. The other three powers pressured the sultan to appoint an Ottoman commission of inquiry into the Sassoun affair. The commission proceeded to whitewash the government's responsibility. However, the European representatives who attended the hearings reported that the Sassoun Armenians had taken up arms in self-defense, that there had been no rebellion, and even if there had been, the ruthless liquidation of innocent women and children was morally reprehensible.[10]

The Sassoun incident marked the beginning of a steady succession of Armenian killings throughout Turkey, especially in the eastern *vilayets*. As the crescendo of mass murder accelerated, Lord Salisbury in England was under growing pressure from evangelical Christians to stop the massacres and enforce the "reforms" of the Treaty of Berlin. Salisbury proposed to the European powers, with the concurrence of Germany's Emperor Wilhelm II, that Sultan Abdul Hamid II be replaced, using collective military force, if necessary. However, Russia's Tsar Nicholas II at first would hear none of it. Preoccupied with Japan's ascendancy in the Far East, Russia refused to support any attempt of England to enforce the Berlin Treaty "reforms" in Turkish Armenia. Without unanimous support of the European powers, England could only periodically send innocuous protests to the sultan.[11]

On May 11, 1895, however, after a crescendo of reliable reports of the Sassoun massacre had reached Europe, the major European powers renewed their long-standing demand upon the sultan to adopt their proposed "Scheme of Reforms" for the six eastern provinces of Erzerum, Van, Bitlis, Diarbekir, Harpoot, and Sivas. Essentially, these internal reforms were drawn to protect the religious freedom of the Christian Armenians. By October, the arrival of European warships in Turkish waters stirred the sultan to contrive a duplicitous scheme in retaliation. First, in order to buy time, he would execute the reform agreement; next he would execute the Armenian people. The European powers could hardly insist that the Ottoman Empire respect its Armenian-Christian minority if such a minority no longer existed.[12] These seemingly contradictory policies were implemented at once.

Realizing that the European powers had no intention of interfering internally with Ottoman-Armenian relations, the sultan proceeded apace with his plan to incrementally massacre Armenians. To prevent news of the massacres from reaching the outside world, the Turkish government restricted reporters and merchants from traveling in the eastern provinces. The government also imposed strict postal and telegraphic censorship. Henry and the other missionaries felt the tightening of the control of information. Letters and mailed books were opened. Foreign newspapers and periodicals, including *The Missionary Herald*, were no longer delivered to them. If a newspaper was delivered, any references to Turkey were cut out. To prevent effective resistance to attacks made upon them, the Armenians were systematically disarmed throughout Turkey.

On September 30, 1895, a group of Armenians in Constantinople planned to petition the Grand Vizier concerning certain grievances, giving him the customary advance notice. However, before they could reach the Sublime Porte, the police stopped them. A riot broke out in which twenty Armenians were injured and three died. A few of the Armenians belonged to the *Hunchagist* activists. This gave the Turkish government the excuse to brand the whole ethnic group as seditious, thus justifying their policy of cruelty, impoverishment, and extermination. Many Armenians were arrested, and several hundred were killed during the week by Mohammedan civilians and *Softas* (religious students).

News and rumors of violence sent fear into the hearts of many of the Armenians. Henry pulled from his files a sermon on "The Abiding Peace of the Son of God." He had first preached this sermon on John 14:27 in Afton, New York, just three weeks before his mother's death. Jesus had comforted the disciples and promised them, "Peace I leave with you: My peace I give unto you: not as the world giveth give I unto you. Let not your heart be troubled neither let it be fearful." It seemed just the message for the fearful Armenians in Sivas. Henry preached his sermon to them on September 15, 1895. He encouraged his congregation to think about the kind of peace Christ had. Jesus was overtaken by the persecuting Jews, betrayed by His own disciples, rejected by His own people, accused unjustly at His trial, deserted by His followers, and taunted by His crucifiers. Later His own followers were persecuted, and all but one of His apostles died a martyr's death. What kind of peace could Jesus offer? Jesus gave an intimation of the source of His peace when He said, "I have food to eat that you know not of," and "My meat is to do the will of my father and to finish His work." By His complete oneness with the Father's will, by His obedient, submissive will and devotion to His divine work, Jesus was able to have victory in suffering. Henry encouraged the Armenians to learn their Father's heart through prayer as Jesus did at Gethsemane. Following His will rather than their own, they could have Jesus' peace, whatever trials life might bring. The best paintings show not only light, but also shadows. The Armenians might face much suffering, but Christ could keep them in perfect peace:

> It is settled calm happiness, more quiet and lasting than joy. More noble than pleasure. Worldly people seldom talk of Peace. Thy look upon it as an impossible condition and plunge into the turmoil of business and politics. Oh! They will not find the Lord's peace there. This Peace, built in absolute obedience and the deepest love of sonship in God; the "My Peace" of our Lord; he <u>gives to you</u>. Do you want it? "Not as the world giveth gives <u>He</u> to <u>you</u>"
>
> I close with a prayer ...Lord God Almighty, Christ the King of Glory, who art our true Peace, and Love Eternal, enlighten our souls with the brightness of thy Peace and purify our Conscience with the sweetness of thy love, that we, with peaceful hearts, may wait for the Author of peace, and in adversities of this world may we have Thee for our guardian and protector, And so being fenced by thy care, May we give ourselves to the love of thy peace.[13]

On October 5, 1895, Henry noted in his journal there was "news of violence at Trebizond," the port city on the Black Sea in northeastern Turkey. An American eyewitness wrote this account of the Trebizond massacre, a pattern of the killings that soon followed throughout the eastern provinces:

> On Saturday, October 5th, the excitement in town (over news of the attacks on Armenians in Constantinople) was very intense.
>
> The [European] Consuls had a consultation, and going in a body to the Governor, earnestly pressed him to arrest those who were exciting the people to acts of outrage. The Governor declined to do so but promised in his own way to do "the right thing."
>
> Suddenly like a clap of thunder in a clear sky, the assault began at about 11 A.M... Unsuspecting people walking along the streets and merchants sitting quietly at their shop doors were shot ruthlessly down. Some were slashed with swords until life was extinct. They passed through the quarters where only old men, women, and children remained, killing the men and large boys, generally permitting the women and younger children to live. For five hours this horrid work of inhuman butchery went on. Then the sound of musketry died away and the work of looting began. Every shop of an Armenian in the market was gutted. For hours bales of broadcloth, cotton goods, and every conceivable kind of merchandise passed along without molestation to the houses of the spoilers. The intention evidently was to impoverish and as near as possible to blot out the Armenians of this town. So far as appearances went, the police and soldiers distinctly aided in this savage work, their only care being to see that the right ones--that is, Armenians--were killed.
>
> [Oct. 13, 1895] Many, who even promised to accept the religion of Islam, were still most cruelly hacked to pieces. In this city and vicinity the killed numbered 1,000, almost exclusively males. When you consider that the adult males of the Armenian community did not number more than 2,000, the frightful mortality is at once understood. On the other hand, not one of the rioters has been arrested; not one has been disarmed. Apparently all this wholesale murder of peaceable and law-abiding subjects of the Sultan is no crime worthy of notice. The Armenians are now so prostrated that they can do nothing. Relief must come from abroad.[14]

Later in October 1895, Henry's journal reported disturbing rumors that the Turkish Government was considering possible "massacre of the Armenians in Sivas."[15] Such news would not have surprised Henry or any of the other missionaries. They were familiar with the Ottoman Empire's long history of ethnic cleansing. They knew that between 1822 and 1895 the Turkish Government had periodically liquidated over 100,000 Armenians, Greeks, Nestorians, and Bulgarians.[16] In recent weeks, the missionaries also knew the details of the Sassoun, Constantinople, and Trebizond massacres from the direct observations of American missionaries in the area at the time. Even as Henry wrote in his journal, the likeness of William Gladstone looking down on him from the wall of his study perhaps reminded him of the previous December, when the English Prime Minister had summarized the horror of the Turkish sultan's massacre of the Bulgarian Christian minority twenty years earlier in 1876:

> Let me endeavor very briefly to sketch, in the rudest outline, what the Turkish race was and what it is. It is not a question of Mohammedanism simply, but of Mohammedanism compounded with the peculiar character of race. They are not the mild Mohammedans of India, nor the chivalrous Saladins of Syria, nor the cultured Moors of Spain. They were, upon the whole, from the black day when they first entered Europe, the one great anti-human specimen of humanity. Wherever they went, a broad line of blood marked the track behind them; and as far as their dominion reached, civilization disappeared from view. They represented everywhere government by force as opposed to government by law. For the guide of this life they had a relentless fatalism; for its reward hereafter, a sensual paradise.
>
> What happened in Bulgaria? The Sultan and his government absolutely denied that anything wrong had been done...but the force of facts shattered their denial. ...I said [then] "It is time that the Turk and all his belongings should go out of Bulgaria bag and baggage." They did go out of Bulgaria.... [C]ommon sense and ommon prudence ought to have taught [the Turks] not to repeat the infernal acts which disgraced the year 1876....[T]he intelligence which has reached me tends to a conclusion ... that the outrages...and abominations of 1876 in Bulgaria have been repeated in 1894 in Armenia. ...I have lived to see the Empire of Turkey in Europe reduced to less than one half of what it was when I was born, and why? Simply because of its misdeeds. ...[S]uch a government as that which can countenance and cover the perpetration of such outrages is a disgrace in the first place to Mohamet the Prophet whom it professes to follow, ...a disgrace to civilization at large, and ...a curse to mankind.[17]
>
> We may ransack the annals of the world; but I know not what research can furnish us with so portentous an example of the fiendish misuse of the powers established by God 'for the punishment of evil-doers, and for the encouragement of them that do well.' No government ever has so sinned; none has so proved itself incorrigible in sin, or...so impotent for reformation.[18]

On October 17, 1895, Henry's journal noted "Reports of an ultimatum at Constantinople and acceptance of the reforms by the Sublime Porte." The massacre in Trebizond actually occurred while the sultan was agreeing to the "reforms" that were presented to him by the European powers of England, France, and Russia. After learning the truth about the Sassoun Massacre, the powers had renewed more forcefully their long-standing demand that the sultan adopt their proposed "Scheme of Reforms" for the six eastern *vilayet*s. The sultan agreed to the reforms protecting the freedom of Christian Armenians, and the European powers seemed satisfied. A.W. Terrell, U.S. Minister in Constantinople, was not persuaded of the sultan's sincerity. In a report to Secretary of State Richard Olney, Terrell noted that the Porte's acceptance of the reforms was not issued with a public proclamation, and there was nothing new in the reforms. Most of the regulations already existed, but were not enforced:

> This "project ... to make some necessary reforms" contains absolutely nothing new of practical value for the security of life or property, and yet the immediate effect upon the fears of all classes have thus far been wonderful, for all hail it as a harbinger of future peace. The Armenian populace here seem delighted; troops have ceased to patrol the street in such force as formerly; the British ambassador and the Serbian minister depart tomorrow for their respective capitals; the French ambassador leaves in a few days and thus this "project" which satisfies the powers, restores confidence.[19]

Minister Terrell did not share the European ambassadors' optimism. Armenian anarchists and revolutionists seemed bent on stirring up conflict, and the religious and racial hatred between the Turks and the Armenians was intense. With the probability of continued violence, Terrell repeatedly pressured the Sublime Porte to ensure the safety of American lives and property in Turkey. He even urged that American navy vessels be brought off the Turkish coast as a show of protective power.

The European pressure to accept the "Reforms" amounted to a demand that the sultan treat Christian Armenians as equal in status to Moslem Turks. If the sultan, as Caliph and head of the national Moslem faith, implemented the reforms by enforcing such religious equality, his Turkish subjects would see him as repudiating Islam and undermining the premise that non-Islamic religions were inferior and not to be tolerated.[20] The sultan settled the issue with his decision that reform by massacre was the order of the day. This policy had already been carried out successfully in the massacres at Sassoun, Constantinople, and Trebizond. More soon followed. The sultan had darkly hinted that this would follow if he were pushed too hard, but no one believed that he would really carry out the threat.[21] In city after city, the Armenians were quickly given over to slaughter and spoliation. In many respects the Trebizond massacre was typical of the wholesale liquidation of Armenian men, women, and children which rapidly followed in Erzerum, Erzinjan, Baiboort, Sivas, Marsovan, Cesarea, Harpoot, Bitlis, Diarbekir, Malatia, Marash, Aintab, Birejik, Ourfa, and other places. However, Trebizond, being a seaport with a large foreign population and European consuls, suffered less than the cities of the interior where there were no such restraining influences.

On October 27, Henry received reports of the "disturbance" at Ourfa, 200 miles southeast of Sivas and 75 miles east of Aintab, Perry's first mission station in Turkey. Two thousand Armenian men, women, and children were massacred by the Turkish soldiers who were appointed to guard them.[22] Two days after the massacre at Ourfa, on Tuesday, October 29, Miss Brewer returned to Sivas from Divrik with reports of killing and plundering by Kurdish irregulars in the region surrounding Pingan, and the destruction of its school buildings.[23]

The American missionaries had little difficulty in concluding that the Ottoman government was planning widespread massacre in the six eastern *vilayets* where Armenians were concentrated. The various foreign consuls had made them aware of the sultan's deliberate efforts to conceal from international scrutiny the earlier massacres at Sassoun and Trebizond. In addition, their daily work brought developments that conveyed the message that the Turkish government in Constantinople was secretly planning more massacres, which the sultan himself was directing.

Perry's co-worker, Albert Hubbard, and his family were in Constantinople, on their way home from furlough in America. They had notified Perry they would be arriving at the Black Sea port of Samsoun, from whence they would proceed south to Sivas. On October 24, several weeks before the massacre of Armenians began in Sivas, Perry noted, "Agop, the zabtea [police escort], leaves today to meet the Hubbard and Larkin families at Samsoun upon their return from the United States." However, the families never arrived at Samsoun. The Turkish government in Constantinople would not permit the missionaries to leave the city and travel to the interior, giving as the reason that there were "reports of serious disturbances."[24] As the plan for massacre unfolded itself in city after city, it became abundantly clear to the missionaries that the Turkish government would do everything in its power to prevent foreigners from witnessing any of the scheduled killings.

Henry concluded a November 6 letter to Reverend Judson Smith in Boston by writing:

> The political shadows deepen upon the northern section of the Sivas *vilayet*. The desperate criminal classes of the Mohammedans, Kurds, Turks, Circassians, Laze immigrants, the "Laz" and "Papahs" are let loose upon the Armenians, raiding villages, taking off whole flesh, and killing many people. The Armenians, you know, have been disarmed. Concerning the result we wait, and pray.[25]

In his diary for November 3, Henry wrote,

> In these times of political confusion, we must trust our Blessed Lord, that He will lead us in His way, which is always the one of safety and confidence. Let his guidance lead us; that we may lead others.

He thought of Luke 5:5, "Master, we have toiled the night and have taken nothing; nevertheless at thy word we will let down the net." Jesus sent the disciples to the very place where they had failed and promised them His help. Henry took encouragement from the story and the truth that God's strength was sufficient and was made perfect in man's weakness.

On Friday, November 8, Henry heard "news of raids and much loss at Derende, Ashude, Albustan, and Kara Enen." The next day further news came of "the sacking of many towns and villages. Diabirkir, Malatia, Erzerum, Albustan, and all the villages in the exposed places between here and Kara Hissar in our field. Only on the surface does this city [Sivas] rest in quiet."[26] There was concern the raiders would soon attack Gürün. A few weeks earlier Henry had preached in the church there, taking as his text John 12: 26, "He that loveth his life shall lose it; and he that hateth his life in this world shall keep it unto life eternal." On November 9, the attack began at Gürün, seventy miles south of Sivas. Only later would Henry and Mary learn the full horror of the massacres and destruction there.

Consul Jewett's reports described the spirit behind the atrocities. On November 9, he wrote assistant Secretary of State Uhl:

> ...the last few weeks have witnessed a demonstration of the lawlessness, fanatical hatred, and brutality of the Mohammedans.
> From Bitlis, Erzerum, Erzinjan, Diabekir, Marash, Palu, Malatia, Trebizond, and other places come reports of serious disturbances in which large numbers of people have been massacred and much property stolen or destroyed.
> Doubtless in some of these cases the Armenians, as the government claims, have taken some initiative in starting the disorder and in all cases it may greatly be claimed that the Armenian revolutionary agitation has prepared the Turk to regard the Armenian as the enemy of the Empire, to kill whom is perfectly justified by the Koran and by Mohammedan sentiment. The battle cry of the Turk today is the same as that of the Janissaries when they slaughtered the "infidel dogs" one hundred years ago. "<u>The head of the infidel for the government and his property to whomsoever seizes it.</u>" And it is the Christian who has been made to suffer chiefly in all these unequal encounters.[27]

Consul Jewett noted that the trouble in the province of Sivas began the day after the sultan issued his reforms. Companies of local Kurds and Turks attacked smaller Christian villages, firing their guns to overawe the people, killing anyone who resisted, and taking off flocks, herds, and other property. As their work continued, they became bolder, and he destruction and killing increased. The government ignored the Armenians' calls for protection. Not a single Turkish village was attacked. Jewett reported that

> The apparent indifference and inactivity of the government almost leads one to suppose that the government allowed the Armenians to be punished and their comparative numbers reduced. It is stated from various sources and I have it on the authority of a telegram from the sub-governor to the Governor General that the Kurds claim that they are acting under orders from high quarters...
> The present state of the whole of this consular district is such as to render life here very weary for all American citizens as well as for the native Christians...

On November 10, Jewett sent in a report that, "Every male adult Christian at Malatia is reported to have been massacred Nov. 3-5 by Kurds and Turks of the city. The Governor is said to have ordered the slaughter and the troops prevented the escape of the Armenians."[28]

On Monday, November 11, there were "bad reports of looting in the villages and suburbs." Next day, Dr. Jewett, the American Consul, called to warn of trouble, and Perry put up the American flag over the missionary compound. Then a special messenger arrived, sent by the Armenian teachers from the mission schools. They asked Perry to attend an emergency meeting at the church to organize relief food and clothing to send to the survivors of the Gürün massacre that had occurred a few days before. After a hasty lunch, Perry started out for the church. It was then, November 12, 1895, he saw first hand that the maelstrom of massacre in eastern Turkey had finally reached Sivas. Suddenly there was shouting in the streets and the Armenian workmen at the mission began to flee. Turks caught an Armenian in the street and started beating him:

> The massacre continued from morning until sunset. It was a veritable cyclone of blood. The Armenians having been assured, in confidence had opened their shops. Suddenly at noon, the buzz of a rush started everywhere. The irregulars commenced with clubs; soon the knifework commenced; and the firearms came into use. It was a rush to kill and plunder the shops and houses of the helpless Armenians. As soon as the soldiers could reach the markets, they commenced to shoot the retreating Armenians. Irregulars rushed all about over the city to cut down doors, small windows, and empty the houses of the Armenians. About 1500 people were killed in the streets and markets of Sivas that p.m. We distributed the remaining students to their homes and heard of the murder of our pastor Garabet.

The killing and pillaging continued all day Wednesday and into Thursday:

> At first in the morning the streets were quiet and we hoped for relief. But soon the firing began. Tho the looters began a rush to plunder houses, the soldiers prevented them, and none were seen in the streets but soldiers. The Consul called. We have three soldiers quartered for our defense whom we must feed. I visited the students shut up now in the new building; examined a case of shooting said to have been done there; and did the best I could to quiet those who are still full of fear. 1500 bodies buried in one grave. ... I went to the government house to get permission to take the body of our pastor Garabet (slain in the city Khan) and bury it in our cemetery. Only the police officers were found there. The officers treated me well but gave no answer. A city government man advised me to do nothing more of it. Miss Brewer went to Bad. [Rev.] Garabet's house for the goods of his wife, now a widow.[29]

During the first days of the massacre, the Perrys' kitchen and dining room quickly filled up with refugees, who wanted to stay with him as long as they could. On Friday, Dr. Jewett called on Perry again, and advised that he was sending "a full report of the tragic massacre in a cablegram to America." Miss Brewer returned to the compound to say that, during the massacre, a man had shot Perry's faithful servant, Neshan, named Mustafa. The Sabbath came,

> a cold rain-piercing day. We could not have any public service. I visited the chapel garrison in the a.m. and the prison in the p.m. to see the Marsovan pastor and take him some food. In our house we held informal services, both A.M. and P.M., among the refugees. Dr. Jewett called and lunched with us. The city is outwardly quiet. Many of our friends are killed.

Other witnesses described the ongoing massacre, which lasted seven days:

> Soldiers, Circassians, and police with their arms, all under command of officers--aided by Moslem women and children, rushed to the market to begin their dreadful work of killing, stripping the dead, and looting the houses. No resistance was made by the Armenians, who seemed overpowered in the suddenness of the onslaught, the number of their armed assailants, and the relentless ferocity with which they were pursued to their death. The shops of the Armenian merchants, whether wholesale or retail, were looted by the rioters and soldiers. Many of the merchants and their clerks were killed; Thus, at one blow the Armenian element was eliminated from the trade at Sivas. The Armenian villagers in the vicinity were robbed of everything, and the people are left to beg and die. A gentleman in high official standing, who has had unusual opportunities for information, uses the following language with regard to this affair: "Don't be deceived by any of the silly government statements which attribute all these massacres to Armenians. It was a deliberate plan on the part of the government to punish the Armenians. The sultan was irritated because he was forced to give them reforms, so he has had 7,000 Armenians killed to show his power, since he signed the scheme of reforms. The government has smashed some Turkish shop windows to show that the Armenians did it.[30]

Henry later wrote the Reverend Smith in Boston:

> It was a sad day as the news came in of the murder of this and that one among our trusted valuable friends. The pastor of our Protestant Church, Bd. Garabet Kulukjian, was killed in one of the khans, whither he had gone for some items of business. His wife, four daughters, and all our congregation deeply mourn his loss. He was a good man and very wise in his dealing with the political questions and especially as a pastor he was loved by all.
>
> The steward of my house, a faithful man by the name of Neshan, who having grown old in our service was familiarly called by our children "Uncle Neshan" was killed by the bullet of a soldier at the blacksmith shop whither I had sent him to get the irons made for some windows.
>
> These two with many others of our Protestant people, were buried on Thursday in a soldier's trench near the Armenian burial ground, prayers being offered by a priest. A careful estimate of Armenian loss of life puts the numbers at about 1500 in Sivas…[31]

A Moslem priest killed many Armenians in the street directly in front of the Normal School.[32]

An article in *The Missionary Herald* described in more detail the death of the Sivas pastor:

> The work of Reverend Garabed Kulukjian, the Protestant pastor at Sivas, was increasingly good. His wife had been for years a much prized and beloved teacher in the Girls' Boarding School at Marsovan, and their own four girls, the oldest not yet sixteen, had profited well by such a mother. On November 10 he preached to his flock an impressive sermon from the text "But there shall not an hair of your head perish." On November 11, at noon, the crash came, shutting him with Armenian companions in an upper room at a khan. They were soon robbed and left, while the storm was raging outside. The pastor led them in prayer and watched till toward evening, when another squad of Mohammedans came to kill them. Something in the composed manner with which the pastor met them made them hesitate and offer him liberty on condition of denying his faith. He thought of his wife in delicate health, and of their daughters, but he answered: "I do not only believe Christ, but also spend my life persuading others." "Then we must kill you," they said; and when he raised both hands toward heaven as a sign of settled trust they shot him twice. Next morning his body was found by friends stripped of nearly all clothing and tossed into the back yard of the khan. As the massacres were still in progress, he could not be taken to the unwalled Protestant burial ground, but joined the 800 who were piled into one huge trench at the Gregorian cemetery, whither an Armenian

priest crept, to read one short prayer and leave them to earth and to God.³³

Ten days after the massacre, Consul Jewett sent a further dispatch to Washington, D.C.:

> Since the scheme of reforms was adopted about 3000 Armenians have been killed [in Sivas province]. The number actually killed represents but a small part of the work accomplished. The property of the Armenians has been very extensively transferred to the Moslems and the spirit has been so strongly crushed out of the remains that the Moslems need not take any account of them even if they are admitted to office.
>
> I think a man must be a blind Turkish apologist who will not admit that the government alone is responsible for all the recent massacres and pillage in this part of the country. An officer of the army admitted to me today that a few soldiers might have stopped the outrages at any time if the government had wished it and ordered it. The Commissioner of Police said it was not stopped because the soldiers, gendarmes, and all the officers were in it.
>
> ... the Turks simply fell upon a helpless and unresisting people and crushed the life out of them. Of course Turkish official reports make it appear differently. A Turk of high rank has told me that Turks have fired at the Governor and accused Armenians of it to make it appear that the Armenians are in revolt and to create more trouble. I am creditably informed that the local government had some Turkish shops damaged and emptied three days after the outbreak of the massacres to show that the rioters were Armenians. The sub-governor of Gürün, I am told on quite good authority, telegraphed to the Governor at Sivas saying, in effect, "you may be assured that no Armenians remain at Gürün."³⁴

Only gradually did Henry begin to learn the stories of individual friends caught up in the massacre. At the end of his 1896 diary he wrote of some of the incidents surrounding people he knew in the massacres. In a May 1901 diary entry, Henry made another list of massacre victims by name and briefly noted where they died. Their faces and deaths were often before him. Nahabet Abdalian, a medical doctor, trusted the government promises and was confident there would be no massacre in Sivas. However, on Tuesday, November 12, his house was attacked and burned. Abdalian spent the night in a Turkish neighbor's house, but they turned him out in the morning. When word came that he was wanted at the government, he went. They said "Take him to the church," the code order to kill him. He was killed in the open street.

Henry learned that the Gregorian monastery at Ashude was burned; the sixty-year old Bishop Sahak was there, and they demanded he become a Moslem. When he refused, the attackers killed him, shooting him and then breaking his skull. His body remained unburied fifteen days; it was partially eaten by dogs. The Ashude priest Mesrope and his son Bedros remained hidden several days. When they were found, they were taken to a café with young Bedros' wife:

> The bride was then openly forced, and then the priest and son were taken out into the street in the night, and shot... Bodies lay in the street and finally taken by the Turks to a stable and left in vile positions. Armenians buried them 10 days later in the yard of the church. Mesrope also openly refused to be a Moslem. They afterwards tried to kill the bride, since they knew that she knew what they did. She was wounded on the way to Derende. Now is living at Albustan. Her child died.

Taman Marashlian, a fourteen-year-old girl, was taken to Azezia by the murderers of her father. An elderly woman found her and cared for her. Hacher Anin was in the street in front of his door when a Kurd demanded his conversion. He replied, "I am 70 and too old now to turn Moslem." The Kurds killed him with an ax:

> His body lay 3 days in the street and was partially eaten by cats. His son Sarkis lived several days...when they killed him in front of his house. He was first shot, when he drew himself upon his knees and commenced to pray. "Praying are you" they said, and seized him killing him with knives. His house was afterward taken by the murderers.

Surrounded by such horrors, it was no wonder that Henry was concerned about Mary, who was "much weakened and I fear she will break down in strength of nerves."[35]

Soldiers guarded the American property and the Sivas Chapel in the weeks following the massacres. The missionaries had to provide for the food and comfort of the soldiers. The Sivas Chapel was closed for worship after the initial killing, and it was not until five weeks later, Sunday, December 22, 1895, that Perry held

...the first service in the Chapel after the massacre. It was nearly as large as those previously; but oh! how many new faces. Many of those whom we were accustomed to see there are gone. In my Sunday School Class, Moses Ammin and Nishan Ammin are no more here to testify for Jesus. Mary addressed the morning congregation using an interpreter. The attention was very good.[36]

Ourfa, two hundred miles southwest of Sivas in central Turkey, endured two massacres, the last being one of the most horrific. Several hundred were killed October 27-28, but at the end of December another reign of terror seemed imminent. Even as Armenian victims in Sivas were returning to their chapel for worship, Turkish forces at Ourfa were converting its worship center into a flaming cauldron of death. First, the authorities advised the people that, since the government was seeking only adult Armenian men, the women and children could find safety in the great Armenian cathedral. Once three hundred of them were inside, the Turks first decapitated many of the children at the altar of the church, then set the cathedral on fire, burning the occupants alive. In this second phase of the Ourfa massacres, a total of eight thousand Armenians were slaughtered.[37]

Reports from the district of Gürün continued to pour into Sivas. Only two months before Henry had described the beauty and prosperity of Gürün in a report to Reverend Smith in Boston. His letter of December 9 told a very different heart-rending tale:

> It is a sickening recital of horrors. No wonder that Mrs. Perry's strength is well-nigh gone from sheer sympathy. It is one thing to hear of the massacre of 1500 people, and quite another to witness the shooting of friends and neighbors, and walk the streets flowing with their blood. Just when we begin to recover breath from the awful scenes at Sivas, the news comes of the repetition of even additional horrors at Manjaluk and Gürün.
>
> From a total population of 9000 Armenians of Gürün it is estimated on good authority that 1200 are killed. All Gregorian and Protestant houses were looted, and 27 also from the Catholics. Of the houses sacked, 1000 were burned, including three Protestant chapels.
>
> The pastor of our Protestant church, Bad. [Rev.] Kevork Demejian, writes that himself and wife are alive, with nothing to eat except a little bread supplied by the Government, having lost all their household goods; and his house was burned. Three priests of the Gregorian church were killed and another saved his life by accepting the Mohammedan faith. Girls and boys were carried off to serve the

vile purposes of the murderers. It is said that mothers to save their children from this end threw them into the river.

Those who attacked the town were chiefly the Kurds aided by the neighboring bad men of all the Mohammedan races. There were soldiers enough to have defended the town against all comers from without. Why they did not do so is the question and mystery which confronts the same situation elsewhere. ...

That there was some plan in the movement of these destroying hordes cannot be doubted. That they carried out that plan without resistance from the soldiers is equally evident. That they claimed to do it by authority given them from high quarters is shown by abundant evidence. However, property and people whom the Government and distinguished individuals wished to have protected were spared without any apparent difficulty even by the most ruthless looters.[38]

With the Hubbards still in Constantinople, Henry could not leave the main mission station in Sivas and the many responsibilities there in the wake of the massacre. Mary, however, was intent on going to Gürün to bring what relief and aid she could to the suffering people there. On January 1, she set out to visit the "remnant" in Gürün, accompanied by Stephan, an Armenian preacher, and two armed policemen provided by the Governor general. Traveling through heavy snowstorms, after four days the little band reached Gürün. They found Pastor Demirjian comfortably housed with a wealthy Moslem, who had vacated six rooms of his house for the Christian family. Mary too was received graciously by the Moslem family who provided every hospitality. The suffering Mary found at Gürün was impossible to describe. Statistics of loss only partially told the story:

> Of our eighty Protestant families, sixty-four were robbed of everything they had on earth. Forty men, five women, and five children were massacred, and ten brides and young girls carried away captive. Thirty-eight houses were totally destroyed...Three hundred survivors have neither homes, daily bread, clothing, bedding nor work, except twenty-five who have a little clothing, bedding, and food saved from the wreckage. For six days the massacring was vigorously pushed in Gürün, and probably 1200 persons were killed, possibly more, though we have not exact figures yet from the Gregorians. In all, about 1600 houses were destroyed, and much wheat, flour, and provisions for the winter were lost by fire. The people are huddled together in Catholic houses, Turkish houses, stables, close to the market (which was protected by the government),

and in the remaining rooms or walls of their ruined homes, if there is one room under roofage.[39]

One Protestant girl, whose name meant "unfading," was captured with her New Testament clasped in her hands. Shortly after her capture she was told she must accept the Moslem faith. She refused. Even when they threatened to kill her, she remained faithful. Repeatedly they insisted, but just as often she resisted, saying, "Kill me now if you must, for I'll never, never become Moslem." She took her New Testament and began reading it in her captors' presence. They actually let the girl go, and she was able to return home unharmed. At least 200 other Armenian brides and girls, however, were carried off and not returned.[40]

Johannes Lepsius, an evangelical pastor from Berlin, later traveled throughout the eastern Turkish provinces reporting on the massacres. He included Mary's account of Gürün in his work:

> The condition of the people there is indescribable. Now, where once lay a charming and fertile district, there is nothing as far as the eye can reach, but an empty desolate coal-black mass to be seen, a picture of what a frightful cannonade can accomplish. The ruined walls, which before were snugly embowered in well-cultivated orchards, remained as a witness of happiness and prosperity destroyed. As I went from one ruined house to another, I heard only thrilling cries from the lips of wives and mothers from whom everything had been taken. The survivors are herded together in isolated stalls, and here and there, in a single room, the only remnant of a once habitable house. The wretched people were dressed in rags which were bound round their loins with a string, and this, their sole clothing, was hardly enough to cover their nakedness. Mothers came and begged me for help to find their captive daughters. Taken altogether, it would be hard to imagine a more heartrending picture than that which I saw. After careful calculation, we find there are 5075 persons in Gürün, who need daily support if they are not to starve. For two and a half months they have received no support from the government, not one grain of corn; and what is true of Gürün, is true also of many other villages, where, besides the famine, many diseases, and especially typhus fever, are said to be spreading.[41]

Mary's heart was breaking as she saw the destruction and suffering everywhere. She did what she could to help Pastor Demirjian organize relief. She also boldly petitioned the city mayor and the highest military officer to show them a house where the 438 remaining Protestants could re-assemble for worship and re-open the school. The officials kindly received Mary and did find a suitable house for Protestant use. Their kindness seemed a direct interposition of Divine favor. Mary also made arrangements for the pastor to rebuild the parsonage as headquarters for the Gospel work. She was able to give the pastor funds for the rebuilding, which would also provide employment for many of the homeless and impoverished Armenians.[42]

As the Ottoman Turks busied themselves with massacre, the European and American consular offices in the six eastern provinces were busy reporting their observations to their principals. Their collective conclusion and judgment was that the 1894-1896 massacres were orchestrated from the sultan's palace. Consular delegates at the Sassoun Inquiry Commission from England, France, and Russia, in a sixty-page report found that refusal of a few Armenians to pay taxes, or some Armenian resistance to Turkish troops, was not an "open revolt" as claimed by the government. British delegate Shipley's separate report referred to the Turkish charges as "pretended outrages."[43] France's Ambassador Cambon described the massacres of 1894-96 as carefully organized. He reported that Turkish foreign minister Tevfik Pasha had stated to him that the Turkish government had condoned the massacres. The French consul at Diarbekir wrote on May 20, 1895, four months before the massacres began, that the Kurds "had received permission to exterminate the Armenians."[44]

British Vice Consul Hampton reported that the massacre at Moush was upon orders from "central authorities" and that prisoners were released from prison to participate in the massacre.[45] In Sivas, Vice Consul Bulman reported that he had "definite proof that the massacres were prearranged."[46] The British Chargé wrote to Lord Salisbury that the 1894-96 "massacres in the Turkish Provinces were the result of secret orders sent by the Palace officials if not the sultan himself" and cited a copy of such an order that had been obtained. In a secret coded message, British Consul Herbert reported that he was "certain that the government organized and armed, for the purpose of killing the Armenians, the mob which committed all the massacres..."[47]

Sir William Ramsay, British classicist and archaeologist, wrote of the massacres of the Armenians:

> ... one must conceive what has been always the character of a thorough-going Turkish massacre. It does not mean merely that

thousands are killed in a few days by the sword, the torture, or the fire. It does not mean merely that everything they possess is stolen, their houses and shops looted and often burned, every article worth a halfpenny taken, the corpses stripped. It does not mean merely that the survivors are left penniless – without food, sometimes literally stark naked. That is only the beginning, the brighter and lighter side of a massacre in Turkey. Sometimes, when the Turks have been especially merciful, they have offered their victims an escape from death by accepting Mohammedanism. But as to the darker side of Turkish massacre – personal outrage and shame – take what the more freespoken historians of former times have told; gather together the details of the most horrible and indescribable outrages that occasional criminals of half-lunatic character commit in this country; imagine those criminals collected in thousands, heated with the hard work of murder, inciting each other and vying with each other, encouraged by the government officials with promises of impunity and hope of plunder – imagine the result if you can, and you will have some faint idea of the massacres in the eastern parts of Turkey.

There has been no exaggeration in the worst accounts of the horrors of Armenia. A writer with the vivid imagination of Dumas and the knowledge of evil that Zola possesses could not attain, by any description, the effect that the sight of one massacre in the Kurdish part of Armenia would produce on any spectator. The Kurdish part of Armenia is the "black country." It has become a charnel house. One dare not enter it. One cannot think about it. One knows not how many maimed, mutilated, outraged Armenians are still starving there.

Further, to rightly appreciate the educative surroundings in which Turks grow up, one must remember that such massacres were preached and roused and led by the priests, who set the example as a holy sacrifice, and who promised special honour in paradise to all who joined in the holy work, teaching that massacre and outrage of Giaours ["cattle"] is a religious merit.[48]

Germany in the 1890s had close ties with Turkey and sent military advisors to the country; the report of its diplomats to Kaiser Wilhelm II generally described the massacres as having been arranged by the sultan. German Ambassador Saurma in one report described the atrocities as "the ongoing mass murder of the Armenians."[49] In another report, the Ambassador said: "...the most diverse sources assure us that the Armenian massacres were enacted mostly as a result of secret orders (*geheime Befehle*) emanating from the Palace.[50] As these consular reports, and those of the eyewitness accounts of the American missionaries, reached America, the outraged U.S. Senate unanimously condemned the Turkish slaughter in its resolution of January 22, 1896. Speaking for the resolution, Senator Cullom said:

> The evidence of the bloody enormities was given by all classes and nationalities until it was beyond the slightest doubt. A Turkish Army had bayoneted, robbed, murdered, and flayed alive the people of Armenia...No event of the centuries called so loudly to the civilized world as the slaughter in Turkey, the greatest in the history of the world.[51]

When the publisher of the *New York Herald* doubted whether the massacres of 1894-96 could have been carried out with such shocking horror, he persuaded Sultan Abdul Hamid to permit a team to investigate the atrocities where they had occurred. In his travels, George Hepworth found that every missionary station was filled with scores of orphans:

> ...made orphans by as base a crime as ever stained the page of history. I have looked into their sad faces, and seen so many widows, that I wonder why the thunderbolts of God have not been hurled at the offenders...The deliberate attempt to exterminate a race is not sanctioned by the spirit of this century. That attempt has been made, and unless all signs fail it will be made again when Europe shall so far forget the past as to render immunity probable.[52]

After a two-month survey, Hepworth wrote carefully documented findings that included an amazing prophecy of future attempts to exterminate the Armenians:

> Way down in the bottom of his heart, the Turk hates the Armenian. He will swear to the contrary, but I am convinced that the statement is true nevertheless. The reasons for this are abundant, as I have tried to show ...in this book. The Turk is extremely jealous of the Armenian, jealous of his mental superiority, of his thrift, and business enterprise. He has, therefore, resorted to oppression, and his steady purpose has been and is now, to keep his victims poor. Equal opportunities for all are a delusion and a snare. They do not exist. ... During my travels in Armenia I have been more and more deeply convinced that the future of the Armenians is extremely clouded. It may be that the hand of the Turk will be held back through fear of Europe but I am sure that the object of the Turk is extermination, and that he will pursue that end if the opportunity offers. He has already

come very near to its accomplishment for the Armenians of today are an impoverished people, hopeless and in despair.[53]

In retrospect, during the 1890s in Turkey, there were a few spontaneous isolated incidents, such as that in Sassoun, where Armenian villagers rose up and resisted intolerable oppression and injustice. During the same decade, revolutionary organizations initiated a few planned uprisings, but none of them accomplished their purpose of enlisting European support for the cause of the Armenian Christians. Regardless of whether Armenian armed resistance was spontaneous self-defense, or an activist group trying to attract European support, the results were tragically the same. In each case, the sultan used the incident as a pretext to launch massive retaliatory execution of thousands of innocent Armenians.[54] Professor H. Anthony Salmone commented on the silence of the western powers at the barbarities of the sultan:

> The darkest record in the page of modern history is unquestionably that of the reign of Abdul Hamid...with all the boasted claim of Western nations to civilization, culture, love of justice and humanity, and the protection of the oppressed, they have of late remained inert witnesses of the most barbaric treatment that a subjugated people ever received from its rulers.[55]

The sultan himself summarized the Ottoman government policy to Turkish Foreign Secretary Said Pasha, when he said: "The Armenian question must be settled not by reform but by blood."[56] This policy of Abdul Hamid II became successful because of the disunity and apathy of the European powers, and their collective unwillingness to enforce the Berlin Treaty reforms. The fact that the Ottoman government could exterminate thousands of innocent and defenseless Armenians with impunity led the sultan to arrive at a horrible truth: Periodic genocide is pragmatically successful.

As Henry and the American missionaries looked back on the sultan's systematic slaughter of Armenians, Gladstone's eloquent appeal the previous year to the conscience of Christendom and humanity took on added meaning :

> There is such a thing as the conscience of mankind at large, and that conscience is not limited even to Christendom. And there is great power in the collected voice of outraged humanity. ... It is time

that one general shout of execration directed against deeds of wickedness should rise from outraged humanity, and should force itself into the ears of the sultan of Turkey and make him sensible, if anything can make him sensible, of the madness of such a course.

The history of Turkey has been a sad and painful history. That race has not been without remarkable and even in some cases fine qualities, but from too many points of view it has been a scourge to the world, made use of, no doubt, by a wise Providence for the sins of the world. If these tales of murder, violation, and outrage be true, then it will ... stand as if it were written with letters of iron on the records of the world that such a government as that which can countenance and cover the perpetration of such outrages is a disgrace... to civilization at large, and that it is a curse to mankind.[57]

U.S. Minister Terrell's reports to the Department of State frequently included reports from missionaries who were experiencing first hand the impact of the massacres. In his January 13, 1896, dispatch, Terrell included the moving statement from a missionary at Harpoot:

I simply wish to state what is made more and more clear to us, that we are confronting a Moslem crusade, the avowed object of which is to leave no Christians here. My responsibility goes no further. I must leave it to the Christian nations to say whether they will permit Islam ruthlessly to invade Christian homes and by force propagate its faith among Christians. I wish I could picture to you one fourth of the wretchedness and woe here in the interior. It is awful, awful, awful! If I should simply take our own students – two have been killed; one has lost 25 relatives, including father and brother; of the family of another only one escaped. Two boys yesterday heard of the death of their father; one girl heard of the death of her father, another of the death of her father and two brothers; and so it goes from day to day. We know of 13 Protestant pastors and preachers who have been killed...the Turks of the city said if war ensued they would slaughter the remaining Christians.[58]

A report from a correspondent in Turkey made an even more impassioned statement and plea in Britain's *Evangelical Christendom*:

The world can never know the thousandth part of the brutality which has been practised in the country districts to destroy Christianity. As one has already said, "It is difficult to find any page of the world's history which is blacker than this, for wide extent of the crime, for diabolical cruelty of the plan, and for inhuman barbarity of its execution."...

The Christian world must no longer disregard the cry of this oppressed and down-trodden people. A wall of despair is heard throughout the length and breadth of the land; the blood of hundreds of martyrs cries to God from the soil; the shrieks of women and maidens is heard as they are dragged into a captivity worse than death. Cannot the eyes of the world be opened to these atrocities, and its conscience aroused to a sense of duty in the direction of causing them to cease? The master's voice still rings in the ears of a generation to whom He appeals. Must it still be in vain? Shall Christians wrap themselves in their comfort and say it falls not to us to interfere... Does not that Voice still sound through the ages, saying,- "Inasmuch as ye did it not unto one of the least of these my brethren, ye did it not unto me?" What answer can we have in that day, if the Church of Christ lifts no voice, and stirs no muscle, to save those who have cried in vain to the soulless politicians of the present decadent age?[59]

The Turkish government, in blaming the uprisings on Armenian revolutionaries, also began to blame the American missionaries for the Armenian disturbances. Minister Terrell advised the missionaries to withdraw from Turkey, fearing their lives were in danger. The missionaries, however, refused to leave. They could not desert their fellow-Christians when they were now needed more than ever. Under pressure from the United States and the European powers, the Ottoman government relented in its attempt to expel the missionaries.

The pressure placed on the missionaries to leave Turkey forced them to evaluate their roll and accomplishments in that country. Reverend Farnsworth, missionary in Caesarea, wrote a detailed evaluation in *The Missionary Herald*. He noted a number of important accomplishments. First, because of the American missionaries, the Scriptures were now available in the several different languages of the people of Turkey for the first time. A change of attitude had occurred as well, and many of the people, even in the older churches, were reading the Scriptures. Secondly, an educational revival had taken place in the land. Many works of Christian literature, such as *Pilgrim's Progress*, had been translated into the vernacular languages. To encourage an interest in education, the missionaries had also published school textbooks. Thirdly, the missionaries were pioneers in educational work in Turkey, including the establishment of schools for girls. Finally, the missionaries in Turkey had added to the growth of the church:

The last published statistics report 111 churches with 11, 835 communicants. Ninety ordained pastors and 125 native preachers are reported as ministering to these churches and the many out-stations. The aggregate native agency, pastors, preachers, teachers, Bible-readers, colporteurs, and other helpers was 800. The number of congregations was 285 and the aggregate worshippers a little more, on an average, than 32,000. There were admitted to the churches in the year (1894-1895) 522. The congregations, despite their chronic poverty and the peculiarly hard times, gave for the support of their preachers, teachers, etc., and for objects of benevolence, $59, 672...Let no one overlook the well-known fact that such statistics represent but a small part of work which missions accomplish. The larger work is the quite unobserved influence of the leaven of the gospel. The leaven is working among the millions of Armenians and Greeks, and to some extent, among the Turks. In very many places the mass of the Armenians, though remaining in their old church connections, are essentially evangelical. A friend of the writer, a very intelligent lawyer, said, a year or two ago: "We have all of us become Protestants and did not know it."[60]

William Wheelock Peet, Treasurer and business agent for the American Board in Turkey, wrote from Constantinople:

It seems to me that we have an unusual opportunity before us; the differences between the Protestant community and the Gregorians are fast melting away. The position taken by the American missionaries in this time of sorrow to the Armenian people is giving them a place in the hearts of the Armenians which they never held before. It is probable that we have before us opportunities without a parallel in the history of these missions, and if we are able and have courage and grace given us to hold on through the present visitation, our position in this land will be such as never could have been gained in any other way. To leave the field now would be to give up the possibility of a stronger position and wider influence than has ever been possible in the history of these missions.[61]

Reverend Judson Smith, foreign secretary for the ABCFM, was the chief correspondent with Henry and the other missionaries in Turkey. He received their firsthand reports of the massacres in their particular regions. In October 7, 1896, he summarized the crisis in Turkey in a report to the ABCFM's Prudential Committee. He began his report by comparing the persecutions in Turkey with the persecutions of the church in its earliest days:

> The events of the past year in Asiatic Turkey have brought us face to face with the greatest disaster which has ever yet befallen any mission of the Board. Indeed, the occasions are few in the whole of Christianity, in earlier or later days, in which the powers of evil have dealt the Church more deadly blows. To a casual view it may seem that the results of all our seventy years in Turkey have gone down in the general crash, and that the only thing left for us to do is to withdraw from the field and count all as lost. But here, as in [the Emperor] Julian's day, the deeper insight will reveal that though much is gone, yet all is not lost; that what remains is the seeds of a nobler, richer growth; that instead of the night of ruin and despair, this also is a little cloud, and will pass away. ...
>
> To withdraw now would be to lose a great opportunity. The calamities of the past year have changed many things. The pressure of common distress has brought Protestants and Gregorians into closer relationships of sympathy and suffering. They have worshipped in the same churches, have met in the same prayer-meetings, have listened now to the Protestant preacher or the missionary, and now to the Gregorian priest. Through large portions of the country this practical unification of the nation is going on. And along with this is the deepened religious feeling that pervades the people. Crushed, humbled, with no help but in God, there is a wide and unwonted turning of heart to the gospel and its great consolations. A new sense of eternal realities, of the privileges of discipleship, of the hopes and joys of the Christian faith has been awakened throughout the whole land....
>
> We must not forfeit the power of the martyr church. For the name of Christ many have met death without dismay; men and women, who could have saved their lives by denying their Lord, have joyfully chosen him at the sword's point, at the musket's mouth. Gathering now in rags from ruined homes, and worshiping in dismantled churches, they wear a glory that time cannot obscure. If it were ever possible for the American churches to retire from these fields, we cannot think of it now, when every heart in the civilized world thrills with admiration of their deeds. Those churches must be sustained at any cost...
>
> We must give great weight to the judgment of the missionaries. They stand at the front. They have faced danger. They have walked in the valley of the shadow of death. They have felt the power of the gates of hell. They know, better than all besides, what has been lost and what still remains. Perils hang about them still, subtle, impalpable, persistent; no man can tell what a day may bring forth. But they

abide in peace, with no thought of fear or retreat. And to a man they urge us to maintain our work and seize the glorious opportunity that lies before us. From the midst of the flames and the ruin they have given thanks to God that they have lived to see this day and have begged us not to recall them. With the vision of faith they have looked beyond this day of fear and desolation, and have seen the kingdom of God coming in power among the people of every name and nation there...[62]

Henry and Mary were both consumed with the massive relief effort to help the now impoverished, starving, and often homeless Armenians. They diligently wrote letters to Christian leaders in the United States and England to raise support for the suffering people. Their house was constantly filled with refugees and those needing aid. Church services too were full as the people realized their need for spiritual food to sustain them in the spiritual struggle. Through it all, Henry and Mary were very protective of eleven year old Jean. Sivas certainly was not the safest place for her, and she was reaching the age when she required more formal schooling. When Dr. and Mrs. Dodd planned to leave Caesarea for the United States, they agreed to take Jean with them. Henry wrote letters and made all the necessary arrangements for her to stay with his sister Sarah in North Adams. It would be difficult and lonely to see his little girl go, but under the conditions it was for the best.

A week before she was scheduled to leave, Jean came down with the mumps! She recovered in time to leave with Henry on April 24 for a rendezvous with the Dodds in Talas. On Sunday, April 26, 1896, Henry gave the sermon in the Talas church. He noted in his diary, "Jean was real good all day, and a great comfort to me." The next day Jean left with the Dodds for Constantinople and the United States. By May 1, Henry was back at Sivas, but noted "Our house was very lonely without our Jean."

---

[1] *Diary*, October 17, 1894.

[2] *Empires in Conflict*, 18; "Armenian Question, 1878-1923," *Crime of Silence*, 16.

[3] A *firman* was an imperial decree or edict, handlettered on parchment and bearing the stylized monogram of the then-reigning Sultan. A *firman* would be needed to build a school, operate a hospital, or carry out any activity which needed government approval.

[4] *Armenian Massacres*, 20-21.
[5] *Armenian Massacres*, 13-14; 20-23. At the time of collecting the eye-witness reports of the massacres, Rev. Greene was careful to verify the identity and veracity of the narrators, but did not publish their names for fear of Turkish retaliation against them or their relatives who still remained alive.
[6] *Armenian Massacres*, 7-8,13; quoting *Blue Book*, Turkey, 1895, No. 1, Part I., 200-206. In November, 1895, the Constantinople papers carried the news that the Sultan had presented high military decorations to Zekki Pasha, the Fourth Army Corps commander who had led the troops during the Sassoun slaughter. The Sultan also had given commendation awards to the Kurdish chiefs whose *Hamediehs* had actively participated in the pogrom.
[7] Greene, *Armenian Massacres*, 8.
[8] British Foreign Office 424/182, Consul Graves to Currie, "Statement of Turkish ex-seargeant Suleiman," 16 March 1895; as quoted in Soumakian, *Empires in Conflict*, p.18.
[9] Judson Smith to H.T. Perry, January 21, 1895. ABC.2.1, Vol. 169, no. 2, p. 2.
[10] "Armenian Question, 1878-1923," *Crime of Silence*, 16 citing documents in the French and British foreign offices.
[11] *Empires in Conflict*, 28-31.
[12] *Armenian Massacres*, 441. Because of their treaty relations with the Ottoman Empire, the European powers were more in a position to seek to enforce reforms on Turkey than was the United States, which was not a party to the same treaties. The United States' ministers and consuls, however, worked closely with the British and other European ministers to protect American lives and property.
[13] Henry T. Perry. *The Abiding Peace of the Son of God*, sermon manuscript in possession of Gordon Bruce Severance.
[14] *Armenian Massacres*, 31-32. See Appendix A for a chart summarizing the 1895 massacres.
[15] *Diary*, October 18, 1895.
[16] *Armenian Massacres*, 96 (citing 4 additional sources).
[17] *London Times*, Weekly Edition, January 14, 1895.
[18] Reprinted from *The Christian Register*, Boston, Dec. 1, 1894, quoted in Frederick Greene, *Armenian Massacres and Turkish Tyranny*, 122-126.
[19] Mr. Terrell to Mr. Olney, October 24, 1895 (No. 651) in *Papers Relating to the Foreign relations of the United States*, Part II. Washington: Government Printing Office, 1896, 1326.
[20] Rev.F.D.Greene, in *Armenian Massacres*, 434, reported that during the last quarter of the nineteenth century, an official prayer of Islam which was used throughout Turkey, and daily repeated in the Cairo Azhar University by thousands of Mohammedan students from many regions of the middle east, was as follows:
> I seek refuge with Allah from Satan, the accursed. In the name of Allah the Compassionate, the Merciful! O Lord of all Creatures! O Allah! Destroy the infidel and polytheists, thine enemies, the enemies of the

religion! O Allah! Make their children orphans, and defile their abodes! Cause their feet to slip; give them and their families, their households and their women, their children and their relations by marriage, their brothers and their friends, their possessions and their race, their wealth and their lands, as booty to the Moslems, O Lord of all Creatures!

[21] *Armenian Massacres*, 32-33.
[22] *Turkey and the Armenian Atrocities*, 471.
[23] *Diary*, October 29, 1895.
[24] Edwin W. Martin, *The Hubbards of Sivas*, 242.
[25] Henry T. Perry to Rev. Judson Smith, November 6, 1895, ABC 16.9.3, Vol. 614.
[26] *Diary*, November 8-9, 1895.
[27] Milo Jewett to Mr. Edwin F. Uhl, November 9, 1895 (T-681, Roll 2). Jewett's reports were generally received in Washington a month after they were sent.
[28] Milo Jewett to Mr. E.F. Uhl, November 10, 1895 (T-681, Roll 2).
[29] *Diary*, November 13-16, 1895.
[30] *Turkey and The Armenian Atrocities*, 465.
[31] Henry T. Perry to Rev. Judson Smith, November 18, 1895, ABC 16.9.3, Vol. 614.
[32] Charles Holbrook, "Turkey Letter No. 3," 24, ABC 16.5, Vol. 6. Writing in 1913, Holbrook included in his letter a photo of the priest and wrote that the fact of his murders was "well known by both Turks and Armenians, and yet he is still an honored priest of Islam!"
[33] "Editorial Paragraphs," *The Missionary Herald*, March 1896, 95; Rev. Ohan Gaidzakian. *Illustrated Armenia and the Armenians*. Boston, 1898, 253.
[34] Mr. Milo Jewett to Mr. Edwin F. Uhl, November 22, 1895 (T-681, Roll 2).
[35] *Diary*, November 18, 1895.
[36] *Diary*, December 17, 22, 1895.
[37] Christopher Walker. *Armenia – Survival of a Nation*. London: Croom Helm, 1980, 158; E.E. Strong. *Asiatic Turkey: A Sketch of the Mission of the American Board*. Boston: Printed for the American Board, 1910, 28-29; *Judgment unto Truth*, 3.
[38] Henry T. Perry to Rev. Judson Smith, December 9, 1895, ABC 16.9.3, Vol. 614.
[39] Mary H. Perry to Rev. Judson Smith, January 21, 1896, ABC 16.9.3, Vol. 614; Mary H. Perry, "Notes on Gurun," ABC 16.9.95, Vol. 3, 51.
[40] "Editorial Paragraphs," *The Missionary Herald*, April, 1896, 137.
[41] J. Lepsius. *Armenian and Europe: An Indictment*, ed. J. Rendel Harris. London: Hodder & Stoughton, 1897, 132-133. Following the massacres in Turkey, in 1895 Lepsius set up the Deutsche Orient Mission to run orphanages for Armenian children who survived the massacres. His writings in 1895 and 1916 documented the atrocities committed against the Armenians. Because of

the Turkophile attitude of the German government, Lepisus had to take refuge in Holland to continue his struggle for the Armenians. http://gariwo.net/armenia/lepsius.htm, 12-30-2002.

[42] Mary H. Perry to Consul Milo Jewett, January 29. 1896 (T-681, Roll 2).

[43] *Blue Book,* Turkey, no.1,(1895) part 1, pp.133-93. Report no. 252, written on 20 July , submitted 15 August 1895, as quoted by Vahakn N. Dadrian. *Warrant for Genocide: Key Elements of Turko-Armenian Conflict.* London (U.K.): Transaction Publishers (1999), 86.

[44] Archives du Ministeré Étrangeéres, N.S.1,Turquie, Politique Interieure Jeuns Turcs. (Paris, 1897), 11 February 1897, as quoted in *Warrant for Genocide,* 87.

[45] British Foreign Office 195/1944, reports of September 25,29,30, and November 8, 1896, folio nos. 224, 228, 253-8,303, quoted in *Warrant for Genocide*, 87.

[46] FO 195/1930, quoted in *Warrant for Genocide*, 87.

[47] FO 195/1870 confidential report no.79, 13 November 1895, as quoted in *Warrant for Genocide, 88.*

[48] *Impressions of Turkey During Twelve Years of Wandering*, 211-212. Sir William Ramsay (1851-1939) was professor of humanity at Aberdeen (1886-1911) and spent many of his long vacations in Asia Minor. He became a specialist in early Christian history, which included the geography and early history of Asia Minor. His works are still classics in the field: *Historical Geography of Asia Minor* (1890), *The Church in the Roman Empire before A.D. 170* (1930), *The Cities of St. Paul* (1907), and *A Historical Commentary on St. Paul's Epistle to the Galatians* (1899). "Sir William Ramsay", J.D. Douglas, et. al. eds. *Who's Who in Christian History* Wheaton, Illinois: Tyndale House Publishers, 1992, 580-581. As a classical scholar and archaeologist, Ramsay believed the Turks had ruined the culture of Asia Minor and had done nothing to elevate the region. He wrote: "The action of the Turks in every department of life has simply been to ruin, never to rebuild. It is not merely the cities, the buildings and the government of old Rome that they destroyed. Their work was far more thorough and far more dangerous. They destroyed the intellectual and moral institutions of a nation; they broke up and dissolved almost the entire social fabric; they annihilated every educative and humanising influence in the land; and they brought back great parts of the country to the primitive simplicity of nomadic life. There was left just enough of the ancient institutions to make an Empire possible…in general, there is hardly a social institution in Asia Minor showing any degree of legal or social constructiveness that is not an older Anatolian creation, Moslemised in outward form, and usually degraded in the process." (*Impressions of Turkey,* 264-265).

[49] German Foreign Ministry Archives, 1871-1914, *Akten des Auswärtigen Amtes,* 1871-1914, vol. 10. *Das Turkische Problem 1895,* (Berlin: Deutsche Verlagsgesellschaft für Politik und Geschichte, 1923, report no. 162/2444, October 26, 1895, 84-5, as quoted in *Warrant for Genocide,* 91-91.

[50] *Ibid.,* report no. 165/2456, 101, cited in *Warrant for Genocide,* 89.

[51] *Congressional Record,* 54th Cong.1st Sess., vol.28, part 1 as quoted in Dadrian *Warrant for Genocide,* 96.

[52] George H. Hepworth. *Through Armenia on Horseback.* New York: E.P. Dutton, 1898, 56.

[53] *Through Armenia on Horseback,* 339-40, 146-147. England's well-known ethnographer, W.M. Ramsay made a similar forecast in 1897: "The Armenians will in all probability be exterminated except the remnant that escapes to other lands." *Impressions of Turkey,* 156-7.

[54] The Turkish ethnocide of Armenians for the years 1894-97 claimed 200,000 victims, according to the estimate of W.M. Ramsey, a noted British ethnographer.

[55] "The Massacres in Turkey," *The Nineteenth Century* No. CCXXXVI, October 1896, 671.

[56] R. Douglas, "Britain and the Armenian Question 1894-7, "*Historical Journal, Vol 19, no.1 (1976),* 125; quoted from Salisbury Papers, A/135, fos. 249-56, Currie to Salisbury, 11 Dec. 1895; cited by Soumakian, *Empires in Conflict,* 21.

[57] *The London Times,* Weekly Edition, Jan. 14, 1895.

[58] Mr. Terrell to Mr. Olney, December 29, 1895 in *Papers Relating to Foreign Relations of the U.S., Part II, 1896,* 1424.

[59] The Massacres and Outrages in Asia Minor," *Evangelical Christendom,* Vol. 37, March 2, 1896.

[60] W.A. Farnsworth," Some Results of Missionary Work in Turkey," *The Missionary Herald,* March 1896, 99-102.

[61] "Editorial Paragraphs," *The Missionary Herald,* April, 1896, 136.

[62] Rev. Judson Smith. "The Crisis in Turkey," *The Missionary Herald,* November, 1896, 443-451.

10
A BRUISED REED
(1896-1901)

*"A bruised reed he shall not break,
and the smoking flax he shall not quench."*
Isaiah 42:3

Throughout the nineteenth century, American missionaries were the prime contact the United States had with foreign countries. The American consular corps remained small, and, following the advice of George Washington in his Farewell Address, the United States had steered clear of foreign alliances. As late as 1912, Nicholas M. Butler, President of Columbia University and a leader in the world peace movement, recognized that:

> Foreign missions are largely responsible for the development of whatever international mind the United States now possesses. ... foreign missions also have no inconsiderable share in exploration and investigation; and what is more, missions have taught us to care for these people with whom we have become acquainted.[1]

Though the American diplomatic and economic presence in Turkey was weak, the American missionary presence was strong; and during the crisis in Turkey after the Armenian massacres, the American missionaries did more for the people in Turkey than all the European powers combined.

The massacres at Sivas and throughout Turkey created "a reign of terror which destroyed confidence, paralyzed industry and seriously affected all business." In Sivas province alone, the November 1895, massacre destroyed "about 5,400 lives and 2,000 houses, caused a loss to the Armenian of about $20,000,000 worth of property and rendered 18,000 or 20,000 children orphans or fatherless."[2]

American and British residents at Constantinople, under the patronage of the British ambassador, formed a relief committee. Within a month of the massacre, the American mission at Sivas was authorized to draw on relief moneys held by the Bible House. Soon funds from every corner of America and England began to pour into the relief effort administered by the American Board in Constantinople. The missionaries at Sivas quickly organized their own regional relief committee, naming British Consul Bullman as chairman, with American Consul Jewett as alternate chairman. Perry, already Treasurer for the Sivas mission, was appointed custodian of incoming relief funds for the region. The American missionaries throughout Turkey, in addition to regular duties, now assumed the staggering challenge of caring for thousands of widows and orphans in the six *vilayets* of Turkish Armenia. Providence qualified the missionaries ideally for the task. With more than a half-century of serving among the Armenians and fluency in their language, the American missionaries tirelessly plunged into the relief effort.

Relief was of two kinds. The first priority was to distribute food and clothing to simply keep the surviving victims of the massacres alive. Then, to help them work toward self-sufficiency, seed, oxen, and farm equipment were distributed. Very little money was given directly to the people. American Consul Jewett estimated that at least 20,000 people in the Sivas province were saved from starvation or death by cold because of the relief assistance.

Donations continued to flood in from many sources, and they all crossed Henry's desk before the funds were converted into goods for the relief of the needy. Many Armenians abroad sent personal checks to their relatives and friends, which were paid directly to the persons for whom the money was sent. The Armenian patriarch had called on William Peet, ABCFM Treasurer in Constantinople, and asked him to take complete charge of money sent to him for relief. He said, "I have no means of distributing this fund with the assurance that it will, in any large part, reach the people, but I know that through the missionaries every dollar will go to the suffering poor." Years later, Dr. James Barton noted that the confidence the Patriarch placed in the missionaries was an indication that:

> The absolute integrity of the life and dealing of the missionaries with the people has done perhaps as much in that land of deceit and dishonesty to commend the simple gospel of Jesus Christ to all classes as any other single phase of missionary work.[3]

Among the many other contributors to general relief were the Duke of Westminster relief committee in London, the Armenian National Relief Association in America, the Armenian Relief Fund, and the American Red Cross.

The American Red Cross relief team was personally headed by seventy-five year old Clara Barton, who had led in the founding of the American society in 1881. This was only the second overseas relief mission for the American Red Cross (the first was during the 1891 Russian famine). Shortly after the massacres, the Reverend Judson Smith in Boston, Secretary of the ABCFM, and Reverend Henry Dwight of Constantinople had requested the aid of the Red Cross to help the suffering Armenians. With Turkey's strict laws and the strong religious differences between Moslems and Christians, distributing relief was difficult. However, since Turkey had been one of the signatory powers to the Red Cross Treaty of Geneva in 1865, it was thought that the government would accept a Red Cross team of workers. The treaty clearly stated: "all national controversies, racial distinctions, and differences in creed must be held in abeyance and only the needs of humanity considered." It was in this spirit that the Red Cross always worked.

However, the American outpouring of aid from groups who denounced the Turks caused the Turkish minister in Washington, D.C. to prohibit the American Red Cross team from coming to Turkey. Even knowing of this prohibition, the Red Cross team optimistically sailed to Turkey aboard the steamship *New York* on January 22, 1896. In London the team learned the American Red Cross was definitely prohibited, but individuals appointed by Minister Terrell at Constantinople would be allowed into the country for relief purposes. With that proviso, Minister Terrell thought he would be able to appoint the individuals of the Red Cross team as relief agents in Turkey. It took more negotiation, however, before Turkey finally agreed to the relief mission.

By mid-February Clara Barton and her five-member Red Cross team were in Constantinople meeting with ABCFM Treasurer Peet and Dr. Washburn of Robert College on how best to proceed in Armenian relief. Dr. William Peet and Dr. Washburn were important representatives of the American Christians in Turkey. Dr. Peet was a businessman who for seven years had been with the Chicago, Burlington, and Quincy Railroad. In 1886, he became diplomatic and business head of the American Board's work in the Near East. He was a devout Christian layman who served the Board admirably in Turkey. To better carry out his duties, he studied Turkish law for four years. His wisdom and training made him highly respected and trusted in American diplomatic circles.[4] Dr. Washburn, as President of the American Robert College, was also highly respected by American and Turkish diplomats.

Miss Barton was somewhat discouraged that Turkey had not yet agreed to the Red Cross relief mission and feared further delay would only accelerate the death rate and increase suffering among the Armenians. At the same time, she was full of admiration for the relief work the American missionaries had already done in Turkey:

> I will always feel it a privilege and an honor to have been called, even in a small way, to assist the efforts of this chosen body of our countrymen and women, whose faithful and devoted lives are made sacred to the service of God and their fellow men.[5]

At last, Minister Terrell and Miss Barton were able to have an hour-long interview with Tewfik Pasha, Turkish Minister of Foreign Affairs, and Turkey agreed to allow the proposed aid mission. Turkish escorts were provided for the five expeditions the Red Cross sent out into the country. The Red Cross had $116,000 to distribute in Turkey. Its aid primarily took the form of seed, tools, and farm equipment. All the Armenian cattle and farm animals had been driven into the Kurdish mountains, but the Red Cross bought them back and restored them to the people.

Clara Barton stayed in Constantinople for six months, overseeing the relief effort. She took no time out for sightseeing, but worked tirelessly to help the suffering Armenians. During her stay she took only two days for any social relaxation – a picnic on July 4th and a farewell dinner with friends in August. Celebrating Independence Day among Americans while in a land lacking in liberty made a deep impression on Miss Barton. Reflecting on the blessings of liberty America had achieved in 1776, she recognized that in the ensuing century the United States had become an important beacon of liberty to people throughout the world.

The Hubbard family had returned to Turkey from their furlough just at the time of the massacres and had to remain at Constantinople some months before they were allowed to continue on to Sivas. Albert returned to Sivas February 1896, but many friends agreed it might not yet be safe for Emma, Mary, Hugh, and Theodore, so they remained in Constantinople. In May 1896, on her way to the United States, twelve-year-old Jean Perry stayed for two weeks with Mrs. Hubbard and the children in Constantinople. One day Mrs. Hubbard took Jean to visit Clara Barton; it was a visit Jean remembered the rest of her life.[6]

As the Red Cross worked with the missionaries to bring aid to the Armenians, Clara Barton's admiration for the missionaries only increased. In a letter from Constantinople dated May 9, she wrote:

> It seems to me that the blessing of heaven is resting on the work we are all trying, however inadequately, to do. My sympathies go out to these worn, tired missionary men and women who have struggled so long, borne so much, so bravely, and so well. It cannot be all in vain; and again daily and hourly I thank our heavenly Father for the little temporary help that it may have been in the power of myself and mine to bring them.[7]

J.B. Hubbell, a medical doctor, was general field agent in charge of the Red Cross expeditions into the interior of Anatolia. In the Red Cross's summer tour, Hubbell's team visited Sivas and made Henry Perry the Red Cross agent for distributing funds in the Sivas province and areas to the south. The Red Cross gave Henry and Albert a splendid Arabian horse to help them in their relief work. The missionaries fittingly named the horse "Hubbell," after the Red Cross doctor. Later the Red Cross left an emergency fund of $15,400 with Reverend Peet in Constantinople, and Henry Perry became one of the major distributors of those funds.[8]

The Red Cross had found that the American missionaries and U.S. government officials throughout Turkey, such as Consul Jewett, were the most effective means of distributing relief. Clara Barton summarized the importance of the relief effort among the Armenians:

> ...the facts are, that between the Archipelago and the Caspian Sea, the Black and the Mediterranean, are today living a million and a half people of the Armenian race, existing under the ordinance of, at least, semi-civilization, and professing the religion of Jesus Christ; that according to the stated estimate of intelligent and impartial observers of various countries and concurred in by their own agents, whose observations have been unrestricted, from 100,000 to 200,000 of these persons, men, women, and children, are destitute of shelter, raiment, fire, food, medicines, and comforts that tend to make human life preserva-

ble, or any means of obtaining them, save through the charitable beneficence of the world.⁹

Without such support, 50,000 more people would die of starvation by May 1897.

About the same time as the Red Cross team was in Turkey, Dr. J. Rendell Harris and his wife Helen were traveling in Turkey as distributors of relief funds collected by Quakers in England. A Biblical scholar and orientalist, Dr. Harris was a Cambridge professor and author of numerous studies on early Christian texts and primitive Christianity. While primarily in Turkey for humanitarian purposes, Dr. Harris availed himself of every opportunity to visit the Armenian monasteries and churches and learn of any early manuscripts that might be in their possession. In spite of the unstable political and social state of Turkey, Dr. Harris and other scholars and archaeologists found over six hundred early Greek and Syriac works which had been translated into Armenian within forty years after the creation of the Armenian alphabet at the beginning of the fifth century A.D. Many of the original works had perished, making the preserved translations even more important. These works included several books by Philo of Alexandria on providence and reason, the *Chronicle* of Eusebius, and the epistles of Ignatius.¹⁰

The Harrises arrived in Constantinople March 25, 1896, at a time when the American and European community there was alarmed at the sultan's plans to expel all the missionaries from Turkey. The sultan had already sent orders to Bitlis for all the American missionaries to leave. The American Charge d'Affaire and British Ambassador Sir Philip Currie immediately took up the cause of the missionaries. The Porte backed down and said there must have been a mistake; certainly the missionaries could remain. The threat of the expulsion of all the American missionaries hung like a Damacles sword over the American and British in Constantinople. There was some evidence that the Russian government was encouraging the sultan to remove the Americans from the country.¹¹

Since the Armenian massacres, the Turkish government had required all foreigners not only to have a passport but also a *tezkirah*, a special local Turkish passport, to travel into the interior of the Empire. As soon as the Harrises had their *tezkirahs* issued, they left for Smyrna, Aintab, and then Harpoot. As they met the orphans and widows and heard the stories of gruesome brutality inflicted on the Armenian Christians, Dr. Harris could not help but be reminded of the many martyrs of the first centuries of the church:

> I begin to see the deeds of Christian heroism which have gone on here, and are still going on, equal anything in the pages of Eusebius (indeed much of it is very like his account of the Martyrs of Palestine in the ninth book of the Ecclesiastical History).[12]

As they traveled, the Harrises also began to realize that conditions among the Armenians were much worse than they had imagined. Destitution was so widespread that the only hope for many Armenians was emigration. Some Armenians had "petitioned the sultan either to give them the means of re-tilling their fields, or to let them leave the country, or to send his soldiers back again to put them out of their misery."

One result of the massacres the Harrises soon noticed, however, was that the horrors had drawn the various bodies of Christians closer together. The common suffering had brought about a Christian unity no church council could have accomplished. Because of their social services to the sufferers, Armenian Protestants were now welcomed into the Gregorian churches. The churches themselves were crowded, and the people would sit for hours listening to the Word of God. One pastor told Dr. Harris, "We were like pieces of cold iron, but this persecution has welded us together."[13]

The massacres had disrupted the entire fabric of society. It reminded the Harrises of what England must have faced after the Black Death. Somehow society had to be rebuilt from the bottom up. It was like trying to piece together a smashed clock. In many villages, whole trades had disappeared as tradesmen were killed. Tools were stolen, and the people did not even have the means of starting to rebuild. The Harrises never gave money directly to the Armenians because the Turks could too easily take it away. They, as had the Red Cross, came to realize it was best to distribute aid and relief through the American missionaries:

> It was wisely decided to make no new organization for relief, no organization can come near to the fitness of the American Missions. If the country can be saved, the foci of its salvation are the mission stations, and in a lesser degree the consulates. No one knows the needs of the people like the Americans, and no one is so busy and so wise in giving aid as they are. They at all events have come to the kingdom for such a time as this.[14]

Wherever the Harrises went, the American missionaries were always completely cooperative and doing all in their powers to bring relief to the suffering Armenians.

In August 1896, Dr. Harris arrived in Sivas on his way to Constantinople and England; Mrs. Harris remained longer in Harpoot to continue helping the relief effort. After traveling for several days through barren, rock-strewn land, as Dr. Harris approached Sivas, he found the scenery "becoming more beautiful, the vegetation richer, and the towns and villages...more and more Swiss in their appearance. Pretty tiled roofs begin to appear, ornamental balconies and the like."[15] The Hubbards and Perrys gave Dr. Harris the warmest of welcomes, and he stayed with the Hubbards for several days. British Consul Major Bulman was not quite pleased with the Harrises' decision to stay with the American missionaries, thinking the Professor should have wrapped himself "in the folds of his hospitable Union Jack." On Sunday, August 2, Dr. Harris preached an excellent sermon in the Protestant church on casting out fear. He felt greatly honored to be standing in the pulpit when he learned the circumstances surrounding Pastor Garabed Kulukjian's death during the massacres. The pastor's steadfastness in the face of death reminded the Professor of the second century martyr Polycarp, who in his old age was burned in the arena after refusing to renounce Christ, proclaiming, "Eighty-six years I have served Him. He had never done me wrong. How then can I blaspheme my King who has saved me?"[16]

In October Albert Hubbard went to Egin, southeast of Divrik on the road to Harpoot, to escort Mrs. Harris to Sivas. Egin had been spared the 1895 massacres because a large bribe was paid to the Turkish officials. Egin was a beautiful village and among the wealthiest. Many Armenian merchants retired there after making their wealth in Constantinople. Egin's reprieve from atrocities was not permanent, however. Near noon on September 15, 1896, the days of planned massacres began. The Egin massacres had their roots in a disturbance at Constantinople.

In 1896, the Dashnaktsutiun Revolutionary Party activists seized the Imperial Ottoman Bank in Constantinople, which was actually owned by Anglo-French investors. Holding 181 hostages, the Party threatened to blow up the bank unless the sultan actually put into effect the reforms he had promised in the Treaty of Berlin. The Revolutionary Party's seizure of the Bank was a last desperate attempt to spur active

European support for Armenian rights. With the European powers applying diplomatic pressure, the Sublime Porte negotiated to guarantee the revolutionaries safe passage out of the country in exchange for release of the hostages. Learning that the leader of the raid was a native of Egin in the Harpoot province, the Palace in Constantinople sent a telegram to the Military Commandant in Harpoot ordering them "to take the necessary action." The Commandant, already overseeing massacres in the Harpoot region, immediately issued telegraphic orders to officials in Egin, and at the firing of a gun a two-day massacre ensued, slaughtering more than 2000 Armenians and burning down 980 of their homes. A Turk employed at the state telegraphic office furnished these details. Vice Consul Hampton concluded, "many Turkish notables here were deploring the massacres...and declaring that the Armenians gave no excuse for the crime."[17]

When news of the tragedy reached Mrs. Harris in Harpoot, she determined to go to Egin and offer what relief she could. An influential Turkish colonel friendly to the Christians lived next to the American Protestant mission and protected its property during the massacres. The other Armenian sections of the town were destroyed and reduced to ruins. Once wealthy and prosperous gentlemen were either butchered or reduced to abject poverty. Few men remained, and the widows and orphans were left with only tales of horror. Most of those killed had their throats cut or were killed with axes. Many of the women saw their husbands, fathers, or sons murdered before their eyes. A month after the massacre Helen Harris wrote friends in England:

> The leading Protestants were, as usual, of all the Christians the most hated by the Turks, and were hunted to the death with hardly an exception, - some shot, others killed with sword and axe, and one of the noblest of all, who had eluded detection during the three days given for the massacre, was killed openly by having his head crushed by heavy stones beaten against it, when he was in the street and supposed himself safe, after the massacre was over. "But you may not kill me now," he said; "orders have come to stop the killing." "We may no longer kill with guns," was the reply, "but stones are different, and so we may use them;" so he died.[18]

As Mrs. Harris visited the women, they invariably welcomed her into their despoiled homes with outbursts of tears. Only the Lord Himself could bring healing and relief to such grieving souls.

Mrs. Harris had spent two weeks in Egin when Albert Hubbard came to escort her to Sivas, where she stayed briefly before continuing her journey home. She was much impressed with the relief work at Sivas and was willing to find more funds in England to rebuild the school there. Mary Perry was absolutely exhausted from work and decided to accompany Mrs. Harris to Marsovan, giving herself a much-needed change. When the party set out from Sivas, it made quite an imposing appearance. As Helen Harris wrote, Mary was protected

> by a Circassian cavass belonging to the American Consulate, armed with ornamental dirk, dagger and pistol...I and an onbashoo (an officer over ten men) and a common zaptieh to take care of me.[19]

Each woman had an araba in which to ride, a sort of small springless covered wagon, but it was so bitterly cold they could not easily sleep in the araba. On the road twelve or thirteen hours a day, the ladies varied their mode of travel by alternating riding on Mardin, the horse the Harrises had bought to use in their relief work. Before the women parted, Helen sold Mardin to Mary and had "the pleasure of thinking that he will remain in the Lord's work and in loving hands."[20] The ladies also gave Turkish Bibles to their guards and protectors, who seemed pleased to receive this gift.

Because of Henry's heavy load of relief work, Mary took over the correspondence with the ABCFM's Dr. Judson Smith. Her letters reflect the severe emotional strain on the missionaries as they dealt with the horror of the massacres and the unspeakable desolation and suffering left in their wake. Now that the massacre in Sivas was over, Mary could see clearly the reason for the Turkish government's order keeping Albert Hubbard in Constantinople. The order was not, as the government had claimed, to protect the missionaries from uprisings in the interior. The real reason for the travel restriction was plain for all the missionaries to see: Sultan Abdul Hamid's planned killing of Armenians must be witnessed by as few foreigners as possible. But once the massacre was over, Mary wondered, why didn't the Turkish authorities let Albert return to his station? Mary's unexpressed anger at Turkish duplicity began to co-mingle with frustration at her own government's seeming inaction. Couldn't the United States have applied diplomatic pressure to permit Mr. Hubbard to return to Sivas so that he could help with the relief of the women and children the massacre had left in its wake? Mary expressed her pent-up frustrations to Dr. Smith, "God pity the U.S.A. Govt.! We seem to have nobody from Grover Cleveland down—able to open the way for a returning missionary to return to his post!"[21] Although Mary felt overworked, tears came to her eyes when she looked at Henry who had grown worn and thin. Unable to hold back her emotion any longer, she poured out her heart and anguish to Dr. Smith:

> If your eyes had seen what mine have, you would not sleep for rest except in snatches. This heart-pain from sheer sympathy, has run my strength low – and it's only through God's sustaining grace, that I am alive today. If we could not do a little relief work – I would have died – from grief. God has let me help, a little, in spiritual things too – which has been a wonderful comfort to my soul…Now that my secret "questionings" and "reasonings" have been let out freely to you in confidence – I'll feel better!

Mary stayed in Marsovan for a month and was able to rest and regain her strength. She was greatly encouraged by Marsovan's vibrant Girls' School. The course of study was of the highest caliber and the building itself equaled the best that might be found in the United States. Mary longed for the funds and Turkish permission to build such a facility in Sivas, but even more importantly, she most wished for more dedicated teachers and workers to help in the Sivas field.

Every day Henry received over one hundred applications for relief from the suffering men, women, and children of Sivas and the surrounding villages. The missionaries also organized relief for many Gregorian villages, not just those where the Protestants had established churches and schools. Though he had a very efficient corps of native helpers, the bulk of the work fell on Henry's shoulders. At least twice he was forced to remain in bed because of the severe back pain caused by his lumbago. He had been able to employ an able amanuensis who could read both Armeno- and Arabo-Turkish and was also able to work fairly well in English. Relief had been divided into four departments – food supply, clothing supply, the city poor, and the sick and destitute. Miss Brewer took charge of a team of women to sew clothes and also went house to house visiting the city's poor. Mary took responsibility for nursing the sick. Dr. Jewett made arrangements with two native doctors for a free medical clinic to be held once a week. With his medical background, Dr. Jewett became the "druggist" of the company. The relief committee paid one half of the doctor's fees if the doctor was sent to a specific patient. One of the Armenian doctors, " …was robbed of <u>every</u> surgical instrument, and his house was stripped of <u>everything</u> from attic to cellar – and his wife and boy two years old shot at, the shot cutting off the ends of two of the little one's fingers!"[22]

A year and a half after the massacres, the Sivas mission had provided substantial aid to over 6000 families without any remuneration for administration of the funds. Frequently, when the bags of gold arrived from the relief agencies, Henry literally spread them out on the treasury room table as he carefully determined the best distribution for the funds.[23] He used trusted pastors, teachers, and colporteurs to distribute aid in their own local communities. Bags of gold were sent by Turkish post to the villages of Tocat, Divrik, Gürün, Derende, and Kara Hissar. None of the gold was ever lost, and the Turkish government never made any resistance to the relief program.[24]

While Mary was in Marsovan, Henry mounted Hubbel and went to Gürün to better coordinate relief in the stricken city. Gürün had been the most promising of all the Sivas outstations and the most self-supporting. Shortly before the massacres the Christians had paid over $500 for two additional school buildings, receiving only $88 of aid from abroad. During the massacres the church and several school buildings were burned, and 1100 people were killed. Miraculously the pastor and teachers escaped death and were able to help in the relief of the people, 5000 of whom were listed as destitute.[25] Henry reported at length to the ABCFM on his December visit to the town:

> The recollection of Gürün, as I had seen it in previous years, and the pictures in my mind of quiet, intelligent, thrifty homes, where I had often been a guest, made the present ruin very sad to me; and 800 houses burned in a small town, these being selected from the best, make a great change in appearance.
>
> The Protestant churches where we had so frequently preached, the school buildings, their books, and fine outfit of school maps and Bibles, with all the personal property of the teachers, both at their schoolrooms and in their homes, had been a total loss. The children were left homeless, hungry, and scattered. In pity for them, Mrs. Perry, when visiting Gürün by a winter's journey over the mountains last year, presented her plea to the local governor, going in person to the government house for this purpose, that permission be given to rent rooms, and gather the children in a comfortable place, where they could also be instructed. The plea was accepted, and an official ordered to accompany her to find a suitable place. The rent for the schoolrooms, books, stores and wood, windows, in fact everything

needful, had to be supplied *de novo*, this including the daily food for the children.

By the aid of relief funds, especially by the *Christian Herald*, the schools were opened in the large, partially lighted rooms of an old house. One of the teachers came back to his work as though having risen from the dead. A succession of hairbreadth escapes, in very trying circumstances, was the proof that the Lord was with him, to spare him for his work. Much to my delight, at the time of my visit there, in December, I found these schools in good condition, and their numbers increased by many orphans who had been received into homes, to be cared for and instructed.

The pastor's own house and personal effects having been burned, after his escape with his wife by the aid of the Catholics, they were received as guests in the house of a Turkish friend. He has since told me that he was never more surprised than when he received from me the suggestion to employ the labor of refugees to clear away the rubbish of a burned house, which had been used for a school (situated in a fine location near the centre of town), and to collect there materials with which to build a house...Our design was to use it for a parsonage, and shelter for teachers, and also perhaps as headquarters for relief work. It was completed last summer, consisting of eight rooms, the work being done chiefly by breadless men; and all materials purchased at a very cheap rate. The total cost was $440; all paid by relief funds, of which the *Christian Herald* bore the chief part. The influence of this building to impart hope as well as help to the stricken people was very great from the first. It is now used as a parsonage; and from it...the larger part of all relief for Gürün has been issued.[26]

Henry also used relief funds given him by the English Consul, Major Bulman, to establish a rug-weaving factory in Gürün. In this way the people could become productive again and not be dependent on handouts for bread.

One result of the persecutions was the people were much more interested in Gospel preaching than they were before. On Sundays Henry preached three times to crowded congregations eagerly gathered together in a large open shed.

When Henry returned to Sivas, Mary was still in Marsovan, but upon her return she immediately wanted Henry to come with her to Tocat. In stopping briefly at the town on her way home, she sensed a great openness and opportunity for ministry. So, as 1896 turned to 1897, the Perrys were happy to be in Tocat where there were large opportunities for work in the gospel. It was a brief respite of intensive relief ministry for Henry, and he was able to spend his time encouraging the leaders of the Tocat church. Mary held numerous meetings with the women of Tocat. Neither Mary nor Henry realized what trying times were to come to the town in barely two months.

Back in Sivas by the end of January, on the last Sunday of the month Henry preached on Moses, also developing Romans 8:39 in his sermon, "The love of God which is in Christ Jesus our Lord." That day Henry wrote in his journal of his passionate desire that

> we may have more of this love in the midst of all this rush and care. We seem to have so little time for meditation and prayer! How much of our time is taken for what seems to be of small account! Reach out to the ministries of holy fellowship and the exploration of the boundless wealth of the love of God which is in Christ.[27]

Henry reflected on I Peter 4:11, "That God in all things may be glorified." Amidst the drudgery and monotonous round of daily duty and the trivial things which so often made up a day's work, he prayed that the "high purpose and intent of this life, ennoble all its details! Do we have the foreglow here of the glory which is to be revealed at the Lord's coming again at His appearing?"[28]

In February, Henry supervised getting the orphanage at the monastery in working order. He also directed the orphan boys in the carpentry shop he had established to help them learn a trade and help in their support. He ordered materials for looms in Gürün, thinking these would help the numerous widows there get on their feet again. The tremendous demands for relief, the supervision of the rebuilding, the keeping of accounts, and teaching Bible in the boys' school consumed Henry's days. All was done in service for his Lord.

Henry continued to have a concern for his Moslem associates as well as for the Armenians to whom he directly ministered:

> Our position in Turkey seems to be many sided. While we officially preach and teach the Gospel only to the Armenians and Greeks, we can live it for a really Gospel result among the Moslems. We do, and speak that which is right and true. We keep our promises; our calls to Moslems here have an evangelistic character.[29]

On one occasion Henry went to visit the *Vali* Pasha about a colporteur, a good man who was in prison simply for continuing to sell the Christian "Holy Book." Though the case had not yet come to the *Vali*

Pasha, he was very open to all Henry had to say and kept him a long time in simple conversation while others were waiting. The *Vali* did Henry the favor of using the simple Turkish Henry used and listened carefully as Henry explained "our work of love with the Holy Book." Henry felt that the Pasha was ready to listen to what he had to say because of the way the missionaries had lived their lives in Sivas. To live the Gospel was one way to preach it in a Moslem country.[30] Within two weeks after Henry's conversation with the *Vali* Pasha, he was removed and replaced with a man more easily swayed by political forces.

The *Vali*'s gracious reception of Henry showed how his life of integrity and honor had gained him the respect of leading Moslems. Throughout his life, Henry believed that the exemplary lives of the missionaries in Turkey witnessed to the truth of Christ before the Moslem people more effectively than any arguments against Mohammed as the false prophet. The selflessness of the missionaries was incomprehensible to the Turks. Why would anyone endure war, massacres, famine, and plagues in a land so far from their homes? Every missionary grave "was an added argument which no Oriental could answer, that the missionaries were there to minister and not to be ministered unto, and to give even their lives for others."[31] When Henry and the other missionaries established homes and reared their families in Turkey, the Mohammedans would

> ...be made to see in the lives of the follower of Jesus that which will give him a clear vision of the Son of man, and lead him to cry out, 'My Lord, and my God.'
> ...The absolute integrity of the life and dealing of the missionaries with the people has done perhaps as much in that land of deceit and dishonesty to commend the simple gospel of Jesus Christ to all classes as any other single phase of missionary work.[32]

The political situation remained tense in Sivas, and rumors of impending outbursts of violence continued to sweep through the villages. Rumor turned to reality on March 19, 1897, when massacre came to Tocat. Until that time Tocat had escaped the ongoing slaughter, due largely to the attitude of the military commander of the city. The fact that it had escaped disaster thus far was all the more reason for anticipating trouble sooner or later. The good military commander had been removed, and the new commander seemed to have made no effort to check the massacre until it had gone on for some hours. U.S. Consul Jewett reported that:

> According to the best information I can obtain, 137 Armenians, including two bishops and a dozen women and children, were killed and thirty-six wounded. Newspaper reports have stated the number killed as high as 400. About 27 shops and 150 houses were looted in the city and some others in the near vicinity.
> The work was commenced by Turks of the city and carried on by the aid of soldiers and police, but the latter stopped the disorder after it had continued about eight hours. The Armenians gave no special provocation and made no resistance. They had been forewarned of the proposed massacre: they closed their shops and sought places of hiding: hence the small number killed.[33]

Moslem neighbors protected the American mission property in Tocat as well as the pastor and his family and the Bible reader from Sivas. Both by their influence and their armed men the Moslems defended the street during the worst time of danger. The Bible reader had been out on the street when the attack began. One of the looters told her to escape quickly to a house, which she did, and then fainted from fear. From the Protestant congregation, only one man was killed and one house was looted. The Monastery of St. Chrysostom near Tocat was robbed. An investigation committee was called in Tocat to examine the incident, and 300 Turks were arrested. British Consul Major Bulman was called in to be part of the military court as was a Russian representative.[34]

When Henry was able to visit Tocat in May, he found the small Protestant congregation continuing strong and attracting many Gregorian young men. These men, interested in Bible study, attended regularly, bringing their testaments and sitting three hours through two services. They often remained for the prayer meeting that followed.

Whatever confidence the Armenians in the Sivas *vilayet* had regained in the government was gone with the massacre at Tocat. Fear of attack was everywhere, and many more made plans to leave the country. Henry was saddened that the Tocat preacher, Pastpor Kaspar Turadian, was seriously talking about emigrating; he was an excellent preacher with a good ministry among the people. Fear continued to grip the people, and Henry noted in his diary:

> As we are acknowledged to be the leaders among the people, in the days of political excitement and the horrors of massacre, we must take care to be in open contact with the people and let them see our

trust in God. Therefore the gates of our house yard are open, our zaptieh guard being there as usual.[35]

On Friday, March 26, Miss Brewer rushed in to see Henry, all excited with reports about detailed plans for a massacre in Sivas that day, including the burning of all the mission buildings. Consul Jewett was out of town, so Henry immediately went to see the British Consul with the news, only to find Major Bulmann even more excited than Henry was. He busily made preparations for a possible attack, providing guards for the mission and coming himself with his gun under his cloak. The various precautions Major Bulman took in cooperation with the French Consul undoubtedly saved the city from attack, and the day passed without incident.[36]

Surrounded by suffering and destitution, the hearts of the weary missionaries were most drawn to the needy orphans. As many as possible were placed in the homes of surviving friends and relatives, but hundreds remained, needing housing and loving care. Evangelical Christians in Switzerland sent funds especially to care for the orphans. The Swiss committee was led by Professor Godet of Neuchâtel, son of Professor Frédéric Louis Godet whose New Testament commentaries had been translated into English and continued to have influence for years. In 1896, Mr. Leopold Favre was sent by the Swiss Committee for Armenian Relief to confer with Mr. Peet in Constantinople on where and how their funds might be used for the greatest good. Mr. Peet recommended Sivas and its orphans. Henry was notified that he might gather 280 children into orphanages, and the Swiss would guarantee their support for five years. Beginning in 1897 the Swiss sent thousands of dollars to Sivas, not only for general relief, but also specifically for work among the orphans in Sivas and Gürün. The Swiss expressly stipulated that the orphanages should be under the control of the American missionaries, yet another tribute to their efficiency and integrity. With the praise also came one more responsibility and burden for the missionaries. There was already more missionary work in the Sivas field than the Perrys and Hubbards could handle, but the massacres had created numerous orphans. Who but the missionaries could provide for them? Both Albert and Henry thoroughly enjoyed teaching the orphan boys in school, and one of Emma Hubbard's childhood dreams was "to be a matron of an orphan asylum."[37] Albert and Emma Hubbard were chosen to supervise the orphanages.

Six orphanages were finally established in the Sivas region, including one at Gürün for over 100 children. 276 children were cared for in the orphanages, 163 of whom were girls. Ninety orphans had been placed with private families. The missionaries worked with native people to provide food, clothing, and schooling for the children. The widow of Sivas' martyred pastor, who had taught in the Sivas school before the massacres, dedicated her life to working among the orphans. Emma Hubbard supervised and kept the accounts for the orphan work. Besides their school lessons, the children were taught Bible and practical skills. Both boys and girls were taught how to care for the sick. Girls were also taught sewing, cooking, weaving, rug making, and teaching. Boys learned trades of carpenter, cabinetmaking, tailor, bookbinding, and shoemaking. The boys in cabinetmaking learned to make folding chairs with cane seats and carved backs. One of the boy's skill at carving came to the notice of the *Vali* Pasha, and he had the boy help his cabinet man make furniture for the *Vali*'s Constantinople house.[38] The children were loved and cared for and happy to be in the orphanage.

Of course Henry and Albert were most interested in the children's spiritual welfare, and the two alternated in teaching Bible in the schools. Henry enjoyed presenting the simple truths of the Bible to the youngsters, from Genesis to Revelation. Albert delighted in the orphan's Sabbath school. He wrote *The Missionary Herald*:

> I've been on mission ground twenty-six years and have never seen anything that fills me with satisfaction as the sight of these contented, obedient, enthusiastic children gathered in their large school-room for Sabbath-school, for they have one all to themselves, our Board schools being already crowded. They are specially open to spiritual leading and teaching.[39]

Many of the orphans had seen relatives and loved ones brutally murdered before their eyes and had been left alone to endure pangs of hunger, cold, and neglect. The mission orphanages were able not only to provide physical needs, but also were able to show the little ones the love of Jesus. Many had never known a prayer in their native tongue or heard any of the Bible. Soon they were praying and eagerly memorizing Scripture.

Some of the older girls who had been carried off by the Turks and then rescued had even more difficult problems. Many had been raped, and they came with tears streaming down their faces begging doctors to rid them of the children they would bear in a few months. Children themselves, how would they be able to care for or love these babes? Albert wrote ABCFM leaders in Constantinople and Boston to see if some Europeans and Americans would want to provide for these children yet to be born.[40]

In November, Miss Marie Zenger and Miss Stuckey, nurses from Switzerland, arrived to work in the Sivas orphanages the Swiss supported. They lived in the American mission compound, and the Hubbards and Perrys welcomed these devoted Christians among them, though both of the Swiss ladies spoke French and neither spoke English. Two months before, Milo Jewett arrived back from Constantinople where he had gone to meet and marry Mrs. Dudley, a widow from the U.S.A.. She had for many years presided over a training school for nurses. Quite a little foreign colony was growing in Sivas – with the five American missionaries, the American Consul and his wife, the British Consul, the French consul and his wife, and the two Swiss orphanage workers! The Hubbards and Perrys started taking weekly French lessons in order to communicate better with the international community. Albert, however, was losing his hearing, and he sometimes found learning a new language under such a handicap especially difficult.

Care for the many orphans and suffering in Sivas did not lesson Henry's care for his own dear children, far away though they might be. Alvan, now a young man in his mid-twenties, had become a successful businessman in New York. He had his own apartment in New York City and was active in the New York militia and a member of the Union League Club. Though a fine young man, he did not share his father's spiritual interests.

Jean was having a more difficult time. When Jean first arrived in the United States in 1896 (after having recovered from a case of the measles crossing the Atlantic!), Alvan met her in New York. Up to this time, Jean hardly knew she had a brother, since he was ten years older than she, and the two had lived separately for so long. After a month's stay with Aunt Harriet White in Mt. Vernon, New York, Jean went to spend the summer in Fredonia with her Grandma Jones and Aunt Emilie Barker. The Barker estate was like a Paradise to the twelve year old girl "with its eleven acres of fruit trees and six acres of Concord grapes, the big house, the two helper houses, and back of all the deep dense woods full of ferns and flowers, birds and butterflies."[41] It was like living in a fairyland. When it came time for school to start, Jean went to North Adams to stay with her father's sister, Sarah Ann. Henry and Mary had made arrangements for Sarah Ann's maiden daughter, Almira, to care for Jean. Mary and Henry had tutored Jean so well that she had no trouble entering the sixth grade at North Adams' Mark Hopkins Elementary School. Living with Aunt Sarah and her two spinster daughters was lonely for Jean. Aunt Sarah was very strict and showed little understanding for her young niece so far away from her parents. She wouldn't even allow Jean a candle to take up to her room at night, fearing she would set the room on fire. Often Jean would find her way up the dark stairs, lie down, and cry herself to sleep at night.[42] There was much illness in the Porter family, and finally Almira had to be hospitalized because of "nervous prostration." Finding it impossible to care for her niece and her own family, Sarah Ann arranged for Jean to live with Reverend Milton and Emily Augusta Severance in Bennington, Vermont.

Emily had been a classmate of Sarah's at Mount Holyoke, and the two had remained friends over the years. Milton was pastor of the Congregational Church in Bennington, and the Severances lived in the manse across the street from the Bennington Monument, which commemorated that important battle of the American Revolution. The Severances had five children of their own, four boys and a girl, but they were all grown when Jean arrived. Mrs. Severance had an abundance of love to shower on Jean. She was a former schoolteacher and loved to encourage others in paths of knowledge and learning. Her heart ached at the thought of the suffering and outrages in Armenia, and she welcomed the opportunity to help a missionary family who had done so much for the afflicted Armenians. She agreed to take Jean for two years, with Henry paying $10 a week board for her. After that time, the plans were for Jean to enter the girls' school at Northfield, Massachusetts.

Emily Severance loved literature and undoubtedly shared this love with Jean. As a friend later wrote:

> The choicest gems of all the great poets were stored in her mind. At one time I think she could recite from memory at least one half of Milton's "Paradise Lost." The most beautiful hymns of all the ages were treasured in her memory to be called up at any time. In the twilight she would sit down with her family and repeat the choicest passages from Tennyson, Longfellow, Whittier, Lowell and others. She apprehended the beautiful everywhere, whether in nature, in litera-

ture, in art, or in character. Her own mind was singularly pure, and she wanted to find only purity in others. There was no sham about her, what she seemed to be, she was in reality.[43]

Jean flourished under Emily Severance's care, and she enjoyed the warmth of family in the Bennington manse. Emily's daughter Maude, a graduate of Wellesley and a teacher in Elmira, New York, came home at Christmastime and immediately established a bond with Jean. She became like an older sister to her. Son Carlton, a newspaper reporter, came home just before enlisting in the army to serve in the Spanish American War. Jean prepared a bag of chestnuts for him to take on his journey.

These were happy days for Jean. Then tragedy struck. She was taken ill with diphtheria on May 13, 1898. Emily carefully nursed Jean as one of her own, but within a week she too took ill. Emily died on May 25, after only six days of illness. Jean was still dangerously ill, and a nurse was hired to care for her. She was kept in quarantine twelve weeks. Once recovered, she went back to stay with Aunt Sarah in North Adams. It was an unpleasant time for her, since Aunt Sarah was not temperamentally or physically capable of sympathizing and caring for the strong-willed adolescent.

It was also a difficult time for Mary and Henry. Mary wrote Dr. Barton in Boston:

> It is a great sorrow to us – that Mrs. Severance has been so suddenly taken away. We feel as if Jean had been orphaned the second time. We feel dazed, by the suddenness of it all. Such experiences make a parent question – what his personal duty is – in such a case – but the circumstances here are such – that we cannot see it to be our duty to give up the missionary work and go home to take charge of the child. There is far too much upon those who are here – to admit of Mr. Perry's laying down his part. We are praying for the Lord to open the right door to our little girl.[44]

The additional expenses from Jean's illness (the nurse cost $15 per week, plus all the doctor's care), forced Henry to request additional funding from the ABCFM to cover Jean's expenses. Missionary salaries across the board had been cut 10 percent in 1898, and this additional expense was difficult. Normally the board granted $120 annually for missionary children in the states. The ABCFM granted Henry an additional $10 a week effective January, 1898, which still meant he had to somehow cover the unexpected medical expenses in 1897.[45]

In the spring of 1898, Henry spent five weeks in Divrik. He had hoped to be able to close down the relief work by that time, but after the exceptionally cold winter, the suffering and need continued unabated. Distribution of clothes, bedding, and seed for sowing continued. In a report to Dr. Barton, Henry described conditions in Divrik two and a half years after the massacres:

> Our congregation at Divrik numbers more than forty families, among whom the work of the Gospel is more hopeful than it has been in former times, being even aided by the terrible trials through which the people have passed. They were all robbed and shaken up by fright. The pastor and many others were killed. The fine chapel building, put up under the direction of Dr. Wheeler, when Divrik was a part of the Harpoot system, with the accompanying school rooms and parsonage, were all totally destroyed by fire. Now the large congregation is crowded here and there in small classrooms. The school has no abiding place; and no permission is yet given to rebuild what the rioters so wantonly destroyed. But the daily morning meetings during the four weeks of our stay there, were made precious by the evident tokens of the Lord's presence. The church was revived, and many were added to it. A preacher sent there for relief service was induced to remain at least for one year, and has removed his family from Sivas. The people are giving for his support what we consider to be well in their circumstances. Can we depend on some aid for them from our American Board?[46]

Henry was concerned that United States' war with Spain might interfere with the American churches' contributions to the mission efforts in Turkey. As usual, he kept up with all the developments of the war and noted in red in his diary the dates when key events occurred. In his diary he also similarly briefly noted events in the Sudan campaign and the Boer War in South Africa. Henry was always keenly interested in world events, for they all affected missionary efforts and the spread of the gospel. It was the gospel's spread that was always uppermost in his mind, and it was this concern which compelled him to return to Divrik in the January cold of 1899. Henry remained there for six weeks.

The Christians at Divrik had continued to suffer after the massacres, and Henry hoped to encourage them in their faith by being with them during the January Week of Prayer. The first pastor at Divrik had been a faithful man who had served the church for many years. Weak in body, though not in faith, he was harmless politically. Nevertheless, he was shot in the massacres, then cut up with knives. Pastor Rafriel Tashkjian became Divrik's preacher after the massacres, but the strain of the times and the extreme losses he had endured caused him to fall sick, and he died of a fever. Then, in the spring of 1898, the church had called Pastor Simone Dzermian, a graduate of Marsovan Theological Seminary. He had worked as a relief worker after the massacres, and Henry had found "His thorough honesty, good judgment, patience in sympathy with the poor, and reliable Christian character, made him invaluable."[47] He had moved his family to Divrik in May, but died suddenly the following fall. Within three years the congregation had lost one pastor and two preachers. During his time with them, however, Henry was able to strengthen the faith of the fifty-one families in the church.

Besides the spiritual ministry, Henry enjoyed the adventure of traveling to Divrik and back in the winter's snows. He wrote Dr. Smith in Boston:

> On the journey over the mountains and in the snow-path the cold and storm were severe, but I was accompanied by strong men who took good care of me, and the Lord brought me in good time, and without harmful exposure...The week of my return was fortunately a very pleasant one, for during both the previous and subsequent week, the deep snow and storms upon the mountains had blocked the roads. When open it was only a mule path a few inches wide, in which each animal steps exactly in the foot-track of the one before him, the treading and filling of this path keeping it up even with the piling snow. Mounted on one of these mountain trained mules I quite enjoyed the hard work of alternate riding and walking in the passes of the Anti-Taurus.

When he returned to Sivas, Mary was coming down with influenza, and Albert Hubbard was also ill with influenza and carbuncles on his back. Though Mary gradually recovered, Albert's condition worsened. By February he had pleura-pneumonia and a fever of 104°. Dr. Jewett and the Swiss Dr. Zatisky attended him constantly; the Swiss nurses Misses Stucky and Zenger were a bulwark of strength for Emma Hubbard. Many prayers were offered for Albert's recovery, and the entire market place of Sivas was talking about "How is Mr. Hubbard?"

In his severe illness Albert asked Emma, "I want to know, if anything happens to me, if you are going to pick up and get off to America as soon as you can?" Emma assured him that there was too much work depending on her for her to leave; Albert sank back on his pillow satisfied. When the violence of the pneumonia was passed and his fever was down, Albert told Emma that during the early days of his sickness he was deeply burdened for his family and all the work of the mission. Then, he said,

> I caught, for an instant, a glimpse of Jesus just above me, just as though he would take the burden from me, and I said, I have given them all to Thee. Thou lovest them even more than I do. And he took the whole burden from me and vanished...he knows, the Father knows. He loves the work better than I do, and it is His work.[48]

Though very weak, Albert appeared to be recovering. The plan was for the Hubbards to go to the mountains during the summer months for complete rest and recovery. Henry and Mary had not been to an annual meeting since coming to Turkey in 1892, and they had planned to go together. With Albert unable to work, however, Henry decided to remain in Sivas and send Mary to the annual meeting accompanied by missionaries from Tocat and Marsovan. Mary was about to break under the pressure of work and the emotional strain of dealing constantly with so much suffering. Hopefully the two-month trip to Constantinople and the annual meeting would be a time of refreshment for her.

In April 1899, Henry and Mary set off for Tocat together, with Mary accompanied by Dr. Jewett's *cavass*. Mary continued on to Marsovan, while Henry stayed in Tocat to preach on Sunday. There he received a telegram from Dr. Dodd, who had come to Sivas from Caesarea to care for Albert. Albert's condition was worsening. Henry returned to Sivas shortly before Albert died on April 13th. Emma was glad Henry had been able to return; she was also thankful Mary, in her nervous state, was away. Emma wrote her brother:

> The whole city has been moved by his death. There was never such a funeral. We had a quiet service in English here at the house, and then they took the body to the church, which the brethren had draped in black, for a service in Turkish and Armenian...The Pasha sent a special messenger with his sympathy and offered to do anything he could for the funeral arrangements, so we asked him for some of the police, that order might be maintained, and he sent officials to the

church and they accompanied us to the grave. The Bishop of the Armenians sent his sympathy and wished to send some one to represent him in taking part in the services. Five priests came and one of them gave a eulogy in the church, and all five went to the grave. Almost all Europeans and leading Armenians were there, and Armenian shops were closed although it was Saturday and a busy day. The flags of different nationalities were at half mast, and the number of people who followed the body to the grave must have been 3000...[Albert] would have been much surprised in his life time to know what a deep hold he had in the hearts of the people...[49]

Reverend J.L. Fowle, missionary at nearby Caesarea, had known Albert since he was a senior at Amherst in 1866. He always appreciated his good-humored way of facing problems, but believed that

> to see him at his best one should be at his Sunday school in Sivas on a Sunday afternoon, when his face just shone with delight and spiritual earnestness. The quality of the audience, as well as its quantity, was a surprise to me, at least 400 souls, most of them young men, would hang on his words and on those of his faithful co-laborers...Eternity alone can show us how great and how helpful was his life work.[50]

Though Henry and Albert were very different temperamentally, they had come to work together well in the Lord's service. On Albert's death, Henry wrote to the ABCFM's Reverend Smith in Boston:

> I need not say to one who knows our work here as you do, that the loss of Mr. Hubbard from it is very severe to us who remain, for he had been here a long time, was well known by all the people of every class of the residents of this vicinity, as one who gave all his service and influence positively to the Lord's work; was aggressive in it, and stable, knowing well in whom he trusted, and was thus unmoved by any fear or criticism of men.
> I have always enjoyed him as an associate, for he was first of all a <u>Christian,</u> and did not shrink from doing the hard things which it might be necessary to attend to. He could always be relied upon to be satisfied with nothing which was not substantial and true. He could work very near to the life of the people, developing their interest in personal service to the Lord, and win them even after they had differed from him. His special line, and one in which he won many to righteousness was among the children...The success of our Sunday School work at Sivas is largely due to his personal and continuous effort.[51]

The last sermon Albert had preached was on making the choice between life and death. The many school children, orphans, and Sunday school students were especially reminded of Mr. Hubbard's words as they said their last good byes.

Both Henry and Emma insisted that Mary continue on to the annual meeting in Constantinople. Meeting the other missionaries and focusing on the Lord's work without the constant responsibility of caring for the sick and suffering did help renew Mary's strength and weary spirit. Along with Dr. H.S. Barnum of Harpoot, Mary helped prepare the mission letter summarizing the meeting. It was a letter full of encouragement at the new doors opened for ministry and at the removal of some of the travel restrictions that the missionaries had worked under. Education was recognized as one of the strong points of the missions. In much of the interior of Turkey, including Sivas, the only thorough and systematic education that could be found was in the mission schools,

> where Christ is presented to every pupil, and where each one is urged to accept him as Savior and Master. And as class after class goes forth under such molding influences, and as the doors of our schools are besieged by a yearly increasing number of applicants, larger in many cases than can be received, we cannot but look forward with large hopefulness to the ultimate result in preparing the way for a widespread religious reformation in the land.[52]

By the end of 1899, it was decided that the foreign-supported relief work in Sivas should be closed, and Henry worked closely with Consul Jewett to file a final report. Though the poor were still among them, the crisis following the massacres had passed, and it seemed best for the poor to be cared for by normal local benevolence. Of course, the orphanages would continue to require special support. The Swiss were continuing in that effort and were also planning to open a hospital in Sivas. The tabular report Consul Jewett submitted to the Department of State showed that during the four years of relief work, $141,751 were received and distributed by the Sivas Relief Committee. In the conclusion of his report on Armenian relief work, Consul Jewett wrote:

> While it is true that the Armenians have recovered wonderfully from the crushing blow of this great disaster, poverty and sickness as remote results are still abundantly present and funds in hand are only

too small to meet the numerous and pressing demands for help. Still it is the opinion of the committee that no more funds for general relief should be solicited and that the Armenians should be forced to rely upon themselves and help one another. The danger of cultivating a feeling of dependence and thus pauperizing instead of elevating a poor community through charity, is always present in such work....[53]

Though the Relief Committee had formerly closed its activities, the poor continued to appear at Henry's door for help, and he continued to help with whatever funds and means were at hand. Albert Hubbard's death had placed even more responsibilities on Henry's shoulders. Not only did Sivas need a replacement for Albert, but Mary Brewer needed someone to assist in administering the Girls' School. Miss Brewer's special talent was in one-to-one evangelism and ministry among the women of Sivas and the outlying stations, but she was limited in this by her responsibilities in the schools.

In February, Henry and Mary received letters from sister Sarah Ann and Grandma Jones "with heavy tidings of Jean's continued misconduct." Henry's diary does not reveal what the "misconduct" was, but it was obvious sixteen-year-old Jean was too much for Sarah Ann to handle. Mary spent time in fasting and prayer about what to do with Jean. Henry wrote to Mrs. Allen of Oberlin, Ohio to see if Jean would be accepted into her missionary children's home. Mary finally decided she needed to return to the United States to take care of Jean until she was ready to attend a good boarding school. Both the mission station and the ABCFM in Boston approved her emergency furlough. In April, Mary left Sivas for the U.S.A.

Henry accompanied her as far as Tocat, from whence she was able to proceed on her way in the company with other missionaries. Henry was more encouraged than he had ever been by the evangelical work in Tocat. Many of the young men who had been regularly studying their Bible for several years had a zeal for service and Christian work, "not only in the congregations of our people, but in the markets and byways of the city." Henry wrote,

> At the Lord's table it was my delightful privilege to receive two persons to the communion of the church and to baptize a young Hebrew convert, who is now in Tocat as an exile from Bulgaria. His confession of Jesus of Nazareth as the one fulfilling all the prophecies of the Old Testament Scriptures and the Saviour of sinners, was clear, decided, and we hope born of the Holy Spirit.

> I am glad to say also of our schools at Tocat that they are doing a good work with the children. There are four teachers, of whose salaries and of all expenses the people of Tocat promptly paying one-half.[54]

At the same time as he sent his favorable report on the work at Tocat to the ABCFM in Boston, Henry also reported on the importance, success, and needs of the schools in Sivas:

> In Sivas we are in the center of a large and populous province. Taken in connection with the two colleges at Aintab and Marsovan (one on each side of us) to which we send annually our graduates, we hold an unquestioned leadership in education. Not to mention now the fundamental character of our thorough instruction in Biblical studies...There are now on duty six teachers having in charge 265 pupils, of whom only ten are boarders. The reason why there are no more boarding pupils is that we cannot receive them, since we have no room for a boarding department.

For twenty-five years the missionary residences at Sivas and the Female Boarding School had been in the same location in a very desirable location in the city. The growth of the work now required more room. Henry was able to buy additional adjoining property and sought funds for additional buildings for the missionary families and for the schools.

He was also most pleased when the long asked for additional workers began coming to Sivas in the fall of 1900. Miss Lina Zenger came from Switzerland to join her sister Marie in working in the Girls Orphanage in Sivas. Miss Ellsworth came from Harpoot to help Miss Brewer in the Girls' Boarding School. Unfortunately for Miss Brewer, Miss Ellsworth soon accepted the marriage proposal of the British consul in Sivas and relinquished her schoolwork. In September, Reverend and Mrs. Margot transferred from Marsovan to take charge of the Swiss orphanages in Sivas and Gürün, freeing Emma Hubbard to resume her general mission work. In November Henry rode to Samsoun to meet the new missionary family assigned to Sivas, Reverend Ernest Partridge, his wife Winona, and little baby Robert. Both Ernest and Winona had graduated from Oberlin College in 1895, and Ernest went on to Andover for theological studies. Ordained in October 1898, Reverend Partridge preached for two years in Shareham, Vermont, before being assigned to Sivas by the ABCFM. As soon as they were settled in Sivas and "with commendable zeal," the Partridges set about learning Armenian. Henry, at 62, was quite pleased to have a younger man now with him in the mission. The infant Robert also warmed Henry's heart. Henry wrote Reverend Smith, "I need not mention what a delight it is to us all, that we have again a baby missionary in our station. With these reinforcements we are anticipating a more vigorous campaign of work in our great field, of which there is an open door, and very peculiar need."[55]

Since he was new to the field, Ernest Partridge studied something of the Sivas mission's history and sent to the ABCFM a table illustrating the growth of work in Sivas over the past twenty-five years, since Henry had come to the station. The table showed that the church members

> ...have increased from none to 106; the average congregation from 120 to 450; the Sunday School scholars from 135 to 477 or (including the orphans in their own buildings) to 750. The pupils in the day schools have increased from 100 to 581, or (including the orphans) to 824.[56]

Ernest immediately took an interest in the Sivas schools and realized what an immense Christian influence the missionaries had in the education of these young people.

The Partridges for a time stayed and dined with Henry, and he welcomed their company, especially with Mary and his own children away in the States. In his diary Henry wrote, "The baby Robert is a delight to us all. I catch him up as often as I can."[57] When Thanksgiving Day arrived, Emma Hubbard had eighteen people at her table for dinner. Ernest Partridge preached on the teaching of the Psalms, and Henry thought it "the best service of the kind that I have attended in Sivas."[58] In the midst of all the business of the mission work, Henry never wanted to lose sight of the importance of daily thanksgiving and prayer. Repeatedly in his diary he noted Scriptures on prayer and commented on the importance of prayer in the daily life:

> November 18, 1900 - II Chronicle 30:27, "Their prayer came up to His holy dwelling place, even unto heaven": How much we are dependent on prayer. We find it hard in the rush of daily duties to take the time needed for prayer. General Gordon took daily two hours in the morning alone in his tent. No messenger could disturb him. This

is the gate of Heaven which we here do so much need. Let us enter by it.

November 22, 1900 – I Timothy 1:18, "This charge I commit unto thee ... that ... supplications, prayers, intercessions, and giving of thanks, be made for all men." Are we fully yielded to the Holy Spirit for the ministry of prayer as the Lord requires us to be? These services are laid upon us for this people to whom we are sent. Let us not fall short by failure to do the <u>work of intercession</u> which Timothy enjoins.

With the coming of the New Year, Henry left the warmth and comfort of the mission station to cross the snowy mountains to Divrik and minister to the Christians there. Difficult though the winter travel might be, the ministry opportunities were always greater in the winter cold. In better weather the people would be working the fields; in winter, they had more time to listen to the Scriptures.

When Henry returned to Sivas at the end of January, Ernest Partridge told him that in his absence the mission station had voted he should have a vacation to the United States during the summer and return to Sivas with Mary in the fall. Henry began the process of preparing for the furlough by transferring the treasury account books to Emma Hubbard. He made arrangements with the British Consul Anderson to oversee the Gürün Rug Company in his absence. He assigned some of his other responsibilities over to Mr. Partridge.

On April 4, Henry said his good-byes to his Sivas friends, and left with Marie Zenger for Tocat and Samsoun, where they were joined by the Wingate family of Caesarea who would be journeying with Henry to the United States. Often during the exhausting relief work, Henry had felt himself the bruised reed of Isaiah 42:3, and it did seem as if his lamp would burn out. He cried out, "O! May the Lord repair the worn out 'reed', and restore the light of the 'lamp'."[59] His prayer had been answered, and his furlough in the United States would strengthen him for even further ministry in Sivas.

---

[1] Alfred L.P. Dennis. *Adventures in American Diplomacy 1896-1906*. N.Y.: E.P. Dutton, 1928, 447. Nicholas Butler, President of Columbia University and active in international movements for world peace, served as president of the Carnegie Endowment for International Peace from 1925-1946 and received the Nobel Peace Prize in 1941.

[2] Milo A. Jewett. "Armenian Relief Work at Sivas, Turkey," report submitted to David J. Hill, Asst. Secretary of State, April 6, 1900 (National Archives Microfilm Publication T681).
[3] *Daybreak in Turkeyi, 216-217.*
[4] *They Lived Their Faith*, 316-317; Louise J. Peet, ed. *No Less Honor: The Biography of William Wheelock Peet*, n.d. As Treasurer of the Sivas Station, Henry Perry was in frequent corrrespondence with Dr. Peet.
[5] Clara Harlowe Barton. *The Red Cross*. Washington: American National Red Cross, 1898, 278.
[6] Jean Perry Severance's typed reminiscences for her son Gordon Severance, n.d. In possession of authors.
[7] "Editorial Paragraphs," *The Missionary Herald*, July, 1896, 266.
[8] *The Red Cross*, 316, 327, 346; "Report of J.B. Hubbell, M.D.," report Dr. Hubbell sent to Clara Barton, August 1, 1896, from American Red Cross Archives, Hazel Braugh Records Center, Falls Church, Va.
[9] *The Red Cross*, 320.
[10] "Harris, James Rendell," *Oxford Dictionary of the Christian Church* (ed. F.L. Cross & E.A. Livingstone), Oxford University Press, 1997, 737; Rev. Oxen Gaidzekian. *Illustrated Armenia and the Armenians*, Boston, 1898, 138-139.
[11] J. Rendell and Helen Harris. *Letters from Armenia*. London: James Nisbet & Co., Ltd., 1897, 11-15; *Hubbards of Sivas*, 259.
[12] *Letters from Armenia*, 18. Eusebius, known as the "Father of Church History" wrote his *Eccesiastical History* in the fourth century. His work includes many accounts of persecution and martyrdom in the first centuries of the church.
[13] *Letters from Armenia*, 43.
[14] *Letters from Armenia*, 158. In their allusion to Esther 4:14 ("Yet who knows whether you have come to the kingdom for such a time as this?"), the Harrises were making an interesting comparison between Esther saving the Jewish people from an attempted massacre and the American missionaries saving the Armenians from a similar genocidal massacre.
[15] *Letters from Armenia*, 219.
[16] *Letters from Armenia*, 219; *Diary*, August 2, 1896.
[17] FO 195/1944, 7 September 1896 report, as quoted in *Warrant for Genocide*, 87-88.
[18] *Letters from Armenia*, 241.
[19] *Letters from Armenia*, 249-250.
[20] *Letters from Armenia*, 251.
[21] Mary H. Perry to Rev. Judson Smith, from Sivas, February 4, 1896, ABC 16.9.3, Vol. 25, Part 2, No. 443.
[22] Mary H. Perry to Dr. Judson Smith, from Sivas, March 31, 1896. ABC 16.9.3, Vol. 25, Part 2, No. 448.
[23] Henry T. Perry to Rev. Judson Smith, from Sivas, March 31, 1897, ABC 16.9.3, Vol. 25, Part 2, No. 426.

[24] *Diary*, additional notes from November 27, 1924 placed at end of 1897 diary.
[25] "Editorial Pragraphs," *The Missionary Herald*, February, 1897, 47.
[26] Henry Perry. "Gurun," *The Missionary Herald*, July, 1897, 273-274.
[27] *Diary*, January 23, 1897.
[28] *Diary*, February 2, 18, 1897.
[29] *Diary*, March 6, 1897.
[30] *Diary*, May 7, 11, 1897.
[31] *Daybreak in Turkey*, 215.
[32] *Daybreak in Turkey*, 114, 217.
[33] Milo Jewett to W.W. Rockhill, Asst. Secr. Of State, from Sivas, April 27, 1897 (National Archives Microfilm Publication T681).
[34] Henry T. Perry to Rev. Judson Smith, from Sivas, March 31, 1897., ABC 16.9.3, Vol. 25, Part 2, No. 426.
[35] *Diary*, March 24, 1897.
[36] *Diary*, March 26, 28, 1897.
[37] "Editorial Paragraphs," *The Missionary Herald*, August, 1897, 301; *Hubbards of Sivas*, 271.
[38] *Helping Hand Series*, Vol. 1, no.1, December 1898, 26; Vol. 1, no. 4, September, 1899, 19-20; Vol. 2, no.2, March 1900, 7.
[39] Albert Hubbard. "Orphan Work at Sivas," *The Missionary Herald*, January, 1898, 24.
[40] *Hubbards of Sivas*, 264-265.
[41] Jean Perry Severance's typed reminiscences, 2.
[42] Diana Lynn Severance interview with Carlton Spencer Severance, October 25, 2000. Carlton, Jean Perry Severance's oldest son, remembered this story from his mother.
[43] Obituary of Emily Augusta Severance," *Middlebury Register*, June 17, 1898.
[44] Mary H. Perry to Dr. Barton, from Sivas, July 8, 1898, ABC 16.9.3, Vol. 25, Part 2, No. 452. James L. Barton, who in 1906 became foreign secretary for the ABCFM, had been a missionary in Harpoot from 1885-1894. He served as Foreign Secretary of the Board from 1894 through 1927. After the 1915 deportations and holocaust, Dr. Barton became head of Near East Relief.
[45] Henry T. Perry to Rev. Judson Smith, from Sivas, January 22, 1898, ABC 16.9.3, Vol. 25, Part 2.
[46] Henry T. Perry to Rev. J.L. Barton, from Sivas, May 18, 1898, ABC 16.9.3, Vol. 25, Part 2, No .
[47] H.T. Perry to Rev. Judosn Smith, from Divrik, Turkey, Jan. 28, 1899, ABC 16.9.3, Vol. 25, Part 2, No.
[48] Emma Hubbard's letter to brother, April 17, 1899, in *Hubbards of Sivas*, 306.
[49] *Hubbards of Sivas*, 307-308.
[50] "Rev. Albert W. Hubbard, of Sivas, Turkey," *The Missionary Herald*, June, 1899, 226.

[51] H.T. Perry to Rev. Judson Smith, from Sivas, April 19, 1899, ABC 16.9.3, Vol. 25, Part 2, No 432.
[52] "Western Turkey Mission – the Annual Meeting," *The Missionary Herald*, August, 1899, 337.
[53] Milo A. Jewett to the Department of State, "Armenian Relief Work," Sivas, Turkey, April 6, 1900 (National Archives Microfilm Publication T681).
[54] Henry T. Perry, "Advance at Tocat," *The Missionary Herald*, October, 1900, 403.
[55] Henry T. Perry to Rev. Judson Smith, from Sivas, Nov. 23rd, 1900, ABC 16.9.3, Vol. 37, No. 11.
[56] "Sivas and Outstations," *The Missionary Herald*, June, 1901, 251.
[57] *Diary*, November 20, 1900.
[58] *Diary*, November 29, 1900.
[59] *Diary*, June 16, 1896.

11
BUILDING THE WALL IN TROUBLOUS TIMES
(1901-1909)

"...the street shall be built again, and the wall, even in troublous times." Daniel 9:25

As the *S.S.Pennsylvania* approached New York, Henry stood on the deck gazing out at the bustling harbor. The harbor itself seemed to reflect all the boisterous energy of the United States at the dawn of the twentieth century. The country had greatly changed since Henry and Jeanne first left for Turkey shortly after the Civil War. Many of the trans-Atlantic steamships in the harbor were bringing new immigrants to the U.S. These new immigrants, including an increasing number of Italians, were passing through Ellis Island at a rate of 100 an hour. In the city streets electric trolleys and automobiles were replacing the horse and buggy. Alexander G. Bell, Thomas Edison, and Henry Ford were changing American life with their inventions of the telephone, electric lighting, motion pictures, and affordable automobiles. The country was moving at a faster pace than when Henry had been there just nine years before. Yet, the cause of missions was still an important one for the nation.

Just a year before, in April 1900, an eleven-day Ecumenical Missionary Conference had been held in New York City with 400 missionary boards and societies from around the world represented. Former President Benjamin Harrison was Chairman of the Conference. In his opening address he called missions "the most influential and enduring work that is being done in the day of great enterprises." All of man's scientific advances could not compare with the important advances being made in Christian missions. Harrison said that man cannot produce peace and unity of himself: "Christ in the heart and His gospel of love and ministry in all the activities of life are the only cure."[1] President McKinley and New York Governor Teddy Roosevelt also gave opening-day addresses at the conference. The United States' leaders spoke to encourage the spread of Christianity throughout the world, believing that the country's and the world's peace and security depended on the Christian principles found in the Word of God.

The *S. S. Pennsylvania* docked at 10 P.M. May 10, 1901, and Henry looked for Alvan as he made his way through the custom lines. At twenty-eight Alvan was a successful real estate broker in New York City. What joy when father and son met again after nine years! After Henry cleared customs, Alvan took his father to his office and then to his rooms at 130 West 34th Street. Mary came that evening, and they had a most enjoyable reunion together. The ensuing days became a blur of visiting friends and relatives, eye doctor appointments, writing financial reports to the ABCFM, and very special days with Alvan. Alvan was active in the National Guard and often took Henry with him to the Armory on Park Avenue when he went for his drill and marching exercises. Henry enjoyed visiting several New York churches and hearing their famous preachers. The Broadway Tabernacle had originally been built by the Tappan brothers for the famous evangelist Charles G. Finney. Henry Van Dyke was pastor of Fourth Avenue Presbyterian Church. Several times Henry and Mary were asked to speak at missionary meetings and at Christian Endeavor meetings for the young people.[2] Though Alvan sometimes accompanied Henry to church, it was obvious that his prime interest was not in spiritual things. It grieved Henry that Alvan had not yet come to recognize the importance of the truths of Scripture and a relationship with Christ in his own life.

Henry and Mary had hoped they would be able to spend some of their time in the United States visiting churches whose contributions to the ABCFM had fallen and encourage them to make additional contributions to the Sivas mission schools. An expansion of the school facilities in Sivas was desperately needed, yet the ABCFM was not providing the funds. Boston's Prudential Committee, however, thought personal solicitation of funds by the missionaries was unwise and told the Perrys not to pursue that course.

When Mary had returned to the United States in the early summer of 1900, she picked up Jean from Sarah Ann's at North Adams, and the two went to Fredonia to visit Grandma Jones and Aunt Emilie. Jean loved her summers at Fredonia and was happy to be away from the somber confines of the ailing Porter family in North Adams. Mary had a sister in Indiana who suggested she place Jean in Asbury College's preparatory school in nearby Kentucky. Established in 1890, Asbury was a Christian college which emphasized the importance of the Bible in the curriculum and the experience of the Christian life. In September, Jean began boarding at Asbury College in Wilmore, Kentucky and did quite well there. She was eager, however, to be with her father, whom she had not seen in five years.

Henry and Mary and Jean spent much of the summer at Bay View, a retreat in Michigan. Originally the grounds for a Methodist camp meeting, Bay View at Petosky on Lake Michigan was a popular Chautauqua site. The air was delightful, and every morning the singing of birds awakened the Perrys. It was a beautiful place and a very special time for Henry and Jean. Often they took walks together in the evening, either along the beach or in the woods. One area along the beach still had at least 25 of the primeval pine trees standing. Jean learned to make bread that summer and baked whatever the family needed. They all attended the various lectures and Bible studies as well as occasional concerts. One Sunday Mary gave a talk on the Syro-Phoenecian woman. Henry noted in his diary that it was "a fine talk. She spoke long – 80 minutes. The audience seemed to be interested."[3]

While at Bay View, Henry wrote a letter to Williams College to be included in the "Class of 'Sixty Two'" report:

>My dear Noble of '62, Sec.:
>
>Thanks for your letter. I very much regret that this vacation in America comes on this year, so near to that of our next class-meeting. The Passage of the years makes the classmates more and more dear to me. How much I should enjoy meeting with you again!
>
>This long residence abroad, since 1866, gives some peculiar experiences upon every return for a brief vacation. So widely apart are the civilizations of America and Turkey that they do not easily mix. Both here and there I must hitch on where I last left off. I seem to live along two lines parallel to each other: and cannot even now wear off the surprise of hearing English spoken in the streets and pales [districts] of business.
>
>I do not envy my classmates['] ... fine opportunities in America. While rejoicing that you have them, let me confess to you my content

to minister to the peculiar needs of many peoples confused by race and language, who are yet under the shadow. Supreme as are the difficulties of such work as mine, in the Mohammedan countries, ... [it] opens out to the Light...[4]

Enjoyable and restful as the weeks were, Henry became increasingly impatient with the inactivity and longed for his work at Sivas; but he and Mary still were unsure what to do with Jean in the fall when they were scheduled to return to Turkey. Though they spent much time in prayer, the way did not seem clear. At one of the Chautauqua meetings in the middle of August, the Perrys met Mr. and Mrs. Jordan. Mr. Jordan was professor of Greek at Albion College in Michigan, a Methodist school founded in 1835. Mrs. Jordan volunteered to be a mother to Jean and invited her to stay with them while attending Albion's preparatory school. After much prayer, this seemed to be the Lord's directions. Jean was both tearful and cheerful when she said goodbye. She looked forward to attending Albion, but how long would it be before she saw her father again?

On the Perrys' return journey to Ashfield, the news came that President McKinley had been shot at the Pan-American Exposition in Buffalo, New York. He died eight days later, and on September 14, 42-year-old Teddy Roosevelt was sworn in as President. Anarchists and revolutionists had a way of affecting government in the democratic United States as they did in the more chaotic Balkan and Turkish lands.

In October, Henry and Mary attended the ABCFM annual meeting in Hartford, Connecticut. One of the reasons Henry had come to the United States was to give an address at the Annual Meeting, hoping to expand the work of evangelization among the Moslems. The population of Turkey was about sixteen million. One fourth, or about four million, were Christian, including Armenians, Greeks, Bulgarians, Syrians, Jacobites, and Nestorians. Twelve million, or three quarters of the population, were Moslems, including Turks, Circassians, Arabs, and some Kurds. Henry believed the ABCFM should develop a Gospel mission to the vast Moslem population of Turkey.[5] He was among the first to encourage a greater emphasis on evangelization among the Moslems in Turkey.

Henry met some of his Williams classmates at the Hartford convention, and they were fascinated to hear about his work and experiences in Turkey. They encouraged him to write up an account of his work among the Armenians and Greeks for the Williams' alumnae, but he told his classmates that he "hardly thought the fellows would be interested in that."[6]

After another hurried week with Alvan in New York, filled with numerous last-minute preparations, Henry and Mary boarded the ship to return to Sivas on Saturday, October 19. The rough sea on the first day out sent Mary to bed with seasickness. As usual, Henry was unaffected by the rolling waves. In the early days of the voyage he took time to write a list of needed supplies:

> 2 copies of Dwight's *Constantinople* (Beal & Tenny)
> 4 #153 T. Diary, 1902 Reg.
> 6 American B. Almanac
> 6 American Brooms
> 2 Garden Hoes (Blades strong)
> 2 Farmers' Lanterns
> 1 Rattan Rug Beater
> ½ pint Liquid Glue[7]

The Perrys spent several days in London, shopping and making last-minute purchases for Turkey. On Sundays they enjoyed attending F.B. Meyer's Christ Church.[8] Since the ABCFM did not wish them to specifically solicit funds for Sivas in the United States, Henry and Mary decided to approach Rendell and Helen Harris, their friends in England, for the needed funds to expand the Sivas school buildings. On November 5, they spent the day at Cambridge with the Harrises, enjoying conversation totally focused on Christian ministry. Professor Harris took them through King's Chapel and Trinity dining hall, and Mrs. Harris agreed to provide the needed funds for the Sivas school.

Since Mary was prone to seasickness and there was now a rail line all the way from Vienna to Constantinople, Henry and Mary decided to go to Constantinople by train. It would also be faster, taking only four days from London. Henry and Mary found traveling through the countryside very interesting and enjoyed the changing scenes from their car windows as they passed through fields, towns, and villages. In Vienna they stayed in the Erzharjag Carl Hotel before boarding the Vienna Express for Constantinople (the Perrys did not take the more expensive and luxurious Orient Express). The changing scenes of Hungary, Serbia, Bulgaria, and the Balkan mountain passes were captivating. The Perrys again reached Constantinople on November 15, 1901.

The *U.S.S. Kentucky* was off the coast in Turkish waters by the time the Perrys arrived in Constantinople, putting pressure on Turkey to finally repay American claims from the 1895-1896 massacres. Though the sultan never admitted any liability for American missionary property destroyed in the "disturbances," by December 1898, he had agreed to pay the claims. However, in order to "save his face" and avoid difficulties with other countries which also might have claims, he proposed that the amount of the indemnity be added to a cruiser he proposed to buy from the United States. But, there had been constant delays in the sultan's paying up. After the navy's show of force in Turkish waters, the contract for the cruiser was signed December 25, 1900, and the following summer, $95,000 was paid to settle the American claims.[9]

Henry was eager to return to work after eight months away from Sivas, so the Perrys quickly continued on their journey. Outside Tocat their travels were slowed by a caravan of at least 100 camels, "which gave some trouble, as the path was wanted by both the camels and the wagon."[10] Even so, the Perrys reached Sivas on December 5. As they approached the bridge into the city, they were met by Mr. & Mrs. Partridge, Miss Brewer, Miss Graffam, the Sivas pastor, the teachers from the school, and a street full of welcomers in wagons and on horseback. It was good to be home.

Mary Graffam, Winona Partridge's sister, had come to Sivas while the Perrys were in the United States. She assumed oversight of the Girls' School, freeing Miss Brewer for more evangelistic work among the women. Henry continued to teach the Bible classes in the Normal School, but with Ernest Partridge eagerly teaching in the schools and assuming supervision of them, Henry was able to spend more time visiting the outstations and building up the Christians there. In 1902, Henry spent 152 days, almost half a year, traveling and ministering in Divrik, Gürün, Kara Hissar, and the villages along the way. As always while visiting the outstations, Henry not only personally taught the Scriptures and prayed with the people, but he encouraged the church leaders in their work of ministry. The ultimate goal of the missionary was for the people to be self-sufficient and self-supporting in their own churches, and Henry encouraged the people in those goals. He examined converts for church membership, performed baptisms and weddings, and served communion to the people. Church membership was not taken lightly. Applicants were carefully interviewed and observed to ascertain if they were genuine Christians. If a church was experiencing discord and strife, Henry would not administer communion unless peace was restored.

Henry and Mary did not spend the winter in Tocat, as the Christians there had requested, but in January 1902, Henry spent the Week of Prayer there. Every morning the church leaders met with Henry at dawn to pray. In the evenings, prayer meetings were held in the chapel for the congregation. Special prayer was made for a pastor needed at the Tocat church. Many of the Armenian ministers had immigrated to America, and it was difficult to find qualified pastors. The Harrises in England were major contributors for the rebuilding of the Tocat parsonage, which Henry helped supervise during his three weeks in Tocat.

The Tocat church was notable for the large number of Armenian young men who remained Gregorian, but were also evangelical and attended the Protestant chapel. They were hoping for an evangelical revival in the Gregorian church. There was also an important women's ministry in the town. Miss Brewer accompanied Henry to Tocat in January and later wrote about the day she spent with the Bible reader:

> I wish you could have seen one of the narrow, steep stony streets we passed through. Really, I considered it a risk to life and limb. We went slowly. I kept one hand on the wall on one side, and we ascended and later descended in safety. The women to whom the Bible reader gives lessons are many of them married and mothers of families, but they gladly put aside their work, and read the Bible, and learn its meaning. [11]

After only a few days back in Sivas, Henry left to visit Divrik. In spite of the cold and hazardous travel crossing the mountains, Henry regularly visited Divrik in the winter because then the men were at home. Most of the men were traders who traveled during the summer. Perched on a mule, sitting on his saddlebags and bedding, covered with a shawl and lined cape, Henry set off in the sub-zero weather over snow bound roads, stopping for the night at the house of a Mohammedan. Part of the way Henry traveled with a caravan of Kurds. On Sunday he stayed at the village of Sinjan. As usual for a Sunday, Henry noted in his diary, "The day is a pleasant one." He also wrote:

> I had a good rest in the house of Abraham, the son of Mado, our friend from the former years, who is no more here to great me. I feel his loss as though he was my own father, even though he was a Gregorian, and knew little of the Bible, he always loved to hear it preached, and left a good record of faith in Christ, and loyalty to Him. I am glad to notice that his son, Abraham, is the best reader of the Bible in all the village. He sat by me all the day and aided me in

preaching to successive audiences of from 20 to 30 people, who in coming and going changed every two or four hours. I enjoyed the day very much in the village.[12]

On his way back to Sivas, Henry stopped at a number of villages that did not have Protestant churches, but where evangelical circles for the reading of the Scriptures had been established. Such Scriptural reading circles had become quite common, and many from the Gregorian church participated.

Back in Sivas, the missionary families were going through a time of transition. Emma Hubbard had decided to return to the United States with her two children at the beginning of summer. Her supervision of the orphanages would need to be taken over by someone else. In addition, Miss Brewer suffered an almost fatal case of typhoid fever. At times she was delirious, violent, and suicidal. The women and Dr. Jewett watched her constantly, but her recovery was extremely slow. She did finally recover enough to plan to return to America with the Hubbard trio in June. Miss Brewer had been an indefatigable worker among the women and children of Sivas and the outstations, as well as in the Sivas schools. Both she and Emma would be sorely missed.

Before Emma left, however, she wanted to visit the Gürün orphanage one last time. In April, Henry accompanied Emma and her daughter, Mary, to Gürün. In May the previous year the Swiss had withdrawn from their work in the Gürün orphanage, and Emma wanted to make certain the re-organized institution was being properly administered. The orphanage was in great part supported by the Gürün Rug and Weaving Company, which Henry had organized in 1897. The Company had 150 looms and provided steady employment for many of the women. The profits from the Company entirely supported the Boys' Orphanage of twenty-eight pupils.

Emma was pleased with the orphanage's continued good management. The boys were not only given a good basic education, but were also taught an industrial skill. Most important to Emma and Henry was the moral and religious development of the boys. The Swiss had done a greatly beneficial work in establishing the orphanage. Surrounded by the ruins and still evident signs of destruction from the massacre, Henry found it "interesting to note how the orphans receive Christian training for the building of God, whose foundation can never be destroyed."[13]

Emma had to return to Sivas to help in the care of Miss Brewer, but Henry continued in Gürün another week. Pastor Demirjian continued to be a stalwart leader of his congregation scattered across the six-mile valley of the town. The pastor held daily sunrise prayer meetings at two places in the town. Henry wrote that in helping the pastor in the services during the week, "I found that a horseback ride and a prayer meeting before breakfast was quite conducive to vigorous health, and also a pleasant reminder of the itinerant preaching in the pioneer work of the American churches."[14]

The church at the Shoghl community of Gürün, which was burned in 1895, was being rebuilt. A shepherd told them that if they wanted stone for the church, there was a lot of cut stone at an old farm stable one and a half-hour away. The pastor and congregation made an agreement with the Moslem owner, and for a small price they were allowed to take away all the stone they wanted. When they began to dig down, they found that the stable was upon the remains of a Greek church, which had been buried by a wash of loose stones and soil coming from the mountains in the spring. There was enough hewn stone for the entire outside walls of the Protestant church. Henry found it

> ...interesting to watch the excavation of the old Greek church to see the stone transported, retrimmed, and placed in position for the new Christian temple. That the old ruin was of a Greek church was evident from the peculiar construction about the altar, the frequent appearance of a Greek cross, and some fragments of Greek inscriptions.[15]

On his way back from Gürün to Manjaluk, Henry was enjoying a quiet ride across the plains when

> Suddenly 3 horsemen were seen, coming in to cut off my way from the right. I joined some Olin donkey men, four in number, who were just in front of me. The Papak horsemen stopped and let me pass in silence. I did not know if they had a bad intention.[16]

By the first of June, Emma Hubbard with Theo and Mary had settled all of their affairs and were ready to leave Sivas, Emma's home for twenty-nine years. She and Albert had especially dedicated their lives to the children of Sivas province, and Emma's departure was a day of sadness for the community. On June 3, the orphans filled the yard of the mission compound to say good bye to Mrs. Hubbard. June 4 was departure day, and many came to see Emma and the children out of the city with much sadness. The mission house and yards were very quiet when the Perrys returned from the emotional departure.

When in Sivas, Henry's time was most often involved in administration. Sivas now had an excellent native pastor, which freed Henry's oversight somewhat. Though he realized the business side of the mission work was important, Henry's first love was evangelistic work and bringing the Word of God to the people. He felt his real work of ministry lay in the outstations. Traveling between the villages, he liked to stay in private homes, especially Moslem ones, where he used these hospitable contacts as an opportunity to share the gospel. He took his traveling bed with him, so he could bed down almost anywhere. He willingly put up with the ubiquitous flies and fleas, always forearmed with his flea powder, for the sake of the Word of God.

In the winter of 1903, although his friends tried to persuade him not to visit Divrik because of the severe snow and ice, Henry persisted in making the trip. The church was pastorless and poor:

> The people have the appearance of being hungry [for the Scriptures]. They crowd in on Sundays filling the room almost to suffocation. We have prayer meetings every weekday morning, and before breakfast...In this way we get the business men, who at another hour would find it difficult to leave their shops...
>
> These are the days of winter fog with severe cold. In nearly all the houses of the poor there are no stoves; the place of it being occupied by a covered frame of wood, under which are deposited a few coals. Around this the family and guests sit, warming their feet and hands from the coals within the cover. The corner seat is usually given to the missionary, who reads the Gospel Word by dim light, and in prayer invokes upon the people the heavenly gift...
>
> Though progress here is slow, it is better that the believers be well established, for the temptations are very great in a Moslem country. The unstable are many who fall back from the truth. Divisions constantly arise, which need to be healed. It is only by the aid of the Paraclete [or Comforter, a name for the Holy Spirit] that the Gospel work is done.
>
> Were it not for the cooperation of the Holy Spirit we should indeed despair of these Protestant churches. The whole course of the matter of this world seems to be against them. When every other hope fails, and they are driven back to the Lord, may it be that their faith in Him may be strengthened, and that He may give them courage! Were it not for the continued reduction of our appropriations, we would have a grant in aid here, sufficient to secure the services of a good preacher or pastor; but in this we are again disappointed.[17]

Not only was the mission budget restricted by ABCFM cuts in funds, but the Turkish government was unfairly taxing and requiring permits for American church property. Most of the American schools and institutions had been established before new rules for permits had been passed. The Turkish government wanted all the American schools closed to seek new permits. This included about four hundred schools and nearly thirty thousand students. Treaty relations with France, Britain, and Russia did not require new permits for any institution they had established, and the United States required the same treatment. The situation so threatened the American missionary activity in Turkey that at the end of 1902, a delegation consisting of Dr. George E. Post, of the Syrian Protestant College in Beirut, Reverend W.W. Eddy, of the Presbyterian Board of Missions in Syria, and Dr. W.W. Peet, Treasurer in Constantinople of the ABCFM, traveled to Washington D.C. to meet with President Teddy Roosevelt and Secretary of State John Hay. Both the President and Secretary were very supportive of American missionary work in Turkey. The President told the delegation, "If we take up this case we shall do so with the determination to push it through to success, and if force is needed to get success, force shall be used."[18]

In February 1903, the American Minister at Constantinople filed with the Turkish government a list of American religious, educational, and benevolent institutions within the Empire. Such institutions under the auspices of France, Russia, or other countries were not taxed, and the American Minister required the same for those sponsored by Americans. The sultan ignored the issue until the American fleet appeared in the harbor of Smyrna. The sultan then said the Americans already enjoyed such exemption rights and no further action on his part was necessary. In October 1904, the United States instructed Americans in Turkey to take the sultan at his word and refuse to pay any taxes for these institutions. However, it was not until May 1907, that the Turkish government officially issued a proclamation recognizing the treaty rights of Americans already granted to European nations. For the first time, corporate ownership was recognized in Turkey and the American Board was able to hold property in its own name, not simply in trust by an individual. President Roosevelt and the State Department had worked diligently to secure this agreement. Roosevelt had always been particularly interested in "the extraordinary work done by the American schools and colleges in the Turkish Empire, both Turkey in Europe and Turkey in Asia."[19]

At the end of November 1903, Henry left for a visit to Caesarea. He delayed his departure for a time because of Ernest Partridge's bout with typhus fever. When Mr. Partridge improved, Henry began his journey. One day out of Sivas, the wind on the mountains increased to a gale, piling up drifts of snow. Passing them, the driver of the carriage let the front wheel fall into a culvert, tearing the spring. Henry helped lift the wagon and tie the spring, but was exposed to the cold and received a severe attack of lumbago. The next day he could barely turn himself over in bed, and when he did try to get on his feet, he fell with a severe spasm in his back. He stayed a week at the khan, cared for by the Moslems, when Mr. Fowle came from Talas to take him back to Sivas, lying in a wagon. Even when back in Sivas, it took three more weeks of careful rest for Henry to get over his back problem. Without complaint, Henry took his hardship as from the Lord. He believed the Lord had made him helpless to teach him not to be so caught up in the rush of work that he no longer held on to the Lord for his entire strength.

In spite of the lumbago and sometimes debilitating headaches, at 65 Henry's health was quite good, and he relished the adventuresome, rough traveling needed in visiting the outstations. He continued to spend at least a third of the year in evangelistic service away from Sivas. Ernest Partridge's excellent care of the schools freed Henry to do more of this work he so enjoyed: "constant exposition and testimony, daytime and evening daily, among Protestants, Gregorians, Greeks, Kurds, and Moslem-Turks. Our great field of more than a half million of people is peculiarly open for this kind of work."[20]

Throughout his life, Henry realized the danger of becoming so involved in the work of the mission that the more important life and work of prayer and communion with the Lord was neglected. His journal was filled with Scriptures that guided every important decision and with comments addressed to himself constantly exhorting a higher and holier standard of godly conduct in his daily life:

> "If ye abide in me and my words abide in you, ye shall ask what ye will and it shall be done unto you." John xvi.7. How much we need to pray! We rush in haste from one piece of work to another. O, let us pray that our Lord may show us His more effective way for results. (August 26, 1902)

> "Thou art near, O Lord." (Psalm cxix:151). O, be thou near to us and help us to live near to thee! When we are tempted and feel our need,

let us keep close, ever so close to the living Christ, and may he make us strong!... In this work we need to love because Jesus loves the needy people and the orphans. "I will love them freely." Hos. xiv.4. How wondrous is His love! Let our love be like His! (September 2, 1902).

It is impossible to live the life of abiding without being full of the Holy Spirit. "The anointing which ye have received of Him abideth in you." I John ii.27. Be sure to take time in prayer to dwell at the footstool of the throne of God and the Lamb whence flows the river of water of life. It is there and only there that we can be filled with the Spirit. O let me not fail to do this, and make our work effective in result of souls born into the Kingdom of God in this Mission at Sivas! (September 16, 1902).

Although we see much as the result of our preaching and schools work, which gives us encouragement, we are anxious to have many more souls brought into the Kingdom of our precious Lord. The ability of God is beyond our largest prayers! What have I asked for? I have asked and even pleaded for a cupful; and the ocean remains. I have asked for a sunbeam and the sun abides. "The Lord is able to give thee much more than this." II Chron. xxv.9 (November 25, 1902).

Henry spent much time in prayer for the specific needs of the Sivas mission, his own family and friends, and the advance of the gospel through the progress of worldwide missions. His extensive correspondence with family, friends, and missionaries throughout the world was an extension of his life of prayer. When the ABCFM appointed Dr. Clark to the Sivas station in 1903, Henry saw the doctor's medical work as a tool for Moslem evangelization. After a long list of Armenian names for whose conversion Henry was praying, he wrote out the following prayer list:

Prayer for the Moslems
1. Drs. Marden [in Marsovan] and Clark: that they may do healing mercies for the Moslems.
2. That a hospital may be given to them and to us for this purpose;
3. That the Sivas Government Hospital may be opened to Dr. Clark.
4. Ask this not for the Glory or Success of our Sivas Mission, but for the Glory of God. Nothing but this can reach to secure answered prayer for the Turks. Let them see that God heals in answer to pray-

er. Let them know that we know that it is because Jesus the Son has gone to the Father. So we ask He who is the source of power and healing.[21]

Of course Henry often wrote long letters and prayed for his children, Jean and Alvan. During a visit to Kara Hissar, Henry wrote Jean and reflected on the time spent there with her mother and Alvan during the winter of 1883-1884:

> There were difficulties about the work on which account we had an occasional "fasting and prayer" day. I remember very distinctly the earnest pleading of the prayers of your own Mamma, and how interested she was in all the parts of our work, and especially that souls might be converted to the Lord. Do you know also how she prayed for Alvan and for you, that you might be indeed the children of the Lord; converted by His grace to do his will; and be numbered among His chosen ones to bear His Gospel message in the world? Though you may oft times be tempted, do not forget the precious inheritance of faith, which you have received. Yours should not be a life of pleasure, but of duty, and service, "sent of God," to gather the needy sin-sick ones in His Kingdom and glory. Ours you must remember is a God-serving ancestry. Our fathers and mothers entered into the church covenant with God concerning their children. Their prayers are stored for you. Let me lay it upon you to lay these things upon your heart and life, and to walk "In the steps" of Our Lord and Master, the Risen and Present Savior."[22]

Jean was preparing to enter Wellesly College and was receptive to her father's admonitions. Alvan was financially prospering, but Henry prayed for his spiritual life:

> ...that the Lord may awaken him, and that he might receive Him...
> I prayed as best I could gather myself for Alvan. "Lord, I believe in thy promise which I preached this morning (Mark xi.22-24). I have no trouble about this doctrine of it that thou wilt grant whatsoever will be sought by those who pray in faith. I do need the experience and joy of it."[23]

When the Russo-Japanese war broke out in 1904, Henry followed its developments carefully. Consul Jewett helped him keep informed, as did the *London Times*. Henry read Dr. Gordon's *Missionary in Japan*, and spent time in prayer, with the map of Russia, China, and Japan before him. International events were not simply interesting political occurrences, but calls for prayer for the advancement of the Gospel of Christ throughout the world. As 1904 drew to a close, Henry prayed with Mary for the issue of the war: "That the Lord will by it open the Gospel to the great countries involved: And that the proud look of man—anywhere—may be taken down."[24]

On January 18, 1905, the Tocat church had a Jubilee celebrating its 50 years. The church had been founded in 1854, by Dr. Van Lennep, flourished for a time, then fell into a decline for about twenty years. Henry and the Hubbards had continued to minister to the people, and once more Christian work there began to grow. Henry wrote Reverend Smith that a perspective of history allowed Christians to better assess the Tocat church at the time of the Jubilee:

> The study of perspective in making the true picture of history is very important. Many of the faults of the time fade away and disappear. There is then revealed in the distance the clear path by which the overruling Hand of the Lord has led His people on to victory... at this distance looking at the perspective of the past, we do not at all clearly see the crooks and narrow places through which the advance was made. On the contrary there appears a clear broad coarse to the glory of Him upon whom as the foundation the church now so useful has been built.[25]

At the time of the Jubilee the Tocat Church had forty-four members, with an average congregation of 150. There were two schools, having sixty-three pupils. On the occasion of the Jubilee Pastor Kartozian and the church leaders sent a letter in English to the ABCFM, thanking the board for the Gospel the missionaries had brought, and the funds contributed to the Tocat church, and asking for continued prayer for the Christians at Tocat.

There was so much to be done in the mission work that Henry did not take summer vacations. He had found that simply varying the work done was as good as a vacation. In June 1905, he varied his work by traveling to Hadjin, to give the graduation address for the eighteen girls graduating from the school there. Such travel and the scenery it brought was still invigorating to the sixty-seven year old missionary:

> I left Sivas on May 29th traveling southwest, during two days on the western and then on the eastern slopes of the Anti-Taurus Mountains, among the numerous fountains which send

their waters afar to the west, the south, and the east. On one night I was in an Armenian village: another with a Circassian boy; a third at the half way town of Azezia; the fourth was spent with some interesting people of the Avshan tribe; and I lingered to meet some old friends of 30 years ago at Shar, famous for its ruins of the Cappadocia Comana.

Finally, making a descent into what from a distance seemed to me to resemble a gristmill hopper with a little grain remaining at the bottom, I went up through the closely built town to a nook among the vineyards on the steep above it...There in what appears to be a complete unit, are the Dormitory and School rooms of the Home and Mission House and Parsonage, all in a setting of trees and vines. What a quiet attractive place for 16 teachers, with their 250 girls, about one third of whom are boarders.[26]

Henry arrived in Hadjin a few days before the graduation to be a part of the Farewell meeting for Mrs. Coffing, who was leaving Turkey after forty-eight years. Henry could not help but think back to thirty-six years earlier, when he and Mr. Montgomery first visited Hadjin after the expulsion of the Coffings. He met a few of the "greybearded fathers" who had attended the Sunday worship under a tent so many years ago: "Surely the hand of the Lord hath rested in blessing, establishing the churches and the schools."[27] Henry was very pleased with the cleanliness of the school, the neat appearance of the girls, and the thorough work done in their studies. About 500 people attended the graduation, held in an open auditorium of a grape arbor. It was a joyous day, though also a sad one with Mrs. Coffing's departure.

When he left Hadjin, Henry joined the muleteers and eighteen girl graduates returning to their homes in Zeitoun and Marash. Henry had not been to Zeitoun since the seventies. Before that, Mr. Montgomery and Reverend Avedin Gastantian had been beaten by a mob when they first visited the town. Now, forty years later, there was a flourishing Protestant church in Zeitoun.

As the muleteers approached Zeitoun, they pointed out the walnut and poplar trees encircling the town some distance outside the city. The trees marked the outside limit of the Armenian defense during the siege of 1895. Some of the Armenians of Zeitoun had been forewarned of potential Turk attacks and had organized a stiff resistance. For three and a half months, 1500 Armenians with flintlock and 400 Martin rifles were able to hold off the "24 battalions, 12 canons, reinforced by 8000 men of a Zeibek division from Smyrna, and about 30,000 Kurdish, Turkish, and Circassian irregulars."[28] During the massacres, Zeitoun successfully resisted, held at bay the town's attackers, and caused the Turks to meet with a serious defeat. Every tree and grapevine inside the town had been used for firewood during the siege.

Sunday, Henry preached three times at the Zeitoun church to a congregation of about 350. At Marash too, Henry was welcomed by the Christians and asked to preach on Sundays. Some of the leaders of the church had been his students in earlier days. What memories these places held for him, and how he could rejoice in the Lord's work in building His church over the years.

On June 19th, Henry left Marash for the return to Sivas, ascending the range of the Akhir Dagh and descending the other side. A huge cloud-burst covered the pass of Koch Dagh and followed Henry throughout the afternoon: "Soon we became entangled in the ash from the mountainside, the torn devastated road, and the flood streams, almost impassable." At nightfall Henry came to the barracks of the Imperial Soldiers at the Zeitoun bridge over the Jehan. When Henry entered, the twenty-five soldiers were seated for dinner and invited Henry's party to join them. They sat down to eat at a table loaded with so many large, cooked fish even the hungry soldiers couldn't eat them all. The soldiers had picked the fish out of the shallow Jehan with their bare hands! Henry was not accustomed to telling fish stories, but that one he recounted several times![29]

The Sivas missionaries had often been hosts to the missionaries of eastern Turkey as they traveled through Sivas on their journeys to and from Constantinople. Henry was especially fond of Reverend Browne of Harpoot, of whom he once wrote, "He is one of the few missionaries after my own heart. He keeps his spiritual mind steady, and preaches with power, gains a great influence over the native people."[30] Henry and Mary, however, had never been to Harpoot or the mission stations in eastern Turkey. At the end of September 1906, the Perrys hosted a number of visitors at once – Mr. Favre of Geneva, Switzerland, and the missionaries Messrs. Browne and French, and Mrs. Waite returning from America. Mrs. Waite had come to Turkey to visit her daughter, the wife of the American consul at Harpoot. She was a delicate woman and became very sick at Sivas. When she recovered somewhat, Mary arranged to accompany her and Mr. Browne to Harpoot, where Henry and Mr. Favre would meet them. The timing was not the best for Mary.

She had just finished supervising re-plastering the house and had "filled about 100 quart lightning jars" with apricots, plums, and tomatoes, besides making the currant jelly and putting away 10-15 bushels of harvested potatoes.

After Henry and Mr. Favre arrived in Harpoot, Henry and Mary journeyed to visit places associated with Henry's earliest missionary labors in Turkey forty years before – Diabekir, Ourfa, Aintab, Marash, and Zeitoun. Along the way, Mary collected wildflowers and pressed them to send Jean for use in her studies. Mary carefully noted the location where each plant had been found: "On the plain in sight of Mardin," "Sunday camps, west of Ourfa," "Near the Euphrates," "from the Antioch plain," "In the Beilan Pass, in sight of the Great Sea." Henry had many opportunities to preach and visit old friends. It was good to be able to share these early associates and places with Mary. It was especially a joy to be with Miss Shattuck in Ourfa and see the wonderful ways the Lord had blessed her in the orphanage and school. She had built several industrial programs in the schools to teach the students useful skills in farming, sewing, and machine work.

Though Henry's work among the Armenians bore the most fruit, he continued to reach out to the various Moslem groups in the Sivas field. One group that especially interested him was the Kuzzle-bash Kurds. He had first encountered them in 1874, when touring among the Hadjin Mountains. When Henry visited them they listened attentively to the Bible, but seemed to lack a settled faith. In 1876, about fifty families of Kurds who declared themselves "Protestants" had been imprisoned in Sivas during impending problems with Russia. Though Henry had many conversations with them, there was some spiritual barrier to a full Christian commitment with them. Whenever possible, Henry tried to stay with them in his travels, using every opportunity to press home the gospel message.

In a March 1907, journey home to Sivas from Divrik, after crossing the Anti-Taurus Mountains at the Gezbel Pass, Henry wrote:

> ...we turned aside for an hour's rest with a friend who is a Sheik of the Kuzzle-bash Turks. He received us with true Oriental hospitality: carpets were immediately spread under the grateful shade of some trees on the banks of a stream; a beautiful meal set before us by which we were soon refreshed, after which we entered into earnest conversation with our host.

The host spoke of their great Shiah leader, Ali, whose great virtue was evident by the great battles

> he had won by the destruction of thousands of lives. I waited my opportunity to draw a contrast between Jesus Christ and my host's champion by telling of what Jesus, our Lord, did when he met the funeral procession near the gate of the city of Nain. Instead of destroying life, he restores life. The penalty of sin is death. He takes us in the condition of death – "dead in trespasses and sin" – and gives us life through his resurrection. Who could be blind to the nobler deed? That the Lord was with me in giving this testimony, I was conscious, for the rattle of tongues was stopped, and a hush came over that little audience that showed me the point was understood... For the next hour "Christ" was our theme, and it seemed as if no one cared to mention any other subject.
>
> The Sheik was a genial fluent man of great dignity, courteous in manner, and kindly in disposition. He reads our Bible with reverence: speaks freely of the typical characters of the Old Testament, and of Christ, of the New Testament: accepts the doctrine of the Resurrection of our Lord, and the New Birth of Believers; but is inclined to question the "General Judgment." A few months later he called upon me in Sivas; and together, with Bibles in hand, we went over the same subjects, I preaching Christ, and he assenting to and accepting whatever he believed to be true, but winding up with the affirmation that "whatever our Lord, the Christ was to the Christians, his 'Ali Hazret-lere' is the same to them," that Ali and Christ are one and the same.[31]

Though these Kurds were willing to listen to the Gospel, in practicality they rejected Christ. They agreed that Jesus was God manifest in the flesh and that he brought salvation from sin, but they also believed Jesus and Ali were one. They were pantheists, and with their belief in the transmigration of souls, Perry finally came to the conclusion that they are much farther away from the Gospel, than are the monotheists of Islam.

Henry completed his report to the ABCFM on his preaching to the Kurds by noting:

> It would seem that the Lord has put them and ourselves into such close contact that in His own time, He may bring them to Himself. But as the years pass quickly by, and we see no visible fruit among them, we are saddened by the thought of their continued rejection of the Truth. Yet we would not give way to discouragement. If any of

the Lord's servants in America are willing to join us in special prayer for these Moslem Pantheists, we shall rejoice in the encouragement of such cooperation, remembering that our Lord declared that in response to <u>faith</u> "nothing shall be impossible to you."

In the midst of the constant rounds of preaching, teaching in the school, visiting the outstations, and keeping the books for the treasury accounts, Henry and Mary received exciting news from Alvan in April 1907. Alvan was doing quite well in his business, and he had arranged for him and Jean to take a European tour and visit Constantinople in the summer. Could Henry and Mary meet them there in July? Henry especially was thrilled at the prospect of being with his children. The only regret was that they would be in Constantinople during the July heat.

Alvan's successful New York business in real estate and mortgages allowed him to help his younger sister Jean through college. Jean had first gone to Wellesley, where Aunt Emilie was the physician, but severe asthma made the damp air of Boston unsuitable for her. Her second year she transferred to Smith in Northampton, only twenty miles from Ashfield. There she studied hard, planning on becoming a Latin teacher. She also studied Greek, having promised her father she would learn to read the New Testament in Greek. The summer of 1907, Jean had just completed her junior year at Smith. July 2 she and Alvan left New York for their grand tour, visiting Paris, the Chateau country of France, Switzerland, Vienna, and Budapest as they made their way to Constantinople.

Henry fell terribly ill in June and was doubtful whether he would be able to make the trip to Constantinople; but he was on the mend when it came time to leave, and he and Mary made the ten-day trip comfortably. They arranged to be in Constantinople to have some dental work done before the children arrived. Henry had three broken teeth that needed capping. The Perrys stayed with Dr. and Mrs. Washburn of Robert College while waiting for the children. What joy it was when Henry and Mary met Alvan and Jean at the train station July 27th. It had been seven years since they had been together. Jean especially was eager to see the land of her birth with adult eyes, for she had grown up since she had left Turkey eleven years before.

The Perrys took rooms on the Black Sea at the Palace Hotel at Therapia on the eastern Bosphorus, one hour from Constantinople.[32] It was much cooler at Therapia than in the city. Up until July 27th, Jean had kept a detailed diary of all she had seen and met during her trip, but once in Constantinople her diary entries are briefer. She wrote that she was so happy to be with her father that she would not take time away from him to write in her diary.

For twelve precious days Henry, Mary, Alvan, and Jean visited, sharing details of their lives, thoughts, and feelings that their frequent letters could not convey. On Sundays they went to the church at Robert College, afterwards visiting and enjoying the hospitality of the missionary families, some of whom Jean had known as a girl in Sivas. Jean especially loved the well-prepared Turkish food – the pilaf, roast lamb, and modzoon. In the evenings they enjoyed each other's company sitting on the hotel balcony overlooking the sea.

Boats carried them from Therapia to either the European or Asiatic side of the Bosphorus. All boats anchored at the Galata Bridge connecting Stamboul and Pera. Jean was fascinated by the sights around her and wrote in her diary:

> The bridge acts as a dock from which everything starts and fills in. It is a most interesting place full of all kinds of people and all nationalities seem to be well represented. Beggars are in abundance.[33]

Alvan and Jean enjoyed shopping in the bazaars together. They learned there was an art to bargaining for purchases. Henry and Alvan visited the U.S. minister one day. Another time they went to visit the sultan's stables. One evening the four hired a boat and rowed on the Bosphorus for an hour. A special occasion for Jean was when she and Alvan accompanied Congressman Bennett to a Selamlik to watch the sultan at his prayers. Jean did describe this with some detail in her diary:

> Its lots of fun to go to Selemliki and see the old Sultan go to prayers. When we reached the shore we all took carriages and drove to the vicinity of the mosque. We were accompanied by Dragoman Mr. L_____ and were admitted by the officers to the little terrace from which we could see the monarch pass. The soldiers quickly closed in upon us and filled up the entire place all around the mosque. Infantry and cavalry came out in full force. The Harem came down from the palace first and then the sultan and crown prince and some generals. It was a great sight. He entered the mosque and was there about half an hour and then returned driving himself – a beautiful span of white horses.[34]

All too quickly the days passed; on August 5th Alvan and Jean boarded the train for Munich. They would travel through Germany, Holland, and Britain before reaching home the first of September. Henry and Mary remained another week in Constantinople before beginning their trip back to Sivas. They both felt invigorated by their visit with Jean and Alvan. It was a good as a furlough for them, and they were ready to resume their work in Sivas. Jean and Alvan wrote detailed letters to them throughout their return trip to the United States, so Henry and Mary could follow them in their imaginations. Henry was thankful to the Lord for making this special meeting with his children possible.

Ernest Partridge's father had been in serious health, so the Partridges had left for the United States earlier in the spring. When Henry and Mary returned to Sivas, more than the usual amount of missionary work awaited them. One of the problems which was especially a burden to Henry was the indebtedness of the mission station that had accumulated over the past decade. Growing taxes and two years of poor harvests continued to impoverish the people. The Sivas schools were growing, but expenses could not be covered by ABCFM allocations. Though he had been able to obtain grants from other sources, including the Harrises in England and Reverend W.A. Essery of England's Bible Lands Missionary Aid Society, the station was still $500 in arrears. Henry explained the causes of the debt in detail and asked the ABCFM's Prudential Committee for a grant to relieve the station of the debt. A great burden was lifted from all the Sivas missionaries when the Prudential Committee agreed to cancel the shortfall.

In October 1907, the Central Evangelical Union held its meetings in Sivas. Dr. and Mrs. Charles Tracy of Marsovan attended and wrote glowingly of Sivas and the Christians there to the home office in Boston:

> The place itself furnished a stimulus to the meetings. There is in Sivas a deep and prevailing religious earnestness. The people generally seem hungry for the Word of Life.
>
> The crowds coming to listen are out of all proportion to the accommodations – 500 crowded into a room not calculated to hold comfortably over two hundred; and this happens day after day, night after night, with increase rather than diminution. The sermons preached on Sunday and in the evenings were gospel sermons, and were listened to with fixed attention and silence. Scarcely have I felt my preaching going so straight to the mark as when uttered to that

crammed and intent audience. *Earnest work has been done by missionaries and preachers at Sivas, and the effects are visible.* [emphasis added].

Mr. Tracy added that the schools at Sivas were woefully overcrowded and in need of twice as much space as available. With 1000 students, the Sivas schools were recognized as the best in the city, and some of the oldest families in the city sent their children there, even if they had little sympathy for the religious instruction given. The library had over a thousand books and was in constant use by the children as well as the ministers of surrounding areas. While Mr. Tracy was in Sivas, a meeting was held to raise money among the people for an expansion of the school facilities. The school had the opportunity to buy a large tract of land outside the city, and Ernest Partridge hoped to build a large high school there.[35]

In the first decade of the twentieth century, political changes affected the Sivas missionaries in a number of ways. For several decades the United States had a consul general in Constantinople as head of the American legation. American consuls were based at Alexandretta, Beirut, Trebizond, Harpoot, Jerusalem, Sivas, Smyrna, and Baghdad. In 1906 the legation at Constantinople was elevated to an embassy, and G.A. Leishman was appointed the first American ambassador to the Ottoman Empire.[36] The next year Consul Milo Jewett was transferred from Sivas to Trebizond, and the Sivas Consul came to an end. The missionaries felt deeply the loss of Consul Jewett. He not only had provided important political protection for the Americans during times of great difficulty, but his medical background and strong Christian commitment had made him an integral part of the Protestant community.

Sultan Abdul Hamid's rule in many ways was Janus-like. With one face he modernized and westernized the bureaucracy, administration, and army of the empire. While showing a desire to be part of western advances in some areas, with another face he resisted any reform that might give freedom and equality to his subjects in the Empire. Though the constitution had been nominally reformed in 1876, the only changes actually implemented were those which re-arranged the bureaucracy and expanded the prerogatives of the absolute monarch. In 1878, the sultan had dissolved the Parliament that had been part of the new constitution.

However, the memory of the Parliament was kept alive as an ideal, and a number of societies were formed to secretly work for the establishment of western-style freedoms in Turkey. Because of censorship and repression within the Empire, most of these organizations had to operate abroad, sending their books and pamphlets into the empire through the foreign mails, which under the capitulations were not subject to Ottoman government control. In the 1880's, Mehmed Talaat Bey and Rahmi Bey organized the secret Committee of Union and Progress (C.U.P) in Salonika. Also known as "Ittihad," the organization was patterned after Freemason lodges and aimed to establish a constitutional monarchy in Turkey. The C.U.P was closely linked with Turkish revolutionary societies in Paris.[37]

Discontent rose within Turkey when, in early 1906, the government instituted new taxes, one on individuals and a poll tax on domestic animals. The Armenian and Moslem populations united in tax revolts in numerous commercial centers, including Sivas. The harshness of the new taxes was intensified by several years of poor crops and a particularly harsh winter in 1905-1906. In January 1906 the Tigris froze at Mosul and temperatures at Sivas dropped to -25^0 F. Many people froze to death at Van, Baghdad, Amasia, Derende, Konya, and Sivas. The C.U.P. tried to organize the popular dissatisfaction and coordinate the widespread protests against the government. On July 24, 1908, Abdul Hamid restored the 1876 constitution, and the Young Turks, as the revolutionaries came to be called, were able to bring a more democratic government to Turkey. The Ottoman Empire was gradually being dismembered. In October, Austria annexed Bosnia and Herzegovina while Bulgaria declared independence. When Abdul Hamid attempted a counter-revolution, the Young Turks dethroned him and placed his brother Mohammed V on the throne, but the new sultan reigned with little power.

It would be some time before the full nature and impact of the Young Turk Revolution could be properly assessed. Henry, however, was soon affected by the revolutionary changes. At Sivas, there had been a consciousness that with the pressure building up on the government, something, somewhere must break, but no one knew when and how the break would come. Henry tried to describe his sense of things to Dr. Barton:

> What we of the interior only knew was, that on one night the wires flashed; and the rusted iron bands were broken and gone. New words

before unheard were uttered; and as quickly written in dazing white upon the red banners, were borne aloft in the street.[38]

Words like "liberty" and "equality" were freely spoken. Obnoxious government officials were forced to resign, and never heard from again. Once the chief officers were removed, however, they were not always replaced. Support from Constantinople was lacking, and many offices in local government remained vacant for months. It was during this lax period that a number of Gregorians organized a mob in Gürün to attack the Protestant pastor, Reverend Kevork Demirjian. An Armenian priest, Demesrobian, brought a charge in criminal court against the Protestant Pastor for "Misuse of Trust Funds." Apparently some of the Gregorians resented Demirjian's administration of the relief funds and sought to attack him in this way. The police searched Demirjian's house and seized all of his account books.

What the jealous Gregorians did not realize fully was that Demirjian was simply Henry Perry's agent in Gürün and that they were attacking Perry himself. The trial was held in the Turkish criminal court in Sivas, and Henry was able to assemble a powerful case against the Gregorians. His carefully recorded and audited account books, support of American and British consuls, and an excellent Greek lawyer made the Gregorian case look especially weak. Henry clearly had all the evidence on his side of the case. More important, however, was the fact that public opinion remained firmly on the side of Henry and the Gürün pastor:

> Just here in my judgment is the rock on which the case against us was hurled in vain. The reasonable people both at Gürün and Sivas held stedfast in my support, to the extent that other than from the Gürün sore-headed agitators and their lawyers, not one word of suspicion has reached me from any quarter to trouble and hinder me; and this clear verdict of Public Opinion, for faithful honest work done in the Relief business, was that which finally neutralized the venom of accusation against our Pastor Mr. Demirjian.[39]

An even more amazing evidence of the hopeful freedom coming to Turkey was the large and honorable funeral of the Protestant pastor Marderos Kalousdian.[40] Kalousdian was an 1882 graduate of Marsovan college and pastored the Sivas church for three years after his graduation. He then went to pastor a church in Gemerek. When many Armenians were arrested over the revolutionary placards in 1893,

Kalousdian was among them. He endured the horrors of a secret tribunal in Sivas. When others were finally released, Kalousdian was exiled to a Turkish fortress in Akka, Syria. English intervention finally brought about his release. Physically broken, Kalousdian was unable to resume his pastoral work, but his spirit remained strong. He never hesitated to speak "of Christ as the source of all true liberty." Though a Protestant and not a physician, he was appointed Superintendent of Sivas' Gregorian hospital. Unfortunately, he soon contracted typhus fever and died. Thousands attended his funeral, and the Gregorians insisted on honoring him in their church before his burial in the Protestant cemetery. At the memorial service, many Turkish officials as well as Gregorians touchingly spoke of Kalousdian as "our brother." Pastor Kalousdian's funeral itself seemed to be a harbinger of a new Turkey. After describing the funeral to Dr. Barton, Henry wrote:

> After July 24th, 1908, his [Kalousdian's] heart burned within him for the emancipation of Turk and Armenian from the thralldom of ignorance and sin; and for a government that would admit of the enlightenment of all its subjects, and also the release from the oppression of taxation from which so many millions of Asiatics have suffered, till they could bear no more.[41]

During the many troubles Henry had seen in Turkey, he had often taken comfort from a sermon on Daniel 9:25 by Dr. E.D. Griffin:

> That sermon treats of "the wall built in troublous times;" and the application to our case was clear, that no matter what troubles come, the Lord's hand is in them to "build the wall" of his Church in these Lands of the Covenant Promise...
> while we missionaries endeavor to work straight ... along the direct lines of service, the Lord makes use of us in many circuitous ways which we know not, and in connection also, with these far reaching results. Out of the very things that often seemed to us only failure, he has brought some peculiar ingathering from the far distant fields, which were perfectly inaccessible to us...[42]

The life and witness of Marderos Kalousdian was a beautiful example of "the wall built in troublous times."

---

[1] *Ecumenical Missionary Conference, 1900.* New York: American Tract Society, 1900.

² Christian Endeavor Society was an interdenominational and evangelical youth ministry founded in 1881. Its purpose was to train young people for future leadership and incorporate them into the life of the church.
³ *Diary*, September 1, 1901.
⁴ "Class of 'Sixty-two," *We Report Progress to 1902*. Lake Helen, Florida, 1902, 68-69.
⁵ *Diary*, October, 8, 1901.
⁶ "Class of 'Sixty-two", 68.
⁷ *Diary*, October 25, 1901.
⁸ Frederick Brotherton Meyer was a popular Baptist pastor and Bible conference speaker who befriended Dwight L. Moody and Ira Sankey during their first evangelistic tour of England in 1873. At Moody's invitation, Meyer traveled and spoke extensively in America. His books on Bible characters and devotional subjects were popular on both sides of the Atlantic. "Meyer, Frederick Brotherton (1847-1929)," *Dictionary of Christianity in America*, 736.
⁹ *Adventures in American Diplomacy, 1896-1986*, 451-452; Sir Edwin Pears. *Forty Years in Constantinople*. London: Herbert Jenkins, Ltd., 1916, 172-173.
¹⁰ *Diary*, December 3, 1901.
¹¹ "Progress at Tocat," *The Missionary Herald*. April 1902, 165.
¹² "Divrik," *The Missionary Herald*, July 1902, 291.
¹³ Henry T. Perry to Rev. Judson Smith, April 28, 1902, ABC 16.9.3, Vol. 37, No. 32.
¹⁴ Henry T. Perry to Rev. Judson Smith, April 28, 1902, ABC 16.9.3, Vol. 37, No. 32.
¹⁵ Henry T. Perry to Rev. Judson Smith, April 28, 1902, ABC 16.9.3, Vol. 37, No. 32.
¹⁶ *Diary*, May 2, 1902. Papak was a founder and leader of an Iranian Moslem sect. "Papak," *Encyclopedia Britannica*, www.britannica.com.
¹⁷ Henry T. Perry to Rev. Judson Smith, January 20, 1903, ABC 16.9.3, Vol. 37.
¹⁸ *No Less Honor*, 106, 104-111; *Adventures in American Diplomacy*, 458-459; William J. Hourikan. "The Big Stick in Turkey: American Diplomacy and Naval Operations Against the Ottoman Empire, 1903-1904," *Naval War College Review*, Vol. XXXIV, No. 5, 287, 78-88; *Annual Report of the American Board of Commissioners for Foreign Missions*, 1906, 18.
¹⁹ "Editorial Paragraphs," *The Missionary Herald*, April 1905, 156; July 1907, 316. The March 1909 issue of *The Missionary Herald*, pp. 130-131, contains a portion of President Roosevelt's address in the Metropolitan Memorial Methodist Episcopal Church in Washington, D.C., in which he praised the American missionaries in Turkey:
> Now in speaking tonight I wish to lay stress upon the missionary side of the general work in the foreign lands. America has for over a century done its share of missionary work, We who stay at home should as a matter of duty give cordial support to those who, in a spirit of

devotion to all that is highest in human nature, spend the best part of their lives in trying to carry civilization and Christianity into lands which have hitherto known little or nothing of either. The work is vast, and it is done under many and widely varied conditions. Personally, I have always been particularly interested, for instance, in the extraordinary work done by the American schools and colleges in the Turkish empire, both Turkey in Europe and Turkey in Asia; a work which has borne such wonderful fruit among the Bulgarians, among Syrian and Armenian Christians, and also among Mohammedans; and this, although among the Mohammedans there has been no effort to convert them, simply an effort to make them good citizens, to make them vie with their fellow-citizens who are Christians in showing those qualities which it should be the pride of every creed to develop. And the present movement to introduce far-reaching and genuine reforms, political and social, in Turkey, an effort with which we all keenly sympathize, is one in which these young Moslems, educated at the American schools and colleges, are especially fitted to take part.

[20] Henry T. Perry to Rev. Judson Smith, January 11, 1904, ABC 16.9.3, Vol. 37, No. 35.

[21] *Diary*, August 16, 1903. Increasingly missionaries with the American Board were considering how to reach the Moslem peoples of Turkey. Because of racial antipathies, it had become clear that the earlier hope that the Armenians might be a missionary people to other ethnic groups in the Ottoman Empire was not to be realized. In an address to the ABCFM annual meeting in 1906, Dr. James Barton recognized that medical work among the Moslems was probably the best way to demonstrate to that people true Christian love and brotherhood. *Annual Report of the American Board of Commissioners for Foreign Missions*, 1906, 296.

The 1905 Annual Report of the Sivas station reports a growing missionary enterprise on all fronts: in the medical work, in evangelistic work among the outstations, in spiritual growth of the Sivas church, the work of the Christian Endeavor Society, in Sunday School growth, in work among the women, and in the self-support of the Armenians themselves. The report noted that, "For the first time in many years Sivas has its full number of missionaries, among them Dr. Clark, a physician who took the place standing vacant since the death of Dr. West in 1879." *Annual Report of the American Board of Commissioners for Foreign Missions*, 1905, 46-47. The 1906 report noted that in spite of the province's poverty, in seven years its donation to Christian work had doubled. $2472 donated in 1905, compared with $1093 in 1899. *Annual Report of the American Board of Commissioners for Foreign Missions*, 1906, 69.

[22] Henry T. Perry to Jean Perry, December 27, 1905. Letter in possession of authors. Jeanne was pregnant with Jean while in Kara Hissar during that win-

ter; Jean was born in April. Perry's diary indicates Jeanne prayed for her children's spiritual development even while they were yet in the womb.
[23] *Diary,* April 24, 1904, August 7, 1904.
[24] *Diary,* December 18, 1904.
[25] Henry T. Perry to Rev. Judson Smith, March 1, 1905, ABC 16.9.3, Vol. 37, No. 36.
[26] Henry T. Perry to Rev. Judson Smith, July 29, 1905, ABC 16.9.3, Vol. 37.
[27] Henry T. Perry to Rev. Judson Smith, August 2, 1905, ABC.16.9.3, Vol. 37.
[28] *History of the Armenian Genocide,* 128.
[29] Henry T. Perry to Rev. Judson Smith, August 2, 1905, ABC.16.9.3, Vol. 37.
[30] *Diary,* May 30, 1902. Henry thought Mr. Browne was much like Giles Montgomery at Marash.
[31] Henry T. Perry to Rev. Enoch F. Bell (Asst. Secr. ABCFM), March 8, 1907, ABC 16.9.3; "Using a Guest's Privilege," *The Missionary Herald,* June 1907, 300-301.
[32] Therapia, the elegant summer resort on the Bosphorus, is today called Tarabya.
[33] Jean H. Perry "An account of her trip abroad in summer of 1907," July 29th. Manuscript diary in the possession of Gordon B. Severance.
[34] "An account of her trip," August 2nd.
[35] "A Significant Meeting in Sivas," *The Missionary Herald,* December 1907, 598-599; Ernst C. Partridge. "The Sights of Sivas," *The Missionary Herald,* May 1909, 216-219.
[36] John A. De Novo. *American Interests and Policies in the Middle East, 1900-1939.* Minneapolis: University of Minnesota Press, 1963, 18-20, 56.
[37] "Bey" was a title of courtesy given to high government officials, colonels, and distinguished persons. For the C.U.P. and the Young Turks, see "Turkey," *Encyclopedia Britannica,* 1958 ed., vol. 22; Aykut Kansu. *The Revolution of 1908 in Turkey.* Leiden: Brill, 1997; M. Sükrü Hanioglu. *The Young Turks in Opposition.* New York: Oxford University Press, 1995.
[38] Henry T. Perry to J.L. Barton, December 22, 1908, ABC 16.9.3, Vol. 37.
[39] Henry T. Perry to J.L. Barton, December 22, 1908, ABC 16.9.3, Vol. 37.
[40] See pp. 187-188 for earlier account of Kalousdian.
[41] Henry T. Perry to J.L. Barton, December 22, 1908, ABC 16.9.3, Vol. 37.
[42] Henry T. Perry to Rev. J.L. Barton, January 1909, ABC. 16.9.3, Vol. 37. Perry noted that the book of sermons was printed in 1844, and had been given to him by Benjamin Schneider, his early mentor during his first days as a missionary in Aintab. The book was Edward Dorr griggin's (president of Williams Colelge and Pastor of Park Street Church, Boston). *Sermons, not before published, on various practical subjects.* M.W. Dodd, 1844.

12
A VESSEL UNTO HONOR
(1909-1914)

---

*"...he shall be a vessel unto honour, sanctified,
and meet for the master's use, and prepared unto every good work."*
II Timothy 2:21

As the first decade of the twentieth century came to a close, there was an optimism throughout much of Turkey. The Constitution established by the Young Turks guaranteed religious liberty, freedom of the press, and a Parliament. Many Turks and Armenians were hopeful about the newly announced freedoms and were ready to cooperate together in the markets and public assemblies. They recognized that without these needed reforms in the Ottoman government, the dismemberment of the Empire by radical groups seeking independence would continue.

The liberty, equality, and fraternity longed for by so many now brought a temporary peace among previously distrustful peoples. For the first time in five or six hundred years, Moslems meeting men of other faiths used the greeting confined to fellow believers, "Peace be unto you!" to be answered with, "And upon you may peace also rest." In Constantinople, many Turks accompanied Armenians to the graves of those killed in earlier massacres and expressed sorrow for the loss of so many Armenian lives. Armenians and Moslems went into Constantinople's churches and together expressed thanks to God for this coming day of peace. Political prisoners were released on the promise that they would abjure all crime. The new constitution established that all subjects of the Empire were Ottomans. No longer was there to be a division of citizenship between Ottoman Turks, Syrians, Macedonians, or Armenians. It was as if the country were ready to leave behind the Middle Ages and enter the modern world.[1]

Henry was very hopeful about the new government. Though the missionaries did not participate in political affairs, they hoped that at last the repressive government of Turkey would provide equality, respect, and justice for all its citizens. Many of those trained in the missionary schools would have the education and training to serve the new government responsibly. Following the Revolution of 1908, Dr. Barton and the Prudential Committee encouraged the missionaries to organize an "All-Turkey Conference" to plan how they could best minister in Turkey's changing political climate. With the increased freedom, it seemed as if many new opportunities were opening up for Christian work. However, a cholera epidemic and renewed unrest prevented the plans for the conference from ever materializing.

There were some who, from the beginning, believed the new government was just as corrupt as the old.[2] There were danger signs that the freedoms promised by the Constitution were a cloak for the Committee of Union and Progress, or at least a faction within the Committee, to establish power for the Turks at the expense of the Greeks, Armenians, and other Christian minorities. Events at Adana dampened the hopes of many.

In the Cilician province of Adana, Armenians made up almost one half of the 40,000 population of the city. The educated among them were especially pleased about the increased self-determination of the people and the possibilities of sharing in the local government. The Turks, however, were angry that their dominance in government might be eroded. In April 1909, at the same time Sultan Abdul Hamid was leading a counter-revolution against the Young Turks in Constantinople, violence broke out in Adana, a city which had been spared the massacres of the 1890's. The precise cause and background of the outbreak has never been determined, but after forty-eight hours of killing, burning, and looting, 2000 in Adana and between 15,000-20,000 in the surrounding villages were dead. 4,407 Armenian homes were burned. Miss E.S. Webb, missionary in Adana, described something of the scene:

> The awful extent of the destruction here in Adana and in all this region grows more apparent every day and hour. One is almost stunned by the misery around us. Most of the people are in utter desolation – homes, business, clothing, household furniture all gone. Most have left only the clothes on their backs. Many have most hor-

rible wounds, and not even a mat to lie on except as we find something for them.

Each wounded person averages at least four wounds. One woman had eleven, and eight or nine is not at all uncommon. Some had been cut in a perfectly fiendish manner, and others shot again and again. A woman came in this afternoon from a village ten miles distant, every member of whose family had been killed, husband, father-in-law, mother-in-law, three children, the youngest of these being a baby two days old. She herself was badly shot, and the wound had remained without care for five days.[3]

Death and destruction spread rapidly to surrounding towns. British vice-consul Wylie was shot in the arm, and two American missionaries were killed. The annual meeting of the Central Turkey Mission American Board was scheduled to meet in Adana, and many of the native pastors, preachers, and delegates on the way to the meeting were slain. In a single day, twenty-eight leaders of the thirty-five churches in the Central Turkey mission were "cruelly slain, and the bleeding, staggering churches are left as sheep without a shepherd."[4]

The Ottoman government investigated the uprising and executed both Turks and Armenians as instigators, but many felt those executed were wrongly convicted and the real culprits remained only lightly punished. Some Turks were astonished that a Turk could be punished for the killing of a Christian. Europe and the United States, wanting to establish the Young Turks in power, only weakly protested the Adana massacres, even though two American missionaries were killed and a British vice-consul injured.[5]

Many Armenians began to feel less hopeful about meaningful reform, and many left the country. By 1910, at least 100,000 Armenians had left Turkey. Though most went to the United States, many also settled in France, South America, Persia, Egypt, the Sudan, and Abyssinia. All of the Christian races, including the Greeks, Syrians, and Bulgarians, were aware of the increasing dangers and uncertainties in the Ottoman Empire. Unfortunately, usually the more energetic and resourceful emigrated. This affected not only church membership, but also meant a loss of leadership in the church. It also affected the ability of the churches to support themselves.[6]

1910 was the Centennial of the ABCFM, and the Sivas station report for that year gave an overview of the station's history, as well as the usual report for the year. In one way the report was easier to assemble this year, since both Henry and Mary now had typewriters for their mission work. As Henry assembled the report, he undoubtedly rejoiced in all the Lord had done in Sivas since the evangelical church was organized there in 1851. In spite of factions and persecutions over the years, the Sivas church was well established and self-supporting. Though in the last decade it had lost 75 members through emigration, it still had a solid membership of 130. Of the 4000 Armenian pupils in the Sivas schools, 900 were in the American mission schools:

> Since the underlying ideal is the formation of character, we strive to secure the best possible teachers, who by their example, the daily Bible Lessons, and Sunday School instruction, give to our schools a spiritual tone not found elsewhere. We believe that these pupils representing 500 families are a strong influence for the Christian elevation of the people.[7]

The Normal School had 100 boys who were being trained as teachers. Graduates of the Normal School taught in the eight out-station schools. These graduates were usually the best educated men in their villages and could have tremendous influence in shaping Turkey's future:

> If he has Christian character, tact and initiative he will organize and superintend a Sunday School, and lead in every movement for good. For years we have prayed for a wider opportunity to help the village people and now it is opened before us. Applications for teachers, more than we can supply, come from school committees, Priests, and Bishops. There never was a time when this call and the need for well educated Christian teachers were so great as the present. The success of the Constitutional Government depends upon raising the general level of education and character, and this is conditioned on the supply of educated leaders.[8]

During its thirty years, the Sivas Normal School had graduated 155 men; 75 percent of them became teachers. Ernest Partridge had enthusiastically taken over superintendence of the school and was working to raise funds for a new building. There even was a Sivas Normal School alumni group in New York that was sending support. The new building would allow an expansion of the industrial shops where the boys learned bookbinding, tailoring, and carpentry skills while also helping to support their education.[9]

Miss Mary Fowle supervised the Girls' Schools while Miss Graffam was on furlough. Nina Rice had also come to Sivas in 1904, to fill the place of Miss Brewer in the schools and evangelistic work. The schools employed twenty-five teachers, fifteen in Sivas and the others in outstation schools. Many of the graduates became teachers. When they married they had a better understanding of home making and child rearing, and many took a firm stand as Christians. Perry rejoiced to see how the missionary work among the girls had expanded and even influenced the Gregorians, who had never had schools for girls before the missionaries came:

> In taking a retrospective view of the outgrowth of the work for the girls begun by one Armenian young woman in 1864 in the city of Sivas, with a group of ten little pupils, we see something parallel to the parable of The Grain of Mustard Seed. There are at present in Sivas city alone, 560 girls under the direct care of the American Missionaries, not to speak of hundreds more gathered in Gregorian schools. Gürün, Tocat, Divrik, Enderes, Zara, Manjaluk, and Derende all have schools for girls under the care of the American Missionaries; and stimulated by this example, Gregorians have founded and carried on schools for girls in Tocat, Gürün, Divrik, and other places that far outnumber our girls' attendance.[10]

Sunday Schools and a Christian Endeavor Society brought Christian teaching to those young people unable to attend the schools. In 1907, the YMCA of Sivas organized an "Industrial Work for Women and Girls" to provide a means of children and young women to earn some food. The young men contributed capital for the girls to begin a "Needlework" program. Samples of embroidery work for handkerchiefs and other items were ordered from Aintab, and material was ordered from England. The Partridges and Mary Graffam encouraged the Association and helped find markets for the girls' handiwork. Though the earnings had been small, they were a great help to the girls in the impoverished society. The girls were taught cleanliness, the importance of self-support, and were kept out of bad company. They also had the opportunity to hear the Scriptures read and have a weekly service of prayer. With liberty being talked about increasingly under the new Constitution, Henry realized the importance of a Christian education for the people, to help them "to understand that their liberty is not freedom from all restraint, or license to do wrong, but a thorough understanding and following of the laws of God."

The Sivas hospital also had become an important Christian outreach in the community. When Dr. Charles Clark came to Sivas in

1903, he rented a small house near the town market and set up four beds for a hospital. The Government objected, however, since he did not have a *firman*. The doctor then moved the beds and dispensary into part of his house at the missionary compound, where there would be no objection to his receiving "guests," whether they were sick or well. When the work expanded, the Clarks rented a house outside the compound, and nurse Lillian Cole took care of the many "guests." By 1910, there were 20 beds in the hospital, and the doctor and nurse treated at least 5000 patients in the previous year. The patients represented all classes, "from the beggar on the street, to the wealthy Government officer. Turkish, Moslem, Circassian soldiers, Kourds, Armenians — both Gregorians and Protestants."[11] In the hospital, prayers were held with the patients morning and night, and the school girls came to sing to the patients. Scriptures were read, and even the Moslem patients looked forward to the Gospel reading and prayers. With such an expanding work, a new hospital was needed; and while Dr. Clark was on furlough in the United States, he hoped to raise funds for the building. According to Turkish plans, Sivas was soon to become a major railroad center, and a major hospital in the town would be a powerful means of ministering to the physical and spiritual needs of the people.

The growth of the many facets of the mission work in Sivas never obscured for Henry the central importance of preaching Christ. Even as the people began to enjoy greater political liberty, they had had three years of bad harvests that caused food prices to rise:

> Poverty and the wave of fear which swept the land in April 1909 made hard conditions, for which the Gospel affords the only true comfort. We thank God that our Station Force has been able to meet the special emergency by more touring than usual, amounting to 161 days during the twelve months, in this particular line of service. We have seen another practical and vivid illustration of the fact that "Fear hath torment." We have been able to witness how the Lord uses this agency to bring His own wandering ones back to Himself, renewing their faith in and dependence upon Him. We have also seen what a separating power "fear" has upon those refusing to recognize God's methods of discipline, driving those so-called Christians, who possess nothing but the name, into the by-ways of infidelity, or the horrors of insanity. During our touring, with a satisfaction that we cannot express, we preached Christ, the once suffering but now triumphant Saviour, waiting to forgive the wanderers and restore them to favor. The people crowded around us daily for the comfort of the Gospel of Christ to their torn hearts. The Lord was with us at the Communion

tables of our branch churches, and we could sing to His praise "Thou preparest a table before me in the presence of mine enemies." We were in a position to call a halt to "fear", reprove "unbelief," and admonish the people to lay hold upon God by faith, for in Him alone is their hope of deliverance.[12]

Once he turned 70, Henry tried to redirect some of his labors, not to cut down on the amount of work but the type of work! Ernest Partridge had so enthusiastically taken over the supervision of the Normal School that in 1910, Henry no longer taught classes there. He was able at last to relinquish his Treasurer position to another, so he freed up more time to travel to the villages and engage in the personal evangelism he loved so much. The Sivas pastor, Mehran Kazanjian, was away in America for two years, going to school; Henry and Ernest Partridge divided much of the preaching among them. After 50 years of use, the Sivas chapel was being renovated inside and out, and Henry oversaw the entire work. He also continued to be the main negotiator with the Turkish government on any difficulties that arose either over missionary property or over the government's treatment of fellow Christians.

It had been nine years since Henry and Mary had a furlough, and the Sivas station encouraged them to apply for one. The station promised to ask for their return. Both Henry and Mary were ready for a rest. Mary wanted to return to the United States by way of Bangkok and California. She wanted to see and share with Henry her former mission in Siam. Henry would have preferred traveling east, since Mary wished it and because the long voyage would do him good. He was tired and often troubled by a confusing headache. Henry was concerned, however, about his older sister Sarah. He had written her several times, but had received only one brief note. He had asked Alvan to look after her, but she might require more of his attention back in Ashfield.

On June 8, 1911, Henry and Mary arrived in New York on the North German Lloyd steamer the *Koenigin Luise* and were met by Alvan, Jean, and Emma Hubbard. They had had a very quiet journey from Constantinople to Naples and directly to New York. For ten days they stayed in New York, basking in the joy of seeing family and friends again. Jeanne's sister and mother, Emilie Jones Barker and Mrs. Jones, came for a visit. Mrs. Jones was 89, and

> ...as bright as a pink and as clear in her faith and hope as when she gave her youngest daughter to me in marriage in 1866, which was the yielding of her also for the foreign service. Not far away do we

seem to be from the dear ones, who have gone hence before us; and the precious memories of the past have become the alluring hope to a more glorious future.[13]

Henry's sister Sarah, however, had fallen into financial difficulties. Her house in North Adams had been taken over by the South Falls Bank, and she had to find somewhere else to live. When Henry arrived, all her furniture was still in the house, and the bank had the key. Henry had to settle the affair with the bank and made arrangements for Sarah's furniture and property to be moved to his house in Ashfield. Sarah too moved into the Ashfield house. Her hearing and eyesight were fading, and she seemed to have become embittered by her shifting fortunes. She only joined the family for the noon meal. Breakfast and dinner were served to her in her room. Henry's diary hints she was not easy to live with:

> My sister Sarah Anne is in good health, but had no pleasant side for me (May 9, 1912).

> What a rich consolation we have in prayer, in the Name of our Blessed Lord Jesus! In the case of my sister, I do what I can for her, and throw off anxiety, in my prayer, that He will care for her in our absence in Turkey! (May 14, 1912).

After several weeks in Ashfield, Henry and Mary attended the annual meeting of the American Board in Milwaukee. It was an invigorating time, as Henry wrote Reverend Barton:

> The old-time feeling of forty-five years ago was stirred in me to press again for the firing line of the front. Especially did I enjoy the subdued calling voice, as it came to us by the quartet, and the earnest, trustful words of the newly appointed missionaries.[14]

The Thursday session was devoted to the ABCFM's work in Turkey. Rev. Haskell of Salomea opened the session and was optimistic about the opportunities in Turkey since the young Turks overthrew Abdul Hamid II and gave more liberty to the people. Henry Perry described work among the Moslem villages. He gave an account of a young Moslem student, Hamdi Effendi, who had read the New Testament and came to him seeking more light about Christianity. Hamdi eagerly accepted Jesus Christ and regularly visited with Perry. One day, after they had their Bible reading together, the young man said, "This is my last visit with you, for I am going to prson. I am called by the officers, and I am sure that they will detail me." He was indeed imprisoned, but released on his promise that he would go to Constantinople. When he arrived, he was imprisoned and later died in prison. Perry recounted how the case of this young student enlarged Perry's efforts to bring the gospel to the Moslems. The Moslems welcomed the American missionaries as neighbors, and the gospel could best be given to them through these neighborly relations.[15]

On the way back east, Henry and Mary spent four weeks traveling and visiting numerous friends and relatives along the way – at Chicago and Danville, Illinois, and East Aurora, West Falls, Auburn Seminary, Binghamton, and Afton, NewYork. It was a refreshing time, and as Henry became rested, he began to think about returning to his work in Turkey. He was 73; but his health was good, and he loved the work in Sivas.

He had noticed his hearing was not as good as it once was and sometimes he had difficulty reading. Reverend Barton recommended a specialist, Dr. Berry of Worcester, for Henry to see. After a very careful examination, Dr. Berry reported that the trouble Henry was having with his eyes, ears and a "left side-headache" was due to a "worn out nervous condition." The rest provided by the furlough should cause these problems to fade, and Henry should be ready to return to the mission field in August.

In Ashfield Henry made repairs on his house and arrangements for Sarah Anne's care for when he returned to Turkey. There was time to read over the correspondence from his parents while he was in college and during those early years in the mission field. He was always thankful the Lord had led him into such a work. Whatever he was doing, Henry's thoughts were on the mission field. He especially thought and prayed much about how to reach the Moslems and worked on an address on missions in Moslem countries to deliver at a meeting of the Presbytery in Courtland, New York. That fateful week in 1912, the papers were full of the disaster of the *Titanic*.

Mary was asked to give several addresses at various women's missionary societies, and in March Henry accompanied her to New York City and Washington, D.C. They had some good visits with Alvan and many friends in the area. In New York Alvan took Henry to an evening meeting of the Union League Club. The Union League Club was one of the elite service clubs of New York. Founded in 1863, by a group of citizens to help preserve the Union, the Club had been instrumental in establishing the Metropolitan Museum of Art and the American Red Cross. It helped erect the Statue of Liberty in New York Harbor as well as the Lincoln monument in Union Square. Its members helped bring down the "Boss" Tweed ring, and Teddy Roosevelt managed his early political career from the Club's rooms. J. Pierpoint Morgan was a regular at the Club, along with Chester A. Arthur and Thomas Nast. Presidents, Senators, many Congressmen, diplomats, cabinet members, and scores of chief executive officers of major corporations were among the members.[16] Alvan was also a regular at the club. Though Henry enjoyed seeing the moving picture "Dunbar of India" at the evening meeting, with such illustrious company, it was understandable that he enjoyed the table conversation even more.

In Washington, Henry went to the Capitol building and sat in the Senate and House galleries. At a church prayer meeting he met Mr. Doremus, who invited him to visit the Smithsonian. There he showed Henry the new African "Roosevelt" collection, an exhibit of animals Teddy Roosevelt brought back from his 1909 African hunting and collecting tour. Henry noted in his diary:

1. The Harte Beest: long-nosed, crooked horned, thin, sharp back.
2. The Lion family, dusty cream color, the case 12 x 18 feet and four plate glass. They have a spring dug in the sand.
3. The Zebra group.
4. Rhinoceros
5. Antelope
6. Gnu (2 horns).[17]

For four months Mary traveled in New York and Illinois, visiting friends and relatives and speaking in churches and to missions organizations. Henry stayed close to Ashfield, taking care of business affairs and making arrangements for the care of his sister. In May Henry again went to New York to have nasal surgery done by Dr. Harris. He had one of the bones removed in his left nostril. The surgery was not too painful, but hopefully would relieve some of the pressure causing his headaches. The following week, Alvan and Henry went to the Armory early to see the troop muster for Memorial Day. Alvan gave his father a ticket for the reviewing stand at 89th Street Riverside Drive, and for two hours Henry watched the cavalry, National Guard, Spanish War Veterans, and Marines march past. There were over fifty marching bands in the parade. Father and son then enjoyed dinner together at the Union Club. In New York Henry was able to do some shopping in preparation for Sivas. He bought a Scofield Reference Bible, which had just been published in 1909, a 12-volume "Dictionary and Cyclopedia" in pigskin for $98, footwear, a soft hat for $5, and a saddle overcoat for $25.[18]

A most unexpected and unsolicited event was Henry receiving a Doctor of Divinity degree from Williams College. Reverend Barton of the ABCFM helped provide the College with information about Henry's many accomplishments. The following information on "Rev. H.T. Perry of Sivas" from the ABCFM files is a keen analysis of Henry's work and character:

> Mr. Perry has been engaged throughout his missionary life in the direct evangelistic work...He has given much time and effort to touring, in which he has had much strenuous and trying experience, but with it the privilege of bringing the gospel in direct contact with the people, to many of whom it came as a new revelation. In the central station he has borne much of the burden of the business administration, including the charge of the treasury, the correspondence with local laborers, and the decision of the great variety of questions relative to policy and methods. First and last, no little portion of his time has gone to what may be called the diplomatic affairs of the Station, - dealings with Turkish officials, and incidentally with foreign consular and other officers, both officially and socially. His extended experimental knowledge of oriental character, and of the Turkish language gave him special fitness for such relations, and he seems to have had a fair average of success in this risky and trying field of effort.
>
> In all these departments of work Mr. Perry has, together with warm Christian devotion and earnestness, manifested a rather rare degree of discretion and shrewdness. Among his personal characteristics may be mentioned, caution and persistence, patience, and self-control. The last mentioned he seemed to have cultivated to a very fine point. He was able not only to check all demonstration of sudden rising emotion, but successfully to hide his own views and judgments, even while taking part in the discussion, until he had sufficiently drawn out the positions of others, and thus to shape his own policy deliberately and independently, under the accumulated light of the views of others, reserving his own decisive expressions until the critical moment, when the ammunition of the enemy was exhausted.
>
> He is not much given to expression of humor, nor to indulgence in amusement, and so has been considered by some as austere and sombre. But in this there is danger of misjudging him, for under an exterior of apparent severity or indifference, there is much of the ge-

nial and truly sympathetic, and he has a gift of doing his kindnesses in an unobserved and unexpected way.[19]

In June Henry went to Williamstown for the Baccalaureate and Commencement ceremonies and to receive his doctoral degree from the College President, Harry A. Garfield, son of the former U.S. President Garfield. Alvan and Jean proudly accompanied their father. In the citation, Henry's biographical and educational background was given and his numerous contributions in Turkey were emphasized, especially the founding of the Sivas Normal School, his evangelistic work, and the establishment of the orphanages:

> ...In 1879, Mr. Perry founded the Sivas Normal School, the primary purpose of which was to supply the educated native teachers and missionaries, who could work among their own people. The School has had a remarkable growth, until at the present time, it has over 1000 resident pupils...giving...the children of Turkey their first opportunity for a real primary school education.
> In its thirty years of existence, the Normal School has graduated many teachers, clergymen, physicians, lawyers and leaders of political thought, and many of the leaders of the present reform movement in Turkey owe their education to the Normal School, and the strides toward religious tolerance and civic freedom which Turkey has made in the last two years have been largely due to influences which have been silently working through the mediums thus established...
> Despite the exacting duties of the administration of the Normal School with its allied primary schools, Mr. Perry has throughout his life, been actively engaged in Evangelical work, continuing to travel throughout the State of Pontus founding churches and missions and preaching the gospel as it came to him from Mark Hopkins.
> Perhaps a single incident in Mr. Perry's life will show the scope of his manifold activities. Thousands of Mr. Perry's Armenian parishioners were being massacred in the Sivas region. Mr. Perry immediately set on foot a movement to provide for the orphans of the murdered Armenians. He raised the needed funds largely through English and Swiss Societies, and founded an Orphan Asylum which gave succor to over 800 orphans. He organized trade schools in which the orphans were educated, and as a result, practically all of these children became self-supporting...[20]

Though Henry appreciated the honor of receiving his D.D. and enjoyed seeing his classmates at the '62 reunion, he would never have sought out the attention which the honor brought him.

Alvan returned to New York, but Jean returned with her father to Ashfield, where she helped him pack and prepare for his return to Turkey. It was a great comfort to Henry to have Jean with him. Unlike Alvan, she shared his interest in spiritual things and delighted in Bible study. Father and daughter enjoyed the days of working together at Ashfield and set aside special Bible study times together. They began a study of the book of Zechariah.

After graduating from Smith in 1909, Jean had taught for a year at Oakwood Seminary, a Quaker school at Union Spring on Cayuga Lake, New York.[21] She was the only non-Quaker at the school, and it took some getting used to the "Thee" and "Thou" in everyone's speech. Jean taught all the sciences and Bible at the school. Realizing she needed more study in the biological sciences, Jean studied for a year at Columbia College. She lived with Alvan in New York and took time to enjoy the theater, especially the plays of Shakespeare and Marlowe and operas starring Caruso. In 1911, Jean secured a teaching job at The Woolcott School in Denver, Colorado. It was a fine private school and paid higher salaries than the eastern schools. During the summer of Henry's furlough, Jean was happy to spend her days with her father. She realized it was likely she would never see him again. When he returned to Turkey he would be 74 and not due for another furlough until he was 81. Both Henry and Mary planned to work and die in Turkey.

In mid-August Jean accompanied Henry and Mary to New York for their return to Sivas. Alvan, Mrs. Hubbard, Mrs. White, and Rebecca Racoubian saw them off. The Racoubians were from Sivas; Rebecca's husband, Roupon, was attending Columbia Teacher's College to better prepare him for teaching in the Sivas Normal School. August 13 the Perrys boarded the *S.S. Rotterdam* for London. From London they went to Kehl in Bade, Germany, where Dr. Milo Jewett was then a Consul. They had a heart-warming visit with Dr. and Mrs. Jewett, who had become dear friends during Dr. Jewett's thirteen years in Sivas. From Germany they went to Geneva, Switzerland, where they were guests of Mr. Leopold Favre, whose Christian Association had helped organize support for the Sivas and Gürün orphanages. It was a stimulating visit and time to learn more of the work of the Christian Association.

September 7, Henry and Mary arrived in Constantinople. The following day was Sunday, and as Henry attended church in the Bible House and listened to the sermon by Mr. Krekorian, he was impressed anew with the vastness of the reach of the Gospel in Turkey and the need for the missionary to live a life of prayer. During the journey home to Sivas, Henry spent as much time as possible in prayer for the work of the mission.

When they left on furlough, the Perrys had given over Dr. West's house to Dr. and Mrs. Clark. They now rented a house near the Swiss orphanage from Garabed Agha Topbashian. Located in an Armenian quarter, the upper floor had a lovely view of the surrounding mountains. By the first of October the Perrys had cleaned the chimneys, moved their furniture, unpacked trunks, and were settled into their new home. While they were getting settled, rumblings of war stirred up excitement in the city. In the Balkans, Bulgaria, Serbia, and Greece had allied themselves with Montenegro against the Ottoman Empire. Troops were called up, and by October 18, war had begun.

The war did not directly affect the Sivas province, and in mid-October Henry left for Tocat to attend the Henry Martyn Centennial Memorial Celebration. Martyn had been an indefatigable worker for the Gospel, with a special facility for languages and had translated the Bible into Hindustani and Persian. He was traveling from India, through Persia and Turkey, on his way home to England, when he died at Tocat on October 16, 1812, at the age of thirty one, alone and surrounded by strangers. Perry had again read Martyn's life before the Centennial meeting and found many lessons to be learned from him – his recognition of the Lord's presence with him continually; his consecration to the cause of missions, to "Go! Teach all nations!;" and his submissive will.

Pastors and missionaries came from Marsovan, Angora, Chakmiah and Caesarea. Perry had been appointed to lead the Martyn memorial meeting at the chapel and the cemetery. Reverend Avedis Kevorkian gave a biographical address; Reverend Mehran Kazanjian of Sivas described Martyn's character as a "man of God;" the Gregorian Vartabed or preacher described Martyn's meeting with the Patriarch at Etchmiatzen and his burial by the Armenian church in its cemetery.[22] After some prayers, the congregation formed a procession across the terraced garden, at the foot of which was Martyn's grave. Reverend Kevork Demirjian of Marsovan led in prayer and gave an address on the spirit of missions. Perry further described the scene to Dr. Barton:

> The day was warm and bright, and in the genial atmosphere of the declining sun, when its softened rays touched so kindly the as-

sembled audience, and lit up the city and mountains in the farther perspective, Dr. Tracy gave the final address with great solemnity and power. It was "The Message of Henry Martyn to the young men of the East." [23]

Dr. Tracy challenged the young men as Martyn himself might have, "Here, in Christ's presence, I regret not that on earth I left all to follow him. Young men of Asia! Choose the Master that I chose and walk with him wherever he may lead. All your loss shall be gain, your reward a hundredfold, and the end life everlasting."[24] In the photo of the pastors around the Martyn monument, Henry's white hair and beard stand out. How many in that crowd could imagine on that beautiful day the horrors they would face within three years? How many of those pastors would indeed, like Henry Martyn, lose all for the sake of following Christ, only to receive an everlasting reward?

Before the winter snows set in, Henry returned quickly to Sivas and set off again on a three-week trip to Zara, Enderes and Kara Hissar. Accompanied only by his Moslem gatekeeper Hallel, Henry relished stopping at the towns and villages to share the Gospel. Years of traveling to the many outstations had made him well known in the villages. His age, highly revered in the Middle East, and white hair now gave an added aura of respect to his majestic six feet height. The people, believer and unbeliever alike, eagerly heard him. At Zara, fifty boys from the school came out to meet Henry. Though the boys' school flourished there, the Protestant church itself was weak. Without a pastor and effective teaching, the church had dwindled. The church had further split into factions of Campbellites, Seventh Day Baptists, and Mormons.

At Kara Hissar, many were concerned about the political situation. Bands of soldiers were constantly moving in opposite directions, some to the Black Sea, and others eastward to Erzinjan. Henry encouraged the people that their resource and strength could only be in their God, the God of the heavens and the earth.

As Henry studied the prophetic passages of Scripture, it seemed obvious to him that the Turkish Empire must retire not only from Europe, but also from Asia Minor and the land of the Jews. He did not know the timing of such events, however, and prayed for peace that the Protestant churches and missions could continue their witness to the Lord. It seemed clear that Constantinople would continue to be an important political center, and it was amazing to watch the various nations vying for power in the region. Though the nations of Europe were secretly vying for portions of a dismembered Ottoman Empire, it was clear to all that the United States had no territorial interest in Turkey. The American missionaries grew in respect among the people, since their work in Turkey was obviously apolitical and unselfish.

By April, the Balkan war came to an end. Turkey gave up all of its lands in Europe and ceded the island of Crete to Greece. It was a stunning blow for Turkey and a further dismemberment of the once great Ottoman Empire. The Liberal Union of the Young Turks seized power and formed a new cabinet, ready to adopt repressive measures to strengthen the Empire. When they first achieved power, the Young Turks had adopted a policy of "Ottomanism," aimed at uniting all of the racial and religious elements of the Empire. The war in the Balkans had led to Turkey losing most of its Greek subjects, as well as its Albanian, Serbian, and Bulgarian ones. The French seemed to be inciting the Arabs in the south to revolts as well. Ottomanism was a failure, and the Young Turks began to return to Abdul Hamid's Pan-Islamist policy. The Ottoman Empire would be for Moslems only. All others must convert, be deported, or eliminated.

Ismail Enver Pasha, who led the Young Turks in Pan Islamism, became minister of war in 1913. Talaat Bey became minister of the interior, and Ahmed Djemal became governor of Constantinople. Enver, Talaat, and Djemal became the triumvirate that would hold power in Turkey during the next tumultuous years. Enver had spent time in Berlin and had a great respect for the German military. A military mission was brought from Germany under Gen. Otto Liman von Sanders to modernize the Turkish army. England's Admiral A.H. Limpus was given the task of building up the Turkish navy. A detailed program for the eastern *vilayet*s was also prepared. Its implementation would produce horrors unknown to the previous century.

Whatever the political changes, the eleven missionaries at Sivas continued their work among the people. Dr. Clark, along with his wife, was assisted in his medical work by Lillian Cole, superintendent of the hospital. C. Henry Holbrook had come to help Ernest and Winona Partridge at the Normal and Boarding Schools.[25] Winona's sister, Mary Graffam, was principal of the Girls' School and the industrial work. Nina Rice and Mary Fowle taught in the schools. The schools continued a major part of the ministry of the Sivas missionaries. As C.H. Holbrook wrote in the station report for 1912:

Every year it becomes increasingly evident that our greatest usefulness as missionaries lies in living and preaching the Christ-life as teachers of these boys and girls, who shall go out from our schools by scores and hundreds to do a missionary work we could never hope to do. It is our conviction that the vast Mohammedan and heathen populations will never be won to Christianity, until those who bear his name shall bear also his Spirit and witness to the power of his purpose in all the social relationships of life.[26]

The American schools had become a great strength of the American mission in Turkey. By 1913, there were "10 colleges with 1,748 students; 46 boarding and high schools, with 4,090 students; 3 theological seminaries, with 24 students; 8 industrial schools; 2 schools for the deaf and blind; and 369 other schools directly or indirectly connected with the American Board, with 19, 361 students."[27]

Both Henry Holbrook and Ernest Partridge were ordained ministers and took part in some of the preaching ministries of the mission. Being younger men, they were ready to use the newer audio-visual techniques to supplement their preaching. Mr. Partridge used a magic lantern show on the life of Christ to help present the gospel in the villages. One Sunday, Mr. Holbrook gave a sermon in the Girls' Hall on sacred music, playing key selections on his gramophone. Henry thought this was good in its place, but thought it no substitute for a Scriptural sermon for the young people. Henry was concerned that the reverence for the power of the Bible was not as it should be. Even in the missionary schools, too many teachers used the Bible only as a reference book, rather than as the living Word of God.

Henry's passion for sharing the gospel seemed to only intensify with age. He renewed his earlier study of Arabo-Turkish so he could better distribute and recommend tracts in this language to the Moslems. He also spent time in prayer:

I was about my studies and writing in the AM, taking occasion (since I was alone) to continue my prayer before the Lord for humility of spirit, and such a way of presenting truth, that He may count me worthy to bear fruit, in turning souls for His service and Kingdom! What is wrong, let Him reveal that I may put it right.[28]

Though now 75, Henry continued to travel among the outstations, taking trips for weeks at a time. Though he probably never took the time to calculate, Henry had traveled on horseback over 30,000 miles bringing the Gospel to the people of Turkey. Fording streams and climbing mountain cliffs, he shared the Gospel with all he met and strengthened the faith of the churches. Many orphans he had helped after the massacres of the 1890's now were leaders in the churches. Others had left the country, many for the United States. When he visited the village of Pingian, Henry noted that the village's 200 houses were reduced to 130 because of emigration. Though many Armenians were leaving, Henry recognized the Greeks, Kurds, and Moslems needed the message of Christ too. Henry wrote a full, descriptive account of his 1913 trip to Divrik. Little did he suspect that this would be his last journey to the Sivas outstations:

> An Armenian Bible Society colporteur and myself got into our saddles on the morning of June 3. The day was cold and windy, with premonitions of a storm. In the late afternoon, the cold having continued to increase, we were glad to seek shelter in a village of Orthodox or Sunni Moslems. Reshid, a stalwart farmer, welcomed us cordially, and soon had a cheerful fire, for which we were exceedingly thankful, as we had barely escaped being thoroughly chilled. Reshid also welcomed his neighbors, who, after the manner of the Orient, quickly flocked in to see who the strangers were and what news they brought. To me was deferentially given the guest privilege of introducing conversation, and when retiring time arrived, my host with his own hands prepared for me a good bed for the night—a service which is only personally performed by the 'man of the house' when he wishes to be understood as holding his guest in distinguished honor.
>
> The little audience that evening was composed entirely of Moslems, twelve of whom were present. The first inquiries were concerning the war and political events. It was not difficult to pass quickly and easily from the statements of our daily bulletins to what is being done by the Great Dispenser.
>
> For several hours the conversation went on, each man freely taking part in the discussions of various topics, but especially in that exhaustless subject, "Our Sacred Books." We did not chide them for the loyalty they expressed to their "Prophet," nor controvert any remarks made about their "Four Books;" but rather went on to show that our sacred Book has for us an amazing record, that we most firmly hold to the unity of God, his righteousness and judgments, and that all men by repentance of their sins may find forgiveness therefor. As we ourselves so much enjoyed that interview with these Moslem villagers, we may infer that their pleasure was not less than our own.
>
> Returning three weeks later by a different route, we visited two Kuzzlebash Turks, each a sheik of great influence among the tribes of

his constituency. In previous years we had several times enjoyed their hospitality, and were now received as old friends. Their village teachers and other prominent men came in, or gathered about us in the comfortable shade. The burden of their hearts was soon revealed as they spoke with deep feeling of their brothers and sons, who are still absent, being soldiers in this war. We were much touched by their sorrows, and did our best to show the sympathy we really felt. Some of the brothers and sons were men we personally knew, and our interest being genuine was doubtless appreciated.

In conversation with these Shi'ah Moslems (heterodox), we have perfect liberty to speak boldly and frankly...The doctrines of the Immortality of the Soul, the Personality of Man, and God the Spirit are points on which our testimony is needed. The Shi'ah exalts 'right living' and demands 'reform.' We show that no real reform and right living can be attained except through the new birth, as explicitly taught by our Saviour.

In Divrik it was my privilege to preach three Sundays to the pastorless Protestant congregation. About one hundred persons made up the audience, most of whom were women. On the third Sunday we celebrated the Lord's Supper, and also had some baptisms. Between Sundays we spent four days of each week visiting neighboring Armenian villages. Prejudice against the gospel truth as taught by Protestants is much less than in former years, and the gospel is much better understood. The field before us is now not only opened, but there are a cordiality and simplicity of at least nominal acceptance, which is certainly encouraging. In certain places there are people who in one respect give us much annoyance and disappointment: their political leaders have thrown off their allegiance to the Bible and now reject the Christ as the true, living and abiding Leader. The attack made by them on our Biblical position was strong and defiant; but intrenched in the Word of God, our colporteur could not be worsted. The Moslem neighbors present gave a verdict in our favor for a 'just reply.'

The second trip out from Divrik was on the west side, to a group of seven villages, all Gregorian and not a solitary Protestant among them. In these places the cordiality with which we were received surprised us. They had not forgotten my services in matters of 're-lief,' when they were struggling to regain possession of the lands of their ancestral homes. Especially did the Gregorian priests sit with us, as if to make the most of every hour of our stay, and repeatedly thanked us for having taken the pains to visit them. At one of these villages an evening was spent in a sharp discussion with the leader in unbelief.

As was the case with Paul, the great apostle, constraint is laid upon us to preach the gospel to these Gregorian, Greek, Moslems, and Kurdish people, who in their distress are vainly seeking for what they call a "Reformation."[29]

After three weeks of traveling, Henry returned to Sivas quite tired. Touring was much more exhausting work than teaching in the schools. Henry finally decided his tours of recent years had become more tiring than earlier years because, "All the people, especially the Moslems and the Kourds, have more reverence for aged, white-haired men: They give more attention to me closely and keep me talking."[30] Days after his return, Henry had one of his "left-sided" headaches that he could not shake off. Neither headache remedies nor bedrest were of any avail. Dr. Clark was at Kara Hissar, but Dr. Sewny recommended a course of quinine. Henry complied and tried to exercise in the open air more. Though he followed the doctors' treatments, Henry's confidence was "not in them; but it is in the Great Physician, My Precious Lord the Healer."[31]

Yet the headache, now accompanied by night chills, continued without relief. Henry noted in his diary that the earliest promise of healing in the Scriptures was in Exodus 15:25-26, "I am the Lord thy God which healeth thee." Other Scriptures referring to healing included:

Bless the Lord...who forgives all thine iniquities, who healeth all thy diseases. Psalm 103:2,3.
He healed all that were sick. Matthew 8:16,17.
They shall lay hands on the sick and they shall recover. Mark 16:18.

Henry spent much time at home in prayer, patiently waiting for the Lord's healing hand. Psalm 25 became his constant prayer.

After six weeks without any abatement of his headache, Henry asked Dr. Sewny if he could go to Dr. Marden's hospital at Marsovan for further care. Dr. Sewny immediately telegraphed Dr. Marden to receive Henry and accompanied him on the five-day journey.

The day Henry left Sivas, his colleague Charles Holbrook was murdered eighty miles east of the city. It was decided not to tell Henry the news. Only a month before, Reverend Holbrook had preached the sermon at the annual meeting of the Western Turkey Mission on the Bible text, "But then face to face," expounding the truth that at death the believer would meet Christ face to face. These words seemed fulfilled in his own sudden death. Holbrook was touring with a group of native teachers in the hill country east of Sivas. He was shot while camped at night. Turkish officials claimed the shot was intended for one of the Armenian teachers, an enemy of the owner of the campsite. For the next several months, Ernest Partridge's time was consumed in working with the State Department and government officials on the trial. In his thirteen years in Sivas, Ernest did not think he had ever seen as rotten a government as that in Sivas. Though he could not prove it, he suspected the government knew of the plans to kill Holbrook. In the trial, the murderers were acquitted of any wrongdoing.[32]

Once in Marsovan, Henry stayed at Dr. Marden's house, where he was given complete rest. Dr. Marden's father had served with Henry in Marash in the earliest days of his mission work. Henry remembered when Jesse Marden had been born in Aintab in 1872. Now that little boy had grown and was serving in the Marsovan mission, building a recognized hospital for the community. Even under Dr. Marden's care, however, Henry's night sweats continued. Often he would wake from visions of crushing machinery with his nightshirt totally drenched. Nurses came to rub him with alcohol, but Henry remained very weak. After two weeks at Marsovan, he was little improved. The Partridges and Mary thought Henry should go to Switzerland for the winter to rest. Henry didn't favor that suggestion. After some resistance, he decided to follow Dr. Marden's opinion, "that in view of my years, and present infirmity, it is better to give up further active work in the Station at Sivas, and withdraw without delay to prepare for their return to America."[33] Though he was still weak, it was a severe blow to Henry to think of giving up his beloved work at Sivas. Mary, who had returned to Sivas, began packing for their final return to the States.

On October 3, 1913, Henry and Mary left Constantinople and their beloved Turkey for the last time. The trip home was relatively uneventful, though Henry suffered from stiffness and lameness in his joints even worse than when at Marsovan. His restless, sleepless nights were gone, however, and the return of good sleep seemed to presage a return to health. On October 27, the Perrys arrived at New York and went to stay with Emma Hubbard at White Plains, a suburb of New York City. Being again with Emma was like being home. Henry was allowed to rest, was given regular massages for his sore muscles, and received regular visits from Alvan. Recovery was slow. Crescent Hubbard was now a lawyer in New York, and on weekends he often came out to visit along with Alvan. Years later Henry noted in his diary that

> My physical trouble by which I was forced to leave the mission was neuritis, an inflammation of the nerve or nerves which connect with the muscles of the left of the shoulder backbone. The place of it has been the same from the time of the first attack; and until the present time when I am tired the ache of it commences there.[34]

Henry was under no medication; the doctors advised a program of rest to allow healing to take place. Though the Lord did not grant him immediate healing, Henry was content with the slower way. He spent much time in Bible study, and by the end of November was able to begin writing a lecture on the Moslems' relation to the Holy Lands since the time of the crusades. He recognized that world events made many people at the time interested in Turkey, since it held the Promised Land and many other Bible areas, was losing much of its territory, and was a place of great need and suffering because of the war and cholera. Though now in the United States, Henry's thoughts continued to be in the land of his missionary service.

Henry and Mary continued to stay with Emma Hubbard in White Plains until spring. Everyone thought a winter in Ashfield would be too cold for Henry in his enfeebled condition. Besides, Henry's invalid sister Sarah Ann occupied the first floor of the Ashfield home, and the second floor had been rented out. Henry continued to slowly recover. By May he was eager to attend the International Mission Union annual meeting at Clifton Springs, New York. It was here Henry and Mary had met twenty-five years ago. One hundred and thirty-five missionaries from fifteen different countries, representing sixteen missionary organizations, attended the conference. Henry was able to attend two out of three of the daily sessions, and especially welcomed participating in the session devoted to work among the Moslems. For the rest of his life, Henry maintained an extensive correspondence with many of the missionaries he met at the conference. Clifton Springs also had a Christian sanatorium that the American Board gave the Perrys certificates to attend. For two and a half weeks the Christian fellowship and treatments there refreshed both Henry and Mary.

Henry's sister Sarah Ann died June 1914. Henry and Mary, whose health was now much improved, were able to move into their Ashfield home. Jean came from Colorado to help them settle in. It was good to be back once again among the western hills of Massachusetts.

---

[1] Howard S. Bliss. "Sunshine in Turkey," *The National Geographic Magazine*, Janaury 1909, 66-76.

[2] In his *Diary*, April 2, 1910, Henry wrote, "Political matters hopeful for the new government, but the people say the Government is as bad as it was before but I do not believe it. There are many who wish to find fault."
[3] *Helping Hand Series*, vol. 11, no.3, June 1909, 6.
[4] "The Roll Call In Armenia," *Evangelical Christendom*, Jan.-Feb. 1910, 93. One such pastor martyred was Rev. Nazareth Heghinian. A graduate of Central Aintab College and Marash Theological Seminary, Rev. Heghinian had spent three years in Edinburgh, Scotland completing his seminary education. When he returned, he was imprisoned by the Turkish government as a spy and condemned to hard labor for five years. Two years later, when the Young Turks came to power, Rev. Heghinian was released. He returned to Azdere Church in Marash, where he had pastored before going to Scotland. Here he at last was reunited with his wife and two daughters. The reunion was short lived, however. Rev. Heghinian was among those pastors martyred on the way to the Adana Armenian Evangelical Church Conference. His family left Turkey and moved to New Jersey. Mrs. Heghenian had a great desire to return to Turkey and preach the Gospel to the Turks, but she died at the age of 36 before fulfilling her wish. Karl Vartan Avakian. "The Armenian Evangelical Church 1846-1946: A Historical Overview," www.cacc-sf.org/c-aehistory.htm.2.
[5] Lillian K. Etmekjian commented on the American press's muted protest: "The reaction of the American press to the Adana massacres and their aftermath could not have been lost on the Young Turk leaders. Despite initial indignation over atrocities, the press did not insist on justice or challenge the obvious lies. Even the killings of the two American missionaries and destruction of American property were swept under the rug. "Turkey for the Turks" and "Death to the Giavours" were widespread sentiments among the Turkish populaton. Only an opportunity was needed to finish the job, and World War I provided that opportunity." Lillian K. Etmekjian. "The Reaction of the Boston press to the 1909 Massacres of Adana," *Armenian Review*, Winter, 1987, Vol. 40, No. 4- 160, 61-74. For more on the Adana disturbance, see Rouben Paul Adrian. "Adana Massacre" in *Encyclopedia of Genocide* (ed. Israel W. Clarney). Santa Barbara, CA: ABC-CLIO, 1999; *Survival of a Nation*, 182-188; Robert Melson. "Provocation or Nationalism: A Critical Inquiry into the Armenian Genocide of 1915," The *Armenian Genocide in Perspective* (ed. Richard G. Hovannisian). New Brunswick: Transaction Books, 1986, 69-70.
[6] The best summary of the political and social situation in Turkey and how it affected ABCFM missions is the unpublished manuscript of H.H. Riggs, *ABCFM History, 1910-1942: Sections on the Turkey Missions*, ABC 88. H.H. Riggs was a grandson of Elias Riggs. Born in Turkey, he became a missionary in Harpoot in 1902. He worked diligently with Near East Relief after World War I, when the Eastern Turkey mission was closed.
[7] "Report of the Sivas Station for the Year 1910, and Survey and Outlook for the Centennial Year of the American Board of Missions", 8, ABC 16.9.3, Vol. 39.

[8] "Sivas Station for the Year 1910," 9.
[9] Rev. E.C. Partridge. "Industries and Self-Help in Education," *Helping Hand Series*, Vol. 10, No. 1, March 1908, 3-29; Ernest Partridge. *Self-Help in Education: Sivas, Turkey in Asia*, pamphlet published by the ABCFM, c. 1911. After describing the industrial work in the Sivas schools, Mr. Partridge concluded, "In calling the attention of friends to this phase of our educational work in Sivas, we desire to express to all who have aided this industrial work our heart gratitude. In the absence in America, of our associate, Rev. H.T. Perry, it may be said that but for his faith and persistence this industrial work would not have continued to the present."
[10] "Sivas Station for the Year 1910," 13.
[11] "Sivas Station for the Year 1910," 16-17.
[12] "Sivas Station for the Year 1910", 7.
[13] Henry T. Perry to Rev. J.L. Barton, June 21, 1911, ABC. 16.9.3, Vol. 43. Grandma Elizabeth Shearer Jones died August 6, 1912, at East Aurora, New York. She would have been 90 on December 10.
[14] Henry T. Perry to Rev. J.L. Barton, Nov. 17, 1911, ABC 16.9.3, Vol. 43, No. 449.
[15] "The Challenge of Opportunity: Sessions of Big Body of Miolitant Christians Nearing Close – All Lands Heard From." *The Milwaukee Journal*, Thursday, October 12, 1911.
[16] "The Union League Club," www.wgba-business.com/pages/symposium-programs/unionleagueclub.html.
[17] *Diary*, March 9, 1912.
[18] C.I. Scofield was a lawyer and Congregationalist minister whose Reference Bible, first published by Oxford University Press in 1909, became enormously popular in the early twentieth century. The Scofield Reference Bible helped establish the dispensational, pre-millennial interpretation of Scripture as the most prominent one among American evangelicals. "Scofield," and "Scofield Reference Bible," *Dictionary of Christianity in America*, 1057-1058.
[19] "Rev. H.T. Perry of Sivas" (exclusively for the private Information of Rev. E.E. Strong, D.D.). February 10, 1911. ABC Ind. Bio. Coll. 47.13. It is not known who wrote this memorandum or for what occasion. Since Williams College originally planned to give Henry a D.D. in 1911, but he could not leave Sivas at that time, it is possible it was part of the preparatory documentation for that honor.
[20] "Rev. Henry Thomas Perry, B.A., M.A. Williams '62, Founder and Ranking Executive of the Sivas Normal School, Turkey in Asia," document in possession of Gordon B. Severance.
[21] After graduating from college, Henry's daughter began using the name "Jean" instead of her given name of "Jennie." Since in that day "Jennie" was a name often given to a mule or a donkey, she did not like that name. She chose to be called "Jean." Authors' conversation with Carlton and June Severance, April 2001.

[22] Etchmiatzen, in the Caucasus Mountains, was the center of the Armenian Church. The old cathedral there was built around 1100.
[23] Henry T. Perry to Dr. James Barton, ABC 16.9.3, vol. 44, no. 22, October 29, 1912, 3.
[24] "The Martyn Memorial at Tocat," *The Missionary Herald*, January 1913, 31-33.
[25] Charles Henry Holbrook's interest in missions was a product of the Student Volunteer Movement (SVM) organized by John Mott. In the 1890s and early 1900s, thousands of students signed the pledge: "It is my purpose, if God permit, to become a foreign missionary." The SVM's goal was "the evangelization of the world in this generation."
[26] "Sivas Station Report", 1912, ABC 16.9.3, Vol. 39, no. 118, 21.
[27] Vahan H. Tootikian. "Armenian Congregationalists flee from genocide and find a home in the U.S.," *Hidden Histories in the United Church of Christ*, at http://www.ucc.org/aboutus/histories/chap4.htm, 12/14/2000.
[28] *Diary*, April 2, 1913.
[29] "Moslems and Gregorians Receive the Message," *The Missionary Herald*, October 1913, 459-462.
[30] *Diary*, July 11, 1913.
[31] *Diary*, August 2, 1913.
[32] Ernest Partridge to Dr. James Barton, ABC 16.9.3, vol. 44, no. 279, February 5, 1914; "Face to Face," *The Missionary Herald*, October 1913, 447.
[33] *Diary,* September 4, 1913.
[34] *Diary*, notes from 1920's made after entry of November 30, 1913.

13
TO LIVE IS CHRIST, TO DIE IS GAIN
(1915-1930)

"...with all boldness, as always, so now also Christ will be magnified in my body, whether by life or by death. For to me, to live is Christ, and to die is gain."
Philippians 1:20-21

As Henry and Mary quietly settled into their Ashfield home, war erupted in Europe. The murder of Austrian Archduke Francis Ferdinand at Sarajevo on June 28, 1914 exploded the Balkan powder keg, embroiling Europe in a war that swiftly swept around the globe, drawing thirty-two nations into its vortex. The Ottoman Empire itself would become one of the casualties of the war. When war broke out with Germany and Austria on one side and England, France and Russia on the other, Turkey declared neutrality. Secretly, however, the Young Turks' leaders Enver and Talaat made an alliance with Germany and began mobilizing for war. By joining Germany against the Allies, including Russia, Turkey hoped it might regain some of its territories lost in earlier wars. When the warships *Breslau* and *Goeben,* part of the Turkish navy but under German command, attacked Russian ships and ports in the Black Sea, Russia declared war on Turkey, and England and France soon followed.

The outbreak of the war immediately affected all missionary operations in Turkey. The first effect was financial. All banks in Turkey were closed. The Boston and New York banks could no longer pay funds to Constantinople. Regular expenses of the American Board in Turkey required $18,000 a month from America. Henry Morgenthau, the American Ambassador, advanced $17,000 of his personal funds to partially meet the crisis and arranged for the Standard Oil Company's agency in Constantinople to receive other funds for the Board.

On September 8, 1914, Turkey unilaterally abolished the capitulations under which Europe and the United States had operated for centuries. The special legal protection the American missionaries had once enjoyed under the capitulations was now removed. Further, the German ambassador had warned the American ambassador that if hostilities broke out between Germany and the United States, every American institution in Turkey would be seized at once. The missionaries faced a choice. If they all withdrew, the Christian population would be without help and at the mercy of a hostile government. If the missionaries remained in Turkey, and Germany and the United States broke off diplomatic relations, their own lives would be endangered. The missionaries chose to remain.[1]

Since 1913, a triumvirate of the Young Turk leaders Enver, Talaat, and Djemal had controlled the empire. Even before the war these men had dreamed of a Turkish state with a homogeneous Turkish population, free from the frictions caused by ethnic minorities. By January 1915, they concluded the time had come to implement their plan.

The Turkish government had a history of killing unwanted portions of its population. In 1822, it was the Greeks on the island of Chios; in 1850, the Nestorians; in 1860, the Marionites and Syrians; in 1867, the Greeks in Crete; in 1876, the Bulgarians; in 1877, 1894-1896, and 1909, the Armenians. No other country in history had so used mass killings as a method of government administration. Under cover of war, the government decided to remove the Armenians from Turkey and to orchestrate the brutal butchering of its Armenian population of more than a million and a half souls.[2] The atrocities would become the twentieth century's first genocide, and one of the most systematic massacres of all time.[3] One *Vali* saw the liquidation of the Armenians as a quick solution to irreconcilable disunity between the nation's Islamic majority and an infidel Christian minority:

> We are determined to get rid, once and for all, of this cancer in our country. It has been our greatest political danger, only we never realized it as much as we do now. It is true that many innocent are suffering with the guilty but we have no time to make any distinction. We know it means an economic loss to us, but it is nothing compared with the danger we are hereby escaping.[4]

The elimination of the Armenians would also provide homes and lands for the thousands of Moslem refugees who had fled from Europe during the Balkan wars and who were even then fleeing to central Turkey from the advancing Russian armies in the east. The logic was simple. If the Armenians were forced out of their homes, the Moslem-Turks could move in.

The Armenians of Van furnished the excuse used to justify the "deportations" throughout all Turkey. Jedvet, the *Vali*, plundered outlying villages, and the Armenians, in self-defense, fortified themselves in the city. Before Turkish forces could retaliate, the advancing Russians, led by Russian-Armenian volunteers, captured the city. The Armenians in Van thus escaped extermination, but news of the Van uprising gave the leaders of the Committee of Union and Progress (C.U.P., also known as *Ittihad*) in Constantinople the pretext they needed. On April 24, the C.U.P. seized several hundred Armenian writers, poets, lawyers, doctors, priests, and political leaders, imprisoned them, and systematically executed them in succeeding months. April 24 has ever since been the day of national mourning for Armenians throughout the world. Through the rest of 1915, adhering to a precise schedule, the Turkish government issued orders to deport all Armenians from the six eastern *vilayet*s of Sivas, Trebizond, Harpoot, Erzerum, Bitlis, and Diarbekir. Later deportations were from the width and breadth of the Empire.[5]

In the early spring of 1915, the Turkish government had placed a strict censorship on all correspondence, and the missionaries were specifically warned not to report on local conditions. Even American Ambassador Morgenthau did not know what was happening in the interior of Turkey, but rumors of atrocities began to spread. Missionaries cryptically referred to literature to tell their stories and wrote that the story of *Evangeline* "seems to be applicable to the circumstances under which we live here."[6] Others wrote that conditions of 1895 prevailed. Only in July did the real stories of massacre and deportation begin to be known. Once known, it was a story that shocked the world.[7]

The Armenian Soldiers in Turkey were disarmed in the fall of 1914. Early in 1915, they were regrouped into work brigades of 500 to 1000 men, assigned to work on road maintenance or to function as pack animals carrying supplies.[8] Then, at convenient times, they were taken to remote locations and shot.[9] Older men were arrested, briefly imprisoned in local jails, tied neck-to-neck with ropes and marched into the country-side in small bands, slaughtered and buried--sometimes first digging their own graves. The Minister of Internal Affairs, Talaat Pasha, claimed that an imminent nationwide Armenian rebellion threatened the rear of the Turkish army and ordered the deportation of the Armenians away from the war zones. In truth, Armenians far from battle areas everywhere in Turkey, except those in Constantinople and Smyrna, were forced to move. All remaining men, women, children, and old people, often without notice, were rounded up and told they were being "deported." In reality they were being forced into death caravans.[10] The Turks adopted the system of marching the Armenians without food, water, or adequate clothing through the cold in the mountains or the heat of the desert until they died or were killed along the way.[11]

A Special Organization (*Teshkilati Mahsuse*), consisting of 12, 000 men recruited from prisons, was created by the *Ittihad* Central Committee to direct the marches throughout the country. These ex-convicts were under the command of a "Committee of Three" consisting of Dr. Mehmed Nazim, Dr. Behaeddin Shakir, and Midhat Shükrü.[12] To ensure efficient massacre, the Special Organization had command over two other agencies: The Butcher Battalions (*Kassab Taburu*) and the Terrorist Irregulars (*Chete*), mostly made up of extremist Muslims who were incited to apply the *Sharia* command to treat Christian infidels like cattle.[13] These groups served both as escorts and murderers.[14]

The *Ittihad* Central Committee in Constantinople issued directives to the *valis, kaimakans*, and all Special Organizations charged with carrying out the genocide. Deportation orders were posted or announced publicly in each city and town, usually with a day or two advance notice. Generally, families were allowed to bring only what property they could carry. Sometimes gendarmes ordered immediate evacuation with only one or two hours notice. The Turkish government confiscated all personal and real property left behind and quickly sold it or otherwise disposed of it. "Deportation" was a disguised form of confiscation and execution.[15]

Once the Armenians were forced out onto the roads, paramilitary troops and local police herded them from village to village in a nationwide series of death marches. In some of the caravans, younger men were permitted to start out with the women and children. Generally, however, the adult and teenage males were swiftly separated from the others and killed under the direction of Young Turk officials, the gendarmeries, Butcher Battalions, the Terrorist Irregulars, nomadic groups of Kurds and Circassians, or in some cases the townspeople in the villages through which the Armenians were marched.[16] Tashin Bey, Governor-General of

Erzerum, testified that the leaders of the Committee on Union and Progress systematically ordered the deportation and atrocities:

> During the deportations, they issued orders to the Governors of the provinces to commit crimes. When some members of the government in the provinces refused to serve their criminal purposes, they had them dismissed immediately, particularly Jemal Bey, Mutesarif of Yozgat, Reshid Pasha, Governor-General of Kastamuni; and Mazhar Bey, Governor-General of Ankara.... The Committee took in hand the direction of the government of ...[Erzerum] by means of similar measures and threats and imposed its will on all of them.[17]

The British Archives contain a decoded telegram of orders from the Special Organization President, Behaeddin Shakir, dated 10 July 1915:

> To His Excellency Sabit Bey, Governor-General of El-Aziz: Are the Armenians deported from there wiped out? Inform me of their massacre and extermination. Are the dangerous persons massacred or only expelled from the town and deported? Let me know clearly, my brother.

On the same day, the Third Army Commander, Mahmoud Kiamit sent this decoded telegram from the Sublime Porte to the *Vali*s and local leaders throughout Turkey:

> We have learned that some Moslems are protecting Armenians in areas where the people are being exiled to the interior. Being against the decision of the Government, the Moslem home owners who dare provide protection for them in their homes must be hanged in front of their homes and it will be necessary to burn the houses. Communicate this order in a suitable manner to whomever it may concern, taking care that not a single Armenian be saved from exile.[18]

Many of the marches were directed south toward the Syrian desert. But numerous other caravans were pointed at random in any direction that would ensure extermination of the marchers. The government authorities in control were well aware that women, children, and old people, walking without food or water would die by the wayside long before traveling even a hundred miles. All along the way the Armenians were robbed, beaten and, in the case of the younger women, raped. Many victims took their own lives and those of their children by leaping into rivers or off cliffs. Sometimes geography made the grisly task of genocide easier. Thus in Trebizond and along the Black Sea coast, hundreds of children were taken out in the ocean and disposed of by drowning.[19] From every region in the Ottoman Empire an entire race of Armenian people melted away into nameless graves, or their tortured corpses were left by the side of the road to be disposed of by vultures, dogs, and wild beasts.[20]

It was not possible to keep secret a nationwide crime of such vast proportions. As the reports of atrocities began to reach Constantinople, American ambassador Henry Morgenthau lost no time in testifying that what the Young Turks intended was the total annihilation of all Armenians in the empire:

> The Central Government now announced its intention of gathering the two million or more Armenians living in the several sections of the empire and transporting them to this desolate [desert] and inhospitable region. Had they undertaken such a deportation in good faith it would have represented the height of cruelty and injustice. As a matter of fact, the Turks never had the slightest idea of reestablishing the Armenians in this new country. They knew that the great majority would never reach their destination and that those who did would either die of thirst and starvation, or be murdered by the wild Mohammedan desert tribes. The real purpose of the deportations was robbery and destruction; it really represented a new method of massacre. When the Turkish authorities gave the orders for these deportations, they were merely giving the death warrant to a whole race; they understood this well, and, in their conversations with me, they made no particular attempt to conceal the fact...."[21]

He went on to say that from April to October 1915, the death marches could be seen

> ... winding in and out of every valley and climbing up the sides of nearly every mountain--moving on and on [the marching deportees] scarcely knew whither, except that every road led to death. ...In a few days, what had been a procession of normal human beings became a stumbling horde of dust-covered skeletons, ravenously looking for scraps of food, eating any offal that came their way, crazed by the hideous sights that filled every hour of their existence, sick with all the diseases that accompany such hardships and privations, but still prodded on and on by the whips and clubs and bayonets of their executioners. And thus, as the exiles moved, they left behind them another caravan-- that of dead and unburied bodies, of old men and women dying in the last stages of typhus, dysentery, and cholera, of little children lying on their backs and setting up their last piteous wails for food and water.

> There were women who held up their babies to strangers, begging them to take them and save them from their tormentors.[22]
>
> .... I am confident that the whole history of the human race contains no such horrible episode as this. The great massacres and persecutions of the past seem almost insignificant when compared to the sufferings of the Armenian race in 1915.[23]

On May 24, 1915, a month after the deportations began, the Allied powers declared:

> In view of these new crimes of Turkey against humanity and civilization, the Allied governments announce publicly to the Sublime Porte that they will hold personally responsible [for] these crimes all members of the Ottoman Government and those of their agents who are implicated in such massacres.

Three months later, on August 15, even Germany, Turkey's ally in the war, protested directly to the Sublime Porte in Constantinople, that the deportations "had been accompanied in many places by acts of violence such as massacres and plunders which could not be justified... " These brutalities were referred to as "acts of horror" for which Germany " decline[s] all responsibility of all consequences which can result."[24]

In the entire *vilayet* of Sivas the total Armenian population was around 165,000. As elsewhere, the "deportation" was in well-orchestrated stages, beginning in Marsovan, northwest of Sivas. On April 29, 1915, the community leaders had all been arrested. In May, all the young men not mobilized as part of the army were formed into workgangs. On June 26, all remaining able-bodied men were arrested and murdered with axes in the outlying country. The "Deportation" orders were first announced at Marsovan on July 22. The deportees, now mostly women and children, were organized into convoys of 500 to 1000 and marched off toward Malatia to the southeast, where they were murdered on the banks of the Euphrates river. The residents at Amasia, to the south of Marsovan, were charged with rebellion and summarily executed there or in the surrounding mountain gorges. At Tocat, midway between Sivas and Samsoun, the men were first killed in the city, then the women and children were deported. southwest of Sivas, at Guemerek, on the Halys River, the Armenians were herded along the road to Sivas and executed en route. In Zileh the men were tied together in small groups, marched into the mountains and killed. The women who refused to convert to Islam were disemboweled with bayonets.[25] Children were auctioned off to

Turkish buyers. At Sivas Armenian leaders were arrested between April and June. Then in July, the rest of the men were arrested and murdered. The women were assembled into groups of 1000 to 3000 and sent to Malatia, one of the major staging areas for the death marches 100 miles to the southeast of Sivas. There they joined the convoys from Samsoun and the northern villages of the *vilayet*. Evacuation and liquidation of the Armenians in the grain-growing areas was deferred until after the harvest.[26]

Missionary Mary Graffam, Perry's former associate at Sivas and sister of Winona Partridge, became a heroine during this trying time.[27] Her strength and wisdom to stand up for the oppressed even caused the Turkish officials to hold her in esteem. Late in the fall of 1914, a colonel in the German army who also was a Christian passed through Sivas. He warned the missionaries that the Armenians were going to be deported. War was raging around Erzerum, but there were no doctors or hospitals there. The Pasha urged the missionaries to help. Dr. Clark, Miss Zenger, and Miss Graffam volunteered to go. Mary Graffam hoped to build up the good will of the Turks for later use in Sivas! She helped open the Red Crescent Hospital in Erzerum before returning to Sivas in time for her school's commencement. Passing through Erzinjan on the way home, she heard the first rumor of deportations. Armenian men were being imprisoned and homes were searched. Armenians were forced to turn in all of their weapons. If they didn't have any, they had to buy them from the Turks and then turn them in to the government.

Mary learned that at Kara Hissar Armenian prisoners were taken to the nearby fields and shot. The people then tried to defend themselves, but were finally forced to surrender. The massacres in the streets were horrible. Women from nearby villages began coming to Sivas with stories about the Armenian men being taken from their homes and killed outside of the villages. Soon, without any warning, officials began imprisoning the Armenian men in Sivas. At first they imprisoned the merchants and the richest men in town. Mary, who spoke Turkish fluently, went to the *Vali* about the imprisonments, and he told her the men would be released in a few days. One of the teachers at the school was then called for, and Mary thought about trying to hide him. The Turks, however, told her that if the men were not given up, their houses would be burned and their families hanged in front. Once the men were all imprisoned, the *Vali* said the deportations would begin, with the men taking one road and the women and children another. Mary went to the *Vali* and asked if a few couldn't be left behind. He told her they were all going safely, and asked, "Why should they be separated from their families?" Mary said if they were all going to be safely cared for, she was going with them. This surprised the *Vali*, but he said nothing.

Before they left, many of the Armenians brought their jewels and other possessions to the missionaries for safe keeping. Some were so excited and crazed that they had to be shaken to tell their names. Ernest and Winona Partridge decided to leave Sivas, go to America, and tell the story of what was happening. Mary Graffam, Winona's sister, was determined to stay.

The Sivas deportations began July 5th, and 3000 people were led out of the city.[28] The government gave forty-five oxcarts and eighty horses for the Protestant townspeople to use, but none for the missionary teachers and children. The missionaries bought ten oxcarts, two horse arabas, and five or six donkeys. Since the Sivas people had not participated in any revolutionary activity, as a special favor, the *Vali* allowed any men not imprisoned to leave with their families. The students and teachers from the American schools stayed together as a group during the journey. This included Mary Graffam, all the Armenian teachers from the college, about twenty boys from the college, and about twenty girls from the girls' school.

The first day and night out were exhausting, but uneventful. Once further out from Sivas, however, the gendarmes went ahead to the villages, encouraged the villagers to rob and steal from the refugees, then stood back and watched the pillaging. Rugs, donkeys, and other valuables quickly disappeared.

The third day out, the people were told the men would soon be separated from them. Mary asked one of the teachers from the college, "How does it feel when death is approaching you?" He told her, "It is nothing, but when I think of this whole nation, I cannot stand it or see the right and justice in it all." Mary asked him how old he was. When he said he was thirty-three, Mary told him 1900 years ago a man was sacrificed at that age, yet his death and resurrection became a cornerstone of faith for people all over the world. To encourage him, she added, "Who knows but this tragedy of today will mean the beginning of a new future?"[29] Mary Graffam and many other American missionaries dreamed that on the ashes of this hideous injustice there would arise a new nation of Armenia.

That night, the Turkish officials came and took the men, over two hundred of them, into the village of Hassan Chalebe and placed them in a stable for the night. In the morning, at least six were suffocated. The rest were taken into a valley and killed with every sort of implement and in every sort of way.[30] At noontime the gendarmes came back to the women and children and set them on the march again. Anyone who lagged behind was killed. Mary saw hundreds die in one day. Some died of thirst; others went crazy. Mary went between different groups of people trying to help. She too was in rags by this point, and the nervous strain was tremendous. Kurds carried off women and young girls for their own use; others attacked the Armenians with stones as they trudged along. The roadsides were strewn with the dead and the dying. The young people from the American schools acted like heroes as they tried to help others along the way.

After crossing the bridge of the Tokma Su, the officials made Mary leave the Sivas deportees and go to Malatia. She was told the deportees, who by now included Armenians from Samsoun, Amasia, Tocat, and other places, would go to Ourfa to build villages and cities. The next day, Mary stood at the window of the German orphanage in Malatia and saw her girls and people file by. She remained in Malatia for three weeks and thought the place a counterpart of the worst description of hell:

> The sky was black with birds and there were hosts of dogs, feeding on the bodies. You could tell where a massacre had taken place by the migration of birds and dogs. I went to the market one day, but the sights I saw were so terrible that I never went again. At first they killed them in the streets, but there was so much blood that they strangled them with ropes and the bodies were taken out during the night. The place they were taken was directly opposite our house, and every afternoon you could see two or three thousand Armenians file past us.[31]

Through the terrible suffering and torment, Mary was amazed at the optimism and hopefulness of many Armenians when everything seemed so hopeless. One day on the march, when people were dying all around, a man came up to her and said, "When we come to our last place, you will open a school, won't you? We don't want our children to be without schools." A German observer later reported that "out of 18,000 persons who were deported from Harpoot and Sivas, only 350 arrived at Aleppo."[32]

On her return journey to Sivas, Mary was given a cart, an old woman as a servant, and an Armenian driver. The sights along the way were grim:

> There are regular places along the road where the official records of those who were killed were kept. Accurate records were kept and when the Kurds killed the Armenians, they kept a record, and then went to these officially designated places to collect their money which the government had promised.[33]

When she reached Sivas, Mary was told the Armenians in the Swiss orphanage were to be deported the next day. The Swiss had supported the orphanage for over twenty years. Mary immediately went to the *Vali*, and he told her that if she remained, the orphans could remain too. Mary also was able to visit the many Armenian men still imprisoned in Sivas. Daily, hundreds were taken out of the prison and killed. One of the Armenian teachers from the missionary schools was promised a position in a Turkish school if he would turn to Islam. It was a struggle for him, but he finally told his captors he represented a principle he had taught all of his life and now he must die for it. When Mary went to the prison the next morning, it was empty. On the way home she met the Greek carriage driver returning with only the men's clothing in the wagon. There had been about 1000 men in the Sivas prison. By this time, Mary was a skeleton and looked like a refugee herself. Yet, through all she had endured and seen, she could testify that "God has come very near to many during these days."[34]

In the *vilayet* of Aleppo all Armenians were evicted from Hadjin, Shar, Albustan, Goksoun, Tasholouk, Zeitoun, and the villages of Alabash, Geben, Shivilgi, Furnus, Fundadjak, Hassan-Beyli, Harni, Lappashli, and others. From 1867 to 1875, Henry Perry had often ridden circuit, preaching in these villages to some of the poor souls who were now being marched off to their death. They were herded along the line of the Baghdad Railway, and at Tel-Armen, near Mosul, 5,000 of them were massacred. They had been told they were going to colonize desert land fifteen miles from the railway. However, since the men had already been separated out and killed, and the women and children were dying from thirst, hunger, and hardship, the Turks would tell them any convenient lie, simply to keep hope alive up to the very moment of execution and death.[35] For a whole month, corpses were observed floating down the Euphrates River nearly every day, often in batches of from two to six bodies bound together. The male corpses were in many cases hideously mutilated. Dogs and vultures devoured the corpses stranded on the bank. A Baghdad Railway employee reported that the prisons at Biredjik were filled regularly every day and emptied every night--into the Euphrates. Aleppo and Ourfa were the assembling-places for the convoys of exiles into the desert. From April to July 1915, more than 50,000 passed through Aleppo. A woman bore twins in the vicinity of Aintab, but was ordered to move on the next day. Soon she had to leave the children under a bush and a little later, she collapsed and died.[36]

Sadly, history was being repeated at Gürün, where Perry had planted a church, discipled the minister, and where Mary had worked tirelessly among the survivors of the 1895 massacre. Now, in 1915, a German national, Dr. Graetner, reported that a convoy of 2800 Armenians was organized and marched in a southeasterly direction toward Malatia. When they arrived at Airan-Pounar (12 hours to the northeast of Marash) the gendarmes joined army officers in robbing everyone in the convoy. 200 were killed. Dr. Graetner

> met the convoy, then consisting of about 2,500 persons at Karaboyuk.... Those who were exhausted were left lying on the road; corpses can be seen lying on both sides of it. .... All the males over the age of 15 were taken away...and were probably killed. These Armenians were intentionally transported over circuitous routes and over dangerous paths. By the direct road to Marash they would have arrived in four days, and they have been on the road for over a month. They had to travel without animals, without beds, without food; once in every day they received a thin slice of bread.

When the Armenian convoy left Gürün, the *Kaimakam* demanded they pay him a bribe to ensure their safety on the road. Then at Albustan, the *Kaimakam* demanded another bribe to ensure their safety en route to Aintab. The soldiers and civilians in the villages through which the convoy passed violated women in the convoy regularly at night.   Dr. Graetner reported that

> ... Mohammedan travelers, who came along this way, report that the roads are impassable owing to the many corpses lying unburied on both sides of the road, the smell of which is poisoning the air. ...At Ras-el-Ain a convoy of 200 girls and women arrived in a state of complete nudity; their shoes, their chemises, everything ...had been taken away from them, and they were made to walk for four days under the hot sun--the temperature was 122 degrees in the shade–in their condition of nakedness, jeered at and derided by the soldiers of their escort....

Whenever the wretched exiles appealed to the humanity of the officials, the reply was: "We have strict orders from the Government to treat you in this way."

On Sunday, the 12th of August 1915, I had to go to the station of the Damascus railway at Aleppo, and was able to see the loading into cattle trucks of about 1,000 women and children. With us in Germany the cattle are allowed more space than those wretched people; 90 per cent of them had death written on their faces. There were people among them who literally had no time allowed them for dying. On the previous evening a convoy had been taken away, and on the next morning the dead bodies of two children, about half grown up, were found, who had died during the loading of the trucks and had been left lying on the platform...

On the road between Marash and Aintab the Mohammedan population of a village wanted to distribute water and bread among a convoy of 100 families, but the soldiers escorting the convoy prevented this. Four-fifths of the deported persons are women and children....

A Turkish police commissary said to me: "We have lost all count of the numbers of women and girls who were taken away by the Arabs and Kurds, either by force or with the connivance of the Government. This time we have carried out our operations against the Armenians according to our heart's desire; not one of ten has been left among the living."[37]

Aleppo was a main railroad junction. From this city, whatever Armenian deportees had survived the death marches could be sent in cattle cars on the Berlin-to-Baghdad railroad east 200 miles as far as Ras-el-Ain. On September 3, 1915, Talaat telegraphed the Aleppo officials specific coded instructions:

> We recommend that the operation which we have ordered you to undertake shall first be carried out on the men of the said people [Armenians] and that you subject the women and children to them also. Appoint reliable officials on this.

Apparently the city officials in Aleppo couldn't quite believe that the *Ittihadist* plan for genocide was intended even to encompass orphans. On September 21, Talaat sent them a coded message to clarify this point:

> There is no need for an orphanage. It is not time to give way to sentiment and feed the orphans, prolonging their lives. Send them away to the desert and confirm back to us.[38]

As soon as news of the massacres reached America, there was an outpouring of aid and support. In October 1915, the American Committee for Armenian and Syrian Relief was organized. A forerunner of Near East Relief, it quickly raised $2.5 million. President Wilson proclaimed October 21-22, 1916, as days of special contributions for the suffering Armenians and Syrians.

Back in Ashfield, Henry learned first hand about the massacres and deportations from Ernest and Winona Partridge, who had returned to the United States. From his correspondence with other missionaries, including Mrs. Fowle, whose daughter Mary was in Sivas with Mary Graffam, he learned details of the suffering afflicting the people there. At one point in his diary he lists names of Armenians deported from Sivas to the south. How many survived? These were not numbers in a statistic of deaths, but people with names, hopes, and dreams whose faces and lives Henry clearly remembered. Garabed Topbashian, whose house he and Mary had rented their last year in Sivas, was deported with his family. Reverend Kevork Demirjian of Marsovan, a beloved friend, was killed. Henry hoped that all remained "faithful until the end, whatever it was; and that the end was a victorious one." In prayer Henry went over the Sivas field:

> Recalling the friends and prayed along the course of the present unknown: were they alive or dead, happy or depressed. <u>May the Lord care for whoever of them may now remain living; spare such as He will, and raise them for his service. May He overturn to use for good our efforts in the past!</u>[39]

Henry's days were now filled with a restful activity. He and Mary were repairing and remodeling the Ashfield house. They added the latest modern improvements, an indoor toilet and electricity, as well as enlarged a sunny sitting room on the second floor. Alvan, now on the staff of Governor Whitman of New York, regularly came to visit and helped financially with the refurbishing of the Ashfield home.[40]

Jean was teaching in the Wolcott school in Denver and corresponding with Maude Severance, whose mother had so lovingly taken in 12-year old Jean when Henry and Mary were carrying on the relief work in Sivas. Jean and Maude had kept in touch over the years. Maude shared one of Jean's letters with her brother Carlton, a newspaper reporter in Salt Lake City. Carlton and Jean began a correspondence that led to their marriage on June 5, 1915. Jean Hannah Perry was thirty, and Carlton Severance was forty-seven. It was too expensive to go to

Ashfield for the wedding, so the couple had a quiet wedding with friends in Denver before moving to Salt Lake City. Aunt Emilie came out for the wedding, but Alvan had to be in California with Governor Whitman. Finances prevented Henry from attending, but he carefully packed a number of pieces of family furniture, some of which had belonged to colonial ancestors, to help his precious Jean set up housekeeping.

In June 1916, Alvan, as a captain in the New York National Guard, was called for six months service in the First Field Artillery and sent to Texas as part of General John Pershing's punitive expedition against the Mexican leader Pancho Villa. In March, Villa had attacked Columbus, New Mexico, killing eighteen people and burning the town. Pershing's expedition unsuccessfully attempted to capture Villa. The First Field Artillery was stationed at McAllen, where Alvan briefly experienced life on the Texas border – with its heat, humidity, drought, tarantulas, mesquite, cactus, and occasional hurricane.[41] While Alvan was on the border with Pershing, his fiancé, Molly, went to stay with Jean and Carlton in Salt Lake City. The following spring, Molly and Alvan were married and made their home in New York City.

Henry was quite content with retirement in Ashfield. He became most interested in Biblical prophecy and how events unfolding in Turkey and the Near East might relate to the coming Kingdom of Christ. He had recovered his health enough to regularly work in his garden, which supplied Mary and him with enough beans, cucumbers, potatoes, cabbage, carrots, turnips, and other vegetables for their own use. Mary carefully put up the vegetables in "lightning jars" for use in the cold winter months. Henry also taught a Sunday school class and maintained a wide correspondence with missionaries all over the world, as well as with his dear Jean, Alvan, and relations closer to home. He was content in his retirement:

> Shall I lament the absence of direct, strenuous work? No! Unless by the Lord's will some work and the ability to do it, shall be shown me. Meantime I have a tack which is imperative and agreeable. I will study the Word of God, to get the fullest light possible on the preparation which the Lord is making for His return to this earth, to receive His own, and with them inaugurate the Coming Kingdom, which He will establish in this world.[42]

Both Henry and Mary remained active in Ashfield's Congregational church. In October 1915, Mary went to Mt. Herman to attend the countywide church conference as a delegate from Ashfield. Henry went to Williamstown to attend the 150th Anniversary of the First Congregational Church and enjoyed the Sunday with Williams College's President Carter. Later in the month Henry attended the 106th meeting of the American Board at New Haven. Ernest Partridge was there, as was Emma Hubbard from White Plains, along with many of the missionaries from Turkey. The addresses by Dr. Barton and Reverend MacNaughton from Bardezag recounted the death and suffering of the Armenians in Turkey. One evening, Booker T. Washington attended, and the Jubilee Singers performed, which Henry thoroughly enjoyed.

Though Henry was no longer on the mission field, his heart and passion remained with the missionary work. When Jean and Carlton moved to Hawaii as part of Carlton's new job with Wayne Oil Tank and Pump Company, Henry carefully traced their travels on a map. He recalled the history of the early Hawaiian missions and the missionary work the family of Samuel Armstrong, his Williams' classmate, had done there. He was full of questions for Carlton about the Hawaiian missionary work and church.

In spite of the disastrous news from Turkey, Henry was optimistic about the effect of missions there. As he wrote to Professor Snowden of Williston Seminary:

> There is no vocation in all the world, which can compare in the fullness of joy and blessing with that to which the Heavenly King and Master calls those who wish to work with Him. Among the vast multitudes of the Near East we have not been left hidden. The Word of our testimony must and does permeate the devious and mystic ways of Moslem life and thought. We are builders which the Master uses, to herald the coming King in Asia.[43]

Throughout his life, Henry's assurance that Christ had won the victory at Calvary gave him a confidence that adverse circumstances could not destroy.

Finances as well as insufficient strength prevented Henry and Mary from visiting Jean and Carlton in Hawaii or Arizona and California, where they later settled. Yet, Henry's frequent letters are full of fatherly advice and interest in the details of his daughter's life. When Jean's first son, Perry Williston, lived only a day, Henry wrote a letter full of comfort, recalling the death of little Harriet on the day she was born, " I found that the only comfort which really availed, was that of the Dear LORD JESUS, which He gave us by the HOLY SPIRIT the

COMFORTER; and this up-bearing hope, may you experience in its full blessing!"[44] When Carlton, Jr. was born two years later, Henry wrote his son-in-law:

> In memory of my own experience I can well imagine how you begin to feel the tender and urgent responsibility, to care for this little, dependent, personal, human life, committed in a peculiar way to you. I believe also that you appreciate the fact, that this child is given to you in trust to nourish and train for the Great Giver. His kingdom is broad enough to include all of us and our children. Of its amazing possibilities we know only a very little, but it is all on the side of blessed fruition. What a privilege therefore to have a new born soul put in our charge![45]

Henry rejoiced too with Jean and Carlton at the birth of their second son, Gordon Barker, in April 1921.

During this time, Turkey was in a state of chaos. In May 1916, the Turks commandeered American Board buildings in Sivas. Because of the Russian invasion, Sivas was considered in a military zone. Mary Graffam, Nina Rice, and Mary Fowle remained at Sivas and found other buildings in which to help the refugees and orphans flooding the town. Dr. and Mrs. Clark worked in the hospital. Since Sivas was at a crossroads, refugees from many other places found their way to the town. Though Miss Graffam was awarded the Red Crescent in 1917, for her hospital work, the government continued to harass her, twice searching her house and once trying her for treason. In the spring, 1916, all the missionaries were ordered out of Marsovan and Sivas; only Misses Graffam and Fowle were allowed to remain. Disease was rampant. November 24, 1916, Mary Fowle died of typhus, leaving Mary Graffam very much alone in her relief work. During the war, the relief work could only be carried on secretively and with much subterfuge.

The Bolshevik Revolution of 1917 led Russia to make peace with the Ottoman Empire March 3, 1918. According to the Treaty of Brest-Litovsk, the territory Turkey had lost to Russia in earlier wars was returned. On October 30, 1918, Turkey signed an armistice with the Allies at Mudros. Though this aimed to end World War I, war continued in Turkey for four more years. Allied navies and armies occupied the straits and Istanbul, but they could not agree on what governing arrangements were best for Turkey. Was the country to be divided among British, French, and Italian protectorates? Would the United

States, with its large missionary interest in Turkey, accept a League of Nations' mandate over the country? Would the Armenians be allowed a separate nation in their homeland? With Turkey's defeat in the war, leaders of the C.U.P. fled to Germany.

A British high commission in Constantinople began conducting hearings and receiving testimony of witnesses relating to a variety of issues—Turkey's noncompliance with armistice terms, insolence to British officers during the occupation, abuse of prisoners of war, looting, and outrages against the Armenians. Its proceedings were awkward and ineffective because the Allies had not established a uniform policy of dealing with postwar issues, as they later did at the Nuremberg trials after World War II. Wanting to show the world that Turkey could conduct its own criminal trials, the sultan authorized a separate tribunal, the Extraordinary Courts Martial, which was charged with trying the leaders of the *Ittihad ve Terakki* party. The trials were held from April 27 to June 28, 1919. Talaat, Enver, Djemal, Nazim, Shakir, and other government leaders were tried in absentia. The court found that "criminal acts that took place at various times and in various places, during the deportations of the Armenians, were not isolated, local incidents but were premeditated and realized by the oral instructions and secret orders of the Special Center."[46] All seven defendants in July 1919 were sentenced to death, but none of the defendants was in custody, and Germany refused extradition. When it appeared that the sentences would not be carried out, a small, secret group of Armenian activists within the *Dashnatsutium* party decided upon assassination. Talaat was found in Germany and killed by Soghomon Tehlirian in Berlin in 1921. Tehlirian had seen his family killed on the forced marches. He himself had been struck on the head with an ax and left for dead, but later escaped. During Tehlirian's trial in Berlin for Talaat's murder, Reverend Johannes Lepsius testified in detail concerning the genocide of 1915 that Talaat, Enver, and the other Young Turks had planned and executed. After deliberating one hour, Tehlirian was acquitted. Subsequently, the secret Armenian activists killed Behaeddin Shakir, Djemal, and others convicted by the tribunal while in hiding.[47]

In many respects, Abdul Hamid's massacres of 1894-96 had served as a pilot program for the later genocide in 1915-1917. Both slaughters were directed by the central Ottoman government in Istanbul; both encouraged local religious groups (Moslem Kurds, Circassians, Turks) to join in the persecution and plunder of the Armenian Christians; both depended upon carefully supervised local governments and military-gendarme forces to administer executions or death marches. In both the government conducted aggressive propaganda campaigns to quiet victims' fears before a pending massacre, and to placate other nations. Both exploited religious hatreds with atrocities against priests, ministers, the burning of churches, and forced conversions to Islam.[48] One important difference between the two, however, was this: Abdul Hamid used massacre to keep Armenians from challenging his status quo, a corrupt and oppressive feudal Islamic theocracy in which they would never be allowed citizenship. The Young Turks used genocide to liquidate all Armenians as part of a drastic change of the status quo into a secular (but nevertheless, Islamic) Turkish state with no Christian minorities.[49]

After the war, England's David Lloyd George, France's Aristide Brand and George Clemenceau, Italy's Orlando, and other Allied leaders were unanimous in affirming the horror of the genocide, promising punishment for the perpetrators, and declaring that the surviving Armenians should have self-rule. One of United States President Woodrow Wilson's Fourteen Points stated, "other nationalities which are now under Turkish rule should be assured an undoubted security of life and an unmolested opportunity of autonomous development."[50] One of the first decisions at the Paris Peace Conference in January 1919, declared, "because of the historical misgovernment by the Turks of subject peoples and the terrible massacres of Armenians and others in recent years, the Allied and Associated Powers are agreed that Armenia, Syria, Mesopotamia, Palestine and Arabia must be completely severed from the Turkish Empire."[51]

The view that Armenia should be a separate nation persisted through 1920. The Treaty of Sèvre in that year between the Allies and the sultan's representatives appeared to solve the Armenian question. In it Turkey recognized a new Armenian republic, and even renounced claims to large sections of the eastern provinces of Trebizond, Van, Bitlis, and Erzerum. It nullified all religious conversions of Armenian Christians to Islam which were under duress during the war, and set up a commission which, in effect, would oversee Armenian families seeking the return of children kidnapped during the death marches. Turkey agreed to help locate and return wives and children that had been forced into Muslim households, to cooperate in the prosecution of war crimes, and to repeal the laws which had confiscated Armenian properties after their owners had been deported.[52]

One of the ironic tragedies of history is that after the war had been "won," the Allied armies all wanted to go home and not assume the responsibility of protecting an inchoate state. None of the Allies was willing to provide the funds to repatriate Armenian refugees or to loan the necessary resources to establish a new nation. The United States, led by what Wilson had referred to as "a small group of willful men" in the Senate, had retreated into isolation, even to the point of declining to accept the League of Nations' mandate for the United States to oversee a new Armenian country, as England accepted in Palestine.

Confusion, indecision, and anarchy reigned until Mustafa Kemal organized the nationalistic forces to establish a free and independent government for Turkey. On September 4, 1919, a national congress met at Sivas. Led by Mustafa Kemal, the congress reasserted its determination to resist both the Allies and the sultan and organize a new Turkey. The nationalists strongly resisted any formation of a Greek or Armenian nation from Turkish lands. In January 1920, a new Parliament assembled in Istanbul, with the nationalists controlling the majority. However, as fighting continued in many places in Anatolia, atrocities, murder, and pillaging of the Turks against the Greek and Armenian Christians continued. Many of the remaining Armenians fled the country.

By 1918, the flourishing missionary work among the Armenians in Turkey was gone. Only 36 missionaries remained of the 151 who had been there in 1914. Of the 1204 native workers in 1914, possibly 200 were still alive. All of the schools were closed, and the hospitals had been taken over by the government. The Eastern Turkey mission stations of Van, Bitlis, Erzerum, Diabekir, and Harpoot were abandoned, never to be reopened. There were no Armenians left in those regions. The missionaries who remained elsewhere in Turkey did all they could to care for the 10,000 orphans left behind.[53]

In spite of the anarchy, the ABCFM did not think it time to withdraw from Turkey and called for prayer, relief funds, and 175 more workers for Turkey. With the encouragement of American Ambassador Morgenthau, the Near East Relief agency had been organized, with the ABCFM's Dr. James Barton at its head. In existence for fourteen years, Near East Relief raised $85 million for the suffering Armenians.[54] Food, clothing, medical assistance, and orphanages were brought to the beleaguered people of Anatolia. Even when the United States was at war with Turkey, the agency continued its relief work.

There was no precedent for a country continuing such humanitarian work within an enemy nation, and the missionaries were indispensable to the work of relief:

Without this large force of experienced men and women available for immediate service, without expense to the general funds, familiar with the language and local conditions, the relief work during the war would have been impossible, even though ample funds had been generously contributed, for the country was closed under stress of war to new workers.[55]

After the Armistice, there was a freedom and openness as help came to the beleaguered country. Seventeen Americans engaged in relief work in Sivas, including Mary Hubbard, the youngest Hubbard daughter who had left Sivas when she was eight.[56] Ernest and Winona Partridge also returned, as did Nina Rice. Nina felt called to "help the Armenians all my life, if only there are any left to be helped."[57] The Sivas relief workers cared for over 1100 orphans, operated a hospital, two farms, and industrial shops to train the orphans in a skillful work.

In 1919 Woodrow Wilson sent Major General James G. Harbord to investigate conditions among the Armenians in Turkey. Dr. Barton had encouraged the plan of a United States mandate in Turkey under the League of Nations and an independent Armenia as an U.S. protectorate.[58] Major General Harbord's report on Turkey and Armenia favored such a United States protectorate. Harbord and his team of military, economic, and political experts spent several days in Sivas. In his report, Harbord extensively praised Mary Graffam's achievements, writing:

Her experiences have never been duplicated in the history of womankind. Her

> knowledge of Turkish, Armenian, and German enabled her to play a part in the stirring events of the past six years which has probably never been equaled by any other woman in the chronicles of missionary effort.[59]

Mary Graffam hoped to establish an agricultural school on farmland leased from the German government. The waterpower on the farm operated several gristmills for the community. However, Mary died in 1921. The schools, closed at the time of the deportations, were never reopened. The Near East Relief used the buildings for the orphans.[60]

In 1923, Turkey became a republic and, under the Treaty of Lausanne, vast populations were exchanged between Turkey and Greece.[61] The Treaty of Lausanne repudiated the Treaty of Sèvres, which had recognized a newly established republic of Armenia. Nowhere in the Lausanne Treaty was Armenia even mentioned. The international community had abandoned the Armenian question, and Turkey's attempted extermination of an entire race of Armenians within its boundaries went unpunished.

In spite of the precision and the efficiency of the Turkish death marches, there were Armenian survivors. In the massacres, some who were not fatally wounded escaped after their executioners had gone. The missionaries saved some families from death. Government officials spared a few highly skilled Armenians; Kurdish or Turkish friends hid others. Constantinople's Armenians were not deported. On the eastern frontier, many thousands of Armenians fled to Russia. In some cases, Armenian resistance, such as that at Musa-Dagh, led to successful escape. Finally, there were hundreds of Armenian orphans taken in by the missionaries and eventually sent abroad to safety.[62]

With the exchange of populations brought about by the Treaty of Lausanne, Nina Rice was able to re-establish many of the Armenian orphans from Sivas in Athens, Greece. When Nina had first cared for many of these little ones, they did not remember their parents, did not know their own names, and did not know how to sleep in beds. With the removal of Nina Rice and the Sivas orphans to Greece, sixty-five years of Protestant missionary work in Sivas came to an end.

The conditions of the ABCFM's work changed under Turkey's new government. The government under Mustafa Kemal struggled to throw off foreign influence, and strict restraints were placed on foreign schools. Gone were the days of evangelistic missions to the villages of Turkey, in which Henry Perry had so delighted. No longer could there be open evangelism and Christian teaching in the schools. Nevertheless, the ABCFM presence continued in Turkey. Though unable to openly proclaim the Gospel, by their humanitarian and educational work, as well as by their lives, the remaining missionaries hoped in some way to make Christ known.

The debate over whether or not the ABCFM should try to continue any work in Turkey was on-going. Ernest Partridge wrote an article in the October 1924, *The Missionary Herald*, "Should We Stay or Go?" He began the article with a probable reference to Henry Perry: "A few days ago, in conversation with a missionary associate now retired by age from service in the field, I found him disposed to protest against the attitude of those who believe in the great commission yet remain in the field under restrictions which seem to hamper their freedom of religious work."[63] Undoubtedly for Henry, it was inconceivable to be a missionary and not preach Christ. Some of the missionaries, however, hoped that a continued presence in Turkey, muted though it was, might in the future open the door for them to again clearly present Christ to the Turks.[64]

In June 1922, Henry attended the Williams College graduation and the sixtieth reunion of his graduating class. Alvan drove his father to the reunion and stayed with him to enjoy the activities. Six others from the class of 1862 also attended the event. Father and son enjoyed staying in one of the new college buildings and eating in the dining hall, served by the students. There was plenty of opportunity to visit with old friends and make new acquaintances before returning to Ashfield along the picturesque Mohawk Trail.

Though in his mid-eighties, Henry's strength and health were good. He kept a garden on his own property as well as on two other pieces of land in order to raise enough food for Mary and him. He regularly walked to visit many of the people in Ashfield. During the summer months, the little town became a bustling resort, and Henry made many friends among the visitors and townspeople. He also spent much time in Bible study, prayer, letter-writing, and teaching Bible studies at church. Alvan came up from New York regularly, but Jean was at the other end of the continent. A steady stream of letters kept father and daughter close, however. Henry's letters are full of love, as well as spiritual advice and counsel.

In 1923, Carlton became seriously ill and had to be hospitalized for some time. He never was able to fully regain his strength and could no longer work, forcing Jean to assume much of the family's support by teaching school in Sacramento. Henry was concerned she tried to do too much. He encouraged her not to waste energy in worry, but to find her spiritual strength in the Lord:

> I deeply sympathize with you in the strait through which you are now passing, and must repeat what I have already written in the previous letters, that you are to hold you and your family steady by your faith in God, your prayers being in the name of our most blessed Leader and Guide, - our Lord Jesus, Who is our Intercessor and Guide. Study Your Bible much, and lay hold by faith on the gracious promises. You know that we also are to bear the Cross with Him. No other road avails anything to us. Let us not get restive along this the very best road for us![65]

Henry prayed daily for Jean and encouraged her to pray so that "according to the need of every day, 'so shall thy strength be' (Deut. 33:25)." He was pleased when Jean's letters showed less worry and more restfulness, even in the midst of a busy life teaching and caring for Carlton and her two boys:

> I wonder how you can carry such a load of work as you have in hand. Doubtless your constant trust in the Lord is one more important source of your supply. It seems to me you have learned the great secret of this. Continue to take all your <u>Burdens</u> to the Great Burden-Bearer. He is able to make the most difficult situations to be easy.[66]

Henry thought Jean's aptness for teaching was inherited from her mother, or at least God had gifted them both in that way. He hoped that her very life and influence would show forth the Gospel to her students. In some ways, her method of teaching in the Sacramento schools was similar to the current missionaries in Turkey. Though she could not preach Christ, she must reveal, "Him to your pupils, without reading to them the Bible or openly teaching His Word. Is your life with <u>Him</u> so deep and strong, that the Holy Spirit can use it, in ... your ... classes?"[67]

Jean and her family attended Pioneer Congregational Church, across the street from Sutter's Fort, and Henry hoped the pastor was not a modernist. He had followed closely the modernist controversy that was dividing the Congregationalist and Presbyterian churches of the 1920's, and he was definitely not in the modernist camp. As he wrote Jean:

> Of course I am a strong Conservative in doctrine, firmly holding on to the Virgin Birth of Christ; and that He rose from the dead, and ascended into Heaven from whence He will come again "in power and great glory" to bring with Him all the glorious changes for the Millennium.[68]

The winter of 1927, when Henry was 89, both he and Mary were quite ill. The doctor had little hope for Mary's recovery, and she disposed of her small funds between Henry, her sister in Chicago, and Miss Brandon's Missionary Society. However, Mrs. Billingsly, a trained nurse hired by the American Board to care for the Perrys in their last years, nursed both Mary and Henry to improved health. Mrs. Billingsly took care of the housekeeping and meals as well as the

Perrys' physical care. After their severe illness, Mary required much rest, and Henry began walking with a cane. That spring was the first time he did not put in a garden himself, but hired a man to do the work for him. He no longer went to church, since his hearing was failing and he could not hear the sermon.

His eyes too were failing, forcing him to limit his reading and correspondence. By using two sets of glasses he could see with difficulty. Nevertheless, Henry spent several months rereading and carefully adding notes to his years of missionary diaries. Dr. Barton had asked if he would give these diaries to the ABCFM as a record of his missionary years in Turkey. After adding his explanatory notes, Henry had the diaries rebound before donating them to the American Board. The Board was making arrangements to house its immense and valuable archives at Harvard University. Henry did keep one of the diaries, however, and gave it to Jean. This was the diary for 1884, the year she was born and her dear mother died.[69]

June 13, 1928, Alvan took Henry to an alumni banquet at Williston Academy. At 90, Henry was the oldest alumnus there. He knew none of the other people at the event, but he was happy to lead the group in prayer before the dinner began. Henry's years at Williston had been important preparation for his years at Williams College and his missionary service.

Though Henry's last few years at Ashfield were marked by waning health, there was never a complaint from his lips. His letters were always filled with the joy of the Lord and a peaceful trust in His care and provision. Repeatedly he expressed thankfulness that he was able to devote his life to the cause of Christian missions.

In the spring of 1930, Henry and Mary eagerly looked forward to a visit from Jean and ten year old Gordon. Gordon needed an eye operation, and Alvan and Aunt Emilie helped pay for the trip east and the surgery in New York. After the surgery, they would spend time in Ashfield. At least, those were the plans. However, on March 30, a month before Jean and Gordon arrived, Henry died peacefully at his Ashfield home. He was 92. The day was Sunday, and if Henry had been writing in his diary, he would undoubtedly have written, "A very pleasant day." His battle against the gates of hell was over, and he had gone on to the treasures laid up in Heaven. Though he left behind few earthly riches, he gave a rich inheritance to his dear Mary and his Alvan and Jean. As Henry wrote in his will:

I wish first of all to commend to my children the blessed inheritance of holy living, in loyalty to our Saviour, the Lord Jesus Christ. Our fathers and mothers of the past were noble, Christian, God-fearing men and women, whose faith in The Unseen Lord, was clear and strong. Such was my father, whose legacy of faith was better for his children than all the riches of this world. For this I prize him more and more, as the years go on.
"Faith of our fathers! Holy faith!
We will be true to Thee till death."[70]

For the living, Henry had earlier written this challenge to trust Christ:

Our part now is to range ourselves entirely on His side, to stand with Him by faith for the present need, that the Holy Spirit may prove its power...God's way is perfect. His weapons are mighty, His powers supreme; and His Church in Christ will be "powerful as an army with banners." There is deliverance through the Name of the Lord. Not by might, nor by power, but by My Spirit, saith the Lord of Hosts.[71]

---

[1] James L. Barton. *Story of Near East Relief*. New York: The MacMillan Co., 1930, 4-8; *The American Board Missions in Turkey*, from the Annual Report of 1914. Dr. Barton noted that American interests in the Near East "measured by the money invested in missionary institutions and in American schools, hospitals, and colleges," together with their upkeep and support, "would amount to more than $40 million."

[2] A part of the denial of Armenian genocide by Turkey consists of its understatement of the Armenian population in 1915. There are many population estimates from many sources. Richard G. Hovannisian estimated there were between 15 million and 2 million Armenians in Turkey (Richard G. Hovannisian. *Armenia on the Road to Independence*. Los Angeles, University of California Press, vol.1 1971, 419-29. Michael J. Arlen. *Passage to Ararat*. New York: Farrar, Straus & Giroux, 1975, 243-244 stated:

...in the course of the 1915-1916 massacres and deportations close to one million Armenians--more than half the Armenian population of Turkey--disappeared; which is to say, were killed, outright by police or soldiers, or by roadside massacres, or by forced marches, or by starvation, or by sickness, or by condition in the concentration camps.

While the genocide was still in progress, in September 1915 the German Consuls at Alexandretta, Aleppo and Mosul estimated that "about a million Armenians have perished by the massacres of the last months. Women and children, who either were killed or died from starvation, probably formed one half of this number." Throughout the First World War, Germany and Turkey were allies and her

Consuls had relative freedom of access to information and relative freedom to communicate it. Since these consulates were in Southern Turkey, the estimates probably do not reflect the large numbers of victims killed in the northern *vilayets* which were heavily populated with Armenians. *Germany, Turkey, and Armenia.* London: J.J. Keliher & Co., Ltd. 1917, 102. Other estimates of the genocide's death toll are much higher. G.S. Graber stated that in 1915 "it is estimated that some 2,076,000 Armenians lived in the Ottoman Empire, about 2,054,000 in the Russian Empire, and an additional 390,000 in the other countries of the world. Cf. *Caravans to Oblivion, The Armenian Genocide, 1915.* New York, John Wiley & Sons, Inc. 1996, 58. See also C.J.Walker. *Armenia, The Survival of a Nation.* London: Groom Helm, 1980, 230. For a detailed analysis of the statistics of the genocide, see Sarkis J. Karajian, "An Inquiry into the Statistics of the Turkish Genocide of the Armenians 1915-1918." *The Armenian Review*, vol. 25, 4-100, Winter, 1972.

[3] Dickran Kouymijian, "The Destruction of Armenian Historical Monuments as a Continuation of the Turkish Policy of Genocide," *Crime of Silence,* 173-177. "Genocide" was a term first coined by Polish scholar Raphael Lemkin in 1944, for the crime of destroying a group of people because of its ethnic, national, racial, or religious identity. Though the word was coined to describe Nazi Germany's attempted annihilation of the Jews, the practice of genocide has an ancient history. Often when a group or nation conquered another group, the men and soldiers as well as many of the civilians were killed or placed into slavery. The Assyrians, Babylonians, Attila the Hun and Genghis Khan all used genocide as a political tool in their conquests. In the twentieth century, mass killings were used to achieve political goals not only in the case of Turkey and the Armenians and Nazi Germany and the Jews, but also in Yugoslavia, Cambodia, Rwanda, Uganda, and Guatemala.

[4] *Story of Near East Relief,* 11.

[5] *Crime of Silence,* 215.

[6] *The American Board Missions in Turkey and the Balkans,* from the Annual Report of 1915, 13. Henry Wadsworth Longfellow's *Evangeline* is a poem about the deportation in 1755, of the French Acadians from British Nova Scotia to new homes along the east coast of North America. The poem describes the harshness of a people's unjust separation from their homes and families.

[7] Sources for information on the Armenian genocide of 1915 are seemingly endless. A few of the most notable references are listed in the bibliography. Many of the missionary accounts as well as ambassador and consular reports are found in the National Archives, especially the following: *Records of Department of State Relating to the Internal Affairs of Turkey. 1910-1929.* RG 59. 867.40 Social Matters, Reels 43-45, 47, Microcopy No. M353. The National Archives and Record Service, General Services Administration. Washington, 1961. A statistical analysis of the contents of the "Race Problems" portion of the Internal Affairs of Turkey can be found in Armen Hairapetian, "'Race

Problems' and the Armenian Genocide: The State Department File," *Armenian Review*, Spring 1984, vol. 37, no. 1-145, 41-59.

[8] *Crime of Silence*, 215.

[9] *Caravans to Oblivion*, 62.

[10] *Crime of Silence*, 20. For a detailed eyewitness account of the horror of the death marches by an American missionary who was born in Sivas, Turkey, see Henry H. Riggs. *Days of Tragedy in Armenia: Personal Experiences in Harpoot 1915-1917.* Ann Arbor, Michigan: Gomidias Institute, 1997.

[11] This mechanism for mass liquidation was even more cruel than the later horrors of the Jewish Holocaust. Being more technologically advanced, the Nazis, had a national railway network to transport victims to a central location (such as Auschwitz) and facilities (the gas chambers) to liquidate the deportees, once they arrived at their destination. Lacking such, the Turks forced the Armenians to wander on endless marches in the desert to bring about their demise.

[12] In February 1915, Nazim warned the Secret Committee of the *Ittihadists* that one remaining Armenian represented a danger to the future of Turkey. *Caravans to Oblivion*, 140. For British Archives excerpts quoting the direct organization of the deportations by Committee of Union and Progress leaders, see monograph of Gerard J. Libaridian,"The Ideology of the Young Turk Movement," *Crime of Silence*, 43-44.

[13] G.S.Graber. *Caravans to Oblivion*, 89. These were similar in function to Nazi Germany's parallel organizations that executed holocaust plans: the *Schutzstaffel, Einsatzgruppen,* and *Totenkopfvierbande*. See Appendix B. See also "A Testimony by Viscount James Bryce," (extract from speech in House of Lords of Great Britain, on October 6, 1915), *An Anthology of the Historical Writings of the Armenian Massacres of 1915.* Beirut, Lebanon: Hamaskaine Press, c. *1970,* 11-13.

[14] R. Hrair Dekmejian, "Determinants of Genocide: Armenians and Jews as Case Studies," *The Armenian Genocide In Perspective*, 87-93.

[15] *Crime of Silence*, 216.

[16] Rev. Johannes Lepsius traveled throughout Turkey at the time of the massacres and documented the details of the genocide wherever he went. By tracing reports of German consulates throughout Turkey to the German embassy in Constantinople, he reconstructed the roundup schedule for each *vilayet* as follows:

Date (1915)	Place
June 14-July 15	From Erzerum
June 24	From Shabin-Karahissar
June 25	From Mamuret-ul-Aziz
June 26	From Sivas
June 26	From Trebizond
June 26	From Samsoun
June 27	From Ezroom (again)
July 1	Massacre at Bitlis
July 10	Massacre at Mush
July 15	Massacre at Malatia

July 27	Coastal region, Cilicia & Antioch
July 28	From Aintab, Killis and Adiaman
July 30	From Suedije
August 12-19	From western Anatolia (Ismid, Brusa, Adabasar, etc.)
August 16	From Marash
August 16	From Konya
August 19	Massacre in Urfa

Johannes Lepsius. *Deutschland und Armenien; Sammlung diplomatischer Aktensteuken.* Bremen: Donat & Temmen, 1986, xxv; cited *Caravans to Oblivion*, 120.

[17] *Crime of Silence*, 44.

[18] *Crime of Silence*, 48-49. For twenty-two sworn eyewitness accounts by American missionaries who wrote immediately after the 1915 genocide of what they observed in Adana, Bitlis, Caesaria, Diabekir, Erzerum, Harpoot, and Mardin, see James Barton, ed. *Turkish Atrocities: Statements of American Missionaries on the Destruction of Christian Communities in Ottoman Turkey, 1915-1917.* Ann Arbor, Michigan: Gomidas Institute, 1998.

[19] *Caravans to Oblivion*, 89; *Crime of Silence*, 216.

[20] *Crime of Silence*, 20.

[21] *Ambassador Morgenthau's Story*, 309. The two most prominent leaders of the Young Turks' Committee on Union and Progress (C.U.P.), were Enver Pasha and Talaat Bey, both of whom openly boasted of the massacres as their personal achievement. Talaat Bey, on receiving news of the assassination of Vartkes, a prominent Armenian leader, said: "There is no room in the Empire for both Armenians and Turks. Either they had to go or we." *Germany, Turkey, and Armenia*, 50.

[22] *Ambassador Morgenthau's Story*, 314-317. One such dying woman in Sivas handed her baby, Araxi, to Mary Hubbard, who adopted her. She later wrote her story: Araxi Hubbard Palmer. *Triumph from Tragedy*, privately printed, 1997.

[23] *Ambassador Morgenthau's Story*, 321-322.

[24] U.S. Department of State, *Papers Relating to the Foreign Relations of the United States, 1915 Supplement* (Washington, D.C.: G.P.O., 1928), 981, as quoted in Vigen Guroian, "Collective Responsibility and Official Excuse Making: The Case of the Turkish Genocide of the Armenians," *The Armenian Genocide In Perspective*, 137; note, p.150.

[25] In the massacres of 1894-1896, women who converted to Islam and agreed to marry their captor were spared from death. In the earlier stages of the genocide of 1915, Moslem villagers along the routes of the convoys sometimes followed this custom. However, sometime after June 1915, Talaat's Ministry of the Interior issued a circular banning the conversion to Islam by the Armenians, thus closing one more door of escape from death. *Caravans to Oblivion*, 192.

[26] Yvres Ternon, "Report on the Genocide of the Armenians of the Ottoman Empire, 1915-1916." *Crime of Silence*, 94.

[27] Mary Graffam's moving, courageous story of the deportation from Sivas can be found in "Miss Graffam's Own Story", taken stenographically by Dr. Richard's secretary, June 28, 1919, ABC 16.5, Vol. 6, no. 274; Mary L. Graffam. "On the Road with Exiled Armenians," *The Misionary Herald*, vol. 111, December 1915, 565-568; "A Lone Sentinel of the Near East," *Churchmen Afield Boston Evening Transcript*, September 3, 1921, ABC 16.5, Vol. 5, 128-E; Henry H. Riggs. *Days of Tragedy in Armenia*, 211-212. Doctor Clark corroborated her story. His report can be found as an enclosure in Henry Morgenthau to Secretary of State, June 12, 1916, RG 59, M353 Records of the Department of State Relating to Internal Affairs of Turkey, 1910-1929, roll 45, (867.4016/288).

[28] Dr. Lepsius (see footnote 12) had stated that deportations from Sivas vilayet began June 26. This would have included the outlying villages. Deportations from the town of Sivas began July 5th.

[29] "Miss Graffam's Own Story," 2-3.

[30] This account corresponds with that given earlier of Mrs. Captanian from Samsoun. It shows a uniform method of handling the deportees on the road to Malatia.

[31] "Miss Graffam's Own Story," 3.

[32] *Germany, Turkey, and Armenia*, 71.

[33] "Miss Graffam's Own Story," 3. Accounts of survivors from the Sivas deportations can be found in Donald E. and Lorna Touryan Miller. *Survivors: An Oral History of the Armenian Genocide*. University of California Press, 1993, 94-97, 145-147; Garabed Kapikian. *Yeghernabadoum (Story of Genocide)*. New York: Pan-Sebastia Rehabilitation Union, 1978; John Minnassian. *Many Hills Yet to Climb*. Santa Barbara, California: Jim Cook, Publisher, 1986; Viscount Bryce. *The Treatment of Armenians in the Ottoman Empire*, 1915-16. Sir Joseph Couston & Sons, Ltd., 1916, 301-325. Araxi Hubbard Dutton Palmer. *Triumph from Tragedy*. Privately printed, 1997. A historical novel that includes events from Sivas is Adam Bogdasarian's *Forgotten Fire*. New York: Dorling Kindersley Publishing, Inc., 2000.

[34] "On the Road with Exiled Armenians," 568; Ternon, "Report on the genocide of the Armenians of the Ottoman Empire." *Crime of Silence*, 127.

[35] Only twenty-five years later, Turkey's German allies would use a similar deception, telling their Jewish victims they were going through a "decontamination shower" which in reality was a lethal gas chamber.

[36] *Germany, Turkey, and Armenia*, p.71.

[37] *Germany, Turkey, and Armenia*, 71-73.

[38] British Foreign Office Documents, ref. 371/6501, as quoted in *Caravans to Oblivion*, 107-108. See also, Tessa Hofman, "German Eyewitness Reports of the Genocide of the Armenians, 1915-1916." *Crime of Silence*, 61-87. For more than 80 years the Turkish government has, with ostrich-like abandon,

denied that the Young Turks directed the 1915 Armenian genocide, or that it ever happened. Turkish officials and ambassadors have persisted with this untruthful viewpoint, notwithstanding overwhelming evidence from several thousand credible eyewitnesses, including: hundreds of American, German, Swiss, French, and Danish missionaries who were on the scene; the American Ambassador Morgenthau and his consular officers throughout Turkey (since America was not at war with Turkey until 1916); German consuls throughout Turkey; hundreds of officers in the German army stationed as military advisors to Turkey as their wartime ally; government archives of the United States, Great Britain, France , and Germany (Turkey has restricted the use of its archives). In addition, there are hundreds of writings, books, and videotaped oral testimonies of surviving Armenian victims of the death marches. While this book is a biography of Dr. Perry, since he was an eyewitness of the 1895-1896 massacres which were a prelude to the genocide, and his colleagues experienced the genocide first hand, their experiences and observations are a part of Dr. Perry's story. However, because of the persistent and sometimes vehement Turkish denial of the genocide, the well-documented details of that unparalleled era of brutality are set forth in Appendix B.

[39] *Diary*, December 17, 1915.

[40] Henry's *Diary* for September 5, 1915, noted that the estimate for installing the toilet was $190, and Alvan gave his father $100 to help cover the cost.

[41] Lt. William P. Welsh. "The First Field Artillery," *New York Division National Guard War Record* (ed. Henry Hagaman Burdick). New York: Burdick & King, 1917, 71-76.

[42] *Diary*, November 17, 1915. Apparently Henry did not keep a diary after 1915. If he did, it was not preserved. For the last fifteen years of his life, information about his activities can mostly be gleaned from the remaining family letters and a few letters in the archives of Williston Seminary and Williams College.

[43] Henry T. Perry to Professor B.B. Snowden, August 12. 1916, Williston Seminary Archives.

[44] Henry T. Perry to Carlton Severance, April 10, 1917, letter property of Carlton Severance II.

[45] Henry T. Perry to Carlton Severance, February 22, 1919, letter property of Carlton S. Severance II.

[46]*Takvimi Vekayi, May 12, 1919*, as quoted in *Caravans to Oblivion*, 164.

[47]*Caravans to Oblivion*, 174.

[48]Leo Kuper, "The Turkish Genocide of Armenians," *The Armenian Genocide in Perspective*, 55.

[49] It is startling to note how many of the Turkish techniques of holocaust were used by Nazi Germany in the persecution of the Jews. One can only guess how many of the young German officers who witnessed the Armenocide in 1915 returned to Germany and realigned themselves with Hitler's SS troops to plan and execute the holocaust. Twelve of Hitler's top ranking officials and officers,

including the commandant of the death camp at Auschwitz, were stationed in Turkey during World War I and had an opportunity to witness first hand the twentieth century's first "successful" genocide. See Appendix B.

[50] The United States Department of State, *Papers relating to the Foreign Relations of the United States, 1918,* Supplement 1:*The World War* (2 vol; Washington D.C., 1933), I,16. as quoted in *Crime of Silence,* 23.

[51] United States Department of State. *Papers Relating to the Foreign Relations of the United States, 1919: The Paris Peace Conference (*13 vols., Washington, D.C., III, 765, as quoted in *Crime of Silence,* 24.

[52] *Crime of Silence,* 26-27.

[53] *Annual Report American Board of Commissioners for Foreign Missions,* 1918, 170.

[54] Tootikian, "Armenian Congregationalists flee," 3.

[55] *Story of Near East Relief,* 48.

[56] Mary's story is movingly told by her adopted daughter, one of the Sivas orphans, Araxi Hubbard Dutton Palmer, in *Triumph from Tragedy,* privately printed, 1997.

[57] "Notes About the Field," *The Missionary Herald,* vol. 120, January 1924, 24.

[58] Missionary influence, especially Dr. James Barton's role, on American policy in the Near East during this time is well summarized in Joseph L. Grabill. "Missionary Influence in American Relations with the Near East, 1914-1923," *Moslem World.* Janaury 1968, 43-56.

[59] Ethel Daniels Hubbard. "Mary Louise Graffam," *Lone Sentinels in the Near East.* Boston,
Massachusetts: Woman's Board of Missions, 1920, 61.

[60] The deportations virtually closed all of the American Board schools in Turkey. Those at Erzerum, Hadjin, Mardin, Trebezon and Van never reopened. War orphans were sheltered at the former schools of Adapazari, Bagcecik, Harpoot, and Sivas. Only at Adana, Talas, and Tarsus did these develop into schools again. Some of the schools later reopened in new locations as the population moved. Anatolia College closed at Marsovan, but reopened near Salonika, Greece. Aintab and Marash Colleges went with students to Aleppo, Syria. A controversy raged within the American Board over whether or not to continue the educational program in Turkey. The new Turkish government would not allow the schools to require any Christian instruction or worship. Non-Christians would not be allowed to attend Christian worship. Strict censorship of all textbooks was required, and Turks had to be portrayed in a positive light throughout. Nevertheless, some argued the ABCFM should continue its presence in Turkey. Though missionary activity was not allowed, there was a strong humanitarian need the Board could fill. Though they could not call for conversion to Christ, American Board educators could teach "character-building" in the schools. They began to teach Jesus' way of a life of service without teaching about Him. They taught the ethical ideals of toleration, mutual respect, family life, a sense of vocation, civic duties and responsibilities. In

1927, there were still nine American Board schools operating in Turkey. All were in coastal cities; none were in the interior. The schools became model schools for the new Turkey. *Academies for Anatolia*, 263-297.

[61] The Greeks endure their own death marches during the population "exchanges." Their story is movingly told in Thea Halo's *Not Even My Name*. New York: Picador, 2001.

[62] *Crime of Silence*, 217. See Appendix C for an account of the Armenian Evangelical Church and its survival after the genocide.

[63] Ernest Partridge, "Should we Stay or Go?," *The Missionary Herald*, October 1924, 480.

[64] For example, the American Board's Dr. H.H. Riggs, as late as 1938, expressed the view that continuing with humanitarian work, even without preaching the gospel, would eventually convince the individual Turk that studying the Gospel and knowing Christ would in no way hinder him from being a loyal citizen or from realizing the full benefits of participation in the national life of Turkey. H.H. Riggs. "The Missionary Situation in Turkey," *The International Review of Missions*, vol. 27, 1938, 200.

[65] Henry T. Perry to Jean Severance, December 6, 1923. Letter property of Carlton S. Severance, II

[66] Henry T. Perry to Jean Severance, November 24, 1927. Letter in possession of Carlton S. Severance, II.

[67] Henry T. Perry to Jean Severance, September 29, 1926. Letter in possession of Carlton S. Severance, II.

[68] Henry T. Perry to Jean Severance, April 20, 1925. Letter in possession of Carlton S. Severance, II.

[69] This diary is in the possession of Gordon B. Severance, Jean's youngest son. When Gordon and his wife, Diana, found in this diary a receipt from the American Board for other diaries, they began the quest for the diaries and other information on Henry Perry, which led to this book!

[70] *Last will and testament of Henry T. Perry*, June 24, 1916. In possession of authors.

[71] *Diary*, later notes from 1920's added after July 5, 1886. Henry quotes from II Chron. 20 and Zech 4:6 in this passage.

EPILOGUE:
CAST DOWN
BUT NOT DESTROYED

"We are hard-pressed on every side, yet not crushed; we are perplexed, but not in despair; persecuted, but not forsaken; struck down, but not destroyed – always carrying about in the body the dying of the Lord Jesus, that the life of Jesus also may be manifested in our body."
II Corinthians 4:8-10

The opening day of school in 1924, Jean Perry Severance sat at her desk in Sutter Junior High, named after John Sutter, whose famous fort was only blocks away in Sacramento. Eighty-four years earlier, John Marshall, Sutter's sawmill operator, had discovered in a nearby river the intriguing yellow pebbles that triggered California's gold rush and statehood. But Jean was not thinking about history at that moment; she was reviewing her science lesson for the new class that would start in a few moments. Just before the bell rang, the principal came in, followed by a new student.

"This young man recently came to us from Ellis Island," he said. "He's still working on his English. My thought is to put him in your class until we see what grade would be best suited for him. Let me know what you think."

When they were alone, Jean turned to the boy: "What's your name?" she asked.

"Franklin Ohanesian," he respectfully answered.

"I'm happy to have you in my class," Jean replied. At once she recognized the *"ian"* in Ohanesian as the characteristic ending of an

Armenian name, and became curious: "Where did you come from, Franklin?"

"From Turkey."

"What part of Turkey?" Jean asked.

"I don't think you would know where it is," Franklin quietly replied.

"Yes, but I'm still very much interested to know what part of Turkey you came from," Jean pressed.

"I came from Erzerum," he answered.

Jean gently touched his shoulder, "I was born not far away in Sivas. *Intcbess es?"* (How are you?) she said in Armenian.

Quickly, Franklin's serious expression broke into a warm smile. *"Shad lav, shenorhagal em?"* (I'm fine, thank you, how are you?) he said, astounded to find an American teacher who spoke his native tongue.

In the days that followed, Jean learned that Franklin and his family had been victims of the Turkish genocidal death marches of 1915. She suggested that Franklin write out his experiences, promising that as he wrote, she would help him with his English grammar and spelling. Often, she invited him to her home to share dinner with her husband and her own two boys, then reviewed his ongoing essay in the evening. This was his story:[1]

> I was born January 5, 1908 in Bitlis. A few years later, my mother and father moved to the village of Khorasan, about 50 miles east of the city of Erzerum, Turkey. My first boyhood memories were in that village which was on the Aras River. Most of the people living there were Turks. My father, Satrak Der Ohanesian, had a dry goods store in the village and sold yardage goods and clothing. We lived in a big two-story house built against the side of a hill. It had a flat roof, so if you went up the hill next to the house, you could get on the roof. My brothers, sister, and I used to play on it.
>
> Our home had a big kitchen and two big bedrooms upstairs. My cousin and his mother and grandmother lived in one bedroom, and our family lived in the other. There was a big fireplace in the kitchen for the cooking. Outside, not far from the kitchen was the barn where we kept our horse and donkey. Here we also washed our clothes, and there was a platform where guests could sleep. My brother and father rode the horse, but sometimes, I would ride on the donkey. My older brothers, Haigaz and Yervant, used to help my father in the store. On Sundays we would all go to the Armenian church.
>
> In the winter we had much snow, which would last a long time into the spring. In the summer of 1915, there were fourteen in our family living in our house: my grandmother; my father, Satrak Oahanesian; my mother, Lucien; my brothers, Haigaz, Yervant, Saragan, Mushegh, and

my two baby brothers; my sister Saramush; my cousin with his mother and grandmother; and me. When the war started the government came and took our horse. They also took over the room where my cousin and his family lived, and a soldier stayed there.

I was seven years old in the spring of 1915 when some gendarmes came to our home and told my mother and father that we had to leave our home the next day and march to a new home in the south. I later learned that we were part of the Turks' 1915 "deportation."[2] My father quickly took all his yardage goods to the church, hoping that someday he could return to claim them. Then the gendarmes told us to "get going," and we started marching. As we walked along the road the gendarmes walked behind us. When we reached Erzerum we walked right through the eastern gate, on through the city, and out the western gate and camped there for several days to wait for Armenians from other villages to arrive for the march. While we were there, more and more Armenians came to join our group. Then we all started walking together. We took turns riding on the donkey. I had a shoulder bag that my mother made for me in which I carried food and other things.

Some families had ox-carts; some as many as 5 or 6 carts loaded with their household goods.[3] My family left with only the donkey. There were big crowds in our group, but I don't remember how many.[4] As we went along there were soldiers and gendarmes with guns and bayonets that went ahead of us and behind us to keep us moving. If we Armenians lagged behind or walked too slowly, the armed policemen pushed us along. After we had been on the road for several days, we noticed my grandmother couldn't keep up with us, and lagged behind. When we could not see her in our group, my older brothers, Haigaz and Yervant, went back to the end of the group looking for her. They tried to go further back to find her, but the gendarmes would not permit it. We never saw her again. She must have died along the road. As we moved along, we saw many swollen bodies of Armenians that had died along the roadside. We were hungry, thirsty, and many were sick.

After we were on the road several days, we came to a narrow bridge, high above the Euphrates River.[5] Just after we crossed the bridge, some soldiers separated out all of the educated men.[6] They took my father and my oldest brother, Haigaz, and put them in a barn with the other men. Then they made us go on. I never saw them again. We were later told that all the Armenian men were tied together in two's, their heads were cut off, and they were thrown into the Euphrates River.

After we crossed the Euphrates, the Turkish gendarmes and soldiers turned our caravan over to Kurdish tribesmen.[7] As one of the Turkish soldiers was leaving, he caught me up on his horse and began to ride away. I started crying and screaming so loudly that he finally put me down, and I ran to my mother.[8] That night we camped again, and Kurdish people brought things to the group to sell. After a day or two, the road narrowed to a foot trail.[9] There was no water for a whole day. We all were suffering from thirst and in terrible shape. But we tried to keep going. Suddenly, as we came around a sharp turn in the path, the Kurds took my cousin who was around 18 years old, and my brother Yervant, who was 14, and the rest of the men in the group in a second separation. We never saw my cousin again, but the next day, Yervant suddenly joined our group dressed as a woman. Yervant and I both spoke good Kurdish and that may have helped him to escape from the Kurds.

The Kurdish soldiers wouldn't let us stop very often. Every little while more people dropped by the wayside. Each one of us had to take care of himself. My poor mother had to hang on to my two little brothers who were only 2 and 4 years old. Finally the struggle and lack of water was too much for them, and they died. Yervant buried them. After the Kurds had taken my cousin away, only his mother and grandmother were left. In the days that followed, they were not able to keep up with the group and either died or were killed. We never saw them again. My mother, my sister and three brothers and I were fortunate. We were healthy enough to keep going. When we finally came to a place where there was a lot of water, everyone was so desperate for it, they all just piled in.

After two or three weeks on the road, we finally came to Djerablous, a little railroad town next to the Euphrates River. The group we were with crossed the bridge over the Euphrates to go to Aleppo. But the Turks took us from the group and put my mother and my two brothers to work on the railroad. They had a small room for us to live in and my sister and I stayed there during the day until my mother and three brothers came home from work.[10] They must have worked there for six months. It was only much later that I learned that working in the railroad labor camp probably saved us from starvation in Aleppo where there were thousands of Armenians without food.[11] Finally, they put us on a train and moved us to Aleppo. The war was still going on. I remember Arabs riding camels through Aleppo. The Turks took Yervant in the Army, but he lived through it.

In Aleppo there were several international relief agencies attempting to help the refugees.[12] My older brother Moushef worked for a relief program, and Serigan worked as a porter. Food was very scarce. My mother would sew and sell things, but sometimes she had to beg for food. She wasn't able to make enough money to buy food for us, so she took my sister and me to an orphanage where there were Armenian boys and girls. They told my mother they didn't have any more room, but she just left us there outside the door and we were there all day. In the evening, they took us in. They had no room there so they took us to a hospital. The sick people there were mostly ailing from leprosy and trachoma eye trouble. We slept in the basement with their regular patients. Before long I had trouble opening my eyes and found I had trachoma too. My sister also had it, but not as bad as I. The nurse would wash my eyes with warm water and boric acid.

Each day about three or four kids died in the orphanage. They would put them in a sack and bury them. Soon there was room for me and my sister, so they took us from the hospital and put us in the orphanage with the other boys and girls. There were no grown-ups there.[13] Soup or bread once a day was all we had to eat, and we were always hungry. We were so hungry that another kid and I would climb over the wall and go down to the market and steal food and eat it right there. Sometimes we would get caught, and the owner of the vegetable stall would beat us, but the next day we would go somewhere else. If they caught us sneaking back into the orphanage, they would also whip us. But we didn't care. We were so hungry it was worth the beatings to get something to eat.

Sometimes I would jump the orphanage wall and go visit my mother. I didn't have any shoes and always went around barefoot. One day at the market, I felt something in the dust with my toes. It was a gold coin. I ran to the room where my mother lived and gave it to her. She looked stern and asked if I had stolen it, but was pleased when I told her that I had found it in the dirt. We all were so poor, it was like a fortune to her.

My sister and I stayed in the orphanage for two years until the war ended. Then we were put in a refugee camp. There were Mother, Mushegh, Seragan, my little sister, Saramush and myself. After a few weeks Yervant came and joined us. At last, all six of us were together as a family! Only six were left of the fourteen from our house who had left Kohrasan. We were in the camp for months, and the hardship of the deportations continued to take its toll. A lot of people became sick and died. But with the war over, things slowly began to look better. Some of the young folks in the camp would get married, and there was much joy and singing. There would even be music and dancing.

Eventually, in 1919, we were taken to Constantinople in a ship that was crowded with people. They put hundreds of us Armenians in a big 3-story building called "Pasha's House." It was supervised by Armenians. Each room had three families in it. I remember that across the street, the sultan would come to worship at a mosque. When his carriage came along, the soldiers lined up on both sides of the street. Yervant helped me make a shoebox, and I started going out into the street alone, shining shoes in the street to earn money. Now that I was 11, for the first time I was also able to attend a church school class for boys and girls. I learned to read and write Armenian. The Near East Relief people also sent my sister and me to Dr. Hoover, an American, to treat our trachoma. He put drops in my eyes that made them burn.

My grandfather had emigrated to Fresno, California in the 1890s. Through him and Armenian friends we were able to get visas and become immigrants to America. But they would not let me go until I was cured of trachoma. Mushegh and Seragan left first for America in 1920. Yervant stayed with Mother, sister, and me until my eyes were better and I had permission to leave. Yervant married while we were in Istanbul. Finally, in 1922, we were allowed to go to America. Outside of Gibraltar, the ship started listing, and we were delayed with repairs. During that time, I had an appendicitis attack and had my appendix removed on board the ship. When we arrived at New York in 1922, my eyes were again infected.[14] The immigration people at Ellis Island said that, since my eyes were so bad, and we were all on the same passport, we all had to go back to Turkey. Finally, with the help of a California Congressman, we were able to persuade the authorities to let me stay at Ellis Island until my eyes healed. Meanwhile, Mother, Yervant and my sister, Saramush took a train to California.

Waiting for my eyes to heal on Ellis Island, I rigged up a shoebox and I began shining shoes. There were many people there, including the immigration officers who were willing to give me a penny or two for a shine. It took almost a year for my eyes to heal. I wrote letters in Armenian to my family in California, and they wrote to me. At last, in 1923, they said I could leave, and I took a train to Chicago. A relief worker met me there and helped me transfer to a train bound for Sacramento. How happy I was to see my family again!

Although my grandfather and grandmother were still living on their farm in Fresno, my family decided to live in Sacramento. There was steady employment available for them there, and Mother and my three brothers all went to work in the big Libby, McNeil, & Libby cannery. We decided that since we were living in America, we needed first names that sounded familiar to Americans. Yervant became "Joe," Mushegh was now "George," and Seragan became "Sam." My sister Saramush was now "Blanche."

I was 15 and had learned a little English on Ellis Island, but had no schooling. As soon as I arrived in Sacramento, I started out in the second grade of an elementary school. Three months later they moved me to the 6th grade. After that I went up one grade at a time. When I finish Sutter Junior High in the ninth grade in 1926, I'll be 18 years old.

Jean was moved by Franklin's story, and she thought again of the many suffering Armenians her father had helped during his missionary years in Turkey. She became a close friend of the Ohanesians and many other Armenian families in Sacramento. Hard working and thrifty, the Ohanesians saved enough from working at the cannery to buy a big house on Q street. Mushegh had enough savings left over to buy a market, which he named "Pioneer Grocery." Before school, Franklin rose early in the morning, went to the wholesale market, and bought produce. After school he also worked in the store. Soon, Seragan had saved enough to buy another grocery store on 7th and A streets. Mother Lucin finally was able to stay home and not work in the cannery.

After finishing junior high school, where Jean helped him with his lessons, Franklin entered Sacramento Senior High. He graduated in 1929 at the age of 21. He had completed in six years an education that for most Americans requires twelve. He went on for the next forty years to be a successful life insurance agent for Prudential Insurance Company. In 1944, Franklin married his wife, Elsie. Their two sons rose in the professions – one a lawyer, the other a governmental official. Their daughter became an attorney and later a Judge of the Superior Court of California for the County of Sacramento. At Jean Severance's invitation, the Ohanesians joined the Pioneer Congregational Church. Back in Ashfield, Henry Perry was pleased to hear that Jean had made many Armenian friends in Sacramento.

The Ohanessian family was only one of thousands who survived the 1915 genocide and fled to America. In the 1920s, Mustafa Kemal's armies continued to sweep across southern Turkey, burning Smyrna, and butchering Christian Armenians wherever they were found.[15] Thousands of refugees came streaming into Ellis Island. Brave and industrious, they interwove themselves into the fabric of American society. Turkey's loss became America's gain. The same people who the Ottoman Turks contemptuously had called "cattle," fit only for slaughter, now became farmers, factory workers, craftsmen, merchants, bankers, doctors, lawyers, artists, inventors, writers, film directors, and leaders in every profession. From Ellis Island to the Golden Gate their names became symbols of success, such as Governor George Deukmejian of California and novelist-playwright William Saroyan.

Wherever the Armenians settled in a community, they established an Armenian church. By the turn of the twentieth century, there were numerous Armenian Evangelical and Gregorian churches throughout America. Strong in faith, the Armenian body of believers--the Church--had marched through the gates of hell, and true to the promise of its Leader the "gates of hell had not prevailed against it."[16]

This amazing first Christian nation in history, small yet great, "persecuted but not forsaken; cast down, but not destroyed, troubled on every side, yet not in despair," [17] had survived. From the rubble, ashes, and horror of destruction, the Armenians, like the Christ whom they had embraced, emerged the real victors--"Not by might, nor by power, but by His spirit"[18] explained Reverend Edward Tovmassian in a sermon delivered at his United Armenian Congregational Church of Hollywood, California:

> The impact and influence of Christianity on this [Armenian] nation has been nearly total and decisive. Christianity changed the entire course of Armenian history.... Armenia became the first nation to adopt Christianity and stayed a Christian nation and people in spite of sword, fire, and massive massacres. Neither the outright persecutions by ...the fast moving armies of Islamic hordes, ... nor the wholesale massacres of the Ottoman Turks could destroy the will and the determination of this nation to stay a Christian nation and hold on to the Gospel light that came to Armenia through the Apostles.
>
> By becoming a Christian nation we chose the way of the Cross and the Son of God who died on that cross. We relinquished and turned our backs to a pagan religious system which promised us worldly things and material blessings. In turn we accepted a Faith ...demanding sacrifices and hardships only to be compensated by certain spiritual and moral values. ...
>
> Christianity gave us a Christian Culture, something we loved and tried to protect when hordes of infidels, one after the other invaded our country and nearly destroyed everything we built. It took centuries to build but a few months to level everything down. And yet, we built again. We never stopped praying, and singing, and laughing, and creating.
>
> To the Persians, to the Mohammedans, to the Turks and Tartars...we definitely said, "You can kill us with your weapons, you can uproot us, you can destroy our countryside and loot our property, you can defeat us on the battleground, you can even bury millions of us and think that you have done away with the Armenians. But you will never be able to destroy our spirit. You will never be able to separate us from the love of Christ. Someday we will surprise you and beat you and bring about your destruction--not by military strength or political power--but, by ideas, by pen, by books and by doing and creating works of beauty and splendor. You may not like us to stay in your country. You may deport us. We will go anywhere in Almighty God's wide country. We will go to the desert, we will go to the Middle East, to South America and North America, to Australia and Canada, wherever they accept us, and when we go the first thing we will do is to build a small Armenian Church, and by its side a small Armenian school, we will congregate together and will speak our beautiful Armenian language and will sing our age-old chants..."Holy, Holy, Lord God Almighty," ...and

when you ...enjoy your periodic blood baths...and destroy the world with your...missiles, we will come back to you, with the Bible ...and the scars of Christ's wounds in our hands and will show you a better way--the Way of Life in Christ.[19]

If Perry had lived to attend that Armenian church service, he would have been pleased and proud. He might have written in his journal, as he always did on Sunday: "It was a very pleasant day." Then he surely would have added, "The Armenian pastor in our church preached with great freedom. Throughout the sermon he constantly had the King in the background of his mind."

---

[1] This paraphrase of Franklin Der Ohanesian's story is based upon a video recording in the oral history video archives of the Zoryan Institute, Cambridge, Massachusetts, 1987. Other primary sources and documents readily confirm details of Franklin's remembrance of the deportation from Erzerum.

[2] In the *Vilayet* of Erzerum the deportations began at the end of May and during the first days of June. U.S. State Department records state that the Ezeroum deportations were largely between May 15-28. Reports from a particularly trustworthy source state that, by the 19th May, more than 15,000 Armenians had been deported from Erzerum and the neighboring villages, and that, by May 25, 1915, the districts of Erzindjan, Keghi, and Baibourt had also been devastated by forced emigration. On June 9, 1915 Tahsin Bey, the *Vali*, issued an order that the whole civic population of Erzerum must be out of the province. B.H. Khounountz, representative of the "All Russian Urban Union," stated: "There are about 80 and 100 Armenians left in Erzerum...." He reported that in April, 1915, the *hodjas* (religious heads) openly preached massacre, casting the responsibility for the defeat upon the Armenians. ...The *Vali* was rather inclined to spare the Armenians, but the order from Constantinople had tied his hands. Representatives of various relief organizations reported that, out of an Armenian population estimated at 400,000 souls for the *vilayets* of Erzerum and Bitlis, not more than 8,000-10,000 survived--i.e. 98 percent of the Armenians in these *vilayets* were either deported or massacred. *Records of Department of State Relating to Internal Affairs of Turkey, 1910-1929; 867.40 Social Matters*, Reel 43; *Henry Morgenthau to Secretary of State, July 23, 1915; 876.1016/95, M353,* Reel 43; *Treatment of Armenians,* 221-240.

[3] The American Consul-General at Trebizond visited Erzerum on August 12 and was guest of Reverend Robert Stapleton, American missionary at Erzerum. When they visited the *Vali* of Erzerum, he told them that many of the Armenian families that had left the city in June and July had sold their possessions and some families had bought as many as five or more ox-carts (*arabas*) to carry their household goods as they left the city. By July 28, the last Armenian had left Erzerum. *Treatment of Armenians*, 225-229.

[4] About 20,000 Armenians were deported from Erzerum. *Treatment of Armenians*, 222.

[5] The deportation path Franklin described was one of the regular deportation routes used for most of the evacuees from Erzerum. It went east from Khorason through the city of Erzerum, followed along the Euphrates through Erzindjan to Kemakh, and there, turning due south, crossed a bridge over the Euphrates proceeding due south through Malatia, along the western bank of the Euphrates to Djerablous on the Berlin-to-Bagdad railway.

[6] A standard Turkish pattern of the death marches from Erzerum was for soldiers to join the gendarmes west of Erzindjan, separate the wealthy and educated men from the convoy and kill them. Since other Armenian groups might be joining a southbound caravan, there was often a second, or even third separation and execution of the men. *Treatment of Armenians*, 224.

[7] Frequently, the Turkish gendarmes and soldiers would "sell" a caravan to the Kurds on the promise they would kill all the men, and they would then be entitled to all the money, clothes, and other property of the victims. This enabled the Turkish escorts to return to Erzerum for another caravan.

[8] Throughout the death marches of 1915, Turkish soldiers often carried off boys or girls and raised them at home as Moslems. *Treatment of Armenians*, 234.

[9] On June 16, 1915, "About 500 Armenian families left Erzerum, via Baibourt, for Erzindjan; They were allowed time for preparations--a concession granted throughout the deportations from the town itself. At Baibourt there was a halt, and the first party of about 10,000 people was joined by later contingents, bringing the number up to about 15,000. A guard of gendarmes (up to 400) was provided by the *Vali*, and these doubtless took their toll of the Armenians in various ways, licentiously and avariciously.... It is known that about 15,000 reach Erzindjan. Up to this point the roads were good enough to allow transport by bullock cars (*arabas*), but after Erzindjan, instead of being allowed to follow the carriage road *via* Sivas, they were turned aside to the route *via* Kamakh, Egin and Arabkir, where there were only footpaths. The arabas had, therefore, to be left behind, and no less than 3,000 vehicles were brought back to Erzerum by an Armenian in the transport service, whom Stapleton [Rev.Robert Stapleton, an American Missionary in Erzerum] met on his return. ... At Kamakh, 12 hours from Erzindjan, it is reported that the men were separated and killed, their bodies being thrown into the river. Beyond this place letters come from women only, though Stapleton's account leads us to suppose that, from among 30 families of which he has news, 10 men survive. Letters from women to Stapleton [in Erzerum] do not, of course, give details of what occurred; they only indicate what happened by such phrases as: 'My husband and boy died on the road.' The destinations reached by these Armenians, as definitely known to Stapleton in January 1916, were Mosul, on the east; Rakka, on the south; Aleppo and Aintab, on the west. The need in these places has been urgent. German Consuls in Aleppo and Mosul are known to have assisted in distributing relief funds sent by Stapleton, per the Agricultural Bank at

Constantinople, to Mesopotamia--in all about £1000 (Turkish)." *Treatment of Armenians*, 224.

[10] Djerablous was on the Berlin-to-Bagdad railroad, which Germany had been constructing for Turkey, and continued to construct during the war. By 1915, the railway had been completed from Aleppo through Harran (where Abraham's father, Terah, died) and as far as Ras-Ul-Ain. The German engineers constantly complained that their Turkish allies were liquidating their labor supply of Armenians, and special arrangements were made to exempt Armenian railroad workers from the genocide until the railroad construction was completed.

[11] On September 29, 1915, American Consul Jackson reported to American Ambassador Henry Morgenthau that the Turks had brought 32,000 Armenian refugees into Aleppo as of August 31. "In addition, it is estimated that at least 100,000 others have arrived afoot, many having left before Easter, deprived of all their worldly possessions, without money and all sparsely clad and some naked from the treatment by their escorts ...en route. It is extremely rare to find a family intact, ...all having lost members from disease and fatigue, young girls and boys carried off by hostile tribesmen, and about all the men having been separated from the families and suffered fates that had best be left unmentioned, many being done away in atrocious manners before the eyes of their relatives and friends. So severe has been the treatment that careful estimates place the number of survivors at only 15 per cent of those originally deported. On this basis the number of those surviving even this far being less than 150,000 up to September 21, there seems to have been about 1,000,000 lost up to this date. ... The heinous treatment of thoroughly exhausted women and children in the open streets of Aleppo by the armed escorts, who relentlessly beat and kicked their helpless charges along when illness and fatigue prevented further effort, is evidence of what must have happened along the roads of the interior further removed from civilization. The exhausted condition of the victims is further proven by the death of a hundred or more daily of those arriving in this city. Travelers report having seen numberless corpses along the roadside in the adjacent territory, or bodies in all sorts of positions where the victims fell in the last gasps of typhoid fever and other diseases, and of the dogs fighting over the bodies of children. Many are the harrowing tales related by the survivors, but time and space prevent the recital thereof. The movement continues with the arrival of hundreds daily and the problem is what can be done for their relief when they are rapidly pushed on to ...Amman, the railway station furthest South to which Christians have been heretofore permitted to travel. Nearly everything necessary for existence is lacking at most of these places, and at Amman it is reported there is neither food nor drink. ... In order to provide the barest existence for these people a most considerable sum is necessary, say $150,000 a month. This would be at the rate of only a dollar a head, which would hardly furnish bread, to say nothing of clothing, shelter, medical treatment, etc. Each religious community has a relief committee to care for its own, but means at hand are altogether inadequate." Enclosure of Consul

Jackson in Morgenthau to Secretary of State, November 1, 1915 (*Records of Department of State relating to the Internal Affairs of Turkey. 1910-1929*, 876.4016/218) Reel 44.

[12] "Mr. W.W. Peet, Business Agent and Treasurer of the four Turkish Missions of the American Board of Commissioners of Foreign Missions with headquarters in Constantinople, reported to the State Department on March 17, 1916 that there were at least 800,000 refugees in Turkey who needed help. One half [400,000] or more of these are reported by the American Consul at Aleppo to be in the districts of Damascus, Zor and Aleppo." Using these figures, one could estimate that when Franklin's family was in Aleppo, they were part of a group of somewhere in the vicinity of 133,000 Armenian refugees. "The general direction of deportation has been to force the exiles to go by train or on foot to the neighborhood of Aleppo." Viscount Bryce, *Treatment of Armenians*, doc.149, .549 states: "Since the 1st August the German Baghdad Railway has brought nine trains of these unfortunate people to Aleppo, each of fifteen truck-loads and each truck (car) containing 35 to 40 persons. All these in addition to many thousands that came on foot."

[13] American Consul Jackson at Aleppo reported on September 29, 1915 to American Ambassador Morgenthau: "The Protestants have organized an orphanage into which have been gathered the following:

      43 widows, acting as care-takers
      48 orphan boys who have mothers
     132 orphan boys without parents
      46 girls who have mothers
     <u>100</u> girls without parents
     369 Total

Of these 139 are Protestants and 230 are Gregorian Armenians." They came from all parts of Turkey, including Erzerum, Diarbekir, Amasia, Severeg, Marash, Tokat, Gurun, Hadjin, Sivas, Harput, Manjilik, Sassoun, Mardin, Kara Hissar. Enclosure from Consul Jackson of Aleppo in Morgenthau to Secretary of State, November 1, 1915 (876.4016/219) Reel 44.

[14] U.S. immigration records show that Louisa (Lucin), Franklin, and Saramush Ohanesian arrived at Ellis Island on *The Acropolis,* January 24, 1922, along with Yerevant and Vartitair, Yervant's wife. Franklin's older brothers, Mushegh (20 years old) and Seragan (14 years old) arrived there earlier on June 22, 1920 on the *Megali Hellas.* www.ellisisland.org.

[15] Thousands of Greek Christians were killed when Turkish armies under Mustafa Kemal, burned Smyrna in 1922. Cf. Thea Halo. *Not Even My Name.* New York: Picador, 2001.

[16] Matthew 16:18.

[17] 2 Corinthians 4:8-9.

[18] Zechariah 4:6.

[19] www.cacc-sf.org, October 26, 1975.

APPENDIX A: ARMENIAN MASSACRES, FALL 1895[1]

TOWN	DATE	ARMENIANS DEAD*
Trebizond	October 8, 1895	920; 200 in villages
Akhisar	October 15, 1895	31
Erzinjan	October 21, 1895	260; 850 in villages
Bitlis	October 25, 1895	800
Barbiert	October 27, 1895	several hundred men
Ourfa	October 27-28, 1895	several hundred
Erzerum	October 30, 1895	over 350
Diarbekir	November 1-3, 1895	1000
Arabkir	November 1-10, 1895	2800
Malatia	November 4-9, 1895	3000
Harpoot	November 10-11, 1895	500
Sivas	November 12, 1895	1500
Amasia	November 15, 1895	1000
Aintab	November 15, 1895	1000
Marsovan	November 15, 1895	150
Gürün	November 15, 1895	1500 families
Karperi	November 30, 1895	1000
Zeitoon	December 23, 1895 (Armenians put Turkish garrison to flight)	
Ourfa	December 28, 1895	3000 burned in chapel

[1] Compiled from information in Christopher Walker. *Armenia – Survival of a Nation*. London: Croom Helm, 1980, 158.
- Does not count those impoverished who would die later, or those dead in near-by villages.

APPENDIX B:
THE UNRELENTING STRUGGLE AGAINST GENOCIDE

I. IMPORTANCE OF MAINTAINING A TRUTHFUL RECORD OF GENOCIDE

The focus of this biography has been the life and times of Dr. Henry T. Perry, one of hundreds of dedicated American missionaries sent around the world in the nineteenth and twentieth centuries. When Perry and some two hundred of these Christian ambassadors answered the call to the Ottoman Empire, they did not contemplate witnessing the massacre of 300,000 Armenians in 1895, or the unprecedented barbaric genocide of 1915, with over a million and a half Armenian Christian men, women, and children dead. The Armenian victims were the same people to whom the missionaries had brought schools, colleges, seminaries, hospitals, orphanages--and the Bible's gospel message. The missionaries lived through the massacres; helped bury the dead; pled with the Turkish officials to spare the lives of the Armenian orphans; administered food, clothing, and medical relief to the few survivors; and helped them buy passage to America and elsewhere to escape the nightmare of persecution. As long as they were able, ministering to the victims of massacre and genocide was one of the missionaries' major goals in Ottoman Turkey. The brutality of the massacres and genocide could not obliterate the human value of the Armenian lives lost or devastated. Every people has the right to existence; the right to have its cultural, linguistic, and religious identity respected; the right of peaceful possession of its territory; and the right not to be subjected to massacre, torture, persecution, deportation, and expulsion.[1] It is important that the truthful record of genocidal atrocities be preserved.

Genocide must be remembered
to respect its victims and warn future killers

Simple respect for the victims of the massacres demands their deaths be remembered. Most descendants of Anatolia's Armenians do not expect to regain ancient homelands or receive indemnity for property that was confiscated long ago. What they resent, however, is seeing the very soul of an ancient nation being executed. Today, scattered throughout the world, the Armenians refuse to accept Turkey's denial that more than a million and a half of their parents and grandparents suffered horribly in the 1915 genocide. For them, it is extremely painful that the Turkish government, and in some cases nations having beneficial relations with it, refuse to acknowledge the fact that hundreds of thousands of Armenians were taken into the countryside and shot, or that defenseless women and children were forced at bayonet point on brutal and inhuman death marches under cover of World War I. Today's Armenians find the 1915 genocide all the more painful because of Turkey's ongoing effort to rewrite history.[2] The truth about past genocides must not be forgotten; this cover-up and propaganda of denial must be refuted. Potential "ethnic cleansers" must know they will be held accountable, as were Nazi war criminals at the Nuremberg trials. They must know truth will ultimately prevail.

Turkey's on-going denial of the
Armenian genocide must confront the evidence

For more than eighty-five years, every government of the Turkish state has denied the Armenian genocide of 1915 and then offered arguments to justify any actions it did take. More recently, the Turkish government has spent millions of dollars on public relations firms to improve its image in the United States. It has used its ambassadors to apply diplomatic pressure to suppress any mention of the genocide. It has funded university scholars to present Turkey in a more favorable light and used its own scholars in Turkish universities to revise and rewrite history denying the basic truths of the genocide.[3]

For these reasons, the authors deemed it prudent to include in this appendix a more detailed summary of the voluminous reports and eyewitness accounts of the genocide. There are thousands of pages in the diplomatic records of Great Britain, France, Germany, and the United States containing first-hand observations and photographs from ambassadors and consuls who had offices throughout Turkey during the massacres of the 1890s and the holocaust of 1915. In addition, there are eyewitness accounts of approximately 135 American missionaries who were stationed in the eastern *vilayets* where the vast majority of Armenians were residing when the genocide began. There are also accounts by French, Swiss, and Danish missionaries who were in the eastern provinces. There are hundreds of eyewitness reports on the genocide by German missionaries, German schoolteachers, and German officers and soldiers stationed throughout Turkey, Germany's ally in World War I. Perhaps most persuasive of all, there are oral history accounts of survivors of the Armenian genocide. Today, the records that come from these credible sources stand as an overwhelming refutation of Turkey's persistent denial that the Armenian genocide ever happened.

Turkish genocide of Armenians and Nazi-German policy towards the Jews

The very fact of Turkey's persistent denial of responsibility for the 1915-22 genocide directly encouraged Nazi Germany to follow Turkey's trail of "ethnic cleansing." In 1939, when Adolph Hitler was preparing to invade Poland and calling for the mass murder of Poles and Jews, some of his advisors warned that world opinion would never tolerate such actions. Hitler replied: "Who still talks nowadays of the extermination of the Armenians?"[4] It is a matter of record that a number of Hitler's highest ranking military officers, including those in the SS troops, were young German officers stationed in Turkey during World War I Many of them saw first hand how a "successful" genocide could dispose of more than a million and a half Armenian men, women, and children— an entire nation.[5] By establishing the precedent that a nation can commit genocide with impunity, Turkey unwittingly assumed part of the responsibility for the Nazi holocaust and future genocides.

There are remarkable parallels between Turkey's genocide of the Armenians and Nazi Germany's holocaust of the Jews:
1. **The goal of both was the total elimination of a race and nationality of peoples.** In February 1915, Dr. Nazim, at a closed meeting of the C.U.P., stated that, "it is absolutely necessary to eliminate the Armenian people in its entirety, so that there is no further Armenian on this earth and the very concept of Armenia is extinguished."[6] Four years later in 1919, Adolf

Hitler expressed similar sentiments: "The anti-Semitism of reason ... must lead to the systematic combating and elimination of Jewish privileges. Its ultimate goal must implacably be the total removal of the Jews.[7] There were no exceptions to the principle of elimination – young, old, successful, and poor were all included. Like Herod the Great's "Slaughter of the Innocents," babies were killed so they would not grow up to be enemies.

2. **Both Turks and Nazis, as a ruling elite class with absolute power, developed detailed plans, programming, and timing for the mass liquidation of the victims, and an efficient bureaucracy to carry out the plans on schedule.**[8]
3. **Both governmental dictatorships developed a deceptive ideological rationale (German Aryan "super-race" and Turkish Moslem superiority over "inferior Armenian infidels") to justify viewing the victim race as debased, incapable of assimilation as mainstream citizens, and therefore proper subjects for extermination.**
4. **Both Turks and Nazis developed immensely popular political party ideologies (Pan-Turanism and National Socialism) to enlist public support for the entire party program, including genocide.**
5. **Both authoritarian governments developed elaborate propaganda machinery to justify the genocide, to downplay its size, scope, and horror, and to incite public hostility toward the victims.**
6. **A major motive for both nations' genocidal plan was to confiscate the victims' land, homes, personal property, money, gold (including dentistry gold), and bank accounts.** For example, U.S. Ambassador Morgenthau's conversation with Talaat revealed from the outset a preconceived intent on the part of Turkish government officials to kill the Armenians *en masse* so that the government might collect their life insurance:

> One day Talaat made what was perhaps the most astonishing request I had ever heard. The New York Life Insurance Company and the Equitable Life of New York had for years done considerable business among the Armenians..."I wish," Talaat now said, "that you would get the American life insurance companies to send us a complete list of their Armenian policy holders. They are practically all

dead now and have left no heirs to collect the money. It of course all escheats to the State. The Government is the beneficiary now. Will you do so?[9]

7. On the other hand, **both the Young Turks and the Nazis disregarded the economic productivity of their victims. Both the Armenians and Jews had a disproportionately large percentage of people in skilled trades and professions.**
8. **Both the Young Turks and the German Nazis maintained strict party discipline and secrecy during the period when plans for genocide were being developed.**
9. **The Young Turks as well as the Nazis developed extralegal special armed forces (e.g. the Turkish Special Organization and the Nazi SS forces) to execute the genocide with rigor.**
10. **Prior to the genocide, both the Young Turks and Nazis took steps to deceive the victims concerning the intended genocide in order to maintain their vulnerability.**
11. **Both governments dismissed or punished officials who were unsympathetic to genocide and replaced them with agents who had no qualms about torture and execution.**[10]
12. **Both governments enforced laws prohibiting their citizenry from aiding, abetting, or harboring, members of the victim group.**[11]

Henry Morgenthau, American Ambassador to Turkey, discussing the concept of transporting Armenians from Turkey to the Mesopotamia area, wrote:

> It was entirely in accordance with the German conception of statesmanship to seize those people in the lands where they had lived for ages and transport them violently to this hot, dreary desert. I found that Germany had been sowing these ideas for several years; I even found that German savants had been lecturing on this subject in the East.[12]

It became obvious to Ambassador Morgenthau that both German Ambassador Wagenheim and the German Naval attaché Humann favored the policy of eliminating the Armenians. Humann was especially implacable:

> He discussed the Armenian problem with the utmost frankness and brutality. "I have lived in Turkey the larger part of my life," he told me,

"and I know the Armenians. I also know that both the Armenians and Turks cannot live together in this country. One of these races has got to go. And I don't blame the Turks for what they are doing to the Armenians. I think they are entirely justified. The weaker nation must succumb."[13]

There has been much scholarly research on the question: To what extent did the Turkish genocide of Armenians influence the holocaust of Jews a quarter century later? For many years prior to World War I, Germany had close diplomatic, military, and commercial ties with Turkey. German army advisors were invited to assist Turkey in upgrading the Ottoman army. The German emperor William II, ambitious to expand the German Empire, had visited the Ottoman Empire in 1889 and again in 1898, and actively promoted Germany's construction of the Berlin-to-Baghdad railway across the Syrian desert.[14] William II showed a willingness to look the other way during Sultan Abdul Hamid's massacres of Armenians in 1894-96 and persistently refused to join the demands of England, France, and Russia that the sultan initiate reforms to protect the Armenians, as he had promised in the Treaty of Berlin. The number of German diplomatic and military personnel in Turkey increased with the outbreak of the war, and German military officers were part of the military councils that coordinated the Armenian genocide. As witnesses to the genocide, other German soldiers gained first-hand knowledge about conducting genocide under the cover of war. For example, Rudolf Höss served in the German army in Turkey while the genocide was going on; he later became Commandant of Auschwitz extermination camp and Deputy Inspector of Concentration camps at SS Headquarters.[15] A more difficult question is: To what extent did these German officials' first-hand knowledge of genocide find its way into the Nazi blueprints for the Holocaust?[16]

II. PROOF OF TURKEY'S 1915 GENOCIDE OF ARMENIANS

The American investigation and diplomatic records of the genocide

A plethora of witnesses from the governments of Europe and the United States completely refute the Turkish government's persistent attempts at historical revisionism. In 1919, American Major General James G. Harbord was sent by President Woodrow Wilson to Turkey on a fact-finding mission to investigate the genocide. In his report, he stated:

> Massacres and deportations were organized in the spring of 1915 under definite system, the soldiers going from town to town. The official reports of the Turkish Government show 1,100,000 as having been deported. Young men were first summoned to the government building in each village and then marched out and killed. The women, the old men, and children were, after a few days, deported to what Talaat Pasha called "agricultural colonies" from the high, cool, breeze-swept plateau of Armenia to the malarial flats of the Euphrates and the burning sands of Syria and Arabia. Mutilation, violation, torture and death have left their haunting memories in a hundred beautiful Armenian valleys, and the traveler in that region is seldom free from the evidence of this most colossal crime of all the ages.[17]

There is no question that Enver and Talaat of the C.U.P. ordered the deportations. In a conversation with Enver Pasha, when Ambassador Henry Morgenthau suggested that undoubtedly Enver's subordinates had committed far more terrible things on the deportation marches than the Committee of Union and Progress ever intended, Enver quickly corrected him:

> You are greatly mistaken. We have this country absolutely under our control. I have no desire to shift the blame on to our underlings and I am entirely willing to accept the responsibility myself for everything that has taken place. The Cabinet itself has ordered the deportations. I am convinced that we are completely justified in doing this owing to the hostile attitude of the Armenians toward the Ottoman Government, but we are the real rulers of Turkey, and no underling would dare proceed in a matter of this kind without our orders.[18]

Talaat Pasha also admitted the central government's deliberate intent to exterminate all Armenians. When Ambassador Morgenthau asked why, instead of killing <u>all</u> Armenians as traitors, the government did not separate the disloyal from those who had remained innocent, he replied:

> We have been reproached for making no distinction between the innocent Armenians and the guilty, but that was utterly impossible, in view of the fact that those who were innocent today might be guilty tomorrow.

Newspaper accounts and American missionaries' records of the genocide

At the outbreak of World War I in 1914, the United States was neutral; it did not enter the war until 1917. Consequently, most American missionaries remained in Turkey through the war and the genocide. At the beginning of the war, the ABCFM had 551 elementary and high schools, eight colleges, several hospitals, and numerous dispensaries and Protestant churches serving mostly Armenians. Over 200 American missionaries staffed these facilities. They were in regular contact with the American consulates situated in Constantinople and other major cities. These missionaries' witness of the genocide was widely reported in the major American press. As reports of the brutality of the genocide reached America, headlines such as the following appeared in the *New York Times:* "Turks are Evicting Native Christians" (July 12, 1915); "Armenian Horrors Grow--Massacres Greater Than Under Abdul Hamid!" (August 6), "Armenians Are Sent to Perish in Desert" (August 18), with subhead "Turks Accused of Plan to Exterminate Whole Population;" "1,500,000 Armenians Starve" (September 5); "Tales of Armenian Horrors Confirmed" (September 27); "Turkey Bars Red Cross" (October 19); "Million Armenians Killed or in Exile" (December 5).[19]

One of the most riveting eyewitness accounts of the Armenian genocide from the *vilayet* of Sivas is that of Missionary Mary Graffam, who served in the Sivas mission with Dr. Perry for more than a decade. For several days she actually traveled on one of the death marches with the Armenian teachers and students that she knew in Sivas. Miss Graffam's story, found in Chapter 13, is significant because she was highly regarded and honored by the Turks as well as by President Wilson's special fact-finding emissary, Major General Harbord.

In Harpoot, Dr. Atkinson, a missionary for the ABCFM, slipped out of the city one night with the American Consul, riding south on the road toward Lake Guljuk over which the soldiers and gendarmes had driven caravans of Armenians:

> They themselves counted over ten thousand bodies, most of them stripped of clothing and showing that they had been killed by violence, largely with the bayonet. In one place they found where great numbers had been pushed over a precipice and the bodies had piled up at the foot. Others had been drowned in the Lake.

Another ABCFM missionary, Henry H. Riggs, riding from Harpoot to Malatia and then to Sivas, reported that he

> ... saw thousands of skulls and skeletons lying along the road west of Malatia for a distance of some fifteen or twenty miles. While these skeletons were seen all along the way, for months the Government has been attempting to get them out of sight, and has very well succeeded on the road between Harpoot and Malatia, but evidently this spot had not been cleared up.[20]

British documentary records

In 1916, Viscount Bryce, the former British ambassador to the United States, edited documents collected by Arnold Toynbee documenting the 1915 death marches. Printed by the government of Great Britain and titled *The Treatment of Armenians in the Ottoman Empire, 1915-16*, Viscount Bryce wrote in the preface, "an effort to exterminate a whole nation, without distinction of age or sex, whose misfortune it was to be the subjects of a Government devoid of scruples and of pity, and the policy they disclosed was one without precedent even in the blood-stained annals of the East." Writing to Viscount Bryce, Moorfield Storey, former president of the American Bar Association, said:

> Such statements as you print ... come from persons holding positions which give weight to their words, and from other persons with no motive to falsify, and it is impossible that such a body of concurring evidence should have been manufactured...In my opinion, the evidence which you print...establishes beyond any reasonable doubt the deliberate purpose of the Turkish authorities practically to exterminate the Armenians, and their responsibility for the hideous atrocities which have been perpetrated upon that unhappy people.[21]

Stationed throughout Turkey were many foreign diplomats whose chief duty was to report conditions objectively to the home office. Such a report from the Italian consul general in Trebizond described the 1915 death marches and was included in Viscount Bryce's documentary record:

> It was a real extermination and slaughter of the innocents, an unheard-of-thing, a black page stained with the flagrant violation of the most sacred rights of humanity, of Christianity, of nationality... There were about 14,000 Armenians at Trebizond--Gregorians, Cath-

olics, and Protestants. They had never caused disorders or given occasion for collective measures of police. When I left Trebizond, not a hundred of them remained.

From the 24th June, the date of the publication of the infamous ["deportation"] decree, until the 23rd July, the date of my own departure from Trebizond, I no longer slept or ate; I was given over to nerves and nausea, so terrible was the torment of having to look on at the wholesale execution of these defenseless, innocent creatures.

The passing of the gangs of Armenian exiles beneath the windows and before the door of the Consulate; their prayers for help, when neither I nor any other could do anything to answer them; the city in a state of siege, guarded at every point by 15,000 troops in complete war equipment, by thousands of police agents, by bands of volunteers and by the members of the "Committee of Union and Progress," ... the shooting of victims in the city, the ruthless searches through the houses and in the countryside; the hundreds of corpses found every day along the exile road; the young women converted by force to Islam or exiled like the rest; the children torn away from their families or from the Christian schools, and handed over by force to Moslem families, or else placed by hundreds on board ship in nothing but their shirts, and then capsized and drowned in the Black Sea ... these are my last ineffaceable memories of Trebizond ...[22]

Although the death marchers suffered from fatigue, the mountains' freezing cold or the desert's burning sun, even worse was the torture the Armenians received from their Turkish tormentors. These included Moslem peasants, brigands (*chettes*) recruited from prisons to harass the deportees, and Kurds, in addition to the soldiers and gendarmes placed in charge of the convoys. British historian Arnold Toynbee summarized the horror of the death caravans:

It depended on the whim of the moment whether a Kurd cut a woman down or carried her away into the hills. When they were carried away their babies were left on the ground or dashed against the stones. But while the convoy dwindled, the remnant had always to march on. The cruelty of the gendarmes towards the victims grew greater as their physical sufferings grew more intense; the gendarmes seemed impatient to make a hasty end of their task. Women who lagged behind were bayoneted on the road, or pushed over precipices, or over bridges. The passage of rivers, and especially of the Euphrates, was always an occasion of wholesale murder. ... The lust and covetousness of their tormentors had no limit. The last survivors often staggered into Aleppo naked; every shred of their clothing had been torn from them on the way. Witnesses who saw their arrival remarked that there was not one young or pretty face to be seen among them, and there was assuredly none surviving that was truly old. ...[23]

German observations: Dr. Lepsius, missionaries, teachers, military officers, and railway workers

As allies of Turkey, the Germans had great freedom to move about in the Ottoman Empire during the war. Some Germans were so shocked at the brutality of the genocide that they left Turkey and their fatherland as well. Most prominent among the German witnesses was Dr. Johannes Lepsius, a prominent missionary leader. After observing the great slaughter of Armenians, he returned to Germany. Germany had not allowed news of the genocide to be published in its borders, but Dr. Lepsius published and secretly distributed his account of the genocide before the German government was aware of what he was doing.[24]

During the summer of 1915, other credible German missionaries and teachers in Turkey began sending shocking eyewitness reports of the genocide to Berlin. Reacting to these on August 9, Germany issued a formal protest to Turkey, its own wartime ally, concerning "expatriation of the Armenian inhabitants of the Anatolian provinces." The choice of the word *expatriation* (meaning "to drive into exile, to banish") revealed the German government's perception of what Turkey was doing to its Armenian population. Turkey was not just relocating the Armenians away from the war zones, it was *driving the Armenians into exile.* The protest observed that this expatriation "had been accompanied in many places by acts of violence such as massacres and plunders which could not be justified by the aim that the Imperial Government was pursuing." The note also referred to these occurrences as "acts of horror" for which Germany "declines all responsibility of all consequences which can result."[25]

A group of sisters from the German League for Promotion of Christian Charitable Work in the East published their observations of the massacres in the ministry newspaper *Sonnenaufgang*.[26] They reported that in May 1915, in the *vilayets* of Diyarbekir and Mamouret-ul-Aziz, 1,200 of the most prominent Armenians were arrested and "deported" to Mosul in the desert area adjacent to the Tigris River. 674 were embarked on thirteen Tigris barges. The accompanying soldiers stripped the Armenians of all their money and clothes and then threw them in the river.

The gendarmes riding along on the shore saw to it that none survived. The victims' clothes were sold in the market of Diyarbekir.

The German women reported that

> In Besne the whole population, consisting of 1,800 souls, principally women and children, were expatriated; it was alleged that they were to be deported to Ourfa. When they reached the Goksu, a tributary of the Euphrates, they were compelled to take their clothes off, and thereupon they were all massacred and thrown into the river.... One mother, whose eldest daughter was taken away by force, threw herself in despair into the Euphrates with her two remaining children.... The Chairman of the Deportation Commission when I made application in favour of four Armenian children [said]: 'You do not grasp our intentions; we want to destroy the Armenian name. Just as Germany will only let Germans exist, so we Turks will only let Turks.[27]

Another German missionary reported what she observed along the Euphrates, southeast of Aleppo:

> On the 20th of April, 1916, I arrived at Meskene [80 miles due east of Aleppo on the Euphrates River, and 80 miles west of Rakka] and found there 3,500 deported Armenians, and more than 100 orphans. ... In every tent there are sick and dying. Anyone who cannot manage to get a piece of bread by begging, eats grass raw and without salt. Many hundreds of the sick are left without any tent and covering, in the open, under the glowing sun. I saw desperate ones throw themselves in grave-trenches and beg the grave-diggers to bury them. The Government does not give the hungry any bread.... As I was in Meskene, there came a caravan of sick women and children ...in indescribable condition. They cried for water ...[but] no one gave them any water, though they remained a whole day under the hot sun. We had to work the whole night to ameliorate their condition a little....
>
> In Meskene I gathered one hundred children; ...had their hair cut and their rags washed. They received daily some bread and some soup. I found a young widow from Hadjin, who asked me if she might take the children under her care. ... Ten days after my departure they had sent the woman with the one hundred children South. ... In Der-el-Zor I found two of them, the only survivors; they said that all the rest had perished. ... [On the road] I found people dying everywhere exhausted from hunger and thirst. They had remained behind the caravan and must perish painfully. Every few minutes came a stench of corpses. ... In Hama I found 7,000 deported, 3,000 of them hungry and practically naked. ... I saw the people were gathering locusts and eating them raw or

cooked. Others were looking for the roots of grasses. They catch street dogs, and like savages pounce upon dead animals, whose flesh they eat eagerly without cooking. ... In Rakka alone there are 15,000 deported in tents. The camp is situated on both banks of the Euphrates. ... In Sepka there are...6,000 in camps on the banks of the Euphrates. There is great misery here. Some in despair throw themselves into the river. ... In Tibne I found 5,000--everywhere we met caravans of deportees. ... Children and grown-ups search among the garbage heaps for food, and whatever is chewable is eaten. Of every fifty persons who start from Rakka or Sepka on boats, twenty arrive, often even less. [When I was in Der-el-Zor] every day we see caravans going in the direction of Mosul [200 miles of open desert].

Nevertheless, at my departure there were at Der-el-Zor 30,000 Armenians. ...The deported are especially badly treated at the region of Der-el-Zor. The people are driven...forward with whip blows, and cannot even take their most urgent necessities. On my return [from Der-el-Zor] I met new caravans everywhere. ... We see a whole row of ghastly forms rising suddenly out of a grave and asking for bread and water. They have dug their graves and lie waiting for death. ... In Sepka a preacher from Aintab told me that parents have often killed their children.[28]

In Aleppo, the horror of the escalating genocide was so great that Dr. Martin Niepage, a higher grade teacher at the German Technical School wrote an open letter report to "the accredited representatives of the German people." Dr. Niepage contended that the educational work of the German technical School would lose its moral foundation if the German government did not prevent the brutal killing of the Armenians:

How can we teachers read German fairy tales with our pupils, or, indeed, the story of the Good Samaritan in the Bible? How can we ask them to decline and conjugate indifferent words, while round about in the neighbouring yards the starving brothers and sisters of our Armenian pupils are succumbing to a lingering death? In these circumstances our educational work flies in the face of all true morality and becomes a mockery of human feeling.

Those remaining in the caravans passing through Aleppo were almost all women and children. They were driven from place to place until only a remnant of the original thousands was alive. For fun, some Turkish soldiers near Ourfa had one company of peasant women stripped of all their clothes. The women then had to march in the desert for days, with temperatures of 104^0, until their skin was completely burnt. ... Conscience compels us to call attention to these things. Though the Government, by the annihilation of the Armenian people, only intends to further internal political objects, the execution of the scheme has in many respects the character of a persecution of Christians. All the tens of thousands of young girls and women who have been dragged away to Turkish harems, and the masses of children who have been collected by the Government and distributed among Turks and Kurds are lost to the Christian Churches and are compelled to go over to Islam....

Men like Talaat Bey and Enver Pasha have repeatedly said, ... "Certainly we are now punishing many innocent people, but we must protect ourselves, even from those who might become guilty in the future." ... A German Catholic priest reports that Enver Pasha had told Monsignore Doici, the Papal representative at Constantinople, that he would not rest while one single Armenian was still living.

The object of the deportations is the extirpation of the entire Armenian nation. ...The Government did not scruple to deport Armenian pupils and teachers from the German schools at Adana and Aleppo, and Armenian children from the German orphanages; the protests of the Consuls and of the heads of the institutions were left unheeded. The offer of the American Government to take the deported persons to America on American ships and at America's expense was refused. ...I should not perform my duty as a German official and as an authorized representative of German culture if, in face of the atrocities of which I was a witness, I were to remain silent and passively look on while the pupils entrusted to me are driven out to die of starvation in the desert. ....

There are still 1,500 healthy Armenians--men, women and children, including grandmothers 60 years old and many children of six and seven-- who are at work breaking stones and shovelling earth, on the part of the Baghdad Railway between Eiran and Entilli, near the big tunnel. At the present moment Superintendent Engineer Morf, of the Baghdad Railway, is still providing for them, but their names too have already been registered by the Turkish Government. As soon as their work is completed... in two or three months, and they are no longer wanted, "new homes will be assigned to them"--which means that the men will be taken away and slaughtered, the good-looking women and girls will find their way into harems, and the others will be driven about in the desert without food, until the end comes. ...

A short time before my departure from Aleppo in May 1916, all the women and children encamped at Ras-el-Ain, on the Baghdad Railway, whose number was estimated at 20,000 were mercilessly slaughtered.[29]

Many German military advisors and other officials in Turkey during the massacres wrote shocking descriptions of what they saw. A German eyewitness at Moush reported that in November 1914, when Turkish commanders wanted to send food to their soldiers at the Caucasian front, they impressed 300 old Armenian men and boys, many who were crippled, to back-pack the supplies on a three-week trek from Moush to the frontier. These poor souls, who had already been robbed of their possessions, soon died of cold, hunger, or beatings on the way. Only thirty to forty returned.[30] In May 1915, after Russian armies retreated from the area around Lake Van, the Turks massacred all the Armenians in the nearby district of Moush, and pillaged and destroyed their property. In June, the whole Armenian population of Bitlis was killed:

> The *Mutessarif* of Moush, who was an intimate friend of Enver Pasha, declared quite openly that they would massacre the Armenians at the first opportune moment and exterminate the whole race. Towards the beginning of April [1915], in the presence of Major Lange and several other high officials, including the American and German Consuls, Ekran Bey quite openly declared the Government's intention of exterminating the Armenian race. All these details plainly show that the massacre was deliberately planned. In a few villages destitute women come begging, naked and sick, for alms and protection. We are not allowed to give them anything, we are not allowed to take them in, in fact we are forbidden to do anything for them, and they die outside.[31]

A German official of the Baghdad Railway related what he saw and observed during the holocaust in Cilicia [southeastern Turkey] and northern Syria:

> About 400 barefooted women, each with one child on her arm, one child on her back (often enough a dead one) and one held by the hand, passed through Marash during the first days. ... The American mission and the Armenians of Aintab managed to bring bread and money during the night to the convoys which passed Aintab, and which totalled about 20,000 persons, mostly women and children.... While on the march the deported Armenians were at first robbed of their ready money, and afterwards of all their possessions. ...The deported Armenians are specially troubled by the fact that they are unable to bury their dead. They are left dying anywhere on the road. ... The hardest fate is that of the women who are ...[giving birth] on the way.... [After one woman gave birth] she was forced to proceed on her march immediately; she fell down dead.... [Another] woman was surrounded by ladies belonging to the American mission, while she was confined in the neighborhood of Aintab. They only succeeded in obtaining permission for her to ride an animal, and she continued her journey in this manner, holding the child in her lap with a few rags round it. At Aintab the people clearing up a khan, which an hour before had been left by a convoy, found a new-born

child. A Turkish Major, who returned with me three days ago, said that many children were abandoned by their mothers on the way because they could not feed them any more. Older children were taken away from their mothers by the Turks. The Major, as well as each of his brothers, had an Armenian child with him; they intended to educate them as Mohammedans. ...

Corpses drifting down the Euphrates have been observed every day during the last 28 days, pairs of them being tied together back to back, while others are tied three to eight together by the arms. ...A German cavalry captain said he had, in the course of a ride from Diyarbekir to Ourfa, seen innumerable unburied corpses on both sides of the road, all corpses of young men whose throats had been cut. These were Armenians called up for military service and used for mending the roads.

It ought not to be overlooked that there are some Mohammedans who disapprove of the horrible deeds done against the Armenians. A Mohammedan Sheikh, a person of great authority at Aleppo, said in my presence: "When I hear talk about the treatment of the Armenians, I am ashamed of being a Turk." Anyone who wishes to remain alive is compelled to go over to Islam. ...

As regards those [Armenians] sent to Mosul, it is said that they are to be settled at a distance of about 16 miles from the railway; this probably means that they are to be driven into the desert, where their extirpation can proceed without witnesses.[32]

III. CHARACTERISTICS OF 1915 GENOCIDE AND TURKISH PATTERNS OF DENIAL

The 1919 trials of the Young Turks under Sultan Mehmet VI

Even as the genocide of 1915 was in progress, the ruling Young Turk triumvirate of Talaat, Enver, and Djemal often admitted privately that they were responsible for the genocide. When they fled to Germany in 1918, the government of Sultan Mehmet VI established a military tribunal to try Talaat and Enver in absentia for their crimes against the Armenian people. Overwhelming evidence was introduced, including the coded telegraphic instructions from the ruling Young Turks ordering various details of the "deportation" death marches. The defendants were convicted and condemned to death in 1919. The trial and verdict against the Young

Turks settled conclusively that Talaat and Enver had ordered the genocide. Yet at the same time, the growing influence of Mustafa Kemal was directed toward denial.

Turkish slaughter of Armenians after 1918 armistice

The Young Turks' plan was to complete the genocide by October 1915, but massacre of Armenians continued through the closing months of the war and for several years after the Turkish armistice of Mudros on October 30, 1918. In the Syrian desert area in 1916:

> Men, women, and children from Constantinople and the surrounding district... were driven into the desert, where they met people from the six Armenian provinces, and from the shores of the Black Sea, but this latter contingent consisted only of women, girls and boys of seven and under, as every male over seven had been slaughtered. All these were the victims of the three massacres. The first massacre was that of Res-ul-Ain, in which 70,000 people were killed; the second took place at Intilli, where there were 50,000 people assembled, most of them working on a tunnel of the Baghdad Railway; and the third, which was the most fearful of all, at Der Zor [Der-el-Zor], where Zia Bey slaughtered nearly 200,000 Armenians. These figures only give the numbers of people killed by massacre. If we add to their numbers the victims of misery, sickness and hunger, especially in Res-ul-Ain and Der Zor, the number of Armenians who were slain or died in the desert will exceed a million.[33]

By December 1916, the English people and their leaders had formed positive conclusions and judgments about the genocide. The *Manchester Guardian* said, "Another word remains--Armenia--word of ghastly horror, carrying the memory of deeds not done in the world since Christ was born--a country swept clear by the wholesale murder of its people."[34]

In July 1918, as a result of the Bolshevik Revolution, Russian troops rapidly withdrew across the Caucasus, and Enver's Turkish forces rapidly filled the vacuum that was left, campaigning as far as Baku on the Caspian Sea, and butchering between 50,000 and 100,000 Armenians in the process.[35]

Meanwhile, a war hero, Mustafa Kemal, as officer in command of Turkish forces in central Turkey had his own ideas about preventing the loss of any territory to Armenians and Greeks. At conferences in Erzerum and Sivas in 1919 he organized a resistance movement. In 1920 Kemal's armies crossed the eastern frontier and compelled the leaders of the newly formed Armenian republic to repudiate the Treaty of Sèvres and any claims to Turkish Armenia, including the former Russian Armenian districts of Kars, Adahan, Surmalu, and the Armenians' cherished Mount Ararat. It is an irony of World War I that Turkey was the only one among all of the defeated nations that expanded its territory. Forgotten and abandoned by the Allies, the remnant of the Armenian republic had no alternative but to join itself to the Soviet Union and the protection of the Red Army.[36] Next, Kemal's armies massacred the Armenians in Cilicia following the French withdrawal in 1920. With the formation of the Republic of Turkey in 1923, remaining Armenians were forced into exile. When the Turkish army drove out Greek forces in the city of Smyrna I 1922 and burned it, there were virtually no Armenians left in Turkey other than in Constantinople, which the Turks renamed "Istanbul." By 1923, the dream of a free and independent Armenia had died.

Mustafa Kemal's military success in forcing the short-lived independent Armenia in the Caucasus to give up its benefits under the Treaty of Sèvres confronted the Allies with a choice: to challenge Kemal militarily, or to recognized his territorial gains in eastern Turkey. Tired of a four-year war, and viewing Kemal's activities as an unimportant brush fire, the Allies and a new Republic of Turkey led by Kemal, signed the Treaty of Lausanne in 1923. Nowhere in the treaty do the words: "Armenia" or "Armenians" appear. As Dr. Richard Hovannisian summarized: "It was as if the Armenian Question or the Armenian people themselves had never existed."[37] The Lausanne Treaty meant not only that the Turkish genocide of an entire race of Armenians within its boundaries would go unpunished, but also that the international community had abandoned the Armenian Question. Those Armenians who survived the Turkish holocaust dispersed throughout the world, but a large number of them fled to the United States.

Genocide was the work of well-educated leaders

A common misconception is that genocide is planned by inhuman "mad men" and hence will probably not be repeated. Yet it is well-educated leaders, such as the Young Turks' Drs. Nazim and Behaeddin Shakir, or Nazi Germany's Heinrich Himmler, who always are the planners of genocide. There is also a tendency to mistakenly conclude that because genocide is buried in the past, it is unlikely to occur again in a future, more enlightened world. Turkey's massacre of Armenians did not deter Nazi Germany several decades later from liquidating millions of Jews. Likewise, the horror of the holocaust did not prevent later ethnic annihilation of the Tutsis in Rwanda, or the Kosovars in Bosnia, or the Christians in southern Sudan. On the contrary, between World War II and the end of the twentieth century, more lives have been lost through genocide than in all the civil and international wars combined. One source estimates that in the century from 1900-2001, more than 119 million have died as a result of genocide. In the twentieth century, genocide has killed nearly 84 million more people than were killed in both world wars plus all the revolutionary and civil wars in the same century.[38] Not surprisingly, most of the mass murders that have taken place in this period have followed the pattern of the Armenian genocide; a government controlled by a dominant ethnic or religious group decided to eliminate minority opposition by eliminating the minority group.[39]

Turkey's ongoing use of propaganda to deny genocide

In spite of overwhelming evidence that the "deportations" of 1915 were a euphemism for racial genocide, Turkish officials immediately launched a propaganda campaign designed to rebut the crescendo of worldwide protests. The campaign attempted both to *justify* the deportation decision and to present arguments designed to *excuse* any "regrettable occurrences" during the deportations.[40]

Generally, the Turkish justification arguments of the genocide were three-fold: (1) Armenians secretly sought political independence through subversive deals with foreign powers; (2) Armenians had defected to join the Russian army, and were plotting insurrection in the eastern provinces, and (3) the deportation was limited to removal of Armenians from war zones only.[41] Because there was a small grain of truth in each argument, Turkish officials could exaggerate so as to transform a molehill into a mountain. The reckless exaggeration, flawed reasoning, and basic untruth of all three Turkish claims that the genocide was "justified" have been forthrightly exposed by thousands of credible eyewitnesses whose testimony has been recorded and summarized by scholars of high repute.[42] These scholarly studies show the wild exaggeration of the Turkish propagandists. There is a modicum of truth to the observation that there were active Armenian political groups such as the Hunchak and Dashnak parties at the beginning of the war that may have favored the Allied powers. However, Armenians actively participating in such an agenda could not have even been one percent of the two million Turkish Armenians. It would have been easy enough to ferret out and arrest a few hundred subversive activists--unless Turkey's ruling elite concluded they would make a good excuse to liquidate an entire nation of innocent men, women, and children. On the eastern Turkey front against Russia, the vast, overwhelming majority of Armenians serving in the Russian army were Russian citizens, not Turkish. Furthermore, after the Young Turk revolution of 1909, Armenian men were required to serve in the army and demonstrated bravery fighting for the Ottoman cause in the Balkan wars. The final "justification" of "military necessity" is flawed because the "deportation" of Armenians was not confined to persons who might be a threat to Turkey in the war zone, but included helpless women and children throughout the country far away from military operations.

When confronted with undeniable evidence of atrocities, Turkish officials utilized another propaganda approach by offering two kinds of *excuses* for the slaughter of innocent men, women, and children. The first was that the central government could not control or prevent a few irresponsible military officers, local gendarmes, occasional "irregular" troops of Kurds and Circassians, local city leaders, or Moslem townspeople from periodically initiating spontaneous massacres, but none of these was ever part of a centrally, premeditated genocidal plan. Compelling evidence that the death marches were conceived and put into effect by the Young Turk leadership refutes this explanation. During the genocide of 1915, England's General Allenby intercepted Young Turk telegraphic commands to local army units ordering the killing and spelling out how it was to be accomplished. More than one Turkish telegraph operator, shocked by the instructions to commence massacre, later testified to a precisely conceived genocidal plan coordinated by the teleprinter of Grand Vizier Talaat at the Ministry of the Interior in Constantinople.[43] Ironically, when Ambassador Morgenthau suggested to Enver Pasha that over-zealous underlings who exceeded their orders might have carried out the massacres, he insisted he was in control of their activities and would accept responsibility for what was happening. The second type of excuse held that as the pressures of world war disintegrated the Ottoman Empire, both Turks and Armenians were victimized during a period of anarchy. This "everybody-suffers-in-war-argument" naively equated the economic hardship, or even death, suffered by Moslem Turkish civilians in a wartime economy with the horror suffered by more than a million and a half Armenians who were forced to march without food or water until they died.[44]

Turkish destruction of Armenian monuments and renaming of cities

To blot out every vestigial reminder of Armenian homelands, the Turkish government has over the past eighty-five years reassigned Turkish names to roughly 90 peercent of the Armenian villages. Only the largest cities in Turkish Armenia, such as Van, Erzerum, and Bitlis, have retained their names. In similar fashion, the Turkish government has systematically removed or destroyed virtually all of the Armenian statues, monuments, and ruins of ancient Armenian Christian churches in Turkey.[45]

Postwar Germany, prompted by its national conscience as well as international coercion, admitted its responsibility for the holocaust and granted reparations to thousands of holocaust survivors and their families. There has never been a similar Turkish response to the Armenian genocide--no acknowledgment of national responsibility, no admission of national complicity, no cooperation with fact-finding inquiries, and no reparations. It would seem that a major reason for this denial is Turkish governmental fear that significant numbers of Armenians now dispersed throughout the world, expect reparations and restitution of confiscated property.[46]

Phases of Turkish denial of genocide

Turkish government officials carefully constructed the rationale denying the Armenian genocide in incremental steps between the armistice of November 11, 1918 and August 1923, when the Treaty of Lausanne was signed. This "Great Denial" was an indispensable part of Mustafa Kemal's formation of a unified Turkish Republic established in the same year. Without foundation in fact, the Turkish government has consistently contended that the central government did not plan and coordinate the great slaughter of 1915.

As circumstances changed, Turkey's propaganda campaign passed through phases, which are summarized by Dr. Hovannisian:[47]
1. Until the empire-wide character of the deportations became known, there was a short time of *outright denial* of any extermination.

2. When the Allies knew of the atrocities and threatened postwar accountability, Turkish officials admitted ongoing deportations, but said they were justified to avoid "possible Armenian riots against Muslims, seditious actions against the government, or difficulties for the Army."[48]
3. When Russia had occupied most of the eastern provinces, Turkish propaganda claimed the invaders were mostly Armenian soldiers who were inflicting heartless brutalities upon the Kurds and Turks in the area.
4. After the war, Turkish opponents of the C.U.P. shifted blame to the Young Turks and away from the Turkish people. They argued that Russia-backed Armenian subversion in the eastern provinces justified deportations of all Armenians throughout Turkey.[49]
5. Postwar Mustafa Kemal's eviction of the French army from Turkey, as well as Greeks and Armenians that had returned to Cilicia, resulted in the Lausanne treaties of 1923. At that conference, Kemal's spokesman argued that Turkish lands should be free of Armenian claims:

> The responsibility for all the calamities to which the Armenian element was exposed in the Ottoman Empire falls upon their own deeds: the Turkish government, in every case and without exception, only having had recourse to repressive measures or reprisals, and that only after they had exhausted all their patience.[50]

6. Beginning with Hitler's rise to power in the early 1930s and continuing through World War II, the horror and magnitude of the Jewish holocaust eclipsed memories of the Armenian genocide a quarter century earlier. During and after World War II, Turkey's strategic control of the Bosphorus corridor to the Black Sea, and its nearness to the Suez Canal, strengthened its bargaining power and improved its ability to obtain compliance with its diplomatic demands to soft-pedal publicity about the Armenian genocide.

Following World War II, the North Atlantic Treaty organization (NATO) was organized as part of a containment policy creating a bulwark against the spread of communism and the Soviet system. The Soviet Union created what Winston Churchill described as an "iron curtain" from the Baltic to the Black Sea. For a half-century, the southeasterly arc of the iron curtain has been located in the territory of NATO member Turkey. During those years a major U.S. Air Force base has been located at Adana in southeastern Turkey. Although collapse of the Soviet system may have reduced the strategic importance of the iron curtain, other developments continue to make Turkey a desirable ally. Among these, the growing power of military dictatorships such as Iraq and Syria, both of which share boundaries with Turkey and are hostile to Israel, has tended to encourage entente between Turkey and Israel. Here, too, Turkey uses its diplomatic bargaining power to erase all memory and mention of its Armenian genocide. Turkey vigorously supported Jewish efforts to memorialize the holocaust, stressing its close ties to Israel. At the same time, Turkey cautioned Israel and the world that the Armenian community seeks to advance its own political agenda by creating its own imaginary genocide to draw world attention away from the holocaust.[51] Thus, at the 1982 International Conference on the holocaust and Genocide in Tel Aviv, Turkey attempted to suppress discussion of the Armenian genocide. Refusing to be intimidated, the conference stood on principle: free discussion on the moral goal of ending genocide is a universal imperative.[52] Again, in 1985, when Hebrew University had a meeting to commemorate the Armenian genocide, Turkey pressured the mayor of Jerusalem not to participate. This pressure to rewrite history was rejected in a *Jerusalem Post* editorial affirming that "no political considerations can supersede the imperative against joining the forgetters and distorters of the genocide of another people."[53]

To ensure its revisionist version of history is accepted, the government of Turkey has adopted a policy of establishing endowments for Turkish studies at American universities so that a history favorable to Turkey, and denying the Armenian genocide, becomes accepted. Turkish officials even threatened to ban Microsoft products in Turkey and arrest Microsoft officials if Microsoft's *Encarta* on-line encyclopedia kept its entry on Armenian genocide. Using threats of removing military bases from Turkey, canceling weapons contracts and imposing trade sanctions, Turkey put pressure on President Clinton to in turn put pressure on the U.S. Congress not to adopt resolutions condemning the Armenian genocide.[54]

In many quarters, the Turkish atrocities of 1915 were viewed as a horrible nightmare that people (and nations) preferred to conveniently forget. For over eighty-five years, Turkish policy has been to influence and encourage forgetting the genocide with a growing flood of clever and sophisticated propaganda. Gradually, the death marches of 1915 have became the "forgotten genocide," and at times, remembered only by families of the victims or the descendants of the American, German, French, British, and Swiss missionaries who ministered to them. However, the Armenian genocide was an offense of such magnitude against mankind that the voluminous historical record simply cannot be blotted out, or successfully modified by mercenary historical revisionists, no matter how skillfully they twist the *truth,* which is the real issue of the Armenian genocide.

Importance of Turks and Turkey remembering the Armenian genocide

The Turkish government first argued that Armenian misdeeds provoked Turkish reprisals, then denied there was ever an official policy of orchestrated genocide, and finally that the Armenian genocide of 1915 never happened. This falsehood has become a national "truth" promulgated with the persistence reminiscent of a Nazi totalitarian propaganda machine. Today, Turkish government officials, diplomats, journalists, academicians and even university historians zealously assert the nonexistence of the Armenian genocide.[55] The rest of the world, however, has accepted and believed the thousands of officials documents and diplomatic records of the international community, as well as the testimony of eye witnesses, journalists, scholars, consuls, ambassadors, presidents and prime ministers, all clearly establishing hat Turkey's government ordered and directed the extermination of more than a million and a half Armenians under the cover of World War I.[56]

To deny the truth, and refuse to come to terms with it is not in the best interest of the Turkish government.[57] Yet another example of the importance of truth to Turkey involves her increasing effort since the 1990s to lobby for admission to the European Union's Common Market. EU member countries are concerned about Turkey's religious discri-mination. In the 1990s, Turkish police repeatedly arrested American missionaries conducting Bible teaching in their homes. When Sir Fred Catherwood, Vice-President of the European Parliament, protested to the Turkish government, its immediate response was a denial. Catherwood promptly dispatched a reply pointing out to the Turkish minister that he had personally verified the facts and they were true, and that denial of the truth was not a satisfactory or acceptable method of addressing the problem.[58] The most effective way for a nation to build trust in every sphere of internal and international relations is to be truthful. Until such time as Turkey acknowledges the unassailable truth that its leaders directed genocide in 1915, the specter of that horrible event will not be brought to closure. At some point, thoughtful Turkish leaders and intellectuals must see the truth of the genocide clearly and muster the courage to confront their own history.

Armenian genocide and world opinion

Just as African-Americans in the United States played a constructive role in awakening white Americans to moral injustices in the national past, the Armenians "are uniquely able to help the Turks remember the past that they have denied or chosen to forget, but which even denied or unremembered endures." The irony that escapes the present leaders of Turkey is "that the capacity of a nation to transcend its past depends upon its willingness to remember it conscientiously, report it truthfully, and criticize it publicly. When a nation's leadership consistently refuses to do so, it risks burdening itself and its citizens with an uneasy conscience and inflicts upon the nation a deformation of character that will severely hinder its capacity to act rationally and responsibly."[59] For these reasons, Turkey must someday accept the historical truth of the genocide.

Fortunately, organizations have sprung up dedicated to keeping truth alive in the international market of ideas. For example, The Permanent Peoples' Tribunal was formed July 4, 1976, the 200th anniversary of the American Declaration of Independence. At that time it issued a "Universal Declaration of the Rights of Peoples." It has periodically conducted scholarly hearings, and received written reports and evidence on issues of nations unjustly abusing their peoples in violation of the Tribunal's precepts, as well as established principles of international law. In April 1984, the Tribunal addressed the Armenian genocide and formally pronounced a decision that:

- the Armenian population did and do constitute a people whose fundamental rights, both individual and collective, should have been and shall be respected in accordance with international law;
- the extermination of the Armenian population groups through deportation and massacre constitutes a crime of genocide not subject to statutory limitations within the definition of the Convention on the Prevention and Punishment of the Crime of Genocide of December 9, 1948. The aforesaid Convention is declaratory of existing law in that it takes note of rules which were already in force at the time of the incriminated acts with respect to the condemnation of this crime;

- the Young Turk government is guilty of this genocide, with regard to the acts perpetrated between 1915 and 1917;
- the Armenian genocide is also an 'international crime' for which the Turkish state must assume responsibility, without using the pretext of any discontinuity in the existence of the state to elude that responsibility;
- this responsibility implies first and foremost the obligation to recognize officially the reality of this genocide and the consequent damages suffered by the Armenian people;
- the United Nations Organization and each of its members have the right to demand this recognition and to assist the Armenian people to that end.

Various Armenian communities throughout the world have supported this verdict. It is the view of the Peoples' Tribunal that oppressed peoples should know that their cause has been determined to be just, and to hear it said publicly.[60]

There is also a growing body of principles and precedents of international law that condemn genocide. The judgments handed down at the Nuremberg and Tokyo trials established that the genocide committed under the cover of World War II were crimes, for which State organizations and their leaders were punished, sometimes even by death. In the 1970s, the International Law Commission of the United Nations introduced the idea that an *international crime* may result from a serious and large-scale violation of international obligations involving safety of human beings. According to this view, the state is obligated not to tolerate slavery or genocide, and the officials of any state that does so are committing a crime.[61]

The haunting evidence of the 1915 Armenian genocide rises, phoenix-like from the ashes of destruction. Although the 1915 genocide remains unacknowledged by the Turkish government, its horror must not be forgotten. It is only by remembering and talking about such crimes that they can be prevented from happening again.

---

[1] These principles were stated in the "Universal Declaration of the Rights of Peoples' adopted by the Permanent Peoples' tribunal at its meeting on July 4, 1976, the bicentennial of the American Declaration of Independence. *Crime of Silence*, 214.

[2] Terrence Des Pres. "Remembering Armenia," *The Armenian Genocide in Perspective*, 17.

[3] Roger W. Smith, "Genocide and Denial: The Armenian Case and Its Implications," *Armenian Review* Spring, 1999, Vol. 42, No. 1/165, 1-38. Most recently, a few Turkish scholars have begun to admit the undeniable reality of the 1915 Armenian genocide. In March 2001, a two day conference was held in Germany at the town of Muelheim an der Ruhr and was billed as the "First Turkish-Armenian Conference." Seven historians spoke at the conference: three Turkish, three Armenian, and one German. The three Turkish historians agreed that the historical record supports the fact that in 1915 the Ottoman government committed crimes against the Armenians by ordering deportations and mass killings. Gohar Gasparian, "Germany: Turks, Armenians Discuss 'Genocide' at Conference" *Radio Free Europe/ Radio Liberty,* March 2, 2001, www.rferl.org.nca.features/2001/03/27032001105302.asp

[4] *New York Times,* November 24, 1945, 7. See also, U.S. Chief Counsel for the Prosecution of Axis Criminality, *Nazi Conspiracy and Aggression, vol.7.* Washington, D.C.:G.P.O., 1946, 753. For other references by Hitler to the Armenian massacres, see *History of the Armenian Genocide,* 402-409 and Edouard Callic, ed. *Secret Conversations with Hitler,* trans. Richard Barry. New York, John Day, 1971, 81 quoted in R. Hrair Dekmejian. "Determinants of Genocide: Armenians and Jews as Case Studies," *The Armenian Genocide In Perspective,* 95.

[5] *History of the Armenian Genocide,* 424-427.

[6] *Caravans to Oblivion,* 88.

[7] G.S. Graber. *History of the SS.* London: Diamond Books, 1994, 76; quoted in *Caravans to Oblivion,* 89.

[8] R.Hrair Dekmejian. "Determinants of Genocide: Armenian and Jews as Case Studies," *The Armenian Genocide in Perspective,* 86.

[9] *Ambassador Morgenthau's Story,* 336-339.

[10] For example, Shefik Bey, *kaimakam* (commissioner of a subdistrict) of a village in the *vilayet* of Van was known to be lenient to the Armenians. Therefore, on April 5, the *Ittihadists* sent him to the Mosul *vilayet* on the excuse he was needed to settle a quarrel between two Kurd tribes. When he returned May 12 , 1915, he found nearly all Armenian males in the *kaza* (subdistrict) had been massacred. In the twenty Armenian Christian villages in his *kaza,* upon his return there were only 2500 women left, and no men at all--they had all been massacred by the regular Turkish cavalry, the Turkish irregulars, and the Kurds: "The Christian population were peaceable folk....To my knowledge they had not gone over to the Russians and I knew of no treason among them. There were no Christian intellectuals in my *kaza.* There were not even any schools. Few spoke their own racial language...The reason for the massacre was merely the carrying out of the Panturanian policy of the CUP...." Statement made in Turkish, translated into French (and subsequently into English) at the British high commission in Constantinople, *British Foreign Office Documents, ref. 371/6501;* quoted in *Caravans to Oblivion,* 109-110.

[11] *Crime of Silence,* 21-22.

[12] Henry Morgenthau, "Ambassador Morgenthau's Story," *World's Work* (November-December 1918, January 1919); 92-116,221-36, 294-304, quoted in Marjorie

Housepian Dobkin. "What Genocide? What Holocaust? News from Turkey, 1915-1923: A Case Study," *The Armenian Genocide In Perspective*, 102.

[13] *Ambassador Morgenthau's Story*, 374-375.

[14] *Caravans to Oblivion*, 11.

[15] *History of the Armenian Genocide*, 424-427. Contains sketches of careers of twelve of Hitler's highest ranking generals and ambassadors who had served in Turkey during the 1915 genocide.

[16] German complicity in the Armenian deportations and massacres is ably dealt with by Vahakn N. Dadrian in *The History of the Armenian Genocide*, 248-302.

[17] U.S.Congress, Senate, 66th Cong.2d sess., Senate Document no. 266, Major General James G. Harbord, *Conditions in the Near East: Report of the American Military Mission to Armenia* (Washington, D.C.: G.P.O., 1920), 7, quoted in *The Armenian Genocide in Perspective*, 34. General Harbord had been Chief of Staff in France under Pershing at the beginnning of America's war effort in World War I. Later he commanded the Second Infantry Division at the Allied victory at Belleau Woods. Harbord's report was favorable to a U.S. mandate for Armenia, but the Republican Senate at the time found this unacceptable. The government film made of Major General Harbord's investigative expedition is available, unedited, from The Armenian Film Foundation.

[18] *Ambassador Morganthau's Story*, 351-352.

[19] "Articles about the Armenian Genocide" can be found at http://pu1.netcom.com/~kojian/armo10c.html.

[20] *Turkish Atrocities*, xii-xiii. This volume contains eyewitness affidavits of 21 American missionaries stationed throughout Turkey during the 1916 genocide. See also Riggs' *Days of Tragedy in Armenia*, a detailed local history of the Armenian genocide covering the systematic way it was carried out in Harpoot.

[21] Arnold J. Toynbee, ed. *Treatment of Armenians, 1915-16*. London: H.M.S.O., 1916, xxxii.

[22] *Treatment of Armenians*, 290-291. For an analysis of the reliability of Toynbee's work see Lillian Etmekjian, "Toynbee, Turks, and Armenians," *Armenian Review*, Autmn 1984, Vol. 37, No. 3-147, 61-70.

[23] *Treatment of Armenians*, 642-45.

[24] Johannes Lepsius. *Le Rapport secret sur les massacres d"Armenie*. Paris, Payot, 1918, quoted in Marjorie Housepian Dobkin. "What Genocide? What Holocaust? News from Turkey, 1915-1923," *The Armenian Genocide in Perspective*, 97.

[25] U.S. Department of State, *Papers Relating to the Foreign Relations of the United States, 1915 Supplement* (Washington, D.C.: G.P.O., 1928), p. 981; and, Morgenthau Senior Papers, Manuscript Division, Library of Congress, Container 4; also Washington, D.C. National Archives, Department of State, 867.4016/173 and 174; all of the foregoing quoted in, Vigen Guroian "Collective Responsibility and Official Excuse Making: The Case of the Turkish Genocide of the Armenians," *The Armenian Genocide In Perspective*. New Brunswick (U.S.A.), Transaction Books, 1986,159.

[26] *Germany, Turkey, and Armenia,* 61-65. Most of the reports which follow were published in *Sonnenaufgang,* September, 1915.
[27] *Germany, Turkey, and Armenia,* 74-79.
[28] *Germany, Turkey, and Armenia,* 119-122.
[29] *Germany, Turkey, and Armenia,* 93-111. The report of another German schoolteacher, Dr. Graetner, can be found in "Protest of German Teachers against Massacres of Armenians," *Current History Magazine* (November 1916), 335-336, quoted in Marjorie Housepian Dobkin, "What Genocide, What Holocaust? News from Turkey, 1915-1923: A Case Study," *The Armenian Genocide in Perspective,* 101.
[30] *Germany, Turkey, and Armenia,* 23.
[31] *Germany, Turkey, and Armenia,* 23-24, 29.
[32] *Germany, Turkey, and Armenia,* 80-83.
[33] Aram Andonian. *The Memoirs of Naim Bey.* London: Hodder & Stoughton, 1920; second reprinting, Armenian Historical Research association, 1965, pp.xiii-xiv; quoted in Leo Kuper, "The Turkish Genocide of Armenians, 1915-1917," *The Armenian Genocide In Perspective,* 65-66.
[34] *Manchester Guardian,* December 29, 1916, 4, as quoted in *Crime of Silence,* 22.
[35] *Caravans to Oblivion,* 147-148.
[36] Richard G. Hovannisian, "Caucasian Armenia between Imperial and Soviet Rule: The Interlude of National Independence," in *Transcaucasia: Nationalism and Socialism,* ed.by Ronald G. Suny (Ann Arbor, 1983), 277-292, as quoted in *Crime of Silence*.
[37] Richard G. Hovannisian, "The Armenian Question, 1878-1923", *Crime of Silence,* 28.
[38] Samuel Totten. "Teaching about Genocide," *Social Science Record 24* (fall 1987) as quoted *Caravans to Oblivion,* 175.
[39] *Caravans to Oblivion,* ix-x. In the foreword, Roger W. Smith, Professor of Government, College of William and Mary, describes the prototype for massacre established by the Armenian genocide:

> There is a divided (or plural) society in which one ethnic group strives to dominate other distinct groups. This can lead [them] to a quest for autonomy, even separation, and the challenge, real or imagined, to the control of the government by the ruling ethnic group. Such demands are likely to be made at a time of political crisis, whether due to internal or external causes, and in the process there is often an increasing emphasis on nationalism. If civil or international war breaks out, the likelihood of genocide is greatly enhanced; genocide can now proceed under the cover of war, and the victims can be blamed for their own destruction. All of this is followed by denial of the genocide, international bodies speak briefly about war crime, and after a short period, the world forgets about the events.

[40] A seminal document issued in 1916 by the Sublime Porte, entitled *Vérité sur le mouvement révolutionnaire arménien et les mesures gouvernementales,* contained

the basic Young Turk justifications and excuses for the genocide. For the past 80 years most Turkish propaganda has used these arguments as a pattern, expanding and elaborating upon them as needed to justify or excuse the Armenian genocide:

> In order to prevent the Armenians in the military zone from creating difficulties to the Army and the Government, in order to remove the possibility of Armenian riots against Moslem populations, in order to protect the communications of the Imperial Army and to prevent possible coups, it was decided to transfer the Armenians from military zones to other localities. ... The primary necessity to assure internal order and external security of the country, has made indispensable the removal of Armenians from places where their presence was considered to be dangerous. ...During the application of these measures, regrettable acts of violence have sometimes been committed, but however regrettable these acts might have been, they were inevitable because of the profound indignation of the Moslem population.

Quoted in Joseph Guttman, "The Beginnings of Genocide," *Turkish Armenocide.* Documentary Series, vol.2. Philadelphia: Armenian Historical Research Association, 1965, 11.

[41] Vigen Guroian. "Collective Responsibility and Official Excuse Making: The Case of the Turkish Genocide of the Armenians," *The Armenian Genocide In Perspective,* 138-141.

[42] Arnold J. Toynbee. *Armenian Atrocities: The Murder of a Nation.* London, Hodder & Stoughton, 1915; and *Treatment of Armenians,* 593-693. Johannes Lepsius. *Deutschland und Armenien, 1914-1918; Sammlung diplomatischer Aktenstücker.* Potsdam, Tempelveriag, 1919. For more recent studies, cf. Richard G. Hovannisian. *Armenia on the Road to Independence.* Berkeley and Los Angeles, University of California Press, 1967, ch.4; Leo Kuper. *Genocide.* New Haven, Yale University Press, 1982, ch.6; Howard M. Sachar. *The Emergence of the Middle East: 1914-1924.* New York, Alfred A. Knopf, 1969, ch.4; Ulrich Trumpener. *Germany and the Ottoman Empire, 1914-1918.* Princeton, Princeton University Press, 1968, ch.7.

[43] *Caravans to Oblivion,* 128.

[44] For a detailed and convincing analysis of the false assumptions underlying Turkish *excuses* for the Armenian genocide, and the rationalization and self-deception underlying Turkish denial of responsibility for the genocide, see Vigen Guroian, "Collective Responsibility and Official Excuse Making: The Case of the Turkish Genocide of the Armenians," *The Armenian Genocide In Perspective,* 135-149.

[45] Dickran Kouymijian, "The Destruction of Armenian Historical Monuments as a Continuation of the Turkish Policy of Genocide," *Crime of Silence,* 173-177; Robert Melson. "Provocation or Nationalism: A Critical Inquiry into the Armenian Genocide of 1915," *The Armenian Genocide in Perspective,* 67.

[46] Richard G. Hovannisian. "The Armenian Genocide and Patterns of Denial," *The Armenian Genocide In Perspective,* 111.

[47]The following is not a direct quote, but a summary of Dr. Hovannisian's analysis as found in Richard G. Hovannisian. "The Armenian Genocide and Patterns of Denial," *The Armenian Genocide in Perspective*, 111-131. A recent analysis of Turkish denial can be found in Vahakn N. Dadrian. *Key Elements in the Turkish Denial of the Armenian Genocide: A Case Study of Distortion and Falsification.* Cambridge, Massachusetts and Toronto: The Zoryan Institute, 1999.

[48]Vigen Guroian, "Collective Responsibility and Official Excuse Making: The Case of the Turkish Genocide of the Armenians," *The Armenian Genocide in Perspective,* 141.

[49]A few post-war Turkish journalists wrote more honestly about the genocide. Thus, in 1930, Ahmed Emin admitted that the deportation was not a matter of "military necessity" but part of "the horrible practices" that Near Eastern peoples used to crush revolts or achieve unity. He acknowledged that the deportees were mostly women and children given only a "day or two" to sell their belongings, and then intentionally exposed to marauders from the "special organization" set up by the Committee on Union and Progress. He noted that the desert destination of the deportees was "incapable of supporting ...a large mass of people who reached it from a cold mountain climate after endless hardships." Finally, he acknowledged that certain influential Young Turks intended the deportations to bring about "the extermination of the Armenian minority in Turkey with the idea of bringing about racial homogeneity in Asia Minor."Ahmed Emin [Yalman]. *Turkey in the World War.* New Haven, Yale University Press, 1930, 217-221, quoted in Richard G. Hovannisian. "The Armenian Genocide and Patterns of Denial," *The Armenian Genocide In Perspective,* 116-117.

[50] Many viewed Mustafa Kemal as a great reformer who was modernizing the country. American missionaries made peace with the Turkish government in the hopes of spreading an "unnamed Christianity" through educational and humanitarian projects. Reshaping its image as an emerging modern "secular" republic, the new Turkey increasingly used diplomatic pressure and propaganda to deny the genocide and suppress all Armenian attempts to memorialize it in the court of world opinion. Thus, in 1934, Turkey's Ambassador lodged a protest with the American Department of State that Metro-Goldwyn-Mayer's proposed filming of Franz Werfel's novel, *The Forty Days of Musa Dagh*, would bring contempt upon the Turkish people. The screenplay dramatized the desperation of 4,000 Armenian deportees near Antioch and their rescue by Allied naval forces. When Turkey added to her protest the threat to ban all U.S. films in Turkey, MGM dropped plans to produce the film

[51]Richard G. Hovannisian, "The Armenian Genocide and Patterns of Denial,"*The Armenian Genocide In Perspective,* 128.

[52] *Armenian Genocide In Perspective,* 2.

[53]Israel W. Charny. "Preface," *The Armenian Genocide In Perspective,* 6.

[54] Amy Magaro Rubin, "In the United States, Allegations of Manipulation," *The Chronicle of Higher Education*, October 27, 1995; "Hot Type," *The Chronicle of Higher Education*, August 18, 2000. Microsoft did keep its de-

scription of the Armenian genocide with this parenthesis, "The government of Turkey denies Ottoman government responsibility for the deaths of the Armenians and disputes the labeling of these events as genocide. However, these events have been affirmed as genocide by the European parliament and more than ten countries – including Vatican City – and also acknowledged in legislative bodies in the United States and Canada as well as by independent genocide scholars." www.encarta.msn.com. Those who have grown up and been educated in Turkey, are kept in total ignorance of the genocide of the Armenian and Greek Christians. One descendant of an American missionary visiting Harpoot was told by a local Turk that the Armenians were wealthy and took their money and left Turkey. Ziegler. *great need over the water,* preface.

[55]"Preface by Professor Pierre Vidal-Naquet. *Crime of Silence: The Armenian Genocide,* 3-4.

[56]Some writers have referred to the steadfast negation of Turkish officials of the massacres of 1894-96 and the genocide of 1915 as "The Great Denial," *Crime of Silence,* 1; Richard Stoneman. *A Traveller's History of Turkey (3rd ed.).* New York: Interlink Books, 1998, 171.

[57] In June 2001, Turkey, in financial crisis, sought a $7 billion loan from the International Monetary Fund, which considers and awards such loans on the basis of a borrowing nations' application setting forth required factual information. It appears difficult for lenders to attach credibility to a loan application seeking billions of dollars when the borrower for more than eighty-five years has denied as false the facts of the Armenian genocide which the world knows are true.

[58]Sir Fred Catherwood. *The Cutting Edge.* London: Hodder & Stoughton, 1995, p.198-199. The facts surrounding these arrests are also based upon confidential interviews by the authors with the affected missionaries in 1990, and with Sir Fred Catherwood in the summer of 1994.

[59]Vigen Guroian. "Collective Responsibility and Official Excuse Making: The Case of the Turkish Genocide of the Armenians," *The Armenian Genocide In Perspective,* 149.

[60]*Crime of Silence,* 227, 242.

[61]*Crime of Silence,* 9-10.

BIBLIOGRAPHY

MANUSCRIPTS AND ARCHIVES

ABCFM archives in the Houghton Library of Harvard University, Boston, Massachusetts, including the following:
    Biographical Collection (ABC 77.1)
    Central and Western Turkey Missions (ABC 16.9).
    Miscellaneous Papers Relating to the Near East Mission (ABC 16.5)
    Mission to the Armenians (ABC 16.7).
    Picture Collection: Missions (ABC 78.2)
    Ms. Histories of Missions (ABC 88)
Ashfield store account books, 1820s-1850s. In possession of Norma L. Harris.
Evangelical Alliance Archives, including Board Minutes and *Evangelcal Christendom*, London, England.
First Presbyterian Church of Rolla, Missouri: Session Minutes of 1865-1866.
Franklin County Registry of Deeds for John, Alvan, and William Perry, Franklin County Court House, Greenfield, Massachusetts.
Franklin County Probate Court Records for John Perry (Case No. 3-596) and Henry T. Perry (Case Nos. 22-879 & 23-907).
Hubbell, J.B. "Report of J.B. Hubbell, M.D.," report Dr. Hubbell sent to Clara Barton, August 1, 1896, from America Red Cross Archives, Hazel Braugh Records Center, Falls Church, VA.
Mount Holyoke College Archives, Mount Holyoke, Massachusetts: Letters and records of Sarah Anne Perry and Emily Spencer Severance; *Twenty-first Catalogue of the Mount Holyoke Female Seminary, 1857-8.* Northampton: Thomas Hale & Co., 1858.
National Archives and Record Service, including the following:

Dispatches from the United States Consuls in Sivas, 1886-1906, National Archives Microfilm Publication T-681, Rolls 1 & 2, G.S.A., Washington, 1962.

"Jewett, Milo," RG 59, Stack 250, Row 19, Compt. 29, Shelf 1, Box 1462, REF. 123J55, United States State Department Archives. Microfilm Publication M862, Numerical and Minor films of the Department of State, Roll 232, File Case No. 2309, United States State Department Archives.

Records of Department of State Relating to the Internal Affairs of Turkey. 1910-1929. RG 59. 867.40 Social Matters, Reels 43-45, 47, Microcopy No. M353. The National Archives and Record Service, General Services Administration. Washington, 1961.

New York State Military Museum, Division of Military and Naval Affairs, Watervliet, NY. Records of Alvan W. Perry.

Perry, Henry T. "A Part of the Story of My Youth on the Farm." Manuscript in possession of Dale Severance.

Stone, Frank A. "Armenian Education at American Schools in Western Turkey: 1865-1921." An Inquiry Prepared for the Historic Armenian Cities and Provinces Seminar on Lesser Armenia at UCLA, Los Angeles, CA, May 15-16, 1999.

_____"The Anatolia to Which American Board Educators Went," draft of new chapter for revision of *Academies for Anatolia*.

Tenth Annual Catalogue of the Western Female Seminary. Oxford, Ohio, 1865.

Union/Auburn Theological Seminary Library Archives, New York, NY, miscellaneous correspondence and notes with Henry T. Perry.

Williams College Archives in Williamstown, Massachusetts, includes college catalogues, commencement brochures, some private correspondence with Henry T. Perry, and *Mills Theological Society Proceedings, 1848-1878*.

The Williston Northampton School Archives in Easthampton, Massachusetts. Contain an ample collection of student letters and class documents from the beginning of the school.

Zoryan Institute Oral History Archive, Cambridge, Massachusetts.

Additional miscellaneous letters, photographs and documents of Henry T. Perry are in the personal possession of Carlton Spencer Severance, Gordon B. Severance, and Gordon Bruce Severance.

EARLY LIFE & BACKGROUND

Adams, John Quincy. *A History of Auburn Theological Seminary, 1818-1918*. Auburn, New York: Auburn Seminary Press, 1918.

Anderson, Virginia DeJohn. *New England's Generation: The Great Migration and the Families of Society and Culture in the Seventeenth Century*. Cambridge University Press, 1993.

Ashfield Bicentennial. *Ashfield, Massachusetts, 1965*.

"Ashfield Church Observes 200th," *Greenfield Recorder-Gazette*, August 10, 1963.

"Auburn Theological Seminary," *Encyclopedia of the Presbyterian Church in the United States of America* (Alfred Nevin, Ed.). Philadelphia: Presbyterian Publishing Co., 1884, 44-46.

Brownson, Lydia B. and McLean, Maclean W. "Ezra Perry of Sandwich, Massachusetts," *New England Genealogical Register*, April, 1961, 86-96, 183-185, 278.

Carroll, Rev. George. "Memorial Tribute to Rev. Williston Jones, Our First Pastor," *Fortieth Anniversary of the First Presbyterian Church of Cedar Rapids, Iowa*. Cedar Rapids, Iowa: Daily Republican Printing and Binding House, 1888, 17-26.

Douma, Grace Hartzwell and Catherine Covert Stepanek. "Coe College: An Informal History, 1851-1041," *The Coe College Courier*, Vol. 52, No.2, December 1951, 7-9.

Durfee, Rev. Calvin. *History of Williams College*. Boston: A. Williams & Co., 1860.

Eriksson, Erik McKinley. *Cedar Rapids Collegiate Institute and Its Founders, 1853-1866*. Cedar Rapids, Iowa: Coe College, 1928, 63-66.

"First Presbyterian Church of Rolla," *Phelps County Missouri Heritage*, Vol. 2, 1994, 117-118.

Garrison, J. Ritchie. *Landscape and Material Life in Franklin County, Massachusetts, 1770*-Knoxville: University of Tennessee Press, 1991.

General Biographical Catalogue of Auburn Theological Seminary, 1818-1918. Auburn, NY: Auburn Seminary Press, 1918, 152.

Hewitt, John H. *Williams College and Foreign Missions*. Boston: The Pilgrim Press, 1919.

"History of Presbyterian Church," *The Rolla Times*, Rolla, Missouri, May 29, 1924.

History of the Connecticut Valley in Massachusetts, Vol. 2. Philadel-

phia: Louise H. Everts, 1879.
Holland, Josiah Gilbert. *History of Western Massachusetts*, Vol. 2, Part 3. Springfield: Samuel Bowles & Co., 1855.
Howe, M.A. DeWolfe. *Classical Shades: Five Leaders of Learning and Their Colleges*. Boston: Little, Brown, & Co., 1928.
Howes, Frederick G. *History of the Town of Ashfield, 1746-1910*. Ashfield, Massachusetts: Ashfield Historical Society, 1983 reprint of 1910 edition.
Inventory of Town and City Archives of Massachusetts. No. 6 – Franklin Co., Vol. 1 – Ashfield. Boston, Massachusetts: Historical Records Survey (WPA), 1940.
Marsden, George. *The Evangelical Mind and the New School Presbyterian Experience*. New Haven and London: Yale University Press, 1970.
Norton, A.T. *History of the Presbyterian Church in the State of Illinois*, Vol. 1. St. Louis: W.S. Bryan, 1979, 353-355.
One Hundred Year Biographical Directory of Mount Holyoke College, 1837-1937. Bulletin Series 30, No. 5. South Hadley, Massachusetts: Alumnae Association of Mount Holyoke College, 1937.
Phelps County: Our Centennial Book – Yesterday Lives Again. Phelps Co., MO, 1957.
Porterfield, Amanda. *Mary Lyons and the Mount Holyoke Missionaries*. New York: Oxford University Press, 1997.
Rosa, Joseph G. *Wild Bill Hickok: The Man and His Myth*. University Press of Kansas, 1996.
Rudolph, Frederick. *Mark Hopkins and the Log*. New Haven: Yale University Press, 1956.
_____, ed. *Perspectives: A Williams Anthology*. Williamstown, Massachusetts: Williams College, 1983.
Sawyer, Joseph H. *A History of Williston Seminary*. Published by the Trustees, 1917.
_____ *Williston Seminary, Easthampton, Massachusetts. Alumni Records from 1852 to 1874*. Springfield, Massachusetts: Clark W. Bryan & Co., Printers, 1875.
Severance, Jean Perry, "Application for Membership to the National Society of the Daughters of the American Revolution," National number 246887, August 27, 1928.
Sheriff, Carol. *The Artificial River: The Erie Canal and the Paradox of Progress. 1817-1862*. Hill & Wong, 1996.
Smith, Elwyn Allen. *The Presbyterian Ministry in American Culture*

(1700-1900). Philadelphia: Westminster Press, 1962.
Spring, Leverett Wilson. *A History of Williams College*. Boston & New York: Houghton Mifflin Co., 1917.
Vital Records of Ashfield, Massachusetts to the Year 1850. Boston, Massachusetts: New England Historic Genealogical Society, 1942.
Western Massachusetts: A History, 1636-1925, Vol. 2. New York & Chicago: Lewis Historical Publishing Co., Inc., 1926.
The Williams Quarterly, Vol. IX. Williamstown, Massachusetts, 1862.

GENERAL HISTORICAL BACKGROUND

Appleton's Cyclopedia of American Biography. N.Y.: D. Appleton & Co., 1887.
Barton, Clara Harlowe. *The Red Cross*. Washington: American National Red Cross, 1898.
Churchill, Winston. *History of the English-Speaking People* (one vol. Ed. By Henry Steele Commager). N.Y.: Pocket Books, 1966.
Cross, F.L. and E.A. Livingstone, eds. *Oxford Dictionary of the Christian Church*. Oxford University Press, 1997.
Douglas, J.D., et al, eds. *Who's Who in Christian History*. Wheaton, Illinois: Tyndale House Publishers, 1992.
McGee, Irving. *"Ben Hur" Wallace: The Life of General Lew Wallace*. Berkeley and Los Angeles: University of California Press, 1947.
Moorhead, Alan. *The White Nile*. New York: Harper and Brothers, 1960.
Morrison, Theodore. *Chautauqua*. University of Chicago Press, 1974.
Reid, Daniel G., Robert D. Linder, Bruce L. Shelley, Harry S. Stout. *Dictionary of Christianity in America*. Downers Grove, Illinois: Intervarsity Press, 1990.
Waller, John H. *Gordon of Khartoum*. New York: Athenum, 1988.
Welsh, William P., "The First Field Artillery," in Burdick, Henry Hagaman, ed. *New York Division National Guard War Record*, by the Officers and Men of the Division. New York: Burdick & King, 1917, 71-76.

ABCFM IN TURKEY & 19TH CENTURY MISSIONS

In addition to the ABCFM archives in the Houghton Library of Harvard University:

American Board Missions in Turkey and the Balkans. Issued annually from the Annual Report of 1915, 1916, 1917, 1918.

Anderson, Rufus. *Republication of the Gospel in Bible Lands: History of the Mission of the American Board of Commissioners for Foreign Missions to the Oriental Churches.* Boston: Congregational Publishing Society, 1872.

Annual Report of the American Board of Commissioners for Foreign Missions, annual issues 1866-1930.

Bartlett, Samuel C. *Historical Sketches of the Missions of the American Board.* New York: Arno Press, 1972 reprint of 1876 edition.

Barton, James L. *Christian Approach to Islam.* Boston: Pilgrim Press, 1918.

_____*Daybreak in Turkey.* Boston: The Pilgrim Press, 1908.

_____, ed. *The Mohammedan World of Today,* being papers read at the First Missionary Conference on Behalf of the Mohammedan World, Held at Cairo, April 4-9, 1906. New York, Toronto, and London: Fleming H. Revell, c. 1906.

Brady, Steve and Harold Rowdon, ed. *For Such a Time as This.* Scripture Union, 1996.

Buchanan, Claudius. *Christian Researches in Asia.* Boston: Samuel F. Armstrong, 1811.

The Constitution and By-Laws of the Mission of the American Board of Commissioners for Foreign Missions to Western Turkey. New York: John A. Gray & Green Printers, 1865.

Dodge, Bayard. "American Educational and Missionary Efforts in the Nineteenth and Early Twentieth Centuries," *The Annals of the American Academy of Political and Social Science,* Vol. 401, May, 1972, 15-22.

Dwight, Rev. H.G.O. *Christianity Revived in the East; or a Narrative of the Work of God among the Armenians of Turkey.* New York: Baker and Scribner, 1850.

_____*Christianity in Turkey: A Narrative of Protestant Reformation in the Armenian Church.* London: James Nisbet & Co., 1854.

_____*Constantinople.* New York: Young People's Missionary Movement, 1901.

_____, Rev. H. Allen Tupper, and Rev. Edwin Munsell Bless, ed. *The Encyclopedia of Missions.* New York & London: Funk & Wagnalls Co., 1904.

Earle, Edward Meade. "American Missions in the Near East," *Foreign Affairs*, April 1929, Vol. 7, 400-417.

Ecumenical Missionary Conference, New York, 1900. New York: American Tract Society, 1900.

Eddy, David Brewer. *What Next in Turkey: Glimpses of the American Board's Work in the Near East.* Boston, Mass.: The American Board, c. 1910.

Evangelical Christendom. Monthly publication of the Evangelical Alliance in England.

Ewing, J.W. *Goodly Fellowship: A Centennial Tribute to the Life and Work of the World's Evangelical Alliance, 1846-1946.* London: Marshall, Morgan, & Scott, Ltd.

Finnie, David H. *Pioneers East.* Cambridge, Mass.: Harvard University Press, 1967.

Goodsell, Fred Field. *They Lived Their Faith: An Almanac of Faith, Hope, and Love.* Boston: American Board of Commissioners for Foreign Mission, 1961.

_____. *You Shall Be My Witnesses.* Boston: ABCFM, 1959.

Grabill, Joseph L. *Protestant Diplomacy and the Near East.* Minneapolis: University of Minnesota Press, 1971

_____ "The 'Invisible' Missionary; A Study in American Foreign Relations," *Journal of State and Church,* Vol. 14, No. 1, Winter, 1972, 93-105.

Greene, Rev. Joseph K. *Leavening the Levant.* The Pilgrim Press, 1916.

Harris, Paul William. *Nothing but Christ: Rufus Anderson and the Ideology of Protestant Foreign Missions.* Oxford University Press, 1999.

Helping Hand Series. After the Massacres, this periodical was published monthly by the National Armenia and India Relief Association. It regularly contained articles about the Sivas orphans and the work being done in Sivas to help the children.

Hubbard, Ethel Daniels. *Lone Sentinels in the Near East.* Boston, Massachusetts: Woman's Board of Missions, 1920.

Hutchison, William P. *Errand into the World: American Protestant Thought and Foreign Missions.* Chicago: University of Chicago Press, 1987.

Latourette, Kenneth Scott. *A History of the Expansion of Christianity*, Vol. 6: The Great Century in North Africa and Asia (1800-1914). New York: Harper & Bros., 1944.

Lybyer, Albert Howe. "America's Missionary Record in Turkey," *Current History*, XIX (Feb. 1924), 802-810.

Makdisi, Ussama. "Reclaiming the Land of the Bible: Missionaries, Secularism, and Evangelical Modernity," *American Historical Review*, June 1997, 680-711.

Marden, Lucy Harriet Morley. *Jesse Krekore Marden*. Claremont, California: The Courier Press, 1950.

Martin, Edwin W. *The Hubbards of Sivas*. Santa Barbara, CA: Fithian Press, 1991.

Minasian, S.M. *Correspondence and Other Documents Relating to Troubles in the Turkish Missions of the American Board CFM*. N.Y.: Atkin & Prout, 1883.

The Missionary Herald. Monthly periodical of the ABCFM.

Nordmann, Bernhard Frederick. *American Missionary Work Among Armenians in Turkey (1830-1923)*. Ph.D. Thesis, University of Illinois, 1927.

Partridge, Rev. E.C. *Mary Louise Graffam, Sivas, Turkey*. Present Day Worker Series, 1917.

_____ *Self-Help in Education: Sivas, Turkey in Asia*, pamphlet published by the ABCFM, c. 1911.

Peet, Louise, ed. *No Less Honor: The Biography of William Wheelock Peet*, n.d.

Phillips, Clifton Jackson. *Protestant America and the Pagan World: First Half Century of ABCFM, 1810-1860*. Harvard University Press, 1968.

Porterfield, Amanda. *Mary Lyons and the Mount Holyoke Missionaries*. New York: Oxford University Press, 1997.

Prudential Committee. *Memorandum for the Missions in the Turkish Empire*. Boston: Beacon Press, 1881.

Putney, Clifford and Burlin, Paul T. *The Role of the Merican Board in the World: Bicentennial reflections on the Organization's Missionary Work, 1810-2010*. Eugene, Oregon: Wipf & Stock, 2012.

Riggs, H.H. "The Missionary Situation in Turkey," *The International Review of Missions*, vol. 27, 1938, 195-200.

Robert, Dana L. *American Women in Missions – A Social History of Their Thought and Practice*. Macon, Georgia: Mercer University Press, 1996.

Stone, Frank Andrews. *Academies for Anatolia*. Lanham, Maryland: University Press of America, 1984.
Strong, E.E. *Asiatic Turkey: A Sketch of the Mission of the American Board*. Printed for the American Board, 1910.
Strong, William Ellsworth. *The Story of the American Board*. Boston: Pilgrim Press, 1910.
Trumbull, Rev. H. Clay. "Bible House Building in the Levant," *The Christian Herald: An Illustrated Family Magazine*, June 18, 1902, 527.
Ussher, Clarence D. *An American Physician in Turkey*. Boston: Houghton Mifflin Co., 1917.
Wheeler, Rev. C.H. *Ten Years on the Euphrates*. Boston: American Tract Society, 1868.
White, Rev. G.H. *Mrs. Coffing of Hadjin*. Chicago: Woman's Board of Mission of the Interior, 1888.
Ziegler, Theresa Huntington. *great need over the water*. Ann Arbor, MI: Gomidias Inst,. 1999.

ARMENIANS

Arpee, Louis. *A History of Armenian Christianity*. New York: Armenian Missionary Association of America, Inc., 1946.
Avakian, Krl Vartan, "The Armenian Evangelical Church 1846-1996, A Historical Overview," http://www.cacc-sf.org/c-aehistory.htm, 12/14/2000.
Bedikian, Dr. Armand. "Pilgrimage to Sebastia in 1993 and 1994," *Nor Sebastia*, Vol. 59, No. 180, 1995.
Bedikian, Rev. Antranig. "The Review of the Evangelical Movement among Armenians," 1946, English translation published by Armenian Missionary Association of America, 1970. http://www.cacc-sf.org/c-riseAAB.html, 12/14/200.
Bournoutian, George D. *A History of the Armenian People*, Vol. II, 1500 A.D. to present. Costa Mesa, California: Mazda Publishers, 1993.
Buchanan, Claudius. *Christian Researches in Asia*. Boston: Samuel F. Armstrong, 1811.
Burnaby, Capt. Fred. "On Horseback Through Asia Minor (excerpt from 1877)," *Nor Sebastia*, Vol. 59, No. 180, 1995.
Chakmakjian, Rev. Hagop A. "The Armenian Evangelical Church and the Armenian People," presented at the Annual Retreat of the

Armenian Evangelical union of California in Yettem, California, fall 1956, http://www.cacc-sf.org/c-aecHAC.html, 12/14/2000.

Chalabian, Antranig. *Armenia After the Coming of Islam.* Southfield, Michigan, 1999.

Childs, W.J. "Across Asia on Foot, (1917 excerpt)" *Nor Sebastia*, Vol. 59, No. 180.

Darakjian, Rev. Barkev. "Armenian Evangelical Identity Historical and Theological Perspectives," first published by the Armenian Evangelical union of North America in the 1980's, http://www.cacc-sf.org/c-aeidentityBND.html, 12/14/2000.

Gaidzakian, Rev. Ohan. *Illustrated Armenia and the Armenians.* Boston, 1898.

Heilig, Matthias R. *The Story of Armenia.* Dansville, N.Y.: F.A. Owen Publishing Co., 1920.

Hovannisian, Richard G., ed. *Armenian Sebastia/Sivas and Lesser Armenia.* Costa Mesa, California: Mazda Publishers, Inc., 2004.

Jaequemyns, M. Rolin. *Armenia, the Armenians, and the Treaties.* London: John Heywood, 1881.

Janbazian, Movses B. "Armenian Evangelical Church's Statement at the Armenia-Diaspora Conference," held in Yerevan, Armenia, September 22-23,1999, http://groong.usc.edu/Adconf/soeeches/amaa.html, 12/14/2000.

Jenkins, Hester Donaldson. "Armenia and the Armenians," *The National Geographic Magazine*, October 1915, 329-359.

Krikorian, Meshob. *Armenians in the Service of the Ottoman Empire.* London & Boston: Routledge Direct editions,

Muncherian, Pastor Stephen, Considerations for the Future of the Armenian Reformation in North America, paper presented at the Armenian Evangelical Union of North America Biennial Convention in San Francisco, August 24, 1996, http://www.cacc-sf.org/c-aeconsider.htm, 12/14/2000.

Redgate, A.E. *The Armenians.* Oxford: Blackwell Publishers, Ltd., 1998.

Robin-Jaequermyns, M. *Armenia, the Armenians, and the Treaties.* London: John Heywood, 1881.

Russo, Jean B. The Nineteenth Century Armenia an Armenians: As Seen Through Western Eyes," *The Armenian Review*, winter 1983, 27-39.

Sarafian, Krikor. *Information about the Armenian Apostolic Church.*

Jerusalem: St. James Press, 1998.
Scipio, Lynn A. *My Thirty Years in Turkey*. New Hampshire: Richard R. Smith, Publisher, Inc., 1955.
Tootikian, Vahan H. "Armenian Congregationalists flee from genocide and find a home in the U.S.," Hidden Histories in the United Church of Christ, http://www.ucc.org/aboutus/histories/chap4.htm, 12/4/2000.
Tovmassian, Rev. Edward S. "The Blessed Nation," sermon delivered at the United Armenian Congregational Church of Hollywood, California, October 26, 1975, http://www.cacc-sf.org/c-blessedEST.html, 12/14/2000.
Tozer, Henry F. "Turkish Armenia and Eastern Asia Minor (excerpt from 1886)," *Nor Sebastia*, Vol. 59, No. 180, 1995.
Walker, Christopher J. *Armenia: The Survival of a Nation*. New York: St. Martin's Press, 1980.
_____*Visions of Ararat: Writings on Armenia*. London: I.B. Touris Publishers, 1997.

OTTOMAN EMPIRE & TURKEY

Barber, Noel. *The Sultans*. New York: Simon & Schuster, 1973.
Bliss, Howard S. "Sunshine in Turkey," *The National Geographic Magazine*, January 1909, 66-76.
Bournoutian. George A. *A History of the Armenian People, Vol. II, 1500 A.D. to the present*. Costa Mesa, California: Mazda Publishers, 1993.
Boulanger, Robert and Margaret Case. *Turkey*. Paris: Hachute World Guides, 1960.
Broude, Benjamin and Bernard Lewis, ed. *Christians and Jews in the Ottoman Empire: The Functioning of a Plural Society*. New York: Holmes & Meier Publishers, Inc., 1982.
Bryce, James. "Two Possible Solutions for the Eastern Problem," *The National Geographic Magazine*, November 1912, 1149-1157.
Cadogan Guide to Turkey. Chester, Conn.: The Globe Pequot Press. 1988.
Ceram, C.W. *The Secret of the Hittites*. N.Y.: Schochen Books, 1973.
Chester, Colby M. "The Young Turk," *The National Geographic Magazine*, January 1912, 46-89.
"The Christians under Turkish Rule," *American Catholic Quarterly*, 1896, 399-409.

Courbage, Youssef and Philippe Fargues (trans. Judy Mabro). *Christians and Jews under Islam*. London & New York: I.B. Tauris Publishers, 1998.

Cox, Samuel S. *Diversions of a Diplomat in Turkey*. New York: Charles L. Webster & Co., 1887.

Dennis, Alfred L.O. *Adventures in American Diplomacy, 1896-1906*. New York: E.P. Dutton, 1928.

DeNovo, John A. *American Interests and Policies in the Middle East, 1900-1939*. Minneapolis: University of Minnesota Press, 1963.

Dugdale, E.T.S., ed. *German Diplomatic Documents, 1871-1914*. London: Methuen & Co., Ltd., 1929, Vol. II, 109-114, 211-235, 327-347, 431-445.

Dwight, H.G. "Life in Constantinople," *The National Geographic Magazine*, December 1914, 521-545.

"Eastern Question," "Berlin, Congress and Treaty of," "Turkey," and "Russo-Tukish War," *Encyclopedia Britannica*, 1958 ed.

Facaros, Dana and Michale Pauls. *Turkey*. Chester, Connecticut: The Globe Pequot Press, 1988.

Garnett, Lucy M.J. *Turkish Life in Town and Country*. London: George Newton, Ltd., n.d. (c. 1890's).

Garstang, John. *The Land of the Hittites: an Account of Recent Explorations and Discoveries in Asia Minor*. New York: E.P.Duton & Co., 1910.

Gillard, David, ed. *British Documents in Foreign Affairs: Reports on Papers from the Foreign Office Confidential Print*, vol. 19.

Grabill, Joseph L. "Cleveland Dodge, Woodrow Wilson and the Near East," *Journal of Presbyterian History*, Vol. 48, No. 4, Winter 1970, 249-264.

_____ "Missionary Influence on American relations with the Near East, 1914-1923." *Muslim World*, January 1968, 43-56.

Grosvenor, Gilbert H. "A German Route to India," *The National Geographic Magazine*, May 1900, 201-204.

Hall, William H. "Under the Heel of the Turk," *The National Geographic Magazine*, July 1918, 51-69.

Hanioglu, M. Sükrü. *The Young Turks in Opposition*. New York: Oxford University Press, 1995.

Heilig, Matthias R. Heilig. *The Story of Armenia*. Dansville, N.Y.: Owen Publishing Co., 1920.

Hourikan, William J. "The Big Stick in Turkey: American Diplomacy and Naval Operations Against the Ottoman Empire, 1903-1904,"

Naval War College Review, vol. xxxiv, No. 5, 287, 78-88.
Huntington, Ellsworth. "The Fringe of Verdure Around Asia Minor," *The National Geographic Magazine*, September 1910, 761-774.
Jaber, Kamel S. Abu. "The Millet System in the Nineteenth Century Ottoman Empire," *Muslim World*, Vol. 57, No. 3, July 1967, 212-223.
Jefferson, Margaret M. "Lord Salisbury and the Eastern Question, 1890-1898," *The Slavonia and East European Review*, December 1960, 44-60.
Kansu, Aykut. *The Revolution of 1908 in Turkey*. Leiden: Brill, 1997.
Kark, Ruth. *American Consuls in the Holy Land, 1832-1914*. Detroit: Wayne State University Press and Jerusalem: Magness Press, Hebrew University, 1994.
Kazamias, Andreas M. *Education and the Quest for Modernity in Turkey*. University of Chicago Press, 1966.
Kenross, Lord. *The Ottoman Centuries: The Rise and Fall of the Turkish Empire*. New York: Morrow Quell Paperbacks, 1977.
Levonian, Lootfy. "The Millet System in the Middle East," *Muslim World*, Vol. 42, 1952, 90-96.
Marsh, Peter. "Lord Salisbury and the Ottoman Massacres," *Journal of British Studies*, Vol. XI, no. 2, 1972, 63-83.
Marashlian, Levon. *Politics and Demography: Armenians, Turks, and Kurds in the Ottoman Empire*. Cambridge, MA: Zoryan Institute, 1991.
"Our Relations with Turkey: Notes of a Conversation with Sir A.H. Layard," *Contemporary Review*, Vol. XLVIII, May 1885.
Pears, Sir Edwin. *Forty Years in Constantinople*. London: Herbert Jenkins, Ltd., 1916.
_____ "Grass Never Grows Where the Turkish Hoof Has Trod," *The National Geographic Magazine*, November 1912, 1132-1147.
Ramsay, W.M. *Impressions of Turkey During Twelve Years of Wanderings*. New York: G.P. Putnam's Sons, 1897.
_____ "A Sketch of the Geographical History of Asia Minor," *The National Geographic Magazine*, November 1922, 553-570.
Salt, Jeremy. *Imperialism, Evangelism, and the Ottoman Armenians 1878-1896*. London: Frank Cass & Co., Ltd., 1995.
Sarlissian, A.O. "Concert Diplomacy and the Armenians, 1890-1897," *Studies in Diplomatic History and Historiography*. London: Longman, Green & Co., Ltd., 1966, 48-75.
Simsir, Bilâl N., ed. *British Documents on Ottoman Armenians*. An-

kara: Türk Tarih Kurumu Basimevi, vol.1, 1982, vol. 2, 1983, vol. 3, 1989, vol. 4, 1900.

Terrell, Honorable A.W. "An Interview with Sultan Abdul Hamid," *The Century Illustrated Monthly Magazine*, vol. LV, New Series, Vol. XXXIII, Nov. 1897 to April 1898, 133-138.

Trowbridge, Stephen van Rensselaer. "Impressions of Asiatic Turkey," *The National Geographic Magazine*, December 1914, 598-608.

Wilson, Keith M. "Constantinople or Cairo: Lord Salisbury and the Partition of the Ottoman Empire, 1886-1897," in Wilson, Keith M., ed. *Imperialism and Nationalism in the Middle East*. London: Mansell Publishing, Ltd., 1983, 26-55.

Y'eor, Bat. *The Decline of Eastern Christianity under Islam: From Jihad to Dhimmitude*. Fairleigh Dickinson University Press, 1996.

ARMENIAN MASSACRES/HOLOCAUST

Addrian, Rouben Paul. "Adana Massacre," *Encyclopedia of Genocide* (ed. Israel W. Clarney). Santa Barbara, CA: ABC-CLIO, 1999.

Balakian, Peter. *The Birning Tigris: The Armenian Genocide and America's Response*. HarperCollins, 2003.

Barton, James L. *Story of Near East Relief (1915-1930)*. New York: The Macmillan Company, 1930.

Bliss, Edwin M. *Turkey and the Armenian Atrocities*. Fresno, California: Meshag Publishing, 1982 reprint of 1896 ed.

British Documents on Foreign Affairs: Reports and Papers form the Foreign Office Confidential Print (David Gillard, ed.), vol. 19: The Ottoman Empire: Nationalism and Revolution, 1885-1908.

Bryce, Viscount James, Arnold Toynbee, Herbert Adams Gibbons, Henry Morgenthau, Fridjhof Nansen. *An Anthology of Historical Writings on the Armenian Massacres of 1915*. Beirut, Lebanon: Hamaskaïne Press, n.d.

Bryce, Viscount. *The Treatment of Armenians*. London: Sir Joseph Causton & Sons, Ltd., 1916.

Charny, Israel W., ed. *Encyclopedia of Genocide*. Santa Barbara, California, 1999, available at http://www.armenian-genocide.org/encyclopedia.

"The Constantinople Massacre," *Contemporary Review*, October 1896 (vol. LXX), 457-465.

Dadrian, Vahakn N. *The History of the Armenian Genocide*. Providence & Oxford: Berghahn Books, 1995.

_____Key Elements in the Turkish Denial of the Armenian Genocide: A Case Study of Distortion and Falsification. Cambridge, MA and Toronto: The Zoryan Institute, 1999.
_____Warrant for Genocide: Key Elements of Turko-Armenian Conflict. London: Transaction Publishers, 1999.
Davis, Leslie. *The Slaughterhouse Province: An American Diplomat's Report on the Armenian Genocide, 1915-1917.* New Rochelle, New York: Aristide D. Caratzas, 1989.
El-Ghusein, Faiz. *Martyred Armenia.* London: C. Arthur Pearson, Ltd, 1917.
Etmekjian, Lillian K. "The Evidence for the Armenian Genocide in the Writings of Two Prominent Turks," *The Armenian Review*, 183-191.
_____"The Reaction of the Boston press to the 1909 Massacres of Adana," *The Armenian Review*, winter 1987, vol. 40, no. 4-160, 61-74.
_____"Toynbee, Turks, and Armenians," *The Armenian Review*, vol. 37, no. 3-147, autumn, 1984, 61-70.
Gasparian, Gohar. "Germany: Turks, Armenians Discuss "Genocide' at Conference. *Radio Free Europe/Radio Free Liberty*, March 27, 2001, www.rferl.org/nca/features/2001/03/27032001105302.asp.
"Genocide and Collective Responsibility," bulletin from symposium held April 24, 1980, within framework of Israel Interfaith Committee's Program on Oriental Churches.
Germany, Turkey, and Armenia. London: J.J. Keliher & Co., Ltd. 1917.
Ghusein, Faizel. *Martyred Armenia* (translated from the original Arabic). New York: George H. Doran Co., 1916.
Graber, G.S. *Caravans to Oblivion, The Armenian Genocide, 1915.* New York: John Wiley & Sons, Inc., 1996.
Greene, Frederick Davis. *Armenian Massacres or Sword of Mohammed.* Philadelphia & Chicago: International Publishing Co., reprinted by J.D. & A.L. Fawcett, 1990.
Gürün, Kamuran. *The Armenian File: The Myth of Innocence Exposed.* London, Nicosia, Istanbul: K. Rustem & Bro. An Weidenfeld & Nicholson Ltd., 1985.
Hairapetian, Armen. "'Race Problems' and the Armenian Genocide: The State Department File," *The Armenian Review*, vol. 37, no. 1-145, Spring 1984, 41-59.
Halo, Thea. *Not Even My Name.* New York: Picador USA, 2001.

Harris, J. Rendell and Helen. *Letters from Armenia*. London: James Nisbet & Co., 1897.

Hepworth, George H. *Through Armenia on Horseback*. New York: E.P. Dutton & Co., 1898.

Horton, George. *The Blight of Asia*. Indianapolis, Kansas City, New York: Bobbs-Merrill Company, Inc., 1926.

Hovannisian, Richard G., ed. *The Armenian Genocide in Perspective*. New Brunswick and Oxford: Transaction Books, 1986.

Jernazian, Ephraim K. Jemazian (trans. Alice Haig). *Judgment unto Truth*. New Brunswick: Transaction Publishers, 1990.

Kapikian, Garabed. *Yegernabadoum [Story of Genocide]*. New York: Pan-SebastiaRehabilitation Union, Inc., 1978.

Karajian, Sarkis. "An Inquiry into the Statistics of the Turkish Genocide of the Armenians 1915-1918, *The Armenian Review*, vol. 25, 4-100, winter 1972, 3-44.

Knadjian, H.M. *The eternal Struggle: a word picture of Armenia's fight for freedom*. Fresno: Republican Printing, n.d.

Lepsius, Johannes (ed. J. Rendel Harris). *Armenian and Europe: An Indictment*. London: Hodder & Stoughton, 1897.

___*Germany, Turkey & Armenia*. London: J.J. Kelihor & Co., Ltd., 1917.

"Massacres in Turkey," *The Nineteenth Century*. No. ccxxxvi, October, 1896, 671.

Miller, Donald E. & Lorna Teuryan. *Survivors: An Oral History of the Armenian Genocide*. University of California Press, 1993.

Minassian, John. *Many Hills Yet to Climb: Memoirs of an Armenian Deportee*. Santa Barbara, California: Jim Cook Publishers, 1986.

Morgenthau, Henry. *Ambassador Morgenthau's Story*. New York: Doubleday, Page, & Co., 1918.

Narmark, Norman M. *Fires of Hatred*. Cambridge: Harvard University Press, 2001.

Nazer, James. *The Armenian Massacre*. New York, N.Y.: T & T Publishing, Co., 1970.

Papers Relating to the Foreign Relations of the United States, Part II. Washington: Government Printing Office, 1896.

Palmer, Araxi Hubbard Dutton. *Triumph from Tragedy*, privately printed, 1997.

Permanent Peoples' Tribunal. *The Crime of Silence: The Armenian Genocide*. London: Zed Books, Ltd., 1985.

Sarafian, Ara. "The Ottoman Archives Debate and the Armenian

Genocide," *Armenian Forum*, 2, no. 1, Spring 1999, 35-44.

Slide, Anthony. *"Ravished Armenia" and the Story of Aurora Mardiganian*. Lanham, MD. & London: The Scarecrow Press, Inc., 1997.

Smith, Roger W. "Genocide and Denial: The Armenian Case and Its Implications," *Armenian Review*, Vol. 42, No. 1/165, Spring 1989, 1-38.

Somakian, Manoug. *Empires in Conflict: Armenia and the Great Powers, 1895-1920*. New York: I.B. Tauris Pub., 1995.

Ternon, Yves, ed. *The Armenian Genocide: Facts and Documents*. St. Vartan Press, 1984.

Toynbee, Arnold Joseph, ed. *The Treatment of the Armenians in the Ottoman Empire, 1915-16; documents presented to Viscount Grey of Falloon, secretary of state for foreign affairs, by Viscount Bryce*. London: H.M. Stationery off., Sir J. Causton, 1916.

"Turks urged to end denial over 'genocide,'" *Houston Chronicle*, April 26, 1999.

Walker, Christopher J. *Armenia: The Survival of a Nation*. New York: St. Martin's Press, 1980.

About the Authors

Gordon B. Severance, Ph.D., J.D., is emeritus professor of business law from California State University at Los Angeles and the University of Nevada, Reno. He received an M.A. in economics from Stanford University, and a Ph.D. in economics and J.D. from the University of Southern California. In 1988-89, as Fulbright Scholar, he taught constitutional law at Makerere University in Uganda, where he was also an advisor to the Constitution revision Commission. A member of the California and federal bar, Gordon has practiced law for 50 years. With a lifelong involvement in Chrsitian missions, in 1999 Gordon was executive producer (India) of an award-winning full length dramatic film, *Candle in the Dark*, a biography of William Carey, the nineteenth century missionary to India. Currently he is President of Media4Kids (http://www.media4kidsintl.org).

Diana L. Severance received her Ph.D. in history from Rice University. She is Director of the Dunham Bible Museum at Houston Baptist University. She was a major contributor to contributed to *Faith of Gods and Generals* and is the author of *Feminine Threads: Women in the Tapestry of Chrsitian History* and *A Cord of Three Strands:Three Centuries of Chrsitian Love Letters*.

The Severances make their home in Houston, Texas.

INDEX

Adana, Turkey, 64, 71, 83, 397, 406
  massacre, 310-311, 331n
Afton, New York, 178-182, 216, 317
Aintab, Turkey, 10-11, 62-75, 78n, 81-82, 87, 162, 221, 251, 272, 296, 313, 328, 331n, 346-347, 380n, 381, 396, 398-399
Albustan, Turkey, 87, 93-94, 113, 163, 222, 228, 345-346
Aleppo, Turkey, 62, 64, 68, 72-73, 97-98, 344-347, 373, 380n, 394-397, 399
Alexandretta, Turkey, 55, 62, 73, 83, 89, 95-97, 99, 301
Amasia, Turkey, 92, 184, 189, 341, 344, 381
American Board of Commissioners of Foreign Missions (ABCFM)
  Annual meetings, 44, 80n, 90, 105n, 125, 141, 144, 159, 169, 268, 270-271, 282-283, 316, 350
  Centennial, 312
  Central Turkey Mission, 38, 68-69, 70, 74, 82, 84, 87, 90, 98, 162, 311
  debate over mission work in Turkey, 134-136, 237-240, 336, 354-357
  history in Ottoman Turkey, 56-62, 78n, 192-193, 360n
  Jubilee Celebration, xx, 6-12, 20, 28, 37-38, 43, 91
  mission policy, 37-38, 40, 59-60, 68, 123, 134-136, 283, 356-357, 367n
  Memorandum for Missions in Turkish Empire, 134-136, 142
  origin, ixx, 6-8, 20n
  Prudential Committee, 53, 59, 68, 134-136, 142, 239, 280, 300, 310,
  schools, 10, 37, 59-61, 64, 66, 69, 94, 97, 113, 115-118, 134-135, 144-146, 164, 192, 196-197, 201-202, 237, 255, 263, 270-274, 280, 289-291, 294, 300, 301, 310, 312-313, 320, 324-325, 328, 354-356, 367n, 390
  relief work, 246-247
American Civil War, 32-40, 65, 82, 91, 144, 169
American Red Cross, 247-251, 317, 392
Anderson, Rufus, 9, 37, 48n, 138n
Andover Seminary, 6, 35, 47n, 273
Antioch, Turkey, 1-2, 9, 64, 74, 89, 143, 296
Arabian desert, 1-2, 73
Ararat, Turkey, 2, 57, 401
Armenakan party, 199
Armenian Evangelical Church (Protestant), 59-62, 66-68, 74, 82, 97, 145, 238, 251, 300, 330-331n, 337-378

Armenian Gregorian church, 58,
    60, 61, 64, 78n, 144-145, 164,
    205, 228-229, 238, 246-247,
    251, 261, 285-286, 303-304,
    313, 322
Armenian Question, 122, 193, 198-
    199, 215, 235, 353, 356, 400
Armenians
    and missionaries, 57-60, 144-
        145, 390-391
    deportation and genocide, 129-
        130, 135, 190-203, 336-348,
        356, 360n, 361n, 363n, 369-
        376, 378n-381n, 383-415,
        407-408
    early history, 57
    education, 58, 64, 345. See
        ABCFM schools.
    emigration, 135, 198-199, 251,
        285, 311-312, 325, 354, 374-
        375, 400
    first Christian nation, 57-58
    massacre of, 212-237, 245-
        246, 251, 266-267
    native pastors, 37, 61-64, 68,
        71, 73-75, 86, 88, 90, 93-94,
        124, 131-134, 143, 145-147,
        190-191, 203, 211, 230, 238,
        256, 267, 288, 293, 311, 322-
        323, 330, 331n. See also
        Beshguturyan, Demirjian,
        Kalousdian, Kazanjian, Kev-
        orkian, and Kulukjian.
    persecution and imprisonment
        of, 129-130, 190-192, 212,
        290-292, 342-343, 345
    political reform movements,
        189, 199-201
    village life, 118-120
Armstrong, Samuel C., 33-34, 47n,
    350
Ashfield, Massachusetts, xx, 7, 11-
    19, 20n, 23, 28-34, 52-53, 87,
    91, 95-96, 99-103, 136, 162,
    172-173, 174, 178-181, 282,
    316-318, 320, 330, 335, 348-
    350, 357, 359, 376
Ashude, Turkey, 125, 148, 222,
    228
Auburn Seminary, 35-36, 48n, 51,
    182, 316
Balkan Wars, 323-324
Barton, Clara, 247-250
Barton, James, 123, 136, 246, 259-
    260, 266, 277n, 303, 304, 310,
    317-318, 322, 350, 354-355,
    359, 360n
Beshguturyan, Marderos, 133, 149
Berlin to Baghdad Railway, 215,
    345-347, 373, 381n, 388, 396-
    399
Bible, 16, 37, 42, 53, 57-58, 61, 63-
    64, 67, 70, 73-74, 78n, 82, 97,
    113, 120, 145, 162-163, 205,
    231, 237, 254, 261-262, 272,
    297, 318, 325, 327, 417-418
    translation, 60, 78n, 87, 90,
        237, 322, 417-419
Bible House, 91, 104n, 141, 246,
    321
Bible readers, 79n, 143, 146, 260,
    285
Bingham, Hiram, 10
Biredjik, Turkey, 1, 71, 221, 346
Blake, Susan, 146, 148-149, 159
Bliss, Daniel, 74, 80n
Bliss, Flavia, 92, 116, 127
Bliss, Isaac, 90-91, 104n, 170
Bolshevik Revolution, 352, 401
Bosnia, 109, 302, 403

Brewer, Mary, 184, 204, 221, 225, 255, 261, 271-273, 269, 284-287, 311
Brookes, Dr. James Hall, 182
Bulgaria/Bulgarians, 109, 121, 144, 162, 169, 197, 199, 201, 218-219, 272, 282, 302, 311, 322, 324, 336
Bushnell, Horace, theology of, 68, 75
Byzantine Empire, 56, 71, 81, 111, 144
Capitulations, 108, 136n, 302, 336
Central Turkey Mission. *See* under Amercan Board of Commissioners
Chamberlin, Laura, 127-129, 146, 155-156, 159, 165, 169
Chautauqua, 177, 186n, 281-282
Cholera, 39, 42, 64, 183, 187n, 204-205, 310, 330, 340
Christian Endeavor Society, 280, 305n, 313
Circassians, 122, 194, 198, 225, 294-295, 402
Clark, Dr. Charles, 291, 314, 316-321, 324, 327, 342, 351, 364n
Clark, Rev. N.G., 40, 43, 85, 96, 101-102, 117, 120, 161, 173, 175
Clifton Springs, New York, 179-180, 182, 330
Coe College, 42
Coffing, Josephine, 68, 82-83, 86, 88-89, 93, 294
Colporteurs, 64, 73, 79n, 118, 120, 130, 190-191, 237, 256, 259, 326-327
Committee of Union and Progress (C.U.P.), 302, 310, 336, 352, 363n, 385, 389, 392, 404, 410n
Congregational Church, 7-8, 10, 12-15, 20n, 54, 59, 66, 264, 350-351, 358, 376-377
Constantinople, Turkey, 10, 28, 55-56, 58-61, 63-64, 67, 72, 77n-80n, 89-92, 97, 100, 103, 104n, 109-112, 115, 121, 125, 129, 138n, 141, 144, 159, 166n, 169-170, 183, 191, 193, 216, 218-221, 230, 238, 240, 250-254, 252-254, 259, 262-263, 269-270, 283, 289, 295-301, 303, 309-310, 315, 321, 323-324, 329, 335-338, 340-341, 352, 358, 374, 391, 397, 400-401, 403, 412-413
  Bosphorus, 55, 90, 166n, 197, 298-300, 402
  Sublime Porte, 60, 78n, 190, 195, 210, 212, 216, 249, 334, 336
Crimean War, 61, 108, 195
Dashnaktsutiun, 199, 252-253, 352, 398
Davis, Dr., 127
Dawes, Electra, 46n, 52, 178, 181
Dawes, Henry, 32, 34, 46n, 181
Demirjian, Kevork, 229-231, 287, 303, 322
Derende, Turkey, 113, 125, 145, 222, 256
Dhimmi system, 194
Disraeli, Benjamin, 109, 122, 157
Divrik, Turkey, 113, 116, 131-133, 147, 156, 188, 204, 220, 252, 256, 274, 280-285, 288, 297, 313, 326,

Djemal, Ahmed, 324, 337, 352, 397
Dodge, William, 52, 76n
Doodoo, Anna, 149, 154-156, 160, 165, 169
Doremus, Sarah, 96
Dwight, H.G.O., 58-59, 110
Dwight, Henry Otis, 247, 283
Earthquakes, 89, 189
Eaton, Dr. Horace, 37-38, 52, 101
Ecumenical Missionary Conference (1900), 279-280
Enderes, Turkey, 120, 131, 142-143, 147, 156, 313, 323
Enver, Ismail, 324, 335-337, 352, 363n, 389, 392-393, 395-97, 398-400
Erdman, Rev. W.J., 182
Erie Canal, 36-37, 51
Erzerum, Turkey, 59, 91, 112-113, 120-121, 193, 212, 221-223, 297, 331-332, 334, 337, 348-349, 370-371, 379n, 381, 399, 402
Evangelical Alliance, 54, 76n, 97, 109, 205n
Favre, Leopold, 262, 296, 317, 321
Fisk, Pliny, 56-58
Fowle, Mary, 313, 324, 348, 351
Garfield, Harry A., 319
Garfield, James, 31, 319
Genocide, 235, 336-348, 361n, 369-376, 383-414
  and Nazi Germany, 362n, 366n, 387-390, 406-410
  proof of, 362n, 388-398
  Turkish denial, 360n, 365n, 384-385, 398-408, 413n-414n
  See also Armenians, deportations, massacre.

Gladstone, William, 109, 157-158, 214, 219, 235
Goodell, William, 28, 58, 138n
Graffam, Mary, 284, 313, 324, 337-338, 342, 348, 351, 355-356, 364n, 390
Greek Christians, 74, 164, 199, 336
Greek Orthodox Church, 60, 130, 132, 164
Greene, Frederick, 118, 183, 187n, 213-214, 241n
Grosvernor, Edwin, 160
Gürün, Turkey, 87, 92, 113, 125, 132-133, 146-147, 149, 203, 222, 224, 227, 230-232, 256, 284, 286-287, 303, 309
  massacre, 222-223, 230-232, 379
  relief, 224, 232, 256-257, 262, 269, 282, 317
  rug company, 258, 275, 286
  deportation, 341
Hadjin, Turkey, 82, 93, 98, 294-295, 297, 340, 390
Hamlin, Cyrus, 59, 166n, 205
Haran, Turkey, 2, 71
Harbord, Maj. Gen. James G., 355, 389, 410n
Harpoot, Turkey, 141, 143, 200, 213, 221, 232, 251, 253-254, 270, 295-296, 354, 381, 390-391
Harris, J. Rendell and Helen, 250-254, 283, 285, 300
Harrison, President Benjamin, 279-280
Hatti Humayoun, 195-196, 201
Hatti Sherif, 195-196
Haystack Jubilee, xx, 5-11, 19n, 37-38, 43

Haystack Meeting, 6-8
Hepworth, George, 234
Herzegovina, 109, 302
Hittites, xx, 55, 71, 78n, 81, 162-163
Holbrook, C. Henry, xiv-xv, 324-325, 328, 332n
Hopkins, Albert, 8, 19n, 30-31
Hopkins, Mark, xx, 8, 19, 20n, 30-34, 33, 38, 47n, 103, 260, 316
Hubbard, Albert, 110, 113-116, 125, 127, 134, 136, 145-146, 156, 164, 184, 187, 202-205, 221, 230, 249-250, 252, 254, 262-263, 293
Hubbard children, 111, 123, 184, 199, 202, 249, 287, 329, 359n
Hubbard, Emma, 110-111, 113, 122-124, 127, 146, 152, 156-157, 164, 184, 202, 249, 262, 268-270, 275, 274-275, 286-287, 315, 321, 329-330, 345
Hubbel, Dr. J.B., 249
Hunchakian Revolutionary Party, 199, 216
Ittihad. See Committee of Union and Progress
Jewett, Milo, 184-185, 188, 202, 212, 222-227, 246, 249, 255-256, 260, 263-264, 269-271, 282, 301, 321
  Reports on massacres, 222-227
Jones, Elizabeth, 41-45, 49n, 73, 96, 264, 272, 281, 316
Jones, Emilie [Barker], 41-42, 44, 96, 264, 281, 298, 316, 344, 354
Jones, Williston, 39, 41-42
Jubilee Singers, 178, 186n, 350
Kaimakam, 129, 139n, 212, 338, 346
Kalousdian, Marderos, 190-191, 206n, 304-305
Kara Hissar, Turkey, 113, 120, 142-147, 156, 165n, 172, 222, 256, 284, 292, 323, 326, 342
Kazanjian, Mehran, 315, 322
Kerkhan, Turkey, 72, 75, 85
Kemal, Mustafa, 354, 357, 371, 377n, 395-396, 399-400, 413n
Kevorkian, Avedis, 318, 322
Khan, 119-120
Koran, 153, 191-192, 219
Kulukjian, Garabed, 224, 226, 252
Kurds, 74, 98, 119, 121-122, 130-131, 143, 194, 197-200, 212-214, 221-223, 228, 230, 241n, 278, 285, 290, 296-298, 325, 333, 339-340, 348, 353, 372, 392, 396, 398, 402
  Hamidieh Regiments, 198, 212-213, 241n
Lancasterian educational plan, 116-117, 138n
Layard, A.H., 61
Lepsius, Johannes, 231, 352, 363, 393
Lyon, Mary, xx, 13
Marash, Turkey, 2, 64, 68, 71-72, 74-75, 79n, 81-101, 116, 145, 151, 162-163, 190, 223, 219, 295-296, 328, 331n, 341-342, 393
Marden, Dr. Jesse Krekore, 287, 328-329
Marden, Henry, 75, 162-163
Marsovan, Turkey, 92, 100, 110, 124, 184, 189-194, 221, 254-256, 267, 269, 272-273, 292, 300, 303, 322, 328-329, 341,

343, 346, 379
Martyn, Henry, 66, 92, 124, 322-323
Masonville, New York, 173-178, 180, 182
Millet system, 60-61, 78n, 88, 212
Missionary influence, 61-62, 67, 115-116, 123, 135, 145, 205, 237-240, 245-247, 249, 252, 259-260, 269, 280, 313, 323-324
    and diplomacy, 105n, 145, 237, 245, 259, 289-290
Montenegro, 109, 121, 196, 318, 322
Montgomery, Giles and Emily, 68, 71, 74-75, 83, 93-94, 96-97, 151, 294
Moody, Dwight L., 103
Mt. Holyoke College, xx, 13, 32, 43, 46n, 265
Morgenthau, Henry, 336, 337, 340-341, 359, 380n, 386-387, 389, 398
Moslems
    H.T. Perry's concern for, 94, 98, 130-131, 258-259, 282, 291-292, 296-298, 317, 325-327
    houses, 94, 127, 230
    missionary activity among, 88-89, 94, 98, 258-260, 306n, 324
    persecution of Christians, 97-98, 110, 226-228, 231, 236-237, 241n-242n, 251, 253, 354, 376, 396
    protection of persecuted, 253, 257, 261, 331, 356
mutassarif, 88-89, 197

Nazim, Dr. Mehmed, 338, 352, 387
Near East Relief, 348, 355-356, 374
Neshan (Perry's servant), 111, 156, 184, 189, 225
Nutting, Dr., 68, 71-72
Ohanesian, Franklin, 369-376
Ottoman Empire. *See also* Sublime Porte, Young Turks, Committee on Union and Progress, and Sultans.
    Armenian deportations and genocide, 336-348, 356, 363n, 369-376, 378-381n, 383-414
    Armenian massacres, 212-237
    Armenian oppression, 135, 190-203, 206-207n, 213, 234
    capitulations, 108, 136n, 302, 336
    Committee on Union and Progress, 302, 310, 336, 352, 363n, 385, 389, 392, 404, 410n
    dhimmi system, 194
    dismemberment, 107-110, 121-122, 302-303, 310, 322-324
    early history, 56, 60-61
    eastern question, 107-110, 121-122, 193
    European powers, 107-110, 193, 195, 198-199, 214-216, 218, 220, 232, 235, 237, 241n, 323, 341, 353
    forced population exchanges and executions, 109, 218-219, 336, 356, 402
    German alliance, 335, 385
    imprisonment of Armenians,

212, 388-390
millet system, 60-61, 78n, 88, 212
Moslem law, 61, 108, 194-196, 220, 247
   reforms under, 109-110, 121-122, 129, 195-196, 198, 214, 220, 225, 227, 235, 253, 302
   relations with
      Britain, 108, 121, 169-170, 192, 200, 214-215, 324, 352, 391-393
      Greece, 56, 58, 169-170, 199, 322-323
      Russia, 58, 61, 107-109, 115, 121, 170, 176, 194, 197-198, 200, 215, 335-337, 352
      United States, 169-170, 215, 220, 234, 250, 284, 289-290, 301, 311, 336, 353-355
   taxation, 69, 82, 109, 120-121, 129, 164, 179, 194, 196, 198-200, 206n-297n, 211-212, 231, 289, 300, 302, 304
   treatment of non-Moslems, 97, 103, 105n, 108-110, 192-197, 236, 304, 309-310, 324
Ourfa, Turkey, 1, 64, 68, 71-72, 74, 79n, 221, 229, 296, 344, 346, 381, 390-391, 394, 398
Paris Peace Conference, 348
Parsons, Levi, 56-57
Partridge, Ernest and Winona, 273-274, 284, 290, 300-301, 312-313, 311, 324-325, 328-329, 342, 348, 350, 355, 357
Peet, W.W., 238, 246-247, 247, 262, 289, 381n

Perry, Alvan, 13-19, 28-30, 32, 34-35, 40, 47n, 52-53, 67-68, 84-85, 87-88, 96, 172, 179
Perry, Alvan Williston, 96-97, 99-103, 114, 122-125, 131-132, 141-142, 147-150, 152, 156-157, 159-160, 171, 173-174, 179, 183, 264, 280, 283, 292, 298-300, 315, 317-321, 329, 348-349, 357, 360
Perry, Henry T.
   Haystack Jubilee, 7-11, 19, 20n, 28
   interest in missions, 8-9, 10, 27, 32, 34, 47n, 90, 281-282, 316, 349, 350-351
   ancestors, 11-15, 21n, 22n, 29
   youth, 15-19
   respect for parents, 87-88, 96, 172, 366
   early schooling, 18
   Williston Academy, 19, 23-30, 51
   and Civil War, 32, 34-37
   Williams College, 30-35, 51, 282-282
   Auburn Seminary, 35-37, 51
   Erie Canal, 36
   ABCFM, 37-38, 40-41, 44, 52, 84, 100, 103, 173, 266, 300, 350, 359
   ordained, 38
   Rolla, Missouri, 38-40
   marriage to Jeanne Jones, 43-45
   honeymoon, 51-53
   Old South Church, 53
   travels to and from Turkey, 54-55, 95-97, 99-100, 103, 183-184, 279, 283

language study, 65-66, 68-71, 77-78n, 92, 325
setting up housekeeping, 66, 114, 185, 322
periodicals read, 66, 157, 177, 293
books read, 16, 28, 66, 103n, 133, 151, 153, 160-161, 177, 181-182, 293
and prayer, 25-26, 28, 32, 54-55, 66, 68, 70, 72, 86, 96, 99, 114, 160, 165, 171-172, 174, 177, 181, 183, 185, 211-212, 258, 274, 282, 285, 290-291, 293-295, 298, 313, 321, 325, 328, 348, 357-359
and horses, 1, 66, 92, 132, 164, 249, 256
Aintab, Turkey, 65-75
and Lord's Day (Sabbath), 16, 26, 62, 66-67, 157, 225
Mission Treasurer, 68-69, 84, 114, 185, 246, 256, 275, 298, 315, 319
outstation travels, 71, 84, 94, 97, 113, 118-121, 125, 130-134, 156, 164, 203-204, 268, 274-275, 284, 288, 290, 294-298, 314-315, 319, 323
captured by robbers, 131-132
love and respect for Jeanne, 43, 54, 63, 70, 72, 85, 90, 94, 126, 146, 253
Kerkhan, 72, 75, 85
dentistry, 73-74, 80n, 298-299
seminary teaching, 75, 83-84, 94, 98
in Marash, 75, 81-87, 93, 95-99
death of daughters, 70, 85-86, 125-127, 351
death of father, 87-88
on Christian suffering, 94, 146, 161-162, 161-173, 290, 358
descriptions of Turkey, 69, 71, 125, 142, 164, 203, 294
and Moslem opposition, 88-89
malaria, 90
annual meetings, 44, 90-92, 141-142, 144, 159-160, 282-283, 350
quarantined, 99-100, 183-184
and Alvan Williston Perry. *See* Perry, Alvan Williston.
furloughs, 100-103, 279-284, 315-321
American Centennial, 102
in Sivas, Turkey, 193, 114-118, 122, 124-125, 147-165, 211, 272-273, 284, 312-315
Sivas Normal School, 115, 117, 202, 312, 320
interest in Africa, 125, 157-159, 166n, 177, 267
holidays and celebrations, 66, 122, 274
grief at Jeanne's death, 150-153, 160-162, 171-172, 177-179
and daughter Jean, 154-155, 160, 169-171, 211, 240. *See* also Severance, Jean Perry.
revisits Central Turkey Mission, 162-164
resigned from mission, 164-165, 173
revival in Masonville, 174-178, 186n
pastoring in Afton, N.Y., 178-181

marries Mary Hartwell, 180
lumbago, 170, 180, 185n, 255, 290
headaches, 47n, 90, 147-148, 150, 171, 290, 315, 317-318, 328
visits Washington, D.C., 181
returns to Sivas, 184
and Bible prophecy, 182-183, 187n, 323, 349-350
and Scripture, 16, 25-26, 38, 53, 85-86, 90, 95, 98, 101, 149, 151-152, 157, 163, 172, 182, 212, 216-217, 222, 258, 274-275, 290-291, 304, 320, 328, 330, 358
sermons, 53, 152, 159-160, 165, 176, 216-217, 222, 258, 304-305
teaching, 83-84, 94, 98-99, 115-116, 258, 284, 298, 315
work in vegetable/fruit gardens, 24, 29, 124, 147, 178-179, 181, 349, 357, 359
Sivas massacre, 224-228
Gürün massacre, 229-230
relief work, 246-247, 249, 254-258, 262-264, 266-267, 271, 317
oversees construction, 124, 202, 204, 258
industrial school, 202, 258, 262-263, 312-313, 320, 332n
interest in Chautauqua, 177, 281-282
concern for Moslems, 94, 153-154, 165, 258-259, 282, 288, 291-292, 317, 325-327, 330
work among Kurds, 74, 98, 130-131, 296-298

to Harpoot, 296
visit with Jean and Alvan in Constantinople, 298-300
diplomacy with government and *Vali*, 73, 88-89, 147, 190, 192, 202, 259, 315, 319
perspective of history, 293, 304-305
love of preaching, 65, 75, 83-84, 87, 91, 94, 118, 130, 172, 288, 314-315, 325, 356, 359
hearing/sight loss, 317, 359
visit to Smithsonian, 318
D.D. from Williams College, 318-320
at H. Martyn Centennial, 322-323
retirement from mission, 329
correspondence, 28, 72, 74, 84, 98, 143, 146-147, 180, 240, 291, 317, 330, 348-349, 357, 359
concern over Bible liberalism, 75, 325, 359
Williams' 60th Reunion, 357
Williston Alumni banquet, 359
death and will, 360
Perry, Jeanne Hannah
 ancestry, 41, 49n
 Western Female Seminary, 43
 marries Henry Perry, 43-45
 honeymoon, 51-53
 children
  Harriet, 70
  Elizabeth Eunice, 73, 85, 162
  Alvan Williston. *See* Perry, Alvan Williston.
  Mary Schneider, 86, 162
  Edith Wilsheimer, 124-125

Carrie Williams, 126
Jean Hannah, 148. *See* Severance, Jean Perry.
missionary heart, 43-44, 54, 72, 84, 101, 118, 124, 126, 143, 147, 151, 153, 292
poor health, 84-87, 90, 92, 95, 99-102, 124, 126, 131, 141-142, 146-148
singing, 42, 53, 65, 84, 101, 116, 122, 131, 143, 153
personal ministry, 116, 122, 143, 152
travels to Turkey, 54-55, 95, 43
death, 148-149, 159
eulogies, 151-153
Perry, Mary Hartwell
Western Female Seminary, 179-180
missionary in Siam, 180, 187n
marries Henry Perry, 179-180
cholera relief, 205
and Gürün massacre, 230-232, 256
complains to Judson Smith, 254-255
speaking, 180, 229, 280-281, 317-318
prepares annual meeting letter, 270-271
returns to U.S. to care for Jean, 272, 281
preserving food, 296, 349
death
Perry, Sarah Ann Sanderson, 14, 16-17, 19, 21n, 28, 32, 52-53, 84, 87, 92, 95-102, 103, 116, 132, 136, 156, 162, 164, 171-174, 177-179, 181,

Porter, Sarah Ann Perry, 15-16, 18, 28, 32, 46n, 52-53, 101-102, 180, 236, 264-266, 272, 281, 316-319, 330
Porter, William Pitt, 32, 46n, 52-53, 66, 101
Post, Dr. & Mrs. George E., 73, 79n, 289
Powers, Philander, 67-68, 70-71, 113
Pratt, Andrew, 68, 90, 100
Puritan(s), 12-14, 16, 18, 157, 292
Great Migration, 12, 14
Racoubian, Rebecca and Roupon, 317, 321
Ramsey, Sir William, 115, 232-233, 243n-244n
Relief work. *See* American Red Cross, Near East Releif, Henry Perry relief work, J. Rendall Harris, and Swiss orphanage.
Rice, Nina, 313, 324, 346, 356-357
Riggs, Edward, 87, 92, 100, 110-111
Riggs, Elias, 10, 87, 91, 104n, 415
Robert College, 89, 90-91, 134, 144, 160, 166n, 198, 247-248, 294-295
Rolla, Missouri, 38-40, 42, 44, 173
Roman remains. 1-2, 111, 132
Roosevelt, Theodore, 20n, 280, 282, 289-290, 306n, 318
Russo-Turkish War, 58, 121, 135, 197-199
Samsoun, Turkey, 92, 141, 159, 165, 183, 221, 273, 275, 342
Sanderson Academy, 7, 14, 19
Sassoun massacre, 212-215, 217, 219-221, 231, 235, 241n

Schneider, Benjamin, 64-66, 70, 72, 81-82, 86, 90, 139n, 142, 308n
Schneider, Susan, 64-66, 70-72, 86, 90-91, 141-142, 159
Schools for girls, 116, 134, 149, 166n, 294, 313, 324-325, 342
Second Great Awakening, 37
Seljuk Turks, 56, 71, 81, 111
Sennekerim, King, 111
Serbia, 109, 121, 169, 283
Severance, Carl, 265, 349-351, 357
Severance, Emily Augusta, 265
Severance, Jean Perry, 148-150, 154-156, 160, 162, 164, 169-174, 176-185, 211, 240, 250, 264-266, 271-272, 279, 281-282, 292, 296, 298-300, 315-316, 319-321, 330, 349-351, 357-360, 369-370, 376
Shaftsbury, Earl of, 61-62
Sharia, 194-195, 338
Shelburne Falls, Massachusetts, 13, 14, 19, 20n, 21n, 30
Sivas, Turkey, xiv-xv, xxi, 86, 92, 100, 103, 110, 120, 122-123, 127, 155, 184, 249, 300-302, 306-307n, 312-315, 337, 347, 341, 351
  description of, 111-113
  history, 111-112, 113
  church disputes in, 114-115, 134
  schools, 115-118, 146, 204, 271-273, 284, 301, 324-325, 331-332n
  industrial school, 202, 258, 262-263
  Normal School, 116, 202, 226, 312. 320-321, 324
  hospital, medical work, 291, 314
  J. Rendell Harris visit, 252-254
  massacre, 218, 221, 223-229, 245-246, 381
  summary of mission work in, 312-315
  Red Cross visit, 249
  YMCA, 313
  relief, 249, 254-258
  Swiss orphanage, 262-263, 271, 273, 286, 321-322
  Valis, 129-130, 202
  National Congress, 354, 401
  Near East Relief in, 355-356
  end of missionary presence, 354-356
Smith, Eli, 58-59, 77n
Smith, Judson, 187n, 215, 222, 229, 238-239, 247, 273, 293
Smyrna, Turkey, 55-57, 89, 95, 97-100, 103, 124, 163, 169, 183, 250, 289, 295, 301
Stewart, Col. John, 158, 166n
Sublime Porte, 60, 78n, 122, 193, 198, 214, 216, 220, 339, 341
Sultan Abdul Aziz, 109, 195
Sultan Abdul Hamid II, xxi, 110, 144, 193-195, 219, 234-235, 241n, 250-254, 299-300, 353
  diplomacy and reform, 107-110, 121, 130, 196-197. 214-215, 220, 223, 225, 289-290, 302-303, 324
  massacres, 194-195, 193, 213-214, 218, 221, 225, 234-235, 254, 353-354, 388
  paying American claims, 284
Sultan Abdul Medjid, 60, 195

Sultan Mehmed, 60
Sultan Murad V, 109
Swiss orphanage, 262-263, 271, 273, 286, 321-322, 340
Talaat. 302, 324, 330, 337, 352, 363n, 386, 389, 392, 395, 398, 402
Tamerlane, 111-112
Taylor, Hudson, 182
Terrel, A.W., 67, 220, 236-237, 247-248
tezkirah, 246
Thoumaian,Harautune and Shemarian, 189-191
Thoumaian, Professor, 190-192
Tocat, Turkey, 92, 113-114, 124, 131, 145-146, 165, 184, 186, 212, 256-258, 260-261, 269, 272, 275, 285-286, 293, 303, 322-323, 336, 339
Topbeshian, Garabed Agha, 321, 348
Travel descriptions, 2, 63, 125, 127-129, 142, 155-156
Treaty of Berlin, 121-122, 157, 169, 198-201, 214-215, 253, 390
Treaty of Lausanne, 356-357, 396, 399, 400
Treaty of San Stefano, 121
Treaty of Sèvres, 353
Trebizond, Turkey, 59, 61, 159, 217-218, 221, 223, 337, 340, 353, 381, 392-393
Trowbridge, T.C. & Margaret, 72, 75, 83, 85
Turkey. *See* also Ottoman Empire. history, 55-56
travel descriptions of, 63, 125, 127-129, 142

Turkish Mission Aid Society (British), 54, 61, 78n, 300
Union League Club, 264, 317-318
Unitarian, 32, 35
Vali, 111, 118, 129-130, 137n, 190-191, 197, 202, 259, 263, 336-339, 342-343
Van Dyke, Henry, 280
Van Lennep, Dr., 124, 293
Vilayet, 122-123, 129-130, 137n, 189, 193, 198-200, 215, 220-222, 246, 261, 324, 337, 342-343, 345, 386, 391, 394
Wallace, Lew, 144
Wasburn, Dr. George, 90-91, 247-248, 300
Washburn, Emory, 10
Week of Prayer, 203, 208n, 267, 285
West, Dr. Henry, 86, 89, 95, 110-111, 114, 116, 127, 156, 164, 321
Western Female Seminary (Oxford, Ohio), 43, 179
Williams College, 6-12, 20n, 30-35, 51, 173, 282-283, 318-319, 350, 357, 386, 394
Williams, Daniel & Almira, 18, 29
Williams, Mary, 83, 86
Williamson, New York, 101-102
Williamstown, Massachusetts, 5, 30, 32, 95, 173, 319, 350,
Williston Academy, 19, 23-25, 29-30, 45n-46n, 59, 350, 359
Williston, Samuel, 23, 28
Wilson, Lt. Col. C.W., 123, 129-131, 158-159, 166n
Wilson, Woodrow, 348, 353-355, 389
World War I, 56, 193, 197, 335,

351-352, 385, 390, 400-401,
404-406, 408, 419
Young Turks, 302-303, 309-311,
324, 331n, 335, 340, 352-353,
363n, 387, 398-399, 401, 404
zaptieh, 118, 212, 254, 261
Zara, Turkey, 113, 120, 131-132,
143, 162, 203, 313, 323
Zeitoun, Turkey, 87, 294-296, 345,
381
Zenger, Lina, 273
Zenger, Marie, 263, 268, 273, 275,
342

www.ingramcontent.com/pod-product-compliance
Lightning Source LLC
Chambersburg PA
CBHW052046290426
44111CB00011B/1642